INTERACTIONS

A THEMATIC READER

W9-AXX-263

INTERACTIONS

A THEMATIC READER

Fifth Edition

ANN MOSELEY

Texas A&M University–Commerce

JEANETTE HARRIS

Texas Christian University

HOUGHTON MIFFLIN COMPANY   Boston   New York

For my husband, Fred—A. M.
For Henry—J. H.

Senior Sponsoring Editor: Mary Jo Southern
Associate Editor: Kellie Cardone
Associate Project Editor: Claudine Bellanton
Editorial Assistant: Shelley Dickerson
Senior Production/Design Coordinator: Carol Merrigan
Senior Manufacturing Coordinator: Marie Barnes
Senior Marketing Manager: Annamarie Rice

Cover image: © 2002 csaimages.com

Interactions
A Thematic Reader
Ann Moseley   Jeanette Harris

© 2002 csaimages.com

Copyright © 2003 by Houghton Mifflin Company. All rights reserved.

No part of this work may be reproduced or transmitted in any form or by any means, electronic or mechanical, including photocopying and recording, or by any information storage or retrieval system without the prior written permission of the copyright owner unless such copying is expressly permitted by federal copyright law. With the exception of nonprofit transcription in Braille, Houghton Mifflin is not authorized to grant permission for further uses of copyrighted selections reprinted in this text without the permission of their owners. Permission must be obtained from the individual copyright owners as identified herein. Address requests for permission to make copies of Houghton Mifflin material to College Permissions, Houghton Mifflin Company, 222 Berkeley Street, Boston, MA 02116-3764.

Printed in the U.S.A.
Library of Congress Control Number: 2001133315

ISBN: 0-618-21424-0

123456789-FFG-06 05 04 03 02

As part of Houghton Mifflin's ongoing
commitment to the environment, this text
has been printed on recycled paper.

Contents

❁

Brackets indicate grouped readings.

Rhetorical Table of Contents

❧

CLASSIFICATION AND ANALYSIS

DESCRIPTION

NARRATION

PERSUASION AND ARGUMENT

Preface

❀

OVERVIEW OF THE TEXT

Like the previous four editions of *Interactions: A Thematic Reader,* this fifth edition is designed to help students discover meaning in what they read and to convey meaning in what they write. The text's readings and accompanying apparatus, thoroughly class-tested and proven effective through four previous editions, move students from a consideration of self to an awareness of how the self interacts with other people and phenomena. We hope that the diverse selections in this thematic reader will foster a stimulating context for reading and writing. By providing a number of perspectives on individual identity within an increasingly diverse and technological society, the focus on self helps students find their own voices.

FEATURES OF THE FIFTH EDITION

The following features of the fifth edition of *Interactions* deserve special attention:

- Thematic focus on the self
- Strong reading/writing connections
- Emphasis on critical thinking and writing
- Emphasis on collaborative learning
- A variety of genres and writing styles
- Diverse and timely readings
- At least one student essay in each unit
- At least one set of paired readings in each unit (designated by brackets in the table of contents)
- Revised introduction with increased emphasis on the writing process

READING SELECTIONS

The reading selections, more than 30 percent of which are new to this edition, are organized into eight thematic units. In Unit One, "The Self," students are guided through an exploration of themselves as they react and interact with the readings. Unit Two, "Self with Family," and Unit Three, "Self with Friends and Mates," encourage students to examine their relationships with those people closest to them—their family members, friends, and mates. In Unit Four, "Self with Work," students are asked to think about not only their own career plans but also the role of work in their lives and how the concept of work has changed in our society. Units Five through Eight help students to examine their relationship to society, the environment, technology, and heroes. These units encourage students to consider and respond critically to larger issues that concern them.

As in previous editions, the reading selections represent a wide range of voices, topics, and sources. Half of the selections are by women, and a substantial number are by culturally diverse writers. This authorial diversity allows students to hear different voices and to identify with familiar ones. The many genres represented—essays, poetry, fiction, editorials, speeches—provide various models and styles of writing. Finally, each unit includes paired readings that present different, often contrasting, viewpoints and thus encourage students to view subjects from different perspectives.

APPARATUS

The text's *Introduction* explains the process and interdependence of reading and writing, stressing the connections students can make between their lives and what they read. It introduces them to writing techniques such as freewriting, brainstorming, mapping, clustering, and journals. Finally, it emphasizes the importance of considering audience and purpose in all reading and writing activities.

Each reading selection includes the following apparatus:

- *Headnotes* precede and provide context for each selection, helping students understand and enjoy the selection.
- *Before You Read* activities involve students in important prereading and prewriting techniques. Before each selection students are asked to:

    THINK critically about the selection's primary theme in relation to their own beliefs, values, or previous experiences.

EXAMINE specific elements of the text such as the title, the format, particular sentences or paragraphs, or potentially difficult vocabulary.

WRITE a reaction, usually in the form of a journal entry, to the topic they are going to read.

- *As You Read* activities help students interact with the selection and make it their own by determining the main idea, annotating the text, focusing on specific information, or by relating what they read to their own personal experiences.

- *After You Read* sections echo the format of the *Before You Read* sections, encouraging students to *THINK* about the ideas and opinions presented in the reading, *EXAMINE* specific features of the text, and *WRITE* a response to what they have read. These activities are more analytical than those for prereading, taking students several steps further in developing their critical thinking capacities.

CRITICAL THINKING
AND WRITING ASSIGNMENTS

This section includes two types of assignments. **Exploring Ideas Together** asks students to collaborate on a topic suggested by the readings in the unit, synthesizing and analyzing information orally or in collaborative writing activities. **Writing Essays** asks individual students to elaborate on ideas derived from the readings, making connections with the readings themselves and/or with their own observations and experiences.

SUPPORT FOR INSTRUCTORS

The Instructor's Resource Manual for *Interactions* offers instructors supplemental instructional material:

- Background information on the selection's author and/or topic
- Suggestions for activities based on the *Before You Read, As You Read,* and *After You Read* sections
- Strategies for teaching vocabulary not covered in the text
- Additional reading and writing activities
- Two additional tables of contents, one emphasizing genre and one identifying alternate themes

For additional resources for instructors and students, visit the *Interactions* web site at: http://developmentalenglish.college.hmco.com.

ACKNOWLEDGMENTS

We would like to thank our colleagues at Texas A&M–Commerce and at Texas Christian University who offered helpful suggestions and responded to the manuscript. We are also indebted to the following persons for their suggestions in revising *Interactions:*

Linda Clegg, Cerritos College, California
Laura Soldner, Northern Michigan University, Michigan
David Winner, Hudson County Community College, New Jersey
Linda S. Weeks, Dyersburg State Community College, Tennessee
Pamela Kincheloe, Rochester Institute of Technology, New York

Finally, we would like to thank our students who inspired the first edition of *Interactions* and who continue to teach us how to teach.

—Ann Moseley and Jeanette Harris

INTERACTIONS

A THEMATIC READER

Introduction

This book is about you—about the individual self that you are and how you *interact* with other people and the world. Each unit explores a different relationship. Beginning with the first unit, which focuses on your relationship to yourself, the book moves from close, intimate relationships with family and friends to more distant, abstract relationships with the society and environment in which you live. We hope you will enjoy the readings in this book and will learn more about yourself and your relationships from them.

But this book has another purpose as well: to help you become a better reader and writer. We believe that you can do this by reading, discussing, and writing about the selections in this book.

BECOMING A BETTER READER

Reading, like writing, is a process of constructing meaning. When you read, you do not merely take meaning from the text by recognizing the words on the page; you *create* meaning. That is, your ideas and the information and experiences you already have *interact* with the ideas and information you discover in the text. No one knows exactly what happens when a person reads, but we do know that discovering meaning in what you read is more likely if you view reading as a process that includes what you do *before you read*, *as you read*, and *after you read*.

Before You Read

Although you may think of reading and writing as lonely tasks, neither readers nor writers operate in isolation. A piece of writing is a site where readers and writers interact. Thus, before you even begin to read something, you should consider the *purpose* and intended *audience* of the writer. Becoming aware of the writer's purpose and audience, as well as your own purposes for reading, will automatically make you a better reader. For example, in the following paragraph from *How to Study in College*, Walter Pauk writes to an audience of college freshmen to convince them of the importance of establishing a study schedule that suits their particular needs:

> It is important for each individual to choose the type of schedule that fits his or her circumstances best. Some students work better with a detailed schedule, whereas others work better with a brief list of things to do. Circumstances also influence the type of schedule a student should make. There are on-campus students, commuting students, married students, employed students, night-class students, and part-time students, and each has different scheduling requirements. Every student should *adapt* the principles of schedule building to his or her personal circumstances, rather than *adopt* some ideal model which fits hardly anybody.

Notice that the writer of this paragraph makes no attempt to amuse or entertain his readers or to reveal anything of himself in his writing. His tone and style are clear, matter-of-fact, and direct because his purpose is primarily to instruct and advise.

Although he is also writing about schedules, the writer of the following paragraph about Larry McMurtry, the well-known Texas writer, has a very different purpose and intended audience. In this paragraph, David Streitfeld provides an entertaining description of McMurtry's daily work schedule.

> He gets up very early in the morning, reads for a bit—he's now working his way through a large chunk of the critic and diarist Edmund Wilson— then writes briskly, without notes or anguish. ("Some writers are bleeders. I'm not.") Then he likes to drive out to a restaurant in one of the surrounding towns. Before an early bed, he reads a little more. "A perfect life," he calls it.

The purpose of this paragraph is not to teach readers the importance of making a schedule but to give them insight into McMurtry as a writer by focusing on his daily schedule. Its purpose is thus to inform and entertain rather than to instruct. And, because the article appeared in a newspaper, it is obviously intended for a more general audience.

As a reader, you will have a better understanding of what you read if you are aware of the writer. In fact, one of the major differences between experienced and inexperienced readers is not level of skill (how many words are in their vocabulary or how many words a minute they can read or how much grammar they know) but awareness of purpose and audience.

Before you read, you should also clearly understand your own purpose for reading. In performing different reading tasks, your purposes will vary widely. If you are looking for an apartment, you will read the want ads by scanning them very quickly, looking for certain words or phrases (furnished, 2 bedrooms, washer/dryer, and so on). You do not need to read every word or to remember everything you read in such cases. Rather, because you are searching for specific information, you will read in a highly selective fashion. If you are reading a letter from a friend, instructions for operating a new video player, an article in a magazine, a best-selling novel, or a biology text, you will read in very different ways because in each case your purpose for reading is different.

When you are assigned a selection to read in a textbook, you do not always have a real purpose for reading (other than complying with the teacher's assignment). In fact, you often have no idea of what you are going to read until you have begun to read it. In this text, we give you some information about each selection so that you will know in a general way what it is about before you begin reading. We also suggest activities that will help you relate what you are about to read to your own experiences.

Any method of retrieving information (writing, discussing, thinking) is valuable to you as a reader because it enables you to make connections and see relationships that you would not otherwise recognize. For example, suppose your history professor has assigned a section of your textbook that discusses the beginning of labor unions in this country. If you write a journal entry about working conditions you have observed or experienced before you begin to read the assignment, you will comprehend and retain more of what you read because your mind will immediately connect the new information in your textbook with your previous experiences. In fact, what you do before you read an assignment can be the key to understanding what you read. Thus, one of the most effective ways to begin reading is to recall what you know about the subject before you even begin to read the new material.

As You Read

As you read, you will need to distinguish between *main ideas* and *supporting ideas*. Readers, like writers, need to recognize what is primary, or most important, and what is secondary, or less important. Every sentence has a main idea, which we call the *subject and verb;* well-structured paragraphs have a main idea, which we often call a *topic sentence;* and larger pieces of discourse, such as essays or reports, have a main idea, which we call a *thesis.* For example, look at the passage below. These paragraphs are from nature writer Edward Abbey's book *Desert Solitaire: A Season in the Wilderness* (1968), which recounts Abbey's experiences as a ranger in Utah's Arches National Park. Although it is part of a longer work, this passage is a miniature essay in itself. Notice, as you read, that we have underlined the main ideas for you.

> I like my job. The pay is generous; I might even say munificent: $1.95 per hour, earned or not, backed solidly by the world's most powerful Air Force, biggest national debt, and grossest national product. The fringe benefits are priceless: clean air to breathe (after the spring sandstorms); stillness, solitude and space; an unobstructed view every day and every night of sun, sky, stars, clouds, mountains, moon, cliffrock and canyons; a sense of time enough to let thought and feeling range from here to the end of the world and back; the discovery of something intimate—though impossible to name—in the remote.
>
> The work is simple and requires almost no mental effort, a good thing in more ways than one. What little thinking I do is my own and I do it on government time. Insofar as I follow a schedule it goes about like this:
>
> For me the work week begins on Thursday, which I usually spend in patrolling the roads and walking out the trails. On Friday I inspect the campgrounds, haul firewood, and distribute the toilet paper. Saturday and Sunday are my busy days as I deal with the influx of weekend visitors and campers, answering questions, pulling cars out of the sand, lowering children down off the rocks, tracking lost grandfathers and investigating picnics. My Saturday night campfire talks are brief and to the point. "Everything all right?" I say, badge and all, ambling up to what looks like a cheerful group. "Fine," they'll say; "how about a drink?" "Why not?" I say.

<u>By Sunday evening most everyone has gone home and the heavy duty is over</u>. Thank God it's Monday, I say to myself the next morning. Mondays are very nice. I empty the garbage cans, read the discarded newspapers, sweep out the outhouses and disengage the Kleenex from the clutches of cliffrose and cactus. In the afternoon I watch the clouds drift past the bald peak of Mount Tukuhnikivats. (*Someone* has to do it.)

<u>Tuesday and Wednesday I rest</u>. Those are my days off and I usually set aside Wednesday evening for a trip to Moab, replenishing my supplies and establishing a little human contact more vital than that possible with the tourists I meet on the job. After a week in the desert, Moab (pop. 5500, during the great uranium boom) seems like a dazzling metropolis, a throbbing dynamo of commerce and pleasure. I walk the single main street as dazed by the noise and neon as a country boy on his first visit to Times Square. (Wow, I'm thinking, this is great.)

You cannot count on finding all main ideas expressed in exactly the same place in everything you read. Often the main idea occurs as the first or second sentence of a paragraph (as in the first paragraph in this passage), but it may also be a middle sentence or even the last sentence in a paragraph. And the main idea of a paragraph or the thesis of a longer piece may not be stated at all but merely implied. In such instances, you must infer the main idea from the information given. For example, Abbey states several main ideas but doesn't supply an explicit thesis for the passage as a whole. However, the main reason he likes his job is clearly not money or prestige but his undemanding, relaxed schedule, which permits him to lead an isolated, uncomplicated life. Thus this idea functions as the thesis for the passage. And, by extension, Abbey may be suggesting that everyone should choose a job (or career) on the basis of values other than money or prestige.

As both a reader and a writer, you need to be aware of the importance of main ideas and to understand how all discourse is a series of relationships between main ideas and the more specific details that support and develop them. You probably noticed as you read the selection by Abbey that his main ideas are supported by specific details about what he does on his job and when he does these different tasks. These specific details explain and develop his more general main ideas and elaborate on why Abbey likes his job.

As a reader of textbooks, you not only need to distinguish between main ideas and supporting details but also to write as you read—to underline, highlight, circle, and draw pictures; to mark between the lines; to write in the margins. If you are going to get your money's worth from the books you buy and the courses you take, you must be willing to write in your books. In this book, you will find much white space and plenty of room to mark the text and write in the margins. We designed the book in this way because we want you to annotate, or mark, your text (the original Latin meaning of *annotate* is "to mark," "note," or "write").

How you choose to annotate is, of course, up to you. You may want to draw illustrations, to highlight with colored markers, to circle words you do not know, to number information, to underline or put asterisks beside ideas you consider important, or to write notes to yourself about what you are reading. You may want to write notes connecting your reading with previous experiences or to write questions to ask your instructor. You may certainly read some selections that do not require a written response, but if you want to improve as a reader, it is essential that you communicate in writing with yourself as you read. The more difficult the material you are reading, the more important it is that you respond to it in writing.

Ideally, you should read the material through once and then annotate it on a second reading when you have a better sense of which ideas and information are significant. But even on a first reading, you will better understand what you are reading if you annotate as you read. We have annotated the following paragraphs, condensed from *The Secrets Our Body Clocks Reveal,* by Susan Perry and Jim Dawson, to illustrate how a reader might respond to a given passage:

> *Main idea*
> All living organisms, from mollusks to men and women, exhibit biological rhythms. Some are short and can be measured in minutes or hours. Others last days or months. The peaking of
>
> *Types of biological rhythms*
> (1) body temperature, which occurs in most people every evening, is a daily rhythm. The (2) menstrual cycle is a monthly rhythm. The increase in (3) sexual drive in the autumn—not in the spring, as poets would have us believe—is a seasonal, or yearly, rhythm.
>
> *State of change*
> The idea that our bodies are in constant (flux) is fairly new—and goes against traditional medical training. In the past, many doctors were taught to believe the body has a relatively
>
> *Stable*
> stable, or (homeostatic) internal environment. Any fluctuations were considered random and not meaningful enough to be studied.

Annotations are the tracks a reader leaves in the text. They reveal something about what was going on in the reader's mind. The annotations we have made reflect our reading of these paragraphs—the ideas that were important to us, the statements that related to our knowledge from experience and reading, the words we needed to define, the information we wanted to remember. Different readers discover different meanings as they read, and even the same reader may discover different meanings upon rereading the same material. But annotating what you read enables you to understand and remember what is most useful and important to you at the time. Your annotations also provide you with a record of your reading so that you can easily review the material at a later time. Even more important, annotations force you to think about what you are reading as you read.

After You Read

When you write, you often go back and rewrite what you have written, editing and revising your ideas so that they are more accessible to your reader. When you read, you also need to revise—to reconstruct and add to the meaning that you created as you read. After each reading selection, we provide questions and writing activities that help you in this process of revising your understanding of what you have read. The suggestions below will also help you rethink and remember what you have read.

Write about what you have read.   Writing in response to what you have read is one of the most effective ways of making it your own. For example, after reading the selection on biological rhythms by Susan Perry and Jim Dawson, you could summarize it or write a journal entry about your own biological rhythms. Or you could outline it or map the relationships among the main ideas and the major supporting ideas as shown below:

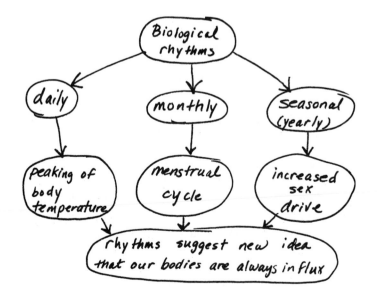

Discuss what you have read with others.   Discussing what you have read with others nearly always helps you to discover meaning in what you read. Therefore, we suggest that you talk frequently with your classmates about what you have read. After reading the selection by Abbey, for example, you could compare your own experiences and schedules with those of a group of your classmates and then discuss how schedules give shape to a person's life. Talking, like writing, helps you to see new connections, arrive at different interpretations, and discover new meanings.

Reread what you have read.   Rereading is another effective way of ensuring that your interaction with a text is productive. Each time you read something, you gain a new understanding of it; rereading what you have already read enables you to build on your prior knowledge of the text as well as your own increased knowledge of the subject. So do not hesitate to reread. Whether it is a single word, a line or sentence, a paragraph, or even an entire selection, rereading not only clarifies and reinforces the meaning you discover in a text but also helps you discover new meanings.

BECOMING A BETTER WRITER

Writing begins as an idea. The most informal note, like the most complex report or essay, originates as an idea that anticipates and shapes the completed piece of writing. But writing is not as simple as this statement suggests. You do not simply come up with an idea and then transfer it directly onto paper or a computer screen. Writing, like reading, is a process—often messy and nonlinear—but still a process. In order to become a better writer, you need a general understanding of this process— what you should do *before you write, as you write,* and *after you write.*

Before You Write

Before you begin to write, you usually need to plan—to think about what you are going to write, discover new ideas, make connections with what you already know, perhaps even look for additional information, and generally organize your thoughts. One of the most important parts of this preliminary process is to think about your purpose and audience—your own purpose in writing and the knowledge and reading skills of those who will read what you write.

Purpose.   Writers have multiple reasons for writing. When you have a writing assignment, you probably write primarily because the assignment is required, but you may also have other purposes—to communicate information, to express your ideas, to impress your teacher and classmates, to demonstrate knowledge, and to improve your skills as a writer. These multiple purposes inform your writing process and shape the resulting piece of writing. But you also have more specific purposes for writing that are often determined by the assignment or your choice of a topic. For example, you may write to explore (journal writing), to reconstruct your own experiences (memoir or personal experience essays), to teach or advise (instructions), to inform (reports), or to persuade (editorials or argumentative essays). These different purposes do not usually exist in isolation. You may write to inform *and* instruct or to explore *and* reconstruct your own experiences. And, because all writing is to some extent persuasive, you are always trying to persuade your reader to accept your point of view. The writer of a set of instructions for assembling a product is not only providing you with the information you need to put the product together but may also be trying to persuade you to perform the task in a specific way, to take certain precautions, and to value and trust the company that produced the product.

Because all writing is at some level persuasive, you also need to consider your *thesis* (the particular point you are trying to make or the primary impression you want your reader to gain from reading what you have written). Thus before you begin to write anything, you need to formulate your thesis. Even if, later in the process of writing, you decide to change your thesis or not to state it explicitly, it is a good idea to begin writing with a thesis clearly in mind to guide your writing.

Audience.   Your audience consists of the people for whom you are writing—those who will read what you have written. Audience, like purpose, shapes the form a piece of writing takes. Good writers not only begin a writing project by identifying who their readers will be but also by *analyzing* their readers. For example, they think about how much information their readers have as well as their educational level, their interests, the time they will devote to reading, and their purpose, or purposes, in reading. In other words, they write *for* specific readers.

When faced with a writing assignment, you may need to spend some time before you actually begin to write your paper or essay thinking about what you want to write and how to structure your ideas. If this is the case, you may benefit from some preliminary writing activities—some warm-up exercises to help you collect your thoughts and focus on the writing project at hand. A few of the most common of these preliminary writing strategies are defined and illustrated for you below:

1. **Freewriting.** In its purest form, freewriting is the practice of writing whatever comes into your head on a topic without worrying about form or correctness. Because this technique is a loosening-up exercise, it is important to continue writing even if you write only meaningless phrases such as "I can't think of anything to write." As you write, you should not be concerned with formal matters of organization, sentence structure, spelling, or punctuation. When you freewrite, you are letting associations lead you from one idea to another, drifting back in time to retrieve information and sensations that are buried in your long-term memory. These long-buried, half-forgotten ideas and experiences can often be recalled once you begin writing.

    As illustrated below, a related strategy is focused freewriting, which helps prepare you to read or write about a particular subject by rapidly recording as many ideas as you can think of about the topic.

    Lets see, schedules, schedules. What kind of schedules do I know about? I check plane schedules when I visit dad or get ready to go back to campus. I had to follow a really strict schedule when I worked at McDonald's last summer. The boss really lost it when I came in late! Just looked at the spring schedule to figure out what classes I want to take next semester. I really don't think I like schedules. I'm not sure if I even have a schedule. Guess I better start thinking about one.

2. **Journal entries.** Writing a journal entry differs from freewriting in that you are exploring a topic rather than giving immediate reac-

tions to it. Journal entries allow you to examine a topic and to discover not only what you think but also how you feel. As illustrated in the example below, a journal entry also has more structure than does freewriting, and the ideas in it are more closely connected. Thus, producing a journal entry will take more time and thought than freewriting. In fact, in a journal entry, you often express ideas that you can later use in compositions to be written for audiences other than yourself. Like freewriting, however, a journal entry is personal and unstructured, and most instructors simply respond to journal entries with comments rather than evaluating such entries for organization, spelling, and punctuation.

My life seems to be run by schedules. Each morning when I get up I have to think about what day it is and then I know the schedule I have to follow. I have one schedule for Mondays, Wednesdays, and Fridays and another one for Tuesdays and Thursdays. On MWF days I go to class from 9:00 to 12:00 and work at the library from 1:00 to 5:00. On TTH days I go to class from 9:30 to 12:15, but I've got a lab from 2:00 to 4:30 so I have to work at the library from 6:00 until 10:00. Needless to say, I have to study at every night. Since I usually go to church on Sunday mornings and study in the afternoons, Saturday is the only day that I have that isn't run by a schedule. Perhaps it's the freedom of that day that makes it so great to me. I can visit friends, go to the movies, or just sleep in if I want. If it wasn't for this day, I couldn't face another week of schedules.

3. **Brainstorming.** Brainstorming works in much the same way as freewriting. Instead of writing connected ideas, however, when you brainstorm, you merely select a topic and make a *list* of ideas

related to that topic. As shown in the following brainstorming on schedules, it is important to generate as long a list as possible—everything that comes into your mind.

time   *busy*

no extra time   *Tina's ballet schedule*

school schedules   *Brad's soccer schedule*

rigid   *daily schedule*

class schedules   *weekly schedule*

MWF classes   *study schedule*

TTH work schedule   *study nights/weekends*

no time to sleep   *study 2 hrs/1 hr class*

After you have generated a fairly lengthy list, you can discard some of the ideas and/or connect related ideas. Or you might select one of the ideas, such as "school schedules" above, that seems especially relevant or interesting to you and brainstorm again, this time focusing on the new narrowed topic.

4. **Mapping.** Mapping, or clustering, ideas is a means of visualizing relationships. If you are mapping a topic, you begin with the topic itself in the center of a blank piece of paper and then branch out from the topic with related ideas. You can continue this branching process as long as you can think of related ideas, examples, and details. A map is a good way of generating ideas because after you get your map started, you can select one idea from the map that interests you or triggers other ideas and continue to develop that idea while ignoring the rest. This technique—which is illustrated in the following figure—encourages you to delve deep into your memory to discover specific ideas.

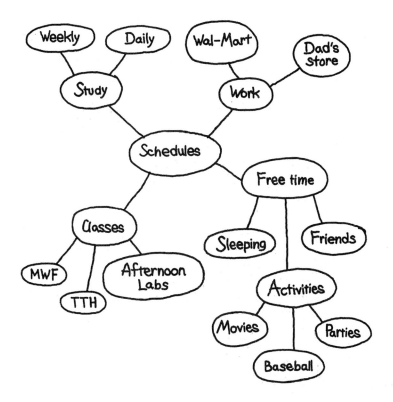

As You Write

Neither writing nor reading is a neat, orderly process. Although the final product may appear to be neat, writing is a process in which the writer's mind shuttles back and forth between a mental image and the written text emerging on the page. Both reading and writing involve going backward (retrieving information from your mental data bank) as well as going forward (discovering new information and making new connections).

Although the messiness of these processes is often hidden from view, discreetly tucked away inside the reader's or writer's mind, there are times when the mess needs to show, times when it needs to spill out on the clean white page. Writers often need to rewrite what they have written. They may need to create several disorganized drafts before they can produce something they want to share with a reader.

When you have some idea of what you want to write, you are ready to begin drafting your paper. Throughout this part of the writing process you will often move backward as well as forward. For example, even though you have formulated a thesis before you begin to write, you may discover when you actually begin to write that you need to revise your thesis or even change it completely. Because writing often leads to new insights and discoveries, these early drafts are sometimes referred to as *discovery drafts*. Don't be concerned if your initial mental image of your paper changes significantly as you continue to write. The early part of this process often involves reading and revising as well as writing. As you write, you will be rethinking what you want to write. This is a normal, productive part of the process. Ultimately, you will produce a piece of writing that satisfies you.

After You Write

Once you have a completed draft, you should try to put it aside for awhile and then focus on revising the entire paper. Even as you write, you are rethinking and revising what you want to say. However, you always need to revise the completed draft as well. Revising involves rereading a draft carefully and critically. To do this, you must try to see your paper through the eyes of your reader. You must also be willing to make major changes—to generate new material, to move information from one place to another, and even to delete large portions if necessary. In general, at this point you want to focus on the following questions:

- Do I have a clear thesis and is my paper focused on this thesis?
- Have I supported my thesis adequately?
- Are my major supporting points effectively organized?
- Are my paragraphs unified and well structured?
- Are my introduction and conclusion effective?

After you have written and revised your paper, you need to turn your attention to preparing the final draft—the one you will submit to a reader (even, or especially, if that reader is your instructor). This final stage in the process involves editing, proofreading, and formatting what you have written so that it is as readable and correct as possible. By the time you begin this stage, you are primarily focusing on the accuracy and appearance of your paper. This is the time to make sure that each sentence is well structured, each word correctly used, and each mark of punctuation appropriate. If you are using a computer, you will need to make final decisions about format and run the spell check. Do not underestimate the importance of this final effort to make your paper as readable and correct as possible.

CONCLUSION

You not only use your own experiences to discover meaning when you read and write, but you also make sense of your experiences and yourself through reading and writing. As you read the selections and do the assignments given in this book, we hope you will increase your understanding of yourself and how you interact with other people and other phenomena in your world. In this process of self-discovery, we believe, you will also become a more experienced reader and writer.

The Self

It is not always easy to know yourself—to know who you are and how you came to be that person. And just when you think you know yourself, you change. You get older, form different relationships, develop new interests, go to college, change jobs, or move to a new community, and the process of knowing yourself begins all over again. So your entire life is spent trying to figure out who you are and how to be happy being that person.

One of the ways in which you can examine who you are is to look at the important relationships in your life—especially the relationships with your family and friends. Another way to gain insight into yourself is to think in terms of the experiences you have had and how these have shaped who you are. In addition to the relationships and experiences in your life that help to define and create you, the language and culture of your particular community determine in a very real sense who you are. From birth, you absorb and are shaped by the language, values, and patterns of behavior that characterize your own small, immediate group. Thus to know yourself you must understand that concepts of self are grounded in language and culture.

This first unit focuses on these factors and how they may shape a person. The unit also includes readings that explore issues of self-esteem—how factors such as your name, age, gender, family, ethnic background, and physical appearance influence the way you perceive yourself. As you read these selections, think about your image of yourself. How would you describe yourself to someone who does not know you? Compare yourself to the child you once were, analyze why you have become the person you are today, or predict the kind of person you will be in the future.

As you read the selections in this unit, also keep in mind the similarities between reading and writing discussed in the Introduction. Remember that the process you go through in reading these selections is much like the process the writers went through in writing them. Both you and the writers are discovering and constructing meaning. When you read, you are adding to and modifying what you already know. You are also evaluating another person's ideas and information and opinions. Therefore, you need to be aware of the writer's purposes in writing, his or her knowledge about the subject, and the possible biases that may have influenced what was written.

Also remember that reading, like writing, is a messy process. Reading a selection through once without marking the text in any way does not usually result in your gaining much from it. So underline the sentences that are important to your understanding, circle the words you don't know, and write notes to yourself (and to the author) in the margins. Don't just read these selections; *interact* with the ideas and information in them. You will not understand yourself any better or improve yourself as a reader unless you actively engage in a dialogue with the writers and the ideas they present in their texts.

Finally, remember that you need to write in response to what you read if you really want to make the information and ideas your own. In addition to annotating the text itself, you may want to write a brief summary of some of the selections; others you may want to outline or map or merely respond to—perhaps in journal entries—by writing your reaction to what you have read. We have suggested writing activities for each selection, but you need to discover for yourself the forms of writing that best help you to understand what you read.

My Name

SANDRA CISNEROS

❀

Sandra Cisneros, the only daughter in a large Mexican-American family, writes stories and poems that reflect her own experience with conflicting cultures and languages. She addresses such issues as poverty, cultural suppression, self-identity, and gender roles in her poetry and fiction. This reading selection is taken from The House on Mango Street, *a collection of related narrative sketches about a Mexican-American family struggling to adjust to life in an English-speaking culture. Loosely based on the life of the author, this selection tells of a young girl's reaction to her name, Esperanza, which means "hope."*

BEFORE YOU READ

▪ *THINK* about your given name, the one you "go by." Is it a family name? Or were you named after a famous person? Do you know why your parents chose to name you as they did? Do you have a nickname? If so, what is its origin?

▪ *EXAMINE* the words *esperanza* and *hope,* both of which have been used as female names. Although both words mean the same thing, they look and sound very different. The Spanish word *esperanza* is much longer and more musical; the English word *hope* is not only shorter, but almost curt sounding.

▪ *WRITE* in your journal the name you would have chosen for yourself and tell why you would have chosen this name.

AS YOU READ

Think about the importance we attach to names and why.

In English my name means hope. In Spanish it means too many letters. It   1
means sadness, it means waiting. It is like the number nine. A muddy
color. It is the Mexican records my father plays on Sunday mornings when
he is shaving, songs like sobbing.

It was my great-grandmother's name and now it is mine. She was a   2
horse woman too, born like me in the Chinese year of the horse—which
is supposed to be bad luck if you're born female—but I think this is a
Chinese lie because the Chinese, like the Mexicans, don't like their women
strong.

My great-grandmother. I would've liked to have known her, a wild   3
horse of a woman, so wild she wouldn't marry until my great-grandfather
threw a sack over her head and carried her off. Just like that, as if she were
a fancy chandelier. That's the way he did it.

And the story goes she never forgave him. She looked out the window   4
all her life, the way so many women sit their sadness on an elbow. I wonder
if she made the best with what she got or was she sorry because she couldn't
be all the things she wanted to be. Esperanza. I have inherited her name,
but I don't want to inherit her place by the window.

At school they say my name funny as if the syllables were made out of   5
tin and hurt the roof of your mouth. But in Spanish my name is made out
of a softer something like silver, not quite as thick as sister's name
Magdalena which is uglier than mine. Magdalena who at least can come
home and become Nenny. But I am always Esperanza.

I would like to baptize myself under a new name, a name more like   6
the real me, the one nobody sees. Esperanza as Lisandra or Maritza or Zeze
the X. Yes. Something like Zeze the X will do.

❁ ❁ ❁

AFTER YOU READ

▪ *THINK* about the young girl's reaction to her name. Why does she want
another name? Does a person's name make a difference in the way you
perceive that person? Does your own name affect how you feel about
yourself? Do the names of others affect how you react to them? Why does
exchanging names seem important when you first meet someone? Could
you feel that you really knew someone whose name you did not know?

▪ *EXAMINE* the name *Zeze the X* the girl chose for herself. Why do you
think she liked this name?

▪ *WRITE* about your own name—where it came from, whether you like it, how you think others perceive it, and what other name you might choose for yourself if you were free to do so.

The Name Is Mine

ANNA QUINDLEN

❀

*Anna Quindlen formerly served as deputy metropolitan
editor for the* New York Times *but is now retired from that
position in order to devote her time to writing. She is best
known as a columnist but is increasingly recognized as a
successful novelist. One of her novels,* One True Thing,
*was made into a movie starring Meryl Streep and William
Hurt. In the following essay, Quindlen tells the story of
her name and how that name has helped to shape her
various identities.*

BEFORE YOU READ

▪ *THINK* about the custom of married females adopting the surnames of
their husbands. What problems or advantages are associated with this
custom?

▪ *EXAMINE* the preceding essay, "My Name" by Sandra Cisneros. Even
though the purpose, content, and tone of the selections by Cisneros and
Quindlen differ significantly, both authors clearly believe that names play
an important role in a person's sense of identity.

▪ *WRITE* in your journal an entry stating your opinion on the issue of
married women keeping their own names rather than taking their husband's surnames.

AS YOU READ

Indicate in the margins how Quindlen's feelings about her name compare
with those of Cisneros.

I am on the telephone to the emergency room of the local hospital. My   1
elder son is getting stitches in his palm, and I have called to make myself

feel better, because I am at home, waiting, and my husband is there, holding him. I am 34 years old, and I am crying like a child, making a slippery mess of my face. "Mrs. Krovatin?" says the nurse, and for the first time in my life I answer "Yes."

This is a story about a name. The name is mine. I was given it at birth, 2 and I have never changed it, although I married. I could come up with lots of reasons why. It was a political decision, a simple statement that I was somebody and not an adjunct of anybody, especially a husband. As a friend of mine told her horrified mother, "He didn't adopt me, he married me."

It was a professional and a personal decision, too. I grew up with an 3 ugly dog of a name, one I came to love because I thought it was weird and unlovable. Amid the Debbies and Kathys of my childhood, I had a first name only my grandmothers had and a last name that began with a strange letter. "Sorry, the letters I, O, Q, U, V, X, Y and Z are not available," the catalogues said about monogrammed key rings and cocktail napkins. Seeing my name in black on white at the top of a good story, suddenly it wasn't an ugly dog anymore.

But neither of these are honest reasons, because they assume rational 4 consideration, and it so happens that when it came to changing my name, there was no consideration, rational or otherwise. It was mine. It belonged to me. I don't even share a checking account with my husband. Damned if I was going to be hidden beneath the umbrella of his identity.

It seemed like a simple decision. But nowadays I think the only simple 5 decisions are whether to have grilled cheese or tuna fish for lunch. Last week, my older child wanted an explanation of why he, his dad and his brother have one name, and I have another.

My answer was long, philosophical and rambling—that is to say, 6 unsatisfactory. What's in a name? I could have said disingenuously. But I was talking to a person who had just spent three torturous, exhilarating years learning names for things, and I wanted to communicate to him that mine meant something quite special to me, had seemed as form-fitting as my skin, and as painful to remove. Personal identity and independence, however, were not what he was looking for; he just wanted to make sure I was one of them. And I am—and then again, I am not. When I made this decision, I was part of a couple. Now, there are two me's, the me who is the individual and the me who is part of a family of four, a family of four in which, in a small way, I am left out.

A wise friend who finds herself in the same fix says she never wants 7 to change her name, only to have a slightly different identity as a family member, an identity for pediatricians' offices and parent-teacher conferences. She also says that the entire situation reminds her of the women's movement as a whole. We did these things as individuals, made these decisions about ourselves and what we wanted to be and do. And they were good decisions, the right decisions. But we based them on individual choice, not on group dynamics. We thought in terms of our sense of ourselves, not our relationships with others.

Some people found alternative solutions: hyphenated names, merged 8 names, matriarchal names for the girls and patriarchal ones for the boys, one name at work and another at home. I did not like those choices; I thought they were middle grounds, and I didn't live much in the middle ground at the time. I was once slightly disdainful of women who went all the way and changed their names. But I now know too many smart, independent, terrific women who have the same last names as their husbands to be disdainful anymore. (Besides, if I made this decision as part of a feminist world view, it seems dishonest to turn around and trash other women for deciding as they did.)

I made my choice. I haven't changed my mind. I've just changed my 9 life. Sometimes I feel like one of those worms I used to hear about in biology, the ones that, chopped in half, walked off in different directions. My name works fine for one half, not quite as well for the other. I would never give it up. Except for that one morning when I talked to the nurse at the hospital, I always answer the question "Mrs. Krovatin?" with "No, this is Mr. Krovatin's wife." It's just that I understand the down side now.

❀ ❀ ❀

AFTER YOU READ

• *THINK* about the different perspectives Quindlen includes in her essay. She is careful to say that her decision about keeping her own name is not the only or necessarily the best answer to this complex problem. What are some of the factors that she includes in her discussion? Is her essay more or less satisfactory because she does not argue strongly for a single answer? Would you describe Quindlen as a militant feminist because she has refused to take her husband's name? Why or why not?

• *EXAMINE* the second sentence in paragraph 6 ("What's in a name?"), which is an allusion to a line in Shakespeare's *Romeo and Juliet*. Did you recognize the line or at least find it familiar? In Shakespeare's play, the response to the question is "A rose by any other name would smell as sweet." Does Quindlen include this reference to Shakespeare's words because she agrees with the sentiment expressed in them? What other reasons might she have for including this allusion to Shakespeare?

▪ *WRITE* a paragraph or essay in which you argue for or against the custom of women taking their husbands' names. Or *WRITE* a comparison of the Cisneros and Quindlen essays, focusing on their attitudes toward their names.

I'm Just Me

LYLAH M. ALPHONSE

❀

This brief essay, which first appeared in the Boston Globe *in 1996, is by a young woman whose mother is Persian and whose father is Haitian. Like names, ethnic backgrounds shape people's perceptions of who they are. People like Alphonse, who belong to more than one ethnic group, may find it especially difficult to define themselves. But in this essay, Alphonse makes it clear that she is very comfortable with who she is and points out that it is our society that has difficulty in accepting people who do not belong to a single ethnic group.*

BEFORE YOU READ

▪ *THINK* about what it is like to be part of two different cultures and to have physical characteristics derived from both. How does a mixed racial heritage complicate life for a person? How do other people react to someone whom they cannot assign to a single race?

▪ *EXAMINE* the title of this essay. Although the author seems proud of her mixed background, she is eager to be perceived as an individual—someone who is unique and distinctive. Why do you think she is determined to be perceived as an individual rather than simply as the product of the two cultures represented by her parents?

▪ *WRITE* a journal entry in which you analyze the different ethnic, religious, and/or racial elements of your own background. Try to determine how each of these elements is reflected in you—what it contributes to your appearance, physique, intelligence, personality, and so on.

AS YOU READ

Try to distinguish among the concepts of culture, ethnicity, and race.

This is me: caramel-colored skin, light-brown eyes, brown-black hair 1
with a few silver threads just to the right of my temple. I have a few
freckles, like cocoa powder dusted under my right eye. I'm 5 foot 3, 115
pounds, was a field hockey goalie, still am a fencer.

This is me: I have my mother's Persian features, my father's Haitian 2
coloring, and curly hair that's somewhere in between. When I was little, I
desperately wanted my younger brother's graceful hands and my youngest
brother's huge green eyes.

This is me: On census forms, aptitude tests, and applications, whenever 3
possible I check the box for "other" after the question about race. When
there's no "other" option, I check four boxes: white (German and French
on my father's side), Asian (Persian Indian on my mother's side), Native
peoples (Arawak Indian on my father's side), and black (an African
great-grandfather on my father's side). If the instructions limit me to only
one box, I skip it entirely.

One would think that institutions could have come up with a different 4
method of classifying people by now. According to 1990 census information, the number of "other" people has grown to 9.8 million—a 45 percent
increase since 1980—and it's still on the rise. "Mixed" marriages doubled
between 1980 and 1992, when 1.2 million were reported. And "mixed" is
more than just black and white, though those unions have increased
also—by 50 percent, to 250,000, since 1980.

"Mixed" relationships are nothing new, even though the media still some- 5
times treat[s] them as though they are. My family's been doing it for four
generations. Five, if you count me and my blond-haired, blue-eyed boyfriend.

There's a massive push to include a "mixed-race" box on the census 6
for the year 2000, but SATs, GREs, and other aptitude tests can surely
rethink their designations more than once a decade. Why isn't there a
"mixed" box on all those other forms yet? Or instructions that tell us to
"check all that apply?" Or, better still, a new question "What group do you
identify with?"

Natives of Zimbabwe, which used to be Rhodesia, who are descended 7
from that country's British settlers are just as African as natives of Ethiopia,
but in the United States we wouldn't call them African Americans. Yet we
would give that label to the child of a Caucasian woman and a man from
the West Indies, even though the child's connection to the African continent
is distant, if it exists at all.

Why do we call mixed marriages "interracial?" Isn't it your ethnicity— 8
the culture in which you are raised—that defines who you are more so than
your race? Race is part of the equation, of course, but the color of your

skin doesn't necessarily dictate the culture and traditions that surround you while you're growing up.

I grew up in Princeton, N.J. It was very sheltered—kind of like growing   9 up wrapped in cotton, which I think was a good thing. When I left Princeton to go to college in Syracuse, N.Y., I was naive about racial matters. I still think I am. I was surprised by the looks I'd get when I walked around on campus at night with my friends and by the fliers I got year after year inviting me to attend the "African American Orientation" at the student center. I didn't understand why, when I was reporting a stalker, the campus police officer told me that I spoke English very well.

Then I realized that people were looking at my skin and deciding that   10 I was African American; or looking at my features and deciding I was Indian; or listening to me talk and not being able to place me at all.

People still try to figure out my background. But now, instead of just   11 looking at me and wondering, they ask me questions like "So, were you born here?" Or "Where in India are your parents from?" And "What do you consider yourself?" A friend's father once asked, point-blank, "What exactly *is* Lylah?" ("Female," my friend replied.)

These are the answers I give them: I was born and raised in Princeton,   12 N.J. My mother is from India. My father is from Haiti. As for what I consider myself . . .

I'm just me.   13

❀   ❀   ❀

AFTER YOU READ

• *THINK* about the two arguments that Alphonse includes in her essay. The first, and most explicit, is her argument that race is not a simple concept and that many people derive from not only more than one race but also from more than one ethnic or cultural background. But she is also, implicitly, arguing for acceptance of people as they are—for not classifying people according to their racial or ethnic backgrounds. Which argument do you think is stronger and why?

• *EXAMINE* the distinctions Alphonse makes among race, ethnicity, and culture in paragraph 8. Do you agree with these distinctions? Look these three terms up in a dictionary and see if the definitions support Alphonse's distinctions.

• *WRITE* an essay entitled "I'm Just Me" in which you describe yourself in terms of your own ethnic, racial, and/or cultural background.

The Jacket

GARY SOTO

❀

Gary Soto, a writer and university professor, is perhaps best known for his poetry. He received the 1976 U.S. Award of the International Poetry Forum for his book-length poem The Elements of San Joaquin, *and his more recent collections* Black Hair *and* Neighborhood Odes *have also been praised highly for their portrayal of Soto's Mexican-American childhood. Soto is also increasingly well known for his collections of autobiographical essays, including* Baseball in April, Buried Onions, *and* Small Faces, *from which this selection was taken. In this essay he tells of an extremely ugly jacket he was forced to wear when he was a child and the effects, both real and imagined, that this jacket had on his life.*

BEFORE YOU READ

- *THINK* about some article of clothing you wore as a child but did not like and how wearing this garment made you feel. Do the clothes you wear still affect the way you feel about yourself on a particular day or occasion?

- *EXAMINE* the first sentence of this essay: "My clothes have failed me." What do you think Soto means by this statement. How can clothes "fail" someone? What functions do clothes have beyond covering our nakedness and protecting us from the elements?

- *WRITE* in your journal a description of some garment you remember wearing as a child and tell how that garment made you feel.

AS YOU READ

Underline clues that reveal the author's ethnic and economic background. Think about whether these factors may have influenced his feelings about himself.

My clothes have failed me. I remember the green coat that I wore in 1
fifth and sixth grades when you either danced like a champ or
pressed yourself against a greasy wall, bitter as a penny toward the happy
couples.

When I needed a new jacket and my mother asked what kind I wanted, 2
I described something like bikers wear: black leather and silver studs with
enough belts to hold down a small town. We were in the kitchen, steam on
the windows from her cooking. She listened so long while stirring dinner
that I thought she understood for sure the kind I wanted. The next day
when I got home from school, I discovered draped on my bedpost a jacket
the color of day-old guacamole. I threw my books on the bed and
approached the jacket slowly, as if it were a stranger whose hand I had to
shake. I touched the vinyl sleeve, the collar, and peeked at the mustard-
colored lining.

From the kitchen mother yelled that my jacket was in the closet. I 3
closed the door to her voice and pulled at the rack of clothes in the closet,
hoping the jacket on the bedpost wasn't for me but my mean brother. No
luck. I gave up. From my bed, I stared at the jacket. I wanted to cry because
it was so ugly and so big that I knew I'd have to wear it a long time. I was
a small kid, thin as a young tree, and it would be years before I'd have a
new one. I stared at the jacket, like an enemy, thinking bad things before I
took off my old jacket whose sleeves climbed halfway to my elbow.

I put the big jacket on. I zipped it up and down several times, and rolled 4
the cuffs up so they didn't cover my hands. I put my hands in the pockets
and flapped the jacket like a bird's wings. I stood in front of the mirror,
full face, then profile, and then looked over my shoulder as if someone had
called me. I sat on the bed, stood against the bed, and combed my hair to
see what I would look like doing something natural. I looked ugly. I threw
it on my brother's bed and looked at it for a long time before I slipped it
on and went out to the backyard, smiling a "thank you" to my mom as I
passed her in the kitchen. With my hands in my pockets I kicked a ball
against the fence, and then climbed it to sit looking into the alley. I hurled
orange peels at the mouth of an open garbage can and when the peels were
gone I watched the white puffs of my breath thin to nothing.

I jumped down, hands in my pockets, and in the backyard on my knees 5
I teased my dog, Brownie, by swooping my arms while making bird calls.
He jumped at me and missed. He jumped again and again, until a tooth
sunk deep, ripping an L-shaped tear on my left sleeve. I pushed Brownie
away to study the tear as I would a cut on my arm. There was no blood,

only a few loose pieces of fuzz. Damn dog, I thought, and pushed him away
hard when he tried to bite again. I got up from my knees and went to my
bedroom to sit with my jacket on my lap, with the lights out.

That was the first afternoon with my new jacket. The next day I wore 6
it to sixth grade and got a D on a math quiz. During the morning recess
Frankie T., the playground terrorist, pushed me to the ground and told me
to stay there until recess was over. My best friend, Steve Negrete, ate an
apple while looking at me, and the girls turned away to whisper on the
monkey bars. The teachers were no help: they looked my way and talked
about how foolish I looked in my new jacket. I saw their heads bob with
laughter, their hands half-covering their mouths.

Even though it was cold, I took off the jacket during lunch and played 7
kickball in a thin shirt, my arms feeling like braille from goose bumps. But
when I returned to class I slipped the jacket on and shivered until I was
warm. I sat on my hands, heating them up, while my teeth chattered like
a cup of crooked dice. Finally warm, I slid out of the jacket but a few
minutes later put it back on when the fire bell rang. We paraded out into
the yard where we, the sixth graders, walked past all the other grades to
stand against the back fence. Everybody saw me. Although they didn't say
out loud, "Man, that's ugly," I heard the buzz-buzz of gossip and even
laughter that I knew was meant for me.

And so I went, in my guacamole jacket. So embarrassed, so hurt, I 8
couldn't even do my homework. I received Cs on quizzes, and forgot the
state capitols and the rivers of South America, our friendly neighbor. Even
the girls who had been friendly blew away like loose flowers to follow the
boys in neat jackets.

I wore that thing for three years until the sleeves grew short and my 9
forearms stuck out like the necks of turtles. All during that time no love
came to me—no little dark girl in a Sunday dress she wore on Monday. At
lunchtime I stayed with the ugly boys who leaned against the chainlink
fence and looked around with propellers of grass spinning in our mouths.
We saw girls walk by alone, saw couples, hand in hand, their heads like
bookends pressing air together. We saw them and spun our propellers so
fast our faces were blurs.

I blame that jacket for those bad years. I blame my mother for her bad 10
taste and her cheap ways. It was a sad time for the heart. With a friend I
spent my sixth-grade year in a tree in the alley waiting for something good
to happen to me in that jacket, which had become the ugly brother who
tagged along wherever I went. And it was about that time that I began to

grow. My chest puffed up with muscle and, strangely, a few more ribs. Even my hands, those fleshy hammers, showed bravely through the cuffs, the fingers already hardening for the coming fights. But that L-shaped rip on the left sleeve got bigger; bits of stuffing coughed out from its wound after a hard day of play. I finally scotch-taped it closed, but in rain or cold weather the tape peeled off like a scab and more stuffing fell out until that sleeve shriveled into a palsied arm. That winter the elbows began to crack and whole chunks of green began to fall off. I showed the cracks to my mother, who always seemed to be at the stove with steamed-up glasses, and she said that there were children in Mexico who would love that jacket. I told her that this was America and yelled that Debbie, my sister, didn't have a jacket like mine. I ran outside, ready to cry, and climbed the tree by the alley to think bad thoughts and watch my breath puff white and disappear.

But whole pieces still casually flew off my jacket when I played hard, 11 read quietly, or took vicious spelling tests at school. When it became so spotted that my brother began to call me "camouflage," I flung it over the fence into the alley. Later, however, I swiped the jacket off the ground and went inside to drape it across my lap and mope.

I was called to dinner: steam silvered my mother's glasses as she said 12 grace; my brother and sister with their heads bowed made ugly faces at their glasses of powdered milk. I gagged too, but eagerly ate big rips of buttered tortilla that held scooped up beans. Finished, I went outside with my jacket across my arm. It was a cold sky. The faces of clouds were piled up, hurting. I climbed the fence, jumping down with a grunt. I started up the alley and soon slipped into my jacket, that green ugly brother who breathed over my shoulder that day and ever since.

❁   ❁   ❁

AFTER YOU READ

• *THINK* about Soto's reaction to his jacket. Do you think the jacket caused other people to shun him or think less of him as he believed? Or did Soto simply blame the jacket for every problem he had during those years?

• *EXAMINE* the following definition of the word *symbol.*

> *Symbol:* Something that represents something else by association, resemblance, or convention, especially a material object representing something invisible (*The American Heritage College Dictionary,* 3rd ed. Boston: Houghton Mifflin, 1993).

Does the jacket in Soto's story function as a symbol? That is, does it represent something more than simply an article of clothing? If so, what do you think it represents?

- *EXAMINE* also the last sentence of the essay:

> I started up the alley and soon slipped into my jacket, that green ugly brother who breathed over my shoulder that day and ever since.

What do you think Soto is implying in this sentence?

- *WRITE* a paragraph or essay describing in detail an article of clothing that you either liked or disliked and tell how that particular garment made you feel.

Salvation

LANGSTON HUGHES

✤

*Langston Hughes lived from 1902 to 1967, and during the
last forty-five years of his life, he was considered by many
to be America's foremost African-American literary figure.
From his beginnings as a poet in Harlem to his later success
as a playwright and fiction writer, Hughes depended on his
personal experiences and the racial and cultural history of
African-Americans as his primary sources. The story below, which is taken from his autobiography* The Big Sea,
*tells of a rite of passage he experienced at a revival meeting
he attended when he was twelve years old.*

BEFORE YOU READ

▪ *THINK* about a time in your life when you experienced an important rite
of passage—an occasion or ceremony that marked your passing from one
stage of your life to another.

▪ *EXAMINE* the first two sentences of this story. Notice that the second
sentence somewhat contradicts the first. Which sentence do you think is
more accurate and why?

▪ *WRITE* in your journal an objective account of some event that marked
a rite of passage for you. Describe the setting, what happened, who was
there, what was said, and so on.

AS YOU READ

Notice that this story can also be interpreted as an account of how the
author became acquainted with sin.

I was saved from sin, when I was going on thirteen. But not really saved. 1
It happened like this. There was a big revival at my Auntie Reed's church.

Every night for weeks there had been much preaching, singing, praying, and shouting, and some very hardened sinners had been brought to Christ, and the membership of the church had grown by leaps and bounds. Then just before the revival ended, they held a special meeting for children, "to bring the young lambs to the fold." My aunt spoke of it for days ahead. That night I was escorted to the front row and placed on the mourners' bench with all the other young sinners, who had not yet been brought to Jesus.

My aunt told me that when you were saved you saw a light, and 2 something happened to you inside! And Jesus came into your life! And God was with you from then on! She said you could see and hear and feel Jesus in your soul. I believed her. I had heard a great many old people say the same thing and it seemed to me they ought to know. So I sat there calmly in the hot, crowded church, waiting for Jesus to come to me.

The preacher preached a wonderful rhythmical sermon, all moans and 3 shouts and lonely cries and dire pictures of hell, and then he sang a song about the ninety and nine safe in the fold, but one little lamb was left out in the cold. Then he said: "Won't you come? Won't you come to Jesus? Young lambs, won't you come?" And he held out his arms to all us young sinners there on the mourners' bench. And the little girls cried. And some of them jumped up and went to Jesus right away. But most of us just sat there.

A great many old people came and knelt around us and prayed, old 4 women with jet black faces and braided hair, old men with work-gnarled hands. And the church sang a song about the lower lights are burning, some poor sinners to be saved. And the whole building rocked with prayer and song.

Still I kept waiting to *see* Jesus.   5

Finally all the young people had gone to the altar and were saved, but 6 one boy and me. He was a rounder's son named Westley. Westley and I were surrounded by sisters and deacons praying. It was very hot in the church, and getting late now. Finally Westley said to me in a whisper: "God damn! I'm tired o' sitting here. Let's get up and be saved." So he got up and was saved.

Then I was left all alone on the mourners' bench. My aunt came and 7 knelt at my knees and cried, while prayers and songs swirled all around me in the little church. The whole congregation prayed for me alone, in a mighty wail of moans and voices. And I kept waiting serenely for Jesus, waiting, waiting—but he didn't come. I wanted to see him, but nothing happened to me. Nothing! I wanted something to happen to me, but nothing happened.

I heard the songs and the minister saying: "Why don't you come? My 8
dear child, why don't you come to Jesus? Jesus is waiting for you. He wants
you. Why don't you come? Sister Reed, what is this child's name?"

"Langston," my aunt sobbed.   9

"Langston, why don't you come? Why don't you come and be saved? 10
Oh, Lamb of God! Why don't you come?"

Now it was really getting late. I began to be ashamed of myself, holding 11
everything up so long. I began to wonder what God thought about Westley,
who certainly hadn't seen Jesus either, but who was now sitting proudly
on the platform, swinging his knickerbockered legs and grinning down at
me, surrounded by deacons and old women on their knees praying. God
had not struck Westley dead for taking his name in vain or for lying in the
temple. So I decided that maybe to save further trouble, I'd better lie, too,
and say that Jesus had come, and get up and be saved.

So I got up.   12

Suddenly the whole room broke into a sea of shouting, as they saw me 13
rise. Waves of rejoicing swept the place. Women leaped in the air. My aunt
threw her arms around me. The minister took me by the hand and led me
to the platform.

When things quieted down, in a hushed silence, punctuated by a few 14
ecstatic "Amens," all the new young lambs were blessed in the name of God.
Then joyous singing filled the room.

That night, for the last time in my life but one—for I was a big boy 15
twelve years old—I cried. I cried, in bed alone, and couldn't stop. I buried
my head under the quilts, but my aunt heard me. She woke up and told my
uncle I was crying because the Holy Ghost had come into my life, and
because I had seen Jesus. But I was really crying because I couldn't bear to
tell her that I had lied, that I had deceived everybody in the church, that I
hadn't seen Jesus, and that now I didn't believe there was a Jesus any more,
since he didn't come to help me.

※   ※   ※

AFTER YOU READ

▪ *THINK* about what is meant by the term *saved*. What are the different
ways in which a person can be saved? What is the. meaning of the term as
it is used by Hughes in this story? Do you think the term has more than
one meaning for Hughes?

- *EXAMINE* the author's thesis statement: "I was saved from sin when I was going on thirteen." Does this statement reflect accurately the story that follows? Can the narrative also be viewed as a rite of passage—a transition from one phase of life to another—in which the young man actually becomes acquainted with sin rather than being saved from sin? Which of these interpretations corresponds more closely to your reading of this story? What other interpretations are possible?

- *WRITE* a story about a rite of passage you have experienced. You can use the same event you described in your journal entry or select another one that you have remembered as a result of reading "Salvation." However, in your essay, rather than just describing the event objectively, make some point about what the experience meant or the impact it had on you.

Nobody Listens When I Talk

ANNETTE SANFORD

❁

This story, which appeared in The Best American Short Stories 2000, *is about an uneventful but significant summer in the life of a teen-aged girl who lives in a small town. The author, Annette Sanford, herself lives in a tiny south-Texas town. A native Texan, Sanford has published in both popular magazines and literary journals and has authored two collections of short fiction:* Lasting Attachments *and* Crossing Shattuck Bridge.

BEFORE YOU READ

- *THINK* about how it feels when no one seems to be listening to you or understanding you.

- *EXAMINE* the first paragraph, in which the author sets the scene for her story. Notice especially where the girl in the story is and what she is doing. Notice also the direct way in which the author speaks to her reader in the first sentence and the short, fragmented sentences she uses in this paragraph.

- *WRITE* in your journal about a time when you felt isolated—cut off from or misunderstood by other people.

AS YOU READ

Notice how often the author refers to the swing and to the girl's being in the swing. Think about the motion of swinging and try to determine why swinging is such an important image in this story.

Locate me in a swing. Metal, porch type, upholstered in orange-striped 1 canvas by my mother. I am spending the summer. My sixteenth, but the first I have spent in a swing. I could say I'm here because I have a broken leg (it's true I do have pain) or ear trouble or a very strict father. I could say I like to be alone, that I'm cultivating my mind, that I'm meditating on the state of the universe. I could say a lot of things, but nobody listens when I talk, so I don't. Talk. Not often anyway. And it worries people.

My mother, for instance. She hovers. She lights in a wicker chair by 2 the banister and stares at me periodically. She wears a blue-checked housedress or a green one under the apron I gave her for Christmas with purple rickrack on the hem. She clutches a dustcloth or a broom handle or the Woman's Section of the *Windsor Chronicle*.

"Marilyn," she says, "a girl your age should be up and doing things." 3

Doing things to her is sweeping out the garage or mending all my 4 underwear. Doing things to me is swimming, hanging on the back of a motorcycle, water-skiing. To her, a girl my age is an apprentice woman in training for three meals a day served on time and shiny kitchen linoleum, but she would be happy to see me dancing the Funky Chicken if it would get me on my feet.

I stay prone. I don't want to do her kind of thing, and I can't do mine. 5 The fact is I don't fit anywhere right now. Except in a swing. So here I am, reading.

My father arrives in the evening. He has worked all day in an office 6 where the air conditioner is broken, or with a client who decides at five minutes to five to invest with another company. He flops in the wicker chair and communes with my mother's ghost.

"Marilyn," he says, "a pretty girl like you ought to realize how lucky 7 she is."

Lucky to him is being sixteen with nothing to worry about. My father 8 grew up in Utopia where everyone between two and twenty dwelt in perpetual joy. If he were sixteen now he would have a motorcycle and a beautiful girl riding behind him. But it wouldn't be me. If he were sixteen and not my father, he wouldn't look at me twice.

From time to time my friend comes. I give her half the swing and she 9 sits like a guru and pops her gum. She can do that and still look great. When she blinks, boys fall dead.

"Marilyn," she says, "a girl like you needs a lot of experience with 10 different men."

She will get me a date with her cousin. With her sister-in law's brother. 11 With the preacher's nephew from Syracuse. She will fix me up in the back seat of a car with someone like myself, and we will eat popcorn and watch the drive-in movie and wish it were time to go home.

I could say, "*I'm not that kind of girl at all.* I could say, *someone should* 12
be kissing me madly, buying me violets, throwing himself in front of Amtrak
for want of my careless glance."

Who would listen?   13

So I say, "No." I say, "Maybe next week." Then I lie in the swing and 14
watch the stars come out and wonder why I didn't go.

When you lie in a swing all day you remember a lot. You close your 15
eyes and listen to the locusts humming in the elm trees and you think of
who you are.

You think of you at six, crying into a blue corduroy bedspread because 16
your uncle has laughed at your elephant which has no tusks. You have
drawn it as a gift for him. You have never heard of tusks before.

You think of lying in the big iron bed at Grandpa's house, listening to 17
the cistern water tapping on the stones outside the window, knowing you
are safe because you are the baby and everybody loves you. You think of
the Dancing Class Grand Ball when you are twelve in a pink dress with
ribbons in your hair and a head taller than the boy who brought you. His
mother has made a corsage for you and when you dance it rubs against his
nose. You pretend he pulls away because of this, but when you are sixteen
lying in a swing, you know it was the scent of your own self-doubt mingling
with the rose and lavender that sent you to the chairs waiting by the wall.

When you lie in a swing all day, you live in the world you read about. 18
You drag a bare foot back and forth across the floor and hear the song the
chains sing, but you aren't really you.

You are a woman standing by a table, reading a letter from a box of 19
other letters. A dead man wrote them. His face, as young as yours, he has
given to the baby sleeping by the window where the boats pass. He has
dreamed his own death and written a passage from the Psalms . . . *his days*
are as grass, in the morning they flourish, in the evening they wither and are
cut down.

You are a father counting cracks in the sidewalk passing under your 20
feet. You have waited a long time in a railroad station for a train carrying
the child who walks beside you, who says: *my mother made me come even*
though I hate you.

You are a girl, pregnant, alone in a car you have parked on a country 21
lane. You are kin to the brown cow chewing across the fence. *You are wet*
and sticky and blind, curled in the cow's stomach waiting for your birth.
You are sick in the ditch.

You are a boy in a room with bars on the window, an old woman on 22
white sheets looking at the Good Shepherd trapped in a frame, a child with
a scar on his face.

When you aren't really you, then the who that you are is different 23
somehow: strong, and part of everything . . . sure of a harvest for every
season . . . glad to be sad. You are a riddle with hundreds of answers, a song
with a thousand tunes.

When you lie in a swing all summer, fall comes before you notice. 24
Suddenly elm leaves pave the street, and you have been seventeen for three
days.

It is time to get up. 25

In the kitchen my mother is still in her apron, frying the supper steaks. 26
I sit at the table and eat a grape. I could say, *don't worry about the
underwear. When the time comes, I can mend it. I can cook and clean a
house and love a lonely daughter. I was watching all summer.*

Instead, I yawn, and she looks at me. "A whole summer," she says, and 27
shakes her head.

In the den the weatherman is promising rain. I kiss the top of my 28
father's head where the hair doesn't grow anymore and lay my cheek on
his whiskers. I could say, *I really am, like you said, beautiful.*

"Try something light for a change," he says, and hands me the funnies. 29
I curl on the couch and call my girl friend. She tells me she has kissed a
trumpet player. He has an incredible lip. She tells me bikinis are on sale,
blond men get bald first, mud is good for the skin.

I could tell her, *summer's over.* I could say, *men are born and die and* 30
are born again. The rest is only details. I could say,

roses are red, 31
violets are blue.
I grew up,
But nothing happened to you.
I don't though. It hurts too much. And besides, nobody listens when I 32
talk.

Sometimes not even me. 33

❀ ❀ ❀

AFTER YOU READ

▪ *THINK* about what happens in this story. Are the outward events and
activities the most important elements of the story? What happens in the
story that the author does not explicitly describe? How would you describe
the plot of this story?

- *THINK* also about the image of the swing. How does the girl's swinging all summer reflect what is happening to her? How is this summer a rite of passage for the girl? Compare her rite of passage to that which Langston Hughes describes in "Salvation."

- *EXAMINE* the following paragraph:

> When you lie in a swing all day, you live in the world you read about. You drag a bare foot back and forth across the floor and hear the song the chains sing, but you aren't really you.

In the following four paragraphs (paragraphs 19–22), the girl imagines herself as different characters she has read about. Following these musings, she says:

> When you aren't really you, then the who that you are is different somehow: strong, and part of everything . . . sure of a harvest for every season . . . glad to be sad.

What purpose do you think the girl's dreams of being other people serve?

- *EXAMINE* also the following sentence near the end of the story:

> It is time to get up.

Why is this sentence a significant clue to what happens in this story? What does it indicate about the girl?

- *WRITE* an essay about the passage, or change, from being a child to being an adult. You can focus on your own experiences, or you can generalize about why this transition is significant or difficult for everyone.

Lives on the Boundary

MIKE ROSE

❀

Mike Rose teaches writing at the University of California at Los Angeles and has published scholarly articles about how to teach writing and several books about education, including Lives on the Boundary. *In this book Rose writes about his own life as a member of a struggling family of poor Italian immigrants living in Los Angeles in the 1950s and 1960s. In this selection from that book, he tells about his early childhood, how it shaped his perception of the world, and how different it was from the academic world he later entered.*

BEFORE YOU READ

- *THINK* about how your own environment shaped your life as you were growing up. How was that environment similar to or different from the world in which you now live?

- *EXAMINE* the specific images from the childhood memories Rose identifies: a gnarled lemon tree, thin rugs, a dirt alley, concrete in the sun. What do these images tell you about his life in Los Angeles when he was a child?

- *WRITE* a journal entry in which you describe several specific images you remember vividly from your own childhood environment.

AS YOU READ

Notice the specific details Rose uses in describing his house and neighborhood. Underline those details that provide you with the clearest, most vivid images of this neighborhood that shaped his early view of reality.

Between 1880 and 1920, well over four million Southern Italian peas- 1
ants immigrated to America. Their poverty was extreme and hope-
less—twelve hours of farm labor would get you one lira, about twenty
cents—so increasing numbers of desperate people booked passage for the
United States, the country where, the steamship companies claimed, prosperity was a way of life. My father left Naples before the turn of the century;
my mother came with her mother from Calabria in 1921. They met in
Altoona, Pennsylvania at the lunch counter of Tom and Joe's, a steamy diner
with twangy-voiced waitresses and graveyard stew.

For my mother, life in America was not what the promoters had told 2
her father it would be. She grew up very poor. She slept with her parents
and brothers and sisters in one room. She had to quit school in the seventh
grade to care for her sickly younger brothers. When her father lost his leg
in a railroad accident, she began working in a garment factory where
women sat crowded at their stations, solitary as penitents in a cloister. She
stayed there until her marriage. My father had found a freer route. He was
closemouthed about his past, but I know that he had been a salesman, a
tailor, and a gambler; he knew people in the mob and had, my uncles
whisper, done time in Chicago. He went through a year or two of Italian
elementary school and could write a few words—those necessary to
scribble measurements for a suit—and over the years developed a quiet
urbanity, a persistence, and a slowly debilitating arteriosclerosis.

When my father proposed to my mother, he decided to open a 3
spaghetti house, a venture that lasted through the war and my early years.
The restaurant collapsed in bankruptcy in 1951 when Altoona's major
industry, the Pennsylvania Railroad, had to shut down its shops. My
parents managed to salvage seven hundred dollars and, on the advice of
the family doctor, headed to California, where the winters would be mild
and where I, their seven-year-old son, would have the possibility of a
brighter future.

At first we lived in a seedy hotel on Spring Street in downtown Los 4
Angeles, but my mother soon found an ad in the *Times* for cheap property
on the south side of town. My parents contacted a woman named Mrs.
Jolly, used my mother's engagement ring as a down payment, and moved
to 9116 South Vermont Avenue, a house about one and one-half miles
northwest of Watts. The neighborhood was poor, and it was in transition.
Some old white folks had lived there for decades and were retired. Younger
black families were moving up from Watts and settling by working-class
white families newly arrived from the South and the Midwest. Immigrant
Mexican families were coming in from Baja. Any such demographic mix is

potentially volatile, and as the fifties wore on, the neighborhood would be marked by outbursts of violence.

I have many particular memories of this time, but in general these early years seem a peculiar mix of physical warmth and barrenness: a gnarled lemon tree, thin rugs, a dirt alley, concrete in the sun. My uncles visited a few times, and we went to the beach or to orange groves. The return home, however, left the waves and spray, the thick leaves and split pulp far in the distance. I was aware of my parents watching their money and got the sense from their conversations that things could quickly take a turn for the worse. I started taping pennies to the bottom of a shelf in the kitchen.

My father's health was bad, and he had few readily marketable skills. Poker and pinochle brought in a little money, and he tried out an idea that had worked in Altoona during the war: He started a "suit club." The few customers he could scare up would pay two dollars a week on a tailor-made suit. He would take the measurements and send them to a shop back East and hope for the best. My mother took a job at a café in downtown Los Angeles, a split shift 9:00 to 12:00 and 5:00 to 9:00, but her tips were totaling sixty cents a day, so she quit for a night shift at Coffee Dan's. This got her to the bus stop at one in the morning, waiting on the same street where drunks were urinating and hookers were catching the last of the bar crowd. She made friends with a Filipino cook who would scare off the advances of old men aflame with the closeness of taxi dancers. In a couple of years, Coffee Dan's would award her a day job at the counter. Once every few weeks my father and I would take a bus downtown and visit with her, sitting at stools by the window, watching the animated but silent mix of faces beyond the glass.

My father had moved to California with faint hopes about health and a belief in his child's future, drawn by that far edge of America where the sun descends into green water. What he found was a city that was warm, verdant, vast, and indifferent as a starlet in a sports car. Altoona receded quickly, and my parents must have felt isolated and deceived. They had fallen into the abyss of paradise—two more poor settlers trying to make a go of it in the City of the Angels.

Let me tell you about our house. If you entered the front door and turned right you'd see a small living room with a couch along the east wall and one along the west wall—one couch was purple, the other tan, both bought used and both well worn. A television set was placed at the end of the purple couch, right at arm level. An old Philco radio sat next to the TV, its speaker covered with gold lamé. There was a small coffee table in the center of the room on which sat a murky fish-bowl occupied by two listless guppies. If, on entering, you turned left you would see a green Formica dinner table with four chairs, a cedar chest given as a wedding present to my mother by her mother, a painted statue of the Blessed Virgin Mary, and a black trunk. It also had a plastic chaise longue between the door and the table. I would lie on this and watch television.

A short hallway leading to the bathroom opened on one side to the   9 kitchen and, on the other, to the bedroom. The bedroom had two beds, one for me and one for my parents, a bureau with a mirror, and a chest of drawers on which we piled old shirt boxes and stacks of folded clothes. The kitchen held a refrigerator and a stove, small older models that we got when our earlier (and newer) models were repossessed by two silent men. There was one white wooden chair in the corner beneath wall cabinets. You could walk in and through a tiny pantry to the backyard and to four one-room rentals. My father got most of our furniture from a secondhand store on the next block; he would tend the store two or three hours a day as payment on our account.

As I remember it, the house was pretty dark. My mother kept the blinds   10 in the bedroom drawn—there were no curtains there—and the venetian blinds in the living room were, often as not, left closed. The walls were bare except for a faded picture of Jesus and a calendar from the *Altoona Mirror.* Some paper carnations bent out of a white vase on the television. There was a window on the north side of the kitchen that had no blinds or curtains, so the sink got good light. My father would methodically roll up his sleeves and show me how to prepare a sweet potato or avocado seed so it would sprout. We kept a row of them on the sill above the sink, their shoots and vines rising and curling in the morning sun.

The house was on a piece of land that rose about four feet up from   11 heavily trafficked Vermont Avenue. The yard sloped down to the street, and three steps and a short walkway led up the middle of the grass to our front door. There was a similar house immediately to the south of us. Next to it was Carmen's Barber Shop. Carmen was a short, quiet Italian who, rumor had it, had committed his first wife to the crazy house to get her money. In the afternoons, Carmen could be found in the lot behind his shop playing solitary catch, flinging a tennis ball high into the air and running under it. One day the police arrested Carmen on charges of child molesting. He was released but became furtive and suspicious. I never saw him in the lot again. Next to Carmen's was a junk store where, one summer, I made a little money polishing brass and rewiring old lamps. Then came a dilapidated real estate office, a Mexican restaurant, an empty lot, and an appliance store owned by the father of Keith Grateful, the streetwise, chubby boy who would become my best friend.

Right to the north of us was a record shop, a barber shop presided over 12 by old Mr. Graff, Walt's Malts, a shoe repair shop with a big Cat's Paw decal in the window, a third barber shop, and a brake shop. It's as I write this that I realize for the first time that three gray men could have had a go at your hair before you left our street.

Behind our house was an unpaved alley that passed, just to the north, 13 a power plant the length of a city block. Massive coils atop the building hissed and cracked through the day, but the doors never opened. I used to think it was abandoned—feeding itself on its own wild arcs—until one sweltering afternoon a man was electrocuted on the roof. The air was thick and still as two firemen—the only men present—brought down a charred and limp body without saying a word.

The north and south traffic on Vermont was separated by tracks for 14 the old yellow trolley cars, long since defunct. Across the street was a huge garage, a tiny hot dog stand run by a myopic and reclusive man named Freddie, and my dreamland, the Vermont Bowl. Distant and distorted behind thick lenses, Freddie's eyes never met yours; he would look down when he took your order and give you your change with a mumble. Freddie slept on a cot in the back of his grill and died there one night, leaving tens of thousands of dollars stuffed in the mattress.

My father would buy me a chili dog at Freddie's, and then we would 15 walk over to the bowling alley where Dad would sit at the lunch counter and drink coffee while I had a great time with pinball machines, electric shooting galleries, and an ill-kept dispenser of cheese corn. There was a small, dark bar abutting the lanes, and it called to me. I would devise reasons to walk through it: "'Scuse me, is the bathroom in here?" or "Anyone see my dad?" though I can never remember my father having a drink. It was dark and people were drinking and I figured all sorts of mysterious things were being whispered. Next to the Vermont Bowl was a large vacant lot overgrown with foxtails and dotted with car parts, bottles, and rotting cardboard. One day Keith heard that the police had found a human head in the brush. After that we explored the lot periodically, coming home with stickers all the way up to our waists. But we didn't find a thing. Not even a kneecap.

When I wasn't with Keith or in school, I would spend most of my day 16 with my father or with the men who were renting the one-room apartments behind our house. Dad and I whiled away the hours in the bowling alley, watching TV, or planting a vegetable garden that never seemed to take.

When he was still mobile, he would walk the four blocks down to St. Regina's Grammar School to take me home to my favorite lunch of boiled wieners and chocolate milk. There I'd sit, dunking my hot dog in a jar of mayonnaise and drinking my milk while Sheriff John tuned up the calliope music on his "Lunch Brigade." Though he never complained to me, I could sense that my father's health was failing, and I began devising child's ways to make him better. We had a box of rolled cotton in the bathroom, and I would go in and peel off a long strip and tape it around my jaw. Then I'd rummage through the closet, find a sweater of my father's, put on one of his hats—and sneak around to the back door. I'd knock loudly and wait. It would take him a while to get there. Finally, he'd open the door, look down, and quietly say, "Yes, Michael?" I was disappointed. Every time. Somehow I thought I could fool him. And, I guess, if he had been fooled, I would have succeeded in redefining things: I would have been the old one, he much younger, more agile, with strength in his legs.

The men who lived in the back were either retired or didn't work that 17 much, so one of them was usually around. They proved to be, over the years, an unusual set of companions for a young boy. Ed Gionotti was the youngest of the lot, a handsome man whose wife had run off and who spoke softly and never smiled. Bud Hall and Lee McGuire were two out-of-work plumbers who lived in adjacent units and who weekly drank themselves silly, proclaiming in front of God and everyone their undying friendship or their unequivocal hatred. Old Cheech was a lame Italian who used to hobble along grabbing his testicles and rolling his eyes while he talked about the women he claimed to have on a string. There was Lester, the toothless cabbie, who several times made overtures to me and who, when he moved, left behind a drawer full of syringes and burnt spoons. Mr. Smith was a rambunctious retiree who lost his nose to an untended skin cancer. And there was Mr. Berryman, a sweet and gentle man who eventually left for a retirement hotel only to be burned alive in an electrical fire.

Except for Keith, there were no children on my block and only one or 18 two on the immediate side streets. Most of the people I saw day to day were over fifty. People in their twenties and thirties working in the shoe shop or the garages didn't say a lot; their work and much of what they were working for drained their spirits. There were gang members who sauntered up from Hoover Avenue, three blocks to the east, and occasionally I would get shoved around, but they had little interest in me either as member or victim. I was a skinny, bespectacled kid and had neither the coloring nor the style of dress or carriage that marked me as a rival. On the whole, the days were quiet, lazy, lonely. The heat shimmering over the asphalt had no snap to it; time drifted by. I would lie on the couch at night and listen to the music from the record store or from Walt's Malts. It was new and quick paced, exciting, a little dangerous (the church had condemned Buddy Knox's "Party Doll"), and I heard in it a deep rhythmic need to be made whole with love, or marked as special, or released in some rebellious way. Even the songs about lost love—and there were plenty of them—lifted me right out of my socks with their melodious longing:

> Came the dawn,
> and my heart and her love and the night
> were gone.
> But I know I'll never forget
> her kiss in the moonlight Oooo . . .
> such a kiss Oooo Oooo such a night . . .*

In the midst of the heat and slow time the music brought the promise of its origins, a promise of deliverance, a promise that, if only for a moment, life could be stirring and dreamy.

But the anger and frustration of South Vermont could prove too strong 19 for music's illusion; then it was violence that provided deliverance of a different order. One night I watched as a guy sprinted from Walt's to toss something on our lawn. The police were right behind, and a cop tackled him, smashing his face into the sidewalk. I ducked out to find the packet: a dozen glassine bags of heroin. Another night, one August midnight, an argument outside the record store ended with a man being shot to death. And the occasional gang forays brought with them some ill-fated kid who would fumble his moves and catch a knife.

It's popular these days to claim you grew up on the streets. Men tell 20 violent tales and romanticize the lessons violence brings. But, though it was occasionally violent, it wasn't the violence in South L.A. that marked me, for sometimes you can shake that ugliness off. What finally affected me was subtler, but more pervasive: I cannot recall a young person who was crazy in love or lost in work or one old person who was passionate about a cause or an idea. I'm not talking about an absence of energy—the street toughs and, for that fact, old Cheech had energy. And I'm not talking about an absence of decency, for my father was a thoughtful man. The people I

Such a Night by Lincoln Chase. Copyright © 1953, 1954 (Renewed) by Embassy Music Corporation (BMI) International Copyright Secured. All rights reserved. Reprinted by permission.

grew up with were retired from jobs that rub away the heart or were working hard at jobs to keep their lives from caving in or were anchorless and in between jobs and spouses or were diving headlong into a barren tomorrow: junkies, alcoholics, and mean kids walking along Vermont looking to throw a punch. I developed a picture of human existence that rendered it short and brutish or sad and aimless or long and quiet with rewards like afternoon naps, the evening newspaper, walks around the block, occasional letters from children in other states. When, years later, I was introduced to humanistic psychologists like Abraham Maslow and Carl Rogers, with their visions of self-actualization, or even Freud with his sober dictum about love and work, it all sounded like a glorious fairy tale, a magical account of a world full of possibility, full of hope and empowerment. Sindbad and Cinderella couldn't have been more fanciful.

❀   ❀   ❀

AFTER YOU READ

▪ *THINK* about the life that Rose had as a child, which he describes as "short and brutish or sad and aimless or long and quiet." Rose later escaped this life by excelling in school. What would his adult life have probably been like if he had not had the opportunity to go to college?

▪ *EXAMINE* the contrast that Rose suggests between the life he knew in Los Angeles and the glamorous image of Los Angeles that most people have.

▪ *WRITE* a description of the place where you grew up and tell how that environment shaped who you are today.

Living in Two Worlds

MARCUS MABRY

❊

*Until he went away to boarding school in the ninth grade,
Marcus Mabry lived in New Jersey, part of a poor, over-
crowded household. When he was a student at Stanford
University, a prestigious private school on the West Coast,
Mabry wrote this essay about a trip back to his home in
New Jersey—a journey that he describes as "travel be-
tween the universes of poverty and affluence." His essay
was published in* Newsweek *as part of its "Newsweek on
Campus" series.*

BEFORE YOU READ

▪ *THINK* about the transitions you faced when you started college. Are
transitions also required when you return to your previous life?

▪ *EXAMINE* the title of this essay. How many different worlds do you live
in, and how do these worlds differ from one another?

▪ *WRITE* a journal entry comparing and contrasting your life as a college
student with your life before you started college.

AS YOU READ

Indicate in the margin beside each paragraph whether it focuses on Mabry's
experiences at home or at school.

A round, green cardboard sign hangs from a string proclaiming, "We 1
built a proud new feeling," the slogan of a local supermarket. It is a
souvenir from one of my brother's last jobs. In addition to being a bagger,
he's worked at a fast-food restaurant, a gas station, a garage and a textile
factory. Now, in the icy clutches of the Northeastern winter, he is unemployed. He will soon be a father. He is 19 years old.

In mid-December I was at Stanford, among the palm trees and weighty 2
chore[s] of academe. And all I wanted to do was get out. I joined the rest
of the undergrads in a chorus of excitement, singing the praises of Christmas break. No classes, no midterms, no finals . . . and no freshmen! (I'm a
resident assistant.) Awesome! I was looking forward to escaping. I never
gave a thought to what I was escaping to.

Once I got home to New Jersey, reality returned. My dreaded freshmen 3
had been replaced by unemployed relatives; badgering professors had been
replaced by hard-working single mothers; and cold classrooms by dilapidated bedrooms and kitchens. The room in which the "proud new feeling"
sign hung contained the belongings of myself, my mom and my brother.
But for these two weeks it was mine. They slept downstairs on couches.

Most students who travel between the universes of poverty and 4
affluence during breaks experience similar conditions, as well as the guilt,
the helplessness and, sometimes, the embarrassment associated with them.
Our friends are willing to listen, but most of them are unable to imagine
the pain of the impoverished lives that we see every six months. Each time
I return home I feel further away from the realities of poverty in America
and more ashamed that they are allowed to persist. What frightens me most
is not that the American socioeconomic system permits poverty to continue, but that by participating in that system I share some of the blame.

Last year I lived in an on-campus apartment, with a (relatively) modern 5
bathroom, kitchen and two bedrooms. Using summer earnings, I added
some expensive prints, a potted palm and some other plants, making the
place look like the more-than-humble abode of a New York City Yuppie. I
gave dinner parties, even a *soirée française*.

For my roommate, a doctor's son, this kind of life was nothing 6
extraordinary. But my mom was struggling to provide a life for herself and
my brother. In addition to working 24-hour-a-day cases as a practical nurse,
she was trying to ensure that my brother would graduate from high school
and have a decent life. She knew that she had to compete for his attention
with drugs and other potentially dangerous things that can look attractive
to a young man when he sees no better future.

Living in my grandmother's house this Christmas break restored all 7
the forgotten, and the never acknowledged, guilt. I had gone to boarding
school on a full scholarship since the ninth grade, so being away from
poverty was not new. But my own growing affluence has increased my
distance. My friends say that I should not feel guilty: what could I do
substantially for my family at this age, they ask. Even though I know that
education is the right thing to do, I can't help but feel, sometimes, that I
have it too good. There is no reason that I deserve security and warmth,

while my brother has to cope with potential unemployment and prejudice. I, too, encounter prejudice, but it is softened by my status as a student in an affluent and intellectual community.

More than my sense of guilt, my sense of helplessness increases each 8 time I return home. As my success leads me further away for longer periods of time, poverty becomes harder to conceptualize and feels that much more oppressive when I visit with it. The first night of break, I lay in our bedroom, on a couch that let out into a bed that took up the whole room, except for a space heater. It was a little hard to sleep because the springs from the couch stuck through at inconvenient spots. But it would have been impossible to sleep anyway because of the groans coming from my grand-mother's room next door. Only in her early 60s, she suffers from many chronic diseases and couldn't help but moan, then pray aloud, then moan, then pray aloud.

This wrenching of my heart was interrupted by the 3 A.M. entry of a 9 relative who had been allowed to stay at the house despite rowdy behavior and threats toward the family in the past. As he came into the house, he slammed the door, and his heavy steps shook the second floor as he stomped into my grandmother's room to take his place, at the foot of her bed. There he slept, without blankets on a bare mattress. This was the first night. Later in the vacation, a Christmas turkey and a Christmas ham were stolen from my aunt's refrigerator on Christmas Eve. We think the thief was a relative. My mom and I decided not to exchange gifts that year because it just didn't seem festive.

A few days after New Year's I returned to California. The Northeast 10 was soon hit by a blizzard. They were there, and I was here. That was the way it had to be, for now. I haven't forgotten; the ache of knowing their suffering is always there. It has to be kept deep down, or I can't find the logic in studying and partying while people, my people, are being killed by poverty. Ironically, success drives me away from those I most want to help by getting an education.

Somewhere in the midst of all that misery, my family has built within 11 me, "a proud feeling." As I travel between the two worlds it becomes harder to remember just how proud I should be—not just because of where I have come from and where I am going, but because of where they are. The fact that they survive in the world in which they live is something to be very proud of, indeed. It inspires within me a sense of tenacity and accomplish-ment that I hope every college graduate will someday possess.

❀ ❀ ❀

AFTER YOU READ

- *THINK* about how this experience of going back and forth between two worlds has shaped the person Mabry has become. Which world has influenced him most? Why?

- *EXAMINE* the number of paragraphs that focus on New Jersey and those that focus on Stanford. Which place does Mabry describe in more detail? Why?

- *EXAMINE* also the following statement, which is found in paragraph 10:

  Ironically, success drives me away from those I most want to help by getting an education.

Explain what you think Mabry means by this statement. Do you agree or disagree with him? Why?

- *WRITE* an essay in which you compare and contrast two different "worlds" in which you live or between which you travel.

Hearing the Sweetest Songs

NICOLETTE TOUSSAINT

✿

Nicolette Toussaint, who lives in San Francisco, describes herself as "a writer, a painter, a slapdash housekeeper, a gardener who grows wondrous roses," as well as a hearing-disabled person. In this article, she describes what it is like to have a hearing disability and argues that an understanding of how disabled people function can benefit everyone.

BEFORE YOU READ

- *THINK* of some way in which you are "disabled"—some way in which you have difficulty functioning.

- *EXAMINE* the title of this essay. Predict why Toussaint chose this title.

- *WRITE* in your journal about someone you know who is disabled in some way, focusing especially on what you have learned from this individual.

AS YOU READ

Try to determine the difference between the terms *unable* and *disabled* as they are used by Toussaint.

Every year when I was a child, a man brought a big, black, squeaking machine to school. When he discovered I couldn't hear all his peeps and squeaks, he would get very excited. The nurse would draw a chart with a deep canyon in it. Then I would listen to the squeaks two or three times, while the adults—who were all acting very, very nice—would watch me raise my hand. Sometimes I couldn't tell whether I heard the squeaks or just imagined them, but I liked being the center of attention. 1

My parents said I lost my hearing to pneumonia as a baby; but I knew 2
I hadn't *lost* anything. None of my parts had dropped off. Nothing had
changed: if I wanted to listen to Beethoven, I could put my head between
the speakers and turn the dial up to 7, I could hear jets at the airport a
block away. I could hear my mom when she was in the same room—if I
wanted to. I could even hear my cat purr if I put my good ear right on top
of him.

I wasn't aware of *not* hearing until I began to wear a hearing aid at the 3
age of 30. It shattered my peace: shoes creaking, papers crackling, pencils
tapping, phones ringing, refrigerators humming, people cracking knuckles,
clearing throats and blowing noses! Cars, bikes, dogs, cats, kids all seemed
to appear from nowhere and fly right at me.

I was constantly startled, unnerved, agitated—exhausted. I felt as 4
though inquisitorial Nazis in an old World War II film were burning the
side of my head with a merciless white spotlight. Under that onslaught, I
had to break down and confess: I couldn't hear. Suddenly, I began to
discover many things I couldn't do.

I couldn't identify sounds. One afternoon, while lying on my side 5
watching a football game on TV, I kept hearing a noise that sounded like
my cat playing with a flexible-spring doorstop. I checked, but the cat was
asleep. Finally, I happened to lift my head as the noise occurred. Heard
through my good ear, the metallic buzz turned out to be the referee's
whistle.

I couldn't tell where sounds came from. I couldn't find my phone under 6
the blizzard of papers on my desk. The more it rang, the deeper I dug. I
shoveled mounds of paper onto the floor and finally had to track it down
by following the cord from the wall.

When I lived alone, I felt helpless because I couldn't hear alarm clocks, 7
vulnerable because I couldn't hear the front door open and frightened
because I wouldn't hear a burglar until it was too late.

Then one day I missed a job interview because of the phone. I had 8
gotten off the subway 20 minutes early, eager and dressed to the nines. But
the address I had written down didn't exist! I must have misheard it: I
searched the street, becoming overheated, late and frantic, knowing that if
I confessed that I couldn't hear on the phone, I would make my odds of
getting hired even worse.

For the first time, I felt unequal, disadvantaged and disabled. Now that 9
I had something to compare, I knew that I *had* lost something; not just my
hearing, but my independence and my sense of wholeness. I had always
hated to be seen as inferior, so I never mentioned my lack of hearing. Unlike

a wheelchair or a white cane, my disability doesn't announce itself. For most of my life, I chose to pass as abled, and I thought I did it quite well.

But after I got the hearing aid, a business friend said, "You know, Nicolette, you think you get away with not hearing, but you don't. Sometimes in meetings you answer the wrong question. People don't know you can't hear, so they think you're daydreaming, eccentric, stupid—or just plain rude. It would be better to just tell them."

I wondered about that then, and I still do. If I tell, I risk being seen as *un*able rather than *dis*abled. Sometimes, when I say I can't hear, the waiter will turn to my companion and say, "What does she want?" as though I have lost my power of speech.

If I tell, people may see *only* my disability. Once someone is labeled "deaf," "crippled," "mute," or "aged," that's too often all they are. I'm a writer, a painter, a slapdash housekeeper, a gardener who grows wondrous roses; my hearing is just part of the whole. It's a tender part, and you should handle it with care. But like most people with a disability, I don't mind if you ask about it.

In fact, you should ask, because it's an important part of me, something my friends see as part of my character. My friend Anne always rests a hand on my elbow in parking lots, since several times, drivers who assume that I hear them have nearly run me over. When I hold my head at a certain angle, my husband, Mason, will say, "It's a plane" or "It's a siren." And my mother loves to laugh about the things I *thought* I heard: last week I was told that "the Minotaurs in the garden are getting out of hand." I imagined capering bullmen and I was disappointed to learn that all we had in the garden were overgrown "baby tears."

Not hearing can be funny, or frustrating. And once in a while, it can be the cause of something truly transcendent. One morning at the shore I was listening to the ocean when Mason said, "Hear the bird?" What bird? I listened hard until I heard a faint, unbirdlike, croaking sound. If he hadn't mentioned it, I would never have noticed it. As I listened, slowly I began to hear—or perhaps imagine—a distant song. Did I *really* hear it? Or just hear in my heart when he shared with me? I don't care. Songs imagined are as sweet as songs heard, and songs shared are sweeter still.

That sharing is what I want for all of us. We're all just temporarily abled, and every one of us, if we live long enough, will become disabled in some way. Those of us who have gotten there first can tell you how to cope with phones and alarm clocks. About ways of holding a book, opening a door and leaning on a crutch all at the same time. And what it's like to give up in despair on Thursday, then begin all over again on Friday, because there's no other choice—and because the roses are beginning to bud in the garden.

These are conversations we all should have, and it's not that hard to 16 begin. Just let me see your lips when you speak. Stay in the same room. Don't shout. And ask what you want to know.

❀   ❀   ❀

AFTER YOU READ

- *THINK* about the following statement, which is found in paragraph 12:

   Once someone is labeled "deaf," "crippled," "mute," or "aged," that's too often all they are.

Do you agree or disagree that people who are disabled are often defined by other people strictly on the basis of their disability? Why or why not?

- *EXAMINE* the following sentence, found in paragraph 15:

   We're all just temporarily abled, and every one of us, if we live long enough, will become disabled in some way.

How does this statement support Toussaint's argument that we can all learn from people who have disabilities?

- *WRITE* an essay in which you identify some "disability" you have and tell how it affects you and other people's perception of you.

Respecting Who You Are

JEFFREY S. NEVID
and
SPENCER A. RATHUS

✿

Who you are depends to a significant degree upon who you think you are—your opinion of yourself. The following "test" is designed to measure your self-concept or self-esteem. Although such tests are never able to measure accurately a complex phenomenon like self-esteem, you may gain some insight into how you feel about yourself from taking this test.

BEFORE YOU READ

- *THINK* about how you feel about yourself. Would you rate your self-esteem as high, average, or low?
- *EXAMINE* the directions carefully before you take the test.
- *WRITE* in your journal about your own self-esteem.

AS YOU READ

Notice the traits that are included in the test and think about why these particular traits were chosen.

Look at each item on the scales below and write the letter *S* in the space 1
that best represents your self-description of that trait. Use the number code 1–7 as your guide, as in the following example of the trait of fairness:

1 = extremely fair	5 = somewhat unfair
2 = rather fair	6 = rather unfair
3 = somewhat fair	7 = extremely unfair
4 = equally fair or unfair, or not sure	

When you have completed your self-description, go back through each 2 of the items and write the letter *I* in the space that best represents your ideal self, or who you think you ought to be. Using the number codes, determine the difference between your *S* score and *I* score on each trait. Your self-esteem is a measure of how well you like and respect yourself. Traits that have low discrepancy scores on this scale most likely make a positive contribution toward your self-esteem. Traits that have a large difference score may indicate areas you should work on to improve your self-esteem.

	1 2 3 4 5 6 7	
fair	___:___:___:___:___:___:___	unfair
independent	___:___:___:___:___:___:___	dependent
religous	___:___:___:___:___:___:___	irreligious
unselfish	___:___:___:___:___:___:___	selfish
self-confident	___:___:___:___:___:___:___	lacking confidence
competent	___:___:___:___:___:___:___	incompetent
important	___:___:___:___:___:___:___	unimportant
attractive	___:___:___:___:___:___:___	unattractive
educated	___:___:___:___:___:___:___	uneducated
sociable	___:___:___:___:___:___:___	unsociable
kind	___:___:___:___:___:___:___	cruel
wise	___:___:___:___:___:___:___	foolish
graceful	___:___:___:___:___:___:___	awkward
intelligent	___:___:___:___:___:___:___	unintelligent
artistic	___:___:___:___:___:___:___	inartistic
tall	___:___:___:___:___:___:___	short
obese	___:___:___:___:___:___:___	skinny

❀   ❀   ❀

AFTER YOU READ

- *THINK* about the results of your test. According to the test, how well do you like yourself? Do you think this test measures your self-esteem accurately? Did you learn anything about yourself by taking the test? If so, what? Compare the results of this test with the journal entry you wrote before you took the test. According to the test, is your self-esteem better or worse than you thought?

- *EXAMINE* the list of traits again. Which three traits do you value most? Why?

- *WRITE* an analysis of your self-esteem based on the results of this test. Try to organize your individual responses into several broad categories so that you can make two or three generalizations about your self-esteem. Then explain each of these generalizations in some detail, using information from the test as well as your general knowledge of yourself to support each generalization.

A Thanksgiving Feast in Aburi

MAYA ANGELOU

❀

*The well-known African-American writer Maya Angelou
has written several autobiographical works, and her poems
have appeared in various collections. In this excerpt from*
All God's Children Need Traveling Shoes, *which was
published in 1986, Angelou describes a celebration that
took place in Aburi, Africa, while she was visiting there.
Her narrative account also suggests the change that occurs
in her as she first observes and then participates in this
celebration of thanksgiving.*

BEFORE YOU READ

▪ *THINK* about a time when you gained a new sense of identity or a new
perception of yourself as a result of an experience you had.

▪ *EXAMINE* the first paragraph of this narrative, which is only one sentence: "The music of the Fanti language was becoming singable to me, and
its vocabulary was moving orderly into my brain." Notice how calm,
detached, and analytical Angelou's language is in this sentence. Here she
is obviously assuming the role of observer—one who is interested in but
not a part of what is occurring.

▪ *WRITE* a brief account of some event you participated in as an observer
rather than a true participant (for example, a family reunion, parade,
ballgame, party, or religious ceremony).

AS YOU READ

Notice the change that occurs in Angelou as the celebration progresses. Pay
particular attention to the image of the handkerchief that Angelou uses to
suggest the change she undergoes.

The music of the Fanti language was becoming singable to me, and its 1
vocabulary was moving orderly into my brain.

Efua took me to a durbar, a thanksgiving feast in Aburi, about thirty 2
miles from Accra. Thousands of gaily dressed celebrants had gathered,
waving, singing and dancing. I stood on the edge of the crowd to watch
the exotic parade. Hunters, rifles across their shoulders, marched in rhythm
to their own drummers. Soldiers, with faces set in grim determination,
paced down the widened roads behind their drummers while young girls
screamed approval. Farmers bearing scythes and fishermen carrying nets
were welcomed loudly by the throng.

The annual harvest ritual gave each segment in the society its oppor- 3
tunity to thank God and to praise its workers and their yield.

I was swaying to the rhythm when the drums stopped, and the crowd 4
quieted. The restless air steadied. A sound, unlike the other sounds of the
day, commenced in the distance. It was the harsh tone of hundreds of giant
cicadas grinding their legs together. Their rasping floated to us and the
crowd remained quiet but edgy with anticipation. When men appeared out
of the dust scraping sticks against corrugated dry gourds, the crowd
recovered its tongue.

"Yee! Yee! Awae! Awae!" 5

The scrapers, like the paraders who preceded them, gave no notice to 6
the crowd or to the small children who ran unceremoniously close to their
serried ranks.

Rasp, Rasp. Scrape! Scrape, Scour, Scrunch, Scrump. Rasp, Rasp! 7
Scree! The raspers faded into a dim distance.

The deep throb of royal drums was suddenly heard in the distance and 8
again the din of celebration stopped. The people, although quiet again,
continued to move, sidle, exchange places and wipe their brows. Women
adjusted the clothes which held babies securely to their backs. Rambunctious children played tag, men and women waved at each other, smiled,
but kept looking toward the sound of the drums.

Efua touched my shoulder and offered me a large white handkerchief. 9

I said, "Thank you, but I'm all right." She kept her hand extended. I 10
took the handkerchief.

Men emerged out of the dim dust. One set had giant drums hefted 11
onto their shoulders, and others followed in splendid cloth, beating the
drums with crooked sticks. The powerful rhythms rattled my bones, and I
could feel the vibrations along the edges of my teeth.

People began clapping, moving their feet, their hands, hips and 12
heads. They shouted clamorously, "Yee! Yee! Aboma!" And there was still

a sense of anticipation in the turbulence. They were waiting for a climax.

When the first palanquin hove into view, I thought of a Chinese junk 13 on the Yangtze (which I had never seen), and a ten-ton truck on a California freeway (which I knew well). Long poled hammocks, sturdy as Conestogas, were carried by four men. In the center of each conveyance sat a chief, gloriously robed in rich hand-woven Kente cloth. At his side (only a few chiefs were female) sat a young boy, called the Kra, who, during an earlier solemn ceremony, had received the implanted soul of the chief. If the chief should die during the ritual, there would be no panic, for his people would know that his soul was safe in the young boy's body and, with the proper ritual, could be placed into the body of the chief's successor.

The drums beckoned, the kings appeared, and the air nearly collapsed 14 under the weight of dust and thudding drums and shouting jubilation.

Each chief was prouder than the one preceding him. Each dressed in 15 more gold and richer colors. Each black beyond ebony and shining with oil and sweat. They arrived in single file to be met by the adoring shouts of their subjects. "Na-na. Na-na." "Yo, Yo, Nana." The shouting united with the thumping of the drums and the explosion of color. Women and men bounced up and down like children's toys, and children not tall enough to see over the crowd were lifted by the nearest adults to see their passing royalty.

A flutter of white billowed over that excited scene. Thousands of 16 handkerchiefs waving from thousands of black hands tore away my last reserve. I started bouncing with the entranced Ghanaians, my handkerchief high above my head, I waved and jumped and screamed, "Na-na, na-na, na-na."

❀   ❀   ❀

AFTER YOU READ

▪ *THINK* about the change that occurs in Angelou as she observes the celebration. She obviously changes from an observer to a participant, but what does this change in roles suggest? Remember that Angelou is African-American and that this trip to Africa was a journey into her ethnic origins.

▪ *EXAMINE* the last sentence in this narrative and compare its emotional tone and content with the detached tone and content of the first sentence.

▪ *EXAMINE* also the descriptive details that Angelou includes in her narrative. Her account of the celebration consists of a series of vivid images. To what senses (sight, sound, etc.) do these images appeal? Which is the strongest image for you as a reader?

▪ *WRITE* a description of the change that occurs in Angelou as the narrative progresses. Conclude your description by discussing why you think these changes occurred and what they mean.

Getting Started

JANET CAMPBELL HALE

Janet Campbell Hale is a member of the Coeur d'Alene
tribe of Northern Idaho. She was born and raised on a
reservation. Most of Hale's books reflect her experiences
as a Native American (for example, Bloodlines, Odyssey
of a Native Daughter, and The Owl's Song). However,
rather than emphasizing her Native American background,
in this poem Hale focuses on the universal dilemma of
wanting to be a special type of person but failing to attain
this goal because of daily concerns and affairs.

BEFORE YOU READ

• *THINK* about your goals for your own life. What do you want to
accomplish? What sort of person do you want to be?

• *EXAMINE* the word *transcend*, which appears in the fifth line of the
poem. The word means "to rise above" (or, literally, "to rise across," since
trans means "across"). As you read the poem, determine what the speaker
wants to transcend.

• *WRITE* in your journal a list of your short-range goals and then a list of
your long-term goals. Beside each goal that is within your control, write
the word *I*. Beside each goal that depends upon the action or attitude of
someone else, write the word *other*. Beside each goal that depends upon
luck or good fortune, write the word *luck*. Then look at your list to
determine how many of your goals depend primarily on your own efforts.

AS YOU READ

Try to determine whether the person in the poem has real reasons for not
achieving her goals or is merely making excuses. Underline the reasons she
gives and decide how valid each is.

Getting Started

It isn't that I've forgotten
Or don't intend to do
With my life what I
Know I should,
That is, transcend the petty concerns　　　5
And live
In truth
And in beauty
according to the
Higher aims of my existence.　　　10
Yet,
I have trouble
getting started
somehow
And day by day,　　　15
Hour by hour,
Wait,
For the spell
to be broken,
And go on,　　　20
Life as usual,
minute by minute,
pulse beat
by
pulse beat,　　　25
paying bills,
doing the laundry,
going to work,
putting band-aids
on little scraped knees,　　　30
watching TV,
Swept along
　　and along.

❀　❀　❀

AFTER YOU READ

▪ *THINK* about the goals the woman has set for herself. Is it realistic to expect to live "In truth/And in beauty/according to the/Higher aims of . . . existence?" Would less ambitious, less abstract goals be more attainable?

▪ *EXAMINE* through a careful rereading the details of the woman's daily life. Are these daily tasks unimportant? For example, is "putting band-aids on little scraped knees" unimportant? Mark other daily tasks mentioned in the poem and evaluate each one in terms of its importance.

▪ *WRITE* an essay in which you evaluate your goals. Are they realistic and attainable? Are they within your own control, or do they depend on others or good fortune? Are you, like the woman in the poem, focusing on future plans and failing to enjoy the life you are now living—the life that sweeps you along day by day?

Unit One: Critical Thinking and Writing Assignments

❀   ❀   ❀

EXPLORING IDEAS TOGETHER

1. Using the selections from this unit as examples, discuss with a group of your classmates the concept of self-esteem and how it is formed.

2. With a group of your classmates, discuss the effects of physical appearance on a person's self-image. Do you know an attractive person who has low self-esteem or an unattractive person who has high self-esteem? Is it important that others consider a person attractive, or is it only how the person feels about his or her own appearance that matters? Consider in your discussion the essays by Gary Soto and Lylah M. Alphonse.

3. In a small group discuss whether a person should set extremely high, perhaps even unattainable, goals or realistic goals that can be attained. You may want to reread the poem "Getting Started" by Janet Campbell Hale.

4. Compare the selection by Sandra Cisneros with the one by Anna Quindlen. Focusing on the attitudes of the two writers toward their names, make two lists: one the ways in which the two writers agree, and the other the ways in which they disagree.

5. There are different theories about how human personalities are constructed. Some theorists believe that genetic factors are most important, others believe that parental influence is what shapes a person, and a new theory argues that peer influence is the most important element in determining who a person becomes. Still others argue that people are the products of the language and culture of the community in which they are reared. Discuss these different theories, focusing on which one you find most convincing.

6. Discuss how and why a person may change as he or she passes from one stage of life to another. Consider in your discussion the reading selections in this unit that focus on different rites of passage that mark the transitions from one stage of life to another (e.g., "Salvation" by Langston Hughes, "Nobody Listens When I Talk" by Annette Sanford, "A Thanksgiving Feast in Aburi" by Maya Angelou, and "Living in Two Worlds," by Marcus Mabry).

WRITING ESSAYS

1. Write an essay in which you identify and discuss one or more of the long-range goals you have set for yourself. In your essay examine your goals and show how these goals have affected your life.

2. In this unit several selections share the theme of isolation (for example, those by Sandra Cisneros, Gary Soto, Annette Sanford, and Nicolette Toussaint). Write an essay in which you focus on this theme, using at least one of the selections in this unit as a source.

3. Describe the environment in which you grew up in such a way that you suggest how that environment shaped you and/or your image of yourself. You may want to refer to the essays by Sandra Cisneros, Gary Soto, Mike Rose, and Marcus Mabry.

4. Using the selections by Mike Rose and Marcus Mabry as models, write an essay in which you discuss the role that education plays in shaping a person's life.

5. Write an essay in which you apply the ideas about self-esteem in "Respecting Who You Are" (by Jeffrey S. Nevid and Spencer A. Rathus) to one or more of the following selections: "My Name" by Sandra Cisneros, "The Name Is Mine" by Anna Quindlen, "I'm Just Me" by Lylah M. Alphonse, "Nobody Listens When I Talk" by Annette Sanford, "Lives on the Boundary" by Mike Rose, "Hearing the Sweetest Songs" by Nicolette Toussaint, and "A Thanksgiving Feast in Aburi" by Maya Angelou.

6. Reread the essays by Sandra Cisneros and Anna Quindlen. Then write an essay about the significance of names.

Self with Family

One of the first and most important relationships that you establish is with your family of origin. In fact, to a great extent you are defined in terms of your initial family experiences. Who you become depends on who you were—your position in your family, your relationship with different members of your family, your perception of yourself as part of your family. As you grow older, you will probably establish a new family, but that family will almost certainly be a reflection of the one in which you grew up. Even if you choose consciously and deliberately to change the old patterns, they will still be there at some level.

This unit includes reading selections that encourage you to explore the relationships within your family and to define yourself more clearly in terms of these relationships. You will read about traditional and nontraditional families, about successful and unsuccessful families, and about how families can help you and hurt you. All of the selections encourage you to think about how you define a family and how a family defines you.

For many years, our ideas of family were based on what sociologist Ian Robertson calls the "middle-class 'ideal' family so relentlessly portrayed in TV commercials, one that consists of a husband, a wife, and their dependent children." To incorporate the complexity of modern family structures, Robertson more openly defines a family as "a relatively permanent group of people related by ancestry, marriage, or adoption, who live together, form an economic unit, and take care of their young." How does this definition compare with the way you define a family? Does it describe your own family as well as the families of your friends? Can you think of any family that it does not describe?

Before you begin this unit, take a few minutes to write about your own family. Use one or more of the following questions to guide your writing:

1. Describe the family in which you grew up. Was it traditional or nontraditional, small or large, wealthy or poor, happy or unhappy?
2. If you have already established a family of your own, how is it similar to or different from the one in which you grew up?
3. To what member of your family are you closest? Why?
4. What member of your family do you most resemble? In what way(s)?
5. What would you change about your family if you could?
6. What would you not want to change?
7. What role (s) do you play in your family?
8. How is your family different from other families? How is your family like other families?

As you read the selections in this unit, remember also to annotate the text—to underline important or interesting ideas, to circle words that you do not know, and to write questions and comments in the margins. Your annotations are, in effect, a dialogue with the author that will increase your comprehension, forcing you to think actively and productively about the subject and how it relates to you.

_____

*Robertson, Ian. *Sociology,* 3rd ed. (New York: Worth, 1987), pp. 348–349.

No Snapshots in the Attic: A Granddaughter's Search for a Cherokee Past

CONNIE MAY FOWLER

❁

Connie May Fowler is the author of four novels, including Sugar Cage, Before Women Had Wings, *and* Remembering Blue. *Each of these novels was inspired in some way by her childhood experiences in the St. Augustine area of Florida, but it is her second novel,* River of Hidden Dreams, *that is most closely related to her personal experiences. Her father's early death having left her living in poverty with her alcoholic mother, Fowler looked to her paternal grandmother, Oneida Marie Hunter May, for aid and inspiration not only in her life but also in her writings. Frustrated by her grandmother's having hidden her own Native American past and by the lack of physical and factual evidence of her own personal heritage—both Native American and European, Fowler begins a physical and mental journey that leads her back to the ancient oral art of storytelling.*

BEFORE YOU READ

▪ *THINK* about your own sense of family heritage. Do you feel that you "know" your ancestors—your grandparents and even great-grandparents that you may not have ever met? If so, how did you learn about these ancestors? Do you feel that your life is richer for this knowledge? If you do not feel that you know your ancestors, do you believe that you have lost something valuable? Explain.

▪ *EXAMINE* the title "No Snapshots in the Attic." Fowler expands this idea in the second paragraph when she declares that "our attics are empty."

What do you think she means by these statements? What, besides snapshots, might be missing from her life?

▪ *WRITE* a journal entry about the ancestor who intrigues you the most. Is
your interest piqued more by what you *know* or what you *do not know*
about this person? How have you acquired the information you have?
What additional information would you like to have?

AS YOU READ

Trace the physical and mental journey that Fowler makes in search of her
Cherokee past. What roadblocks does she encounter in this search? How
does she finally achieve a sense of this past?

For as long as anyone can remember, poverty has crawled all over the   1
hearts of my family, contributing to a long tradition of premature deaths
and a lifetime of stories stymied behind the mute lips of the dead. The
survivors have been left without any tangible signs that evoke the past: no
photographs or diaries, no wedding bands or wooden nickels.

This absence of a record seems remarkable to me since our bloodline   2
is diverse: Cherokee, Irish, German, French; you would think that at least
a few people would have had the impulse to offer future generations a few
concrete clues as to who they were. But no; our attics are empty. Up among
the cobwebs and dormer-filtered light you will find not a single homemade
quilt, not one musty packet of love letters.

Lack of hard evidence of a familial past seems unnatural to me, but I   3
have developed a theory. I believe that my relatives, Indians and Europeans
alike, couldn't waste free time on preserving a baby's first bootee. There
were simply too many tales to tell about each other, living and dead, for
them to be bothered by objects that would only clutter our homes and our
minds.

The first time I noticed this compulsion to rid ourselves of handed-   4
down possessions was in the summer of my eighth year when my mother
decided to fix the front screen door, which was coming off its hinges. As
she rummaged through a junk drawer for a screwdriver, she came upon a
dog-eared photograph of her father. He stood in front of a shack, staring
into the camera as though he could see through the lens and into the eyes
of the photographer. "Oh, that old picture," my mother said disdainfully.
"Nothing but a dust catcher." She tossed the photo in the trash, pulled up
a chair, lit a cigarette and told me about how her Appalachian-born daddy

could charm wild animals out of the woods by standing on his front porch
and singing to them.

The idea that my family had time only for survival and storytelling ₅
takes on special significance when I think of my grandmother, my father's
mother, Oneida Hunter May, a Cherokee who married a white man. Hers
was a life cloaked in irony and sadness, yet 30 years after she died her
personal history continues to suggest that spinning tales is a particularly
honest and noble activity.

Throughout her adult life, the only time Oneida Hunter May felt free ₆
enough to claim her own heritage was in the stories she told her children.
At all other times, publicly and privately, she declared herself white. As
both a writer and a granddaughter, I have been haunted by her decision to
excise her Indian heart and I have struggled to understand it. Of course,
her story would work its way into my fiction, but how it did and what I
would learn about the truth of cultural and familial rumors when they
contradict the truth of our official histories would change the way I see the
world, the way I write, and how and whom I trust.

Until I became an adult this is what I accepted as true about my ₇
grandmother: She was a Cherokee Indian who married a South Carolinian
named John May. Early in the marriage they moved to St. Augustine, Fla.
They had three children, two boys and a girl. Shortly after moving to
Florida, John May abandoned his wife and children. The family believed
he joined the circus. (When I was a child my family's yearly pilgrimage to
the Greatest Show on Earth took on special significance as I imagined that
my grandfather was the lion tamer or the high-wire artist.) Grandmama
May was short and round. While she was straightforward with the family
about her Indian ancestry, she avoided instilling in us a shred of Native
American culture or custom. Through the use of pale powder and rouge,
she lightened her skin. Her cracker-box house on the wrong side of the
tracks was filled with colorful miniature glass animals and hats and boots,
all stolen from tourist shops downtown. According to my father, she was
"run out of town on a rail" more than once because of the stealing, and
she even spent time in the city jail. Her laughter was raucous. She tended
to pick me up by putting her hands under my armpits, which hurt, and it
seemed as if every time I saw her she pinched my cheeks, which also hurt.
My grandmother mispronounced words and her syntax was jumbled. I've
since realized that her strange grammar patterns and elocution were the
results of having no formal education and of speaking in a language that
was not her native tongue.

For me, growing up was marked not only by a gradual loss of innocence ₈
but by the loss of the storytellers in my life: grandparents, aunts and uncles,

parents. With them went my ability to believe and know simple truths, to accept the face value of things without needless wrestling. As the cynicism of adulthood took hold, I began to doubt the family stories about my grandmother and I even decided my recollections were warped by time and the fuzzy judgment of childhood, and that the stories were based on oral tradition rooted in hearsay. What is this ephemeral recitation of our lives anyway? A hodgepodge of alleged fact, myth and legend made all the more unreliable because it goes unchecked by impartial inquiry. After all, don't scholars dismiss oral histories as anecdotal evidence?

I told myself I was far too smart to put much stock in my family's 9 Homeric impulses. In choosing to use my grandmother's life as a stepping-off point for a new novel, I decided that everything I knew as a child was probably exaggerated at best and false at worst. I craved empirical evidence, irrefutable facts; I turned to government archives.

I began my inquiry by obtaining a copy of my grandmother's death 10 certificate. I hoped it would provide me with details that would lead to a trail back to her early life and even to her birth. The document contained the following data: Oneida Marie Hunter May was born Aug. 14, 1901, in Dillon, S.C. She died June 8, 1963, of diabetes. But from there her history was reduced to no comment. Line 13, father's name: five black dashes. Line 14, mother's maiden name: five dashes. Line 16, Social Security number: none. The most chilling, however, because it was a lie, was line 6, color or race: white.

Her son, my uncle J. W., was listed as the "informant." Perhaps he 11 thought he was honoring her by perpetuating her longstanding public falsehood. Perhaps, despite what he knew, he considered himself white— and therefore so was she. Perhaps in this small Southern town he was embarrassed or frightened to admit his true bloodline. Did he really not know his grandparents' names? Or did he fear the names would suggest his Indian lineage? Whether his answers were prompted by lack of knowledge or a desire to be evasive, the result was that the "facts" of the death certificate were suspect. The information recorded for posterity amounted to a whitewash. The son gave answers he could live with, which is what his mother had done, answers that satisfied a xenophobic society.

Thinking that perhaps I had started at the wrong end of the quest, I 12 went in search of her birth certificate. I contacted the proper office in South Carolina and gave the clerk what meager information I had. I realized that without a Social Security number, my chances of locating such a document were slim, but I thought that in its thirst for data the government might have tracked Indian births. "No, I'm sorry," I was told over the phone by the clerk who had been kind enough to try an alphabetical search. "South Carolina didn't keep detailed files on Indians back then. You could try the Cherokees, but I don't think it will help. In those days they weren't keeping good records either."

I was beginning to understand how thoroughly a person can vanish   13 and how—without memory and folklore—one can be doomed to oblivion. But I pursued history, and I changed my focus to Florida. I began reading accounts of St. Augustine's Indian population in the last century, hoping to gain insight into my grandmother's experience. There is not a great amount of documentation, and most of what does exist was written by long-dead Roman Catholic missionaries and Army generals, sources whose objectivity was compromised by their theological and military mandates. Nevertheless, I stumbled on an 1877 report by Harriet Beecher Stowe about the incarceration of Plains Indians at Castillo de San Marcos (then called Fort Marion) at the mouth of the St. Augustine harbor.

During their imprisonment, which lasted from 1875 to 1878, the Indians   14 were forced to abandon their homes, religions, languages, their dress and all other cultural elements that white society deemed "savage"—a term used with alarming frequency in writings of the time. Calling the Indians in their pre-Christian state "untamable," "wild" and "more like grim goblins than human beings," Stowe apparently approved of what they became in the fort: Scripture-citing, broken-spirited Indians dressed like their tormentors, United States soldiers. She writes, "Might not the money now constantly spent on armies, forts and frontiers be better invested in educating young men who shall return and teach their people to live like civilized beings?"

The written record, I was discovering, was fabulous in its distortion,   15 and helpful in its unabashedness. It reflected not so much truth or historical accuracy as the attitudes of the writers.

The most obvious evidence of the unreliable nature of history is the   16 cultural litany set down in tourist brochures and abstracted onto brass plaques in parks and on roadsides across America. My family has lived for three generations in St. Augustine, "The Oldest Continuously Inhabited City in America. Founded in 1565." What this proclamation leaves out is everything that preceded the town's European founding. Like my uncle's carefully edited account of my grandmother's life, St. Augustine's official version amounts to historical genocide because it wipes away all traces of the activities and contributions of a specific race. For hundreds of years this spit of land between two rivers and the sea was the thriving village of Seloy, home to the Timucuan Indians. But while still aboard a ship, before

ever stepping onto the white and coral-colored shores of the "New World,"
Pedro Menéndez renamed Seloy in honor of the patron saint of his
birthplace. Then he claimed this new St. Augustine and all of "La Florida"
to be the property of Spain; the Timucuans and their culture had been
obliterated by a man at sea gazing at their land.

These distinctions between European facts and Indian facts are not trivial. 17
The manipulation of our past is an attempt, unconscious or not, to stomp
out evidence of the success and value of other cultures. My grandmother's
decision to deny her heritage was fueled by the fear of what would happen
to her if she admitted to being an Indian and by the belief that there was
something inherently inferior about her people. And the falsehoods and
omissions she lived by affected not just her; her descendants face a personal
and historical incompleteness.

   But when the official chronicles are composed of dashes and distor- 18
tions and you still hunger for the truth, what do you do? For me, the answer
was to let my writer's instincts take over. I slipped inside my grandmother's
skin and tried to sort out her motives and her pain. I imagined her birth
and what her mother and father might have looked like. I gave them names,
Nightwater and Billy. I called the character inspired by my grandmother
Sparrow Hunter. She would bear a daughter, Oneida. And it would be
Oneida's offspring, Sadie Hunter, who would uncover the stories that
revealed the truth.

   But I needed to know how a young Indian woman with three babies 19
to feed survives after she's been abandoned in a 1920's tourist town that
promoted as its main attraction an ancient and massive fort that had served
as a prison for Comanches, Kiowas, Seminoles, Apaches, Cheyennes,
Arapaho, Caddos and others. The writer-granddaughter listened to her
blood-born voices and heard the answers. Her grandmother made up a
birthplace and tried to forget her native tongue. She stayed out of the sun
because she tanned easily, and she bought the palest foundations and
powders available. She re-created herself. For her children and grandchildren never to be called "Injun" or "savage" must have been one of her most
persistent hopes. And what bitter irony it must have been that her children
obeyed and took on the heritage of the man who had deserted them. I was
discovering that my novel would be far better served if I stopped digging
for dates and numbers and instead strove to understand my grandmother's
pain.

My research had another effect, one far more important than causing me 20
to question our written record. It pushed me forward along the circle,

inching me back to where I had started: the oral history. My family has relentlessly nurtured its oral tradition as though instinctively each of us knew that our attics would be empty for generations but our memory-fed imaginations could be filled to overbrimming with our tales of each other. And certainly, while the stories are grandiose and often tall, I decided they are no more slanted than what is fed to us in textbooks.

I have come to view my family's oral history as beautifully double- 21 edged, for in fiction—oral or written—there is a desire to reveal the truth, and that desire betrays my grandmother's public lie. It is in the stories shared on our beloved windy porches and at our wide-planked pine tables, under the glare of naked moth-swept light bulbs, that the truth and the betrayal reside. Had my grandmother not felt compelled to remember her life before John May stepped into it and to relate to little Henry and J. W. and Mary Alice what times were like in South Carolina in the early 1900's for a dirt-poor Indian girl, then a precious link to her past and ours would have been lost forever. And while she raised her children to think of themselves as solely white, she couldn't keep secret who she really was.

Those must have been wondrous moments when she tossed aside the 22 mask of the liar to take up the cloak of the storyteller. It was a transformation rooted in our deepest past, for she transcended her ordinary state and for a brief time became a shaman, a holy person who through reflection, confession and interpretation offered to her children an opportunity to become members of the family of humankind, the family that traces its history not through DNA and documents but through the follies and triumphs, the struggles and desires of one another. So I turn to where the greatest measure of truth exists: the stories shared between mother and child, sister and brother, passed around the table like a platter of hot biscuits and gravy and consumed with hungry fervor.

My attempt to write about my grandmother's life was slow and often 23 agonizing. But turning a tangle of information and inspiration into a novel and into a facet of the truth that would shine was the process of becoming a child again, of rediscovering the innocence of faith, of accepting as true what I have always known. I had to believe in the storyteller and her stories again.

The novel my grandmother inspired is fiction, for sure, but it reinforces 24 the paradox that most writers, editors and readers know: fiction is often truer than nonfiction. A society knows itself most clearly not through the allegedly neutral news media or government propaganda or historical records but through the biased eyes of the artist, the writer. When that vision is tempered by heaven and hell, by an honesty of the intellect and gut, it allows the reader and viewer to safely enter worlds of brutal truth, confrontation and redemption. It allows the public as both voyeur and safely distanced participant to say, "Aha! I know that man. I know that woman. Their struggles, their temptations, their betrayals, their triumphs are mine."

One of my favorite relatives was Aunt Emily, J. W.'s wife. I saw her the night of my father's death in 1966 and—because my aunt and uncle divorced and because my father's death was a catastrophic event that blew my family apart—I did not see her again until 1992. She was first in line for the hometown book signing of my debut novel, "Sugar Cage." We had a tearful and happy reunion, and before she left she said, "I remember the day you were born and how happy I was that you were named for your Grandmother Oneida." 25

I looked at her stupidly for a moment, not understanding what she was saying. Then it dawned on me that she misunderstood my middle name because we pronounced Oneida as though it rhymed with Anita. "Oh no," I told her. "My name is Connie Anita." Aunt Emily smiled and said, "Sweetheart, the nurse wrote it down wrong on your birth certificate. All of us except for your grandmother got a big laugh out of the mistake. But believe me, it's what your parents said: you're Connie Oneida." 26

I loved that moment, for it was a confirmation of the integrity of our oral histories and the frailties of our official ones. As I go forward with a writing life, I accept that my creative umbilical cord is attached to my ancestors. And to their stories. I've decided to allow their reflective revelations to define me in some measure. And I have decided not to bemoan my family's bare attics and photo albums, because as long as we can find the time to sit on our porches or in front of our word processors and continue the tradition of handing down stories, I believe we will flourish as Indians, high-wire artists, animal charmers and writers all. And the truth will survive. It may be obscured occasionally by the overblown or sublime, but at least it will still be there, giving form to our words and fueling our compulsion to tell the tale. 27

❀   ❀   ❀

AFTER YOU READ

▪ *THINK* about Fowler's two different heritages: European and Native American. Does she find these heritages to be complementary or contradictory? How does she become reconciled to both? With which does she ultimately identify? If, like Fowler, you have a mixed heritage, how have you reconciled the different elements of your ancestry?

▪ *EXAMINE* this description of Fowler's grandmother as storyteller:

> It was a transformation rooted in our deepest past, for she transcended her ordinary state and for a brief time became a shaman, a holy person who through reflection, confession and interpretation offered to her children an opportunity to become members of the family of humankind, the family that traces its history not through DNA and documents but through the follies and triumphs, the struggles and desires of one another. So I turn to where the greatest measure of truth exists: the stories shared between mother and child, sister and brother, passed around the table like a platter of hot biscuits and gravy and consumed with hungry fervor. (Paragraph 22)

As this passage suggests, family stories provide not only family history but also important family beliefs and values. Which images in this passage are the most effective and why? What does this passage tell you about Native American life in particular?

▪ *WRITE* a summary of this reading selection. Structure your summary around the four main sections in the reading, but remember to include in your summary only main ideas and not the specific details that you would include in an essay. Or *WRITE* a story about your family—one that reveals something about your family's history, values, or goals. Your story might be one of those "passed around the table like a platter of hot biscuits" from family member to family member, or it might be one that you "make up" from clues that you have about one of your ancestors. Like Fowler in her search for her Cherokee grandmother, you can try to "slip inside the skin" of this person and tell the story through his or her eyes.

Hold the Mayonnaise

JULIA ALVAREZ

❀

Distinguished Latina poet and novelist Julia Alvarez is the author of numerous books of poetry and fiction and the recipient of many awards, including the American Library Association's notable book award for her first book, How the Garcia Girls Lost Their Accents. *As a child, Alvarez and her family were forced to leave the Dominican Republic for political reasons. Her experiences as an immigrant finding her place in America and her interest in family relationships involving different cultures are major subjects in her work. In this selection, Alvarez focuses specifically on the relationship between a Latina stepmother and her American stepdaughters.*

BEFORE YOU READ

• *THINK* about the stereotype of "the stepmother" as found in stories such as Hansel and Gretel. Have such stories caused you to form a negative opinion of stepmothers in general? Have you personally known any "stepmothers"? How do your personal experiences and observations compare or contrast with the stereotype?

• *EXAMINE* the title of this selection. With what culture is mayonnaise most closely associated? Can you think of any Latino foods that use mayonnaise?

• *WRITE* a journal entry in which you discuss your reaction—positive or negative—to a particular cultural food.

AS YOU READ

Note in the margin each time Alvarez uses mayonnaise as a symbol of American culture. How do her reactions to this food parallel her reactions to American culture in general and to her new American stepdaughters in particular?

“If I die first and Papi ever gets remarried,” Mami used to tease when we 1 were kids, “don't you accept a new woman in my house. Make her life impossible, you hear?” My sisters and I nodded obediently, and a filial shudder would go through us. We were Catholics, so of course, the only kind of remarriage we could imagine had to involve our mother's death.

We were also Dominicans, recently arrived in Jamaica, Queens, in the 2 early 60's, before waves of other Latin Americans began arriving. So, when we imagined who exactly my father might possibly ever think of remarrying, only American women came to mind. It would be bad enough having a *madrastra,* but a "stepmother."

All I could think of was that she would make me eat mayonnaise, a 3 food I identified with the United States and which I detested. Mami understood, of course, that I wasn't used to that kind of food. Even a madrastra, accustomed to our rice and beans and tostones and pollo frito, would understand. But an American stepmother would think it was normal to put mayonnaise on food, and if she were at all strict and a little mean, which all stepmothers, of course, were, she would make me eat potato salad and such. I had plenty of my own reasons to make a potential stepmother's life impossible. When I nodded obediently with my sisters, I was imagining not just something foreign in our house, but in our refrigerator.

So it's strange now, almost 35 years later, to find myself a Latina 4 stepmother of my husband's two tall, strapping, blond, mayonnaise-eating daughters. To be honest, neither of them is a real aficionado of the condiment, but it's a fair thing to add to a bowl of tuna fish or diced potatoes. Their American food, I think of it, and when they head to their mother's or off to school, I push the jar back in the refrigerator behind their chocolate pudding and several open cans of Diet Coke.

What I can't push as successfully out of sight are my own immigrant 5 childhood fears of having a *gringa* stepmother with foreign tastes in our house. Except now, I am the foreign stepmother in a gringa household. I've wondered what my husband's two daughters think of this stranger in their family. It must be doubly strange for them that I am from another culture.

Of course, there are mitigating circumstances—my husband's two 6
daughters were teen-agers when we married, older, more mature, able to
understand differences. They had also traveled when they were children
with their father, an eye doctor, who worked on short-term international
projects with various eye foundations. But still, it's one thing to visit a
foreign country, another altogether to find it brought home—a real bear
plopped down in a Goldilocks house.

Sometimes, a whole extended family of bears. My warm, loud Latino 7
family came up for the wedding: my *tia* from Santo Domingo; three
dramatic, enthusiastic sisters and their families; my papi, with a thick accent
I could tell the girls found hard to understand; and my mami, who had her
eye trained on my soon-to-be stepdaughters for any sign that they were
about to make my life impossible. "How are they behaving themselves?"
she asked me, as if they were 7 and 3, not 19 and 16. "They're wonderful
girls," I replied, already feeling protective of them.

I looked around for the girls in the meadow in front of the house we 8
were building, where we were holding the outdoor wedding ceremony and
party. The oldest hung out with a group of her own friends. The younger
one whizzed in briefly for the ceremony, then left again before the
congratulations started up. There was not much mixing with me and mine.
What was there for them to celebrate on a day so full of confusion and
effort?

On my side, being the newcomer in someone else's territory is a role 9
I'm used to. I can tap into that struggling English speaker, that skinny,
dark-haired, olive-skinned girl in a sixth grade of mostly blond and
blue-eyed giants. Those tall, freckled boys would push me around in the
playground. "Go back to where you came from!" *"No comprendo!"* I'd
reply, though of course there was no misunderstanding the fierce looks on
their faces.

Even now, my first response to a scowl is that old pulling away. (My 10
husband calls it "checking out.") I remember times early on in the marriage
when the girls would be with us, and I'd get out of school and drive around
doing errands, killing time, until my husband, their father, would be leaving
work. I am not proud of my fears, but I understand—as the lingo goes—
where they come from.

And I understand, more than I'd like to sometimes, my stepdaughters' 11
pain. But with me, they need never fear that I'll usurp a mother's place.
No one has ever come up and held their faces and then addressed me,
"They look just like you." If anything, strangers to the remarriage are

probably playing Mr. Potato Head in their minds, trying to figure out how my foreign features and my husband's fair Nebraskan features got put together into these two tall, blond girls. "My husband's daughters," I kept introducing them.

Once, when one of them visited my class and I introduced her as such, 12 two students asked me why. "I'd be so hurt if my stepmom introduced me that way," the young man said. That night I told my stepdaughter what my students had said. She scowled at me and agreed. "It's so weird how you call me Papa's daughter. Like you don't want to be related to me or something."

"I didn't want to presume," I explained. "So it's O.K. if I call you my 13 stepdaughter?"

"That's what I am," she said. Relieved, I took it for a teensy inch of 14 acceptance. The takings are small in this stepworld, I've discovered. Sort of like being a minority. It feels as if all the goodies have gone somewhere else.

Day to day, I guess I follow my papi's advice. When we first came, he 15 would talk to his children about how to make it in our new country. "Just do your work and put in your heart, and they will accept you!" In this age of remaining true to your roots, of keeping your Spanish, of fighting from inside your culture, that assimilationist approach is highly suspect. My Latino students—who don't want to be called Hispanics anymore—would ditch me as faculty adviser if I came up with that play-nice message.

But in a stepfamily where everyone is starting a new life together, it 16 isn't bad advice. Like a potluck supper, an American concept my mami never took to. ("Why invite people to your house and then ask them to bring the food?") You put what you've got together with what everyone else brought and see what comes out of the pot. The luck part is if everyone brings something you like. No potato salad, no deviled eggs, no little party sandwiches with you know what in them.

❁   ❁   ❁

AFTER YOU READ

▪ *THINK* about how Julia Alvarez felt not only as a new stepmother but as a stepmother to children of a different culture. Describe her feelings toward her new stepdaughters. During the story, how do these feelings change and why?

▪ *EXAMINE* the phrase "my husband's daughters" that Alvarez uses to introduce her stepdaughters. What does this phrase show about her feelings about herself as well as those about her stepdaughters? What prompts her to change the way she introduces her stepdaughters, and how does this simple change improve her relationship with her stepdaughters?

▪ *WRITE* an essay in which you first identify one or more problems of adjustment that are common to stepfamilies such as Alvarez's family. Then propose a solution for the problem(s) that you have identified.

Keepsakes

STEVE SHERWOOD

❦

*Steve Sherwood has worked as a trash collector in Rocky
Mountain National Park, a reporter in Wyoming, a free-
lance writer in Colorado, and a teacher of composition
and creative writing in Montana and Texas. Reflecting his
interest in the people and landscapes of the modern
American West, this story revolves around a young
woman's attempt to cope with the death of her father—a
Kansas farmer—while her family harvests the wheat he
has planted. The story was originally published in* New
Texas *in 1992. Sherwood's work has also appeared in*
Northern Lights, Outside, Riversedge, Descant, *and other
journals.*

BEFORE YOU READ

• *THINK* about the different relationships that can exist in an extended
family—relationships between grandparents and grandchildren, parents
and children, siblings, and various in-laws. Sherwood's story deals with
several of these complex relationships.

• *EXAMINE* the title of the selection, "Keepsakes." A *keepsake* is an object
that an individual keeps to remember an important person or event. Do
you have a keepsake that is important to you? If so, why is it important?

• *WRITE* a journal entry in which you tell the "story" of a keepsake, either
a family or a personal remembrance. Or *WRITE* a journal entry about one
of your family relationships, perhaps a close relationship with a favorite
family member or a relationship that has changed over the years in some
significant way.

AS YOU READ

Look for the keepsake that Sarah chooses to take with her when she leaves her family farm. Try to determine why she selects this particular item and what it means to her.

S arah's brothers stepped down from the combine and grain truck and 1
brushed wheat chaff out of their dark hair. Sarah threw an arm around each of their necks. Looking bone tired behind paper masks that filtered out enough dust to let them work the harvest, they broke her embrace to use aerosol devices that shot medication into their lungs. Then the older of the two, Lane, came over to shake my hand, doing a little bow as if to apologize for his six feet seven inches of bony angles.

I offered to shake with Rhys, shorter and heavier than Lane, until he 2
showed me the oil on his hands.

"What brings you to Kansas?" Lane asked.   3

"Didn't your mother tell you? We're here to help with the harvest."   4

A look passed between my brothers in-law, and they bent to examine 5
the combine's broken drive chain.

"There must be something we can do to make your jobs easier," I said 6
into the silence.

A master mechanic, Rhys patted the combine. "Know what makes one 7
of these tick?"

I looked at the tangle of machinery, half the size of our apartment in 8
Colorado. "My first guess would be a big engine."

They shared the look again, faces impassive. Lane nodded at the worn, 9
two-story farmhouse, neglected in the nine months since their father died and their mother moved to town. "If you like, you can mow the weeds in the yard."

He had to show me how to operate the riding mower, whose engine 10
complained under my weight. I tried to catch Sarah's eye but couldn't. At the time, she still hoped to re-form me in the image of her male relatives, any one of whom, blindfolded, could rebuild a Chevy.

During courtship, our first fight had come when I insisted on having 11
my Subaru serviced. "We never take our cars to the shop," she'd said. "Dad does all the repairs himself."

"Well, I'm not your father!"   12

"No."   13

"And I don't want to be."   14

"Don't worry," she'd said.   15

Now I mowed a forest of goldenrod, sending her brothers scrambling   16
for their breathers. Long before I finished, they climbed back into their
vehicles and drove away. Sarah came over and made a slashing motion
across her throat. I cut the engine, and she said, "Sorry, honey, but the boys
don't need our help."

"So I gathered," I said, a little surprised at the depth of my disappoint-   17
ment. Pulling together as a family to harvest Graham Roberts's wheat,
planted in the weeks before he died, had become important to me somehow.

"You would have loved harvest in the old days," Sarah said. "We used   18
to ride in the combine with Dad; Mom cooked and drove the grain trucks.
The house was filled with people."

She looked at the homestead—empty but for the few rooms Lane   19
occupied—then out across the fields that stretched to the horizon, the earth
that supported the Roberts family for three generations swept into a distant,
chocolate-colored dust devil.

"The boys know we want to help," she said, "and mowing the yard   20
reminded Lane of the southwest quarter. So tomorrow we'll take the
tractors out and cut weeds in the fallow fields."

I was tense that evening in my mother-in-law's backyard because she was   21
spraying Raid at the bugs that flew over the barbecue.

"Do you think you should do that?" I asked.   22

If I'd used her name, I might have stopped her; but we were on a *hey*   23
basis. A year ago, when Sarah announced our wedding plans, Graham had
welcomed me to the family with a smile and a hug, but Sarah's mother
showed the idea little warmth. Now, I felt uncomfortable calling her
Hannah or Mom, and *Mrs. Roberts* rang too formal. So I said, "Hey, are
you sure you want to eat Raid?" as the horseflies and mosquitoes crash-
landed on our burgers.

Sarah's glance cut through the smoke and insecticide to warn that our   24
marriage of ten months might last longer if I said no more. I joined her
paternal grandmother, Electa, who sat nearby and watched Hannah with
a critical expression. The family matriarch, Electa had a deceptively soft
voice that could harden abruptly. She tightly controlled most of the land
Graham had farmed, in part, according to Sarah, because she never took
to her daughter-in-law. From the occasional sparks between them, I gathered the feeling was mutual.

Electa turned to me. "You know, Sarah was the homecoming queen,   25
the prettiest girl in the county. We always figured she'd find herself a farmer
and settle down here."

[. . .] Instead, she escaped and married me. I glanced at Sarah, whose 26
dark-haired, Midwestern beauty drew me to her, and whose loyalty to
family and quiet strength of will made loving her inevitable. We hardly had
time to get to know one another before Graham died and a small,
undefinable part of Sarah seemed to draw away from me. "Hard to figure,
isn't she?" [I asked.]

Lane and Rhys came in from the fields to eat the poisoned burgers with 27
wolfish gratitude, nodding or shaking their heads at the women's questions
without stopping to talk. Electa brooded as they ate, finally blurting out,
"Young people don't appreciate farming anymore. It's a good life if you're
willing to work. Your father knew that."

Still chewing, the brothers avoided her eyes, which shone beneath her 28
bifocals with the hint of tears. "After supper, I'm going to the cemetery,"
Electa said. "Who'll come along?"

Hannah and the boys agreed to go, but I stopped in mid-nod when 29
Sarah said, "I believe I'll stay here."

Electa's face darkened. "Your mother says you haven't visited the grave 30
since the funeral."

I recalled that day as a blur of sympathetic expressions and homemade 31
pies. Sarah wore a fixed smile as she passed the open casket and Hannah
said, "Well, don't he look nice. They even waxed his mustache." Since then,
Sarah had refused to discuss Graham's death even with me.

"I'm staying here," she said now. "You all go on ahead."   32

"Maybe your mother has something to say about showing respect for 33
the dead," Electa said.

But tending a new batch of hamburgers at the barbecue, Hannah only 34
frowned and gave the bugs another shot of Raid.

Dust marked Sarah's position in the next field. Earlier, as Lane explained 35
my tractor's controls, Sarah climbed aboard hers and checked the gauges
like a pro.

"Nothing to it," Lane said. "Drives like a car, except you use the brakes 36
to make sharp turns like a tank. Oh, and the throttle is beside the steering
wheel and you need to raise your undercutting blades before you back up.
Got it?"

"You mean those things?"   37

He clapped me on the shoulder. "You'll do fine."   38

Now Sarah was making orderly passes, leaving a wake of disturbed 39
earth and slashed weeds. I mimicked her, settling into an uneasy
rhythm, warmed when a passing trucker mistook me for a farmer and
waved.

In choosing our vehicles, Sarah had presented me with the old tractor 40
as if bestowing a gift of love. "It was the first in the county with air
conditioning," she'd said. "It's Dad's favorite."

Her use of the present tense worried me. Did she know what she was 41
saying? Should I confront her? I wondered. But when she talked about
Graham, she looked so happy and so fragile that I didn't dare. And in a
way, she was right. His imprint was everywhere, in the arrangement of
outbuildings, in the shape of the fields. He was a big man, an inch or two
over six feet and close to 260 pounds. As I drove, feeling the engine's
heavy throb, I sat in the hollow he'd left in the seat cushion, not quite
filling it. At our wedding, he'd crushed my hand. "You take care of my
Sarah," he said, and he didn't let go till I swore I would. The next time we
shook, he couldn't speak. Sarah flew to Kansas, and I'd driven all night
to be with her. By the time I arrived, though, she'd done her crying and
seemed resigned, almost cheerful, in spite of the septic smell of the cancer
ward.

The tractor drove more or less like a car, as Lane said, and after cutting 42
weeds for most of the morning, I felt I was mastering the controls. Then,
as I cranked the steering wheel into a tight left turn for another pass, the
tractor's front end seemed to sink into the field. The powerful rear wheels
churned and the engine compartment plowed a furrow. When the entire
vehicle tipped to one side and threatened to roll, I cut the engine and
jumped out.

The tractor leaned at an extreme angle, its front wheel assembly 43
jammed under the rear wheels. I circled, bending to examine the snapped
steering column.

"Christ, what have I done?" I muttered.   44

Why hadn't Lane warned me that I couldn't make a sharp turn without 45
losing the front end? With a dreadful feeling that maybe he had, I sat on
the hot dirt. Sarah found me there. Sunbaked, I passively watched her climb
from her tractor and kneel beside me.

"Are you all right?"   46

"I'm sorry, honey," I said.   47

She studied the wreck of Graham's favorite tractor for a while, then 48
leaned her forehead against my shoulder.

We sat in a grain truck at the edge of a rolling wheat field. "Forget it," Lane 49
said. "It's my fault for not doing the maintenance. If Dad was here, it
wouldn't have happened."

I drank some water that tasted faintly of aluminum and went back to 50
watching Rhys work. A grain-reaping maestro, he cut wheat for hours at a

stretch, grim behind his filter mask. Lane drove to the local elevator whenever Rhys filled one of the haul trucks. Meanwhile, I played water boy or
sometimes Lane let me drive, but we all knew I was nothing but ballast.

"It wasn't your fault," Lane repeated.   51

I looked up at him. "Has Sarah ever talked to you about your dad?"   52
He frowned slightly, and I added, "About his death, I mean."

"No need to," he said slowly. "We know how they felt about each other.   53
He loved us all, but he loved Sarah best. You might have noticed, Mom's
not much for hugging and kissing and all. She handed out the punishment
and the religion. Hugging and kissing and comforting—that was Dad's
job."

"Whose job is it now?" I asked.   54

The question seemed to surprise him. "Nobody's, I guess."   55

Rhys drove up then and sent a stream of grain shooting through a   56
curved auger into the truck's bed. Over the noise, Lane shouted, "You and
Sarah are lucky to have somebody."

After a while, I shouted back, "You dating anyone?"   57

He actually blushed. "You don't meet anybody stuck out here on the   58
farm."

"I guess not."   59

"I'm no good with women anyhow," he added. "Too tall."   60

"Maybe you haven't met the right one."   61

"How did you know Sarah was right for you?"   62

I thought for a long time, unable to come up with an answer I could   63
feel sure he'd understand. Finally, I shrugged. "The way she looked at me,
I guess."

At the top of a low hill, a mile from town, a square of green lay among the 64
ripe wheat fields. People drove here to sit in the dark and watch lightning
storms, Sarah said. Families gathered on Decoration Day to spruce up the
graves of ancestors, and one could nearly always find a loyal widow paying
respects.

Sarah did not explain her decision to visit the cemetery, saying only   65
that she wanted my company. From the funeral, I tried to recall whether
Graham's grave lay under the trees or out in the open, but the headstones
cast long shadows in the fading sunlight and everything looked different
to me.

Earlier, Hannah had retrieved Sarah from the fallow fields and brought   66
us lunch, spreading the food out on the tailgate of her pickup. Sarah and

her brothers ate and talked of other harvests, other tailgate lunches. Slapping bologna slices onto white bread, Rhys laughed and said, "Dad sure loved his bologna. Remember? Just like this, with lots of mayo." Maybe Sarah saw something in her mother's face. Anyway, she went over and put her arms around Hannah's neck, only to back away when Hannah's body stiffened at the touch.

"Well then," Hannah muttered, turning away. "I'll be getting back to 67 town."

It took us an hour to find Graham's headstone. By then the bugs and 68 the heat made dramatics on Sarah's part unlikely, even if she were given to them. We stood looking down at the marker, silently reading and rereading his name.

"It's like I thought," Sarah finally said. "He's not here."   69

I looked at her.   70

"I don't know where he is, but it's not here."   71

By the end of the week, Lane and Rhys had brought in all but twenty-five 72 acres of Graham's wheat. "Three or four hours' work and we'll be done," Lane said. "If you want, you can head for home in the morning."

Having finished the weeding, Sarah sat between us in a pair of cut-offs, 73 her bare leg resting against mine. I watched her pop a handful of raw wheat into her mouth.

"You're not eating that!" I said.   74

"It turns to gum if you chew it long enough."   75

I glanced at Lane, who nodded. "Dad taught us."   76

Sarah's jaw muscles bunched as she chewed. "See?" She opened her 77 lips to show a wad of blond gum plastered against her teeth, then startled me by blowing a bubble. "Want some?"

"I don't think so."   78

"You can have some of mine," she offered and smiled in a way I hadn't 79 seen for a long time. We moved closer together.

Lane watched us with an exasperated look and said, "You two want to 80 cut that out?"

Later, Sarah said, "Lane, Grandma says you're going to quit farming." 81

Lane was silent for so long, I wasn't sure he would reply. Finally, he 82 said, "Wasn't for Dad, I never would've kept at it so long. What I'm really interested in is computers."

"How about Rhys?"   83

"He can't stand the dust."   84

"What's going to happen to the farm?"   85

"Jake Hocklemier tried to buy Mom and Grandma out a week after   86
Dad died," he said. "He's gobbling up the county at bargain prices—mostly
from widows with medical bills."

"Will he get our land?"   87

"Probably," Lane said. "If he's patient."   88

Sarah left us and waded out into the wheat. I followed, meaning to   89
comfort her, but when I touched her shoulder she surprised me by smiling
up at me.

"I used to gallop Princess across this field in the spring," she said. "The   90
wheat grass was soft on her hooves, and it always made me feel so free.
Dad knew we were trampling the crop and costing him money, but he never
stopped me."

We waded deeper into the shoulder-high stalks. Finally, she said, "I'm   91
going to miss him."

Rhys drove by in the combine, spewing chaff into the air. The wind   92
caught it and blew it back in our faces as we walked to the truck. From the
cab we watched him mow down what was left of the wheat, leaving stubble
and bare ground. Within three hours, twenty-five acres of wheat became
three loads of grain, which we took turns driving to the elevator.

On the last trip, as we waited to dump our load, Sarah got out and   93
filled a small jar with wheat. She looked embarrassed as she slipped it into
her purse.

"Just a keepsake," she said.   94

❀   ❀   ❀

AFTER YOU READ

▪ *THINK* about the changes in the Roberts family that occurred after
the death of the father. How has Graham Roberts's death affected his
wife? His sons Lane and Rhys? His daughter Sarah? His son-in-law who is
writing the story? Who seems to be affected most by the father's death and
why?

▪ *THINK* also about the time of year in which the story is set. Harvest time
is linked with the death of vegetation, with the gathering of the seeds that
will be planted for the next year's crop. How is this setting particularly
appropriate for this story?

• *EXAMINE* the last three paragraphs of the selection that describe the harvesting of the last wheat. Why is this harvest significant to the family, especially to Sarah? What does the small jar of wheat that she takes as a keepsake symbolize to her?

• *WRITE* an essay in which you describe and discuss the importance of a particular family keepsake. Or, if you don't have such a keepsake, *WRITE* an essay in which you discuss the effect on you (and perhaps your family) of a change in relationships because a family member has died, married, or moved away.

Sibling Imprints

FRANCINE KLAGSBRUN

❀

A successful editor and writer, Francine Klagsbrun has contributed to both the Encyclopedia Americana *and* The World Book Encyclopedia. *She has written many informative books for children and has published essays in* Ms., Seventeen, *and* Newsweek. *In the following selection, which is an excerpt from* Mixed Feelings: Love, Hate, Rivalry, and Reconciliation Among Brothers and Sisters, *Klagsbrun draws on her personal experiences with her brother Robert Lifton, whose success as a businessman parallels Klagsbrun's own success as a writer.*

BEFORE YOU READ

• *THINK* about your personal experiences with (or observations of) sibling relationships. What feelings were dominant in these sibling relationships—love, jealousy, competition, or some other feeling?

• *EXAMINE* the title of the selection. How can siblings "imprint" one another?

• *WRITE* a journal entry about your experiences with (or observations of) a sibling relationship.

AS YOU READ

Identify and mark in some way each anecdote (brief narrative) that Klagsbrun includes in her essay. What purposes do these anecdotes serve in the essay?

One Sunday afternoon of my childhood stands out in sharp relief from all others. It's a grueling hot day in mid-July. We are on the way home—my father and mother, my brother Robert, and I—from a day at

Jones Beach, about an hour's drive from our Brooklyn apartment. I am around six years old and my brother around ten.

We have been inching along, stuck in a massive traffic jam. Perspiring 2 from the stifling heat (air conditioners in cars as yet unknown), our bodies raw from the mixture of sunburn and dried ocean salt and itching from the tiny grains of sand we have not bothered to wipe away with our towels, Robert and I fight constantly in the back seat. Irritated, my father finally pulls off the road and rearranges the seating, my brother in back with my mother, and I with my father up front. To quiet us, he also buys each a Dixie cup—those little round containers filled with equal amounts of chocolate and vanilla ice cream.

I begin nibbling at my ice cream with the flat wooden spoon that 3 accompanies it, and in nibbling I hatch a delicious plan. I will eat slowly, so slowly that I will finish *last*. I'll have ice cream left after Robert has gulped down all of his, and just when he might be wishing for more, I'll produce mine. "Look," I'll say, "*I* still have ice cream to eat." What I will mean is that I have something he doesn't have, that this time I will have beaten him, this older brother whom I adore and idolize, but who has always bested me.

So I nibble slowly at my ice cream with my wooden spoon, and it begins 4 to melt.

"Are you finished with your ice cream?" I call out every few minutes. 5

"No, not yet," he answers. 6

On we drive, and the heat becomes more intense, and the ice cream 7 melts and melts until the chocolate runs into the vanilla, and the cup turns warm and sticky.

"Are you finished yet?" I turn around to try to see how much ice cream 8 he has left, but he holds his cup close to his chest.

"Not yet." And my ice cream is now warm liquid, the chocolate and 9 vanilla completely blended.

Then, finally, triumph. 10

"I'm finished," he says. 11

"Ha-ha," I shout in glorying delight just as I had imagined it. "*I* still 12 have *my* ice cream." I hold up my cup, crushed and leaking now, to show him. "I scream, you scream, we all scream for ice cream," I chant, and in the next moment quickly gulp down the syrupy mixture. It bears little resemblance to the cool treat it had once been, yet nothing I have ever tasted is as pleasing to me as this victory.

"Ha-ha yourself." My brother's voice, rocking with laughter, rises from 13 the back seat as I swallow the last drop. "I fooled you. I still have mine."

Leaning forward, he shows me the leftover in his own cup, then proceeds to drink slowly, all the while bending close to my face so that my utter defeat will not for one second be lost on me.

Tricked! But worse. He has won again. I cannot make my mark. I 14 cannot get a leg up on him, not even with a cup of ice cream soup. I bellow with the pain only a child knows who has been totally outwitted.

"It's not fair!" I scream. "He always gets what he wants. He always has 15 more than I have. I can never win. I can never have anything of my own."

My brother roars with glee. "I scream, you scream, we all scream for 16 ice cream," he mocks as I bawl uncontrollably. My parents laugh also, scolding me for acting like a baby. Why all this fuss? It's nothing more than ice cream, after all. What difference does it make who ate it first?

But I know what the fuss is about. It's about much more than ice cream. 17 It's about coming out ahead for once. It's about establishing myself and holding my own. It's about being recognized.

Decades pass.   18

I am now a writer and my brother a businessman.   19

"You know, don't you," my husband says to me one evening when I'm 20 describing to him some of my research and findings about adult siblings, "that I make a point of trying to avoid putting myself into situations with you that you would perceive as competitive?"

"What do you mean?" I ask cautiously.   21

Although my husband is a psychiatrist, there has long been an unspo- 22 ken agreement between us that he not apply the tools of his profession to our family life. Little psychological jargon ever gets tossed around our home, and few of our discussions—or arguments—serve as sources for analytic interpretations. Now, however, I feel a worm of suspicion gnawing within. What is he trying to tell me?

"You've been talking about the influence of siblings," he says, "and I 23 was thinking that I try to steer clear of situations that would stir up in you the old feelings of competition you have with Robert."

"First of all," I reply, "Robert and I get along just fine. Secondly, my 24 old competitions with him have nothing to do with anything that goes on between us—you and me. Third of all . . ." I hesitate. "So what kinds of situations have you avoided that you think would make me feel competitive toward you?"

"Well," he says slowly, "I haven't written a book, even though I've 25 thought about doing so from time to time."

"Written a book!" I explode. "Why should you write a book? *I'm* the 26 writer in the family. You run a hospital, you hold academic appointments.

You have everything you want. Why should you move in on my turf? Why can't I ever have anything of my own?" Echoing that long-forgotten wail of childhood, I add with fervor, "It's not fair!"

I stop, astonished at the vehemence of my reaction.   27

"Okay," I say, trying to laugh. "You made your point. Maybe I do repeat 28 with you some of the competitive feelings I had with Robert. Let's drop this subject."

"Sure."   29

"Want some ice cream?"   30

I have never been unaware of the importance my brother holds in my 31 life. That awareness, in fact, motivated this book, with its goal of exploring and unraveling the mysteries of sibling attachments. But it was not until I was well into my investigations, not until my conversation with my husband, that I became truly conscious of the lasting imprint my relationship with my brother has had on all aspects of my existence, including my marriage.

What I discovered in myself I have seen operating in others as well. 32 The effects of our early experiences with brothers and sisters remain with us long after childhood has ended, long after the experiences themselves have faded into the past, influencing us as adults in ways we rarely recognize, from the intimate relationships we establish with lovers and spouses, to the attitudes we carry into the workplace, to our behavior toward our children.

The woman who, twice, married and divorced "exciting, dynamic and 33 irresponsible" men much like her younger brother is an example of the potency of that sibling influence. So is the corporate executive who time and again, without realizing it, stops himself from going after the top position in his company because somewhere within he believes that only his older brother and not he is capable of filling such a role. And so too—to take one more example—is the lawyer who describes growing up with a domineering older sister who physically and emotionally grabbed everything from her: clothes, toys, eventually even her friends.

"My sister dominates my life," the lawyer says, although they live miles 34 apart and have little contact. She explains: "I still can't deal with any kind of rivalry. If I know someone else is competing with me for a client, I pull back. But at the same time, I feel despondent if the client doesn't come to me, as if I've lost out to my sister again. I have the same reaction to love triangles. I get into a terrible state if I think another woman is at all interested in a man I'm going out with. I don't want someone I care about to be taken away from me the way my sister took everything that meant something. But neither can I fight for what I want."

More aware of such inner conflicts, perhaps, than many people, she 35 says, "In every relationship that I encounter, I reenact what I had with my sister."

We usually associate such reenactments with our parents, and certainly 36 both professional and popular literature have made us conscious of the dominant and lasting impact of our parents on our lives. Yet the more closely one examines the sibling experience, the more evident it becomes that the bond between brothers and sisters leaves its own stamp, separate and apart from the mark parents make, and, in turn, demands scrutiny on its own.

Unlike the ties between parents and children, the connection among 37 siblings is a horizontal one. That is, sibs exist on the same plane, as peers, more or less equals. Although one may be stronger or more dominant than others, brothers and sisters rarely exert the kind of power and authority over one another that parents hold over their children. Nor are there rules, codes of behavior for different stages of life or biblical commandments mandating siblings to respect and honor one another as they must respect and honor parents. As a result they are freer, more open, and generally more honest with each other, than they are with parents, and less fearful of punishment or rejection. As children, they say what is on their minds, without censoring their words or concerning themselves about the long-range effects of their emotions on one another. Even as adults, many sibs speak more bluntly to each other than they dare to friends or colleagues.

The freedom siblings enjoy with one another and the peer status they 38 hold also allow them greater intimacy than they have with their mothers or fathers. In growing up, sisters and brothers often spend more time alone together than they do with parents, and they get to know each other in ways that their parents never know them. An older child reexperiences her own past in playing with a younger one. The younger learns from sharing the older's activities, and in the process comes to understand both his sib and himself.

Together, siblings become experts in penetrating each other's thoughts 39 and feelings. Studies of empathy among young children have found that toddlers as young as two or three are able to interpret for their parents baby siblings' expressions and noises and explain a baby's wishes that a mother or father doesn't understand. "He wants to go out," an older child will say, or, "She's hungry," or, "Pick her up, Mommy," and usually the information will be correct.

Siblings have a compelling need to accumulate the knowledge they 40
have of each other. Each *wants* to know what makes the other tick. Each
wants to know which buttons to press to make the other cry or cringe. Each
also wants to know how to make the other laugh and how to win the other's
love and approval. In its intensity, their mutual knowledge becomes
all-embracing—a naked understanding that encompasses the very essence
of the other's being.

Once gained, that gut understanding remains a crucial part of the link 41
between siblings for life. Even after years of separation, an adult brother
or sister may quickly, intuitively, pick up on another's thoughts, sympathize
with the other's needs, or zero in—unerringly—on the other's insecurities.

The intimate knowledge siblings hold is not limited to themselves; it 42
also includes knowledge of their parents. Sibs are able to validate for one
another realities about their parents. They may be the only ones who know,
for instance, that beneath the wit and charm the world sees in their parents
lies a cold, mutual anger that causes the family great suffering. More
important, children often blame themselves for a parent's cruel or disturbed behavior. A brother or sister helps free the other from his guilt and
blame, helps define family conditions for the other.

Discussing the pain of growing up with an abusive, alcoholic father, 43
one man said, "My older sister was like an oasis I could escape to. I could
bounce things off her and say, 'Hey, what's happening?' and she would
reassure me that none of it was my fault, that it had nothing to do with
me. I'll always be grateful to her for that."

But even in happy homes young siblings become allies. They may 44
fight and scream at each other, but they also offer one another solace and
safety in a world that appears overwhelmingly stacked in favor of adults.
They share secrets parents never hear, and communicate with each other
through signals and codes, private languages whose meanings only they know.

One of my sweetest recollections of the past is that of lying in bed late 45
at night, speaking to my brother through the wall of our adjoining rooms.
We speak loudly, oblivious of our parents in their bedroom down the hall.
We imitate characters on the radio shows we listen to addictively, or we
talk "silly talk," making up nonsense words and sounds that send us into
peals of laughter and affirm for me that nobody is as clever and funny as
my big brother.

"Shush," my mother quiets us angrily. "Go to sleep, both of you."   46

We snort as we try to squelch the waves of giggles that envelop us, 47
dizzyingly conscious of our superiority to the parents we have excluded
from our club.

"Are you asleep?" we continue to call out to each other in stage 48
whispers until the voice down the hall sounds as though it means business,
and one of us drifts off.

Through their clubby confidences and shared secrets, through the time 49
they spend alone and the knowledge they gain, siblings learn to cooperate
and get along together. They discover the meaning of loyalty, and master
skills in defending one another against the outside even in the midst of their
own angers or vicious battles. They cultivate their ability to have fun, to
laugh and make jokes. They gain their first experiences in knowing
themselves as individuals but also as persons connected to others. In short,
they learn what it means to be "we" and not just "I."

Eventually what siblings learn with each other gets transferred to their 50
dealings with the world beyond the family, to schoolmates and friends, later
to adult peers.

With their learning and knowledge siblings also build a personal 51
history that serves as a reference point through the years. That is not to say
that brothers and sisters have identical histories. Each child in a family
experiences life differently, relates differently to parents, and creates a
different and unique environment for the other. Yet there is a family ethos
and a pool of memories—of parental attitudes, of humor and expectations,
of vacations and hard times—that transcend individual experiences and
form a common past for siblings.

The pull of memory and history and the rewards of sibling compan- 52
ionship draw adult brothers and sisters to each other in spite of their
differences.

❀   ❀   ❀

AFTER YOU READ

• *THINK* about how one sibling can "imprint" or influence another sibling's life. In class discussion, give examples of such imprints from the
reading as well as from your personal experience and observation.

• *EXAMINE* the author's conversation with her husband in paragraphs
20–30. What discovery does she make about herself as well as about her
relationships with her brother and her husband?

• *WRITE* a summary of this selection. Or *WRITE* a brief essay describing a
relationship between siblings. Be sure that your essay contains a clear thesis,
or main point, about that relationship.

Brothers

BRET LOT T

❀

*Bret Lott is a writer of both fiction and nonfiction. He has
published six books of fiction, including, most recently,*
The Hunt Club. *But he has also written* Fathers, Sons, and
Brothers: The Men in My Family, *in which he analyzes
the relationships among the male members of his family.*

*Like the preceding essay by Francine Klagsbrun, "Sib-
ling Imprints," Lott's essay focuses on the relationship
between siblings. Both essays emphasize the antagonism
that often characterizes sibling relationships but also the
real affection that siblings usually feel for each other. Both
Klagsbrun and Lott also use anecdotes, or brief narratives,
to develop their essays. However, Klagsbrun is direct and
explicit, stating her arguments clearly, while Lott tends to
be less explicit, merely implying or suggesting his thesis
rather than stating it as Klagsbrun does.*

BEFORE YOU READ

▪ *THINK* about family pictures and how they often constitute a type of
family history, giving us a glimpse of the past and prompting memories that
might otherwise lie buried. How do pictures differ from verbal records?
Which are "truer"?

▪ *EXAMINE* the different sections of this essay. How many sections do you
identify? Why would a writer divide a brief essay into different sections?
Can you determine a purpose for this format?

▪ *WRITE* in your journal about a family picture or photograph that you
remember well. Describe in detail what the photograph reveals.

Try to determine how the author, as an adult, feels about his brother. Make notes in the margins to indicate the clues that help you understand Lott's attitude toward his brother.

This much is fact: 1

There is a home movie of the two of us, sitting on the edge of the 2 swimming pool at my grandma and grandpa's old apartment building in Culver City. The movie, taken some time in early 1960, is in color, though the color has faded, leaving my brother Brad and me milk-white and harmless children, me a year and a half old, Brad almost four. Our mother, impossibly young, is in the movie, too. She sits next to me, on the right of the screen. Her hair, for all the fading of the film, is coal black, shoulder length and parted in the middle, curled up on the sides. She has on a bathing suit covered in purple and blue flowers, the color in them nearly gone. Next to me, on the left of the screen, is Brad in his white swimming trunks, our brown hair faded to only the thought of brown hair. I am in the center, my fat arms up, bent at the elbows, fingers curled into fists, my legs kicking away at the water, splashing and splashing. I am smiling, the baby of the family, the center of the world at that very instant, though my mother is pregnant, my little brother Tim some six or seven months off, my little sister Leslie, the last child, still three years distant. The pool water before us is only a thin sky blue, the bushes behind us a dull and lifeless light green. There is no sound.

My mother speaks to me, points at the water, then looks up. She lifts 3 a hand to block the sun, says something to the camera. Her skin is the same white as ours, but her lips are red, a sharp cut of lipstick moving as she speaks.

I am still kicking. Brad is looking to his right, off the screen, his feet 4 in the water, too, but moving slowly. His hands are on the edge of the pool, and he leans forward a little, looks down into the water.

My mother still speaks to the camera, and I give an extra hard kick, 5 splash up shards of white water.

Brad flinches at the water, squints his eyes, while my mother laughs, 6 puts a hand to her face. She looks back to the camera, keeps talking, a hand low to the water to keep more from hitting her. I still kick hard, still send up bits of water, and I am laughing a baby's laugh, mouth open and eyes nearly closed, arms still up, fingers still curled into fists.

More water splashes at Brad, who leans over to me, says something. 7
Nothing about me changes: I only kick, laugh.

He says something again, his face leans a little closer to mine. Still I 8
kick.

This is when he lifts his left hand from the edge of the pool, places it 9
on my right thigh, and pinches hard. It's not a simple pinch, not two fingers
on a fraction of skin, but his whole hand, all his fingers grabbing the flesh
just above my knee, and squeezing down hard. He grimaces, his eyes on
his hand, on my leg.

And this is when my expression changes, of course: in an instant I go 10
from a laughing baby to a shocked one, my mouth a perfect O, my body
shivering so that my legs kick even harder, even quicker, but just this one
last time. They stop, and I cry, my mouth open even more, my eyes all the
way closed. My hands are still in fists.

Then Brad's hand is away, and my mother turns from speaking to the 11
camera to me. She leans in close, asking, I am certain, what's wrong.

The movie cuts then to my grandma, white skin and silver hair, seated 12
on a patio chair by the pool, above her a green and white striped umbrella.
She has a cigarette in one hand, waves off the camera with the other.
Though she died eight years ago, and though she, too, loses color with each
viewing, she is still alive up there, still waves, annoyed, at my grandpa and
his camera, the moment my brother pinched hell out of me already gone.

This much is fact, too: 13

Thumbtacked to the wall of my office is a photograph of Brad and me, 14
taken by my wife in November 1980, the date printed on the border. In it
we stand together, I a good six inches taller than he, my arm around his
shoulder. The photograph is black and white, as though the home movie
and its sinking colors were a prophecy, pointed to this day twenty years
later: we are at the tidepools at Portuguese Bend, out on the Palos Verdes
Peninsula; in the background are the stone-gray bluffs, to the left of us the
beginnings of the black rocks of the pools, above us the perfect white of
an overcast sky.

Brad has on a white Panama hat, a gray hooded sweatshirt, beneath it 15
a collarless shirt. His face is smooth-shaven, and he is grinning, lips
together, eyes squinted nearly shut beneath the brim of the hat. It is a goofy
smile, but a real one.

I have on a cardigan with an alpine design around the shoulders, the 16
rest of it white, the shawl collar on it black, though I know it to have been
navy blue. I have on a button-down Oxford shirt, sideburns almost to my

earlobes. I have a mustache, a pair of glasses too large for my face, and I am smiling, my mouth open to reveal my big teeth. It isn't my goofy smile, but a real one, too.

These are the facts of my brother: the four-year-old pinching me, the 17 twenty-four-year-old leaning into me, grinning.

But between the facts of these two images lie twenty years of the play 18 of memory, the dark and bright pictures my mind has retained, embroidered upon, made into things they are, and things they are not. There are twenty years of things that happened between my brother and me, from the fist-fight we had in high school over who got the honeybun for breakfast, to his phone call to me from a tattoo parlor in Hong Kong, where he'd just gotten a Chinese junk stitched beneath the skin of his right shoulder blade; from his showing me one summer day how to do a death drop from the jungle gym at Elizabeth Dickerson Elementary, to his watching while his best friend and our next-door neighbor, Lynn Tinton, beat me up on the driveway of our home, a fight over whether I'd fouled Lynn at basketball. I remember—memory, no true picture, certainly, but only what I have made the truth by holding tight to it, playing it back in my head at will and in the direction I wish it to go—I remember lying on my back, Lynn's knees pinning my shoulders to the driveway while he hit my chest, and looking up at Brad, the basketball there at his hip, him watching.

I have two children now. Both boys, born two and a half years apart.   19

I showed the older one, Zeb—he is almost eight—the photograph, 20 asked him who those two people were.

He held it in his hands a long while. We were in the kitchen. The bus 21 comes at seven-twenty each morning, and I have to have lunches made, breakfasts set out, all before that bus comes, and before Melanie takes off for work, Jacob in tow, to be dropped off at the Montessori school on her way to her office.

I waited, and waited, finally turned from him to get going on his lunch. 22

"It's you," he said. "You have a lot of hair," he said.   23

"Who's the other guy?" I said.   24

I looked at him, saw the concentration on his face, the way he brought 25 the photograph close, my son's eyes taking in his uncle as best he could.

He said, "I don't know."   26

"That's your Uncle Brad," I said. "Your mom took that picture ten 27 years ago, long before you were ever born."

He still looked at the picture. He said, "He has a beard now."   28

I turned from him, finished with the peanut butter, now spread jelly   29
on the other piece of bread. This is the only kind of sandwich he will eat
at school.

He said from behind me, "Only three years before I was born. That's   30
not a long time."

I stopped, turned to him. He touched the picture with a finger.   31

He said, "Three years isn't a long time, Dad."   32

But I was thinking of my question: *Who's the other guy?* and of the   33
truth of his answer: *I don't know.*

Zeb and Jake fight.   34

They are only seven and a half and five, and already Zeb has kicked   35
out one of Jake's bottom teeth. Melanie and I were upstairs wrapping
Christmas presents in my office, a room kept locked the entire month of
December because of the gifts piled up in there.

We heard Jake's wailing, dropped the bucket of Legos and the red and   36
green Ho! Ho! Ho! paper, ran for the hall and down the stairs.

There in the kitchen stood my two sons, Jacob with his eyes wet,   37
whimpering now, a hand to his bottom lip.

I made it first, yelled, "What happened?"   38

"I didn't do it," Zeb said, backing away from me, there with my   39
hand to Jacob's jaw. Melanie stroked Jacob's hair, whispered, "What's
wrong?"

Jacob opened his mouth then, showed us the thick wash of blood   40
between his bottom lip and his tongue, a single tooth, horribly white,
swimming up from it.

"We were playing Karate Kid," Zeb said, and now he was crying. "I   41
didn't do it," he said, and backed away even farther.

One late afternoon a month or so ago, Melanie came home with the   42
groceries, backed the van into the driveway to make it easier to unload all
those plastic bags. When we'd finished, we let the boys play outside, glad
for them to be out of the kitchen while we sorted through the bags heaped
on the counter, put everything away.

Melanie's last words to the two of them, as she leaned out the front   43
door into the near-dark: "Don't play in the van!"

Not ten minutes later Jacob came into the house, slammed shut the   44
front door like he always does. He walked into the kitchen, his hands
behind him. He said, "Zeb's locked in the van." His face takes on the cast
of the guilty when he knows he's done something wrong: his mouth was

pursed, his eyebrows up, his eyes looking right into mine. He doesn't know enough yet to look away. "He told me to come get you."

He turned, headed for the door, and I followed him out onto the porch 45 where, before I could even see the van in the dark, I heard Zeb screaming.

I went to the van, tried one of the doors. It was locked, and Zeb was 46 still screaming.

"Get the keys!" he was saying. "Get the keys!"   47

I pressed my face to the glass of the back window, saw Zeb inside 48 jumping up and down. "My hand's caught," he cried.

I ran into the house, got the keys from the hook beneath the cupboard, 49 only enough time for me to say to Melanie, "Zeb's hand's closed in the back door," and turned, ran back out.

I made it to the van, unlocked the big back door, pushed it up as quick 50 as I could, Melanie already beside me.

Zeb stood holding the hand that'd been closed in the door. Melanie 51 and I both took his hand, gently examined the skin, wiggled fingers, and in the dull glow of the dome light we saw that nothing'd been broken, no skin torn. The black foam lining the door had cushioned his fingers, so that they'd only been smashed a little, but a little enough to scare him, and to make blue bruises there the next day.

But beneath the dome light there'd been the sound of his weeping, then 52 the choked words, "Jacob pulled the door down on me."

From the darkness just past the line of light from inside the van came 53 my second son's voice: "I didn't do it."

I have no memory of the pinch Brad gave me at the edge of an apartment 54 complex pool, no memory of my mother's black hair—now it's a sort of brown—nor even any memory of the pool itself. There is only that bit of film.

But I can remember putting my arm around his shoulder, leaning into 55 him, the awkward and alien comfort of that touch. In the photograph we are both smiling, me a newlywed with a full head of hair, he only a month or so back from working a drilling platform in the Gulf of Mexico. He'd missed my wedding six months before, stranded on the rig, he'd told us, because of a storm.

What I believe is this: that pinch was entry into our childhood; my arm 56 around him, our smiling, the proof of us two surfacing, alive but not unscathed.

And here are my own two boys, already embarked.   57

❀   ❀   ❀

AFTER YOU READ

- *THINK* about facts versus fiction. The author begins by saying "This much is fact." What types of facts does he include? Later, he interprets these facts. Is his interpretation also factual? Is it fiction? Even in an essay such as this one that is based on real people and events, is it possible to stick just with facts?

- *THINK* also about the essay by Klagsbrun. Her thesis is that siblings are always competitive. Do you think Lott and his brother were competitive? Why or why not? What other emotions motivated their behavior?

- *EXAMINE* the final sentence of this essay: "And here are my own two boys, already embarked." To embark means to set forth, as on a journey or a venture. Can you identify the venture on which Lott's two sons are embarking?

- *WRITE* an essay comparing and contrasting the sibling relationships described in the essays by Klagsbrun and Lott. Before you write your essay, determine whether you think the two authors are mainly in agreement about sibling relationships or whether they differ significantly in their views. State your opinion clearly in your introduction.

Two Kinds

AMY TAN

❀

Amy Tan is a well-known Chinese-American author. Her most recent publications include The Bonesetter's Daughter, The Hundred Secret Senses, *and the children's books* The Moon Lady *and* The Chinese Siamese Cat. *As in many families, the mother and daughter in this selection have difficulty understanding and communicating with each other, and ultimately the daughter rebels. "Two Kinds" is taken from Tan's best-selling book* The Joy Luck Club, *which describes the changing relationships between four pairs of Chinese-American mothers and daughters. Here, Jing-Mei Woo tells the story of her mother's determined campaign to force her to excel—to become a child prodigy.*

BEFORE YOU READ

▪ *THINK* about the expectations that your mother or father held for you when you were growing up—and even today. Did either parent push you to excel beyond your ability or ambition? If so, was this challenge a positive one? Or did the challenge backfire, causing you to rebel and achieve less than you might have?

▪ *EXAMINE* the introduction to the story. What do these first three paragraphs suggest to you about the mother's character? About her background and about her dreams for the future?

▪ *EXAMINE* also the word *prodigy,* which is introduced in the second paragraph: "'Of course you can be *prodigy,* too,' my mother told me when I was nine." A prodigy is a person, especially a child, with exceptional talents and abilities. The mother's expectation that Jing-Mei Woo can become a prodigy and the daughter's reactions to this expectation provide the major tension in the story.

- *WRITE* a journal entry discussing the expectations that your parent(s) have, or had, for you.

AS YOU READ

Try to determine how the title relates to the main idea of the story. As ideas occur to you, write them in the margins.

My mother believed you could be anything you wanted to be in 1 America. You could open a restaurant. You could work for the government and get good retirement. You could buy a house with almost no money down. You could become rich. You could become instantly famous.

"Of course you can be prodigy, too," my mother told me when I was 2 nine. "You can be best anything. What does Auntie Lindo know? Her daughter, she is only best tricky."

America was where all my mother's hopes lay. She had come here in 3 1949 after losing everything in China: her mother and father, her family home, her first husband, and two daughters, twin baby girls. But she never looked back with regret. There were so many ways for things to get better.

We didn't immediately pick the right kind of prodigy. At first my mother 4 thought I could be a Chinese Shirley Temple. We'd watch Shirley's old movies on TV as though they were training films. My mother would poke my arm and say, "*Ni kan*"—You watch. And I would see Shirley tapping her feet, or singing a sailor song, or pursing her lips into a very round O while saying, "Oh my goodness."

"*Ni kan,*" said my mother as Shirley's eyes flooded with tears. "You 5 already know how. Don't need talent for crying!"

Soon after my mother got this idea about Shirley Temple, she took me 6 to a beauty training school in the Mission district and put me in the hands of a student who could barely hold the scissors without shaking. Instead of getting big fat curls, I emerged with an uneven mass of crinkly black fuzz. My mother dragged me off to the bathroom and tried to wet down my hair.

"You look like Negro Chinese," she lamented, as if I had done this on 7 purpose.

The instructor of the beauty training school had to lop off these soggy 8
clumps to make my hair even again. "Peter Pan is very popular these days,"
the instructor assured my mother. I now had hair the length of a boy's,
with straight-across bangs that hung at a slant two inches above my
eyebrows. I liked the haircut and it made me actually look forward to my
future fame.

In fact, in the beginning, I was just as excited as my mother, maybe 9
even more so. I pictured this prodigy part of me as many different images,
trying each one on for size. I was a dainty ballerina girl standing by the
curtains, waiting to hear the right music that would send me floating on
my tiptoes. I was like the Christ child lifted out of the straw manger, crying
with holy indignity. I was Cinderella stepping from her pumpkin carriage
with sparkly cartoon music filling the air.

In all of my imaginings, I was filled with a sense that I would soon 10
become *perfect*. My mother and father would adore me. I would be beyond
reproach. I would never feel the need to sulk for anything.

But sometimes the prodigy in me became impatient. "If you don't hurry 11
up and get me out of here, I'm disappearing for good," it warned. "And
then you'll always be nothing."

Every night after dinner, my mother and I would sit at the Formica kitchen 12
table. She would present new tests, taking her examples from stories of
amazing children she had read in *Ripley's Believe It or Not,* or *Good
Housekeeping, Reader's Digest,* and a dozen other magazines she kept in a
pile in our bathroom. My mother got these magazines from people whose
houses she cleaned. And since she cleaned many houses each week, we had
a great assortment. She would look through them all, searching for stories
about remarkable children.

The first night she brought out a story about a three-year-old boy who 13
knew the capitals of all the states and even most of the European countries.
A teacher was quoted as saying the little boy could also pronounce the
names of the foreign cities correctly.

"What's the capital of Finland?" my mother asked me, looking at the 14
magazine story.

All I knew was the capital of California, because Sacramento was the 15
name of the street we lived on in Chinatown. "Nairobi!" I guessed, saying
the most foreign word I could think of. She checked to see if that was
possibly one way to pronounce "Helsinki" before showing me the answer.

The tests got harder—multiplying numbers in my head, finding the 16
queen of hearts in a deck of cards, trying to stand on my head without using

my hands, predicting the daily temperatures in Los Angeles, New York, and London.

One night I had to look at a page from the Bible for three minutes and 17 then report everything I could remember. "Now Jehoshaphat had riches and honor in abundance and . . . that's all I remember, Ma," I said.

And after seeing my mother's disappointed face once again, something 18 inside of me began to die. I hated the tests, the raised hopes and failed expectations. Before going to bed that night, I looked in the mirror above the bathroom sink and when I saw only my face staring back—and that it would always be this ordinary face—I began to cry. Such a sad, ugly girl! I made high-pitched noises like a crazed animal, trying to scratch out the face in the mirror.

And then I saw what seemed to be the prodigy side of me—because I 19 had never seen that face before. I looked at my reflection, blinking so I could see more clearly. The girl staring back at me was angry, powerful. This girl and I were the same. I had new thoughts, willful thoughts, or rather thoughts filled with lots of won'ts. I won't let her change me, I promised myself. I won't be what I'm not.

So now on nights when my mother presented her tests, I performed 20 listlessly, my head propped on one arm. I pretended to be bored. And I was. I got so bored I started counting the bellows of the foghorns out on the bay while my mother drilled me in other areas. The sound was comforting and reminded me of the cow jumping over the moon. And the next day, I played a game with myself, seeing if my mother would give up on me before eight bellows. After a while I usually counted only one, maybe two bellows at most. At last she was beginning to give up hope.

Two or three months had gone by without any mention of my being a 21 prodigy again. And then one day my mother was watching *The Ed Sullivan Show* on TV. The TV was old and the sound kept shorting out. Every time my mother got halfway up from the sofa to adjust the set, the sound would go back on and Ed would be talking. As soon as she sat down, Ed would go silent again. She got up, the TV broke into loud piano music. She sat down. Silence. Up and down, back and forth, quiet and loud. It was like a stiff embraceless dance between her and the TV set. Finally she stood by the set with her hand on the sound dial.

She seemed entranced by the music, a little frenzied piano piece with 22 this mesmerizing quality, sort of quick passages and then teasing lilting ones before it returned to the quick playful parts.

"*Ni kan*," my mother said, calling me over with hurried hand gestures, 23 "Look here."

I could see why my mother was fascinated by the music. It was being 24 pounded out by a little Chinese girl, about nine years old, with a Peter Pan haircut. The girl had the sauciness of a Shirley Temple. She was proudly modest like a proper Chinese child. And she also did this fancy sweep of a curtsy, so that the fluffy skirt of her white dress cascaded slowly to the floor like the petals of a large carnation.

In spite of these warning signs, I wasn't worried. Our family had no 25 piano and we couldn't afford to buy one, let alone reams of sheet music and piano lessons. So I could be generous in my compliments when my mother bad-mouthed the little girl on TV.

"Play note right, but doesn't sound good! No singing sound," com- 26 plained my mother.

"What are you picking on her for?" I said carelessly. "She's pretty good. 27 Maybe she's not the best, but she's trying hard." I knew almost immediately I would be sorry I said that.

"Just like you," she said. "Not the best. Because you not trying." She 28 gave a little huff as she let go of the sound dial and sat down on the sofa.

The little Chinese girl sat down also to play an encore of "Anitra's 29 Dance" by Grieg. I remember the song, because later on I had to learn how to play it.

Three days after watching *The Ed Sullivan Show*, my mother told me what 30 my schedule would be for piano lessons and piano practice. She had talked to Mr. Chong, who lived on the first floor of our apartment building. Mr. Chong was a retired piano teacher and my mother had traded housecleaning services for weekly lessons and a piano for me to practice on every day, two hours a day, from four until six.

When my mother told me this, I felt as though I had been sent to 31 hell. I whined and then kicked my foot a little when I couldn't stand it anymore.

"Why don't you like me the way I am? I'm *not* a genius! I can't play 32 the piano. And even if I could, I wouldn't go on TV if you paid me a million dollars!" I cried.

My mother slapped me. "Who ask you be genius?" she shouted. "Only 33 ask you be your best. For you sake. You think I want you be genius? Hnnh! What for! Who ask you!"

"So ungrateful," I heard her mutter in Chinese. "If she had as much 34 talent as she has temper, she would be famous now."

Mr. Chong, whom I secretly nicknamed Old Chong, was very strange, 35
always tapping his fingers to the silent music of an invisible orchestra. He
looked ancient in my eyes. He had lost most of the hair on top of his head
and he wore thick glasses and had eyes that always looked tired and sleepy.
But he must have been younger than I thought, since he lived with his
mother and was not yet married.

I met Old Lady Chong once and that was enough. She had this peculiar 36
smell like a baby that had done something in its pants. And her fingers felt
like a dead person's, like an old peach I once found in the back of the
refrigerator; the skin just slid off the meat when I picked it up.

I soon found out why Old Chong had retired from teaching piano. He 37
was deaf. "Like Beethoven!" he shouted to me. "We're both listening only
in our head!" And he would start to conduct his frantic silent sonatas.

Our lessons went like this. He would open the book and point to 38
different things, explaining their purpose: "Key! Treble! Bass! No sharps
or flats! So this is C major! Listen now and play after me!"

And then he would play the C scale a few times, a simple chord, and 39
then, as if inspired by an old, unreachable itch, he gradually added more
notes and running trills and a pounding bass until the music was really
something quite grand.

I would play after him, the simple scale, the simple chord, and then I 40
just played some nonsense that sounded like a cat running up and down
on top of garbage cans. Old Chong smiled and applauded and then said,
"Very good! But now you must learn to keep time!"

So that's how I discovered that Old Chong's eyes were too slow to 41
keep up with the wrong notes I was playing. He went through the
motions in half-time. To help me keep rhythm, he stood behind me,
pushing down on my right shoulder for every beat. He balanced pennies on top of my wrists so I would keep them still as I slowly played
scales and arpeggios. He had me curve my hand around an apple and keep
that shape when playing chords. He marched stiffly to show me how to
make each finger dance up and down, staccato like an obedient little
soldier.

He taught me all these things, and that was how I also learned I could 42
be lazy and get away with mistakes, lots of mistakes. If I hit the wrong notes
because I hadn't practiced enough, I never corrected myself. I just kept
playing in rhythm. And Old Chong kept conducting his own private
reverie.

So maybe I never really gave myself a fair chance. I did pick up the 43
basics pretty quickly, and I might have become a good pianist at that young

age. But I was so determined not to try, not to be anybody different that I learned to play only the most ear-splitting preludes, the most discordant hymns.

Over the next year, I practiced like this, dutifully in my own way. And 44 then one day I heard my mother and her friend Lindo Jong both talking in a loud bragging tone of voice so others could hear. It was after church, and I was leaning against the brick wall wearing a dress with stiff white petticoats. Auntie Lindo's daughter, Waverly, who was about my age, was standing farther down the wall about five feet away. We had grown up together and shared all the closeness of two sisters squabbling over crayons and dolls. In other words, for the most part, we hated each other. I thought she was snotty. Waverly Jong had gained a certain amount of fame as "Chinatown's Littlest Chinese Chess Champion."

"She bring home too many trophy," lamented Auntie Lindo that 45 Sunday. "All day she play chess. All day I have no time do nothing but dust off her winnings." She threw a scolding look at Waverly, who pretended not to see her.

"You lucky you don't have this problem," said Auntie Lindo with a sigh 46 to my mother.

And my mother squared her shoulders and bragged: "Our problem 47 worser than yours. If we ask Jing-mei wash dish, she hear nothing but music. It's like you can't stop this natural talent."

And right then, I was determined to put a stop to her foolish pride.   48

A few weeks later, Old Chong and my mother conspired to have me play 49 in a talent show which would be held in the church hall. By then, my parents had saved up enough to buy me a secondhand piano, a black Wurlitzer spinet with a scarred bench. It was the showpiece of our living room.

For the talent show, I was to play a piece called "Pleading Child" from 50 Schumann's *Scenes from Childhood*. It was a simple, moody piece that sounded more difficult than it was. I was supposed to memorize the whole thing, playing the repeat parts twice to make the piece sound longer. But I dawdled over it playing a few bars and then cheating, looking up to see what notes followed. I never really listened to what I was playing. I daydreamed about being somewhere else, about being someone else.

The part I liked to practice best was the fancy curtsy: right foot out, 51 touch the rose on the carpet with a pointed foot, sweep to the side, left leg bends, look up and smile.

My parents invited all the couples from the Joy Luck Club to witness 52 my debut. Auntie Lindo and Uncle Tin were there. Waverly and her two older brothers had also come. The first two rows were filled with children both younger and older than I was. The littlest ones got to go first. They recited simple nursery rhymes, squawked out tunes on miniature violins, twirled Hula Hoops, pranced in pink ballet tutus, and when they bowed or curtsied, the audience would sigh in unison, "Awww," and then clap enthusiastically.

When my turn came, I was very confident. I remember my childish 53 excitement. It was as if I knew, without a doubt, that the prodigy side of me really did exist. I had no fear whatsoever, no nervousness. I remember thinking to myself, This is it! This is it! I looked out over the audience, at my mother's blank face, my father's yawn, Auntie Lindo's stiff-lipped smile, Waverly's sulky expression. I had on a white dress layered with sheets of lace, and a pink bow in my Peter Pan haircut. As I sat down I envisioned people jumping to their feet and Ed Sullivan rushing up to introduce me to everyone on TV.

And I started to play. It was so beautiful. I was so caught up in how 54 lovely I looked that at first I didn't worry how I would sound. So it was a surprise to me when I hit the first wrong note and I realized something didn't sound quite right. And then I hit another and another followed that. A chill started at the top of my head and began to trickle down. Yet I couldn't stop playing, as though my hands were bewitched. I kept thinking my fingers would adjust themselves back, like a train switching to the right track. I played this strange jumble through two repeats, the sour notes staying with me all the way to the end.

When I stood up, I discovered my legs were shaking. Maybe I had just 55 been nervous and the audience, like Old Chong, had seen me go through the right motions and had not heard anything wrong at all. I swept my right foot out, went down on my knee, looked up and smiled. The room was quiet, except for Old Chong, who was beaming and shouting, "Bravo! Bravo! Well done!" But then I saw my mother's face, her stricken face. The audience clapped weakly, and as I walked back to my chair, with my whole face quivering as I tried not to cry, I heard a little boy whisper loudly to his mother, "That was awful," and the mother whispered back, "Well, she certainly tried."

And now I realized how many people were in the audience, the 56 whole world it seemed. I was aware of eyes burning into my back. I felt the shame of my mother and father as they sat stiffly throughout the rest of the show.

We could have escaped during intermission. Pride and some strange 57 sense of honor must have anchored my parents to their chairs. And so we watched it all: the eighteen-year-old boy with a fake mustache who did a magic show and juggled flaming hoops while riding a unicycle. The breasted girl with white makeup who sang from *Madama Butterfly* and got honorable mention. And the eleven-year-old boy who won first prize playing a tricky violin song that sounded like a busy bee.

After the show, the Hsus, the Jongs, and the St. Clairs from the Joy 58 Luck Club came up to my mother and father.

"Lots of talented kids," Auntie Lindo said vaguely, smiling broadly.   59

"That was somethin' else," said my father, and I wondered if he was 60 referring to me in a humorous way, or whether he even remembered what I had done.

Waverly looked at me and shrugged her shoulders. "You aren't a genius 61 like me," she said matter-of-factly. And if I hadn't felt so bad, I would have pulled her braids and punched her stomach.

But my mother's expression was what devastated me: a quiet, blank 62 look that said she had lost everything. I felt the same way, and it seemed as if everybody were now coming up, like gawkers at the scene of an accident, to see what parts were actually missing. When we got on the bus to go home, my father was humming the busy-bee tune and my mother was silent. I kept thinking she wanted to wait until we got home before shouting at me. But when my father unlocked the door to our apartment, my mother walked in and then went to the back, into the bedroom. No accusations. No blame. And in a way, I felt disappointed. I had been waiting for her to start shouting, so I could shout back and cry and blame her for all my misery.

I assumed my talent-show fiasco meant I never had to play the piano again. 63 But two days later, after school, my mother came out of the kitchen and saw me watching TV.

"Four clock," she reminded me as if it were any other day. I was 64 stunned, as though she were asking me to go through the talent-show torture again. I wedged myself more tightly in front of the TV.

"Turn off TV," she called from the kitchen five minutes later.   65

I didn't budge. And then I decided. I didn't have to do what my mother 66 said anymore. I wasn't her slave. This wasn't China. I had listened to her before and look what happened. She was the stupid one.

She came out from the kitchen and stood in the arched entryway of 67 the living room. "Four clock," she said once again, louder.

"I'm not going to play anymore," I said nonchalantly. "Why should I? 68 I'm not a genius."

She walked over and stood in front of the TV. I saw her chest was 69
heaving up and down in an angry way.

"No!" I said, and I now felt stronger, as if my true self had finally 70
emerged. So this was what had been inside me all along.

"No! I won't!" I screamed. 71

She yanked me by the arm, pulled me off the floor, snapped off the 72
TV. She was frighteningly strong, half pulling, half carrying me toward the
piano as I kicked the throw rugs under my feet. She lifted me up and onto
the hard bench. I was sobbing by now, looking at her bitterly. Her chest
was heaving even more, and her mouth was open, smiling crazily as if she
were pleased I was crying.

"You want me to be someone that I'm not!" I sobbed. "I'll never be 73
the kind of daughter you want me to be!"

"Only two kinds of daughters," she shouted in Chinese. "Those who 74
are obedient and those who follow their own mind! Only one kind of
daughter can live in this house. Obedient daughter!"

"Then I wish I wasn't your daughter. I wish you weren't my mother," 75
I shouted. As I said these things I got scared. It felt like worms and toads
and slimy things crawling out of my chest, but it also felt good, as if this
awful side of me had surfaced, at last.

"Too late change this," said my mother shrilly. 76

And I could sense her anger rising to its breaking point. I wanted to 77
see it spill over. And that's when I remembered the babies she had lost in
China, the ones we never talked about. "Then I wish I'd never been born!"
I shouted. "I wish I were dead! Like them."

It was as if I had said the magic words. Alakazam!—and her face went 78
blank, her mouth closed, her arms went slack, and she backed out of the
room, stunned, as if she were blowing away like a small brown leaf, thin,
brittle, lifeless.

It was not the only disappointment my mother felt in me. In the years 79
that followed, I failed her so many times, each time asserting my own
will, my right to fall short of expectations. I didn't get straight As. I
didn't become class president. I didn't get into Stanford. I dropped out of
college.

For unlike my mother, I did not believe I could be anything I wanted 80
to be. I could only be me.

And for all those years, we never talked about the disaster at the recital 81
or my terrible accusations afterward at the piano bench. All that remained
unchecked, like a betrayal that was now unspeakable. So I never found a

way to ask her why she had hoped for something so large that failure was inevitable.

And even worse, I never asked her what frightened me the most: Why 82 had she given up hope?

For after our struggle at the piano, she never mentioned my playing 83 again. The lessons stopped. The lid to the piano was closed, shutting out the dust, my misery, and her dreams.

So she surprised me. A few years ago, she offered to give me the piano, 84 for my thirtieth birthday. I had not played in all those years. I saw the offer as a sign of forgiveness, a tremendous burden removed.

"Are you sure?" I asked shyly. "I mean, won't you and Dad miss it?" 85

"No, this your piano," she said firmly. "Always your piano. You only 86 one can play."

"Well, I probably can't play anymore," I said. "It's been years." 87

"You pick up fast," said my mother, as if she knew this was certain. 88 "You have natural talent. You could been genius if you want to."

"No I couldn't." 89

"You just not trying," said my mother. And she was neither angry nor 90 sad. She said it as if to announce a fact that could never be disproved. "Take it," she said.

But I didn't at first. It was enough that she had offered it to me. And 91 after that, every time I saw it in my parents' living room, standing in front of the bay windows, it made me feel proud, as if it were a shiny trophy I had won back.

Last week I sent a tuner over to my parents' apartment and had the piano 92 reconditioned, for purely sentimental reasons. My mother had died a few months before and I had been getting things in order for my father, a little bit at a time. I put the jewelry in special silk pouches. The sweaters she had knitted in yellow, pink, bright orange—all the colors I hated—I put those in moth-proof boxes. I found some old Chinese silk dresses, the kind with little slits up the sides. I rubbed the old silk against my skin, then wrapped them in tissue and decided to take them home with me.

After I had the piano tuned, I opened the lid and touched the keys. It 93 sounded even richer than I remembered. Really, it was a very good piano. Inside the bench were the same exercise notes with handwritten scales, the same secondhand music books with their covers held together with yellow tape.

I opened up the Schumann book to the dark little piece I had played 94 at the recital. It was on the left-hand side of the page, "Pleading Child." It looked more difficult than I remembered. I played a few bars, surprised at how easily the notes came back to me.

And for the first time, or so it seemed, I noticed the piece on the 95 right-hand side. It was called "Perfectly Contented." I tried to play this one as well. It had a lighter melody but the same flowing rhythm and turned out to be quite easy. "Pleading Child" was shorter but slower; "Perfectly Contented" was longer, but faster. And after I played them both a few times, I realized they were two halves of the same song.

❀   ❀   ❀

AFTER YOU READ

▪ *THINK* about the relationship Jing-Mei Woo has with her mother. From the mother's point of view, why is it so important for Jing-Mei Woo to be a success or, at least, *try* to be a success? Why does Jing-Mei Woo rebel as she does?

▪ *THINK* also about the relationship between Jing-Mei Woo and her cousin Waverly. Jing-Mei Woo states, "We had grown up together and shared all the closeness of two sisters squabbling over crayons and dolls. In other words, for the most part, we hated each other." What part does the competition between Jing-Mei Woo and Waverly play in Jing-Mei Woo's struggle with herself and her mother?

▪ *EXAMINE* again the title "Two Kinds." To what does this title refer? Could the title refer to two kinds of children? Two kinds of attitudes? Now, examine more specifically the titles of the two piano pieces that Jing-Mei Woo plays at the conclusion of the story. How do the names of the contrasting musical pieces "Pleading Child" and "Perfectly Contented" relate to the title and to the main idea of the story?

▪ *WRITE* an essay about how you reacted to a particular expectation your parent(s) had for you.

A Parent's Journey Out of the Closet

AGNES G. HERMAN

❀

As a social worker and the wife of a rabbi, Agnes Herman thought she was prepared for being a mother. But discovering that her nineteen-year-old son was gay forced her to come to terms with some difficult issues. In this essay she tells of her "journey"—the long struggle she underwent in order to accept without blame or guilt her son's decision.

BEFORE YOU READ

• *THINK* about what it means to be gay or lesbian in a society such as ours. How do most cultures view homosexuality? Have attitudes toward homosexuality changed in recent years? In what way?

• *EXAMINE* the title of this essay. What does "coming out of the closet" usually mean? How has our perception of this phrase and the process it refers to changed in recent years? From the title, what do you expect the parent's situation to be?

• *WRITE* a journal entry in which you explore your position on the issue of homosexuality. Has your position changed in some way? If so, why and how?

AS YOU READ

Trace Herman's journey out of the closet, indicating in the margins each step forward she makes in her struggle to accept her son's sexual orientation.

When we agreed to adopt seven-month-old Jeff, we knew that his life 1
as a member of a Jewish family would begin the moment we brought
him to our home. We celebrated that joyous homecoming with appropriate
religious ritual, with blessings recited by Jeff's rabbi father as our gurgling,
happy baby teethed on his infant kiddush cup and enjoyed his challah.
There, in the warmth of our extended family circle of grandparents, an
aunt, an uncle, and the Temple Board, our small son passed comfortably
through his bris, his initial Jewish milestone. There would be many more.

By the time he was two, Jeff ate an ice cream cone without spilling a 2
drop; his face came out of the sticky encounter clean. At five, he watched
other kids play ball in the alley, standing aside because he had been told
not to play there. Besides, he seemed more comfortable playing with the
little girl next door. There were awkward moments as he began to grow
up, such as the times when the baseball bat, which his father insisted upon,
was not comfortable in his hands, but the rolling pin, which his father
decried, was. His grandmother, whom he adored, remarked, "Jeff is too
good."

I knew she was right, and privately I felt a nagging fear I could hardly 3
express to myself. Was Jeff a "sissy"? That archaic term was the only one I
dared whisper to myself. "Gay" only meant "lively and fun-loving";
"homosexual" was a label not to be used in polite society and certainly
never to be mentioned in the same sentence with a child's name. Such a
term would certainly stigmatize a youngster and humiliate a family.

Jeff continued to be an eager volunteer in the kitchen and a reluctant 4
participant on the ballfield. We fought the former and pressed to correct
the latter, frustrating our son while we all grew tense. As to our silent fears,
we repressed them.

Jeff developed reading problems in school. We worried, but accepted 5
the inappropriate assurance offered by his teacher. "He is such a good
boy—don't confuse him with counseling." We bought it, for a while. As
the reading problems continued, Jeff did enter therapy and was helped to
become less anxious and learn how to read all over again. At our final
parental consultation with the psychiatrist, I hesitantly asked, "Doctor, I
often worry that Jeff is effeminate. What do you think?" I held my breath
while he offered his reassurance: "There is nothing wrong with your son.
He is a sensitive boy—not aggressive or competitive. So he likes girls! In a
few years you will be worrying about that for other reasons."

Jeff looked forward eagerly to religious school. He accompanied his 6
dad, helped around the temple, and received many kudos. He was quick,
efficient, and willingly took instructions. In later years, even after his father

was no longer in the pulpit, Jeff continued his role as a temple volunteer. He moved chairs and carried books; later, he changed fuses, focused spotlights, and handled sound equipment. Jeff was comfortable; it was "his" temple. Other children there shared his interests and became his friends, later forming the temple youth group.

Bar mitzvah class, however, was a difficult obstacle. When Hebrew 7 became a daily family battle, we withdrew him from Hebrew school to be tutored instead by his father. He spent a substantial amount of time, which otherwise was not available, with his dad. As a result, a potential failure was transformed into another family milestone. Jeff yawned his way through formal bar mitzvah training, but when his big day arrived, he was prepared, and pleased even himself.

During confirmation and youth group years, Jeff seemed to be strug- 8 gling to be like his peers. Temple became the center of his life. He worked and played there, dated, went steady, and attended meetings and dances. He shared with no one—not his parents, his friends, or his rabbi—his own feelings of being "different."

When Jeff was sixteen, we moved from New Rochelle to Los Angeles. 9 It was a difficult move for him, cutting off relationships and sources of recognition and acceptance. As we settled into our new home, Jeff began to explore the San Fernando Valley, enrolled in high school, and tried to make new friends. At our insistence, he attended one meeting of the local temple youth group, but felt rejected by the youngsters there. That marked the unfortunate beginning of Jeff's disenchantment with synagogues and withdrawal from family religious observances and celebrations.

Jeff gradually acclimated to his new environment. He took Amy, a 10 Jewish girl his own age, to the senior prom; he cruised Van Nuys Boulevard on Wednesdays with Ann. He was always on the move—coming home to eat, shower, change clothes, and zip out again. We blamed it on the fast pace of California and the novelty of having his own "wheels": first a motorcycle, and then a car. There were several accidents—none serious, thank heavens! Again, in retrospect, the furious struggle with his identity must have played a part in his fast-paced behavior. At the time, though, we buried our heads in the sand, believing that Jeff was merely behaving like every other teenager.

After high school, the pace seemed to slow down a bit. So when Jeff 11 was nineteen and we decided to leave him in charge for the six months of our sabbatical world tour, we had no hesitation. Conscientious and cautious, he could handle the cars and the checkbook. He would continue in college and be available to his sister Judi, also attending college. We flew off to Europe and Israel, confident and secure.

When an overseas call came three months later in Jerusalem, my heart 12 beat fast, and my sense of well-being faltered slightly. "Everything is fine, no problem. I have quit college. Now don't get excited . . . I want to go to business school and study interior design. Jobs are plentiful; I know a guy who will hire me the minute I graduate."

Jeff had always shown a creative flair for color and design. He 13 constantly rearranged our furniture, changing one room after another. All this raced through my mind as I held the phone, separated from him by 9000 miles. Erv and I looked at each other, wished Jeff luck, and told him to write the check for his tuition.

When we finally returned home, Jeff was obviously depressed. His 14 answers to our questions were surly, clipped, and evasive. Behaving unlike his usual loving self, he ran in and out of the house silently, furtively, always in a hurry. He seemed uninterested in our trip and was clearly trying to avoid us.

One day during Passover, Erv was searching for a favorite cantorial 15 record that Jeff often appropriated. He checked Jeff's record collection and poked about among the torn jeans. Speechless and ashen, Erv returned to the breakfast room and dropped a book into my lap: *Homosexuality in Modern Society.* "This was hidden in Jeff's room." My heart raced and skipped. Confrontation was finally at hand, not only with Jeff, but with my own fears as well.

Then our son came through the front door on the run: "I'm late . . . 16 can't stop . . . talk to you later."

The tone of our response and expressions on our faces stopped him 17 midflight. "Son, stand still! Something is going on, you are not yourself! Are you in trouble? Drugs, maybe? Is one of your girlfriends pregnant? Or, are you, is it possible that you are . . . homosexual?"

I waited, trembling. The faces of my beloveds were creased with anger 18 and worry. I could barely breathe.

"Yes, I am gay." A simple sentence, yet I did not understand. Nothing 19 was "gay"!

We asked in unison, "What does that mean?"   20

"I am homosexual," he explained. After long minutes of uncomfort- 21 able conversation, we sent Jeff on his way with "we'll talk later." I ran from the room to what was to become my comfort zone, the cool tile of the bathroom floor, and I cried my eyes out. I guess Erv went to work. All we can recall now is that neither of us could face the reality right then.

That evening and the next, we did an enormous amount of soul- 22 searching. What did I, a social worker, know about homosexuality? What did my husband, the rabbi, know? Our academic credentials were impressive—professionally we were both well-trained to help other people in pain. But in our personal distress, we felt helpless.

Everything I had ever heard about homosexuality destroyed all my dreams about our son's future. He would never marry and have children. His warmth, caring, good looks, and so many other wonderful traits would not be passed along to a son or daughter, a grandchild. We wondered whether we could keep him in our family circle, or would we lose him to "that other world" of homosexuality, a world that was foreign to us.

We wracked ourselves with self-blame—what did we do wrong? I accepted all the myths about homosexuality. First, the myth of the strong mother—I was a strong mother, but what mother doesn't overexert her influence on her children? Second, the myth of the absent father—Erv spent so much time crisscrossing the country, berating himself for not being at home enough. Third was the myth of seduction—had someone lured Jeff into this awful lifestyle? And then, finally, I believed the myth of "the cure"—that the right therapist could change Jeff's sexual orientation.

We did seek help from a therapist. He was patient, caring, and accepting of Jeff and his lifestyle. He helped us begin to sort out myth from reality and guided us through a tangled web of grief, pain, and disappointment. He gently destroyed our unrealistic hope of "changing" Jeff. Our abiding love for our son was, of course, the key to this difficult yet hopeful journey.

I did not like Jeff's lifestyle at that time, but that did not interfere with my love for him. Understanding and acceptance gradually grew, but the path to real comfort continued to be bumpy.

Jeff sought help, too. At nineteen, he admitted that there was much that he wanted to know about himself. During that time, he offered a comment that we gratefully accepted: "Please stop blaming yourselves. It is not your fault that I have grown up gay." With those words, Jeff erased our most devastating, yet unspoken, anxiety.

Time moved along for all of us. We grieved the loss of deeply held expectations for our son's life. We experienced inner turmoil. Jeff struggled to make peace with himself. We learned to support one another.

Over time, we came to understand that a child who is homosexual needs no less understanding, support, and acceptance than one who is heterosexual. Clearly, our gay son has the same human needs that his straight sister has: for empathy and patience, for security and success, for caring and love. Rejection is difficult for both our children, yet perhaps more so for our gay child. Society has taught him that he will experience less validation and more unnecessary pain. He, and all of us who love him, are vulnerable to that pain.

It became clear that Jeff's sexual orientation was only one part of his 30
life. There remained the ordinary concerns and controversies intrinsic to
raising any child. Jeff rode the roller coaster of financial and vocational
problems. We provided advice, which he sometimes accepted, and loans,
which he often repaid. Jeff's married sister behaved in much the same
manner.

Jeff became ill and required the usual chicken soup and tender care in 31
his apartment. He preferred receiving that attention from friends, but also
expected Mother and Dad to stop by regularly with reassurance and love.
His sister behaved the same way when she broke her leg and was living
alone.

When a love affair went sour, Jeff became depressed and sad. We 32
worried and tried to be especially sensitive to his pain. The same support
was called for when his sister faced divorce with sadness and depression.
We were happier when Jeff was living with a friend who cared about him
and about whom he cared, and we felt the same way about his sister, now
happily remarried.

During all this time, it never occurred to us to turn to the Jewish 33
community for support, though we knew its resources well. We kept our
concerns about Jeff's lifestyle to ourselves: We were in the closet. A child's
homosexuality was not something one discussed in 1969 and throughout
the 1970s. And sharing intimacies with others was not our way—these were
matters we had to work out ourselves. We had decided alone, together, to
marry each other; we decided alone, together, to have children. And we
decided alone, together, to tough out our son's homosexuality, confront it,
embrace him, and then face the world together.

I recall sitting with close friends one evening. Naturally, the conversa- 34
tion turned to our kids. At one point, someone said, "I think we have
something in common." We all agreed, but even then, none of us could
articulate it. In fact, on the way home, Erv asked, "Are you sure their oldest
son is gay?"

Finally we came "halfway out," sharing only with family. We found 35
almost unanimous acceptance; affection for Jeff did not falter. But it was
seventeen long years before we went public in the Jewish community. Even
during the years when my husband was deeply involved in supporting the
establishment of a gay outreach synagogue in Los Angeles, when he was
busy teaching others that Judaism must not turn its back on any of its
children, we did not share our son's homosexuality with the Jewish public.

I "came out" for us, with Jeff's permission, in 1986, with an article in 36
The Reconstructionist, a national Jewish magazine. The response was
overwhelming. Support from rabbis, lay leaders, and friends poured in

from around the country. Even at that late date, comfortable as we had become with Jeff's lifestyle, we found those messages heartwarming and reassuring.

Some of our friends were angry that we had not shared our pain with 37 them. Perhaps we did not trust people to practice compassion and acceptance. Perhaps we did not trust them to understand that we are not failures as parents. We did not want our son to suffer rejection from those we loved. We did not want to be rejected by those we loved!

The pressure was greater on Jeff. Because he is a rabbi's child, he felt, 38 correctly, that the expectations of him were high. Jeff was not alone in fearing the expectations of others; he had learned that sensitivity from us. Every family feels a need to be without flaws: a nonsensical, impossible attitude, but it is real. Among rabbis' families it is often exaggerated.

Should we have trusted our friends and colleagues from the beginning? 39 Could we have dared to test the support of the synagogue leaders with whom Erv worked daily? Should we have risked our own self-image and left the closet earlier? Would any of that have made our son more comfortable at our seder table or at services? I do not have the answers. I believe we came out only when we were ready; getting ready took a long time.

❀   ❀   ❀

AFTER YOU READ

• *THINK* about Herman's reaction to the discovery that her son is gay. What are some of the emotions that she experiences? How does she finally learn to be comfortable with her son's homosexuality? Why would it be difficult for many parents to accept a son or daughter who is gay?

• *EXAMINE* paragraph 29, especially the sentence in which Herman states, "we came to understand that a child who is homosexual needs no less understanding, support, and acceptance than one who is heterosexual." Do you think that Jeff's needs for acceptance may actually have been greater than that of most heterosexual children? Why or why not?

• *EXAMINE* the story "Two Kinds" by Amy Tan, comparing the parent-child relationships in the two situations. How does the point of view differ in these two selections? What are the expectations of the mothers in each story? Who do you think worries more about not meeting parental expectations—Jeff or Jing-Mei Woo?

▪ *WRITE* an essay in which you tell of an experience you have had that involved a lengthy process of acceptance. This experience might be a divorce—your own or that of someone close to you; some type of failure; the loss of a family member; gaining a new sense of identity; the acquiring of a new family member—a younger sibling, stepparent, or stepsibling; a major setback; or a significant disappointment. Briefly describe the experience, but focus on the process of recovering and adjusting rather than on the experience itself.

Silk Parachute

JOHN McPHEE

❀

John McPhee is a New Yorker *staff writer who covers science, especially geology, for that magazine. He is also the author of a number of books, including* Coming into the Country, Basin and Range, Rising from the Plains, *and* Irons in the Fire. *In this essay, which appeared in the* New Yorker, *McPhee recalls several memories of his ninety-nine-year-old mother. Although he begins the essay with some incidents that portray his mother as a strict, somewhat authoritarian parent, McPhee soon reveals his fondness for his mother. Ultimately, the essay is a tribute to her.*

BEFORE YOU READ

• *THINK* about how stories from our childhood continue to shape our feelings even when we are adults. Do we remember stories because we realize their importance in our lives or because it is easier to remember a story than a thought or emotion? Or do you think we remember stories because they are both important to us and easy to remember?

• *EXAMINE* the statement McPhee makes in the first paragraph about the difficulty of remembering any one incident that sums up his mother and their relationship. This statement prepares the reader for the series of anecdotes that follow. Yet the title of this essay refers to the last story he tells, which clearly seems to "exemplify the whole" for him.

• *WRITE* in your journal at least one story from your past that seems to "exemplify the whole" of some relationship you have.

Reprinted by permission; © 1997 John McPhee. Originally published in *The New Yorker.* All rights reserved.

AS YOU READ

Identify each anecdote by numbering it. Notice how the tone of the essay changes as it progresses from light and humorous to thoughtful and serious. Mark the point in the essay at which this change begins.

When your mother is ninety-nine years old, you have so many memo- 1
ries of her that they tend to overlap, intermingle, and blur. It is extremely difficult to single out one or two, impossible to remember any that exemplify the whole.

It has been alleged that when I was in college she heard that I had 2
stayed up all night playing poker and wrote me a letter that used the word "shame" forty-two times. I do not recall this.

I do not recall being pulled out of my college room and into the church 3
next door.

It has been alleged that on December 24, 1936, when I was five years 4
old, she sent me to my room at or close to 7 P.M. for using four-letter words while trimming the Christmas tree. I do not recall that.

The assertion is absolutely false that when I came home from high 5
school with an A-minus she demanded an explanation for the minus.

It has been alleged that she spoiled me with protectionism, because I 6
was the youngest child and therefore the most vulnerable to attack from overhead—an assertion that I cannot confirm or confute, except to say that facts don't lie.

We lived only a few blocks from the elementary school and routinely 7
ate lunch at home. It is reported that the following dialogue and ensuing action occurred on January 22, 1941:

"Eat your sandwich."   8

"I don't want to eat my sandwich."   9

"I made that sandwich, and you are going to eat it, Mister Man. You 10
filled yourself up on penny candy on the way home, and now you're not hungry."

"I'm late. I have to go. I'll eat the sandwich on the way back to school." 11

"Promise?"   12

"Promise."   13

Allegedly, I went up the street with the sandwich in my hand and buried 14
it in a snowbank in front of Dr. Wright's house. My mother, holding back the curtain in the window of the side door, was watching. She came out in the bitter cold, wearing only a light dress, ran to the snowbank, dug out

the sandwich, chased me up Nassau Street, and rammed the sandwich down my throat, snow and all. I do not recall any detail of that story. I believe it to be a total fabrication.

There was the case of the missing Cracker Jack at Lindel's corner store.   15 Flimsy evidence pointed to Mrs. McPhee's smallest child. It has been averred that she laid the guilt on with the following words: "'Like mother like son' is a saying so true, the world will judge largely of mother by you." It has been asserted that she immediately repeated that proverb three times, and also recited it on other occasions too numerous to count. I have absolutely no recollection of her saying that about the Cracker Jack or any other controlled substance.

We have now covered everything even faintly unsavory that has been   16 reported about this person in ninety-nine years, and even those items are a collection of rumors, half-truths, prevarications, false allegations, inaccuracies, innuendos, and canards.

This is the mother who—when Alfred Knopf wrote her twenty-two-   17 year-old son a letter saying, "The readers' reports in the case of your manuscript would not be very helpful, and I think might discourage you completely"—said, "Don't listen to Alfred Knopf. Who does Alfred Knopf think he is, anyway? Someone should go in there and k-nock his block off." To the best of my recollection, that is what she said.

I also recall her taking me, on or about March 8th, my birthday, to the   18 theatre in New York every year, beginning in childhood. I remember those journeys as if they were today. I remember "A Connecticut Yankee." Wednesday, March 8, 1944. Evidently, my father had written for the tickets, because she and I sat in the last row of the second balcony. Mother knew what to do about that. She gave me for my birthday an elegant spyglass, sufficient in power to bring the Connecticut Yankee back from Vermont. I sat there watching the play through my telescope, drawing as many guffaws from the surrounding audience as the comedy on the stage.

On one of those theatre days—when I was eleven or twelve—I asked   19 her if we could start for the city early and go out to LaGuardia Field to see the comings and goings of airplanes. The temperature was well below the freeze point and the March winds were so blustery that the wind-chill factor was forty below zero. Or seemed to be. My mother figured out how to take the subway to a stop in Jackson Heights and a bus from there—a feat I am unable to duplicate to this day. At LaGuardia, she accompanied me to the observation deck and stood there in the icy wind for at least an hour, maybe two, while I, spellbound, watched the DC-3s coming in on final, their wings flapping in the gusts. When we at last left the observation deck, we went downstairs into the terminal where she bought me what appeared to be a black rubber ball but on closer inspection was a pair of hollow hemispheres hinged on one side and folded together. They contained a silk parachute. Opposite the hinge, each hemisphere had a small nib. A piece of string wrapped round and round the two nibs kept the ball closed. If you threw it high into the air, the string unwound and the parachute blossomed. If you sent it up with a tennis racquet, you could put it into the clouds. Not until the development of the ten-megabyte hard disk would the world ever know such a fabulous toy. Folded just so, the parachute never failed. Always, it floated back to you—silkily, beautifully—to start over and float back again. Even if you abused it, whacked it really hard—gracefully, lightly, it floated back to you.

❀ ❀ ❀

AFTER YOU READ

▪ *THINK* about the image of a parachute, picturing in your mind the sight of a billowing silk parachute silently and slowly dropping out of the sky. What connotations does a parachute have? What is its purpose? How does it look? Why is it an appropriate image for McPhee's essay? Try to put into words what you think it means to McPhee.

▪ *EXAMINE* McPhee's tone in the first half of the essay. In this first half, he tells, but playfully denies stories about his mother that show the strength of her love for him. Describe the tone he uses: the words he uses to describe both his mother and himself, the exaggeration he uses for humorous effect, and the mock seriousness of the accusations he makes about his mother. Identify the ways in which his tone gradually changes in the second half of the essay.

▪ *WRITE* a profile, or character sketch, of a family member or some other person you know well. In the essay, do at least one of the following:

1. Modify your tone in some way as the essay progresses.
2. Use multiple anecdotes to portray your subject.
3. Include a strong image, such as McPhee's parachute, that symbolizes the person or the relationship in some way.

Wanted—A Mother

ORVILLE RAWLINS

❀

Born on the island of Puerto Rico, Orville Rawlins grew up on the British West Indian island of St. Kitts, which is the setting for the following essay. A journalism and French major, Rawlins first published this essay in Write-On, *an annual anthology of essays written in a freshman English class.*

BEFORE YOU READ

▪ *THINK* about the title of the essay. Since you discover in the first paragraph that Rawlins does indeed have a mother, what do you think he means by this title?

▪ *EXAMINE* Rawlins's use of the word *bastard* in paragraphs 1 and 4. What does he mean by the word in each case? How do these meanings differ? In your opinion, is the shock value of the word effective?

▪ *EXAMINE* also Rawlins's comment about the "maelstrom of emotions" (paragraph 5) that he felt when he discovered his mother could not read. Literally, a *maelstrom* is a whirlpool, but in this context it means a "great confusion" of emotions.

▪ *WRITE* a journal entry in which you describe a time that you were ashamed of one of your parents or of someone else whom you love.

AS YOU READ

Note in the margin passages that reveal how and why Rawlins's attitude toward his mother changes.

I was born the bastard child of a cop and a maid—born in a foreign land 1
called Puerto Rico to illegals who had no green card. We were always on
the run. Eventually we ran out of Puerto Rico. They named me Orville Ira
Rawlins and I hated them both.

I grew up on a small Caribbean island called St. Kitts where poor 2
niggers lived with rich black folk[s] and stoned-out expatriates afraid to
confront their national demons. My mother did her best by me. I can never
say like other [black] folks that my life was a struggle; in comparison I had
a cruise. She worked at Mr. Blake's plantation house for $30.00 a week,
and we all thought that she had one of the plum jobs. Breakfast, lunch, and
dinner were always prepared for me but still that hatred inside festered. I
could not find cause or escape for it.

Everyone thought that Violet, that's my mom, had a nice child. 3
Everybody said so.

"Laud he look so good," they said in that Caribbean dialect. They 4
always tried to touch me. I hated that, being touched, fondled, and kissed,
especially by these toothless crones. I didn't give a damn that my clothes
were sometimes hand-me-downs from their kids. I just wanted to be left
alone. When I was ten years old, my father left us. No! He left my mother.
I never needed him. However, I still hated him for doing that because Violet
became a simpering sycophant. Kept telling me how I was the only thing
in her world that made sense. I found that scary, because to me, I didn't
make sense. She made me angry by her dependance on other people for
her happiness. I felt that [this] was a dangerous weakness. It seems that I
was an intelligent child. Everybody said so. I was always at the top of my
class. I wanted it that way—not just to be the best that I could be; just better
than all the rest. I was a selfish, arrogant bastard who was trying to prove
himself better than everyone else.

November 25 came. It was a rainy day. Storm clouds and equally foul 5
winds were the order of the day. That year I was about fourteen years old.
I had an assignment for English about increasing your vocabulary. I took it
home to Violet to get her help. When I gave her the book she said nothing,
did nothing; an opaque film seemed to come across her eyes. I looked at
her and then I looked at the book. It was upside down. Then it hit me. My
mother could not read. She could NOT READ. Up to this day it's
impossible to totally explain my feelings, to come to grips with the
maelstrom of emotions that I felt. Shame, shock, anger, pain, disgust—they
all flashed through my mind, heart, and soul; each one more powerful than
the last. God, it hurt. I looked at her and in that one moment, it all came

together; I felt nothing but an insane, powerful disgust at this woman who could NOT READ.

From that day onward, our roles changed in that household. I became 6 a virtual lord. Never again would I eat boiled rice and chicken. I decided the menu. She would ask me daily what I wanted for dinner and I would order only what I liked, and she would cook it. My excesses were a painful price for her to pay, but my pain and shame were excessive. If someone were to ask me what I was doing to Violet, I wouldn't have a coherent clue of a reason fitting my actions. I thought I was making her pay for being dumb and illiterate, but I was paying more. I was becoming a scary specter, not only to Violet, but to myself.

At nights, I would lie down and think about my thoughts. Yes, I would 7 actually ponder a certain situation, my reaction to it, and then wonder why. Why did I want to hurt her so? She never resisted my demands, never refused me anything. She loved me, I knew. God knows I couldn't feel that soulful connection; our lives just never meshed. I hated her. This relationship continued for about three years. During this time, I was becoming something of a farce. Amongst friends, I was friendly toward her, but at home all my disappointments and frustrations imploded. My anger, like an all-consuming bile, flew outward, and in front of it all, covered my mother. So I gained strength, like a demon sucking the will out of a living, breathing soul. Yes, that's what I was, a damned demon. I half-heartedly tried to exorcise these thoughts, but I failed; the truth was, I was enjoying it.

When I graduated from high school at age seventeen, she was there, 8 she was proud, she was crying. I was just hoping that she wouldn't say anything stupid to embarrass me. "If you ain't got anything to say, don't say it," on that we were in total agreement. Man that was a great day, top of my class and valedictorian. I felt good. She gave me a watch that day. My name was inscribed on the back. I'm sure it must have cost her a pretty penny, but she bought it. It's what I had asked for. At that time she must have been hitting forty but still looking all right.

My grandfather came visiting one day. He came down from Nevis for 9 a wedding and was going to stay with us for a couple of days. Violet slept on the couch. He used her bed. It was a beautiful night, the night of his visit.

The next day dawned beautiful. I swear to God it was the most 10 beautiful day that I had ever seen. The flowers were in full bloom. Their scents filled the Caribbean air. Obviously I wasn't the only one to appreciate the blue sky and bougainvillea-perfumed air. People were out changing curtains and taking advantage of the good weather to paint roofs and get rid of old bric-a-brac accumulated in their houses over the years. I was supposed to accompany my grandfather up to our family plot in the mountains. This was the spot where we used to grow our vegetables and animal feed. He wanted to touch base with his youth I guess; anyway, I went along.

The path was long and winding, but the views were magnificent. At 11 some points you could see the beautiful Atlantic in the distance, the coral reef becalming the inner waters. It was so beautiful. I had seen it before, of course, but this day seemed to have made nature look down upon herself and improve on her countenance. We were pretty silent up to that point, content just to take in the vistas. That's when it happened.

A female monkey ran across our path followed by a wild dog foaming 12 at the mouth. Minutes later we heard a shriek of pain and instantly knew the outcome of the chase. We kept on walking. A few yards into the woods, crouched on a rock, was a baby monkey, eyes wide open, trembling with fear. I remember scooping it up and holding it against my chest to comfort it. It relaxed considerably. Grandfather began talking then.

He spoke a lot about when he was rearing his kids. How he could 13 barely feed them all. He recalled the times when mackerel and dumplings constituted dinner for months on end. He told me that he used to beat the hell out of his kids for refusing to eat the same fare. He taught them to be satisfied with what they had by literally beating it into them. As he spoke, tears came to his eyes. He told me of times when there was nothing to eat save for the fruits which grew in the yard: guavas, pineapples, mangoes and the like. His voice broke when he told me how ashamed he was that he couldn't provide for his family which numbered fourteen. Then, with phlegm running from his nose, tears from his eyes, he looked at me and for the next hour told me the story of my life. This story became my linchpin for the future.

"You know," he said, "that monkey reminds me a lot of Violet.   14

"She was my first child. I always wanted a boy for my first, but she 15 came—God's will, I guess. She was a very quiet baby, never complained, yet her eyes always seemed to be laughing at you. Parson said he never saw such a child.

"He said that she was going to be a strong child, long-suffering, and 16 Lawd, that she was. After her I had eleven sons, yes, a whole bunch of them. Everybody said how it was killing my wife young, but back then "frenchies"* weren't around. Every time we did it, a child came along, just like damn guinea pigs.

"When they got to school age that's when the nightmare started. There [17] was no way in God's world that I could feed them, clothe them, and send them all to school. Somebody had to be left out. Somebody had to help with the cattle and sheep and "work the ground."† For days, months even, I pondered my choices; how could a father in good conscience keep some of his children out of school, some half-clothed, and all fed? Who among them should I deny? Believe me, Orville, I loved them all equally.

"One night Violet came to me. She must have been thirteen years old [18] at the time. I tell you, her eyes were wise; she looked as if she knew exactly what I was holding on my chest, what questions were going through my mind. And she said quite clearly, 'Daddy, I'm going to drop out of school and look for a job. You know I don't like school no how.'

"And me, coward that I was, I agreed without pause. And so she got a [19] job at the police cafeteria. That's where she met your father, I suppose. She started selling the eggs from our chickens in the yard. She was very industrious. They paid her well, and the money put her brothers through school. She was the reason they stayed in school. My word, look at them now—two doctors, a cop, a teacher, a minister, Godwin's a lieutenant-colonel in the U.S. Army, one's a lab technician, three of them are registered contractors with their own business, and Bal's an interpreter at Foreign Affairs. Never in my wildest dreams would I have thought such success possible."

I wondered if he ever thought about the eleventh child, the success she [20] had. She was, after all, a successful waitress.

He picked up on his story. "That monkey gave up her life to distract [21] the dog from her young. She gave her child a chance to survive. Your mother gave your uncles that chance, and I'm proud of her for it. I will never be able to repay her; all I can do is love her for who she is."

I fought myself to deflate the pinpricks of pride that I felt then for my [22] mother. I'm not going to say that I rushed home instantly to beg her forgiveness. That would be a gross misrepresentation of the truth. We walked home slowly, silently, our minds on distant oases of times gone by. When I got home I asked mommy to cook boiled rice and chicken. For me, it was a start. I got rid of most of my animosities by starting two gardens:

---

*frenchies: french letters, condoms.
†work the ground: engage in land cultivation.

a vegetable garden in the back yard and a flower garden in front. I loved the flower garden more, and I think mommy did too because she used to cut the flowers every day for the vases inside.

August 3, 1989. This day began very ordinarily. I woke up and 23 showered. I walked out into the dining room, and she was there, preparing breakfast as usual. I walked up behind her and held her around the waist. Her body visibly trembled, then sagged as if it had lost some of its strength. I said, "I hope you have a good day, Mom." And then the tears started. . . .

        ❁   ❁   ❁

AFTER YOU READ

• *THINK* about the different types of shame that Rawlins describes: his shame about his mother's being illiterate, the grandfather's shame about his failure to provide well for his family, and, eventually, Rawlins's own shame about the way he has treated his mother. How are all of these instances of shame similar? How are they different?

• *EXAMINE* Rawlins's reaction to his father's leaving the family (paragraph 4). Do you think Rawlins's feelings toward his father and his father's absence affected his attitude and actions toward his mother? If so, how?

• *WRITE* an essay in which you tell of a time you felt ashamed of someone you love. Explore both the causes and effects of the shame.

Adoption Should Be Color-Blind

KRISTIN ST. JOHN

❀

Transracial adoption—especially the adoption of African-American children by white parents—is an increasingly controversial topic. Opponents argue that parents who do not have the same racial and cultural background cannot give the adopted child a true sense of heritage. Supporters argue that it is better for a child to have loving parents of a different race than to have no parents at all. In the following essay from Parents *magazine, Kristin St. John gives her viewpoint as a child with an African-American father who was adopted by white parents. At the time she wrote the essay, St. John was a student majoring in journalism at the University of Massachusetts.*

BEFORE YOU READ

▪ *THINK* about the question of transracial adoption, the adoption of children from one race or culture by parents of another race or culture. Do you think such adoptions are a good idea? Why or why not?

▪ *EXAMINE* the title and first paragraph of St. John's essay. What does she know about her birth parents? What is her cultural heritage? Do you think her complex heritage jeopardized or helped her chances for adoption? Or do you think her background simply did not matter to her adoptive parents?

▪ *WRITE* a journal entry in which you make two lists, one of the advantages of transracial adoption and another of the disadvantages.

AS YOU READ

Identify and underline at least three positive experiences that led St. John to conclude that "adoption should be color-blind."

In 1974 I was born in Buffalo to a mother who was part Native American 1
and part white, and a father who was African-American. My birth mother
was 16, and her mother essentially forced her to give me up for adoption.
I know practically nothing about my birth father.

Around the time I was born, Judy and Nicholas St. John wanted to 2
adopt a girl. The child's race was of no consequence to them. When they
spoke to a representative of the Erie County Department of Social Services
adoption agency, they were told that under no circumstances could they
cross racial lines in order to adopt a child. They then went to a Catholic
agency, where they heard that I was available.

It's 21 years later, but attitudes toward transracial adoption haven't 3
changed much, if the fuss caused by the Multi-Ethnic Placement Act passed
by the U.S. Congress last year is any indication. This bill directs child
welfare agencies not to judge adoptive parents on the basis of race, color,
or national origin. The bill has been opposed by, among other groups,
the Association of Black Social Workers, which contends that African-
American adoptees should be placed only with same-race parents. To do
otherwise, the group argues, condones what it calls "cultural genocide."

It's interesting to me that whenever I listen to the "debate" over 4
transracial adoption, there's one set of voices that rarely gets the chance to
speak. These voices belong to African-American children of white adoptive
parents. The few of us who do manage to be heard, mostly on syndicated
talk shows, seem to have been chosen precisely because their experiences
have been negative. However, even though I've listened to these transracial
adoptees tell their stories on several occasions, not once have I ever felt
that the person on the screen spoke for me.

So now I'm speaking for myself, as an African-American raised in a 5
white family. I'm proud of my racial and ethnic backgrounds, both the
biological and the cultural ones. And I love and admire my parents. ·

Throughout my childhood, my mother and father—and everyone else 6
in the family, for that matter—freely acknowledged that I wasn't their
biological child. (Not that I wouldn't have figured it out soon enough.) My
two brothers, both of whom had been born to my mother, gave me the
same hard time they would have given any little sister when they thought
I might have a boyfriend, or when I played music too loud.

Far from practicing "cultural genocide," however, my family proved 7
sympathetic and helpful when, as a freshman in high school, I went through
a period of exploring my heritage. When I immersed myself in books and
movies that dealt with Native American and African-American culture and
became involved in the local chapter of the NAACP, my parents responded

by making a conscious effort not only to point out people of color who made positive role models, but also to help me be open to all cultures.

Now I've just finished my junior year at the University of Massachu- 8 setts, Amherst. I'm also a person with a pretty good idea of who I am. That knowledge came in very handy during my freshman year, when an attack on a dormitory resident assistant of color sparked racial tension throughout our campus. I found myself challenged about which "side" I was on. I didn't like these litmus tests and wasn't shy about saying so. When I became the black-affairs editor for the daily campus newspaper, I tried to offer perspectives that made sense to both sides.

My experience with transracial adoption probably won't get me on 9 any talk shows, and it might not sit too well with racial separatists on both sides. That's a shame, really. Everyone—and especially children whose biological parents cannot, for one reason or another, take care of them— should be given the opportunity to see that, as trite as it may sound, love really *is* color-blind.

❀ ❀ ❀

AFTER YOU READ

▪ *THINK* about St. John's strong sense of personal identity, which she describes in paragraph 8. How do you think she developed this sense of identity? What gives her the courage to maintain her identity even when others disagree with her?

▪ *EXAMINE* paragraphs 2, 5, and 7, which describe St. John's relationship with her adoptive parents. How determined were her parents to adopt a girl? How are their responsibilities as St. John's parents similar to that of any other parents? How are they different? What special effort have they made to develop St. John's awareness of her heritage? How would you describe St. John's overall relationship with her parents?

▪ *WRITE* an essay in which you argue for or against transracial adoption. You may refer to this selection in your essay, but be sure to include additional support based on your own ideas, readings, and experiences.

Those Winter Sundays

ROBERT E. HAYDEN

❁

The recipient of numerous awards for his poetry, Robert Earl Hayden (1913–1980) was a member of the American Academy and Institute of Arts and Letters, a Fellow of the Academy of American Poets, and the first African-American poet to serve as Consultant in Poetry to the Library of Congress. His Collected Poems *were published in 1985. Born Asa Sheffey Bundy, he was at eighteen months of age left with neighbors William and Sue Ellen Hayden while his parents pursued separate livelihoods. Although they never formally adopted Asa, the Haydens rechristened him "Robert Hayden" and provided him with a home and an education. The following poem, which was originally published in* A Ballad of Remembrance *in 1962, recalls the fatherly devotion that Hayden learned to appreciate many years later.*

BEFORE YOU READ

▪ *THINK* about your father or about another person who has been in charge of your care. What is your relationship with this person? Are you grateful to this person? Is this person aware of your gratitude?

▪ *THINK* also about what it would be like to get up every winter morning in an unheated house. If you lived in these conditions, would you be willing to get up first and get the house warm for your family?

▪ *EXAMINE* the title of the poem. What connotations, or personal associations, do you have with "winter"? What associations do you have with "Sundays"?

▪ *WRITE* a journal entry about what you do, or would like to do, on a "Winter Sunday."

Underline passages that describe the unselfish actions, or "offices," that the
speaker's father performs.

Sundays too my father got up early
and put his clothes on in the blueblack cold,
then with cracked hands that ached
from labor in the weekday weather made
banked fires blaze. No one ever thanked him.   5

I'd wake and hear the cold splintering, breaking.
When the rooms were warm, he'd call,
and slowly I would rise and dress,
fearing the chronic angers of that house.

Speaking indifferently to him,   10
who had driven out the cold
and polished my good shoes as well.
What did I know, what did I know
of love's austere and lonely offices?

❖   ❖   ❖

AFTER YOU READ

• *THINK* about the commitment that it takes to raise a child. Do you think
it takes an even greater commitment to raise a foster child or an adopted
child? Why or why not?

• *THINK* also about relationships between fathers and sons. Hayden's
foster father was a stern and religious man who no doubt expected his son
to go to church every Sunday morning. The phrase "chronic angers," which
refers to arguments between Hayden's parents, may also suggest some
conflict between Hayden and his father. What other phrases suggest that,
as a child, Hayden may have felt resentful or even rebellious toward his
father and his father's expectations? Are these feelings common between
fathers and sons? Explain.

▪ *EXAMINE* the reaction of the son to the father in lines 10–12. How would you describe this reaction? How do you suppose the son's thoughtless response made the father feel? Why did the father continue to get up early on Sundays as well as on weekdays to get the house warm and his son's clothes ready? Why does Hayden call these duties "love's austere and lonely offices"?

▪ *EXAMINE* also the language of the poem. What words and images suggest the cold most effectively?

▪ *WRITE* an essay about a family member who has performed, or who performs, "love's austere and lonely offices" for you.

Fatherless America

DAVID BLANKENHORN

❀

The founder of the Institute for American Values and chair of the National Fatherhood initiative, David Blankenhorn has edited several books that promote strong marriages and traditional family values. In the following essay from Fatherless America: Confronting Our Most Urgent Social Problem *(1995), Blankenhorn not only documents that our country "is becoming an increasingly fatherless society" but also argues against the growing popular belief that a father is not a necessary component for a strong family.*

BEFORE YOU READ

- *THINK* about Blankenhorn's assertion that our society is becoming "increasingly fatherless." Do you believe his observation is true? In the fatherless homes you know, does the absence of the father cause problems?

- *EXAMINE* the italicized words in the following sentences:

Demographic: "Fatherlessness is the most harmful *demographic* trend of this generation" (paragraph 3).

Demography is the study of characteristics of human population, as in size, density, growth, distribution of gender and race, and the makeup of individual households.

Narcissism, Puerile: "In personal terms, the end result of this process [of devaluing fatherhood] . . . is *narcissism:* a me-first egotism that is hostile not only to any societal goal or larger moral purpose but also to any save the most *puerile* understanding of personal happiness" (paragraph 22).

The context of Blankenhorn's sentence gives a helpful definition of *narcissism*, which derives from the mythic character Narcissus, who fell in love with his own image in the water. *Puerile* means "immature, juvenile, childish."

Anthropomorphic, Paternity: "A good father is a cultural model, or what Max Weber calls an ideal social type—an *anthropomorphized* composite of cultural ideas about the meaning of *paternity*" (paragraph 23).

Because *anthropomorphic* means having human qualities, Blanken-horn is saying that a good father is a human embodiment of a society's ideas about *paternity,* or fatherhood. *Note:* An *anthropologist* (paragraph 18) studies the origin and behavior of human beings.

▪ *WRITE* a journal entry in which you describe the role of the father in today's family. How important is this role? What responsibilities does it—or should it—include?

AS YOU READ

Underline the examples that Blankenhorn uses to support his belief that the United States is becoming "increasingly fatherless" and circle the effects that he believes result from this trend.

The United States is becoming an increasingly fatherless society. A generation ago, an American child could reasonably expect to grow up with his or her father. Today, an American child can reasonably expect not to. Fatherlessness is now approaching a rough parity with fatherhood as a defining feature of American childhood.

This astonishing fact is reflected in many statistics, but here are the two most important. Tonight, about 40 percent of American children will go to sleep in homes in which their fathers do not live. Before they reach the age of eighteen, more than half of our nation's children are likely to spend at least a significant portion of their childhoods living apart from their fathers. Never before in this country have so many children been voluntarily abandoned by their fathers. Never before have so many children grown up without knowing what it means to have a father.

Fatherlessness is the most harmful demographic trend of this generation. It is the leading cause of declining child well-being in our society. It is also the engine driving our most urgent social problems, from crime to adolescent pregnancy to child sexual abuse to domestic violence against women. Yet, despite its scale and social consequences, fatherlessness is a problem that is frequently ignored or denied. Especially within our elite discourse, it remains largely a problem with no name.

If this trend continues, fatherlessness is likely to change the shape of ₄
our society. Consider this prediction. After the year 2000, as people born
after 1970 emerge as a large proportion of our working-age adult population, the United States will be a nation divided into two groups, separate
and unequal. The two groups will work in the same economy, speak a
common language, and remember the same national history. But they will
live fundamentally divergent lives. One group will receive basic benefits—
psychological, social, economic, educational, and moral—that are denied
to the other group.

The primary fault line dividing the two groups will not be race, ₅
religion, class, education, or gender. It will be patrimony. One group will
consist of those adults who grew up with the daily presence and provision
of fathers. The other group will consist of those who did not. By the early
years of the next century, these two groups will be roughly the same size.

Surely a crisis of this scale merits a response. At a minimum, it requires ₆
a serious debate. Why is fatherhood declining? What can be done about it?
Can our society find ways to invigorate effective fatherhood as a norm of
male behavior? Yet, to date, the public discussion on this topic has been
remarkably weak and defeatist. There is a prevailing belief that not much
can—or even should—be done to reverse the trend.

When the crime rate jumps, politicians promise to do something about ₇
it. When the unemployment rate rises, task forces assemble to address the
problem. As random shootings increase, public health officials worry about
the preponderance of guns. But when it comes to the mass defection of
men from family life, not much happens.

There is debate, even alarm, about specific social problems. Divorce. ₈
Out-of-wedlock childbearing. Children growing up in poverty. Youth
violence. Unsafe neighborhoods. Domestic violence. The weakening of
parental authority. But in these discussions, we seldom acknowledge the
underlying phenomenon that binds together these otherwise disparate
issues: the flight of males from their children's lives. In fact, we seem to go
out of our way to avoid the connection between our most pressing social
problems and the trend of fatherlessness.

We avoid this connection because, as a society, we are changing our ₉
minds about the role of men in family life. As a cultural idea, our inherited
understanding of fatherhood is under siege. Men in general, and fathers in
particular, are increasingly viewed as superfluous to family life: either
expendable or as part of the problem. Masculinity itself, understood as
anything other than a rejection of what it has traditionally meant to be
male, is typically treated with suspicion and even hostility in our cultural

discourse. Consequently, our society is now manifestly unable to sustain, or even find reason to believe in, fatherhood as a distinctive domain of male activity.

The core question is simple: Does every child need a father? Increasingly, our society's answer is "no," or at least "not necessarily." Few idea shifts in this century are as consequential as this one. At stake is nothing less than what it means to be a man, who our children will be, and what kind of society we will become. 10

This [essay] is a criticism not simply of fatherlessness but of a culture of fatherlessness. For, in addition to losing fathers, we are losing something larger: our idea of fatherhood. Unlike earlier periods of father absence in our history, we now face more than a physical loss affecting some homes. We face a cultural loss affecting every home. For this reason, the most important absence our society must confront is not the absence of fathers but the absence of our belief in fathers. 11

In a larger sense, this [essay] is a *cultural* criticism because fatherhood, much more than motherhood, is a cultural invention. Its meaning for the individual man is shaped less by biology than by a cultural script or story—a societal code that guides, and at times pressures, him into certain ways of acting and of understanding himself as a man. 12

Like motherhood, fatherhood is made up of both a biological and a social dimension. Yet in societies across the world, mothers are far more successful than fathers at fusing these two dimensions into a coherent parental identity. Is the nursing mother playing a biological or a social role? Is she feeding or bonding? We can hardly separate the two, so seamlessly are they woven together. 13

But fatherhood is a different matter. A father makes his sole biological contribution at the moment of conception—nine months before the infant enters the world. Because social paternity is only indirectly linked to biological paternity, the connection between the two cannot be assumed. The phrase "to father a child" usually refers only to the act of insemination, not to the responsibility for raising a child. What fathers contribute to their offspring after conception is largely a matter of cultural devising. 14

Moreover, despite their other virtues, men are not ideally suited to responsible fatherhood. Although they certainly have the capacity for fathering, men are inclined to sexual promiscuity and paternal waywardness. Anthropologically, human fatherhood constitutes what might be termed a necessary problem. It is necessary because, in all societies, child well-being and societal success hinge largely upon a high level of paternal investment: the willingness of adult males to devote energy and resources 15 to the care of their offspring. It is a problem because adult males are frequently—indeed, increasingly—unwilling or unable to make that vital investment.

Because fatherhood is universally problematic in human societies, 16 cultures must mobilize to devise and enforce the father role for men, coaxing and guiding them into fatherhood through a set of legal and extralegal pressures that require them to maintain a close alliance with their children's mother and to invest in their children. Because men do not volunteer for fatherhood as much as they are conscripted into it by the surrounding culture, only an authoritative cultural story of fatherhood can fuse biological and social paternity into a coherent male identity.

For exactly this reason, Margaret Mead and others have observed that 17 the supreme test of any civilization is whether it can socialize men by teaching them to be fathers—creating a culture in which men acknowledge their paternity and willingly nurture their offspring. Indeed, if we can equate the essence of the antisocial male with violence, we can equate the essence of the socialized male with being a good father. Thus, at the center of our most important cultural imperative, we find the fatherhood script: the story that describes what it ought to mean for a man to have a child.

Just as the fatherhood script advances the social goal of harnessing male 18 behavior to collective needs, it also reflects an individual purpose. That purpose, in a word, is happiness. Anthropologists have long understood that the genius of an effective culture is its capacity to reconcile individual happiness with collective well-being. By situating individual lives within a social narrative, culture endows private behavior with larger meaning. By linking the self to moral purposes larger than the self, an effective culture tells us a story in which individual fulfillment transcends selfishness, and personal satisfaction transcends narcissism.

In this respect, our cultural script is not simply a set of imported 19 moralisms, exterior to the individual and designed only to compel self-sacrifice, It is also a pathway—indeed, our only pathway—to what the founders of the American experiment called the pursuit of happiness.

The stakes on this issue could hardly be higher. Our society's conspicu- 20 ous failure to sustain or create compelling norms of fatherhood amounts to a social and personal disaster. Today's story of fatherhood features one-dimensional characters, an unbelievable plot, and an unhappy ending. It reveals in our society both a failure of collective memory and a collapse of moral imagination. It undermines families, neglects children, causes or aggravates our worst social problems, and makes individual adult happiness—both male and female—harder to achieve.

Ultimately, this failure reflects nothing less than a culture gone awry: 21
a culture increasingly unable to establish the boundaries, erect the sign-
posts, and fashion the stories that can harmonize individual happiness with
collective well-being. In short, it reflects a culture that increasingly fails to
"enculture" individual men and women, mothers and fathers.

In personal terms, the end result of this process, the final residue from 22
what David Gutmann calls the "deculturation" of paternity, is narcissism:
a me-first egotism that is hostile not only to any societal goal or larger
moral purpose but also to any save the most puerile understanding of
personal happiness. In social terms, the primary results of decultured
paternity are a decline in children's well-being and a rise in male violence,
especially against women. In a larger sense, the most significant result is
our society's steady fragmentation into atomized individuals, isolated from
one another and estranged from the aspirations and realities of common
membership in a family, a community, a nation, bound by mutual commitment and shared memory.

[A good father] is a cultural model, or what Max Weber calls an ideal 23
social type—an anthropomorphized composite of cultural ideas about the
meaning of paternity. I call him the Good Family Man. As described by one
of the fathers [I] interviewed [. . .] , a good family man "puts his family
first."

[. . .] A good society celebrates the ideal of the man who puts his family 24
first. Because our society is now lurching in the opposite direction, I see
the Good Family Man as the principal casualty of today's weakening
fatherhood script. And because I cannot imagine a good society without
him, I offer him as the protagonist in the stronger script that I believe is
both necessary and possible.

❁   ❁   ❁

AFTER YOU READ

▪ *THINK* about how not having a father affects a child. What effects does
Blankenhorn discuss in his essay? Do you agree with Blankenhorn's
assessment of the significant negative effects of fatherlessness on a child?
Or do you believe that a mother or other family member can effectively
fulfill the role that Blankenhorn assigns to fathers?

▪ *EXAMINE* Blankenhorn's claim in paragraph 11 that "in addition to
losing fathers, we are losing something larger: our idea of fatherhood.

Unlike earlier periods of father absence in our history, we now face more than a physical loss affecting some homes. We face a cultural loss affecting every home." Do you agree or disagree that fatherhood is less valued in our society than it was a few years ago? How is the role of fathers portrayed in television dramas and situation comedies today? How was it portrayed five or ten years ago? Based on your own experiences and observations, what is the role of most fathers today? Can you describe one or more examples—real or fictional—of what Blankenhorn calls "the Good Family Man" that you have encountered in your life?

▪ *EXAMINE* also Blankenhorn's claim that "fatherhood, much more than motherhood, is a cultural invention" (paragraph 12). Reread paragraphs 12–16, in which Blankenhorn continues his comparison (some of which is implied) of mothers and fathers. Do you agree or disagree with the distinctions he makes? How do you define "motherhood" and "fatherhood"? How do you distinguish between them?

▪ *WRITE* a summary of Blankenhorn's essay. Remember that a summary includes major supporting points, or arguments, but that—unlike an essay—it does not include specific examples and statistics. Or *WRITE* an essay in which you combine your ideas with Blankenhorn's to define "the Good Family Man." Include in your essay several shorter examples or one extended example.

The Perfect Family

ALICE HOFFMAN

❀

*Alice Hoffman's best-known work is probably the screen-
play for the Warner Brothers movie* Independence Day. *A
prolific author, Hoffman has published numerous essays
in* Ms., Redbook, *and other magazines and has written
eleven novels, many of which deal with themes of family
and identity. The title of this essay is an ironic allusion to
what David Blankenhorn and other conservatives would
call "The Perfect Family"—a nuclear family in which the
children are raised by both a mother and a father. Describing her own happy childhood growing up in a divorced
family in which her mother provided for all her needs,
Hoffman suggests that she had "the perfect family" even
without a father.*

BEFORE YOU READ

▪ *THINK* about the title of the selection. In your opinion, what makes a
family "perfect"? Do you think the perfect family exists?

▪ *EXAMINE* the first paragraph of the selection. The names that Hoffman
lists—Princess, Kitten, and Bud—are the children of the 1950s family
television show "Father Knows Best." On this show, the mother stayed at
home, cooked the meals, and took care of the children, while the father
made the living and dispensed thoughtful advice.

▪ *WRITE* a journal entry in which you explain either why your family is or
is not "perfect."

AS YOU READ

Underline the details that Hoffman uses to describe the "perfect" life
represented by the idealized television family and circle those that she uses
to describe her real family life.

W hen I was growing up in the 50's, there was only one sort of family, 1
the one we watched on television every day. Right in front of us, in
black and white, was everything we needed to know about family values:
the neat patch of lawn, the apple tree, the mother who never once raised
her voice, the three lovely children: a Princess, a Kitten, a Bud and, always,
the father who knew best.

People stayed married forever back then, and roses grew by the front 2
door. We had glass bottles filled with lightning bugs and brand-new swing
sets in the backyard, and softball games at dusk. We had summer nights
that lasted forever and well-balanced meals, three times a day, in our
identical houses, on our identical streets. There was only one small bargain
we had to make to exist in this world: we were never to ask questions,
never to think about people who didn't have as much or who were
different in any way. We ignored desperate marriages and piercing loneli-
ness. And we were never, ever, to wonder what might be hidden from view,
behind the unlocked doors, in the privacy of our neighbors' bedrooms and
knotty-pine-paneled dens.

This was a bargain my own mother could not make. Having once 3
believed that her life would sort itself out to be like the television shows
we watched, only real and in color, she'd been left to care for her children
on her own, at a time when divorce was so uncommon I did not meet
another child of divorced parents until 10 years later, when I went off to
college.

Back then, it almost made sense when one of my best friends was not 4
allowed to come to my house; her parents did not approve of divorce or
my mother's life style. My mother, after all, had a job and a boyfriend and,
perhaps even more incriminating, she was the one who took the silver-
colored trash cans out to the curb on Monday nights. She did so faithfully,
on evenings when she had already balanced the checkbook and paid the
bills and ministered to sore throats and made certain we'd had dinner; but
all up and down the street everybody knew the truth: taking out the trash
was clearly a job for fathers.

When I was 10, my mother began to work for the Department of Social 5
Services, a world in which the simple rules of the suburbs did not apply.
She counseled young unwed mothers, girls and women who were not
allowed to make their own choices, most of whom had not been allowed
to finish high school or stay in their own homes, none of whom had been
allowed to decide not to continue their pregnancies. Later, my mother
placed most of these babies in foster care, and still later, she moved to the
protective-services department, investigating charges of abuse and neglect,
often having to search a child's back and legs for bruises or welts.

She would have found some on my friend, left there by her righteous 6
father, the one who wouldn't allow her to visit our home but blackened
her eye when, a few years later, he discovered that she was dating a boy he
didn't approve of. But none of his neighbors had dared to report him. They
would never have imagined that someone like my friend's father, whose
trash cans were always tidily placed at the curb, whose lawn was always
well cared for, might need watching.

To my mother, abuse was a clear-cut issue, if reported and found, but 7
neglect was more of a judgment call. It was, in effect, passing judgment on
the nature of love. If my father had not sent the child support checks on
time, if my mother hadn't been white and college educated, it could have
easily been us in one of those apartments she visited, where the heat didn't
work on the coldest days, and the dirt was so encrusted you could mop all
day and still be called a poor housekeeper, and there was often nothing
more for dinner than Frosted Flakes and milk, or, if it was toward the end
of the month, the cereal might be served with tap water. Would that have
meant my mother loved her children any less, that we were less of a family?

My mother never once judged who was a fit mother on the basis of a 8
clean floor, or an unbalanced meal, or a boyfriend who sometimes spent
the night. But back then, there were good citizens who were only too ready
to set their standards for women and children, factoring out poverty or
exhaustion or simply a different set of beliefs.

There are always those who are ready to deal out judgment with the 9
ready fist of the righteous. I know this because before the age of 10 I was
one of the righteous, too. I believed that mothers were meant to stay home
and fathers should carry out the trash on Monday nights. I believed that
parents could create a domestic life that was the next best thing to heaven,
if they just tried. That is what I'd been told, that in the best of all worlds
we would live identical lives in identical houses.

It's a simple view of the world, too simple even for childhood. 10
Certainly, it's a vision that is much too limited for the lives we live now,
when only one in 19 families are made up of a wage-earner father, a mother
who doesn't work outside the home and two or more children. And even
long ago, when I was growing up, we paid too high a price when we cut
ourselves off from the rest of the world. We ourselves did not dare to be
different. In the safety we created, we became trapped.

There are still places where softball games are played at dusk and roses 11
grow by the front door. There are families with sons named Bud, with kind
and generous fathers, and mothers who put up strawberry preserves every
June and always have time to sing lullabies. But do these families love their
children any more than the single mother who works all day? Are their

lullabies any sweeter? If I felt deprived as a child, it was only when our family was measured against some notion of what we were supposed to be. The truth of it was, we lacked for little.

And now that I have children of my own, and am exhausted at the end 12 of the day in which I've probably failed in a hundred different ways, I am amazed that women alone can manage. That they do, in spite of everything, is a simple fact. They rise from sleep in the middle of the night when their children call out to them. They rush for the cough syrup and cold washcloths and keep watch till dawn. These are real family values, the same ones we knew when we were children. As far as we were concerned our mother could cure a fever with a kiss. This may be the only thing we ever need to know about love. The rest, no one can judge.

❀   ❀   ❀

AFTER YOU READ

▪ *THINK* about the adjustment that Hoffman had to make after her parents' divorce. What are some details that show that divorce in the 1950s was not as fully accepted in society as it is today? How did Hoffman and her mother react to the condescension and criticism they received?

▪ *EXAMINE* paragraph 4, which points out the significance of Hoffman's mother taking "the silver-colored trash cans out to the curb on Monday nights." Why was it embarrassing for Hoffman that her mother had to take out the trash cans? How significant was the absence of the father in Hoffman's home? How successfully did she and her mother cope with this loss? (If you have read the previous selection, "Fatherless America" by David Blankenhorn, relate Hoffman's experience to Blankenhorn's discussion of the effects of fatherlessness.)

▪ *EXAMINE* the last paragraph of the essay in which Hoffman uses the term "family values." What family values does Hoffman admire in her mother? Do you agree with her view of family priorities?

▪ *WRITE* an essay in which you define and give examples of your idea of the "perfect family." Or *WRITE* an essay in which you discuss the effects of fatherlessness on a child or a family.

Unit Two: Critical Thinking and Writing Assignments

❀   ❀   ❀

EXPLORING IDEAS TOGETHER

1. Two of the selections in this unit (Connie May Fowler's "No Snapshots in the Attic" and Bret Lott's "Brothers") explore the importance of family photographs (and home movies) in reconstructing family histories. Discuss the roles that family pictures play according to these two writers. Does the essay by Lott confirm or contradict the essay by Fowler?

2. The poem by Robert E. Hayden and the essays by Amy Tan and Orville Rawlins describe the difficulty that parents and children—especially teenage children—often have in communicating with one another. Discuss with a group of your classmates the different communication problems depicted in each of these selections. Then try to find some common agreement on this topic among the different authors.

3. In their respective essays Alice Hoffman explains how she adjusted to her parents' divorce; David Blankenhorn analyzes the fatherlessness that may arise from divorce; and Julia Alvarez describes a stepfamily that has resulted from divorce. Discuss how these authors view the effects of divorce on a child. Working with a group of your peers, compare the viewpoints of these authors on this issue.

4. Both Amy Tan and Agnes G. Herman write about the expectations parents have for their children. Make a list of expectations that your parents have or had for you. Then compare your list with those of a group of your peers, discussing potential positive and negative effects.

WRITING ESSAYS

1. The essays by Connie May Fowler and Steve Sherwood both focus on family heritage—on searching for or maintaining connections with previous generations as a way of understanding oneself and passing on the family heritage to future generations. Write an essay about your own family heritage. Do you have a special "inheritance" of some sort from a particular family member? Do you have physical evidence of this heritage, or was this knowledge transmitted orally? If you do not have such a heritage, discuss why this heritage is missing in your life and what you have lost or gained as a result.

2. Steve Sherwood and Julia Alvarez discuss families that have been extended and complicated through marriage. Write an essay in which you take a position on the positive or negative effects that relationships with in-laws or step-relatives can have on a family.

3. The readings by Amy Tan and Orville Rawlins focus on a child's rebellion against a parent. In general, does the kind of rebellion described by these writers ultimately have a positive or negative effect on the child? Write an essay in which you argue your position.

4. Francine Klagsbrun and Bret Lott describe the intense competition that they felt with their brothers, and Amy Tan suggests that the competition that Jing-Mei Woo felt with Waverly resembled the competition between sisters. Write an essay discussing competition among siblings or other close family members. What causes such competition? What are the effects? Can this competition have positive as well as negative effects?

5. Kristin St. John's essay describes her personal experience as a child of mixed race adopted by a white family, Herman's essay analyzes the joys and challenges of raising an adopted son who is homosexual, and Robert Hayden's poem reveals the complexity of his relationship with his foster father. Write an essay in which you discuss adoption, focusing on its effects on personal identity and family relationships.

6. A significant relationship exists between families as portrayed on television and family life. Which family models do you see most often on television shows—the model of the traditional family that includes "the Good Family Man" described by Blankenhorn or the model described by Hoffman in which a strong single mother fulfills the roles of both father and mother? Write an essay in which you discuss either (1) the effect the portrayal of the family on television has on actual families or (2) the accuracy with which one or more television families portray real family life.

7. The readings by Francine Klagsbrun, Bret Lott, and John McPhee all rely on anecdotes, or brief stories, to portray a family member. Write an essay in which you use two or three brief anecdotes to characterize one of your family members.

8. Write an essay on *one* particular family relationship: mother-daughter, mother-son, father-daughter, father-son, grandmother-granddaughter, grandfather-grandson, and so forth. Use support from your own experiences, observations, and reading.

Self with Friends and Mates

Although your family relationships may be largely predetermined by biology and circumstances, you reach beyond your family to choose your friends and your mate. These choices are, of course, also influenced by chance meetings and circumstances of college, work, and play. However, most people have a good idea of what they want—and do not want—in a friend or a mate.

Friends are a major influence in your life. At work or in class, you often define yourself in terms of your friends. You may even, consciously or unconsciously, choose friends who match your concept of yourself or of the self you want to be. Or you may choose friends with qualities different from yours—friends of different ages, backgrounds, or interests—to complement your own qualities.

Throughout your lifetime, you will have a great many friends. Unlike your family ties, which remain basically the same, your friendships will change. That is, your friends in college may be different from those you had as a child, or your relationship with a particular friend may change. A friend may move away, or even die. Sometimes a relationship that starts as a friendship may develop into a romantic attachment.

Perhaps the most important "friend" you will select is your mate. Your decision to share your life with a particular person, whether you choose carefully and deliberately or hastily and impulsively, tells more about you and how you perceive yourself than almost any other decision you make. Just as individuals usually have many different friends in life, most people typically date a variety of potential partners, ultimately deciding, on the basis of these experiences, which one is "right." Ideally, this choice results in a long and happy life together—a life in which the two people love and support each other, share an intimate emotional and physical relationship, have children and cooperate in rearing them, and grow old together.

In reality, however, choosing a mate is seldom as tidy and uncomplicated as this description suggests. Finding a partner often involves luck and circumstances as much as, or more than, love and wisdom. In spite of all the time and energy you devote to the process of selecting a mate, your decision will probably be influenced by where you are and whom you know. And although the romantic ideal in our society continues to be that two people meet, fall in love, get married, and live happily ever after, that ideal is often not realized. You will be joining an increasingly small minority if you spend your entire life happily married to one person. It is possible, perhaps even likely, that you will have a series of partners, each of whom will play a significant role in your life. Furthermore, life experiences with mates vary greatly. Some people choose to live together before or instead of marrying, others divorce and remarry one or more times, and still others outlive one mate and then choose another. In addition, some individuals select mates of the same sex, and other individuals—sometimes by chance but often by choice—remain single.

As you read the selections in this unit, you will, naturally, enjoy and comprehend readings you can relate to your own experiences, but you can also gain new information and an understanding of different viewpoints through your reading.

A Small Act

JIMMY CARTER

❁

Jimmy Carter (James Earl Carter, Jr.) was the thirty-ninth president of the United States, but his greatest legacy may well be the work he has done as an ex-president. Since leaving the White House, Carter and his wife Rosalynn have dedicated themselves to working for social justice and basic human rights. The nonprofit Carter Center, based in Atlanta, promotes peace and health in nations around the globe. And each year for one week, the Carters lead the Jimmy Carter Work Project for Habitat for Humanity International. In addition, Carter has written fifteen books, most recently An Hour Before Daylight: Memories of a Rural Boyhood *(2001). The reading selection below is taken from this memoir.*

BEFORE YOU READ

▪ *THINK* of your own early childhood and the playmates you had. Which of these playmates do you remember most vividly and why?

▪ *EXAMINE* the title of this selection. Think of a small act that affected a relationship you had with a friend. Was the effect positive or negative? Was the act intentional or unintentional?

▪ *WRITE* a journal entry about a friendship you had as a child. Include in your account how and why that relationship changed as you grew older.

AS YOU READ

Notice how and why Carter's relationship with his black friends changes as he grows older.

Adapted from *An Hour Before Daylight: Memories of a Rural Boyhood* by Jimmy Carter. Copyright © 2001 by Jimmy Carter. Reprinted by permission of the author.

From the first day we moved to the farm in Archery, my primary 1
playmate was Alonzo Davis, always known as A.D., who lived on our
farm with his uncle and aunt. During my first four years in Plains I had
known only white children, and it must have been quite a change for me
to meet this very timid little black boy with kinky hair, big eyes, and a
tendency to mumble when he talked. I soon learned that A.D.'s bashfulness
evaporated as soon as we were out of the presence of adults and on our
own together, and it took me about an hour to forget, once and for all,
about any racial differences between us. Since our other playmates on the
farm were also black, it was only natural for me to consider myself the
outsider and to strive to emulate their habits and language. It never seemed
to me that A.D. tried to change, except when one of my parents was present.
Then he just became much quieter, watched what was going on with
vigilance, and waited until we were alone again to resume his more carefree
and exuberant ways.

I was soon spending most of my waking hours on the farm with him, 2
except when I was alongside Daddy or Jack Clark. Although his surrogate
parents didn't know exactly when he was born, A.D. was close to my age,
and it was not long after we met that he and his aunt adopted my birthday
as his own, so we could share whatever celebrations there might be. A.D.
was slightly larger and stronger than I, but not quite as fast or agile, so we
were almost equal in our constant wrestling, running, and other contests.
I was perfectly at ease in his house, and minded his uncle and aunt as though
they were my own parents. At least during our younger years, I believe that
he felt equally comfortable in our house; he and I didn't think it was
anything out of the ordinary in our eating together in the kitchen, rather
than at the table where my family assembled for meals.

When I had a choice of companions, I always preferred A.D. We 3
worked, played, fished, trapped, explored, built things, fought, and were
punished together if we violated adult rules. Our other regular playmates
were A.D.'s cousin Edmund Hollis and Milton and Johnny Raven, two
brothers who lived a half-mile down the road. . . .

Until my last two years of high school, the black boys at Archery were my 4
closest friends; I had a more intimate relationship with them than with any
of my white classmates in town. This makes it more difficult for me to
justify or explain my own attitudes and actions during the segregation era.
A turning point in my relationship with A.D. and my other friends occurred
when we were about fourteen years old. Until then, there had never been
any distinction among us, despite the great difference between our eco-

nomic circumstances. I lived in the "big house" and they lived in tenant shacks; I had a bicycle, my parents owned an automobile, and we went to separate churches and schools. I was destined to go to college, and few of them would finish their high school work. But there were no acknowledged differences of rank or status when we were together in the fields, on the creek banks, or playing in our yard or theirs, and we never thought about being of different color.

Around age fourteen, I began to develop closer ties with the white community. I was striving for a place on the varsity basketball team and developed a stronger relationship with my classmates, including a growing interest in dating girls. One day about this time, A.D., Edmund, and I approached the gate leading from our barn to the pasture. To my surprise, they opened it and stepped back to let me go through first. I was immediately suspicious that they were playing some trick on me, but I passed through without stumbling over a tripwire or having them slam the gate in my face.

It was a small act, but a deeply symbolic one. After that, they often treated me with some deference. I guess that their parents had done or said something that caused this change in my black friends' attitude. The constant struggle for leadership among our small group was resolved, but a precious sense of equality had gone out of our personal relationship, and things were never again the same between them and me.

It seems strange now that I never discussed this transition in our lives with either my black friends or my own parents. We still competed equally while on the baseball field, fishing, or working in the field, but I was not reluctant to take advantage of my new stature by assuming, on occasion, the authority of my father. Also, we were more inclined to go our separate ways if we had an argument, since I was increasingly involved with my white friends in Plains. I guess all of us just assumed that this was one more step toward maturity and that we were settling into our adult roles in an unquestioned segregated society.

❀ ❀ ❀

AFTER YOU READ

- *THINK* about the circumstances that led to the change in Carter's relationship with his black friends. Remember that Carter was born in 1924 in a small Southern town. Were friendships between white and black children common at this time? Were such friendships more or less likely to occur in the South than in the North? Why do you think his relationships with his black playmates changed as they grew older? Are relationships between children of different races or ethnic backgrounds more or less common today? Why or why not?

• *EXAMINE* Carter's description of the "small act" that changed his relationship with his black playmates (paragraphs 5–6). What was the act? Why do you think Carter calls this act "deeply symbolic"? What does the act symbolize for him and his friends?

• *WRITE* an essay or memoir about a relationship you have had with someone who was different from you in some way or about a relationship that changed significantly.

A Simple Gift

ROBERT J. MATTHEWS

❀

Robert J. Matthews, a mathematics teacher and free-lance writer who lives in San Francisco, made a trip to Kath-mandu, Nepal, in 1989. After returning from his trip, he wrote this account of an incident that occurred during the last days of his visit. Like the preceding selection by Jimmy Carter, this one is about a friendship between people from two very different worlds. Matthews's relationship is also affected by a small but significant act, but his memoir focuses on a fleeting friendship between two people who know very little about each other and who have no opportunity to get to know each other better.

BEFORE YOU READ

- *THINK* about very brief but memorable encounters with people you have had. How are these fleeting friendships different from more lasting relationships? Are they more or less significant than longer relationships? Does one of these fleeting encounters stand out in your mind more than others?

- *EXAMINE* the following sentence that occurs in the second paragraph of this memoir:

> I certainly did not know these people as one knows a friend or even an acquaintance, but for the past several months they had been my land-marks. . . .

What is the difference between a friend and an acquaintance? What do you think Matthews means by "landmarks"? How can people serve as land-marks in a person's life?

- *WRITE* a description of a brief but significant encounter you had with a person and why it was important to you.

Try to determine why this brief encounter made such an impression on Matthews.

It was almost winter, and nearing the end of my stay in Nepal; much of 1 my time was occupied with saying good-bye. I had gotten to know many new people on this particular visit, but those persons whom I most actively sought out were those whom I had gotten to know the least.

They were waiters, merchants, black-market money changers; they 2 were little children and old women who sold single cigarettes and matches along damp, narrow streets. I certainly did not know these people as one knows a friend or even an acquaintance, but for the past several months they had been my landmarks along countless streets and in innumerable restaurants, and they were by now as familiar to me as any back home. It was this collection of faces, brief greetings and equally brief conversations that always endeared Nepal to me.

Upon finding one of these persons prior to my departure, I rarely 3 would actually say good-bye. Instead, I found that all I really wanted to do was just look at them once more; to memorize them in their world, perhaps foolishly thinking that the moment could later be recalled with the same life and clarity as the original.

Sometimes, in my marginal Nepali, I would say that I am returning to 4 my own country. Most often the reply was simply a smile, accompanied by the characteristic little sideways nod of the head which in Nepal means understanding. And that was all.

One person with whom I did speak was an old man I used to see almost 5 every day. He seemed to spend most of his time just sitting in the sun on a small, raised wooden platform next to an outdoor marketplace where aggressive women with clumps of wrinkled and faded rupees in their fists deftly negotiated the cacophonous buying and selling of fruits and vegetables.

The first time I saw him he smiled at me. He said nothing, nor did I 6 stop to speak with him. I recall giving him a rather cursory smile in return, and then continued on my way without another thought. A few days later I saw him again, still seated in the same place. As I passed him he smiled at me again just as he had before. I was taken by how sincere this man's expression was, and also how peaceful he seemed to be. I smiled back and offered the traditional *namaste,* which he returned. I could not quite explain why, but it was that ingenuous smile of his that many times made me detour just to see him and say hello.

Eventually I found that he spoke a few words of English, and sometimes we would have a cigarette together and exchange pleasantries. Sometimes, after dinner, I would walk through the silent streets that were now only sporadically lit by the weak light filtering through greasy restaurant windows. Then I would come upon him, still seated in the same place. He would be sitting quietly, smoking, and sometimes drinking tea out of the ubiquitous glass tumbler that someone had probably bought for him. 7

One evening, on my way back to my room after dinner, I saw him in his usual spot, and I stopped to say hello. For the first time since I had known him, I glimpsed his feet protruding from under the rough woolen blanket that always covered him. They were severely misshapen and deeply ulcerated, and the toes were unusually short and seemed strangely small for his feet. I remembered having seen similar symptoms during a brief stint of clinical work I had done several years earlier. No doubt it was very difficult for this man to walk, and it was now apparent why so much of his time was spent sitting. He had leprosy. 8

Some time after this I again stopped to greet him. He smiled and appeared glad to see me. We spoke easily now; he in his broken English, and I in my fractured Nepali. Out of respect I now called him *daju,* or "older brother," as is the custom. The first time I addressed him as *daju* his expression did not change, but from then on he called me *bhai,* or "younger brother," as though he had been doing so for years. 9

I cannot explain the feeling, but there has always been something exquisitely heartwarming about being referred to as "*bhai*" or "*daju*" by the Nepalis. Perhaps these words were intended to convey nothing more than simple courtesy to a foreigner, but countless times I have been struck by the intimacy these words implied, and the genuine affection with which they were spoken. 10

We talked for a few more minutes, and when I left I gave him a couple of cigarettes wrapped in a five-rupee note. He accepted this graciously and with dignity. I said good-bye, but resolved to continue to see him until I had to leave. 11

This I did, and in the course of my last few days in Kathmandu we would talk frequently. I would do as much as I could manage in Nepali, but we usually relied considerably more on English. We sometimes had a glass of tea together in the pale afternoon sun, limiting our conversation to superficial things, but enjoying it nevertheless. 12

It gets cold at night in November, and prior to leaving I wanted to 13 bring the old man a pair of heavy woolen socks that I had brought for use in the mountains. On my last night in Nepal, I found him sitting in his usual place. It was a very cold night. I approached him and said that tomorrow I was leaving. I then said that I wished to give him my socks. He said nothing. I felt awkward, and as gently as I could I lifted the blanket that covered his legs. I put the socks on what remained of his feet and tried to explain that I would be pleased if he would keep them.

For a long moment he did not speak. I feared that I might have made 14 him uncomfortable, but then he looked at me with marvelous compassion in his eyes and said, "God bless you, *bhai*. No one has touched me in a very long time."

❀   ❀   ❀

AFTER YOU READ

▪ *THINK* about why Matthews wanted to say goodbye to these "landmark" people who had become familiar to him during his visit to Nepal. How would you characterize the type of relationship he had with these people? Why were they important to Matthews?

▪ *EXAMINE* Matthews's description of his "simple gift" to the leper. Which was the greater gift—the heavy woolen socks he gave the man or the touch? Why had the man not been touched "in a very long time"? Why was this incident significant to Matthews as well as to the leper?

▪ *WRITE* an essay about a brief but significant encounter with someone. Include a detailed description of the person and a clear account of the encounter as well as what you learned about yourself from this experience or how it changed you.

Snapshots of Memory

CHRISTINE CHOI

❀

Christine Choi, who grew up in Cornwall, New York, is currently a student at Northwestern University in Evanston, Illinois, where she is majoring in English and religion. In this essay, Choi describes two high school friends by identifying the images they evoke in her mind when she thinks of them.

BEFORE YOU READ

▪ *THINK* about several of your closest friends. How would you describe them? What one thing about each defines that person in your mind?

▪ *EXAMINE* the first paragraph of this essay. Can you tell from reading this introductory paragraph what the essay is about? What clues does Choi provide to indicate what her focus will be in this essay?

▪ *WRITE* in your journal brief descriptions of several present or past friends.

AS YOU READ

Notice the vivid, descriptive details and images the author uses. Mark the ones that you find most useful in understanding the person she is describing.

Friends are more than their physical stature, width, hair-style, or shoe- size. They are not defined by the styles they wear, their mannerisms, or even the things they say. Our friends' personalities bleed into everyday ordinary objects—smells, textures of fabrics, flavors, sounds, and colors. As we spend longer months and years with the people we enjoy, romping together in good company, making memories while trailing through our physical surroundings, certain images become symbols of those relation-ships, those people, those particular months and years.

This past Fourth of July, my friends Alicia and Tenley and I drove up 2 to Hampton, New Hampshire, from Boston to visit our friend Sally. Since our high school graduation a year ago, we're all eager for moments like this—taking wrong exits and squinting at vague handwritten directions as salty-damp gusts tossed our hair through open windows. This is the summer after our first year apart. At red lights, we frowned and turned up the radio, allowing swanky Latin rhythms to console our lack of direction. Alicia had made jam. The red jam in a flat Tupperware container sat beside me in the back seat. Alicia is the only person I can think of who would make raspberry rhubarb jam for no particular reason and drive to New Hampshire with it. The unique seed-studded crimson color, the super-sweet flavor of it spread on Eggo waffles speak of Alicia. To me, that jam *is* Alicia; it speaks to me of the way she bustles around her kitchen, eager to mark reactions of those who sample her results. It sings of her preference for unique, challenging dishes, for elaborate detail. It reminds me of her sweet-tooth. The raspberry rhubarb jam seated beside me describes Alicia in so many more ways than adjectives in my vocabulary ever would.

The jam is a symbol of the time Alicia and I made cookies using a recipe 3 from her grandmother's Cuban cookbook. It was her idea to follow a recipe in Spanish, for a challenge. We decided on vanilla chocolate spiral cookies, as it was the only one that contained simple ingredients that we could understand and pronounce. Eagerly, we turned to the first line of the directions which, translated literally, read, "Ostracize the chocolate in Maria's bathroom until it forms a paste." An exchanged glance and a moment later, the two of us were rolling around on her kitchen floor, shuddering with uncontrollable laughter as tears streamed down our cheeks. The jewel-red raspberry rhubarb jam symbolizes the way Alicia later covered the plate of perfect spiral cookies with wax paper instead of aluminum foil so that everyone could admire the product of our labors. The sweet jam spread thick on Alicia's Eggos represents the way she likes her French toast with both cinnamon sugar and syrup, as she wasn't allowed to have both when she was little.

By mid-afternoon, we pulled into the driveway of Sally's dad's house 4 in Hampton with our jam, tires crunching on gravel as Latin rhythms flooded through our open windows. "Come see the sheep!" Sally chimed, as she waved a hand and led us around the house to her backyard. The four of us leaned over the fence, squinting in summer heat, watching her dad's sheep chew lazily and occasionally blink in our direction.

Sally is my roommate for the summer. After having been separated 5
nine hundred miles for our first year at college, we spontaneously decided
sometime in the spring to share an apartment and work in Boston. We were
eager to help each other unpack last month, rearranging the random
furniture that had accumulated in the living room that we'd be sharing.
She had an entire box of thick cream-colored wool sweaters. "Sally, it's
June," I remarked. She flashed me a smile as she continued to stack her
sweaters in neatly folded piles. She also brought with her a thick, soft,
sheepskin rug—for petting purposes only. The "sheepy rug" lies carefully
draped at the head of her bed; a silent symbol of the Sally I know. Sheep,
wool, cream-colored sweaters, and the warm soft texture of her "sheepy
rug" have come to represent Sally to me in ways elusive words cannot.
Leaning over her backyard fence listening to her soft, slow-spoken words
describe the lambs that were sold the week before, confirmed my Sally-
sheep metaphor.

Sally speaks slowly and moves deliberately and carefully. When I first 6
met her four years ago, I remember watching her "doodle" beautiful,
intricate leaf patterns and outlines of girls' faces with sunken, shaded eyes
in the margin of her English notes. Her simple, black L.L. Bean bag was
distinguished from others by an indigo beaded swirl that she had stitched
on one idle afternoon. Now she studies Fine Arts in New York, bringing
home the fleece, denim, and silk handbags that she makes herself. "Feel it.
It's so soft," she prompts, as she offers me folds of fabric. Prints and photos
of friends and sheep hang on our walls, as she plods around the apartment
in her wool sweaters and makes pots of apricot tea.

We are surrounded by symbols. Ordinary objects like jam or sheep 7
serve as portholes that transport us to glossy-print moments—snapshots of
memory where friends are squinting or making us laugh in ways that are
so uniquely them but that they may not realize. When Alicia packed her
raspberry rhubarb jam into that little Tupperware container, she had no
idea how much of herself she would be serving up. Sally's love of soft warm
textures and the sheep that graze in her dad's backyard speak of who she
is. When she offers me a piece of fabric to feel, she is offering me her
friendship, her self. And as I feel the fabric, I think of Sally sitting beside
me in Sophomore English, with her fists tucked into the sleeves of her
cream-colored sweater.

❀   ❀   ❀

AFTER YOU READ

▪ *THINK* about the friends you described in your journal. What symbol or image would you assign each of them? Is a symbol or image that you associate with someone an effective way of defining that person? Why or why not?

▪ *EXAMINE* Choi's implicit argument that a symbol or metaphor (something concrete that stands for something abstract or intangible) is a better way to describe a person than is factual information such as physical characteristics, occupation, hobbies, etc. Do you agree or disagree with this argument? Why or why not? What are the advantages of describing someone in this way? What are the disadvantages?

▪ *WRITE* an essay in which you describe one of the friends you wrote about in your journal. Like Choi, choose a dominant symbol, image, or metaphor to represent this friend and to serve as the focus of your essay.

The Difference Between Male and Female Friendships

ELLEN GOODMAN
and
PATRICIA O'BRIEN

❁

Ellen Goodman and Patricia O'Brien are good friends who recently wrote a book together entitled I Know Just What You Mean: The Power of Friendship in Women's Lives *(2000). Although this book focuses on female friendships—how they work and how they affect the lives of women—the authors also explore the differences between male and female friendships. The following reading selection is taken from their book and attempts to answer the question, "Why do men and women, on the topic of friendship, puzzle each other so much?"*

BEFORE YOU READ

- *THINK* about your own perceptions of male and female friendships. Do you see them as different? In what ways?

- *EXAMINE* the last sentence of the first paragraph in which the authors state: "While women tend to *be* together, men tend to *do* together." Do you agree with this statement? Why or why not? If this observation is accurate, what does it indicate in terms of the difference between male and female friendships?

- *WRITE* a journal entry in which you list some of the differences you think exist between male and female friendships.

AS YOU READ

Number the differences between male and female friendships that you find in this selection.

Why do men and women, on the topic of friendship, puzzle each other 1
so much? Let us start with the obvious: women do friendship
differently than men. Among women, friendship is conducted face-to-face.
But as Carolyn Heilbrun once wrote, "Male friends do not always face each
other: they stand side by side, facing the world." While women tend to *be*
together, men tend to *do* together.

We have thought about this friendship divide ever since that dinner 2
back in 1975, a time when sex differences were just beginning to go under
an intense cultural microscope. We know that men's feelings of closeness
and connection are real; that painting a house or watching a ball game
together can be an act of friendship. But we also know we would feel lonely
if we couldn't talk to each other about everything, through good and bad
times.

The two of us have wondered over the years just what is going on 3
between men. And the truth is, we have disagreed with each other about
whether men are missing something so central to friendship that it amounts
to almost a fatal flaw, or whether they are handling friendship just fine—in
their own, mysterious way. Do men, as Letty Pogrebin wrote in *Among
Friends,* deserve "Incompletes" in the subject of friendship? Are women in
the business of grading?

"What on earth do you have to say to each other?" men ask. Women 4
have their own counterquestion for male friends: "You spent all day
together on the golf course and never told him you were worried about
your job?"

When we first began telling people that we were writing about women 5
and friendship, the second or third question would invariably be, "What
about men? Are you writing about them, too?" Sometimes it was asked
with a smile or a teasing challenge; sometimes defensively. We could hear
a distinct subtext: if you're writing only about women, are you saying your
friendships are better than ours?

We answered that we were writing about women because, if you write 6
about what you know, what we know are women's friendships. We would
leave it to men to write about their own friendships. The contradictory,
complex differences between the two sexes in a time of such change is a
topic for a different kind of book. Yet here we are, looking across the gender
divide with curiosity and sometimes bewilderment.

Let's give comedian Rob Becker the first take on this subject. Becker 7
plays Darwin to the sexes in the theatrical hit, *Defending the Caveman.* He
announces to his audiences at one point that—at last—he has the gender-
friendship gap all figured out.

So, here's how it works, he says. Men were the hunters, see? They were 8
required to stand side by side without talking for fear they'd scare off the
prey. Women? They were gatherers, out there foraging in the jungle for
food. So they HAD to talk while they worked, for safety.

You get the picture? "If a woman goes for very long without hearing 9
the voice of another woman, she knows she's been eaten by an animal,"
Becker announces. So women are genetically allotted some five thousand
words a day, while men are allotted only two thousand. No wonder women
talk more, he triumphantly concludes.

Well, hunters and gatherers aside, if there is one prototypical image of 10
women sharing friendship, it's that of two friends sitting across a table from
each other, clutching their coffee cups, talking feelings. If there is a similar
image of men, it is of buddies sitting together watching television, talking
football.

We know these images are simplistic and women and men are both 11
guilty of stretching them to make assumptions about each other's friendships that range from the stereotypic to the bizarre. Men never talk about
anything but sports, women say in frustration. Women talk only about
clothes, men retort. Both sexes get trapped in vast generalizations. But the
differences between the same-sex friendships of men and women are real.
Decades of research can't be ignored.

A long list of studies tell men and women what they already know: 12
men and women talk about different things in different ways. Men are less
likely to talk about personal subjects with other men than women are with
other women. As Pogrebin summed it up, "The average man's idea of an
intimate exchange is the average woman's idea of a casual conversation."

What else do the researchers show? Men's friendships are based on 13
shared activities, women's on shared feelings. Men who do things together,
paint that house, change that tire, feel close; women who share secrets,
troubles, relationships, feel close.

If you had a camera you could videotape the gender gap. Women 14
literally touch each other more; they sit closer together, focus on one-to-
one sharing. But when men talk about what they do with their friends, you
get a different portrait: men doing things together in groups.

The research list goes on. Men do not criticize their friends as much 15
as women, but neither do they communicate the kind of acceptance women
count on from their friends. Men put shared interests highest among the
reasons they bond with a friend, while women first want friends who share
their values. And even men tend to view their friendships with women as
closer and more intimate than those with other men.

And yet—here's the counterweight—at least among grade school boys, 16 a study shows that a relative lack of intimacy and affection doesn't affect the importance or the satisfaction boys get from their friends.

Every friendship is as different as the people involved, and not all men 17 are caveman hunters and not all women are cavewoman gatherers. But differences between male and female friendships have remained constant and consistent. What has shifted are the values placed on those differences. What's striking now is that the culture has gone from seeing men's friendships as superior to seeing women's friendships as superior. Is that just a swing of the pendulum?

It's not surprising that philosophers in the past routinely dismissed 18 women as incapable of true friendship. They were certain that, because women led more "trivial" lives, they had limited capacity for elevated feelings. The classical idea of friendship was heroic, and the greatest thing a man could give a friend was his courage and loyalty. Montaigne once wrote in a spirit of superior regret, "To speak truly, the usual capacity of women is not equal to the demands of the communion and intercourse which is the sustenance of that sacred bond; nor do their minds seem firm enough to sustain the pressure of so hard and so lasting a knot."

Women, on the other hand, often idealized their relationships with 19 each other. Historian Nancy Cott describes how educated women in the nineteenth century passionately poured out their feelings, often expressing their firm belief in the superiority of female relationships. "I do not feel that men can ever feel so pure an enthusiasm for women as we can feel for one another," wrote one woman to another. "Ours is nearest to the love of angels."

The idea that friendship is defined by intimacy has become, in our time, 20 less fervently defined—but more solidly understood. As a result, the gender gap has been focused on the intimacy gap. And men's friendships are indeed often given an "incomplete" grade.

❀   ❀   ❀

AFTER YOU READ

▪ *THINK* about the authors' argument that women friends communicate with each other while men friends simply do things together. In your experience, do you find this to be true? If so, what does it say about men and women?

• *EXAMINE* Pogrebin's assertion that "The average man's idea of an intimate exchange is the average woman's idea of a casual conversation." Do you agree with this assertion? Why or why not? Do you believe that men's friendships are inferior to women's simply because men do not communicate in the way women do? Why or why not? What other significant differences do you think exist between male and female friendships?

• *WRITE* an essay in which you compare and/or contrast male and female friendships. You may want to use the selection by Goodman and O'Brien as a resource in addition to your own experiences and observations. Or *WRITE* an essay in which you agree or disagree with the authors about the differences they claim exist between male and female friendships. Support your argument with examples from your own experiences and observations.

What Friends Are For

PHILLIP LOPATE

❦

Although New Yorker Phillip Lopate thinks of himself as a creative writer—a poet and novelist—he has received high praise for his nonfiction works, which include the selection that follows as well as Bachelorhood: Tales of the Metropolis *and* Portrait of My Body. *In the following essay, originally published in the collection* Against Joie de Vivre, *Lopate uses personal examples and thoughtful analysis to define friendship. Lopate's special interest in personal essays such as "What Friends Are For" is also apparent in his anthology* The Art of the Personal Essay.

BEFORE YOU READ

- *THINK* about the people you consider to be friends, making a list of the three or four who are most important to you. Why did you select these people as friends? Do you and your friends have interests and opinions in common, or are you very different? Do you see a pattern in your friendships?

- *EXAMINE* Lopate's title, "What Friends Are For." In your opinion, what are friends for? That is, what role do they play in your life? How important are friends to you?

- *WRITE* a journal entry in which you explain what friends are for. Include in your entry a discussion of the roles that your friends play in your life.

AS YOU READ

Notice that Lopate's view of friendship challenges that of Goodman and O'Brien, who argue in the previous essay that men "are less likely to talk about personal subjects with other men than women are with other women." Lopate suggests that communication is an important element of all friendships. As you read, identify and mark the references he makes to the role and importance of communication in friendships.

Friendship has been called "love without wings." On the other hand, the ₁ Stoic definition of love ("Love is the attempt to form a friendship inspired by beauty") seems to suggest that friendship came first. Certainly a case can be made that the buildup of affection and the yearning for more intimacy, without the release of sexual activity, keeps friends in a state of sweet-sorrowful itchiness that has the romantic quality of a love affair. We know that a falling-out between two old friends can leave a deeper and more perplexing hurt than the ending of a love affair, perhaps because we are more pessimistic about the affair's endurance from the start.

Our first attempted friendships are within the family. It is here we ₂ practice the techniques of listening sympathetically and proving that we can be trusted, and learn the sort of kindness we can expect in return.

There is something tainted about these family friendships, however. ₃ My sister, in her insecure adolescent phase, told me, "You love me because I'm related to you, but if you were to meet me for the first time at a party, you'd think I was a jerk and not worth being your friend." She had me in a bind: I had no way of testing her hypothesis. I should have argued that even if our bond was not freely chosen, our decision to work on it had been. Still, we are quick to dismiss the partiality of our family members when they tell us we are talented, cute, or lovable; we must go out into the world and seduce others.

It is just a few short years from the promiscuity of the sandbox to the ₄ tormented, possessive feelings of a fifth grader who has just learned that his best and only friend is playing at another classmate's house after school. There may be worse betrayals in store, but probably none is more influential than the sudden fickleness of an elementary school friend who has dropped us for someone more popular after all our careful, patient wooing. Often we lose no time inflicting the same betrayal on someone else, just to ensure that we have got the victimization dynamic right.

What makes friendships in childhood and adolescence so poignant is ₅ that we need the chosen comrade to be everything in order to rescue us from the gothic inwardness of family life. Even if we are lucky enough to have several companions, there must be a Best Friend.

I clung to the romance of the Best Friend all through high school, ₆ college, and beyond, until my circle of university friends began to disperse. At that point, in my mid-20s, I also acted out the dark, competitive side of friendship that can exist between two young men fighting for a place in life and love by doing the one unforgivable thing: sleeping with my best friend's girl. I was baffled at first that there was no way to repair the damage. I lost this friendship forever, and came away from that debacle much more aware of the amount of injury that friendship can and cannot sustain. Perhaps I needed to prove to myself that friendship was not an all-permissive resilient bond, like a mother's love, but something quite fragile. Precisely because best friendship promotes such a merging of identities, such seeming boundarylessness, the first major transgression of trust can cause the injured party to feel he is fighting for his violated soul against his darkest enemy. There is not much room to maneuver in a best friendship between unlimited intimacy and unlimited mistrust.

Still, it was not until the age of thirty that I reluctantly abandoned the   7 best friend expectation and took up a more pluralistic model. At present, I cherish a dozen friends for their unique personalities, without asking that any one be my soul-twin. Whether this alteration constitutes a movement toward maturity or toward cowardly pragmatism is not for me to say. It may be that, in refusing to depend so much on any one friend, I am opting for self-protection over intimacy. Or it may be that, as we advance into middle age, the life problem becomes less that of establishing a tight dyadic bond and more one of making our way in a broader world, "society." Indeed, since Americans have so indistinct a notion of society, we often try to put a network of friendships in its place.

If a certain intensity is lost in the pluralistic model of friendship, there   8 is also the gain of being able to experience all of one's potential, half-buried selves, through witnessing all the spectacle of the multiple fates of our friends. As it happens, the harem of friends, so tantalizing a notion, often translates into feeling pulled in a dozen different directions, with the guilty sense of having disappointed everyone a little. It is also a risky, contrived enterprise to try to make one's friends behave in a friendly manner toward each other. If the effort fails, one feels obliged to mediate; if it succeeds too well, one is jealous.

Whether friendship is intrinsically singular and exclusive or plural and   9 democratic is a question that has vexed many commentators. Aristotle distinguished three types of friendship: "friendship based on utility," such as businessmen cultivating each other for benefit; "friendship based on pleasure," like young people interested in partying; and "perfect friendship." The first two categories Aristotle calls "qualified and superficial friendships," because they are founded on circumstances that could easily change. The last, which is based on admiration for another's good character, is more permanent, but also rarer, because good men "are few." Cicero, who wrote perhaps the best treatise on friendship, also insisted that what brings true friends together is "a mutual belief in each other's goodness." This insistence on virtue as a precondition for true friendship may strike us as impossibly demanding: Who, after all, feels himself good nowadays? And yet, if I am honest, I must admit that the friendships of mine that have lasted longest have been with those whose integrity, or humanity, or strength to bear their troubles I continue to admire. Conversely, when I lost respect for someone, however winning he or she otherwise remained, the friendship petered away almost immediately. "Remove respect from friendship," said Cicero, "and you have taken away the most splendid ornament it possesses."

Friendship is a long conversation. I suppose I could imagine a nonver- 10
bal friendship revolving around shared physical work or sport, but for me, good talk is the point of the thing. Indeed, the ability to generate conversation by the hour is the most promising indication, during the uncertain early stages, that a possible friendship will take hold. In the first few conversations there may be an exaggeration of agreement, as both parties angle for adhesive surfaces. But later on, trust builds through the courage to assert disagreement, through the tactful acceptance that differences of opinion will have to remain.

Some view like-mindedness as both the precondition and the product 11
of friendship. Myself, I distrust it. I have one friend who keeps assuming that we see the world eye-to-eye. She is intent on enrolling us in a flattering aristocracy of taste, on the short "we" list against the ignorant "they." Sometimes I do not have the strength to fight her need for consensus with my own stubborn disbelief in the existence of any such inner circle of privileged, cultivated sensibility. Perhaps I have too much invested in a view of myself as idiosyncratic to be eager to join any coterie, even a coterie of two. What attracts me to friends' conversation is the give and take, not necessarily that we come out at the same point.

"Our tastes and aims and views were identical—and that is where the 12
essence of a friendship must always lie," wrote Cicero. To some extent, perhaps, but then the convergence must be natural, not, as Emerson put it, "a mush of concession. Better be a nettle in the side of your friend than his echo."

Friendship is a school for character, allowing us the chance to study, 13
in great detail and over time, temperaments very different from our own.

These charming quirks, these contradictions, these nobilities, these blind spots of our friends we track not out of disinterested curiosity: We must have this information before knowing how far we may relax our guard, how much we may rely on them in crises. The learning curve of friendship involves, to no small extent, filling out this picture of the other's limitations and making peace with the results. Each time I hit up against a friend's inflexibility I am relieved as well as disappointed: I can begin to predict, and arm myself in advance against repeated bruises. I have one friend who is always late, so I bring a book along when I am to meet her. I give her a manuscript to read and she promises to look at it over the weekend. I prepare for a month-long wait.

Though it is often said that with a true friend there is no need to hold 14 anything back ("A friend is a person with whom I may be sincere. Before him I may think aloud," wrote Emerson), I have never found this to be entirely the case. Certain words may be too cruel if they are spoken at the wrong moment—or may fall on deaf ears, for any number of reasons. I also find with all my friends, as they must with me, that some initial resistance, restlessness, some psychic weather must be overcome before that tender ideal attentiveness may be called forth.

I have a good friend, Charlie, who is often very distracted whenever 15 we first get together. If we are sitting in a café he will look around constantly for the waiter, or be distracted by a pretty woman or the restaurant's cat. It would be foolish for me to broach an important subject at such moments, so I resign myself to waiting the half hour or however long it takes until his jumpiness subsides. Or else I draw this pattern grumpily to his attention. Once he has settled down, however, I can tell Charlie virtually anything, and he me. But the candor cannot be rushed. It must be built up to with the verbal equivalent of limbering exercises.

The friendship scene—a flow of shared confidences, recognitions, 16 humor, advice, speculation, even wisdom—is one of the key elements of modern friendships. Compared to the rest of life, this ability to lavish one's best energies on an activity utterly divorced from the profit motive and free from the routines of domination and inequality that affect most relations (including, perhaps, the selfsame friendship at other times) seems idyllic. The friendship scene is by its nature not an everyday occurrence. It represents the pinnacle, the fruit of the friendship, potentially ever present but not always arrived at. Both friends' dim yet self-conscious awareness that they are wandering conversationally toward a goal that they have previously accomplished but that may elude them this time around creates a tension, an obligation to communicate as sincerely as possible, like actors in an improvisation exercise struggling to shape their baggy material into some climactic form. This very pressure to achieve "quality" communication may induce a sort of inauthentic epiphany, not unlike what sometimes happens in the last ten minutes of a psychotherapy session. But a truly achieved friendship scene can be among the best experiences life has to offer.

Contemporary urban life, with its tight schedules and crowded appointment books, has helped to shape modern friendship into something requiring a good deal of intentionality and pursuit. You phone a friend and make a date a week or more in advance; then you set aside an evening, as if for a tryst, during which to squeeze in all your news and advice, confession and opinion. Such intimate compression may add a romantic note to modern friendships, but it also places a strain on the meeting to yield a high quality of meaning and satisfaction, closer to art than life. If I see busy or out-of-town friends only once every six months, we must not only catch up on our lives but also convince ourselves within the allotted two hours together that we still share a special affinity, an inner track to each other's psyches, or the next meeting may be put off for years. Surely there must be another, saner rhythm of friendship in rural areas—or maybe not? I think about "the good old days" when friends would go on walking tours through England together, when Edith Wharton would bundle poor Henry James into her motorcar and they'd drive to the south of France for a month. I'm not sure my friendships could sustain the strain of travel for weeks at a time, and the truth of the matter is that I've gotten used to this urban arrangement of serial friendship "dates," where the pleasure of the rendezvous is enhanced by the knowledge that it will only last, at most, six hours. If the two of us don't happen to mesh that day (always a possibility)—well, it's only a few hours. And if it should go beautifully, one needs an escape hatch from exaltation as well as disenchantment. I am capable of only so much intense, exciting communication before I start to fade: I come to these encounters equipped with a six-hour oxygen tank. Is this an evolutionary pattern of modern friendship, or just a personal limitation?

Perhaps because I conceive of the modern friendship scene as a somewhat theatrical enterprise, a one-act play, I tend to be very much affected by the "set." A restaurant, a museum, a walk in the park through the zoo, even accompanying a friend on shopping errands—I prefer public turf where the stimulation of the city can play a backdrop to our dialogue, feeding it with details when inspiration flags.

I have a number of *chez moi* friends who always invite me to come to 19
their homes while evading offers to visit me. What they view as hospitality
I see as a need to control the mise-en-scène of friendship. I am expected to
fit in where they are most comfortable, while they play lord of the manor,
distracted by the props of decor, the pool, the unexpected phone call, the
swirl of children, animals, and neighbors. Indeed, *chez moi* friends often
tend to keep a sort of open house, so that in going over to see them—for
a tête-à-tête, I had assumed—I will suddenly find their other friends and
neighbors, whom they have also invited, dropping in all afternoon. There
are only so many Sundays I care to spend hanging out with a friend's
entourage before I become impatient for a private audience.

Married friends who own their own homes are apt to try to draw me 20
into their domestic fold, whereas single people are often more sensitive
about establishing a discreet space for the friendship to occur. Perhaps the
married assume that a bachelor like me is desperate for home cooking and
a little family life. I have noticed that it is not an easy matter to pry a married
friend away from mate and milieu. For married people, especially those
with children, the home often becomes the wellspring of all their nurturing
feelings, and the single friend is invited to partake in the general flow.
Maybe there is also a certain tendency on their part to kill two birds with
one stone: They don't see enough of their spouse and kids, and they figure
they can visit with you at the same time.

From my standpoint, friendship is a jealous goddess. Whenever a friend 21
of mine marries, I have to fight to overcome the feeling that I am being
"replaced" by the spouse. I don't mind sharing a friend with his or her
family milieu—in fact I like it, up to a point—but eventually I must get the
friend alone, or else, as a bachelor at a distinct power disadvantage, I risk
becoming a mere spectator of familial rituals instead of a key player in the
drama of friendship.

A person who lives alone usually has more energy to give to friendship. 22
The danger is investing too much emotional energy in one's friends. When
a single person is going through a romantic dry spell, he or she often tries
to extract the missing passion from a circle of friends. This works only up
to a point: the frayed nerves of protracted celibacy can lead to hypersen-
sitive imaginings of slights and rejections, and one's platonic friends seem
to come particularly into the line of fire.

Today, with the partial decline of the nuclear family and the search for 23
alternatives to it, we also see attempts to substitute the friendship web for
intergenerational family life. Since psychoanalysis has alerted us to regard
the family as a mine field of unrequited love, manipulation, and ambiva-

lence, it is only natural that people may look to friendship as a more supportive ground for relation. But in our longing for an unequivocally positive bond, we should beware of sentimentalizing friendship, as saccharine "buddy" movies and certain feminist novels do, and of neutering its problematic aspects. Besides, friendship can never substitute for the true meaning of family: if nothing else, it will never be able to duplicate the family's wild capacity for concentrating neurosis.

In short, friends can't be your family, they can't be your lovers, they 24 can't be your psychiatrists. But they can be your friends, which is plenty.

When I think about the qualities that characterize the best friendships 25 I've known, I can identify five: rapport, affection, need, habit, and forgiveness. Rapport and affection can take you only so far; they may leave you at the formal, outer gate of goodwill, which is still not friendship. A persistent need for the other's company, for the person's interest, approval, opinion, will get you inside the gates, especially when it is reciprocated. In the end, however, there are no substitutes for habit and forgiveness. A friendship may travel for years on cozy habit. But it is a melancholy fact that unless you are a saint you are bound to offend every friend deeply at least once in the course of time. The friends I have kept the longest are those who forgave me time and again for wronging them unintentionally, intentionally, or by the plain catastrophe of my personality. There can be no friendship without forgiveness.

❀ ❀ ❀

AFTER YOU READ

• *THINK* about some of the qualities that Lopate believes are necessary to maintain friendship, including respect, good conversation, independent thought, character, sincerity, affection, need, habit, and forgiveness. In your opinion, which of these qualities are the most important? Why?

• *EXAMINE* Lopate's reference in paragraph 9 to Aristotle's classification of friends into three basic categories. Underline and number these categories. Do you agree that this classification is logical and realistic? Why or why not? Can you think of friends whom you would place in each category?

• *EXAMINE* also Lopate's statement in paragraph 24 that "friends can't be your family, they can't be your lovers, they can't be your psychiatrists. But they can be your friends, which is plenty." How are friends *different* from your family, from a lover, or from a psychiatrist? How are they *similar*? What ultimately distinguishes a friend from these other people?

▪ *WRITE* an essay in which you define *friendship* or a *friend*. Before writing your essay, review the journal entry that you wrote. As you plan your essay, remember that a definition essay may incorporate various other methods of development, such as the use of examples, comparison and contrast, and, perhaps even, classification.

From Front Porch to Back Seat

BETH BAILEY

❀

This reading selection is the first chapter of a sociological study of changing patterns of courtship in twentieth-century America. The author, Beth Bailey, points out that courtship literally moved from the front porch of the girl's home to the back seat of the boy's car, "from woman's sphere to man's sphere," in the last century. In supporting her thesis, Bailey provides her readers with a wealth of information about dating and what effects it has had on courtship in the United States.

BEFORE YOU READ

▪ *THINK* about the "dating system" that exists today in this country. How would you describe this system? Do you think there is a single, uniform system of dating in this country or different systems based on geographical, social, cultural, and economic factors?

▪ *EXAMINE* the title, "From Front Porch to Back Seat." How would you change this title to reflect where dates typically take place today?

▪ *WRITE* in your journal a brief definition of courtship as it exists today in this country.

AS YOU READ

Compare the dating practices Bailey describes with those you have experienced and observed.

One day, the 1920s story goes, a young man asked a city girl if he might 1
call on her. We know nothing else about the man or the girl—only that, when he arrived, she had her hat on. Not much of a story to us, but any American born before 1910 would have gotten the punch line. "She

had her hat on": those five words were rich in meaning to early twentieth-century Americans. The hat signaled that she expected to leave the house. He came on a "call," expecting to be received in her family's parlor, to talk, to meet with her mother, perhaps to have some refreshments or to listen to her play the piano. She expected a "date," to be taken "out" somewhere and entertained. He ended up spending four weeks' savings fulfilling her expectations.

In the early twentieth century this new style of courtship, dating, had begun to supplant the old. Born primarily of the limits and opportunities of urban life, dating had almost completely replaced the old system of calling by the mid-1920s—and, in so doing, had transformed American courtship. Dating moved courtship into the public world, relocating it from family parlors and community events to restaurants, theaters, and dance halls. At the same time, it removed couples from the implied supervision of the private sphere—from the watchful eyes of family and local community—to the anonymity of the public sphere. Courtship among strangers offered couples new freedom. But access to the public world of the city required money. One had to buy entertainment, or even access to a place to sit and talk. Money—men's money—became the basis of the dating system and, thus, of courtship. This new dating system, as it shifted courtship from the private to the public sphere and increasingly centered around money, fundamentally altered the balance of power between men and women in courtship.

The transition from calling to dating was as complete as it was fundamental. By the 1950s and 1960s, social scientists who studied American courtship found it necessary to remind the American public that dating was a "recent American innovation and not a traditional or universal custom." Some of the many commentators who wrote about courtship believed dating was the best thing that had ever happened to relations between the sexes; others blamed the dating system for all the problems of American youth and American marriage. But virtually everyone portrayed the system dating replaced as infinitely simpler, sweeter, more innocent, and more graceful. Hardheaded social scientists waxed sentimental about the "horse-and-buggy days," when a young man's offer of a ride home from church was tantamount to a proposal and when young men came calling in the evenings and courtship took place safely within the warm bosom of the family. "The courtship which grew out of the sturdy social roots [of the nineteenth century]," one author wrote, "comes through to us for what it was—a gracious ritual, with clearly defined roles for man and woman, in which everyone knew the measured music and the steps."

Certainly a less idealized version of this model of courtship had existed ₄ in America, but it was not this model that dating was supplanting. Although only about 45 percent of Americans lived in urban areas by 1910, few of them were so untouched by the sweeping changes of the late nineteenth century that they could live that dream of rural simplicity. Conventions of courtship at that time were not set by simple yeoman farmers and their families but by the rising middle class, often in imitation of the ways of "society."

By the late nineteenth century a new and relatively coherent social ₅ group had come to play an important role in the nation's cultural life. This new middle class, born with and through the rise of national systems of economy, transportation, and communication, was actively creating, controlling, and consuming a national system of culture. National magazines with booming subscription rates promulgated middle-class standards to the white, literate population at large. Women's magazines were especially important in the role of cultural evangelist.

These magazines carried clearly didactic messages to their readership. ₆ Unlike general-interest (men's) magazines, which were more likely to contain discussions of issues and events, women's magazines were highly prescriptive, giving advice on both the spiritual and the mundane. But while their advice on higher matters was usually vaguely inspirational, advice on how to look and how to act was extremely explicit.

The conventions of courtship, as set forth in these national magazines ₇ and in popular books of etiquette, were an important part of the middle-class code of manners. Conventional courtship centered on "calling," a term that could describe a range of activities. The young man from the neighboring farm who spent the evening sitting on the front porch with the farmer's daughter was paying a call, and so was the "society" man who could judge his prospects by whether or not the card he presented at the front door found the lady of his choice "at home." The middle-class arbiters of culture, however, aped and elaborated the society version of the call. And, as it was promulgated by magazines such as the *Ladies' Home Journal*, with a circulation over one million by 1900, the modified society call was the model for an increasing number of young Americans.

Outside of courtship, this sort of calling was primarily a woman's ₈ activity, for women largely controlled social life. Women designated a day or days "at home" to receive callers; on other days they paid or returned calls. The caller would present her card to the maid (common even in moderate-income homes until the World War I era) who answered the door, and would be admitted or turned away with some excuse. The caller who regularly was "not received" quickly learned the limits of her family's social status, and the lady "at home" thus, in some measure, protected herself and her family from the social confusion and pressures engendered by the mobility and expansiveness of late nineteenth-century America. In this system, the husband, though generally determining the family's status, was represented by his wife and was thereby excused from this social-status ritual. Unmarried men, however, were subject to this female-controlled system.

The calling system in courtship, though varying by region and the status of the individuals involved, followed certain general outlines. When a girl reached the proper age or had her first "season" (depending on her family's social level), she became eligible to receive male callers. At first her mother or guardian invited young men to call; in subsequent seasons the young lady had more autonomy and could bestow an invitation to call upon any unmarried man to whom she had been properly introduced at a private dance, dinner, or other "entertainment." Any unmarried man invited to an entertainment owed his hostess (and thus her daughter[s]) a duty call of thanks, but other young men not so honored could be brought to call by friends or relatives of the girl's family, subject to her prior permission. Undesired or undesirable callers, on the other hand, were simply given some excuse and turned away.

The call itself was a complicated event. A myriad of rules governed everything: the proper amount of time between invitation and visit (a fortnight or less); whether or not refreshments should be served (not if one belonged to a fashionable or semi-fashionable circle, but outside of "smart" groups in cities like New York and Boston, girls *might* serve iced drinks with little cakes or tiny cups of coffee or hot chocolate and sandwiches); chaperonage (the first call must be made on daughter and mother, but excessive chaperonage would indicate to the man that his attentions were unwelcome); appropriate topics of conversation (the man's interests, but never too personal); how leave should be taken (on no account should the woman "accompany [her caller] to the door nor stand talking while he struggles into his coat").

Each of these "measured steps," as the mid-twentieth-century author nostalgically called them, was a test of suitability, breeding and background. Advice columns and etiquette books emphasized that these were the manners of any "well-bred" person—and conversely implied that deviations revealed a lack of breeding. However, around the turn of the century, many people who did lack this narrow "breeding" aspired to politeness. Advice columns in women's magazines regularly printed questions from "Country Girl" and "Ignoramus" on the fine points of calling etiquette. Young men must have felt the pressure of girls' expectations, for they wrote to the same advisers with questions about calling. In 1907, *Harper's Bazaar* ran a major article titled "Etiquette for Men," explaining the ins and outs of the calling system. In the first decade of the twentieth century, this rigid system of calling was the convention not only of the "respectable" but also of those who aspired to respectability.

At the same time, however, the new system of dating was emerging. 12 By the mid-1910s, the word *date* had entered the vocabulary of the middle-class public. In 1914, the *Ladies' Home Journal,* a bastion of middle-class respectability, used the term (safely enclosed in quotation marks but with no explanation of its meaning) several times. The word was always spoken by the exotica, the college sorority girl—a character marginal in her exoticness but nevertheless a solid product of the middle class. "One beautiful evening of the spring term," one such article begins, "when I was a college girl of eighteen, the boy whom, because of his popularity in every phase of college life, I had been proud gradually to allow the monopoly of my 'dates,' took me unexpectedly into his arms. As he kissed me impetuously I was glad, from the bottom of my heart, for the training of that mother who had taught me to hold myself aloof from all personal familiarities of boys and men."

Sugarcoated with a tribute to motherhood and virtue, the dates—and 13 the kiss—were unmistakably presented for a middle-class audience. By 1924, ten years later, when the story of the unfortunate young man who went to call on the city girl was current, dating had essentially replaced calling in middle-class culture. The knowing smiles of the story's listeners had probably started with the word *call*—and not every hearer would have been sympathetic to the man's plight. By 1924, he really should have known better.

❀   ❀   ❀

AFTER YOU READ

• *THINK* about the different roles men and women assumed when dating replaced calling as the primary form of courtship in this country. How have these roles continued to change as dating has evolved?

• *EXAMINE* Bailey's statement that "dating moved courtship into the public world." Is dating still primarily associated with the public rather than the private world, or have there been other changes in recent years?

• *WRITE* an essay in which you explain some new development in the courtship practices of your age group. You may want to compare this new development with the calling and dating practices described by Bailey.

Finding a Wife

GARY SOTO

❊

Gary Soto, whose essay, "The Jacket," appears in Unit One, is known for both his poetry and his fiction. He is also increasingly well known for his collections of auto-biographical essays, including Small Faces *(1986) and* Baseball *(1990). Soto is a member of the Royal Chicano Navy and Distinguished Professor of Creative Writing at the University of California—Riverside. In the following essay, Soto argues that it is easy to find a wife, recounting his own experience as a Mexican-American who fell in love with and married his Japanese-American neighbor.*

BEFORE YOU READ

▪ *THINK* about your image of an ideal mate. Is this image clear and specific? Do you know exactly the kind of person you want to marry? If you are already married, think about the image of a mate you held before you met your husband or wife. Does your spouse conform to the ideal mate you envisioned?

▪ *EXAMINE* the first two sentences of this essay, in which Soto states simply and directly, "It's easy to find a wife. . . . Pick anybody. . . ." Do you think he means exactly what he says? Or is he being ironic, saying one thing when he means something else?

▪ *WRITE* in your journal a list of the characteristics that are important to you in a mate.

AS YOU READ

Try to determine why Soto was attracted to the young Japanese-American woman whom he married. Write brief notes in the margins to help you arrive at your conclusion.

It's easy to find a wife, I told my students. Pick anybody, I said, and they 1
chuckled and fidgeted in their chairs. I laughed a delayed laugh, feeling
hearty and foolish as a pup among these young men who were in my house
to talk poetry and books. We talked, occasionally making sense, and drank
cup after cup of coffee until we were so wired we had to stand up and walk
around the block to shake out our nerves.

When they left I tried to write a letter, grade papers, and finally nap 2
on the couch. My mind kept turning to how simple it is to find a wife; that
we can easily say after a brief two- or three-week courtship, "I want to
marry you."

When I was twenty, in college and living on a street that was a row of 3
broken apartment buildings, my brother and I returned to our apartment
from a game of racquetball to sit in the living room and argue whether we
should buy a quart of beer. We were college poor, living off the cheap
blessings of rice, raisins, and eggs that I took from our mom's refrigerator
when Rick called her into the backyard about a missing sock from his
laundry—a ploy from the start.

"Rick, I only got a dollar," I told him. He slapped his thigh and told 4
me to wake up. It was almost the end of the month. And he was right. In
two days our paychecks from Zak's Car Wash would burn like good report
cards in our pockets. So I gave in. I took the fifteen cents—a dime and five
pennies—he had plucked from the ashtray of loose change in his bedroom,
and went downstairs, across the street and the two blocks to Scott's Liquor.
While I was returning home, swinging the quart of beer like a lantern, I
saw the Japanese woman who was my neighbor, cracking walnuts on her
front porch. I walked slowly so that she looked up, smiling. I smiled, said
hello, and continued walking to the rhythm of her hammer rising and
falling.

In the apartment I opened the beer and raised it like a chalice before 5
we measured it in glasses, each of us suspicious that the other would get
more. I rattled sunflower seeds onto a plate, and we pinched fingersful, the
beer in our hands cutting loose a curtain of bubbles. We were at a party
with no music, no host, no girls. Our cat, Mensa, dawdled in, blinking from
the dull smoke of a sleepy afternoon. She looked at us, and we looked at
her. Rick flicked a seed at her and said, "That's what we need—a woman!"

I didn't say anything. I closed my eyes, legs shot out in a V from the 6
couch, and thought of that girl on the porch, the rise and fall of her hammer,
and the walnuts cracking open like hearts.

I got up and peeked from our two-story window that looked out onto 7
a lawn and her apartment. No one. A wicker chair, potted plants, and a

pile of old newspapers. I looked until she came out with a broom to clean up the shells. "Ah, my little witch," I thought, and raced my heart downstairs, but stopped short of her house because I didn't know what to say or do. I stayed behind the hedge that separated our yards and listened to her broom swish across the porch, then start up the walk to the curb. It was then that I started to walk casually from behind the hedge and, when she looked at me with a quick grin, I said a hearty hello and walked past her without stopping to talk. I made my way to the end of the block where I stood behind another hedge, feeling foolish. I should have said something. "Do you like walnuts," I could have said, or maybe, "Nice day to sweep, isn't it?"—anything that would have my mouth going.

I waited behind that hedge, troubled by my indecision. I started back   8
up the street and found her bending over a potted geranium, a jar of cloudy water in her hand. Lucky guy, I thought, to be fed by her.

I smiled as I passed, and she smiled back. I returned to the apartment   9
and my bedroom where I stared at my homework and occasionally looked out the window to see if she was busy on the porch. But she wasn't there. Only the wicker chair, the plants, the pile of newspapers.

The days passed, white as clouds. I passed her house so often that we   10
began to talk, sit together on the porch, and eventually snack on sandwiches that were thick as Bibles, with tumblers of milk to wash down her baked sweet bread flecked with tiny crushed walnuts.

After the first time I ate at her house, I hurried to the apartment to   11
brag about my lunch to my brother who was in the kitchen sprinkling raisins on his rice. Sandwiches, I screamed, milk, cold cuts, chocolate ice cream! I spoke about her cupboards, creaking like ships weighed down with a cargo of rich food, and about her, that woman who came up to my shoulder. I was in love and didn't know where to go from there.

As the weeks passed, still white as clouds, we saw more of each other.   12
Then it happened. On another Saturday, after browsing at a thrift shop among gooseneck lamps and couches as jolly as fat men, we went to the west side of Fresno for Mexican food—menudo for me and burritos for her, with two beers clunked down on our table. When we finished eating and were ready to go, I wiped my mouth and plucked my sole five-dollar bill from my wallet as I walked to the cashier. It was all the big money I had. I paid and left the restaurant as if it were nothing, as if I spent such money every day. But inside I was thinking, "What am I going to do?"

Scared as I was, I took Carolyn's hand into mine as we walked to the   13
car. I released it to open the door for her. We drove and drove, past thrift shops she longed to browse through, but I didn't want to stop because I

was scared I would want to hold her hand again. After turning corners aimlessly, I drove back to her house where we sat together on the front porch, not touching. I was shivering, almost noticeably. But after a while, I did take her hand into mine and that space between us closed. We held hands, little tents opening and closing, and soon I nuzzled my face into her neck to find a place to kiss.

I married this one Carolyn Oda, a woman I found cracking walnuts 14 on an afternoon. It was a chance meeting: I was walking past when she looked up to smile. It could have been somebody else, a girl drying persimmons on a line, or one hosing down her car, and I might have married another and been unhappy. But it was Carolyn, daughter of hard workers, whom I found cracking walnuts. She stirred them into dough that she shaped into loaves, baked in the oven, and set before me so that my mouth would keep talking in its search of the words to make me stay.

❀   ❀   ❀

AFTER YOU READ

▪ *THINK* about the opening sentences of the essay again. Do you now have a different interpretation of the author's meaning when he says that "it's easy to find a wife"? What was involved in Soto's finding a wife? Would it be possible for a woman to find a husband in the same way? Why or why not?

▪ *EXAMINE* the frequent descriptions of food in this essay. Why do you think these references are included? Why might the author have been particularly interested in food at the time that he was a young student? What kinds of associations do we have with food and with people who feed us or with whom we share food?

▪ *WRITE* an essay (or a set of instructions) in which you tell a specific audience how to find a mate. For example, you could advise people who are shy or who smoke, work nights, or can't afford to date how to find a mate.

Pom's Engagement

VED MEHTA

❀

Although blind since the age of three, Ved Mehta has produced more than a dozen books plus a documentary film. A native of India, Mehta was educated in the United States and England. He is currently a writer for The New Yorker *and teaches writing at Yale University. This story about his sister's engagement comes from his 1984 autobiography,* The Ledge Between the Streams. *It describes the formal, structured courtship ritual of India, which is very different from the informal, almost accidental, process described by Gary Soto.*

BEFORE YOU READ

▪ *THINK* about the informality of the custom of dating in the United States. What role do parents play in a young couple's decision to date? What is the role of parents if a marriage takes place? Is the role of parents in courtship and marriage changing in this country? In what way?

▪ *EXAMINE* the proper nouns the author uses in the first paragraph. Lahore, where the family in the story lives, is a town in the Punjab region, which lies between northwestern India and northeastern Pakistan. Mussoorie, which is at some distance from Lahore, is a scenic hill resort with views of the snowcapped Himalayan Mountains. The words *Daddyji* and *Mamaji* you can probably figure out for yourself.

▪ *WRITE* in your journal an objective description of courtship practice and rituals as they exist in your culture and/or community.

AS YOU READ

Compare the courtship and marriage customs described in this story with those described by Gary Soto in the previous story.

196

Before we moved to Lahore, Daddyji had gone to Mussoorie, a hill 1
station in the United Provinces, without telling us why he was going
out of the Punjab. Now, several months after he made that trip, he gathered
us around him in the drawing room at 11 Temple Road while Mamaji
mysteriously hurried Sister Pom upstairs. He started talking as if we were
all very small and he were conducting one of our "dinner-table–school"
discussions. He said that by right and tradition the oldest daughter had to
be given in marriage first, and that the ripe age for marriage was nineteen.
He said that when a girl approached that age her parents, who had to take
the initiative, made many inquiries and followed many leads. They inves-
tigated each young man and his family background, his relatives, his
friends, his classmates, because it was important to know what kind of
family the girl would be marrying into, what kind of company she would
be expected to keep. If the girl's parents decided that a particular young
man was suitable, then his people also had to make their investigations,
but, however favorable their findings, their decision was unpredictable,
because good, well-settled boys were in great demand and could afford to
be choosy. All this took a lot of time. "That's why I said nothing to you
children about why I went to Mussoorie," he concluded. "I went to see a
young man for Pom. She's already nineteen."

We were stunned. We have never really faced the idea that Sister Pom 2
might get married and suddenly leave, I thought.

"We won't lose Pom, we'll get a new family member," Daddyji said, as 3
if reading my thoughts.

Then all of us started talking at once. We wanted to know if Sister Pom 4
had been told; if she'd agreed; whom she'd be marrying.

"Your mother has just taken Pom up to tell her," Daddyji said. "But 5
she's a good girl. She will agree." He added, "The young man in question
is twenty-eight years old. He's a dentist, and so has a profession."

"Did you get a dentist because Sister Pom has bad teeth?" Usha asked. 6
Sister Pom had always been held up to us as an example of someone who,
as a child, had spurned greens and had therefore grown up with a mouthful
of poor teeth.

Daddyji laughed. "I confess I didn't think of anyone's teeth when I 7
chose the young man in question."

"What is he like?" I asked. "What are we to call him?"   8

"He's a little bit on the short side, but he has a happy-go-lucky nature, 9
like Nimi's. He doesn't drink, but, unfortunately, he does smoke. His father
died at an early age of a heart attack, but he has a nice mother, who will
not give Pom any trouble. It seems that everyone calls him Kakaji."

We all laughed. Kakaji, or "youngster," was what very small boys were 10
called.

"That's what he must have been called when he was small, and the 11
name stuck," Daddyji said.

In spite of myself, I pictured a boy smaller than I was and imagined 12
him taking Sister Pom away, and then I imagined her having to keep his
pocket money, to arrange his clothes in the cupboards, to comb his hair.
My mouth felt dry.

"What will Kakaji call Sister Pom?" I asked.   13

"Pom, silly—what else?" Sister Umi said.   14

Mamaji and Sister Pom walked into the room. Daddyji made a place 15
for Sister Pom next to him and said, "Now, now, now, no reason to cry. Is
it to be yes?"

"Whatever you say," Sister Pom said in a small voice, between sobs.   16

"Pom, how can you say that? You've never seen him," Sister Umi said. 17

"Kakaji's uncle, Dr. Prakash Mehrotra, himself a dentist, has known 18
our family from his student days in Lahore," Daddyji said. "As a student
dentist, he used to be welcomed in Babuji's Shahalmi Gate house. He would
come and go as he pleased. He has known for a long time what kind of
people we are. He remembered seeing you, Pom, when we went to
Mussoorie on holiday. He said yes immediately, and his approval seemed
to be enough for Kakaji."

"You promised me you wouldn't cry again," Mamaji said to Sister Pom, 19
patting her on the back, and then, to Daddyji, "She's agreed."

Daddyji said much else, sometimes talking just for the sake of talking, 20
sometimes laughing at us because we were sniffling, and all the time trying
to make us believe that this was a happy occasion. First, Sister Umi took
issue with him: parents had no business arranging marriages; if she were
Pom she would run away. Then Sister Nimi: all her life she had heard him
say to us children, "Think for yourself—be independent," and here he was
not allowing Pom to think for herself. Brother Om took Daddyji's part:
girls who didn't get married became a burden on their parents, and Daddyji
had four daughters to marry off, and would be retiring in a few years. Sisters
Nimi and Umi retorted: they hadn't gone to college to get married off, to
have some young man following them around like a leech. Daddyji just
laughed. I thought he was so wise, and right.

"Go and bless your big sister," Mamaji said, pushing me in the direction 21
of Sister Pom.

"I don't want to," I said. "I don't know him."   22

"What'll happen to Sister Pom's room?" Usha asked. She and Ashok 23
didn't have rooms of their own. They slept in Mamaji's room.

"Pom's room will remain empty, so that any time she likes she can come 24
and stay in her room with Kakaji," Daddyji said.

The thought that a man I never met would sleep in Pom's room with 25
Sister Pom there made my heart race. A sob shook me. I ran outside.

The whole house seemed to be in an uproar. Mamaji was shouting at Gian 26
Chand, Gian Chand was shouting at the bearer, the bearer was shouting at
the sweeper. There were the sounds of the kitchen fire being stoked, of the
drain being washed out, of water running in bathrooms. From behind
whichever door I passed came the rustle of saris, salwars, and kemises. The
house smelled of fresh flowers, but it had a ghostly chill. I would climb to
the landing of Sister Pom's room and thump down the stairs two at a time.
Brother Om would shout up at me, "Stop it!" Sister Umi would shout down
at me, "Don't you have anything better to do?" Sister Nimi would call to
me from somewhere, "You're giving Pom a headache." I wouldn't heed any
of them. As soon as I had thumped down, I would clatter to the top and
thump my way down again.

Daddyji went past on the back veranda. "Who's coming with Kakaji?" 27
I asked. Kakaji was in Lahore to buy some dental equipment, and in a few
minutes be was expected for tea, to meet Sister Pom and the family.

"He's coming alone," Daddyji said, over his shoulder. "He's come from 28
very far away." I had somehow imagined that Kakaji would come with at
least as many people as we had in our family, because I had started thinking
of the tea as a kind of cricket match—the elevens facing off.

I followed Daddyji into the drawing room. "Will he come alone for 29
his wedding, too?"

"No. Then he'll come with the bridegroom's party." 30

We were joined by everyone except Mamaji and Sister Pom, who from 31
the moment we got the news of Sister Pom's marriage had become
inseparable.

Gian Chand came in, the tea things rattling on his tray. 32

Later, I couldn't remember exactly how Kakaji had arrived, but I 33
remember noticing that his footfall was heavy, that his greeting was
affectionate, and that his voice seemed to float up with laughter. I don't
know what I'd expected, but I imagined that if I had been in his place I
would have skulked in the *gulli,* and perhaps changed my mind and not
entered at all.

"Better to have ventured and lost than never to have ventured at all," 34
Daddyji was saying to Kakaji about life's battles.

"Yes, Daddyji, just so," he said, with a little laugh. I had never heard 35
anybody outside our family call my father Daddyji. It sounded odd.

Sister Pom was sent for, and she came in with Mamaji. Her footsteps 36
were shy, and the rustle of her sari around her feet was slow, as if she
felt too conscious of the noise she was making just in walking. Daddyji
made some complimentary remark about the silver border on her sari,
and told her to sit next to Kakaji. Kakaji and Sister Pom exchanged a
few words about a family group photograph on the mantelpiece, and
about her studies. There was the clink of china as Sister Pom served Kakaji
tea.

"Won't you have some tea yourself?" Kakaji asked Sister Pom.   37

Sister Pom's sari rustled over her shoulder as she turned to Daddyji.   38

"Kakaji, none of my children have ever tasted tea or coffee," Daddyji 39
said. "We consider both to be bad habits. My children have been brought
up on hot milk, and lately Pom has been taking a little ghi in her milk at
bedtime, for health reasons."

We all protested at Daddyji's broadcasting family matters.   40

Kakaji tactfully turned the conversation to a visit to Mussoorie that 41
our family was planning.

Mamaji offered him onion, potato, and cauliflower pakoras. He 42
accepted, remarking how hot and crisp they were.

"Where will Sister Pom live?" Usha asked.   43

"In the summer, my practice is in Mussoorie," Kakaji said, "but in the 44
winter it's in Dehra Dun."

It struck me for the first time that after Sister Pom got married people 45
we didn't know, people she didn't know, would become more important
to her than we were.

Kakaji had left without formally committing himself. Then, four days later, 46
when we were all sitting in the drawing room, a servant brought a letter to
Mamaji. She told us that it was from Kakaji's mother, and that it asked if
Sister Pom might be engaged to Kakaji. "She even wants to know if Pom
can be married in April or May," Mamaji said excitedly. "How propitious!
That'll be the fifth wedding in the family in those two months." Cousins
Prakash and Dev, Cousin Pushpa (Bhaji Ganga Ram's adopted daughter),
and Auntie Vimla were all due to be married in Lahore then.

"You still have time to change your mind," Daddyji said to Sister Pom. 47
"What do you really think of him?"

Sister Pom wouldn't say anything.   48

"How do you expect her to know what her mind is when all that the   49
two talked about was a picture and her bachelor's exam in May?" Sister
Umi demanded. "Could she have fallen in love already?"

"Love, Umi, means something very different from 'falling in love,'"   50
Daddyji said. "It's not an act but a lifelong process. The best we can do as
Pom's parents is to give her love every opportunity to grow."

"But doesn't your 'every opportunity' include knowing the person   51
better than over a cup of tea, or whatever?" Sister Umi persisted.

"Yes, of course it does. But what we are discussing here is a simple   52
matter of choice—not love," Daddyji said. "To know a person, to love a
person, takes years of living together."

"Do you mean, then, that knowing a person and loving a person are   53
the same thing?" Sister Umi asked.

"Not quite, but understanding and respect are essential to love, and   54
that cannot come from talking together, even over a period of days or
months. That can come only in good time, through years of experience. It
is only when Pom and Kakaji learn to consider each other's problems as
one and the same that they will find love."

"But Daddyji, look at the risk you're taking, the risk you're making   55
Pom take," Sister Nimi said.

"We are trying to minimize the risk as much as we can by finding Pom   56
a family that is like ours," Daddyji said. "Kakaji is a dentist, I am a doctor.
His life and way of thinking will be similar to mine. We are from the same
caste, and Kakaji's family originally came from the Punjab. They eat meat
and eggs, and they take religion in their stride, and don't pray every day
and go to temples, like Brahmans. Kakaji knows how I walk into a club
and how I am greeted there. The atmosphere in Pom's new home will be
very much the same as the atmosphere here. Now, if I were to give Pom in
marriage to a Brahman he'd expect Pom to live as he did. That would really
be gambling."

"Then what you're doing is perpetuating the caste system," Sister Nimi   57
said. She was the political rebel in the family. "You seem to presuppose that
a Kshatriya should marry only a Kshatriya, that a Brahman should marry
only a Brahman. I would just as soon marry a shopkeeper from the Bania
caste or an Untouchable, and help to break down caste barriers."

"That day might come," Daddyji said. "But you will admit, Nimi, that   58
by doing that you'd be increasing the odds."

"But for a cause I believe in," Sister Nimi said.   59

"Yes, but that's a whole other issue," Daddyji said.   60

"Daddyji, you say that understanding and respect are necessary for 61 love," Sister Umi said. "I don't see why you would respect a person more because you lived with him and shared his problems."

"In our society, we think of understanding and respect as coming only 62 through sacrifice," Daddyji said.

"Then you're advocating the subservience of women," Sister Nimi 63 said, "because it's not Kakaji who will be expected to sacrifice—it's Pom. That's not fair."

"And why do you think that Pom will learn to respect Kakaji because 64 she sacrifices for him?" Sister Umi said, pressing her point.

"No, Umi, it is the other way around," Daddyji said. "It is Kakaji who 65 will respect Pom because she sacrifices for him."

"But that doesn't mean that Pom will respect Kakaji," Sister Umi 66 persisted.

"But if Kakaji is moved by Pom's sacrifices he will show more consid- 67 eration for her. He will grow to love her. I know in my own case I was moved to the depths to see Shanti suffer so because she was so ill-prepared to be my wife. It took me long enough—too long, I believe—to reach that understanding, perhaps because I had broken away from the old traditions and had given in to Western influences."

"So you admit that Pom will have to suffer for years," Sister Umi said. 68

"Perhaps," Daddyji said. "But all that time she will be striving for 69 ultimate happiness and love. Those are precious gifts that can only be cultivated in time."

"You haven't told us what this ultimate happiness is," Sister Umi said. 70 "I don't really understand it."

"It is a uniting of ideals and purposes, and a merging of them. This is 71 the tradition of our society, and it is the means we have adopted to make our marriages successful and beautiful. It works because we believe in the goodness of the individuals going into the marriage and rely on the strength of the sacred bond."

"But my ideal is to be independent," Sister Nimi said. "As you say, 72 'Think for yourself.'"

"But often you have to choose among ideals," Daddyji said. "You may 73 have to choose between being independent and being married."

"But aren't you struck by the fact that all the suffering is going to be 74 on Pom's part? Shouldn't Kakaji be required to sacrifice for their happiness, too?" Sister Nimi said, reverting to the old theme.

"There has to be a start," Daddyji said. "Remember, in our tradition 75 it's her life that is joined with his; it is she who will forsake her past to build

a new future with him. If both Pom and Kakaji were to be obstinate, were
to compete with each other about who would sacrifice first, who would
sacrifice more, what hope would there be of their ever getting on together,
of their ever finding love?"

"Daddyji, you're evading the issue," Sister Nimi said. "Why shouldn't 76
he take the initiative in this business of sacrifice?"

"He would perhaps be expected to if Pom were working, too, as in the 77
West, and, though married, leading a whole different life from his. I
suppose more than this I really can't say, and there may be some injustice
in our system, at that. In the West, they go in for romantic love, which is
unknown among us. I'm not sure that that method works any better than
our method does."

Then Daddyji said to Sister Pom, "I have done my best. Even after you 78
marry Kakaji, my responsibility for you will not be over. I will always be
there in the background if you should need me."

"I respect your judgment, Daddyji," Sister Pom said obediently. "I'll 79
do what you say."

Mamaji consulted Shambu Pandit. He compared the horoscopes of 80
Sister Pom and Kakaji and set the date of the marriage for the eleventh of
May. . . . "That's just three days after she finishes her B.A. finals!" we cried.
"When will she study? You are sacrificing her education to some silly
superstition."

But Shambu Pandit would not be budged from the date. "I am only 81
going by the horoscopes of the couple," he said. "You might as well protest
to the stars."

We appealed to Daddyji, but he said that he didn't want to interfere, 82
because such matters were up to Mamaji. That was as much as to say that
Shambu Pandit's date was a settled thing.

I recall that at about that time there was an engagement ceremony. We 83
all—Daddyji, Mamaji, Sister Pom, many of our Mehta and Mehra relatives—sat cross-legged on the floor of the front veranda around Shambu
Pandit. He recited the Gayatri Mantra, the simple prayer he used to tell us
to say before we went to sleep, and made a thank offering of incense and
ghi to a fire in a brazier, much as Mamaji did—behind Daddyji's back—
when one of us was going on a trip or had recovered from a bout of illness.
Servants passed around a platter heaped up with crumbly sweet balls. I
heard Kakaji's sister, Billo, saying something to Sister Pom; she had just
come from Dehra Dun bearing a sari, a veil, and the engagement ring for
Sister Pom, after Romesh Chachaji, one of Daddyji's brothers, had gone to

Dehra Dun bearing some money, a silver platter and silver bowls, and sweetmeats for Kakaji. It was the first time that I was able to think of Kakaji both as a remote and frightening dentist who was going to take Sister Pom away and as someone ordinary like us, who had his own family. At some point, Mamaji prodded me, and I scooted forward, crab fashion, to embrace Sister Pom. I felt her hand on my neck. It had something cold and metallic on it, which sent a shiver through me. I realized that she was wearing her engagement ring, and that until then Mamaji was the only one in our family who had worn a ring.

In the evening, the women relatives closeted themselves in the drawing 84 room with Sister Pom for the engagement singsong. I crouched outside with my ear to the door. The door pulsated with the beat of a barrel drum. The pulse in my forehead throbbed in sympathy with the beat as I caught snatches of songs about bedsheets and henna, along with explosions of laughter, the songs themselves rising and falling like the cooing of the doves that nested under the eaves of the veranda. I thought that a couple of years earlier I would have been playing somewhere outside on such an occasion, without knowing what I was missing, or been in the drawing room clapping and singing, but now I was crouching by the door like a thief, and was feeling ashamed even as I was captivated.

❀ ❀ ❀

AFTER YOU READ

▪ *THINK* about the economic and social customs associated with courtship and marriage as described in this story. A marriage in India, at least among people in the middle and upper classes, is a socioeconomic decision that is made by the parents, especially the father, rather than the man and woman to be married. What are the strengths and weaknesses of this system? What are the strengths and weaknesses of our much more casual, informal system?

▪ *EXAMINE* Sister Pom's initial reaction to the news that she is to be married. How does this initial reaction change during the course of the story?

▪ *EXAMINE* also the role of the father in the story. What are his primary considerations in arranging this marriage for his daughter? Do you agree with him that "Love . . . means something very different from 'falling in love'" and that "To know a person, to love a person, takes years of living together"? Why or why not?

▪ *WRITE* an essay in which you argue for or against the custom of arranging marriages as described in this story. Or *WRITE* an essay in which you compare our system, in which "romantic love" is the basis for marriage, with the system described in this story. You may want to use the previous story by Gary Soto as well as the one by Ved Mehta to illustrate your comparison.

How Do I Love Thee?

ROBERT J. TROTTER

❁

The author of Psychology: The Human Science *and* The Father Factor: What You Need to Know to Make a Difference, *Robert J. Trotter is a psychology professor and a former editor of* Psychology Today. *In the following excerpt from his article "The Three Faces of Love," originally published in* Psychology Today, *Trotter discusses intimacy, passion, and commitment. Trotter's discussion of these different aspects of love is based on the theories of love and sexuality developed by psychologist R. J. Sternberg, who is also an expert on human intelligence.*

BEFORE YOU READ

• *THINK* about the title, "How Do I Love Thee?" You might be interested to know that this title is an allusion to a famous poem by Elizabeth Barrett Browning, who wrote to her love Robert Browning:

> How do I love thee? Let me count the ways.
> I love thee to the depth and breadth and height
> My soul can reach, when feeling out of sight
> For the ends of Being and ideal Grace.
> I love thee to the level of everyday's
> Most quiet need, by sun and candlelight.
> I love thee freely, as men strive for Right;
> I love thee purely, as they turn from Praise.

"How Do I Love Thee?" by Robert J. Trotter, from "The Three Faces of Love," *Psychology Today,* September 1986. Reprinted with permission from *Psychology Today Magazine,* Copyright © 1986 Sussex Publishers, Inc.

I love thee with the passion put to use
In my old griefs, and with my childhood's faith.
I love thee with a love I seemed to lose
With my lost saints,—I love thee with the breath,
Smiles, tears, of all my life!—and, if God choose,
I shall but love thee better after death.

▪ *EXAMINE* Trotter's first sentence, which states that "Intimacy, passion and commitment are the warm, hot and cold vertices of Sternberg's love triangle." In geometry, vertices (plural of vertex) means the point at which the sides of an angle intersect. In your opinion, which feeling is the warm, which is the hot, and which is the cold vertex of the love triangle?

▪ *WRITE* in your journal a list of the most important relationships you have had—not including family relationships. In your list, include friendships that have been important to you as well as romantic relationships.

AS YOU READ

Identify and number the eight different kinds of love that can be formed from various combinations of intimacy, passion, and commitment.

Intimacy, passion and commitment are the warm, hot and cold vertices 1 of Sternberg's love triangle. Alone and in combination they give rise to eight possible kinds of love relationships. The first is nonlove—the absence of all three components. This describes the large majority of our personal relationships, which are simply casual interactions.

Nonlove

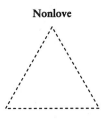

The second kind of love is liking. "If you just have intimacy," Sternberg 2 explains, "that's liking. You can talk to the person, tell about your life. And if that's all there is to it, that's what we mean by liking." It is more than nonlove. It refers to the feelings experienced in true friendships. Liking includes such things as closeness and warmth but not the intense feelings of passion or commitment.

Liking

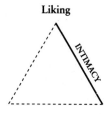

If you just have passion, it's called infatuated love—the "love at first ₃ sight" that can arise almost instantaneously and dissipate just as quickly. It involves a high degree of physiological arousal but no intimacy or commitment. It's the 10th-grader who falls madly in love with the beautiful girl in his biology class but never gets up the courage to talk to her or get to know her, Sternberg says, describing his past.

Infatuation

Empty love is commitment without intimacy or passion, the kind of ₄ love sometimes seen in a 30-year-old marriage that has become stagnant. The couple used to be intimate, but they don't talk to each other any more. They used to be passionate, but that's died out. All that remains is the commitment to stay with the other person. In societies in which marriages are arranged, Sternberg points out, empty love may precede the other kinds of love.

Empty Love

Romantic love, the Romeo and Juliet type of love, is a combination of 5 intimacy and passion. More than infatuation, it's liking with the added excitement of physical attraction and arousal but without commitment. A summer affair can be very romantic, Sternberg explains, but you know it will end when she goes back to Hawaii and you go back to Florida, or wherever.

Romantic Love

Passion plus commitment is what Sternberg calls fatuous love. It's 6 Hollywood love: Boy meets girl, a week later they're engaged, a month later they're married. They are committed on the basis of their passion, but because intimacy takes time to develop, they don't have the emotional core necessary to sustain the commitment. This kind of love, Sternberg warns, usually doesn't work out.

Fatuous Love

Companionate love is intimacy with commitment but no passion. It's 7 a long-term friendship, the kind of committed love and intimacy frequently seen in marriages in which the physical attraction has died down.

Companionate Love

When all three elements of Sternberg's love triangle come together in 8
a relationship, you get what he calls consummate love, or complete love.
It's the kind of love toward which many people strive, especially in
romantic relationships. Achieving consummate love, says Sternberg, is like
trying to lose weight, difficult but not impossible. The really hard thing is
keeping the weight off after you have lost it, or keeping the consummate
love alive after you have achieved it. Consummate love is possible only in
very special relationships.

Consummate Love

COMMITMENT *INTIMACY*

PASSION

❀ ❀ ❀

AFTER YOU READ

▪ *THINK* about the poem by Elizabeth Barrett Browning that you read on
pp. 206–207. Does this poem reflect the consummate love that Trotter and
Sternberg believe to be the ideal? Reread the poem, trying to identify in it
each of the three essential qualities of consummate love: intimacy, passion,
and commitment.

▪ *EXAMINE* carefully the eight triangles illustrated throughout the essay.
As you study these triangles, keep in mind that only "consummate" love is
perfectly balanced. If you could not achieve this type of love, which other
type would be your second choice? Why?

▪ *WRITE* an essay in which you select one type of relationship discussed by
Trotter and illustrate it with an example from your own life.

Sex, Lies and Conversation

DEBORAH TANNEN

❀

Deborah Tannen, a professor of linguistics at Georgetown
University, is well known for her studies of the differences
between male and female speech patterns. Her first book,
You Just Don't Understand, *explains her general theories*
on male/female speech patterns, while later books, such as
Gender and Discourse, Talking from Nine to Five, *and*
the Argument Culture: Moving from Debate to Dialogue,
explore these issues in more specific ways. This article,
which first appeared in The Washington Post, *is based on*
her first book but focuses on the different ways in which
male and female partners communicate and on the prob-
lems these differences cause.

BEFORE YOU READ

▪ *THINK* about your own observations of male/female speech patterns. Do
you think there are significant differences between the way men and
women in general communicate? If so, how do these differences affect
male-female relationships?

▪ *EXAMINE* the anecdote that Tannen recounts in her first paragraph. What
does it tell you about male/female communication patterns?

▪ *WRITE* in your journal a list of the differences you have noticed between
the way men and women communicate.

AS YOU READ

Compare your own observations about male/female speech patterns with
those Tannen makes in this article. Also, as you read, identify and underline
Tannen's thesis.

I was addressing a small gathering in a suburban Virginia living room—a
women's group that had invited men to join them. Throughout the
evening, one man had been particularly talkative, frequently offering ideas
and anecdotes, while his wife sat silently beside him on the couch. Toward
the end of the evening, I commented that women frequently complain that
their husbands don't talk to them. This man quickly concurred. He
gestured toward his wife and said, "She's the talker in our family." The
room burst into laughter; the man looked puzzled and hurt. "It's true," he
explained. "When I come home from work I have nothing to say. If she
didn't keep the conversation going, we'd spend the whole evening in
silence."

This episode crystallizes the irony that although American men tend
to talk more than women in public situations, they often talk less at home.
And this pattern is wreaking havoc with marriage.

The pattern was observed by political scientist Andrew Hacker in the
late '70s. Sociologist Catherine Kohler Riessman reports in her new book
Divorce Talk that most of the women she interviewed—but only a few of
the men—gave lack of communication as the reason for their divorces.
Given the current divorce rate of nearly 50 percent, that amounts to
millions of cases in the United States every year—a virtual epidemic of
failed conversation.

In my own research, complaints from women about their husbands
most often focused not on tangible inequities such as having given up the
chance for a career to accompany a husband to his, or doing far more than
their share of daily life-support work like cleaning, cooking, social arrangements and errands. Instead, they focused on communication: "He doesn't
listen to me," "He doesn't talk to me." I found, as Hacker observed years
before, that most wives want their husbands to be, first and foremost,
conversational partners, but few husbands share this expectation of their
wives.

In short, the image that best represents the current crisis is the
stereotypical cartoon scene of a man sitting at the breakfast table with a
newspaper held up in front of his face, while a woman glares at the back
of it, wanting to talk.

Linguistic Battle of Sexes

How can women and men have such different impressions of communication in marriage? Why the widespread imbalance in their interests and
expectations?

In the April issue of *American Psychologist,* Stanford University's 7
Eleanor Maccoby reports the results of her own and others' research
showing that children's development is most influenced by the social
structure of peer interactions. Boys and girls tend to play with children of
their own gender, and their sex-separate groups have different organizational structures and interactive norms.

I believe these systematic differences in childhood socialization make 8
talk between women and men like cross-cultural communication, heir to
all the attraction and pitfalls of that enticing but difficult enterprise. My
research on men's and women's conversations uncovered patterns similar
to those described for children's groups.

For women, as for girls, intimacy is the fabric of relationships, and talk 9
is the thread from which it is woven. Little girls create and maintain
friendships by exchanging secrets; similarly, women regard conversation as
the cornerstone of friendship. So a woman expects her husband to be a
new and improved version of a best friend. What is important is not the
individual subjects that are discussed but the sense of closeness, a life
shared, that emerges when people tell their thoughts, feelings, and impressions.

Bonds between boys can be as intense as girls', but they are based less 10
on talking, more on doing things together. Since they don't assume talk is
the cement that binds a relationship, men don't know what kind of talk
women want, and they don't miss it when it isn't there.

Boys' groups are larger, more inclusive, and more hierarchical, so boys 11
must struggle to avoid the subordinate position in the group. This may play
a role in women's complaints that men don't listen to them. Some men
really don't like to listen, because being the listener makes them feel
one-down, like a child listening to adults or an employee to a boss.

But often when women tell men, "You aren't listening," and the men 12
protest, "I am," the men are right. The impression of not listening results
from misalignments in the mechanics of conversation. The misalignment
begins as soon as a man and a woman take physical positions. This became
clear when I studied videotapes made by psychologist Bruce Dorval of
children and adults talking to their same-sex best friends. I found that at
every age, the girls and women faced each other directly, their eyes
anchored on each other's faces. At every age, the boys and men sat at angles
to each other and looked elsewhere in the room, periodically glancing at
each other. They were obviously attuned to each other, often mirroring
each other's movements. But the tendency of men to face away can give
women the impression they aren't listening even when they are. A young
woman in college was frustrated: Whenever she told her boyfriend she

wanted to talk to him, he would lie down on the floor, close his eyes, and put his arm over his face. This signaled to her, "He's taking a nap." But he insisted he was listening extra hard. Normally, he looks around the room, so he is easily distracted. Lying down and covering his eyes helped him concentrate on what she was saying.

Analogous to the physical alignment that women and men take in 13 conversation is their topical alignment. The girls in my study tended to talk at length about one topic, but the boys tended to jump from topic to topic. Girls exchanged stories about people they knew. The second-grade boys teased, told jokes, noticed things in the room and talked about finding games to play. The sixth-grade girls talked about problems with a mutual friend. The sixth-grade boys talked about 55 different topics, none of which extended over more than a few turns.

Listening to Body Language

Switching topics is another habit that gives women the impression men 14 aren't listening, especially if they switch to a topic about themselves. But the evidence of the 10th-grade boys in my study indicates otherwise. The 10th-grade boys sprawled across their chairs with bodies parallel and eyes straight ahead, rarely looking at each other. They looked as if they were riding in a car, staring out the windshield. But they were talking about their feelings. One boy was upset because a girl had told him he had a drinking problem, and the other was feeling alienated from all his friends.

Now, when a girl told a friend about a problem, the friend responded 15 by asking probing questions and expressing agreement and understanding. But the boys dismissed each other's problems. Todd assured Richard that his drinking was "no big problem" because "sometimes you're funny when you're off your butt." And when Todd said he felt left out, Richard responded, "Why should you? You know more people than me."

Women perceive such responses as belittling and unsupportive. But the 16 boys seemed satisfied with them. Whereas women reassure each other by implying, "You shouldn't feel bad because I've had similar experiences," men do so by implying, "You shouldn't feel bad because your problems aren't so bad."

There are even simpler reasons for women's impression that men don't 17 listen. Linguist Lynette Hirschman found that women make more listener-noise, such as "mhm," "uhuh," and "yeah," to show "I'm with you." Men, she found, more often give silent attention. Women who expect a stream of listener-noise interpret silent attention as no attention at all.

Women's conversational habits are as frustrating to men as men's are   18
to women. Men who expect silent attention interpret a stream of listener-
noise as overreaction or impatience. Also, when women talk to each other
in a close, comfortable setting, they often overlap, finish each other's
sentences and anticipate what the other is about to say. This practice, which
I call "participatory listenership," is often perceived by men as interruption,
intrusion and lack of attention.

A parallel difference caused a man to complain about his wife. "She   19
just wants to talk about her own point of view. If I show her another view,
she gets mad at me." When most women talk to each other, they assume a
conversationalist's job is to express agreement and support. But many men
see their conversational duty as pointing out the other side of an argument.
This is heard as disloyalty by women, and refusal to offer the requisite
support. It is not that women don't want to see other points of view, but
that they prefer them phrased as suggestions and inquiries rather than as
direct challenges.

In his book *Fighting for Life*, Walter Ong points out that men use   20
"agonistic" or warlike, oppositional formats to do almost anything; thus
discussion becomes debate, and conversation a competitive sport. In
contrast, women see conversation as a ritual means of establishing rapport.
If Jane tells a problem and June says she has a similar one, they walk away
feeling closer to each other. But this attempt at establishing rapport can
backfire when used with men. Men take too literally women's ritual
"troubles talk," just as women mistake men's ritual challenges for real
attack.

The Sounds of Silence

These differences begin to clarify why women and men have such different   21
expectations about communication in marriage. For women, talk creates
intimacy. Marriage is an orgy of closeness: you can tell your feelings and
thoughts, and still be loved. Their greatest fear is being pushed away. But
men live in a hierarchical world, where talk maintains independence and
status. They are on guard to protect themselves from being put down and
pushed around.

This explains the paradox of the talkative man who said of his silent   22
wife, "She's the talker." In the public setting of a guest lecture, he felt
challenged to show his intelligence and display his understanding of the
lecture. But at home, where he has nothing to prove and no one to defend
against, he is free to remain silent. For his wife, being home means she is

free from the worry that something she says might offend someone, or spark disagreement, or appear to be showing off; at home she is free to talk.

The communication problems that endanger marriage can't be fixed 23 by mechanical engineering. They require a new conceptual framework about the role of talk in human relationships. Many of the psychological explanations that have become second nature may not be helpful, because they tend to blame either women (for not being assertive enough) or men (for not being in touch with their feelings). A sociolinguistic approach by which male-female conversation is seen as cross-cultural communication allows us to understand the problem and forge solutions without blaming either party.

Once the problem is understood, improvement comes naturally, as it 24 did to the young woman and her boyfriend who seemed to go to sleep when she wanted to talk. Previously, she had accused him of not listening, and he had refused to change his behavior, since that would be admitting fault. But then she learned about and explained to him the differences in women's and men's habitual ways of aligning themselves in conversation. The next time she told him she wanted to talk, he began, as usual, by lying down and covering his eyes. When the familiar negative reaction bubbled up, she reassured herself that he really was listening. But then he sat up and looked at her. Thrilled, she asked why. He said, "You like me to look at you when we talk, so I'll try to do it." Once he saw their differences as cross-cultural rather than right and wrong, he independently altered his behavior.

Women who feel abandoned and deprived when their husbands won't 25 listen to or report daily news may be happy to discover their husbands trying to adapt once they understand the place of small talk in women's relationships. But if their husbands don't adapt, the women may still be comforted that for men, this is not a failure of intimacy. Accepting the difference, the wives may look to their friends or family for that kind of talk. And husbands who can't provide it shouldn't feel their wives have made unreasonable demands. Some couples will still decide to divorce, but at least their decisions will be based on realistic expectations.

In these times of resurgent ethnic conflicts, the world desperately needs 26 cross-cultural understanding. Like charity, successful cross-cultural com-munication should begin at home.

❀   ❀   ❀

AFTER YOU READ

▪ *THINK* about your own experiences in communicating with people of the opposite sex. Do your experiences confirm Tannen's theory that one of the main problems between partners of the opposite sex is that males do not value conversation as much as females do? What factors other than gender might influence a person's speech patterns?

▪ *EXAMINE* Tannen's statement that "men don't know what kind of talk women want, and they don't miss it when it isn't there." Do you agree with this assertion? Why or why not?

▪ *WRITE* an essay in which you agree or disagree with Tannen's arguments. Use your own experiences or observations to support your thesis.

Let Gays Marry

ANDREW SULLIVAN

❀

Editor of the New Republic *from 1991 to 1996 and a resident of Washington, D.C., Andrew Sullivan writes a weekly column for the* Sunday Times *(London), is a regular contributor to the* New York Times Magazine, *and remains as senior editor of the* New Republic. *A writer who focuses on gay politics, Sullivan has published* Virtually Normal: An Argument About Homosexuality *and* Love Undetectable: Notes on Friendship, Sex, and Survival. *In the book,* Same-Sex Marriage: Pro and Con, *which he has co-edited, Sullivan presents a fuller debate on the issue of same-sex marriage through essays by authors ranging from gay congressman Barney Frank to political conservative William Bennett.*

BEFORE YOU READ

• *THINK* about the idea of same-sex marriages. Do you agree or disagree that members of the same sex should be allowed to "marry" in civil ceremonies and to have the same legal rights as members of the opposite sex who marry? What are some of these "legal rights"?

• *EXAMINE* the title of Sullivan's essay. This title is a brief statement of his thesis, clearly stating his position on same-sex marriage.

• *EXAMINE* also paragraph 5, in which Sullivan discusses his view of the changing definition of marriage. Sullivan begins by giving a brief traditional definition of marriage and then discusses how he believes this definition has "changed." Does he give a clearly stated definition of marriage, or does he give an implied definition? Based on this paragraph, how do you think Sullivan defines marriage?

• *WRITE* two lists, one of reasons *for* same-sex marriages and one of reasons *against* same-sex marriages. (Good persuasive, or argumentative, writing must always recognize the opposing side in order to *refute*, or argue against, it.) You may be able to use these ideas later in a persuasive essay.

AS YOU READ

Underline phrases that suggest Sullivan's definition of marriage and number other definitions of marriage that he includes but refutes.

"A state cannot deem a class of persons a stranger to its laws," declared 1 the Supreme Court last week. It was a monumental statement. Gay men and lesbians, the conservative court said, are no longer strangers in America. They are citizens, entitled, like everyone else, to equal protection—no special rights, but simple equality.

For the first time in Supreme Court history, gay men and women were 2 seen not as some powerful lobby trying to subvert America, but as the people we truly are—the sons and daughters of countless mothers and fathers, with all the weaknesses and strengths and hopes of everybody else. And what we seek is not some special place in America but merely to be a full and equal part of America, to give back to our society without being forced to lie or hide or live as second-class citizens.

That is why marriage is so central to our hopes. People ask us why we 3 want the right to marry, but the answer is obvious. It's the same reason anyone wants the right to marry. At some point in our lives, some of us are lucky enough to meet the person we truly love. And we want to commit to that person in front of our family and country for the rest of our lives. It's the most simple, the most natural, the most human instinct in the world. How could anyone seek to oppose that?

Yes, at first blush, it seems like a radical proposal, but, when you think 4 about it some more, it's actually the opposite. Throughout American history, to be sure, marriage has been between a man and a woman, and in many ways our society is built upon that institution. But none of that need change in the slightest. After all, no one is seeking to take away anybody's right to marry, and no one is seeking to force any church to change any doctrine in any way. Particular religious arguments against same-sex marriage are rightly debated within the churches and faiths themselves. That is not the issue here: there is a separation between church and state in this country. We are only asking that when the government gives out *civil* marriage licenses, those of us who are gay should be treated like anybody else.

Of course, some argue that marriage is *by definition* between a man   5
and a woman. But for centuries, marriage was *by definition* a contract in which the wife was her husband's legal property. And we changed that. For centuries, marriage was *by definition* between two people of the same race. And we changed that. We changed these things because we recognized that human dignity is the same whether you are a man or a woman, black or white. And no one has any more of a choice to be gay than to be black or white or male or female.

Some say that marriage is only about raising children, but we let   6
childless heterosexual couples be married (Bob and Elizabeth Dole, Pat and Shelley Buchanan, for instance). Why should gay couples be treated differently? Others fear that there is no logical difference between allowing same-sex marriage and sanctioning polygamy and other horrors. But the issue of whether to sanction multiple spouses (gay or straight) is completely separate from whether, in the existing institution between two unrelated adults, the government should discriminate between its citizens.

This is, in fact, if only Bill Bennett could see it, a deeply conservative   7
cause. It seeks to change no one else's rights or marriages in any way. It seeks merely to promote monogamy, fidelity and the disciplines of family life among people who have long been cast to the margins of society. And what could be a more conservative project than that? Why indeed would any conservative seek to oppose those very family values for gay people that he or she supports for everybody else? Except, of course, to make gay men and lesbians strangers in their own country, to forbid them ever to come home.

❀   ❀   ❀

AFTER YOU READ

▪ *THINK* about Sullivan's definition of marriage. What is the definition that emerges from the complete essay? Do you agree or disagree with this definition of marriage? Why or why not?

▪ *EXAMINE* paragraphs 4–7, in which Sullivan identifies and argues against some of the reasons for opposing same-sex marriages. Underline three of these reasons, or arguments. How does Sullivan refute, or argue against, each of these opposing positions?

▪ *WRITE* an essay in which you define marriage. In your essay, you may want to refer to Sullivan's definition of marriage, either agreeing or disagreeing with it.

Leave Marriage Alone

WILLIAM BENNETT

❀

A conservative political commentator and a frequent guest on Larry King Live, *William J. Bennett has served as secretary of education, chairman of the National Endowment for the Humanities, director of the National Drug Policy, and codirector of Empower America. His many publications include* The Book of Virtues: A Treasury of Great Moral Stories, Abortion Rites: A Social History of Abortion in America, Death of Outrage: Bill Clinton and the Assault on American Ideals, *and* The Wealth of the West. *Concerned about the education and moral values of the nation's children, he has also written several children's books on such subjects as virtues, heroes, and the nation's founders. As shown in the following essay, Bennett's feelings about same-sex marriages are certainly as strong as those of Andrew Sullivan in the previous selection, but Bennett's opinions on the subject are just the opposite of Sullivan's.*

BEFORE YOU READ

• *THINK* about the title "Leave Marriage Alone." Since this is a companion essay to Sullivan's, what do you think Bennett's title means?

• *EXAMINE* the first paragraph of Bennett's essay. Underline the "two key issues that divide proponents and opponents of same-sex marriage." What are these two issues?

• *EXAMINE* also the word *teleology* in paragraph 5. *Teleology* means "the study of design or purpose in life, whether the source be divine or natural (scientific)."

• *WRITE* your own response to one of the two issues that Bennett identifies in his first paragraph.

AS YOU READ

Compare Bennett's arguments with those of Sullivan. Think about which arguments are more convincing to you.

There are at least two key issues that divide proponents and opponents 1 of same-sex marriage. The first is whether legally recognizing same-sex unions would strengthen or weaken the institution. The second has to do with the basic understanding of marriage itself.

The advocates of same-sex marriage say that they seek to strengthen 2 and celebrate marriage. That may be what some intend. But I am certain that it will not be the reality. Consider: the legal union of same-sex couples would shatter the conventional definition of marriage, change the rules which govern behavior, endorse practices which are completely antithetical to the tenets of all of the world's major religions, send conflicting signals about marriage and sexuality, particularly to the young, and obscure marriage's enormously consequential function—procreation and childrearing.

Broadening the definition of marriage to include same-sex unions 3 would stretch it almost beyond recognition—and new attempts to expand the definition still further would surely follow. On what *principled* ground can Andrew Sullivan exclude others who most desperately want what he wants, legal recognition and social acceptance? Why on earth would Sullivan exclude from marriage a bisexual who wants to marry two other people? After all, exclusion would be a denial of that person's sexuality. The same holds true of a father and daughter who want to marry. Or two sisters. Or men who want (consensual) polygamous arrangements. Sullivan may think some of these arrangements are unwise. But having employed sexual relativism in his own defense, he has effectively lost the capacity to draw any lines and make moral distinctions.

Forsaking all others is an essential component of marriage. Obviously 4 it is not always honored in practice. But it is the ideal to which we rightly aspire, and in most marriages the ideal is in fact the norm. Many advocates of same-sex marriage simply do not share this ideal; promiscuity among homosexual males is well known. Sullivan himself has written that gay male relationships are served by the "openness of the contract" and that homosexuals should resist allowing their "varied and complicated lives" to be flattened into a "single, moralistic model." But that "single, moralistic model" has served society exceedingly well. The burden of proof ought to be on those who propose untested arrangements for our most important institution.

A second key difference I have with Sullivan goes to the very heart of 5 marriage itself. I believe that marriage is not an arbitrary construct which can be redefined simply by those who lay claim to it. It is an honorable estate, instituted of God and built on moral, religious, sexual and human realities. Marriage is based on a natural teleology, on the different, complementary nature of men and women—and how they refine, support, encourage and complete one another. It is the institution through which we propagate, nurture, educate and sustain our species.

That we have to engage in this debate at all is an indication of how 6 steep our moral slide has been. Worse, those who defend the traditional understanding of marriage are routinely referred to (though not to my knowledge by Sullivan) as "homophobes," "gay-bashers," "intolerant" and "bigoted." Can one defend an honorable, 4,000-year-old tradition and not be called these names?

This is a large, tolerant, diverse country. In America people are free to 7 do as they wish, within broad parameters. It is also a country in sore need of shoring up some of its most crucial institutions: marriage and the family, schools, neighborhoods, communities. But marriage and family are the greatest of these. That is why they are elevated and revered. We should keep them so.

❀ ❀ ❀

AFTER YOU READ

▪ *THINK* about the two issues that Bennett identifies in paragraph 1 and the arguments that he develops for each issue. Bennett first recognizes the opposing side and then presents his own position. Which of Bennett's points is more convincing—his argument that same-sex marriage does *not* strengthen and celebrate marriage or his position on the nature, or definition, of marriage? In your opinion, which issue is more important?

▪ *EXAMINE* the definition of marriage that Bennett gives in paragraph 5. What does Bennett say marriage is *not*? What does he say it *is*? Do you agree or disagree with this definition? Why or why not?

▪ *WRITE* a comparison of Sullivan's and Bennett's essays. What are Sullivan's strongest arguments? What are his weakest? What are Bennett's strongest arguments? What are his weakest? Ultimately, which essay is more persuasive to you? Or *WRITE* an essay in which you argue for or against same-sex marriage. You may want to use some of the ideas you wrote in your journal before the Sullivan essay as well as ideas or quotations from the essays by both Sullivan and Bennett. (Remember that a good persuasive essay recognizes and refutes opposing arguments.)

Unit Three: Critical Thinking and Writing Assignments

❀   ❀   ❀

EXPLORING IDEAS TOGETHER

1. Meet with a group of your classmates to discuss and define the term *friend*. Write a group definition of friendship. Then compare your group's definition with definitions composed by other groups in the class. What qualities do all definitions have in common? Keep notes from this discussion for possible use in writing an essay on this subject.

2. As a class, divide into three groups, with each group discussing one type of friendship: friendships between men, friendships between women, and friendships between a man and a woman. What makes each type of friendship unique? What makes each type different from the other types? When your group finishes its discussion, write a brief, collaborative report on the type of friendship your group has chosen to discuss.

3. As several of the essays in this unit suggest, successful communication is essential between friends and mates. Meet with a group of your classmates and write a list of suggestions for successful communication in either type of relationship.

4. Using the various types of love or friendship classified in Robert J. Trotter's essay, identify the relationships portrayed in *three* of the selections you have read in this unit.

5. Although European and American cultures consider romantic love important, other cultures base marriage on other factors. Using the readings in this unit as well as your own experiences and observations, discuss whether you think romantic love is the soundest foundation for choosing a mate. What other foundations can there be for a long-lasting love?

WRITING ESSAYS

1. Write an essay defining the word *friend* or *friendship*. Before you begin your essay, review your notes from Question 1, Exploring Ideas Together (above), as well as from the journal and/or essay you wrote in response to the Phillip Lopate essay (pp. 178–186). You may want to include a formal definition in your introduction ("A friend is

someone who . . ."), but expand your definition with examples, comparisons, and so on.

2. Write an essay in which you use your own experiences and observations as well as some of the essays in this unit to compare friendships between men and those between women.

3. The essays by Phillip Lopate and Robert J. Trotter discuss the connection between friendship and love. Write an essay in which you compare friendship with a romantic relationship. How are these two relationships similar? How are they different? Even more specifically, how is a friend similar to or different from a mate?

4. The selections by Jimmy Carter, Robert J. Matthews, and Christine Choi emphasize the important role that small acts assume in friendships. Write an essay in which you tell about a small thing that defined or enhanced one of your friendships.

5. Write an essay in which you argue whether good friendships (or romantic relationships) are based on similarities or differences between the people involved. Consider ages, careers, interests, and so forth.

6. Interview someone who is considerably older or younger than you about the process of mate selection that existed when this person was selecting a mate. Write an essay in which you compare the process as you know it with the process this person experienced. Write your essay for an audience unfamiliar with either your experience or that of the person you interview.

7. The essays by Gary Soto ("Finding a Wife") and Ved Mehta ("Pom's Engagement") describe two very different types of courtship. Write an essay in which you compare the strengths and weaknesses of these two approaches to marriage.

8. Deborah Tannen ("Sex, Lies and Conversation") and Ellen Goodman and Patricia O'Brien ("The Difference Between Male and Female Friendship") address the important role effective communication assumes in relationships and suggest that males are lacking in these communication skills. Write an essay in which you agree or disagree with the arguments set forth by these authors. Use both your own experiences and observations and the other essays in this unit to support your argument.

9. Write an essay in which you classify your friendships into categories. Be sure to give examples of each category.

10. Write an essay in which you argue why you do or do not think married life is better than single life.

11. Write a persuasive essay in which you argue *for* or *against* same-sex marriage. (You should be able to use the essays by Andrew Sullivan and William Bennett to support your argument.) Remember that the writer of an effective persuasive essay not only presents his or her own arguments effectively but also recognizes and refutes, or argues against, major opposing arguments.

Self with Work

People are often defined by the work they do. Individuals are identified as teachers or lawyers or accountants in the same way they are identified by their names. In fact, once we have asked a person's name, we next want to know what he or she does. Even before children become adolescents, they are asked what they want to do or be when they grow up. In our society it is assumed that everyone, or almost everyone, will work.

However, the nature of work has changed. Relatively few people in this country now engage in work that requires hard physical labor. In contrast, our ancestors often worked long hours at tasks that required great physical strength and endurance. Both men and women (and often children as well) accepted physical labor as a fact of life. Although some people in our society still work in jobs that are physically demanding, most heavy labor has been taken over by machines. Today when we talk about work, we often mean working with our minds and/or our hands. Even though many people still have jobs that require them to work long hours or to be on their feet all day, most of us spend more time operating a machine, thinking, or talking than working physically. But we still call what we do work.

Not only is work less physically demanding than it once was, but it is also less defined in terms of gender differences. Fifty years ago, some types of work were typically performed by males while other types were performed by females. Nurses and secretaries were nearly always females, while doctors, construction workers, and mail carriers were almost inevitably males. Today most of those distinctions have been erased. In fact, it is difficult to think of any job that is associated exclusively with either males or females. Women pilot airplanes while men serve snacks to the passengers; men take care of small children while women serve as presidents of universities. Both men and women are lawyers, doctors, senators, professors, and truck drivers. It is only a matter of time, surely, until a woman becomes president of the United States.

Even though the kind of work we do has changed, working has not become less important. Work is still how we define ourselves and how we spend most of our time. When technology began to make work less physically demanding and production faster, many people predicted that Americans would work fewer hours—but this has not happened. Most people still work eight hours a day, and many people work far more—bringing work home or holding two jobs instead of one. Couples often come home from their jobs to face child rearing and housekeeping responsibilities. Instead of becoming a society in which people work less, we have become a society in which people work more.

We continue to redefine what it means to work: more people work at home as well as at offices and factories; technology plays an increasingly important role in work; and people share jobs. But the importance of work will not change. Children will continue to pretend they are working; young people will continue to worry about what career to pursue; and adults will continue to focus on their jobs as a major feature of their lives. Perhaps most important, people will continue to define themselves in terms of their work.

The reading selections in this unit describe the effect of work on individuals, analyze how the role of work is changing in our society, and predict what jobs and careers will be available in the future. You will be asked to think about your attitude toward work and your choice of a career, to consider the place of work in our culture, and to reflect on why work is so important to us as a society and as individuals.

What You Do Is What You Are

NICKIE McWHIRTER

❀

This essay, first published in The Detroit Free Press, *argues that "Americans . . . tend to define and judge everybody in terms of the work they do, especially work performed for pay." McWhirter further argues that defining a person by how that person "earns his or her rent money" is not always accurate or fair.*

BEFORE YOU READ

▪ *THINK* about someone you know who holds a prestigious job but whom you do not respect. Think also about someone you know who holds a menial job but whom you do respect. If you were describing these two people to someone, would you identify them by their job titles or in some other way?

▪ *EXAMINE* the first sentence of this essay. Do you agree with McWhirter that the practice of defining people in terms of the work they do is prevalent among Americans? If you agree, why do you think this is true? If not, how might you refute this assertion?

▪ *WRITE* a journal entry in which you explore the idea that young people choose a profession on the basis of how it will define them rather than on the basis of their qualifications for or interest in that profession.

AS YOU READ

Underline and number in the margin each of McWhirter's assertions about the effects of defining someone on the basis of how that person earns a living.

Americans, unlike people almost everywhere else in the world, tend to 1
define and judge everybody in terms of the work they do, especially
work performed for pay. Charlie is a doctor; Sam is a carpenter; Mary Ellen
is a copywriter at a small ad agency. It is as if by defining how a person
earns his or her rent money, we validate or reject that person's existence.
Through the work and job title, we evaluate the worth of the life attached.
Larry is a laid-off auto worker; Tony is a retired teacher; Sally is a former
showgirl and blackjack dealer from Vegas. It is as if by learning that a person
currently earns no money at a job—and maybe hasn't earned any money
at a job for years—we assign that person to limbo, at least for the present.
We define such non-employed persons in terms of their past job history.

This seems peculiar to me. People aren't cast in bronze because of the 2
jobs they hold or once held. A retired teacher, for example, may spend a
lot of volunteer time working with handicapped children or raising money
for the Loyal Order of Hibernating Hibiscus. That apparently doesn't
count. Who's Tony? A retired teacher. A laid-off auto worker may pump
gas at his cousin's gas station or sell encyclopedias on weekends. But who's
Larry? Until and unless he begins to work steadily again, he's a laid-off auto
worker. This is the same as saying he's nothing now, but he used to be
something: an auto worker.

There is a whole category of other people who are "just" something. 3
To be "just" anything is the worst. It is not to be recognized by society as
having much value at all, not now and probably not in the past either. To
be "just" anything is to be totally discounted, at least for the present. There
are lots of people who are "just" something. "Just" a housewife immediately and painfully comes to mind. We still hear it all the time. Sometimes
women who have kept a house and reared six children refer to themselves
as "'just' a housewife." "Just" a bum, "just" a kid, "just" a drunk, bag lady,
old man, student, punk are some others. You can probably add to the list.
The "just" category contains present non-earners, people who have no past
job history highly valued by society and people whose present jobs are on
the low-end of pay and prestige scales. A person can be "just" a cab driver,
for example, or "just" a janitor. No one is ever "just" a vice-president,
however.

We're supposed to be a classless society, but we are not. We don't 4
recognize a titled nobility. We refuse to acknowledge dynastic privilege. But
we certainly separate the valued from the valueless, and it has a lot to do
with jobs and the importance or prestige we attach to them.

It is no use arguing whether any of this is correct or proper. Rationally 5
it is silly. That's our system, however, and we should not only keep it in

mind but we should teach our children how it works. It is perfectly swell to want to grow up to be a cowboy or a nurse. Kids should know, however, that quite apart from earnings potential, the cattle breeder is much more respected than the hired hand. The doctor gets a lot more respect and privilege than the nurse.

I think some anthropologist ought to study our uncataloged system 6 of awarding respect and deference to each other based on jobs we hold. Where does a vice-president–product planning fit in? Is that better than vice-president–sales in the public consciousness, or unconsciousness? Writers earn diddly dot, but I suspect they are held in higher esteem than wealthy rock musicians—that is, if everybody older than 40 gets to vote.

How do we decide which jobs have great value and, therefore, the 7 job-holders are wonderful people? Why is someone who builds shopping centers called an entrepreneur while someone who builds freeways is called a contractor? I have no answers to any of this, but we might think about the phenomenon the next time we are tempted to fawn over some stranger because we find out he happens to be a judge, or the next time we catch ourselves discounting the personal worth of the garbage collector.

❀ ❀ ❀

AFTER YOU READ

▪ *THINK* about the American work ethic—the high value we traditionally place on work. Do you see a relationship between this work ethic and the practice of defining people on the basis of what they do to earn a living? What other causes can you identify for what McWhirter believes is a typically American practice?

▪ *EXAMINE* McWhirter's assertion that "We're supposed to be a classless society, but we are not." Do you agree or disagree with this assertion? Do you think McWhirter supports this assertion adequately in this essay? Why or why not?

▪ *WRITE* an essay in which you agree or disagree with one of McWhirter's assertions.

The Way We Worked

TOM BROKAW

❀

Tom Brokaw's face and voice are familiar to millions of television viewers. Since 1983, he has been the anchor and managing editor of NBC's Nightly News with Tom Brokaw. But he is also the author of The Greatest Generation, *a book about the generation that not only fought and won World War II but also survived the Great Depression. In this 1999 article, based on* The Greatest Generation, *Brokaw points out that one of the defining characteristics of the people of this generation was their great capacity for work.*

BEFORE YOU READ

▪ *THINK* about the attitude of your own generation toward work. Do you value work for itself or for what it can provide you? Are you aware of differences between your perceptions of work and those of your parents or grandparents? What are these differences?

▪ *EXAMINE* the term *work ethic,* which appears in this essay. What does it mean to have a work ethic? Are all work ethics the same?

▪ *WRITE* in your journal a definition of your own work ethic.

AS YOU READ

Underline details that indicate the work ethic of the generation Brokaw is describing.

When my father, Anthony "Red" Brokaw, was preparing to retire, all 1
of us in the family were supportive and relieved. After all, he had
been working for almost 50 years, since he was a husky ten-year-old driving
a team of horses for a Swedish homesteader on the plains of South Dakota.

However, as his retirement date drew near, he became uncharacteris- 2
tically emotional at the thought of not having a job to go to every day. He
was almost poetic as he described his love of plowing snow after a harsh
blizzard. "Tom," he'd say, "it's the most beautiful thing when the sun
catches the snowflakes as they come off the big blade of my plow. I would
really miss that."

So we weren't surprised when he postponed his retirement for another 3
year. When he did finally quit, though, we had another worry: What would
he do now?

Work defined him in every way. It was how he made his living and it 4
was his favorite leisure-time activity. When he wasn't plowing snow or
building parks and campsites along the Missouri River for the U.S. Army
Corps of Engineers, he was in his basement workshop restoring antique
furniture or in his garage tuning up the family car. One Father's Day when
I came home from college, he spent that Sunday changing the brake pads
on my car. For him, it was the perfect way to spend the day.

In his generation, he was not unusual. As I researched the lives of the 5
men and women who came of age in the Great Depression, went through
World War II, and built the country we know today, I was struck by how
many of them went to work in their early teenage years. They had to work
because their families needed the extra income for food, for clothing, to
meet that month's rent.

Al Neuharth, the flamboyant publisher who founded *USA Today* when 6
he was CEO of Gannett, worked as a butcher's assistant and soda jerk when
he was a teenager, to help his widowed mother. As a teenager, Charles
Briscoe, who later helped build the first long-range B-29 bombers during
World War II, made a deal with a local dentist: He would clean his offices
in exchange for the dental work Briscoe's mother required. When Bob Bush
returned from the war with the Congressional Medal of Honor, he found
a partner and they started a building-supply business. They both worked
seven days a week; every other week each man would work a full 24-hour
cycle so they could add a day to their workload.

Dorothy Haener left her poor Michigan family to work on Ford's 7
assembly lines during the war. When she lost her job to returning vets, she
became a labor activist to ensure that women got equal opportunity and
pay. "I didn't go to work to find myself," she says. "I needed the money."

When my mother, Jean, graduated from high school, she went to work 8
at the post office for a dollar a day because she couldn't afford the college
tuition of $125 a year.

Lifelong work habits for this generation were formed by more than 9
the bleak economics of the Depression, however. In the '30s and '40s,
America was a much more rural society and there were very few of the
labor-saving devices that we normally take for granted today. The daily
chores of even middle-class homes required shoveling coal into the furnace,
carrying heavy baskets of wet laundry outside to hang on the clothesline,
washing and drying dishes, canning fruits and vegetables from the large
garden, mending socks, and cutting patterns and sewing them into homemade dresses, blouses, and shirts.

Many of the farms of the '30s and '40s had no indoor plumbing. Water 10
was heated atop wood-burning stoves. Cows were milked by hand. Tractors
and motorized combines were available, but they were primitive compared
with the mechanized wonders of the modern farm; many a young farm boy
got tough fast by lifting heavy bales of hay all day long in the hot sun.

As a result of its early experience of developing a work ethic out of 11
necessity, that generation was uniquely ready for the rigors of WWII. Young
men off the farm showed up for basic training already in peak physical
condition. Women who went to work on assembly lines were already used
to working with their hands. Nursing was a popular way out of hard times
for many of them, so when the Army suddenly needed thousands of nurses,
it had a ready supply of women who knew how to cope with difficulties.

When the war ended, that same generation rushed into the task of 12
building modern America: The suburbs became sprawling landscapes of
new homes, Detroit hummed with automobile production after turning
out tanks and jeeps and other military equipment during the war years, and
the interstate highway system laced the country together with great ribbons
of pavement.

The rewards of work in the postwar years went well beyond the meager 13
returns of the '30s. Families were buying new homes, new cars, and modern
appliances, as well as saving for their children's college education. It was
an unheard of experience for many of the WWII generation—to actually
have more than they needed.

Still, they remembered the bad old days, and there was always an 14
underlying anxiety that the Depression could return at any moment. In the
small towns of South Dakota where I grew up, my parents and their friends
managed their new prosperity very carefully.

In the '50s, before credit cards, they paid cash for everything. They   15
made sure there was always a direct connection between what they earned
and what they spent.

If we were going on a family trip to, say, Minneapolis, my father would   16
go to the bank and get one $100 bill to mix in with the fives, tens, and 20s
in his wallet.

He told us it was his insurance against running short. When we asked,   17
he would let me and my brothers have a peek at it, then he'd tuck it away
again. I don't think he ever actually spent one of those $100 bills, but he
did have a certain pride in knowing that he'd reached a stage where he
could have $100 all in one banknote.

Sometimes that conditioning from the dark days of the '30s would   18
seem a little excessive to those of us who were their offspring. The children
of the WWII generation, by and large, have never known really hard times.
The American economy has been expanding since the war ended and that,
in turn, has given birth to a long run of instant gratification in American
society.

Buy now, worry later. Don't like your job? Quit and get another one.   19
Tired of working so hard? Take off for three months to "find yourself."

It is an approach to life that those of the WWII generation, now in   20
their 70s and 80s, cannot fathom. How many have visited their kids'
homes, walked through the yard, garage, and living quarters, and mentally
added up all the luxuries and what they must have cost? How many have
said in a bewildered tone, "He had a good job—but he quit because he had
to work too many Saturdays"?

Every generation is a reflection of the times it has lived through.   21
Modern America is a mélange of experiences, from the extremes of
deprivation to the comforts of material wealth. However, as those of the
WWII generation pass on and the personal memories of the Depression
fade away, we will lose a tempering influence on our common experience
of work and its rewards.

❀   ❀   ❀

AFTER YOU READ

▪ *THINK* about Brokaw's statement about his father: "Work defined him
in every way." Do you know someone who is defined by work? What does

it mean to be defined by work? Do you think it is desirable to define yourself in terms of the work you do? Why or why not?

- *EXAMINE* the following sentence from the essay:

  As a result of its early experience of developing a work ethic out of necessity, that generation was uniquely ready for the rigors of WWII.

In this statement Brokaw clearly suggests that a strong work ethic is an important attribute for citizens. Do you agree with this statement? Why or why not? This statement also suggests that Brokaw idealizes the World War II generation, believing it to be superior to other generations. Do you think that entire generations can be characterized in this way? Is it accurate to generalize about generations and to attribute specific characteristics to them? Why or why not?

- *WRITE* an essay in which you describe or define your own generation's work ethic (or attitude toward money), comparing it to and contrasting it with that of an earlier generation—perhaps that of your parents or grandparents.

The Case Against Chores

JANE SMILEY

❀

Jane Smiley lives in California with her three children, three dogs, and sixteen horses. This essay by Smiley was originally part of a longer essay that appeared in the Hungry Mind Review. *In this selection, the author, who is best known as a novelist, argues that children should not be given chores. Smiley's most recent novels are* Moo, At Paradise Gate, The All-True Travels and Adventures of Lidie Newton, *and* Horse Heaven. *Her 1992 novel,* A Thousand Acres, *won the Pulitzer Prize.*

BEFORE YOU READ

- *THINK* about the types of chores you were asked to do as a child. Do you think doing these chores improved you in any way?

- *EXAMINE* your own attitudes about chores. Do you think children should be given routine chores? Why or why not?

- *WRITE* a journal entry in which you describe in detail a chore you were given as a child, and tell what you learned from performing this chore.

AS YOU READ

Underline Smiley's arguments against giving children chores, and put a check mark by the arguments that you think are most convincing.

I've lived in the upper Midwest for twenty-one years now, and I'm here 1 to tell you that the pressure to put your children to work is unrelenting. So far I've squirmed out from under it, and my daughters have led a life of almost tropical idleness, much to their benefit. My son, however, may not be so lucky. His father was himself raised in Iowa and put to work at an

239

early age, and you never know when, in spite of all my husband's best intentions, that early training might kick in.

Although "chores" are so sacred in my neck of the woods that almost ₂ no one ever discusses their purpose, I have over the years gleaned some of the reasons parents give for assigning them. I'm not impressed. Mostly the reasons have to do with developing good work habits or, in the absence of good work habits, at least habits of working. No such thing as a free lunch, any job worth doing is worth doing right, work before play, all of that. According to this reasoning, the world is full of jobs that no one wants to do. If we divide them up and get them over with, then we can go on to pastimes we like. If we do them "right," then we won't have to do them again. Lots of times, though, in a family, that *we* doesn't operate. The operative word is *you*. The practical result of almost every child-labor scheme that I've witnessed is the child doing the dirty work and the parent getting the fun: Mom cooks and Sis does the dishes; the parents plan and plant the garden, the kids weed it. To me, what this teaches the child is the lesson of alienated labor: not to love the work but to get it over with; not to feel pride in one's contribution but to feel resentment at the waste of one's time.

Another goal of chores: the child contributes to the work of maintain- ₃ ing the family. According to this rationale, the child comes to understand what it takes to have a family, and to feel that he or she is an important, even indispensable member of it. But come on. Would you really want to feel loved primarily because you're the one who gets the floors mopped? Wouldn't you rather feel that your family's love simply exists all around you, no matter what your contribution? And don't the parents love their children anyway, whether the children vacuum or not? Why lie about it just to get the housework done? Let's be frank about the other half of the equation too. In this day and age, it doesn't take much work at all to manage a household, at least in the middle class—maybe four hours a week to clean the house and another four to throw the laundry into the washing machine, move it to the dryer, and fold it. Is it really a good idea to set the sort of example my former neighbors used to set, of mopping the floor every two days, cleaning the toilets every week, vacuuming every day, dusting, dusting, dusting? Didn't they have anything better to do than serve their house?

Let me confess that I wasn't expected to lift a finger when I was growing ₄ up. Even when my mother had a full-time job, she cleaned up after me, as did my grandmother. Later there was a housekeeper. I would leave my room in a mess when I headed off for school and find it miraculously neat when I returned. Once in a while I vacuumed, just because I liked the pattern the Hoover made on the carpet. I did learn to run water in my cereal bowl before setting it in the sink.

Where I discovered work was at the stable, and, in fact, there is no housework like horsework. You've got to clean the horses' stalls, feed them, groom them, tack them up, wrap their legs, exercise them, turn them out, and catch them. You've got to clip them and shave them. You have to sweep the aisle, clean your tack and your boots, carry bales of hay and buckets of water. Minimal horsekeeping, rising just to the level of humaneness, requires many more hours than making a few beds, and horsework turned out to be a good preparation for the real work of adulthood, which is rearing children. It was a good preparation not only because it was similar in many ways but also because my desire to do it, and to do a good job of it, grew out of my love of and interest in my horse. I can't say that cleaning out her bucket when she manured in it was an actual joy, but I knew she wasn't going to do it herself. I saw the purpose of my labor, and I wasn't alienated from it.

Probably to the surprise of some of those who knew me as a child, I have turned out to be gainfully employed. I remember when I was in seventh grade, one of my teachers said to me, strongly disapproving, "The trouble with you is you do only what you want to do!" That continues to be the trouble with me, except that over the years I have wanted to do more and more.

My husband worked hard as a child, out-Iowa-ing the Iowans, if such a thing is possible. His dad had him mixing cement with a stick when he was five, pushing wheelbarrows not long after. It's a long sad tale on the order of two miles to school and both ways uphill. The result is, he's a great worker, much better than I am, but all the while he's doing it he wishes he weren't. He thinks of it as work; he's torn between doing a good job and longing not to be doing it at all. Later, when he's out on the golf course, where he really wants to be, he feels a little guilty, knowing there's work that should have been done before he gave in and took advantage of the beautiful day.

Good work is not the work we assign children but the work they want to do, whether it's reading in bed (where would I be today if my parents had rousted me out and put me to scrubbing floors?) or cleaning their rooms or practicing the flute or making roasted potatoes with rosemary and Parmesan for the family dinner. It's good for a teenager to suddenly decide that the bathtub is so disgusting she'd better clean it herself. I admit that for the parent, this can involve years of waiting. But if she doesn't want to wait, she can always spend her time dusting.

❀ ❀ ❀

AFTER YOU READ

• *THINK* about Smiley's argument against chores. First, review her arguments by reading the sections you underlined as you read the essay. How many of her arguments are based on her own experience? Can you refute these arguments by using your own experiences, or do you agree with Smiley?

• *EXAMINE* Smiley's definition of good work for children is "the work they want to do." Do you agree with this definition? Why or why not?

• *WRITE* a "case for chores" in which you refute Smiley's arguments. You may use your own experiences or the experiences of others as evidence.

W-O-R-K

BRIAN BRAAKSMA

❁

In this student essay, Brian Braaksma describes vividly his experience working on a family farm in Northwest Iowa, where winters are severe and work is taken seriously. Now a senior at Texas Christian University, Braaksma plans to go to medical school and become a doctor. In his essay, he remembers a time when he was expected to do manual labor even on the coldest days.

BEFORE YOU READ

- *THINK* about a time when you did hard manual labor. What did you learn from this experience? Do you consider manual labor more difficult than mental labor? Why or why not?
- *EXAMINE* the reference to the "difference between work and real work" that Braaksma makes in his opening sentence. How would you define "real work"? What is the difference between "work" and "real work"?
- *WRITE* a list of different work experiences you have had and what you learned from each.

AS YOU READ

Notice Braaksma's use of specific details to describe the work on his family's farm. Underline the details that communicate to you most vividly what this experience was like for him.

G rowing up on a family farm in Northwest Iowa, I learned many things, 1 the most important of which was the difference between work and real work. There is the kind of work that my friends would continuously complain about: homework, cleaning their rooms, or passing Super Mario

Brothers 3. I was familiar with their kind of "work," but the work I was more accustomed to was the hard, excruciating, manual labor of farm-work.

"W-O-R-K!" This word was my wake-up call every morning for twelve 2 years. It started when I was old enough to handle a grain shovel at the age of six, and if I had not left for college three years ago at the age of eighteen, I am sure that this morning would be no exception. My father turned on every light in the house at five thirty in the morning, waking up each of my three brothers and me in turn by chanting "W-O-R-K." I would try to ignore him, but with his six foot four inch, two hundred and sixty-pound body looming over me, I knew resistance was futile. So everyday, just like clockwork, the Braaksma brothers would roll out of bed at the crack of dawn to do farm-work. The type of work to be done on any given day depended on the season and the day of the week, but we could always count on two things: getting dirty and doing physical labor.

One such morning was Friday, December 12, 1992. The day before, 3 there was a terrible snowstorm that dropped twelve inches of snow over our area, and school had been canceled. All the kids at school were ecstatic about this fortunate turn of events and were busy planning an exciting day of sleeping in, watching television and sledding. Yet my brothers and I had a very different outlook on the situation—we knew we had a long day of strenuous work ahead of us.

The day started out like any other; dad woke us up at five thirty 4 chanting what has become the family motto: "W-O-R-K!" I reluctantly got up and looked outside. What my friends saw as prime packing snow for snowballs, I saw as a foot of wet, heavy snow that I was going to have to scoop by hand. After eating a quick bowl of Lucky Charms for breakfast, I ran barefoot across the freezing cold floor of our garage to get my "pig clothes" that I had to wear. My pig clothes were multiple layers of clothing that needed to be worn to defend myself against the cold while working outside on the farm in the arctic temperatures of Iowan winter. The pig clothes were kept outside because after being worn for only a single day of chores in the pigpen, the smell of them was so rank that the mere presence of them would fill the house with the rancid stench of pig. Similarly, it would be senseless to wash them after chores because the very next day chores would need to be done again, and the clothes would promptly be soiled. Consequently, they were always ice-cold and dirty.

I shivered as I slid into my frigid long johns and cringed as I put on 5 crusty sweat pants and coverall—stiff with dried and frozen pig manure. As I expected, as soon as we were dressed, dad ordered my brothers and me to march out to the barn and commence cleaning. The pigs were almost large enough to sell, and at that size, they can produce an unbelievably large amount of manure. Consequently, we had the pleasure of removing their poop every week, usually on Saturday, but since we didn't have school, dad knew he had a captive audience, and decided to clean the buildings that Friday instead. When I opened the door to the barn, a wall of dense, moist, dusty, rank air hit me. The stench was so penetrating that it took my breath away. Ammonia, formed when urine and manure mix, burns the nose and mouth and stings the eyes. I immediately closed the door, thinking about hiding to delay the torture, but at the same time I knew that the work needed to be done and wasting time would only perpetuate the suffering, so like lemmings my brothers and I filed into the barn.

Inside the barn, no matter the time of day, it was always dark due to dust particles and steam in the air from sweaty pigs, making the air too thick for the light to travel through. It was impossible to see the length of the fifty-yard barn, and cobwebs hung from the ceiling heavy and thick from a coating of dust. While breathing the filthy, unhealthy dust into my lungs, I began scooping. The task at hand was tremendous—to totally rid the building of manure, while at the same time fighting off aggressive pigs continually trying to bite us. To make matters worse, dad was a slave driver who was never satisfied. We could always be scooping faster or working harder, and he would let us know. As he barked out orders, his teeth were white against his face now black from dust-saturated sweat, but soon his teeth too would be black; nothing could escape being covered by filth.   6

Four hours later, we were finished. As soon as dad gave permission to leave, I ran out of the barn, wanting only to breathe clean air again. I trudged back to the house exhausted and covered inside and out with a film of putrid dust. Inside the house, I tried to clean up. After thirty minutes in the shower rubbing my hands raw with industrial strength soap, my fingers still smelled as if I had just pulled them out of a steaming pile of dung. The stench seemed to seep into my pores. It consumed me, and stayed with me as a constant reminder of the work I had done. The smell of the barn remained in my nostrils for days, and for a week I blew black mucus from my nose. This was the kind of work I did, week in and week out, but that morning, I decided that I did not want to do manual labor all my life. I did not want to become a retired farmer with bones and muscles aching from years of strenuous work, lungs black with soot. I had tasted what real work was like, and I did not like it. I decided that I would much rather live my life working with my mind instead of my muscle.   7

☞ ☞ ☞

AFTER YOU READ

- *THINK* about the difference between Braaksma's work ethic and that of his father. How are they different and how are they alike? Do you think that Braaksma's work ethic was influenced by his father's even though they were different?

- *THINK* also about Braaksma's use of a single anecdote to communicate what working on his family farm was like. Would it have been more effective if he had recounted a series of anecdotes or just a general description of the work rather than focusing on this single event?

- *EXAMINE* Braaksma's last sentence: "I decided that I would much rather live my life working with my mind instead of my muscle." Does this statement suggest that Braaksma does not have a strong work ethic? Why or why not? Can mental work be as rigorous and demanding as physical work? Why or why not?

- *WRITE* an essay in which you describe a single work experience you have had. You may include what you learned from this experience either by stating the lesson explicitly (as Braaksma, does in his essay) or by simply implying the lesson you learned. Try to include the same type of vivid sensory details that Braaksma does in his essay.

Girl in an Oven

SARAH JEANETTE SMITH

❖

Sarah Jeanette Smith is a sophomore interior design stu-
dent from Silver City, New Mexico. During the summer
after her freshman year at college, Smith worked as a
firefighter for the Forest Service in New Mexico. As a rookie
and the only woman on her crew, Smith spent the summer
"trying to act like a girl while working like a man." In her
essay, she describes the danger of firefighting and the
challenge of being the only female in a "man's world" as
well as how this experience helped her to define herself.

BEFORE YOU READ

- *THINK* about different professions that are traditionally associated with either males or females. Are there fewer of these than there used to be? Are there any professions today that are exclusively male or female?

- *EXAMINE* the title of this essay. What image does it evoke? Knowing that firefighters refer to a forest fire as an "oven" may help you understand the title better.

- *WRITE* two lists—one of professions or jobs that have traditionally been associated with females and one of professions or jobs that have tradition-ally been associated with males.

AS YOU READ

Mark the descriptive passages that communicate most vividly to you what it is like to fight forest fires.

I tasted the smoke curling into my lungs, I blinked as the dancing flames 1
tried to snatch my eyelashes, and I felt my boots melt on the smoldering

ground. And then I looked at the guys around me—a hippie boss and his recruits—a redneck cowboy, a gangster, a macho snowboarder and an overweight father. And then there was me: the girl.

I had been hired as a summer wildland firefighter with the Forest 2 Service, and this New Mexico wildfire was my first near-kabob experience. For a split-second, I pondered the unknown impulse that caused me to strap on a pair of massive black boots and confront a flaming force that danced and sparked, daring me to challenge it. Then I heard the urgent yell of my crew boss, jerking my mind back to the char-grilling force.

Evan Sota was a seasoned firefighter, and his beady eyes were just the 3 beginning of his intimidating presence. The hazel points seemed to detach from his face and drill right through me, exposing my naked inexperience beneath the green and yellow Nomex fire wear. Evan's thick gray mustache fell over his mouth, and he seemed to enjoy the ambiguity of his hidden facial expressions. Long summers on the fire line had sculpted a man of solid muscle and big hands, and experience was even tied into the knot of the bandanna covering his bald head. A sense of military formality gave order and precision to his mannerisms and instructions; he was the only person on the fire to have his last name monogrammed on his pack and shirt pocket. If there was anything Evan successfully conveyed to us, it was the sizzling uncertainty of the fire and our need to perform accordingly with "aggressive caution."

Safety was always of utmost concern, and we were loaded down with 4 hard hats, huge black boots, safety glasses, gloves and the most sacred object in the lives and deaths of firefighters: the fire shelter. It could supposedly save your life if you could bury yourself under the taco-like shelter in less than 30 seconds. But if the fire got hotter than 500 degrees Fahrenheit, the aluminum laminate would melt, sealing your baked-potato fate. After practice in training, I was confident about the procedure, but I hoped that I wouldn't ever face the last-resort.

Equipping us with one last encouraging comment, Evan squinted with 5 serious emphasis and pronounced, "This is the closest thing to war you'll see as a civilian. I want you to go out there and rock this oven!"

My crew's first order was to dig a "fire line" down a dry creek bottom, 6 in order to connect with another crew coming to tie in the last corner. Surrounding the fire with a line of fresh dirt put a halt to the blazing furnace, and once the line was dug, it was only a matter of "mopping-up" and watching the flames slowly burn out. We grabbed our *Pulaskis*—the fire axe with a hoe opposite the blade. I lined up with my crew, and we fell into the staccato rhythm of chinking rocks and shoveling dirt. In hunched-over positions, we wore our packs at all times, even when nature called us to take a break. Dehydration was a problem on the line, and the hot sun, hotter fire and dripping sweat made it necessary to carry at least a gallon of water. Not only did I look forward to the refreshing wetness on my lips, but I also guzzled the water to lighten my heavy pack. I took a break after working for an hour, and Evan warned me that we might have to continue digging line until midnight.

It was 10 a.m. I took another drink.   7

I wasn't the only rookie on the crew; all the other guys were first-time 8 forest firefighters, with the exception of Jake. As the token cowboy of the group, Jake had endless stories of ropin' and ridin' across his father's ranch in Wyoming. Jake and I patrolled the fires during late nights, making coffee on the warm smoldering coals and sharing our own stories of college life. Jake had a story about the time he got kicked out of college—he and some buddies stole a pickup-load of fish from a hatchery and then scattered them all over campus—and it was so good that we didn't care if it was a lie. His cowboy background made him the biggest gentleman on the crew, and I spent most of my time working on fires with him. Jake was like a big brother to me; he was encouraging and strong when I needed him to be, made me laugh when tears were beginning to fall, and stood ready to bash anyone who doubted I could "hang."

As I leaned against the sloping creekbed during the break, I remem- 9 bered that frantic morning of loading gear into helicopters and then flying to the fire. It was my first helicopter flight, my first fire and the first time that I didn't have the option of making a collect call home. The helicopter's low flying altitude intensified my anticipation, and the waxy pine smears below me looked almost close enough to touch. The beautiful green shine of the untouched pine needles was in sharp contrast to the burned ruin of charred sticks, drifting smoke and billowing flames. Fires were more than just burning wood, though. In training, I learned about fuel types, weather, the physics of falling trees, wind conditions and topography. Then I had to take the deciding "Pack Test," the endurance test of hiking three miles in less than 45 minutes carrying a pack loaded down with enough water to flood a small country. Then there was "Chain Saw 101." I didn't really meet the prerequisites for this class—I was never a boy who chopped wood with Dad, and I had never used an axe, let alone a chain saw. But it was a great class, complete with a slide show and a step-by-step process for felling, limbing and bucking a tree. The hardest thing for me to do, however, was simply starting the chain saw. I didn't have the upper body strength of the guys, so I was unable to stand up and pull the starter at the same time. But

I was determined to wield my new-found power to end photosynthesis, so I invented my own way of bending down so that I could use my whole body to pull the starter with one furious yank. From knowing nothing about a chain saw but the noise, I progressed to felling a tree 18 inches in diameter. That was a great day—I screamed and all the guys cheered when the tree came crashing down.

As long as the fire was raging, it was not unusual to work 16 to 20 10 hours a day. Sometimes we worked with intense action to quench a fire's roaring character, but other teasing fires demanded more patience. There were nights when we slept on the fire line, and took turns waking up every hour to check on a burning snag that was in danger of falling across the line. Layers of thick tape tried to remedy the blisters and annoying rub of my heavy black boots. In a matter of four days, my painted toenails and soft, moisturized feet seemed to be an extension of the slashing and burning. My morning routine included talking to Evan while he massaged and bandaged my suffering feet. We discussed everything from Florida trailer parks to philosophy to the Civil War. Whenever he took out the Band-Aids from his monogrammed first-aid pack, I saw a more compassionate, caring side of a man who had not yet been completely hardened by fire.

Of the 95 people working at the fire, five were girls. Most of the guys 11 on the fire satisfied Evan's idea of the macho pyromaniac, or "23-year-old brain donor." This was a guy who lived only for beer, Copenhagen and the prospect of single-handedly smothering the blaze. I always laughed at Evan's stories, but never really believed that such a mindless male creature existed.

Then I met Dave. He was a tall kid from Colorado and, from outward 12 appearances, looked like he and his hair came straight out of a rock band. With his Pulaski, Dave would rip through burning wood like a maniac, and one time a chain saw almost severed his arm when he barged in front of the whirling destruction. He would attempt to lift heavy chunks of wood that should take two people to lift, his face turning into a grimace of bulging eyes and popping veins. Dave frequently tried to fill a silence with his own profound thoughts, but once spoken, they materialized as pure ignorance. I couldn't count the number of times he asked me, "Have you seen the girl with the beer cart?"

After we spent innumerable days on a fire, the Incident Commander— 13 the biggest of the fire bosses—called the fire "under control." Of course, the lightning that had caused the fire only seemed to strike in the middle of the wilderness, so fire crews were guaranteed to have a marathon hike back to civilization at the end of each fire. On one occasion, the nearest road was 16 miles away, so we packed our gear and left the dying wisps of smoke behind. My crew guys trekked out at a pace that shouldn't be possible while carrying a heavy pack. I worked to keep up with them, running at times—up mountains, down embankments—and finally stopping near a dry lake for lunch. I sat down to eat with Jake and Evan, but when Dave saw me, he took a long drag of his cigarette and said, "Girl, you kept up with us? You're pretty damn burly."

Even though I thought Dave intended that to be a compliment to my   14
endurance, I was furious. I finished the hike by myself. At the end of the day, I was dead-tired, but at the same time, I was proud of the work that both united and separated me from the guys on my crew. It had been a never-ending summer of trying to act like a girl while working like a man. I didn't want any favors or easy jobs just because I had to work harder to keep up. I wanted the guys to respect me, to laugh with me and to count on me. It wasn't easy. Sometimes it wasn't fun. But no matter how much my feet hurt, how thirsty I was or how badly I wanted to drench my hair in fruity conditioner, I loved working hard and being in the woods. It felt great because I was covered with layers of sticky sweat, black smoke, dried tears and the sense of accomplishment. . . .

That summer, the inferno raged and the smoke swirled, but the girl   15
smothered the red-eyed monster.

❁   ❁   ❁

AFTER YOU READ

▪ *THINK* about the author's motivation for working as a firefighter for the Forest Service. Why do you think this job appealed to her?

▪ *EXAMINE* the author's ambivalent feelings about wanting to be "one of the guys" but at the same time wanting her male colleagues to think of her as a female. How did this job as a firefighter help her to define herself?

▪ *WRITE* an essay in which you argue for or against the proposition that gender should not be a consideration for any job or profession.

My Mother Enters the Workforce

RITA DOVE

❁

Formerly the poet laureate of the United States, Rita Dove is a Pulitzer Prize–winning author. She has written a novel, a play, and six books of verse, including most recently On the Bus with Rosa Parks. *The poem that follows, which is about Dove's mother, tells of her mother's struggle to support her family by working first as a seamstress and later as a secretary.*

BEFORE YOU READ

• *THINK* about who is making your education possible. Are you putting yourself through school, or is someone helping you? Why do parents typically help their children get an education? Should children expect their parents' financial support while they attend college?

• *EXAMINE* the term *seamstress,* usually defined as a woman who is expert at sewing, especially one who makes her living by sewing. The word comes from a Middle English word that referred to both males and females who sewed. Now we usually call a man who sews a tailor. What connotations do the words *seamstress* and *tailor* have? Which is more prestigious?

• *WRITE* a journal entry in which you first describe your image of a seamstress, then your image of a secretary. Analyze why both now seem rather old-fashioned even though people still do these types of work.

AS YOU READ

Think about what it would be like to try to earn a living by sewing clothes for other people.

My Mother Enters the Workforce

The path to ABC Business School
was paid for by a lucky sign:
Alterations, Qualified Seamstress Inquire Within.
Tested on Sleeves, hers
never puckered—puffed or sleek,   5
Leg o' Mutton or Raglan—
they barely needed the
damp cloth
to steam them
perfect.   10

Those were the
afternoons.
Evenings
she took in
piecework,   15
the treadle
machine
with its
locomotive whir
traveling the lit path   20
of the needle
through quicksand taffeta
or velvet deep as a forest.
And now and now sang the treadle,
I know, I know . . .   25

And then it was day again, all morning
at the office machines, their clack and chatter
another journey—rougher,
that would go on forever
until she could break a hundred words   30
with no errors—ah, and then
no more postponed groceries,
and that blue pair of shoes!

❁   ❁   ❁

AFTER YOU READ

▪ *THINK* about what happens in the poem and then identify the poet's thesis. Because Dove does not articulate her thesis explicitly, you will need to infer it from the poem and state it in your own words. Cite evidence from the poem that supports the thesis you identify.

▪ *EXAMINE* the final phrase in the poem, "that blue pair of shoes." Whom are the shoes for? Why is it significant that they are blue?

▪ *WRITE* an essay in which you argue for or against the idea that education is the best means of improving a person's status.

Black Mountain, 1977

DONALD ANTRIM

❀

*In this memoir, Donald Antrim writes of a summer in 1977
when he learned from his grandfather not only to work
with his hands, but also why work is valuable. Antrim,
who lives in Brooklyn, is the author of* Elect Mr. Robinson
for a Better World, The Hundred Brothers, *and* The
Verificationist. *Antrim's work has been described as
"short, elegant, outrageously imagined comic novels"
(Jeffrey Eugenides,* The New Yorker, *June 24 and July 1,
1996). However, in this memoir Antrim's tone is thoughtful rather than comic. This memoir appeared in* The New
Yorker.

BEFORE YOU READ

▪ *THINK* about someone from whom you learned something about work—
someone who passed on to you a valuable skill or taught you the value of
work.

▪ *EXAMINE* the first paragraph of this essay, analyzing the information that
it provides you as a reader. What relationship is going to be the focus of
this memoir? What do you learn about the author's family? Why do you
think the author provides this information about his family?

▪ *WRITE* a journal entry in which you describe a person who taught you
the value of work or influenced your attitude toward work.

AS YOU READ

Notice the changes that occur in Antrim as the summer progresses. Mark
the passages in the memoir that indicate these changes.

When my grandfather was in his seventies and I in my twenties, we 1
created one of those friendships that are sometimes available between nonconsecutive generations in broken or unhappy families. This
friendship was brokered, however inadvertently, and as so many are, by a
third party who functioned largely as an object of worry and distress—common cause and a bond between the new friends. The third party was my
mother, my grandfather's daughter, a woman whose lifelong pursuit of
death was, arguably, a response to severe mishandling by her own mother,
my grandfather's wife, a woman who in later age became a nutritionist and
appeared merely stern, but who during her early years of motherhood
carried out an aggressive campaign against her daughter's body, even going
so far as to advocate unnecessary surgeries for her only child. It is, of course,
pointless to imagine the implications of a revision in past events or
behaviors—to guess at how things might have been. Nevertheless, I hatch
these kinds of daydreams constantly. Had my grandfather been less cowed
by his wife, less meek and alcoholic—had he been able, in other words, to
intercede and protect my future mother—then it is at least likely that she
(his young girl) might not have grown up to become the lonely, distrustful,
ragingly self-obliterative woman she became; it is unclear, in other words,
whether my grandfather and I, during those years right before he began
having his heart attacks, the years of his great anxiety over his daughter's
well-being, the years when everyone was still alive—it is unclear whether
my grandfather and I would have been given the platform on which to
build, out of guilt, sorrow, need, and respect, our real love for each other.

I was a teen-ager when my grandfather retired from his job as a 2
junior-high-school principal in Sarasota, Florida. He and my grandmother
sold their large Spanish-style house on Wisteria Street and moved into a
tiny, unattractive condominium, which they hated. After that, they became
regular visitors to the Great Smoky Mountains, around Asheville, North
Carolina—just east of the part of the world they had both originally come
from—and in 1977, the summer I graduated from boarding school, they
retired from their retirement and bought a truly derelict bungalow in Black
Mountain, intending to restore it and, eventually, move in. Would I like to
join them, to spend my summer before college working on the old house?
My mother's alcoholism was by then reaching its advanced stages—in a
few years she would be forced to attempt sobriety or die—and my parents'
fighting, not only with each other but with me, had escalated to nearly
heroic levels. Yes, I would be happy to come to North Carolina and work
on the house.

And yet, once in Black Mountain, I had a tendency to abandon my 3
grandparents to their painstaking and methodical, stooped-over, Presbyte-

rian labors; every day, I fled the house and drove aimlessly over mountain roads that passed by indigent farms and strange, unpainted churches. I had no concept of work. What was wrong with me? When would my life begin? Looking back on that time, I have an impression of myself performing a kind of fitful, mild-mannered revolt against—what? Anhedonia? Boredom? My family? Or perhaps it was a revolt against Southern Protestantism in general, which I associated with prohibitions and taboos in a variety of forms, perversely expressed in the self-destructive or work-obsessed temperaments of, it seemed to me then, everyone I knew. But protests against the denial of pleasure bring no pleasure. In the spirit of someone with nowhere else to go, I turned the car around and returned to the house in Black Mountain, picked up steel wool or a rag, and found something to scrub.

The day came when we got around to windows. These were painted 4 shut and badly warped. There was, for my grandfather, no question of replacing them; they would be removed, their panes razored clean, and the frames stripped with fine-grade sandpaper, or, if too profoundly rotten, disassembled and rebuilt. This was heartbreakingly deliberate work. The casements were filled with dust, dirt, and dead animals' tiny skeletons. Here, as well, were the windows' rusted pulley wheels and ancient counterweights, canvas sacks stuffed with lead shot and tied off, their ropes broken. I remember my grandfather's old-man hands worrying the wood, delicately touching, like a blind man reading, the surfaces of things; it was slow work that he seemed determined to make slower, as if work of any sort were equivalent to an act of obstinacy. My grandmother's style, by contrast, was all harshness and haste—she attacked her chores. And I remained lazy and sarcastic; the screen door was always slamming behind me. Nonetheless, I was attracted by my grandfather's tremendous patience for what people in romantic moments like to call honest labor. It wasn't that I suddenly understood the value of a job well done. Far from it. It was that for a moment—a romantic moment of my own, destined to resonate and grow in magnitude over the years—I hoped (and this may have been a fantasy that I wanted to have about the man) that my grandfather had something to pass on to me, to teach me. And I imagined (because it did not occur to me to ask him) that what he had to teach me concerned the beauty in labor that remains, at the end of the job, hidden, and that no one except the worker will see or understand or even necessarily appreciate. The windows, when they went back in, slid up or down at a touch.

Years later, when my grandfather was nearing ninety, well after he and 5 I had been brought together by my mother's many hospitalizations, we took drives together along the roads that led over the mountains. Ours were rambling, all-day excursions, little revolts that infuriated my grand-mother, who feared for his health. We'd stop on the shoulder in hollows or valleys, where my grandfather took leaks beside the car—frequent urination caused by his heart medication. Always, he drove. Bourbon was stashed in the tire well in the trunk—his guilty, exciting secret. At some point along the way, generally when we were far from home, out beyond Hendersonville, he'd ask the question we lived with every day in our family: Will your mother be all right? Will she be all right? Since by this time he had long supported not only his daughter but, intermittently over the years, her son, his only grandson, the cash-poor so-called writer living up North, I felt that the question might in some ways be a question not about her, or at least not about her alone, but about me. And what could I possibly tell him? That because of a way he'd once gazed at a window frame, then gradually, stubbornly, lovingly sanded smooth its torn, abused edges, I'd be all right?

❀   ❀   ❀

AFTER YOU READ

▪ *THINK* about how Antrim's account of his family history provides a context for his memoir. Would the lessons Antrim learned about work from his grandfather be as meaningful if the reader did not know something about the relationships and problems within the family?

▪ *EXAMINE* Antrim's statement, "I had no concept of work" (paragraph 3). Compare this statement about himself with his description of other people's "work-obsessed temperaments" (paragraph 3) and then later his admission, "I was attracted by my grandfather's tremendous patience for what people . . . like to call honest labor" (paragraph 4). What do these statements tell you about the change in Antrim's attitude?

▪ *EXAMINE* also the last sentence of the memoir. What did Antrim learn about work from his grandfather that summer in 1977 that would translate into his own life as a writer and would ensure that, in spite of his family history, he would be "all right"?

▪ *WRITE* a memoir about an occasion when you learned something about work from someone.

It's About Time

MARY LEONARD

❀

This article, which first appeared in the Boston Globe, *reports on current trends in people's attitudes toward work and leisure time. The article is based on a number of different sources, all of which focus on the increasing interest in shorter hours and more flexibility in the work-place. Leonard's conclusion is that American workers increasingly value time more than money.*

BEFORE YOU READ

- *THINK* about the forty-hour work week that we have traditionally accepted as a reasonable expectation for a full-time job. Have you ever worked forty hours a week? What was this experience like? How many hours each week do you think should be expected of a full-time employee?
- *EXAMINE* the first sentence of this article: "All that many people want this year is a little more time." Since there are only twenty-four hours in a day, how do people get "more time"?
- *WRITE* in your journal a detailed description of how you spend your time. You might even want to draw a graph or chart that shows how your typical day is divided among various activities.

AS YOU READ

Identify each source that Leonard uses in this article by making a notation in the margin or numbering the different sources.

All that many people want this year is a little more time. 1
Could Americans, swept up in a work-worshiping culture and control- 2
led by the clock, really be serious about taking back time? It's hard to

believe, when a 60-hour week is a marker of making it, and the three-martini meal has been replaced, at least in New York City, by multiple, 20-minute business lunches for some executives on the run.

Yet a recent poll in *U.S. News & World Report* signaled an interesting 3 attitude change. It showed notable jumps from a decade ago in the number of Americans who call leisure important (57 percent vs. 33 percent in 1986) and who say society needs to stop emphasizing work and put more value on free time (49 percent vs. 28 percent).

There's evidence, too, that those attitudes are producing action on the 4 job. So-called work-life issues have become central as businesses in a tight labor market try to recruit and retain employees, luring them not just with money, but with time—flexible time, shared time, compressed time, and even shorter hours at a full-time job.

"Flexibility is the No. 1 business trend right now, growing by leaps and 5 bounds," says Susan Seitel, president of the Work & Family Connection, a Minneapolis-based information service for more than 850 companies. "People want a life, and they are demanding that employers take time out of the traditional 40-hour-a-week box."

Balancing work and personal time is hard enough, but increasingly, the 6 blurring of the two creates the perception that leisure has disappeared. Paradoxically, the same technologies we think save time—computers, cellular telephones, fax machines, beepers—have turned homes and get-aways into workplaces and take up time that otherwise would have been spent alone or with family and friends.

Even now, the debate over how much free time Americans have, and 7 how they spend it, continues.

John Robinson, director of the Americans' Use of Time Project at the 8 University of Maryland, recently published research surprisingly contrary to the end-of-leisure theory. Based on what 10,000 people recorded in precise hour-by-hour time diaries, Americans on average have 40 hours a week of leisure time, more than they had 30 years ago and five hours more than in 1975. Much of the increase comes in bits and pieces of time, and mostly it is used up watching television, Robinson found.

"Like making money, progress in gaining leisure is often hidden, 9 particularly because people have so many choices in how they will spend it that they feel out of control and don't enjoy what leisure time they have," Robinson says.

Consequently, people tend to overestimate how much they work, 10 Robinson said, and the distortions are greater the more they actually do work.

Robinson's research has been pounced on by economists who cite U.S. 11
Labor Department data showing that the average American works a
39.2-hour week, about 1.5 hours more than in 1976. Nearly 20 percent of
Americans work 50 hours a week, and 8.5 percent work 60 hours or more
a week. Robinson said it took five years to sell his book, *Time for Life,*
because editors—particularly women editors—challenged his findings.

Benjamin Hunnicutt, a professor of leisure studies at the University of 12
Iowa, disputes Robinson's conclusion and adds he doubts that work will
ever slip from first place in the cultural hierarchy. Work, he says, is closer
than anything else to a modern religion. Arlie Hochschild, a sociologist
and author of *The Time Bind,* says workers today find relief at work from
the pressures at home, so much so that they reject family friendly corporate
policies.

"At least four times before in this century Americans have questioned 13
the central reality of work and struggled with this strange and frightening
concept of leisure time; in fact, it's not a place we're really comfortable
with," Hunnicutt said. "If we do start dismantling the theology of work,
that represents a change of humongous proportions."

Boston University's Center on Work and Family says there is a change, 14
and it cites its ongoing research on physician work patterns. According to
Lena Lundgren, the center's director, in this group of professionals who
tend to work long hours, there is a clear trend toward: shortening the
workweek to 40 hours; compressing schedules into fewer workdays; and
even choosing specialties that allow for more family time.

"Increasingly, people want to work less; overall there is a greater and 15
greater discrepancy between the number of hours these physicians are
working and the number of hours they want to work," Lundgren says,
noting that many doctors have the independence and income that others
don't to cut their hours. "It holds true for both men and women."

Working women with children were in the vanguard of the flex-time 16
movement, but its appeal quickly spread to men and single people who
also want more control over their lives. Telecommuting is growing; 11.1
million Americans now work that way, up 10 percent from a year ago.
There is no national data on other flexible arrangements, but with the U.S.
unemployment rate at 4.6 percent, employers are scrambling to offer
solutions to the time bind to attract workers.

Since 1988, Barbara Brandt of Somerville, Mass., has headed a na- 17
tional, nonprofit organization devoted to changing corporate and public
policies that contribute to a worker-bee culture. But the Shorter Work-Time

Group didn't get any recognition or respect, Brandt says, until individuals began downshifting and threatening to move on unless businesses responded to their needs not just for flexibility—which potentially can lengthen a workday—but for more personal time.

The urge for the balanced life now is so strong, she said, that she has 18 moved on and founded the Sustainable Living Institute, which is developing strategies to help people slow down, find time and do less.

"People really feel frantic and unfulfilled in a culture that has gone so 19 far in the direction of materialism and workaholism." Brandt says. "This isn't about moving to Vermont or making do with less. It's about reclaiming your life and getting more from what you truly value."

For overtaxed Americans, the issue of time may not be about paid work 20 at all, but rather whether they can stand to lose the status that can come with being busy and turn off the engine, put down the remote control, sign off the computer, or hang up the phone. Leisure—whether it's playing the piano, reading a book, or taking a walk—takes practice and discipline.

"Everybody has the same 24 hours of time in every day," says Jon 21 Kabat-Zinn, who emphasizes the importance of mindfulness as director of the stress-reduction clinic at the University of Massachusetts Medical School. "But which of us can take advantage of the moment and step out of the constant rush of time, pay attention, and learn to be still?"

❀   ❀   ❀

AFTER YOU READ

▪ *THINK* about the following statement made by John Robinson: "Work . . . is closer than anything else to a modern religion." In what ways can work be similar to a religion? In what ways is it different? Do you agree or disagree with this statement? Why or why not?

▪ *EXAMINE* the number of sources you identified in the article as you read. How many different sources did you identify? Which source impressed you as most credible? Why were you impressed by this source? Notice how Leonard identifies in some way each of the sources she uses. Why are these identifications necessary?

▪ *EXAMINE* also Leonard's reference to Barbara Brandt in paragraphs 17–19. Brandt is the author of the next reading selection in this unit, which is also on the topic of the need for shorter work hours. Analyze Brandt's comments in this article, focusing on her attitude toward this subject and how it compares with the other sources included by Leonard.

- *WRITE* a summary of this article. Do not include in your summary any of the source material. Rather, try to summarize clearly the different points made by Leonard. Or *WRITE* an essay in which you analyze how you spend your time. In your introduction or conclusion, state your opinion about whether your use of time is as healthy and balanced as you would like.

Less Is More: A Call for Shorter Work Hours

BARBARA BRANDT

❀

Barbara Brandt is director of a national, nonprofit organization that is trying to change corporate and public policies that encourage what she calls "workaholism." As an organizer and social activist, Brandt champions causes that range from environmental conservation to feminism. She is the author of several books, most notably Whole Life Economics: Revaluing Daily Life. *The following essay by her was first presented as a paper for the Boston-based Shorter Work-Time Group.*

This selection, like the preceding one by Mary Leonard, focuses on the issue of whether Americans need to work less. However, in spite of their basic similarity, the two selections are very different. The one by Brandt is primarily persuasive while the one by Leonard is mainly informative. And, whereas Leonard focuses on the individual, Brandt focuses on society.

BEFORE YOU READ

• *THINK* about the term *workaholism*. How would you define this term? Do you know anyone who is a workaholic? Do you perceive this type of behavior as unhealthy or unproductive? Why or why not?

• *EXAMINE* the first paragraph of this selection. In it the author clearly states her thesis. Underline the sentence that serves as her thesis.

• *EXAMINE* also the chart that appears at the end of this essay. Study the chart to determine which country has the least amount of annual vacation time.

▪ *WRITE* a journal entry in which you explore the two terms *work ethic* and *workaholism*. Define both terms and then describe the terms' connotations—that is, tell what types of associations you have with each. Finally, tell which you think has the more positive connotations.

AS YOU READ

Notice the organization of this essay in which the author presents a problem, discusses it (using sources to support her arguments), and then proposes a series of solutions. Clearly mark the text to indicate each of these sections.

America is suffering from overwork. Too many of us are too busy, trying 1
to squeeze more into each day while having less to show for it. Although our growing time crunch is often portrayed as a personal dilemma, it is in fact a major social problem that has reached crisis proportions over the past 20 years.

The simple fact is that Americans today—both women and men—are 2
spending too much time at work, to the detriment of their homes, their families, their personal lives, and their communities. The American Dream promised that our individual hard work paired with the advance of modern technology would bring about the good life for all. Glorious visions of the leisure society were touted throughout the '50s and '60s. But now most people are working more than ever before, while still struggling to meet their economic commitments. Ironically, the many advances in technology, such as computers and fax machines, rather than reducing our workload, seem to have speeded up our lives at work. At the same time, technology has equipped us with "conveniences" like microwave ovens and frozen dinners that merely enable us to adopt a similar frantic pace in our home lives so we can cope with more hours at paid work.

A recent spate of articles in the mainstream media has focused on the 3
new problems of overwork and lack of time. Unfortunately, overwork is often portrayed as a special problem of yuppies and professionals on the fast track. In reality, the unequal distribution of work and time in America today reflects the decline in both standard of living and quality of life for most Americans. Families whose members never see each other, women who work a double shift (first on the job, then at home), workers who need

more flexible work schedules, and unemployed and underemployed people who need more work are all casualties of the crisis of overwork.

Americans often assume that overwork is an inevitable fact of life—like 4 death and taxes. Yet a closer look at other times and other nations offers some startling surprises.

Anthropologists have observed that in pre-industrial (particularly 5 hunting and gathering) societies, people generally spend 3 to 4 hours a day, 15 to 20 hours a week, doing the work necessary to maintain life. The rest of the time is spent in socializing, partying, playing, storytelling, and artistic or religious activities. The ancient Romans celebrated 175 public festivals a year in which everyone participated, and people in the Middle Ages had at least 115.

In our era, almost every other industrialized nation (except Japan) has 6 fewer annual working hours and longer vacations than the United States. This includes all of Western Europe, where many nations enjoy thriving economies and standards of living equal to or higher than ours. Jeremy Brecher and Tim Costello, writing in Z Magazine (Oct. 1990), note that "European unions during the 1980s made a powerful and largely successful push to cut working hours. In 1987 German metalworkers struck and won a 37.5-hour week; many are now winning a 35-hour week. In 1990, hundreds of thousands of British workers have won a 37-hour week."

In an article about work-time in the Boston Globe, Suzanne Gordon 7 notes that workers in other industrialized countries "enjoy—as a statutory right—longer vacations [than in the U.S.] from the moment they enter the work force. In Canada, workers are legally entitled to two weeks off their first year on the job. After two or three years of employment, most get three weeks of vacation. After 10 years, it's up to four, and by 20 years, Canadian workers are off for five weeks. In Germany, statutes guarantee 18 days minimum for everyone, but most workers get five or six weeks. The same is true in Scandinavian countries, and in France."

In contrast to the extreme American emphasis on productivity and 8 commitment, which results in many workers, especially in professional-level jobs, not taking the vacations coming to them, Gordon notes that "in countries that are America's most successful competitors in the global marketplace, all working people, whether lawyers or teachers, CEOs or janitors, take the vacations to which they are entitled by law. 'No one in West Germany,' a West German embassy's officer explains, 'no matter how high up they are, would ever say they couldn't afford to take a vacation. Everyone takes their vacation.'"

And in Japan, where dedication to the job is legendary, Gordon notes 9
that the Japanese themselves are beginning to consider their national
workaholism a serious social problem leading to stress-related illnesses and
even death. As a result, the Japanese government recently established a
commission whose goal is to promote shorter working hours and more
leisure time.

Most other industrialized nations also have better family-leave policies 10
than the United States, and in a number of other countries workers benefit
from innovative time-scheduling opportunities such as sabbaticals.

While the idea of a shorter workweek and longer vacations sounds 11
appealing to most people, any movement to enact shorter work-time as a
public policy will encounter surprising pockets of resistance, not just from
business leaders but even from some workers. Perhaps the most formidable
barrier to more free time for Americans is the widespread mind-set that
the 40-hour workweek, 8 hour a day, 5 days a week, 50 weeks a year, is a
natural rhythm of the universe. This view is reinforced by the media's
complete silence regarding the shorter work-time and more favorable
vacation and family-leave policies of other countries. This lack of information, and our leaders' reluctance to suggest that the United States can learn
from any other nation (except workaholic Japan) is one reason why more
Americans don't identify overwork as a major problem or clamor for fewer
hours and more vacation. Monika Bauerlein, a journalist originally from
Germany now living in Minneapolis, exclaims, "I can't believe that people
here aren't rioting in the streets over having only two weeks of vacation a
year."

A second obstacle to launching a powerful shorter work-time move- 12
ment is America's deeply ingrained work ethic, or its modern incarnation,
the workaholic syndrome. The work ethic fosters the widely held belief
that people's work is their most important activity and that people who do
not work long and hard are lazy, unproductive, and worthless.

For many Americans today, paid work is not just a way to make money 13
but is a crucial source of their self-worth. Many of us identify ourselves
almost entirely by the kind of work we do. Work still has a powerful
psychological and spiritual hold over our lives—and talk of shorter work-
time may seem somehow morally suspicious.

Because we are so deeply a work-oriented society, leisure-time activi- 14
ties—such as play, relaxation, engaging in cultural and artistic pursuits, or
just quiet contemplation and "doing nothing"—are not looked on as

essential and worthwhile components of life. Of course, for the majority of working women who must work a second shift at home, much of the time spent outside of paid work is not leisure anyway. Also much of our non-work time is spent not just in personal renewal, but in building and maintaining essential social ties—with family, friends, and the larger community.

Today, as mothers and fathers spend more and more time on the job, 15 we are beginning to recognize the deleterious effects—especially on our young people—of the breakdown of social ties and community in American life. But unfortunately, our nation reacts to these problems by calling for more paid professionals—more police, more psychiatrists, more experts— without recognizing the possibility that shorter work hours and more free time could enable us to do much of the necessary rebuilding and healing, with much more gratifying and longer-lasting results.

Of course, the stiffest opposition to cutting work hours comes not from 16 citizens but from business. Employers are reluctant to alter the 8-hour day, 40-hour workweek, 50 weeks a year because it seems easier and more profitable for employers to hire fewer employees for longer hours rather than more employees—each of whom would also require health insurance and other benefits—with flexible schedules and work arrangements.

Harvard University economist Juliet B. Schor, who has been studying 17 issues of work and leisure in America, reminds us that we cannot ignore the larger relationship between unemployment and overwork: While many of us work too much, others are unable to find paid work at all. Schor points out that "workers who work longer hours lose more income when they lose their jobs. The threat of job loss is an important determinant of management's power on the shop floor." A system that offers only two options—long work hours or unemployment—serves as both a carrot and a stick. Those lucky enough to get full-time jobs are bribed into docile compliance with the boss, while the spectre of unemployment always looms as the ultimate punishment for the unruly.

Some observers suggest that keeping people divided into "the em- 18 ployed" and "the unemployed" creates feelings of resentment and inferiority/superiority between the two groups, thus focusing their discontent and blame on each other rather than on the corporations and political figures who actually dictate our nation's economic policies.

Our role as consumers contributes to keeping the average work week 19 from falling. In an economic system in which addictive buying is the basis of corporate profits, working a full 40 hours or more each week for 50 weeks a year gives us just enough time to stumble home and dazedly—almost automatically—shop; but not enough time to think about deeper issues or to work effectively for social change. From the point of view of corporations and policymakers, shorter work-time may be bad for the economy, because people with enhanced free time may begin to find other things to do with it besides mindlessly buying products. It takes more free time to grow vegetables, cook meals from scratch, sew clothes, or repair broken items than it does to just buy these things at the mall. . . .

Many people are experimenting with all sorts of ways to cope with grueling   20
work schedules. Those with enough money use it to "buy time." They find child care, order take-out meals, and hire people to pick their children up from school and do the family shopping. Other options being pursued by both men and women include actively looking for good part-time jobs; sharing jobs; arranging more flexible work schedules; going into business for themselves; working at home; and scaling back on consumption in order to work fewer hours for lower pay. While these ideas work in some cases, they are often stymied by a lack of support from employers, and they aren't available to many people, especially those with lower incomes.

But perhaps the major shortcoming of all these individual responses is   21
precisely that: They are individual. The problem of overwork is a broad problem of our economic system. It cannot be solved by just one individual, family, or business. Individual approaches ignore the many larger causes of the problem. . . .

Now that public attention is beginning to take note of the mounting   22
personal, economic, and social toll of overwork, it is time to treat overwork as a major political and social issue. To accomplish this, the Shorter Work-Time Group of Boston—a multicultural group of women's and labor activists—proposes a national campaign for shorter work hours that could foster a formidable alliance of unions, community groups, women's groups, and workers in all fields. To begin this campaign, we propose a 10-point plan that could help heal the problems of overwork in its many forms and enhance the quality of all our lives—at home, on the job, and in the community.

1. **Establish a 6-hour day/30-hour week**   23
   We propose that a 6-hour day/30-hour week be made the new standard for "full-time work." This new policy would not only give America's workers more time to devote to our families,

friends, and personal and community lives, but would also provide benefits to employers in increased efficiency and productivity, reduced accidents and absenteeism, improved morale, lower turnover, and retention of valuable employees.

So that workers do not suffer financially from reduction of their work-time, we also propose that any reduction in hours be accompanied by a corresponding increase in hourly income—that the six-hour day be compensated by what was formerly eight-hour pay. Since numerous studies have shown shortened workdays improve productivity, this would not be economically unrealistic. 24

2. **Extend paid vacations for all American workers**   25
American workers should enjoy what their counterparts around the world take for granted—four to six weeks of paid vacation each year. Vacation should be based on overall years in the work force rather than tied to the number of years a person has been employed in a particular firm.

3. **Improve family-leave policies**   26
The Family and Medical Leave Act . . . needs broad national support so that politicians would fear reprisals from an angry public if they did not support it. This bill would provide job security for people who have to leave work for extended periods in order to care for newborn children or seriously ill family members. Although it does not provide for pay during such leaves, paid leave should be an eventual goal.

4. **Establish benefits for all workers**   27
At present, employers of part-time and temporary workers are not legally required to provide health insurance, vacations, pensions, or any other benefits. This is especially insidious because women and many low-income workers are most likely to hold part-time and temporary jobs. Congresswoman Pat Schroeder has introduced HR 2575, the Part-Time and Temporary Workers Protection Act, to rectify this situation at the national level.

5. **Discourage overtime work**   28
Since overtime is detrimental to workers, their families, and the other workers it replaces, we would like to see it eliminated as much as possible. This can be done by mandating the elimination of compulsory overtime and raising the pay rate to double time for voluntary overtime.

6. **Support alternative working arrangements**   29
   We encourage business to increase flex-time and other innovative
   work-time arrangements that enable employees to better meet
   their personal and family needs.

7. **Acknowledge workaholism as a social disorder**   30
   In Japan, they even coined a word—*karoshi* (death from over-
   work)—to show this is a serious disease.

8. **Promote awareness that our citizens and our nation as a whole** 31
   will benefit from shorter work-time
   We need a public education campaign to raise public consciousness
   about the devastating effects that overwork is having on our
   health, our families, our communities, and especially on our young
   people. American workers must have more time to care for their
   families and restore their communities. This does not mean sending women back home. It means giving all people the time and
   resources to create their own solutions. If we had more time for
   ourselves, for example, we would probably see a wide variety of
   child-care options. In some families, women would do this exclusively; in others, women and men would share child-care responsibilities; some people would hire paid help; and others would
   develop cooperative or community-based programs for their children; many people would take advantage of a mix of options. The
   same would probably occur with regard to a wide range of family
   and community issues.

9. **Look at how the issue of overwork influences the problems of** 32
   underemployment and unemployment
   Because of increasing economic pressures, many corporations are
   developing a two-tier work force: a core of workers who enjoy
   good salaries, job security, and full benefits, and another group of
   lower paid part-time and temporary workers who have no benefits
   or job security.

10. **Challenge the assertion that we have to enslave ourselves to our** 33
    jobs in order to keep America competitive
    Germany, for example, has mandated shortened work hours,
    and clearly has not lost its competitive edge in the world econ-
    omy.

ANNUAL VACATION TIME (in weeks)

	By law	By bargaining agreement
Austria	4	4–5
Denmark	—	5
Finland	5	5–6
France	5	5–6
Germany	3	4–6
Greece	4	—
Ireland	3	4
Italy	—	4–6
Netherlands	3	4–5
Portugal	4	—
Spain	5	5
Sweden	5	5–8
Switzerland	4	4–5
United States	—	2–4
United Kingdom	—	4–6

Source: From "Reduction of Working Time in Europe," *European Industrial Relations Review,* No. 127, August 1984, pp. 9–13. Used by permission.

❀   ❀   ❀

AFTER YOU READ

▪ *THINK* about Brandt's arguments that workers in other countries (except Japan) have shorter work weeks, more vacation time, better benefits, and more flexibility. Are her arguments convincing? Why or why not?

▪ *EXAMINE* Brandt's claim that the issue of how many hours should be considered a normal work week is a "broad problem of our economic system" and thus a social rather than an individual problem. Do you agree or disagree with this statement? Why or why not? How can an issue such as this be addressed broadly? How can it be addressed by individuals? Do you think it is a significant problem that deserves to be a national public issue?

▪ *WRITE* an essay in which you refute one of Brandt's assertions (for example, that Americans work harder than people of other nations, that women work longer hours than men, that technology has not reduced our workload but has just "speeded up our lives," or that "For many Americans today, paid work is not just a way to make money but is a crucial source of their self-worth."). Begin by *briefly* summarizing the entire essay; then identify the assertion with which you disagree; finally, make your own arguments to refute Brandt's assertion. Or *WRITE* an essay in which you contrast the essay by Brandt with the one by Leonard, focusing on the purpose of each. Begin by *briefly* summarizing both essays (in just a few sentences, or two paragraphs at the most). Then identify the purpose of each essay and discuss how the two purposes differ and how this difference shaped the type of essay each author constructed.

The Workman's Compensation

REG THERIAULT

❀

This essay, which appeared in Harper's Magazine, *is from a book entitled* How to Tell When You're Tired: A Brief Examination of Work. *The author, Reg Theriault, should know about work because for many years he has worked as a longshoreman in San Francisco. In this essay, Theriault defends the practice of "taking it easy" on the job. He argues that workers, especially if their jobs are physically or mentally demanding, need to work "on and off" rather than continuously.*

BEFORE YOU READ

- *THINK* about your own work experiences. Do you take it easy occasionally even though you are being paid for working?

- *EXAMINE* the term *workman's compensation.* Compensation, in terms of working, can simply be wages or can be money paid to an employee who is injured on the job. However, Theriault uses the term in his title to mean another kind of compensation he believes workers deserve.

- *WRITE* a journal entry in which you tell of a time when you "took it easy" while you were being paid to work.

AS YOU READ

Identify the form of compensation that Theriault refers to in his title.

How can someone, hour after hour, day after day, year in and year out, 1 tighten approximately the same nut to the same bolt and not go mad? That most working people do not, in fact, go mad is due in large measure to a phenomenon so common that it is found wherever people labor in industry: taking it easy. It would take some kind of real mental case to do all the work one could all day long. No one expects it. Taking it easy on the job while someone else covers your work, or "working on and off," as it is usually called in America, is an established part of the working life.

Working on and off, however, has its limits. The rules are infinitely 2 varied, subtle, and flexible, and, of course, they are always changing. Management, up to a certain level at least, is aware of the practice, and in some industries employs entire cadres of people to curtail or put an end to it. Simultaneously, the workers are subtly doing their best to keep it going, and to extend it wherever possible.

Every worker has a highly developed sense of how much work is 3 expected of him. When he feels that the expectation is excessive, he tries to do something about it. This instinct has to do with the political nature of work itself, something every modern worker understands. The bosses want more from the worker than they are willing to give in return. The workers give work, and the bosses give money. The exchange is never quite equal, and the discrepancy is called profit. Since the bosses cannot do without profit, workers have an edge. A good worker in a key spot could, so long as he kept up production, take all the coffee breaks he wanted, and the bosses would very likely look the other way. He could also choose to cut down on the coffee breaks, apply himself, and increase production, and then ask for and get more money. But that would be self-defeating, and he knows it. It would also place him in competition with other workers, which would be playing into the bosses' hands. What he would rather do is create some slack for himself and enjoy his job more.

At present on the West Coast, when a gang of longshoremen working 4 on cargo starts a shift, they often divide themselves into two equal groups and flip a coin. One group goes into the far reaches of the ship's hold and sits around. The other group starts loading cargo, usually working with a vengeance, since each one of them is doing the work of two men. An hour later, the groups change places. In other words, although my fellow longshoremen and I are getting paid for eight hours, on occasion we work only four. If someone reading this feels a swelling sense of moral outrage because we are sitting down on the job, I am sorry.

If you *are* that reader, I would recommend that you abandon your 5 outrage and begin thinking about doing something similar for yourself. You probably already have, even if you won't admit it. White-collar office workers, too, have come under criticism recently for robbing their bosses of their full-time services. Too much time is being spent around the Mr. Coffee machine, and some people (would you believe it?) have even been having personal conversations on company time. In fact, one office-system

expert recently said that he had yet to encounter a business workplace that
was functioning at more than about 60 percent efficiency.

Management often strives to set up a situation where work is done in series: 6
a worker receives an article of manufacture, does something to it, and
passes it on to another worker, who does something else to it and then
passes it on to the next guy, and so on. The assembly line is a perfect
example of this. Managers like this type of manufacture because it is more
efficient—that is, it achieves more production. They also like it for another
reason, even if they will not admit it: it makes it very difficult for the worker
to do anything other than work.

 Frederick W. Taylor, the efficiency expert who early in this century 7
conducted the time-and-motion studies that led to the assembly-line process, tried to reduce workers to robots, all in the name of greater production.
His staff of experts, each armed with clipboard and stopwatch, studied
individual workers with a view toward eliminating unnecessary movement.
Even ditchdigging could be made more efficient, they bragged, as if they
had discovered something new in the world. Grasp the shovel, sink it into
the earth with the arch of your boot for a good bite, and heave out the dirt.
Then repeat the steps. Don't lean on that shovel between times! That's an
unnecessary movement! The Taylorites soon found a great deal of opposition from some very tired workers. They discovered that the best shovelers
were mentally retarded young men, who accepted directions readily and
were less bored by repetitious acts. They got some pretty healthy shoveling
done, but even they tended to goof off when a staff member wandered
away.

 Most people not directly engaged in daily work express disapproval 8
when they hear of people working on and off. A studied campaign with
carefully chosen language—"featherbedding," "a full day's work for a full
day's pay," "taking a free ride"—has been pushed by certain employers to
discredit the practice, and their success is such that I rarely discuss it except
with other workers. My response is personal, and I feel no need to defend
it: If I am getting a free ride, how come I am so tired when I go home at
the end of a shift?

❁ ❁ ❁

AFTER YOU READ

▪ *THINK* about the issue of workers taking time off while on the job from an employer's or manager's point of view. Are there reasons for employers and managers to support this form of workman's compensation? Why or why not?

▪ *EXAMINE* Theriault's arguments for "working on and off" rather than working every minute for which you are being paid. Are his arguments sensible, fair, convincing?

▪ *WRITE* an essay in which you summarize Theriault's arguments and then argue for or against his position.

The Future of Work

ROBERT B. REICH

❦

Robert Reich, a political economist and former professor who served as secretary of labor in the Clinton administration, recently published a book entitled The Future of Success. *In this book he not only predicts the economic and labor conditions of the future but also cautions readers to be aware of the price that success may demand of them. This essay focuses on the same general subject but was published earlier, in 1989, in* Harper's *magazine. In it, Reich predicts which careers and occupations will expand in the future and how best to prepare for these careers.*

BEFORE YOU READ

▪ *THINK* about your plans for the future. Have you decided on a career? If so, how did you reach that decision? What do you think is the best way to prepare for future success?

▪ *EXAMINE* Reich's tone in the first paragraph. Notice his use of humor and his directness (including the use of *you* when he addresses his readers). Is his tone what you would expect of an economist and professor? What is your response to his informal, direct tone? Is it appropriate for this essay? Is it effective?

▪ *WRITE* a journal entry in which you predict which careers or occupations Reich will select as the most promising ones for the future.

AS YOU READ

Identify Reich's predictions about the nature of work in the future and indicate those you think are accurate. Also underline Reich's definitions of *complex services* and *person-to-person services*.

It's easy to predict what jobs you *shouldn't* prepare for. Thanks to the   1
wonders of fluoride, America, in the future, will need fewer dentists.
Nor is there much of a future in farming. The federal government probably
won't provide long-term employment unless you aspire to work in the
Pentagon or the Veterans Administration (the only two departments accounting for new federal jobs in the last decade). And think twice before
plunging into higher education. The real wages of university professors
have been declining for some time, the hours are bad, and all you get are
complaints.

Moreover, as the American economy merges with the rest of the   2
world's, anyone doing relatively unskilled work that could be done more
cheaply elsewhere is unlikely to prosper for long. Imports and exports now
constitute 26 percent of our gross national product (up from 9 percent in
1950), and barring a new round of protectionism, the portion will move
steadily upward. Meanwhile, ten thousand people are added to the world's
population every hour, most of whom, eventually, will happily work for a
small fraction of today's average American wage.

This is good news for most of you, because it means that you'll be   3
able to buy all sorts of things far more cheaply than you could if they
were made here (provided, of course, that what your generation does
instead produces even more value). The resulting benefits from trade
will help offset the drain on your income resulting from paying the
interest on the nation's foreign debt and financing the retirement of
aging baby boomers like me. The bad news, at least for some of you, is
that most of America's traditional, routinized manufacturing jobs will
disappear. So will routinized service jobs that can be done from remote
locations, like keypunching of data transmitted by satellite. Instead,
you will be engaged in one of two broad categories of work: either
complex services, some of which will be sold to the rest of the world to
pay for whatever Americans want to buy from the rest of the world, or
person-to-person services, which foreigners can't provide for us because
(apart from new immigrants and illegal aliens) they aren't here to provide
them.

Complex services involve the manipulation of data and abstract symbols.   4
Included in this category are insurance, engineering, law, finance, computer
programming, and advertising. Such activities now account for almost 25
percent of our GNP, up from 13 percent in 1950. They already have
surpassed manufacturing (down to about 20 percent of GNP). Even *within*
the manufacturing sector, executive, managerial, and engineering positions

are increasing at a rate almost three times that of total manufacturing employment. Most of these jobs, too, involve manipulating symbols.

Such endeavors will constitute America's major contribution to the rest 5 of the world in the decades ahead. You and your classmates will be exporting engineering designs, financial services, advertising and communications advice, statistical analyses, musical scores and film scripts, and other creative and problem-solving products. How many of you undertake these sorts of jobs, and how well you do at them, will determine what goods and services America can summon from the rest of the world in return, and thus—to some extent—your generation's standard of living.

You say you plan to become an investment banker? A lawyer? I grant 6 you that these vocations have been among the fastest growing and most lucrative during the past decade. The securities industry in particular has burgeoned. Between 1977 and 1987, securities-industry employment nearly doubled, rising 10 percent a year, compared with the average yearly job growth of 1.9 percent in the rest of the economy. The crash of October 1987 temporarily stemmed the growth, but by mid-1988 happy days were here again. Nor have securities workers had particular difficulty making ends meet. Their average income grew 21 percent over the decade, compared with a 1 percent rise in the income of everyone else. (But be careful with these numbers; relatively few securities workers enjoyed such majestic compensation. The high average is partly due to the audacity of people such as Henry Kravis and George Roberts, each of whom takes home a tidy $70 million per year.)

Work involving securities and corporate law has been claiming one- 7 quarter of all new private sector jobs in New York City and more than a third of all the new office space in that industrious town. Other major cities are not too far behind. A simple extrapolation of the present trend suggests that by 2020 one out of every three American college graduates will be an investment banker or a lawyer. Of course, this is unlikely. Long before that milestone could be achieved, the nation's economy will have dried up like a raisin, as financiers and lawyers squeeze out every ounce of creative, productive juice. Thus my advice: Even if you could bear spending your life in such meaningless but lucrative work, at least consider the fate of the nation before deciding to do so.

Person-to-person services will claim everyone else. Many of these jobs will 8 not require much skill, as is true of their forerunners today. Among the fastest growing in recent years: custodians and security guards, restaurant and retail workers, day-care providers. Secretaries and clerical workers will be as numerous as now, but they'll spend more of their time behind and around electronic machines (imported from Asia) and have fancier titles, such as "paratechnical assistant" and "executive paralegal operations manager."

Teachers will be needed (we'll be losing more than a third of our entire 9 corps of elementary- and high-school teachers through attrition over the next seven years), but don't expect their real pay to rise very much. Years of public breast-beating about the quality of American education notwithstanding, the average teacher today earns $28,000—only 3.4 percent more, in constant dollars, than he or she earned fifteen years ago.

Count on many jobs catering to Americans at play—hotel workers, 10 recreation directors, television and film technicians, aerobics instructors (or whatever their twenty-first century equivalents will call themselves). But note that Americans will have less leisure time to enjoy these pursuits. The average American's free time has been shrinking for more than fifteen years, as women move into the work force (and so spend more of their free time doing household chores) and as all wage earners are forced to work harder just to maintain their standard of living. Expect the trend to continue.

The most interesting and important person-to-person jobs will be in 11 what is now unpretentiously dubbed "sales." Decades from now most salespeople won't be just filling orders. Salespeople will be helping customers define their needs, then working with design and production engineers to customize products and services in order to address those needs. This is because standardized (you can have it in any color as long as it's black) products will be long gone. Flexible manufacturing and the new information technologies will allow a more tailored fit—whether it's a car, machine tool, insurance policy, or even a college education. Those of you who will be dealing directly with customers will thus play a pivotal role in the innovation process, and your wages and prestige will rise accordingly.

But the largest number of personal-service jobs will involve health care, 12 which already consumes about 12 percent of our GNP, and that portion is rising. Because every new medical technology with the potential to extend life is infinitely valuable to those whose lives might be extended—even for a few months or weeks—society is paying huge sums to stave off death. By the second decade of the next century, when my generation of baby boomers will have begun to decay, the bill will be much higher. Millions of corroding bodies will need doctors, nurses, nursing-home operators, hospital administrators, technicians who operate and maintain all the fancy machines that will measure and temporarily halt the deterioration, hospice directors, home-care specialists, directors of outpatient clinics, and euthanasia specialists, among many others.

Most of these jobs won't pay very much because they don't require 13
much skill. Right now the fastest growing job categories in the health sector
are nurse's aides, orderlies, and attendants, which compose about 40
percent of the health-care work force. The majority are women; a large
percentage are minorities. But even doctors' real earnings show signs of
slipping. As malpractice insurance rates skyrocket, many doctors go on
salary in investor-owned hospitals, and their duties are gradually taken over
by physician "extenders" such as nurse practitioners and midwives.

What's the best preparation for one of these careers?   14

Advice here is simple: You won't be embarking on a career, at least as 15
we currently define the term, because few of the activities I've mentioned
will proceed along well-defined paths to progressively higher levels of
responsibility. As the economy evolves toward services tailored to the
particular needs of clients and customers, hands-on experience will count
for more than formal rank. As technologies and markets rapidly evolve,
moreover, the best preparation will be through cumulative learning on the
job rather than formal training completed years before.

This means that academic degrees and professional credentials will 16
count for less; on-the-job training, for more. American students have it
backwards. The courses to which you now gravitate—finance, law, accounting, management, and other practical arts—may be helpful to understand how a particular job is *now* done (or, more accurately, how your
instructors did it years ago when they held such jobs or studied the people
who held them), but irrelevant to how such a job *will* be done. The
intellectual equipment needed for the job of the future is an ability to define
problems, quickly assimilate relevant data, conceptualize and reorganize
the information, make deductive and inductive leaps with it, ask hard
questions about it, discuss findings with colleagues, work collaboratively
to find solutions, and then convince others. And *these* sorts of skills can't
be learned in career-training courses. To the extent they can be found in
universities at all, they're more likely to be found in subjects such as history,
literature, philosophy, and anthropology—in which students can witness
how others have grappled for centuries with the challenge of living good
and productive lives. Tolstoy and Thucydides are far more relevant to the
management jobs of the future, for example, than are Hersey and
Blanchard (*Management of Organizational Behavior,* Prentice-Hall, 5th
edition, 1988).

❁ ❁ ❁

AFTER YOU READ

▪ *THINK* about the advice Reich gives his readers (young people about to launch a career). Because he wrote this article a little over ten years ago, you should be able to judge whether Reich's predictions seem to be on target. Which of his predictions have thus far proved accurate? Are there some that have not proven accurate?

▪ *EXAMINE* Reich's prediction that "hands-on experience will count for more than formal rank" in the future and that "on-the-job training" will count for more than "academic degrees and professional credentials." Do you agree with this viewpoint? Why or why not? Do you think Reich's intention is to discourage young people from going to college? Why or why not?

▪ *WRITE* a summary of this article. You may want to illustrate your summary with a graph or chart. Or *WRITE* an essay in which you make your own predictions about "the future of work."

The Work Ahead

HARPER'S MAGAZINE

❀

This chart, which was called a forecast, appeared in Harper's Magazine. *As the introductory note makes clear, the chart is taken from a bulletin called* The American Work Force: 1992–2005. *The chart is divided into two parts: Positive Job Growth and Negative Job Growth. By studying this chart, you will be able to identify which jobs are likely to increase in number and which are likely to decrease in number.*

BEFORE YOU READ

- *THINK* about the factors that influence your decision about a career. Is availability of jobs one of these factors? Should it be?

- *EXAMINE* the introductory note at the top of the chart. It provides a context for the chart, identifies the information found in the chart, and explains how the chart is organized.

- *WRITE* a journal entry in which you list the factors that have influenced you as you decide on a career.

AS YOU READ

Locate on the chart those jobs in which you are interested. Also, compare the predictions in this article with those in the preceding essay by Reich.

From *The American Work Force: 1992–2005,* a bulletin of employment projections issued last year by the U.S. Department of Labor. The study found that nearly half of the jobs that the economy will gain over the next decade will be in three service industries—retail trade, health services, and educational services—and that most of the jobs lost will be in agriculture and manufacturing. The list on the left shows the professions that will 1 experience the greatest growth over the next decade and the projected number of new jobs; the list on the right shows the professions that will experience the greatest decline and the projected number of jobs that will be lost.

POSITIVE JOB GROWTH		NEGATIVE JOB GROWTH	
Occupation	*Increase (No. of jobs)*	*Occupation*	*Decrease (No. of jobs)*
Retail salespersons	786,000	Farmers	−231,000
Registered nurses	765,000	Sewing-machine operators	−162,000
Cashiers	670,000	Cleaners/servants (domestic)	−157,000
General office clerks	654,000		
Truck drivers	648,000	Farmworkers	−133,000
Waiters and waitresses	637,000	Typists and word processors	−125,000
Nursing aids and orderlies	594,000	Childcare workers (domestic)	−123,000
Janitors and cleaners	548,000	Computer operators	−104,000
Food-preparation workers	524,000	Packaging machine operators	−71,000
Systems analysts	501,000		
Home health aides	479,000	Precision inspectors	−65,000
Secondary-school teachers	462,000	Switchboard operators	−51,000
Childcare workers (institutional)	450,000	Telephone and cable-TV line installers and repairers	−40,000
Security guards	408,000		
Marketing/sales supervisors	407,000	Textile-machine operators	−35,000
		Bartenders	−32,000
Teacher aides	381,000	Forming-machine operators	−32,000
Top executives and managers	380,000	Butchers and meat cutters	−31,000
General maintenance and repair workers	319,000	Bookkeeping-machine operators	−28,000
Elementary-school teachers	311,000	Central communications-equipment installers and repairers	−25,000
Gardeners and groundskeepers	311,000	Telephone operators	−24,000
Fast-food counter workers	308,000	Bank tellers	−24,000

❁ ❁ ❁

AFTER YOU READ

▪ *THINK* about how the information in this chart affects your decision about a career. If you really want to be a farmer, for example, will you change your mind about pursuing that career because this chart indicates a decline of 231,000 farming jobs between 1992 and 2005?

▪ *THINK* also about how this same information might have been presented in an article or essay rather than as a chart. Which format is more useful and accessible? Why?

▪ *EXAMINE* the generalization found in the introductory note that "nearly half of the jobs that the economy will gain over the next decade will be in three service industries—retail trade, health services, and educational services—and that most of the jobs lost will be in agriculture and manufacturing." What other generalizations can you make on the basis of the information included in the chart?

▪ *WRITE* a brief report in which you summarize the information in the chart.

Unit Four: Critical Thinking and Writing Assignments

❀ ❀ ❀

EXPLORING IDEAS TOGETHER

1. Many of the authors included in this unit write about hard work—times when they or someone they knew worked long hours doing something that required significant physical labor. Most often this type of hard work is associated with previous generations rather than present ones. With a group of your classmates, discuss whether people of your generation work as hard as people did in the past. Consider also whether work that does not require physical labor can be "hard work" and what effects working hard has on people. You may want to refer to the reading selections by Dove, Brokaw, Antrim, Braaksma, and Theriault.

2. Role models often influence a person's choice of a career. Review the reading selections by Antrim, Brokaw, and Dove and determine who their role models were and how they were influenced by them.

3. Tom Brokaw suggests in his essay that hard work is a virtue. Which of the other authors in this unit agree with Brokaw? Which ones disagree?

4. Apply the arguments found in Barbara Brandt's essay, "Less Is More: A Call for Shorter Work Hours," to the situations described by Theriault. Would Theriault agree with Brandt? What other selections in this unit directly or indirectly argue for Brandt's theory that Americans work too much?

5 Compare the images of working women found in the essay by Smith and the poem by Dove.

WRITING ESSAYS

1. Research a career in which you are interested by searching for information in your library and/or by interviewing someone in that field. Then write an essay in which you share the information you have collected with other college students who are interested in the same career.

2. Write an essay in which you explore the effects of work and/or a career on a particular person's life. Consider such issues as the effects of working too hard or too much, the effects of not finding a job, the stereotypical way people define those who work in certain professions,

or the role of work in establishing a healthy self-concept. The reading selections by Smiley, Braaksma, Smith, and Antrim will provide you with useful information for your essay.

3. The type of work Americans do has changed dramatically in the last fifty years. Choose one type of work or career. Write an essay in which you describe the changes that have occurred, and identify the factors responsible for these changes. You will find the information in the reading selections taken from *Harper's Magazine* as well as those by Brokaw, Smith, Reich, and Dove useful as sources.

4. Write an essay in which you tell how the roles that males and females assume in the work force have changed in recent years.

5. Write an essay in which you compare and contrast the problems your generation faces in selecting and establishing careers with those faced by earlier generations.

6. Write an essay in which you compare work and play (or leisure) and the roles they assume in a person's life. You may want to reread the selections by Smiley, Leonard, and Brandt before beginning your essay.

Self with Society

The United States has become the most powerful nation on earth—acknowledged widely as a leader not only in global politics but also in business, health, and education. However, it is also known for its diversity because, perhaps more than any nation on earth today or at any time in history, the United States is populated by people from all over the world. These people live and work together in relative harmony and are considered equal in the sight of the law. Never before has a nation accepted such a wide variety of people and given those people an opportunity to become citizens with equal rights and privileges. And never before has a nation made a strength and virtue of diversity. The United States is, in one sense, a great experiment in multiculturalism. And most people today view the experiment as a success. Our nation is known around the world for successfully melding a rich variety of cultures into a single society. For this, we can all be proud.

But the struggle to live together in peace and harmony has not been easy. If we are not watchful, our diverse society can become a divisive society—with each group fighting for its own causes. One of the most effective remedies for divisiveness is learning more about one another. This unit focuses on and celebrates the diversity that has made us unique. But it also recognizes that prejudice and discrimination have been, and continue to be, a serious danger to the ideals of diversity and equality. Some selections highlight different ethnic groups within our society, while others discuss explicitly some of the problems and solutions associated with a multicultural society.

Interactions with specific individuals—even your own family, friends, and mates—can be complicated and at times even difficult, but your relationship with society—with all the diverse people who exist in this country under one government—is even more complex. Because our society is made up not only of different individuals but also of individuals from different cultures and ethnic backgrounds, the task becomes enormous. As a member of such a diverse society, you are called upon to make decisions about people who are very different from you, who live in different parts of the country, who have different religious and ethnic backgrounds, and who have different social and economic conditions. Although such diversity is clearly a strength, giving the American culture a texture and energy that it would otherwise lack, it can also be a challenge.

Before you begin this unit, think about the rights and privileges of citizenship in this country. What rights should every member of a society have? Which groups in our society enjoy the greatest privileges? What tensions are created by the fact that some segments of society enjoy a much better lifestyle than do others?

As you read the selections in this unit, keep in mind that our society consists of a collection of people—different groups with different backgrounds, cultures, and concerns. Each group contributes to our society in different ways—making it a richer, stronger, more interesting society. Ask yourself these questions as you read:

- Can a society such as ours endure if all groups do not have a voice?
- Can problems be solved if we do not understand the people who have the problems?
- How can our society protect its citizenry and yet continue the tradition of opening our doors to newcomers?

Child of the Americas

AURORA LEVINS MORALES

❀

*As this poem makes clear, Aurora Levins Morales is the
product of two cultures—two Americas. The poet's mother
is Puerto Rican and her father is Jewish. Her family moved
to the United States when Morales was thirteen. She now
writes and teaches Jewish studies and women's studies at
the University of California at Berkeley. Her most recent
publication is* Remedios: Stories of Earth and Iron from
the History of Puertorriquenas. *This poem is from a
collection entitled* Getting Home Alive, *which Morales
coauthored with her mother.*

BEFORE YOU READ

▪ *THINK* about the two Americas (North America and Latin America) that
produced Morales. How are these two Americas alike? How are they
different?

▪ *EXAMINE* the following terms, which may be unfamiliar to you:

mestiza: a female of mixed racial ancestry, especially of mixed European
and Native American ancestry

diaspora: the scattering of an originally homogeneous people (often refers
to the dispersion of Jews outside Palestine)

taína: one of the aboriginal people of the Greater Antilles and Bahamas

spanglish: Spanish and English combined

Which of these terms derives from the poet's Latin-American background?
Which from her North American (Jewish) background?

▪ *WRITE* a journal entry in which you explore all of the different cultures
that have contributed to making you who you are. If necessary, interview
family members about your family history before writing in your journal.

AS YOU READ

Identify and underline each image. Try not only to visualize the image but also to understand what Morales was trying to communicate by including it in the poem.

Child of the Americas

I am a child of the Americas,
a light-skinned mestiza of the Caribbean,
a child of many diaspora, born into this continent at a crossroads.

I am a U.S. Puerto Rican Jew,
a product of the ghettos of New York I have never known.   5
An immigrant and the daughter and granddaughter of immigrants.
I speak English with passion: it's the tongue of my consciousness,
a flashing knife blade of crystal, my tool, my craft.

I am Caribeña, island grown. Spanish is in my flesh,
ripples from my tongue, lodges in my hips: 10
the language of garlic and mangoes,
the singing in my poetry, the flying gestures of my hands.
I am Latinoamerica, rooted in the history of my continent:
I speak from that body.

I am not african. Africa is in me, but I cannot return.   15
I am not taína. Taíno is in me, but there is no way back.
I am not european. Europe lives in me, but I have no home there.

I am new. History made me. My first language was spanglish.
I was born at the crossroads
and I am whole.   20

❀   ❀   ❀

AFTER YOU READ

▪ *THINK* about what Morales values most from each of the cultures that has shaped her. What cultures other than the two Americas does she claim as part of her heritage? What is her conclusion about who she is?

▪ *EXAMINE* the word *crossroads,* which Morales uses twice in this poem— once in the third line and again in the next to last line. Why do you think this is an important image for her?

▪ *WRITE* a prose version of this poem, making its meaning more explicit. Or *WRITE* an essay in which you analyze this poem, focusing on its major images and how they reinforce and contribute to the meaning of the poem.

Indian Education

SHERMAN ALEXIE

❀

Sherman Alexie is the author of Reservation Blues, Indian Killer, *and* The Lone Ranger and Tonto Fistfight in Heaven. *His most recent publications include a collection of short stories,* The Toughest Indian in the World, *and a book of poetry entitled* One Stick Song. *He also wrote the screenplay for the successful film* Smoke Signals. *In this reading selection, as in all of his work, Alexie focuses on his experiences as a Native American and the conflicts that Native Americans face as they struggle to live in two very different cultures.*

BEFORE YOU READ

▪ *THINK* about how an "Indian" education might differ from the education that other students receive in public schools. Why do you think Alexie uses the term *Indian* rather than *Native American* in this title?

▪ *EXAMINE* the format of this reading selection, noting especially the headings that divide it into different segments. What is the effect of these headings?

▪ *WRITE* a journal entry in which you write one sentence for each of your twelve years in school. Label your sentences as First Grade, Second Grade, etc., and try to remember one "true thing" about each of the years you were in school.

AS YOU READ

Underline the term *Indian* (or indian) and circle the term *Native American*. Try to determine when and why Alexie uses one term or the other.

Identify also the conflicts that Alexie describes or alludes to in this selection. Number each conflict.

FIRST GRADE

My hair was too short and my U.S. Government glasses were horn- 1
rimmed, ugly, and all that first winter in school, the other Indian
boys chased me from one corner of the playground to the other. They
pushed me down, buried me in the snow until I couldn't breathe, thought
I'd never breathe again.

They stole my glasses and threw them over my head, around my 2
outstretched hands, just beyond my reach, until someone tripped me and
sent me falling again, facedown in the snow.

I was always falling down; my Indian name was Junior Falls Down. 3
Sometimes it was Bloody Nose or Steal-His-Lunch. Once, it was Cries-Like-
a-White-Boy, even though none of us had seen a white boy cry.

Then it was a Friday morning recess and Frenchy SiJohn threw 4
snowballs at me while the rest of the Indian boys tortured some other
top-yogh-yaught kid, another weakling. But Frenchy was confident enough
to torment me all by himself, and most days I would have let him.

But the little warrior in me roared to life that day and knocked Frenchy 5
to the ground, held his head against the snow, and punched him so hard
that my knuckles and the snow made symmetrical bruises on his face. He
almost looked like he was wearing war paint.

But he wasn't the warrior. I was. And I chanted *It's a good day to die,* 6
it's a good day to die, all the way down to the principal's office.

SECOND GRADE

Betty Towle, missionary teacher, redheaded and so ugly that no one 7
ever had a puppy crush on her, made me stay in for recess fourteen days
straight.

"Tell me you're sorry," she said.   8

"Sorry for what?" I asked.   9

"Everything," she said and made me stand straight for fifteen minutes, 10
eagle-armed with books in each hand. One was a math book; the other was
English. But all I learned was that gravity can be painful.

For Halloween I drew a picture of her riding a broom with a scrawny 11
cat on the back. She said that her God would never forgive me for that.

Once, she gave the class a spelling test but set me aside and gave me a 12
test designed for junior high students. When I spelled all the words right,
she crumpled up the paper and made me eat it.

"You'll learn respect," she said.   13

She sent a letter home with me that told my parents to either cut my 14
braids or keep me home from class. My parents came in the next day and
dragged their braids across Betty Towle's desk.

"Indians, indians, indians." She said it without capitalization. She 15
called me "indian, indian, indian."

And I said, *Yes, I am. I am Indian. Indian, I am.*   16

THIRD GRADE

My traditional Native American art career began and ended with my very 17
first portrait: *Stick Indian Taking a Piss in My Backyard.*

As I circulated the original print around the classroom, Mrs. Schluter 18
intercepted and confiscated my art.

Censorship, I might cry now. *Freedom of expression,* I would write in 19
editorials to the tribal newspaper.

In third grade, though, I stood alone in the corner, faced the wall, and 20
waited for the punishment to end.

I'm still waiting.   21

FOURTH GRADE

"You should be a doctor when you grow up," Mr. Schluter told me, even 22
though his wife, the third grade teacher, thought I was crazy beyond my
years. My eyes always looked like I had just hit-and-run someone.

"Guilty," she said. "You always look guilty."   23

"Why should I be a doctor?" I asked Mr. Schluter.   24

"So you can come back and help the tribe. So you can heal people."   25

That was the year my father drank a gallon of vodka a day and the 26
same year that my mother started two hundred different quilts but never
finished any. They sat in separate, dark places in our HUD house and wept
savagely.

I ran home after school, heard their Indian tears, and looked in the 27
mirror. *Doctor Victor,* I called myself, invented an education, talked to my
reflection. *Doctor Victor to the emergency room.*

FIFTH GRADE

I picked up a basketball for the first time and made my first shot. No. I 28
missed my first shot, missed the basket completely, and the ball landed in
the dirt and sawdust, sat there just like I had sat there only minutes before.

But it felt good, that ball in my hands, all those possibilities and angles. 29
It was mathematics, geometry. It was beautiful.

At that same moment, my cousin Steven Ford sniffed rubber cement from 30
a paper bag and leaned back on the merry-go-round. His ears rang, his
mouth was dry, and everyone seemed so far away.

But it felt good, that buzz in his head, all those colors and noises. It 31
was chemistry, biology. It was beautiful.

Oh, do you remember those sweet, almost innocent choices that the Indian 32
boys were forced to make?

SIXTH GRADE

Randy, the new Indian kid from the white town of Springdale, got into a 33
fight an hour after he first walked into the reservation school.

Stevie Flett called him out, called him a squawman, called him a pussy, 34
and called him a punk.

Randy and Stevie, and the rest of the Indian boys, walked out into the 35
playground.

"Throw the first punch," Stevie said as they squared off. 36

"No," Randy said. 37

"Throw the first punch," Stevie said again. 38

"No," Randy said again. 39

"Throw the first punch!" Stevie said for the third time, and Randy 40
reared back and pitched a knuckle fastball that broke Stevie's nose.

We all stood there in silence, in awe. 41

That was Randy, my soon-to-be first and best friend, who taught me 42
the most valuable lesson about living in the white world: *Always throw the
first punch.*

SEVENTH GRADE

I leaned through the basement window of the HUD house and kissed the 43
white girl who would later be raped by her foster-parent father, who was
also white. They both lived on the reservation, though, and when the
headlines and stories filled the papers later, not one word was made of their
color.

Just Indians being Indians, someone must have said somewhere and 44
they were wrong.

But on the day I leaned through the basement window of the HUD 45
house and kissed the white girl, I felt the good-byes I was saying to my
entire tribe. I held my lips tight against her lips, a dry, clumsy, and ultimately
stupid kiss.

But I was saying good-bye to my tribe, to all the Indian girls and women 46
I might have loved, to all the Indian men who might have called me cousin,
even brother.

I kissed that white girl and when I opened my eyes, she was gone from 47
the reservation, and when I opened my eyes, I was gone from the reservation, living in a farm town where a beautiful white girl asked my name.

"Junior Polatkin," I said, and she laughed.   48

After that, no one spoke to me for another five hundred years.   49

EIGHTH GRADE

At the farm town junior high, in the boys' bathroom, I could hear voices 50
from the girls' bathroom, nervous whispers of anorexia and bulimia. I could
hear the white girls' forced vomiting, a sound so familiar and natural to
me after years of listening to my father's hangovers.

"Give me your lunch if you're just going to throw it up," I said to one 51
of those girls once.

I sat back and watched them grow skinny from self-pity.   52

Back on the reservation, my mother stood in line to get us commodities. 53
We carried them home, happy to have food, and opened the canned beef
that even the dogs wouldn't eat.

But we ate it day after day and grew skinny from self-pity.   54

There is more than one way to starve.   55

NINTH GRADE

At the farm town high school dance, after a basketball game in an 56
overheated gym where I had scored twenty-seven points and pulled down
thirteen rebounds, I passed out during a slow song.

As my white friends revived me and prepared to take me to the 57
emergency room where doctors would later diagnose my diabetes, the
Chicano teacher ran up to us.

"Hey," he said. "What's that boy been drinking? I know all about these 58
Indian kids. They start drinking real young."

Sharing dark skin doesn't necessarily make two men brothers.   59

TENTH GRADE

I passed the written test easily and nearly flunked the driving, but still 60
received my Washington State driver's license on the same day that Wally
Jim killed himself by driving his car into a pine tree.

No traces of alcohol in his blood, good job, wife and two kids.   61

"Why'd he do it?" asked a white Washington State trooper.   62

All the Indians shrugged their shoulders, looked down at the ground.   63

"Don't know," we all said, but when we look in the mirror, see the   64
history of our tribe in our eyes, taste failure in the tap water, and shake
with old tears, we understand completely.

Believe me, everything looks like a noose if you stare at it long enough. 65

ELEVENTH GRADE

Last night I missed two free throws which would have won the game against 66
the best team in the state. The farm town high school I play for is nicknamed
the "Indians," and I'm probably the only actual Indian ever to play for a
team with such a mascot.

This morning I pick up the sports page and read the headline: INDIANS 67
LOSE AGAIN.

Go ahead and tell me none of this is supposed to hurt me very much.   68

TWELFTH GRADE

I walk down the aisle, valedictorian of this farm town high school, and my 69
cap doesn't fit because I've grown my hair longer than it's ever been. Later,
I stand as the school board chairman recites my awards, accomplishments,
and scholarships.

I try to remain stoic for the photographers as I look toward the future. 70

Back home on the reservation, my former classmates graduate: a few can't 71
read, one or two are just given attendance diplomas, most look forward to
the parties. The bright students are shaken, frightened, because they don't
know what comes next.

They smile for the photographer as they look back toward tradition.   72

The tribal newspaper runs my photograph and the photograph of my 73
former classmates side by side.

POSTSCRIPT: CLASS REUNION

Victor said, "Why should we organize a reservation high school reunion? 74
My graduating class has a reunion every weekend at the Powwow Tavern."

❀   ❀   ❀

AFTER YOU READ

▪ *THINK* about how Alexie portrays the student in this story. How would
you describe him? Have you known students like him?

▪ *THINK* also about the two schools in this story. How would you describe
them? How are they similar to or different from schools you attended?

▪ *EXAMINE* the conflicts that Alexie includes, comparing those you identified with those your classmates or group members identified. Which
conflicts were physical? Which were with peers? Which were with school
authorities? Which were conflicts in cultures?

▪ *WRITE* an essay in which you identify several differences between your
education and the one Alexie describes. Discuss the significance of these
differences.

The Misery of Silence

MAXINE HONG KINGSTON

❀

Maxine Hong Kingston grew up in Stockton, California, in a Chinese immigrant community where her parents operated a laundry. Later she graduated from the University of California at Berkeley. After living in Hawaii for seventeen years, she returned to California and now teaches writing at her alma mater. Her most well-known novels are Tripmaster Monkey: His Fake Book *and* China Men. *This selection is from her autobiography,* The Woman Warrior: Memoirs of a Girlhood Among Ghosts, *in which she tells of the problems she encountered growing up as part of two very different cultures.*

BEFORE YOU READ

▪ *THINK* about the effect that not speaking the language of the society in which you live would have on your image of yourself.

▪ *EXAMINE* the title "The Misery of Silence." What do you associate with silence? Why do you think Kingston uses the word *misery* to describe silence? When is silence a misery?

▪ *WRITE* a journal entry in which you describe how you felt when you first started school or how you felt on your first day of college.

AS YOU READ

Try to imagine how it would feel if you did not speak the language of your instructor and classmates.

When I went to kindergarten and had to speak English for the first 1 time, I became silent. A dumbness—a shame—still cracks my voice in two, even when I want to say "hello" casually, or ask an easy question in front of the check-out counter, or ask directions of a bus driver. I stand frozen, or I hold up the line with the complete, grammatical sentence that comes squeaking out at impossible length. "What did you say?" says the cab driver, or "Speak up," so I have to perform again, only weaker the second time. A telephone call makes my throat bleed and takes up that day's courage. It spoils my day with self-disgust when I hear my broken voice come skittering out into the open. It makes people wince to hear it. I'm getting better, though. Recently I asked the postman for special-issue stamps; I've waited since childhood for postmen to give me some of their own accord. I am making progress, a little every day.

My silence was thickest—total—during the three years that I covered 2 my school paintings with black paint. I painted layers of black over houses and flowers and suns, and when I drew on the blackboard, I put a layer of chalk on top. I was making a stage curtain, and it was the moment before the curtain parted or rose. The teachers called my parents to school, and I saw they had been saving my pictures, curling and cracking, all alike and black. The teachers pointed to the pictures and looked serious, talked seriously too, but my parents did not understand English. ("The parents and teachers of criminals were executed," said my father.) My parents took the pictures home. I spread them out (so black and full of possibilities) and pretended the curtains were swinging open, flying up, one after another, sunlight underneath, mighty operas.

During the first silent year I spoke to no one at school, did not ask 3 before going to the lavatory, and flunked kindergarten. My sister also said nothing for three years, silent in the playground and silent at lunch. There were other quiet Chinese girls not of our family, but most of them got over it sooner than we did. I enjoyed the silence. At first it did not occur to me I was supposed to talk or to pass kindergarten. I talked at home and to one or two of the Chinese kids in class. I made motions and even made some jokes. I drank out of a toy saucer when the water spilled out of the cup, and everybody laughed, pointing at me, so I did it some more. I didn't know that Americans don't drink out of saucers.

I liked the Negro students (Black Ghosts) best because they laughed 4 the loudest and talked to me as if I were a daring talker too. One of the Negro girls had her mother coil braids over her ears Shanghai-style like mine; we were Shanghai twins except that she was covered with black like my paintings. Two Negro kids enrolled in Chinese school, and the teachers gave them Chinese names. Some Negro kids walked me to school and home, protecting me from the Japanese kids, who hit me and chased me and stuck gum in my ears. The Japanese kids were noisy and tough. They appeared one day in kindergarten, released from concentration camp, which was a tic-tac-toe mark, like barbed wire, on the map.

It was when I found out I had to talk that school became a misery, that   5 the silence became a misery. I did not speak and felt bad each time that I did not speak. I read aloud in first grade, though, and heard the barest whisper with little squeaks come out of my throat. "Louder," said the teacher, who scared the voice away again. The other Chinese girls did not talk either, so I knew the silence had to do with being a Chinese girl.

Reading out loud was easier than speaking because we did not have to   6 make up what to say, but I stopped often, and the teacher would think I'd gone quiet again. I could not understand "I." The Chinese "I" has seven strokes, intricacies. How could the American "I," assuredly wearing a hat like the Chinese, have only three strokes, the middle so straight? Was it out of politeness that this writer left off strokes the way a Chinese has to write her own name small and crooked? No, it was not politeness; "I" is a capital and "you" is lowercase. I stared at that middle line and waited so long for its black center to resolve into tight strokes and dots that I forgot to pronounce it. The other troublesome word was "here," no strong consonant to hang on to, and so flat, when "here" is two mountainous ideographs. The teacher, who had already told me every day how to read "I" and "here," put me in the low corner under the stairs again, where the noisy boys usually sat.

When my second grade class did a play, the whole class went to the   7 auditorium except the Chinese girls. The teacher, lovely and Hawaiian, should have understood about us, but instead left us behind in the classroom. Our voices were too soft or nonexistent, and our parents never signed the permission slips anyway. They never signed anything unnecessary. We opened the door a crack and peeked out, but closed it again quickly. One of us (not me) won every spelling bee, though.

I remember telling the Hawaiian teacher, "We Chinese can't sing 'land   8 where our fathers died.'" She argued with me about politics, while I meant because of curses. But how can I have that memory when I couldn't talk? My mother says that we, like the ghosts, have no memories.

After American school, we picked up our cigar boxes, in which we had   9 arranged books, brushes, and an inkbox neatly, and went to Chinese school, from 5:00 to 7:30 P.M. There we chanted together, voices rising and falling, loud and soft, some boys shouting, everybody reading together, reciting together and not alone with one voice. When we had a memorization test, the teacher let each of us come to his desk and say the lesson to him privately, while the rest of the class practiced copying or tracing. Most of the teachers were men. The boys who were so well behaved in the American school played tricks on them and talked back to them. The girls were not mute. They screamed and yelled during recess, when there were no rules; they had fistfights. Nobody was afraid of children hurting themselves or of children hurting school property. The glass doors to the red and green balconies with the gold joy symbols were left wide open so that we could run out and climb the fire escapes. We played capture-the-flag in the auditorium, where Sun Yat-sen and Chiang Kai-shek's pictures hung at the back of the stage, the Chinese flag on their left and the American flag on their right. We climbed the teak ceremonial chairs and made flying leaps off the stage. One flag headquarters was behind the glass door and the other on stage right. Our feet drummed on the hollow stage. During recess the teachers locked themselves up in their office with the shelves of books, copybooks, inks from China. They drank tea and warmed their hands at a stove. There was no play supervision. At recess we had the school to ourselves, and also we could roam as far as we could go—downtown, Chinatown stores, home—as long as we returned before the bell rang.

At exactly 7:30 the teacher again picked up the brass bell that sat on   10
his desk and swung it over our heads, while we charged down the stairs, our cheering magnified in the stairwell. Nobody had to line up.

Not all of the children who were silent at American school found voices   11
at Chinese school. One new teacher said each of us had to get up and recite in front of the class, who was to listen. My sister and I had memorized the lesson perfectly. We said it to each other at home, one chanting, one listening. The teacher called on my sister to recite first. It was the first time a teacher had called on the second-born to go first. My sister was scared. She glanced at me and looked away; I looked down at my desk. I hoped that she could do it because if she could, then I would have to. She opened her mouth and a voice came out that wasn't a whisper, but it wasn't a proper voice either. I hoped that she would not cry, fear breaking up her voice like twigs underfoot. She sounded as if she were trying to sing though weeping and strangling. She did not pause or stop to end the embarrassment. She kept going until she said the last word, and then she sat down. When it was my turn, the same voice came out, a crippled animal running on broken legs. You could hear splinters in my voice, bones rubbing jagged against one another. I was loud, though. I was glad I didn't whisper.

How strange that the emigrant villagers are shouters, hollering face to   12
face. My father asks, "Why is it I can hear Chinese from blocks away? Is it that I understand the language? Or is it they talk loud?" They turn the radio

up full blast to hear the operas, which do not seem to hurt their ears. And they yell over the singers that wail over the drums, everybody talking at once, big arm gestures, spit flying. You can see the disgust on American faces looking at women like that. It isn't just the loudness. It is the way Chinese sounds, ching-chong ugly, to American ears, not beautiful like Japanese sayonara words with the consonants and vowels as regular as Italian. We make guttural peasant noise and have Ton Duc Thang names you can't remember. And the Chinese can't hear Americans at all; the language is too soft and western music unhearable. I've watched a Chinese audience laugh, visit, talk-story, and holler during a piano recital, as if the musician could not hear them. A Chinese-American, somebody's son, was playing Chopin, which has no punctuation, no cymbals, no gongs. Chinese piano music is five black keys. Normal Chinese women's voices are strong and bossy. We American-Chinese girls had to whisper to make ourselves American-feminine. Apparently we whispered even more softly than the Americans. Once a year the teachers referred my sister and me to speech therapy, but our voices would straighten out, unpredictably normal, for the therapists. Some of us gave up, shook our heads, and said nothing, not one word. Some of us could not even shake our heads. At times shaking my head no is more self-assertion than I can manage. Most of us eventually found some voice, however faltering. We invented an American-feminine speaking personality.

❀ ❀ ❀

AFTER YOU READ

- *THINK* about the similarities and differences in the two schools that Kingston describes. Why did her parents send her to both schools? What did she gain from each? How did this experience affect her sense of identity?

- *EXAMINE* Kingston's statement, "We American-Chinese girls had to whisper to make ourselves American-feminine." How did her struggle to define herself as a female contribute to the silence that characterized her childhood? How does American-feminine differ from Chinese-feminine or Hispanic-feminine? Do sex roles differ from one culture to another?

- *WRITE* about a time when you felt isolated or shut off from the people around you. Or *WRITE* a paragraph in which you compare and contrast the roles of females (or males) in two different cultures.

The Scholarship Jacket

MARTA SALINAS

❀

Marta Salinas is an environmental activist as well as a writer. She has published stories in California Living *and the* Los Angeles Herald Examiner. *In "The Scholarship Jacket," which was originally published in* Growing Up Chicana/o: An Anthology, *Salinas writes about her experience as a Chicana student in a public school in south Texas.*

BEFORE YOU READ

- *THINK* about some award or recognition that you wanted very much or worked very hard to achieve. Why was this goal so important to you? Did you achieve it? Why or why not?
- *EXAMINE* the title, "The Scholarship Jacket," as well as the first paragraph, in which Salinas describes the jacket and its significance. In Salinas's story, earning this jacket becomes not only a personal goal but also a symbol of achievement for her family and for her people.
- *WRITE* a journal entry about a situation in which you feel you were treated unfairly because of your social situation—because you were too poor or too rich; because of your parents or family; or because of your race, nationality, or religion.

AS YOU READ

Try to determine the motivations of the characters in the story.

The small Texas school that I attended carried out a tradition every year   1
during the eighth grade graduation: a beautiful gold and green jacket, the school colors, was awarded to the class valedictorian, the student who had maintained the highest grades for eight years. The scholarship jacket

had a big gold S on the left front side, and the winner's name was written in gold letters on the pocket.

My oldest sister Rosie had won the jacket a few years back, and I fully 2
expected to win also. I was fourteen and in the eighth grade. I had been a straight A student since the first grade, and the last year I had looked forward to owning that jacket. My father was a farm laborer who couldn't earn enough money to feed eight children, so when I was six I was given to my grandparents to raise. We couldn't participate in sports at school because there were registration fees, uniform costs, and trips out of town; so even though we were quite agile and athletic, there would never be a sports school jacket for us. This one, the scholarship jacket, was our only chance.

In May, close to graduation, spring fever struck, and no one paid any 3
attention in class; instead we stared out the windows and at each other, wanting to speed up the last few weeks of school. I despaired every time I looked in the mirror. Pencil thin, not a curve anywhere, I was called "Beanpole" and "String Bean," and I knew that's what I looked like. A flat chest, no hips, and a brain, that's what I had. That really isn't much for a fourteen-year-old to work with, I thought, as I absentmindedly wandered from my history class to the gym. Another hour of sweating in basketball and displaying my toothpick legs was coming up. Then I remembered my P.E. shorts were still in a bag under my desk where I'd forgotten them. I had to walk all the way back and get them. Coach Thompson was a real bear if anyone wasn't dressed for P. E. She had said I was a good forward and once she even tried to talk Grandma into letting me join the team. Grandma, of course, said no.

I was almost back at my classroom door when I heard angry voices and 4
arguing. I stopped. I didn't mean to eavesdrop; I just hesitated, not knowing what to do. I needed those shorts and I was going to be late, but I didn't want to interrupt an argument between my teachers. I recognized the voices: Mr. Schmidt, my history teacher, and Mr. Boone, my math teacher. They seemed to be arguing about me. I couldn't believe it. I still remember the shock that rooted me flat against the wall as if I were trying to blend in with the graffiti written there.

"I refuse to do it! I don't care who her father is, her grades don't even 5
begin to compare to Martha's. I won't lie or falsify records. Martha has a straight A plus average and you know it." That was Mr. Schmidt and he sounded very angry. Mr. Boone's voice sounded calm and quiet.

"Look, Joann's father is not only on the Board, he owns the only store 6
in town; we could say it was a close tie and—"

The pounding in my ears drowned out the rest of the words, only a 7 word here and there filtered through. ". . . Martha is Mexican. . . . resign. . . . won't do it. . . ." Mr. Schmidt came rushing out, and luckily for me went down the opposite way toward the auditorium, so he didn't see me. Shaking, I waited a few minutes and then went in and grabbed my bag and fled from the room. Mr. Boone looked up when I came in but didn't say anything. To this day I don't remember if I got in trouble in P. E. for being late or how I made it through the rest of the afternoon. I went home very sad and cried into my pillow that night so Grandmother wouldn't hear me. It seemed a cruel coincidence that I had overheard that conversation.

The next day when the principal called me into his office, I knew what 8 it would be about. He looked uncomfortable and unhappy. I decided I wasn't going to make it any easier for him so I looked him straight in the eye. He looked away and fidgeted with the papers on his desk.

"Martha," he said, "there's been a change in policy this year regarding 9 the scholarship jacket. As you know, it has always been free." He cleared his throat and continued. "This year the Board decided to charge fifteen dollars—which still won't cover the complete cost of the jacket."

I stared at him in shock and a small sound of dismay escaped my throat. 10 I hadn't expected this. He still avoided looking in my eyes.

"So if you are unable to pay the fifteen dollars for the jacket, it will be 11 given to the next one in line."

Standing with all the dignity I could muster, I said, "I'll speak to my 12 grandfather about it, sir, and let you know tomorrow." I cried on the walk home from the bus stop. The dirt road was a quarter of a mile from the highway, so by the time I got home, my eyes were red and puffy.

"Where's Grandpa?" I asked Grandma, looking down at the floor so 13 she wouldn't ask me why I'd been crying. She was sewing on a quilt and didn't look up.

"I think he's out back working in the bean field." 14

I went outside and looked out at the fields. There he was. I could see 15 him walking between the rows, his body bent over the little plants, hoe in hand. I walked slowly out to him, trying to think how I could best ask him for the money. There was a cool breeze blowing and a sweet smell of mesquite in the air, but I didn't appreciate it. I kicked at a dirt clod. I wanted that jacket so much. It was more than just being a valedictorian and giving a little thank you speech for the jacket on graduation night. It represented eight years of hard work and expectation. I knew I had to be honest with Grandpa; it was my only chance. He saw me and looked up.

He waited for me to speak. I cleared my throat nervously and clasped   16
my hands behind my back so he wouldn't see them shaking. "Grandpa, I
have a big favor to ask you," I said in Spanish, the only language he knew.
He still waited silently. I tried again. "Grandpa, this year the principal said
the scholarship jacket is not going to be free. It's going to cost fifteen dollars
and I have to take the money in tomorrow, otherwise it'll be given to
someone else." The last words came out in an eager rush. Grandpa
straightened up tiredly and leaned his chin on the hoe handle. He looked
out over the field that was filled with the tiny green bean plants. I waited,
desperately hoping he'd say I could have the money.

He turned to me and asked quietly, "What does a scholarship jacket   17
mean?"

I answered quickly; maybe there was a chance. "It means you've earned   18
it by having the highest grades for eight years and that's why they're giving
it to you." Too late I realized the significance of my words. Grandpa knew
that I understood it was not a matter of money. It wasn't that. He went
back to hoeing the weeds that sprang up between the delicate little bean
plants. It was a time-consuming job; sometimes the small shoots were right
next to each other. Finally he spoke again.

"Then if you pay for it, Marta, it's not a scholarship jacket, is it? Tell   19
your principal I will not pay the fifteen dollars."

I walked back to the house and locked myself in the bathroom for a   20
long time. I was angry with Grandfather even though I knew he was right,
and I was angry with the Board, whoever they were. Why did they have to
change the rules just when it was my turn to win the jacket?

It was a very sad and withdrawn girl who dragged into the principal's   21
office the next day. This time he did look me in the eyes.

"What did your grandfather say?"   22

I sat very straight in my chair.   23

"He said to tell you he won't pay the fifteen dollars."   24

The principal muttered something I couldn't understand under his   25
breath, and walked over to the window. He stood looking out at something
outside. He looked bigger than usual when he stood up; he was a tall gaunt
man with gray hair, and I watched the back of his head while I waited for
him to speak.

"Why?" he finally asked. "Your grandfather has the money. Doesn't he   26
own a small bean farm?"

I looked at him, forcing my eyes to stay dry. "He said if I had to pay   27
for it, then it wouldn't be a scholarship jacket," I said and stood up to leave.

"I guess you'll just have to give it to Joann." I hadn't meant to say that; it had just slipped out. I was almost to the door when he stopped me.

"Martha—wait." 28

I turned and looked at him, waiting. What did he want now? I could 29 feel my heart pounding. Something bitter and vile tasting was coming up in my mouth; I was afraid I was going to be sick. I didn't need any sympathy speeches. He sighed loudly and went back to his big desk. He looked at me, biting his lip, as if thinking.

"Okay, damn it. We'll make an exception in your case. I'll tell the 30 Board, you'll get your jacket."

I could hardly believe it. I spoke in a trembling rush. "Oh, thank you, 31 sir!" Suddenly I felt great. I didn't know about adrenaline in those days, but I knew something was pumping through me, making me feel as tall as the sky. I wanted to yell, jump, run the mile, do something. I ran out so I could cry in the hall where there was no one to see me. At the end of the day, Mr. Schmidt winked at me and said, "I hear you're getting a scholarship jacket this year."

His face looked as happy and innocent as a baby's, but I knew better. 32 Without answering I gave him a quick hug and ran to the bus. I cried on the walk home again, but this time because I was so happy. I couldn't wait to tell Grandpa and ran straight to the field. I joined him in the row where he was working and without saying anything I crouched down and started pulling up the weeds with my hands. Grandpa worked alongside me for a few minutes, but he didn't ask what had happened. After I had a little pile of weeds between the rows, I stood up and faced him.

"The principal said he's making an exception for me, Grandpa, and 33 I'm getting the jacket after all. That's after I told him what you said."

Grandpa didn't say anything, he just gave me a pat on the shoulder 34 and a smile. He pulled out the crumpled red handkerchief that he always carried in his back pocket and wiped the sweat off his forehead.

"Better go see if your grandmother needs any help with supper." 35

I gave him a big grin. He didn't fool me. I skipped and ran back to the 36 house whistling some silly tune.

❀ ❀ ❀

AFTER YOU READ

- *THINK* again about the motivations of the people in the story. Why does Martha want to win the scholarship jacket? Why does Mr. Boone make the proposal that he makes? Why does the grandfather refuse to pay the money for the jacket even though he can afford it? And why does the principal make an exception to the new rule in Martha's case?

- *EXAMINE* the conversation between Mr. Schmidt and Mr. Boone in paragraphs 5–7. What does this conversation reveal about racial and economic prejudice? In your opinion, is such prejudice found today in educational and social institutions—even among people in authority such as teachers and administrators?

- *WRITE* an essay in which you use your own experience and observations to identify and analyze a school or college policy that you believe discriminates against some group, such as handicapped students or students of a particular ethnic or religious background. In your analysis, explain why this policy is unfair, and give specific supporting examples.

Getting to Know About You and Me

CHANA SCHOENBERGER

❈

This student essay, which first appeared in Newsweek, *tells of a young Jewish woman's experience, during a summer scholarship program, with a group of people who know nothing about her religion. Schoenberger describes how it feels to be the victim of stereotyping—to be defined on the basis of race, religion, class, gender, or appearance.*

BEFORE YOU READ

▪ *THINK* about a time when you felt stereotyped, when someone judged you on the basis of your race, religion, class, gender, ethnic background, or appearance. How did this experience make you feel?

▪ *EXAMINE* the first paragraph of this essay, which serves as the introduction. How does Schoenberger introduce her subject? On the basis of this introduction, do you want to read the essay? From just reading this first paragraph, do you think you know what the author is going to focus on in the essay and what her main point will be?

▪ *WRITE* a journal entry in which you describe a time when you felt you were stereotyped—judged as a member of a group rather than as an individual. The group can be religious or political, social or economic, racial or ethnic, or a group such as smokers, commuters, pickup truck owners, hunters, athletes, or beauty contestants.

AS YOU READ

Discover what scared Schoenberger most about her experience and what she believes caused the problems she faced. Indicate in the margin those sentences or paragraphs that focus on these subjects.

As a religious holiday approaches, students at my high school who will 1
be celebrating the holiday prepare a presentation on it for an assembly.
The Diversity Committee, which sponsors the assemblies to increase
religious awareness, asked me last spring if I would help with the presentation on Passover, the Jewish holiday that commemorates the Exodus from
Egypt. I was too busy with other things, and I never got around to helping.
I didn't realize then how important those presentations really are, or I
definitely would have done something.

This summer I was one of 20 teens who spent five weeks at the 2
University of Wisconsin at Superior studying acid rain with a National
Science Foundation Young Scholars program. With such a small group in
such a small town, we soon became close friends and had a good deal of
fun together. We learned about the science of acid rain, went on field trips,
found the best and cheapest restaurants in Superior and ate in them
frequently to escape the lousy cafeteria food. We were a happy, bonded
group.

Represented among us were eight religions: Jewish, Roman Catholic, 3
Muslim, Hindu, Methodist, Mormon, Jehovah's Witness and Lutheran. It
was amazing, given the variety of backgrounds, to see the ignorance of
some of the smartest young scholars on the subject of other religions.

On the first day, one girl mentioned that she had nine brothers and 4
sisters. "Oh, are you Mormon?" asked another girl, who I knew was a
Mormon herself. The first girl, shocked, replied, "No, I dress normal!" She
thought Mormon was the same as Mennonite, and the only thing she knew
about either religion was that Mennonites don't, in her opinion, "dress
normal."

My friends, ever curious about Judaism, asked me about everything 5
from our basic theology to food preferences. "How come, if Jesus was a
Jew, Jews aren't Christian?" my Catholic roommate asked me in all
seriousness. Brought up in a small Wisconsin town, she had never met a
Jew before, nor had she met people from most of the other "strange"
religions (anything but Catholic or mainstream Protestant). Many of the
other kids were the same way.

"Do you all still practice animal sacrifices?" a girl from a small town 6
in Minnesota asked me once. I said no, laughed, and pointed out that this
was the 20th century, but she had been absolutely serious. The only Jews
she knew were the ones from the Bible.

Nobody was deliberately rude or anti-Semitic, but I got the feeling that 7
I was representing the entire Jewish people through my actions. I realized
that many of my friends would go back to their small towns thinking that

all Jews liked Dairy Queen Blizzards and grilled cheese sandwiches. After all, that was true of all the Jews they knew (in most cases, me and the only other Jewish young scholar, period).

The most awful thing for me, however, was not the benign ignorance 8 of my friends. Our biology professor had taken us on a field trip to the EPA field site where he worked, and he was telling us about the project he was working on. He said that they had to make sure the EPA got its money's worth from the study—he "wouldn't want them to get Jewed."

I was astounded. The professor had a doctorate, various other degrees 9 and seemed to be a very intelligent man. He apparently had no idea that he had just made an anti-Semitic remark. The other Jewish girl in the group and I debated whether or not to say something to him about it, and although we agreed we would, neither of us ever did. Personally, it made me feel uncomfortable. For a high-school student to tell a professor who taught her class that he was a bigot seemed out of place to me, even if he was one.

What scares me about that experience, in fact about my whole visit to 10 Wisconsin, was that I never met a really vicious anti-Semite or a malignantly prejudiced person. Many of the people I met had been brought up to think that Jews (or Mormons or any other religion that's not mainstream Christian) were different and that difference was not good.

Difference, in America, is supposed to be good. We are expected—at 11 least, I always thought we were expected—to respect each other's traditions. Respect requires some knowledge about people's backgrounds. Singing Christmas carols as a kid in school did not make me Christian, but it taught me to appreciate beautiful music and someone else's holiday. It's not necessary or desirable for all ethnic groups in America to assimilate into one traditionless mass. Rather, we all need to learn about other cultures so that we can understand one another and not feel threatened by others.

In the little multicultural universe that I live in, it's safe not to worry 12 about explaining the story of Passover because if people don't hear it from me, they'll hear it some other way. Now I realize that's not true everywhere.

Ignorance was the problem I faced this summer. By itself, ignorance is 13 not always a problem, but it leads to misunderstandings, prejudice and hatred. Many of today's problems involve hatred. If there weren't so much ignorance about other people's backgrounds, would people still hate each other as badly as they do now? Maybe so, but at least that hatred would be based on facts and not flawed beliefs.

I'm now back at school, and I plan to apply for the Diversity Commit- 14 tee. I'm going to get up and tell the whole school about my religion and the tradition I'm proud of. I see now how important it is to celebrate your heritage and to educate others about it. I can no longer take for granted that everyone knows about my religion, or that I know about theirs. People who are suspicious when they find out I'm Jewish usually don't know much about Judaism. I would much prefer them to hate or distrust me because of something I've done, instead of them hating me on the basis of prejudice.

❀   ❀   ❀

AFTER YOU READ

▪ *THINK* about Schoenberger's argument that ignorance causes prejudice and stereotyping. Do you agree or disagree with her argument? Why or why not?

▪ *THINK* also about the relationship between prejudice and stereotyping. Does stereotyping always involve prejudice? That is, does stereotyping always result from prejudice or can it simply be the result of ignorance?

▪ *EXAMINE* Schoenberger's solution to the problem she has identified (ignorance). What does she plan to do personally to eradicate the ignorance that she believes is at the root of prejudice and stereotyping? What larger, more systematic efforts might be implemented to solve this problem?

▪ *WRITE* an essay in which you begin with a brief anecdote about a time that you were the victim of stereotyping. Then analyze what caused the stereotyping and, finally, what you think should be done to avoid this particular type of stereotypical thinking.

Cultural Diversity

JOAN MARIE SNIDER

❀

When Joan Marie Snider wrote this piece, she was a student at New Mexico Highlands University and editor of the school's student newspaper, La Mecha. *In this editorial, which was clearly written in response to some cultural conflicts on her campus, Snider argues that "it is possible to preserve one's own culture while acknowledging, and maybe even sharing, another's."*

BEFORE YOU READ

▪ *THINK* about the idea of a college campus as a "shared culture." How would you describe your own college culture?

▪ *EXAMINE* Snider's first paragraph. Does she get your attention? Are you offended by her language? Are you surprised by the question she asks: "Can't we all get along?" How effective is this paragraph as an introduction?

▪ *WRITE* a journal entry in which you predict from Snider's title and first paragraph the argument she will make in this editorial.

AS YOU READ

Notice how Snider explores her own cultural identity in an effort to establish common ground with readers from different cultural and ethnic backgrounds.

I haven't figured out how to say this without sounding like some over-privileged whiny white bitch, or a sound-bite-infatuated Pollyanna, but: Can't we all get along?   1

But besides being trite and painfully naive, this is just a dumb question. 2
No, we cannot all get along. People have been not getting along since before
Time. Remember the Barbarian invasions? The Crusades? The Holocaust?
The weight of history impresses on me that differences between people
have always been more important than similarities.

But to be optimistic for a moment: We do seem to be discovering ways 3
to overcome our differences. People now go to conflict resolution work-
shops where once they beat each other with clubs. This is a nice trend, I
think. It means that we are beginning to see our world as something to
share, not something to conquer.

Unfortunately, there are people who are stuck in the old conquering 4
mode. There are people who would say, for example, that Highlands
University should be the private domain of northern New Mexicans. This
doesn't make any sense to me. It seems akin to huddling, each in our
respective caves, afraid to come out or let anyone in lest they wield a club
against us.

It just seems that with all the emphasis on what is "my" culture versus 5
what is "your" culture, the fact that all of us here have more in common
than not is lost. We see each other when we're buying our laundry detergent
at Wal-Mart or renting videos at Furr's or standing in line for new IDs, but
we don't realize that the fact that we're here, together, doing a lot of the
same things, means that we have, at least to some extent, a shared culture.

But maybe it's just this, the specter of cultural amalgamation, which 6
has prompted some to pick up the torch of cultural preservation. But—
here's the whiny part—I'm not threatening anyone's cultural preservation
when I wish someone Gesundheit and I'm not threatening it when I make
tamales, Anglicized and mutilated though they may be. I'm not threatening
it when I choose to be a part of a university which includes people from
other backgrounds. It is possible to preserve one's own culture while
acknowledging, and maybe even sharing, another's.

I have no doubt that my attitude toward culture is shaped in part by 7
the fact that I'm very confused about what "my" culture is. The culture of
my German ancestors was lost more than a century ago, as they respelled
their names, gave up the German language and did everything they could
to assimilate with the dominant culture of the Midwest. Growing up, "my"
culture included Jell-o salads, Barbie dolls, hymns by Henry Wadsworth
Longfellow and the belief that anything pleasant is necessarily sinful. Not
exactly the types of things one might want to claim, let alone preserve. And
I haven't even mentioned that it has been people of roughly my ethnic
makeup who have been the oppressors in much of this planet's history.

When I signed up for a German course in ninth grade, a friend, incredulous, asked me how I could study German after what Hitler had done. What could I say?

I'm glad that other people have more of a sense of their own culture 8 than I do of mine, but I still say it's time we started venturing out and realizing that we can visit neighboring cavedwellers without sacrificing the integrity of our own caves.

Maybe Conflict Resolution 101 should be on the core curriculum and 9 Playing Well With Others a section of the ACT. We could all learn from a friend who said she doesn't care if her professors are green or purple, as long as they are qualified to teach what she wants to learn. It might take a little adjustment, but different as we are, there's no reason we can't be part of the same university, to everyone's benefit. What a concept.

❀   ❀   ❀

AFTER YOU READ

• *THINK* about Snider's tone in this essay. Notice especially her vocabulary and her sentence structure. Is her informal, colloquial tone effective, given the seriousness of the problem she is trying to solve? Would a more formal, serious tone have been more persuasive? Why, or why not?

• *EXAMINE* Snider's description of her own cultural background. Does this information contribute to the effectiveness of her argument? Why, or why not?

• *EXAMINE* also Snider's definition of the problem she is addressing and her solution to the problem. Is her definition of the problem clearly articulated, or does she assume that her readers (other students at the same school) are familiar with the problem? Is the solution she proposes (a required course in conflict resolution and an ACT test that focuses not only on academic achievement but also on how well students get along with others) a serious suggestion? What other, more serious but unstated, solution is implied?

• *WRITE* a problem-solution essay in which you define some problem on your campus and propose a solution. You may focus primarily on the problem, as Snider does, or on the solution. Or you may choose to take a more balanced approach, giving equal emphasis to the problem and the solution.

Anonymous Victims of
Dreams and a River

VICTOR LANDA

❀

*Victor Landa is news director of KVDA-TV in San Antonio
and a contributing columnist for the* San Antonio Express-
News. *In this article he remembers when he was a young
journalist, living and working on the border between Texas
and Mexico, which is created by the Rio Grande. The tone
of his essay is reflective and poetic, but it also includes
some hard facts about the number of immigrants who die
each year attempting to cross the river.*

BEFORE YOU READ

▪ *THINK* about what compels people to leave the place of their birth and
emigrate to a new country. What would motivate you to leave your home
and go to a strange land?

▪ *EXAMINE* the title of the essay. Why are the victims described as anonymous? How can someone be a victim of a dream?

▪ *WRITE* a journal entry in which you explain what it would take to
convince you to emigrate to a new country.

AS YOU READ

Identify the passages that are clearly poetic by underlining them and those
that are clearly informative by circling them.

There are rivers that we shouldn't cross. There are places where we 1
shouldn't go, not because it's prohibited but because we're not prepared. Because it is the end.

319

When I was a young journalist in Laredo, cadavers would regularly ₂
appear on the Rio Grande. We called them "floaters" out of a sharp sense
of cynicism that protected us from the cold reality of death.

They seldom had identification, and if they did, it was of no use. Their ₃
names were entered in some official ledger, and the bodies were buried in
paupers' graves, marked by simple wooden crosses in a remote corner of
the city cemetery.

They came from small towns, farming communities, forgotten enclaves ₄
of industrial centers—they came from families, from homes that saw them
leave and never heard from them again.

The official reports always read the same: Dead for two or three days, ₅
death by drowning.

The Rio Grande is a dangerous river. The current is tricky. One slip ₆
and you lose control. The water pulls you; it suffocates and kills.

The bodies sink to the bottom and stay there until gases form inside ₇
them—gases lighter than water that eventually make the corpses rise to the
surface. The same currents that took their lives deposit them among the
green rushes on the river's edge.

Boys would come on their bicycles from the nearby neighborhoods. ₈
People would emerge from everywhere. Women in housecoats carrying
babies on their hips would arrive, like moths drawn to a light—attracted
by the police, by the television cameras, by the fascination with death.

Death is a part of the risk, the losing end of the gamble. When you ₉
travel among the shadows, death is a constant companion.

Between 1993 and 1996, according to the U.S. Immigration and ₁₀
Naturalization Service, more than 1,000 of these travelers died trying to
cross the border between the United States and Mexico. From San Ysidro,
Calif., to Brownsville, almost 400 die every year now. More than one a day.
Most of them in Texas.

The agents in charge of the macabre count travel to every town along ₁₁
the border, endure bureaucracies, speak with policemen, coroners, cemetery keepers. They comb through registers and record books, looking for
details. And the final result is a simple number. In the end, they are all the
same.

Their efforts, though, should mean something. The impulse to leave ₁₂
everything behind obeys the promise of a light much brighter than the
darkness they came from. They gambled for very human reasons, and the
tragedy of their death is a very human event.

Since I was a young journalist on the border so many years ago, there ₁₃
have been tens of thousands of dreams that have ended floating in the

current, among the rushes. And in all those years, I still haven't been able to understand the misery of the river's end.

All I know is that there are places where we shouldn't go, places that 14 will take your life and your name in a cruel exchange for an empty dream.

❀   ❀   ❀

AFTER YOU READ

▪ *THINK* about Landa's representation of the Rio Grande. How does he describe it? Is it the river's fault that the immigrants drown while trying to cross it? Landa does not refer to the people who die in the river as illegal immigrants, but obviously they are illegal or they would be crossing the river on the bridges at the legal immigration entry points. Why do you think he avoids this term?

▪ *THINK* also about Landa's thesis, which is implicit rather than explicit. Although he does not state his thesis, the essay's purpose is ultimately persuasive. Try to state his thesis in your own words.

▪ *EXAMINE* Landa's statement that "The impulse to leave everything behind obeys the promise of a light much brighter than the darkness they came from." This statement implies that people emigrate to a new land not only because of the problems that characterize their lives in the place where they live but also because of their dreams of what is possible in the new land. Do you agree or disagree with this statement?

▪ *WRITE* an essay in which you argue for or against stronger enforcement of immigration laws, or propose new immigration laws for Mexicans entering the United States.

The Citizenship Boom

NATHAN GLAZER

❀

Nathan Glazer is the author of several books that focus on issues related to diversity (for example, Arguing Immigration: The Debate over the Changing Face of America *and* We Are All Multiculturists Now*). This selection, which first appeared in the* New Republic, *explores the process by which immigrants become citizens of the United States. Nathan Glazer concedes that the process may be antiquated and idealistic but argues that it would be a mistake to change it.*

BEFORE YOU READ

• *THINK* about the difference between being born a citizen and becoming a citizen. What do you know about the process of becoming a citizen of the United States? What should this process accomplish?

• *EXAMINE* the word *fealty* in the following sentence:

> Yet, we do have an exalted idea of what it means to be an American, and we would like *fealty* to our principles to play a larger role in the mix of motives that lead people to become citizens.

Can you figure out from the context what this word means?

• *WRITE* a journal entry about what you think the process of becoming a citizen involves.

AS YOU READ

Underline those sentences that describe the process of becoming a citizen.

It was to be expected that the enormous surge of people applying to 1
become, and becoming, citizens would at some point lead to controversy.
On the one hand, Americans want immigrants to become citizens. (If they
learn that longtime residents are *not* citizens, they are likely to ask, in
surprise, "why not?" The idea that people may be attached to distant,
poorer and less powerful countries is difficult for Americans to understand.) But, on the other hand, it is not surprising that the astonishing rise
in the number of people applying for citizenship (1.3 million in 1996, an
estimated 1.8 million in 1997, compared to an average of 220,000 new
citizens a year in the 1980s) has led to some uneasiness, as well as a widened
scope for error and scandal.

We have had both: the possibility that the Immigration and Naturali- 2
zation Service reduced the long wait between application for citizenship
and completion of the process in order to increase the number of Democratic voters in 1996 has outraged Republicans. In congressional hearings,
witnesses have also attacked the INS for weakening the statutorily required
standards for citizenship—knowledge of English, American history and the
Constitution. Republican congressmen cannot criticize the INS for becoming more efficient and productive. So they have attacked the INS for
granting citizenship before having 180,000 applicants checked for criminal
records by the FBI. (I wonder how many informed Americans even knew
that prospective citizens undergo an FBI check.)

Other scandals have also focused attention on citizenship: it has been 3
charged that persons who applied for citizenship—but were not yet
citizens—voted in the close election for Congress in southern California in
which Democrat Loretta Sanchez defeated Republican Congressman
Robert Dornan by a mere 979 votes. And, of course, there's the scandal
around political contributions from foreign sources, which has allowed
some congressmen to propose that only citizens be allowed to make
political contributions.

But the scandals have not focused on, or brought attention to, what I 4
think really concerns Americans when they see a million new citizens a
year. I believe many people must be asking themselves whether all these
people are becoming citizens for the right reasons. It is clear many are
rushing to citizenship now to escape welfare legislation, which cuts nonci-
tizens off from Supplemental Security Income, Food Stamps and other
benefits. But, then, what are the right reasons for becoming a citizen? After
all, if people become citizens to advance their self-interest, isn't that the
reason they immigrate in the first place? They do not all come to escape
political or religious persecution. Yet, we do have an exalted idea of what

it means to be an American, and we would like fealty to our principles to play a larger role in the mix of motives that lead people to become citizens.

Ideally, we want people to become citizens because they admire the ₅ United States for its highest goals and accomplishments, and wish to become a part of our people, participating as full partners in the governing of the nation. We don't want them to become citizens because they envy our wealth or our standard of living. We want them to become citizens because they want to bind themselves to the United States out of heartfelt agreement with our finest commitments—to the liberty of the individual, to the fullest measure of equality in the status of individuals, to ordered democratic government. Those are the values embodied in the Declaration of Independence and in the Constitution. We want them to be committed to our form of government, as laid down in these documents. We think it works well, and we expect new citizens to accept these arrangements and, indeed, to defend them.

Is this impossibly idealistic? Very likely, and yet our law asks for nothing ₆ less. We ask that prospective citizens be acquainted with American history and government, that they know something of the Constitution, that they be loyal to the United States above any other country, that they know English—with certain exceptions made for age. We make a great deal of becoming a citizen, rather more than other countries. We once celebrated, I recall, an "I am an American day," marking the day when the oath of citizenship was taken. I don't think other countries, however difficult the process of attaining citizenship (and it is rather more difficult in most other countries), have any equivalent to the process by which one becomes a citizen here, or to the final ceremony which marks the attainment of citizenship. In this country, hundreds (or even thousands) participate in a ceremony conducted by a judge, in the presence of friends and family, in locations meant to inspire awe and love of country. In Boston, these ceremonies are conducted in Faneuil Hall, the "cradle of liberty." (In major gateway cities, owing to greater numbers, they have to take place in convention halls and stadiums, which take away some of the dignity provided by an historic space.)

The concern today is that citizenship is being devalued, and I share ₇ that concern. One problem, however, in maintaining the process at an exalted level is that we have become a different country, less chauvinistic, very likely less patriotic, certainly more cynical about our government and its virtues. Indeed, the immigrant may think better of America on the whole than the native.

Undoubtedly, very ordinary motives are at play in the decision to ₈ become a citizen. But there are higher motives, too. We want to shore these up, we want to avoid making the process purely mechanical, bureaucratic, matter of fact. With more than a million new American citizens each year, that is not an easy assignment, and it is understandable that the INS has sped up and shortened—and possibly removed some dignity from—the process. But it is a process now more than two centuries old, with a remarkable degree of continuity to it. Some parts of the oath of citizenship, prescribed by law, may go back almost 200 years. The prospective citizen swears: "I absolutely and entirely renounce and abjure any allegiance and fidelity to any foreign prince. . . . I will support and defend the Constitution and laws of the United States of America against all enemies, foreign and domestic; that I will bear arms on behalf of the United States when required by the law . . ." and so on.

Antique sentiments all, and I am sure many of us feel we could do 9 better today, and we should reshape the oath in more contemporary form, the way ancient prayers are updated. But the making of Americans should always have something special about it. We could not today bring the same exalted tone to the oath. I would vote against trying.

We will undoubtedly continue to debate the process of granting 10 citizenship, but we should be cautious in making changes. Our tendency today would be to strip seriousness from the process, and that would be a mistake, for there is little enough that is taken seriously in our lives today.

❀   ❀   ❀

AFTER YOU READ

▪ *THINK* about the advantages of allowing immigrants to become citizens of the United States. Then think about the disadvantages. What conclusion do you reach on the basis of your comparison of the advantages and disadvantages?

▪ *EXAMINE* the sentences you underlined as you read and summarize the process that Glazer describes. Do you think this process should be more difficult? Should it be less difficult? Are you in favor of revising the process that now exists? If so, in what way?

▪ *WRITE* an essay in which you argue for or against Glazer's conclusion that it would be a mistake to change the process that now exists for becoming a citizen.

The African-American Century

HENDRIK HERTZBERG
and
HENRY LOUIS GATES, JR.

❀

This article was coauthored by two well-known writers and scholars. Hendrik Hertzberg served on the White House staff throughout the Carter administration. From 1979 until 1981, he was President Carter's chief speechwriter. However, he has spent most of his career as a journalist, most recently as editorial director of The New Yorker. *Henry Louis Gates, Jr. is a renowned African-American scholar and cultural critic. A prolific writer who has authored and coauthored several books and numerous articles, he currently directs the W.E.B. Du Bois Institute for Afro-American Studies at Harvard University.*

In this article, which appeared in The New Yorker *toward the end of the twentieth century, Hertzberg and Gates argue that the twentieth century can be characterized as the African-American century because of the progress and accomplishments of black Americans in that time period.*

BEFORE YOU READ

• *THINK* about the progress made by African-Americans during the past century. In what areas have they excelled? How has the progress made by African-Americans benefited the nation as a whole?

• *EXAMINE* the following italicized words, which you will encounter in this reading selection and which may be unfamiliar to you.

1. "An observer from 1900 transported forward in time to this century's end would be astonished at the *ubiquity* of the black presence in artistic, cultural, and quasi-cultural endeavors of every kind, . . ."

The word *ubiquity* means to be, or appear to be, everywhere at the same time.

2. ". . . from the frontiers of modern art (born when Picasso laid eyes on African masks), through the written word . . . , to the *iconography* of mass marketing (with Michael Jordan looking down from giant billboards like some beneficent Big Brother). . . ."

An *icon* is a pictorial representation, illustration, or symbol of a subject (often a sacred subject). Thus, *iconography* is the collected representations of a subject, or a set of icons.

3. "It is *bootless*" to compare African-Americans to 'other' immigrant groups and to speak of '*assimilating*' them. . . ."

As you can probably tell, *bootless* means useless, without advantage or benefit. The word *assimilate* means to make similar, incorporate, or absorb.

▪ *WRITE* in your journal several reasons you think it might be appropriate to designate the twentieth century as the African-American century.

AS YOU READ

Identify the areas in which African-Americans have excelled and those areas in which their progress has been less significant.

The story of America, according to the narrative enshrined in our civic 1
religion, goes something like this. A great wilderness was gradually populated by waves of hardy immigrants fleeing the oppressions of the Old World to build a better life in the New. Throwing off subordination to a distant throne, they made a commonwealth, the first in history to be founded explicitly on principles of self-government and political equality. Over the next two hundred years and more, they worked and sometimes fought to insure that their "new nation, conceived in Liberty, and dedicated to the proposition that all men are created equal," would increasingly live up to its moral and material promise. And they succeeded, creating a nation not only of unparalleled personal and political freedom but also (a recent flourish) of wonderful, enriching diversity—a powerful nation, universally looked to as an example and a protector.

A pretty story; and, like all folk tales, this one tells a kind of truth. 2
But the reality is more complicated, darker (in more ways than one), more painful, and, ultimately, more heroic. The myth ignores the tragic

dimension of the American condition, the dimension that challenges the moral seriousness of American thinkers and makes American art and culture, high and low, the most dynamic and pervasive on the planet— makes American culture American, in fact. Not all Americans' ancestors came here to escape tyranny; many were brought here in furtherance of tyranny. Not all crossed the ocean to better themselves and their families; many were forcibly carried here—their families torn apart, their social structures smashed, their languages suppressed—to labor without recompense for the benefit of their oppressors. Yet those of us whose forebears came here in chains have much deeper roots in American soil, on the average, than do those of us whose forebears came here in and for freedom; the vast majority of African-Americans are descended from men and women who arrived before 1776. Except for American Indians, only a shrinking minority of other Americans can say the same. (And, of course, scores of millions of us—no one knows how many—of every hue are termed "black" or "white" in our country's arbitrary racial shorthand but are in reality a mixture of, at a minimum, both.)

The history of settlement in what is now the United States dates back 3 nearly four hundred years, but the twentieth will be the first century unpolluted by chattel slavery. When the century began, most adult African-Americans were former slaves, and had known not only the degradation of bondage but also the exultation of Emancipation, the giddy hopefulness of Reconstruction, and the calamity of a reactionary and increasingly violent regime of legalized white supremacy. The grandchildren of the grandchildren of those African-Americans are the African-Americans of today. The line is short, the connection between past and present inescapable.

Even so, there have been titanic changes, and they have been accom- 4 panied by unexpected ironies. The most striking change has been the growing centrality of the black experience to the maturing national culture of the United States; the most striking irony has been the degree to which blacks, despite that centrality, have remained economically marginal.

An observer from 1900 transported forward in time to this century's 5 end would be astonished at the ubiquity of the black presence in artistic, cultural, and quasi-cultural endeavors of every kind, from the frontiers of modern art (born when Picasso laid eyes on African masks), through the written word (more books by and about African-Americans will be published this year than appeared during the whole of the Harlem Renaissance), to the iconography of mass marketing (with Michael Jordan looking down from giant billboards like some beneficent Big Brother). The prime example, of course, is music, the most accessible of the arts. In 1900, ragtime was only just coming into its own, beginning the long and steady fusion of African-American themes and form with those of European origin. In the early decades of the century, Negro music came to dominate the new technologies of sound recording and radio so thoroughly that, in 1924, an alarmed music establishment sought out a syncopationally challenged bandleader by the comically apt name of Paul Whiteman and designated him "the King of Jazz." But jazz and its offshoots could not be so easily tamed. The wildly creative creolization of African-American and European-American strains produced a profusion of mulatto musics—one thinks of Ellington and Gershwin, Joplin and Stravinsky, Miles Davis and Gil Evans, Chuck Berry and Jerry Lee Lewis, Jimi Hendrix and Bruce Springsteen—that spread their dominion across the whole world.

Economically, however, African-Americans remain left out. The suc- 6 cesses of integration and affirmative action created a substantial black middle class: there are now four times as many black families with incomes above fifty thousand dollars a year as there were in 1964. But those same successes have contributed to a distillation of ever more concentrated pools of poverty and despair in the inner cities—a process greatly worsened by the catastrophic decline of decent manufacturing jobs and the growing hardheartedness and insolvency of social policy at every level of government. The sufferings and pathologies associated with this process are well known. Half of all African-American children live in poverty. A third of all black men between the ages of twenty and twenty-nine are entangled in the criminal-justice system. The leading cause of death among young black men is gunshot wounds.

Our market economy has shown no ability to solve these problems, 7 and our gridlocked, fragmented political system has shown very little. After a century of struggle, African-Americans have at last achieved more or less equal political rights. But our majoritarian electoral system generally prevents them from attaining real power except in geographic areas where they are a majority or a near-majority. Although African-Americans constitute some thirteen per cent of the population, their representation in state governorships is zero. In the United States Senate it is one per cent. In the House of Representatives, which now has forty African-American members, black progress has come at the price of racial gerrymandering. It's a high price: it drains (liberal) black voting strength from neighboring districts, often tipping them over into the control of politicians indifferent to black interests; it discourages grass-roots interracial coalition-building; and it creates a black political class with a vested interest in patterns of residential segregation. And even this progress, such as it is, is under mortal threat from a Supreme Court piously bent on making the Constitution "color-blind," especially in cases where a bit of color consciousness might do black folks some good.

For African-Americans, the country of oppression and the country of 8 liberation are the same country. Fleeing to some faraway land of liberty is not a possibility, though something like that impulse is implicit in black nationalism, in ironic tribute to the power of the immigrant myth. (Marcus Garvey wanted to call his promised land the United States of Africa.) It is bootless to compare African-Americans to "other" immigrant groups and to speak of "assimilating" them: African-Americans are not an immigrant group, and, as the success of the cultural synthesis shows, the responsibility for doing the assimilating is not theirs alone. The history that is at the root of the "differentness" of blacks—what might be called African-American exceptionalism—cannot be changed. There is only one option, and it is to make our country live up to its nominal creed.

❀   ❀   ❀

AFTER YOU READ

• *THINK* about the distinction the authors make between African-Americans and those immigrants who came to this country by their own choice. What is the significance of this distinction? Do you agree with the authors that this distinction means that African-Americans should not be considered immigrants? Why or why not?

• *EXAMINE* the first paragraph of this essay, in which the authors give a glorified account of U.S. history, which they call "the story of America." Then read the second paragraph, in which they present a less "pretty" but more realistic and complex version of the same story. Which account seems more accurate to you? Is there any justification for an idealized view of history? Why or why not?

• *WRITE* an essay in which you agree or disagree with the authors that integration and affirmative action have helped African-Americans to progress.

The Resegregation of a
Southern School

DOUGLAS A. BLACKMON

❀

This essay first appeared in the Perspective section of the Atlanta Journal-Constitution *and was later reprinted in* Harper's Magazine. *The author, who is a reporter for* The Wall Street Journal, *grew up in Leland, Mississippi, which is located in the fertile, flat, northwestern part of the state known as the Delta. In this essay he tells of the changes that have taken place in Leland since 1982, when he graduated from the high school there.*

BEFORE YOU READ

• *THINK* about the racial makeup of your college. How do the different races get along? Is there much social interaction? If not, why? Are different races represented on the faculty as well as among the student body?

• *EXAMINE* the title of the essay. What does it mean to resegregate? Why would anyone want to resegregate? What connotations are associated in your mind with the word *segregation*? Do you associate these same connotations with the word *resegregate*? Why or why not?

• *WRITE* a journal entry about a significant personal experience you have had with a member of a race different from your own. What did you learn from this experience?

AS YOU READ

Compare the author's racial experiences in high school with your own.

Another long hot summer has ended in the Mississippi Delta, and the   1
students in my hometown are coming back to Leland High School.
Seventy-five seniors are expected to graduate this year, sixty-one of them
black and fourteen white. I entered the first grade in the Leland school
system in 1970—Leland's first year of fully integrated classes. That spring,
sixty white faces peered out from the Leland senior-class portrait. In 1982,
when my class was the first to graduate after twelve full years of black and
white children studying together, only two dozen whites remained in a class
of just under ninety.

Despite the fact that the number of white graduates diminished slowly   2
during the time I was there, the class of 1982's graduation symbolized the
culmination of the struggle to integrate public education in a state long
defined by racial hatred. Our rite of passage was Mississippi's rite of
passage, and when my classmates ventured into the world, Mississippians
who believed in the ideal of integration hoped they had sown the seeds of
a more equal and tolerant society.

But now, ten years later, hardly anyone, black or white, even remem-   3
bers that dream. Integration here in Leland and across much of Mississippi
has largely failed. The Delta school system is almost as segregated today as
it was in 1968, although now it is characterized by mostly black public
schools and all-white private institutions. In many towns, there are virtually
no whites left in the public school system.

At Leland High, extracurricular activities are fading as community   4
support for them diminishes among whites. The school newspaper, started
in the 1970s by my oldest brother, vanished several years ago. Academic
clubs are struggling. When a newspaper story recently reported that Leland
High might no longer be able to afford a yearbook, most townsfolk just
rolled their eyes.

What is most noticeably absent in Leland's schools today is the biracial   5
community spirit that initially made them some of the most integrated in
the Delta—an achievement that was supposed to be a dramatic first step
toward integrating all of society. While desegregation succeeded in easing
overt racial hostility and opening up Leland's restaurants, motels, and
libraries, black and white children today face one another across the same
awkward divide that we did twenty years ago. And they leave high school
on opposite sides of an economic gulf almost as wide as before. Yet Leland
has become a place where few blacks or whites find it objectionable—or
even odd—that there are racially divided schools. And almost no one
believes it will ever change. Integration, born amid outcries of both hope
and excoriation, has withered in virtual silence.

Leland is a rather typical Mississippi Delta town of 6,000 residents,   6
mostly merchants, planters, and laborers. The population is—and has been
for as long as anyone recalls—about 60 percent black. My family moved
there in 1967, into an old, rambling yellow house in a white middle-class
neighborhood. Like the rest of Mississippi, Leland inched its way toward
integration only at the steady prod of the federal government. The tide
turned on October 29, 1969, when the Supreme Court issued a sweeping
ruling that required almost immediate integration in Leland and twenty-
nine other Mississippi school districts. I began the first grade the following
fall.

After the Court's ruling, a flood of hysterical white Mississippi fami-   7
lies fled to newly created private segregationist academies—schools with
Confederate-colonel mascots and rebel-flag logos. But in Leland, a biracial
coalition of school leaders and parents, my own included, began a campaign to encourage whites to stay with the public schools. They handed
out stickers at school board meetings that read, "Think Positive," and
published a full-page ad in the local paper with the names of more than
200 white parents who promised that their children would remain in the
public-school system. In that first year, Leland retained about half of its
white students—a remarkable achievement for a Delta town.

Those were curious times of racial exploration for me. I was com-   8
pletely unaware of the turmoil that had preceded my first day of school,
and, as best I recall, it was a topic that our teachers never encouraged us
to discuss. My parents didn't talk about it either, but they somehow drilled
into me the notion that there was one evil perhaps greater than any other,
this thing called "prejudice."

I wasn't exactly sure what it meant. I just knew I was supposed to avoid   9
it, and that my friends from church who went to "the academy" were
somehow tainted by it. The word was so ominous and omnipresent that it
terrified me. Occasionally a black classmate would suddenly ask me, "Are
you prejudiced?" "Of course not," I would quickly respond, while thinking,
"It's the private-school people who are prejudiced."

But I was receiving other signals that were confusing. I became fast   10
friends with a black classmate, Donald Richardson, and at some point in
the fourth grade we began talking about visiting each other's homes to
combine our GI Joe collections. His parents were schoolteachers, just like
my mother, and his grandfather was a retired school principal.

Donald and I never did visit each other, though. He's a band director   11
at Leland High now, and recently I asked him why he thought we never
spent time at each other's homes—or, for that matter, why black and white

classmates almost never visited each other's homes. He remembers that time the same way I do—no specific recollection of which teacher or parent or classmate had conveyed it, but the sense of getting a clear message: visiting each other was "not a good idea."

By the time I was in junior high school, segregation was evident in almost every facet of my life except the classroom. I earned merit badges in an all-white Boy Scout troop and played Little League baseball on an all-white team, the Planters. My friends and I spent our summers at segregated swimming pools, and our families had picnics in segregated parks. Blacks and whites even played on opposite sides of Lake Monocnoc on the edge of town.

At school, racial tension characterized the daily dynamic. Fistfights on the playground between blacks and whites were routine, and being harassed by blacks as I walked home through their neighborhood after school was so common that I was later amazed to learn that anyone else had grown up differently. The school stopped sponsoring senior proms, student banquets, senior trips, and other social gatherings long before I was old enough to know what they were.

Some of the reluctance to integrate children outside of the classroom came, ironically, from desegregation supporters. Many of these parents believed that the immediate goal was simply to integrate the schools. They feared that sanctioning socializing between black and white students might cause anxious white parents to pull their children out of the schools altogether. But much of the hesitation about social integration was triggered by far more extreme sentiments. Blacks were seething with the anger of decades of humiliation and years of white obstructionism, even after segregation was illegal. Whites were gripped by misgivings about integration: everything from the innocuous "decline in quality education" to more bizarre concerns that whites would no longer be able to compete athletically, or that lecherous black boys would attack innocent white girls.

The anger and fear I witnessed daily, I now realize, reflected a complex set of emotions being vented at dinner tables in every part of town. During the first years of integration, dedicated black and white adults worked within the institutions of church, jobs, and city hall to resolve the fear and anger. But over the long haul, they left it to their children, for the most part, to fight it out around the swing sets.

Despite the racial tension, we whites were well served by the integrated public schools. We gained from the rough-and-tumble mix of cultures and,

Perhaps the lesson to be drawn from a place like Leland is th
the formal institutions of racism has little effect on integra
day-to-day personal lives—or on advancing economic equal
nomic situation for blacks in the Delta today has changed littl
good intentions of the people who pushed for diverse school

Maybe that was inevitable. Maybe it's impossible to eff
change in only a quarter of a century. Maybe desegregation
from its first day. But I can't help thinking that these are litt
excuses. The preachers and teachers and aldermen and gro
search scientists and high-minded farmers of today's Leland co
the coalition that first integrated my school. They could talk b
about schools, but about the broader issues of race and
opportunity. I don't know whether such an effort would as
and Eloise's baby boys of something more than the catfish j
the only thing that might.

※ ※ ※

AFTER YOU READ

- *THINK* about Blackmon's assertion that both blacks an
allowing schools to become resegregated. Do you agree or
this assertion? Why? Do you think that public schools a
resegregated all across the nation or just in the South?

- *EXAMINE* Blackmon's statement that "destroying the form
of racism has little effect on integrating people's day-to
lives—or on advancing economic equality." Do you agree v
ment, or do you find it pessimistic and even cynical?

- *WRITE* an essay or journal entry responding to this essay. `
on the author's main idea or on some specific statement that
WRITE a personal essay about your own experiences with s
resegregation, using Blackmon's essay as a point of departu

I think, were strengthened by the confrontations it sparked. Most of the whites in the class of 1982—generally from wealthier, more educated families than the blacks—finished college and never returned to Leland. My black classmates did not fare as well. A few went to college and then to cities in the North or West; several others went into the military. But the basic threshold of "success" for blacks in the Delta is leaving it, and most of my classmates never did.

Recently, I went back to Leland to see what had become of my 17 classmates who stayed behind during the decade since we graduated. I found that being black in the Delta typically still means a lifetime of barely scraping by in a place where factory jobs are few and the only big industry, farming, is controlled by an old-fashioned white elite. Brandon Taylor, who broke my undefeated spelling-bee record when he entered our class in the sixth grade, briefly played professional basketball in Europe. Now he's back in the Delta struggling to make a living. Elaine and Eloise Chillis, one of two sets of fraternal twins in my class, have worked since graduation for Delta Pride, a catfish company in Indianola, notorious for its oppressive working conditions. With experience and good performance, they told me they can look forward to eventually making top pay at the plant: $5.30 an hour. By Delta standards they are fairly successful, each with steady work and one beautiful boy. They don't particularly want to leave.

Elaine and Eloise were precisely the kind of children—smart, but 18 deprived of opportunity—that integration was supposed to help. No one spelled out exactly what integration was meant to accomplish at the time it was ordered, but there was an overwhelming sense that it was going to bring genuine change for the Elaines and Eloises of this country.

Instead, integration became a game of numbers that fell far short of 19 any real effort to secure civil—and human—rights. In the tremendous and exhausting struggle to prove on paper that public schools no longer discriminated, the larger question of how truly to unite a divided society was forgotten. "We didn't have a really specific vision," my father told me recently. "We thought we were in the midst of some very profound changes. In retrospect, it may have been an overexpectation."

Naive or not, the goals of school integration were doomed when the 20 community leadership that had worked so hard to sustain the public schools slowly melted away: the newspaper editor who had weathered scorn for his pro-integration positions moved to another town; the white school superintendent and the top black school administrator who had worked tirelessly behind the scenes to promote understanding retired; the white school-board members, who despite their political conservatism

believed that good public schools were essential to a smal
after years of frustration.

But why didn't others come forward to replace them? W
present-day counterparts to the white leaders who suppo
gration twenty years ago? Part of the reason, perhaps, i
urgency of the late 1960s—the sense of rapid social chang
people to take strong stands—is gone.

For white Mississippians who considered themselves
idea of sending their children to all-white private schools
ago was taboo. The academies held the torch in those d
old Southern evils against which America was railing.
crude segregationist trappings have largely fallen away. N
est, most retrograde academies have closed, and their stu
consolidated into larger, better schools. Supporters of th
their "quality" educational environment in nonracial term
body may well include the children of one or two black p

Personal convenience has prevailed over community
conviction that integrated my school has given way to an
numbness—the same numbness that allowed me (and mo
to accept abject black poverty just a stone's throw awa
homes. Today, many of the children of the early white grad
integrated public schools are attending private academies

In the black community too, almost no one is comp
resegregation of Leland's schools. In recent months, bla
been more focused on keeping alive the traditions of the
school, which now houses grades four, five, and six. Last f
white principal wanted to replace some athletic trophi
before integration in a display case with the work of curr
black community was outraged.

This acute nostalgia reflects a growing sense among
the cost of giving up schools that they controlled may h
than the benefits of integration. Before desegregation
learned in institutions that, despite all the adversity the
succeeded entirely because of the efforts and talents o
black adults. The schools were woven into the fabric of th
were a sanctuary from the racial denigration that mai
Integration changed all that, removing blacks from to
positions in the schools and raising racial questions ab
promotion and every student disciplinary action.

The Recoloring of Campus Life

SHELBY STEELE

❦

Shelby Steele, a research fellow at the Hoover Institution, has called himself a "classic liberal" who focuses on "freedom, on the sacredness of the individual, [and] the power to be found in the individual" (Time, August 12, 1991). *However, his conservative views on civil rights and affirmative action have drawn sharp criticism from black leaders such as Jesse Jackson. Steele has articulated his ideas in a collection of essays entitled* The Content of Our Character; *the following selection is part of his essay "The Recoloring of Campus Life." It provides an interesting contrast to the preceding essay by Blackmon.*

BEFORE YOU READ

- *THINK* about the racial harmony or disharmony that exists on your own campus. Do you agree or disagree with Steele's assertion that "racial tension on campus is more the result of racial equality than inequality" (paragraph 1)? Why do you feel as you do?

- *EXAMINE* the sentences below to be sure that you understand the meanings of the italicized words.

1. The word *paradox*, which occurs in the following two sentences in the reading, is central to Steele's main point.

   "But there is a *paradox* here: on a campus where members of all races are gathered, mixed together in the classroom as well as socially, differences are more exposed than ever" (paragraph 2).

   "But there is another, related *paradox*, stemming from the notion of—and practice of—affirmative action. . . . What has emerged on campus in recent years—as a result of the new equality and of affirmative action and, in a sense, as a result of progress—is a *politics of difference,* a troubling, volatile politics in which each group justifies itself, its sense of worth, and its pursuit of power, through difference alone" (paragraph 3).

As illustrated in these two sentences, a *paradox* is a statement that seems contradictory but is nevertheless true. Another word in the second sentence that you may not know is *volatile,* which means "explosive" or "violent" in this context.

2. "For members of each race—young adults coming into their own, often away from home for the first time—bring to this site of freedom, exploration, and (now, today) equality, very deep fears, anxieties, *inchoate* feelings of racial shame, anger, and guilt" (paragraph 2).

Feelings that are *inchoate* are immature and/or at an early stage, just beginning.

3. "The politics of difference leads each group to pick at the *vulnerabilities* of the other" (paragraph 4).

A *vulnerability* is a weak spot; to be *vulnerable* is to be defenseless and unprotected.

4. "Universities can never be free of guilt until they truly help black students, which means leading and challenging them rather than negotiating and capitulating. It means inspiring them to achieve academic *parity,* nothing less, and helping them to see their own weaknesses as their greatest challenge" (paragraph 8).

Academic *parity* is academic equality. You should also know that to *capitulate* means "to relent" or "to give in."

▪ *WRITE* a journal entry in which you agree or disagree with Steele's statement that living "with racial difference has been America's profound social problem" (paragraph 2).

AS YOU READ

Evaluate the support that Steele gives for his thesis that "racial tension on campus is more the result of racial equality than inequality."

I have long believed that the trouble between the races is seldom what it appears to be. It was not hard to see after my first talks with students that racial tension on campus is a problem that misrepresents itself. It has

the same look, the archetypal pattern, of America's timeless racial conflict—white racism and black protest. And I think part of our concern over
it comes from the fact that it has the feel of a relapse, illness gone and come
again. But if we are seeing the same symptoms, I don't believe we are
dealing with the same illness. For one thing, I think racial tension on
campus is more the result of racial equality than inequality.

How to live with racial difference has been America's profound social 2
problem. For the first hundred years or so following emancipation it was
controlled by a legally sanctioned inequality that kept the races from each
other. No longer is this the case. On campuses today, as throughout society,
blacks enjoy equality under the law—a profound social advancement. No
student may be kept out of a class or a dormitory or an extracurricular
activity because of his or her race. But there is a paradox here: on a campus
where members of all races are gathered, mixed together in the classroom
as well as socially, differences are more exposed than ever. And this is where
the trouble starts. For members of each race—young adults coming into
their own, often away from home for the first time—bring to this site of
freedom, exploration, and (now, today) equality, very deep fears, anxieties,
inchoate feelings of racial shame, anger, and guilt. These feelings could lie
dormant in the home, in familiar neighborhoods, in simpler days of
childhood. But the college campus, with its structures of interaction and
adult-level competition—the big exam, the dorm, the mixer—is another
matter. I think campus racism is born of the rub between racial difference
and a setting, the campus itself, devoted to interaction and equality. On our
campuses, such concentrated micro-societies, all that remains unresolved
between blacks and whites, all the old wounds and shames that have never
been addressed, present themselves for attention—and present our youth
with pressures they cannot always handle.

I have mentioned one paradox: racial fears and anxieties among blacks 3
and whites, bubbling up in an era of racial equality under the law, in settings
that are among the freest and fairest in society. But there is another, related
paradox, stemming from the notion of—and practice of—affirmative
action. Under the provisions of the Equal Employment Opportunity Act of
1972, all state governments and institutions (including universities) were
forced to initiate plans to increase the proportion of minority and women
employees and, in the case of universities, of students too. Affirmative
action plans that establish racial quotas were ruled unconstitutional more
than ten years ago in *University of California* v. *Bakke*, but such plans are
still thought by some to secretly exist, and lawsuits having to do with
alleged quotas are still very much with us. But quotas are only the most

controversial aspect of affirmative action; the principal of affirmative action is reflected in various university programs aimed at redressing and overcoming past patterns of discrimination. Of course, to be conscious of past patterns of discrimination—the fact, say, that public schools in the black inner cities are more crowded and employ fewer top-notch teachers than a white suburban public school, and that this is a factor in student performance—is only reasonable. But in doing this we also call attention quite obviously to difference: in the case of blacks and whites, racial difference. What has emerged on campus in recent years—as a result of the new equality and of affirmative action and, in a sense, as a result of progress—is a *politics of difference,* a troubling, volatile politics in which each group justifies itself, its sense of worth, and its pursuit of power, through difference alone. . . .

The politics of difference sets up a struggle for innocence among all   4
groups. When difference is the currency of power, each group must fight for the innocence that entitles it to power. To gain this innocence, blacks sting whites with guilt, remind them of their racial past, accuse them of new and more subtle forms of racism. One way whites retrieve their innocence is to discredit blacks and deny their difficulties, for in this denial is the denial of their own guilt. To blacks this denial looks like racism, a racism that feeds black innocence and encourages them to throw more guilt at whites. And so the cycle continues. The politics of difference leads each group to pick at the vulnerabilities of the other.

Men and women who run universities—whites, mostly—participate in   5
the politics of difference because they handle their guilt differently than do many of their students. They don't deny it, but still they don't want to *feel* it. And to avoid this feeling of guilt they have tended to go along with whatever blacks put on the table rather than work with them to assess their real needs. University administrators have too often been afraid of guilt and have relied on negotiation and capitulation more to appease their own guilt than to help blacks and other minorities. Administrators would never give white students a racial theme dorm where they could be "more comfortable with people of their own kind," yet more and more universities are doing this for black students, thus fostering a kind of voluntary segregation. To avoid the anxieties of integrated situations, blacks ask for theme dorms; to avoid guilt, white administrators give theme dorms.

When everyone is on the run from their anxieties about race, race   6
relations on campus can be reduced to the negotiation of avoidances. A pattern of demand and concession develops in which both sides use the other to escape themselves. Black studies departments, black deans of

student affairs, black counseling programs, Afro houses, black theme dorms, black homecoming dances and graduation ceremonies—black students and white administrators have slowly engineered a machinery of separatism that, in the name of sacred difference, redraws the ugly lines of segregation.

Black students have not sufficiently helped themselves, and universities, despite all their concessions, have not really done much for blacks. If both faced their anxieties, I think they would see the same thing: academic parity with all other groups should be the overriding mission of black students, and it should also be the first goal that universities have for their black students. Blacks can only *know* they are as good as others when they are, in fact, as good—when their grades are higher and their dropout rate lower. Nothing under the sun will substitute for this, and no amount of concessions will bring it about.

Universities can never be free of guilt until they truly help black students, which means leading and challenging them rather than negotiating and capitulating. It means inspiring them to achieve academic parity, nothing less, and helping them to see their own weaknesses as their greatest challenge. It also means dismantling the machinery of separatism, breaking the link between difference and power, and skewing the formula for entitlement away from race and gender and back to constitutional rights.

As for the young white students who have rediscovered swastikas and the word "nigger," I think that they suffer from an exaggerated sense of their own innocence, as if they were incapable of evil and beyond the reach of guilt. But it is also true that the politics of difference creates an environment that threatens their innocence and makes them defensive. White students are not invited to the negotiating table from which they see blacks and others walk away with concessions. The presumption is that they do not deserve to be there because they are white. So they can only be defensive, and the less mature among them will be aggressive. Guerrilla activity will ensue. Of course this is wrong, but it is also a reflection of an environment where difference carries power and where whites have the wrong "difference."

I think universities should emphasize commonality as a higher value than "diversity" and "pluralism"—buzzwords for the politics of difference. Difference that does not rest on a clearly delineated foundation of commonality is not only inaccessible to those who are not part of the ethnic or racial group, but also antagonistic to them. Difference can enrich only the common ground.

Integration has become an abstract term today, having to do with little 11
more than numbers and racial balances. But it once stood for a high and
admirable set of values. It made difference second to commonality, and it
asked members of all races to face whatever fears they inspired in each
other. I doubt the word will have a new vogue, but the values, under
whatever name, are worth working for.

❀   ❀   ❀

AFTER YOU READ

• *THINK* about the racial situation on your own college campus. Do the
students and administrators pursue a "politics of difference" or the goal of
"commonality" in regard to race, ethnicity, and gender? How, specifically,
does your institution pursue either goal? With which objective do you
agree? Why do you feel as you do?

• *EXAMINE* paragraph 3, in which Steele discusses the practice of affirmative action on campus. How, according to Steele, is affirmative action
applied on most campuses? What does he believe are the results of the
policy? Do you agree or disagree with Steele? Why do you feel as you do?

• *WRITE* a letter to your college newspaper in which you argue that official
policy at your institution should either follow a politics of difference or
aim for commonality in racial, ethnic, and gender questions. Make specific
suggestions about campus courses, programs, and policies.

I Have a Dream

MARTIN LUTHER KING JR.

Martin Luther King Jr.

GWENDOLYN BROOKS

❀

Throughout his all-too-brief career, African-American civil rights leader Martin Luther King Jr. worked with the Southern Christian Leadership Conference to gain for African-Americans the freedom and justice promised all Americans in the Constitution but denied for many years to its nonwhite citizens. King was assassinated in Memphis in 1968, but he left a rich heritage of courage and faith for his followers. This reading selection combines King's most influential speech with a poetic tribute to him written by Pulitzer Prize–winning poet Gwendolyn Brooks.

BEFORE YOU READ

▪ *THINK* about what life was like for African-Americans in 1963 when this speech was made. What kind of dreams did King and other civil rights leaders have at this time? How has our society changed today? Do you think some of the improvements in civil rights were directly influenced by King? Has our society changed enough?

▪ *EXAMINE* the first two paragraphs of King's speech. In his first paragraph, he states the purpose of the rally and of his speech. What is this purpose? Notice that King begins his second paragraph with the phrase "Five score years ago." This phrase recalls Abraham Lincoln's famous Gettysburg Address, which begins "Four score and seven years ago, our fathers brought forth on this continent a new nation, conceived in liberty, and dedicated to the proposition that all men are created equal." By using a phrase similar to the one Lincoln used, King reminds his hearers and readers of the promises—or at least assumptions—in Lincoln's speech that all people are equal and that liberty and justice belong to all humankind.

▪ *WRITE* a journal entry about your own personal dream for the future of America. If you could have only one dream for this country, what would it be?

AS YOU READ

Think about the line "A man went forth with gifts," the first line of a poem by Gwendolyn Brooks entitled "Martin Luther King Jr." The word *gifts* can suggest positive qualities that an individual has as well as "presents" that he or she gives to others. What personal gifts does King display in his speech? Indicate in the margin those passages that reflect King's gift of effective use of language.

I am happy to join with you today in what will go down in history as the greatest demonstration for freedom in the history of our nation. 1

Five score years ago, a great American, in whose symbolic shadow we stand today, signed the Emancipation Proclamation. This momentous decree came as a great beacon light of hope to millions of Negro slaves who had been seared in the flames of withering injustice. It came as a joyous daybreak to end the long night of their captivity. 2

But one hundred years later, the Negro still is not free; one hundred years later, the life of the Negro is still sadly crippled by the manacles of segregation and the chains of discrimination; one hundred years later, the Negro lives on a lonely island of poverty in the midst of a vast ocean of material prosperity; one hundred years later, the Negro is still languished in the corners of American society and finds himself in exile in his own land. 3

So we've come here today to dramatize a shameful condition. In a sense we've come to our nation's capital to cash a check. When the architects of our republic wrote the magnificent words of the Constitution and the Declaration of Independence, they were signing a promissory note to which every American was to fall heir. This note was the promise that all men, 4 yes, black men as well as white men, would be guaranteed the unalienable rights of life, liberty, and the pursuit of happiness.

It is obvious today that America has defaulted on this promissory note 5 in so far as her citizens of color are concerned. Instead of honoring this sacred obligation, America has given the Negro people a bad check; a check which has come back marked "insufficient funds." But we refuse to believe that the bank of justice is bankrupt. We refuse to believe that there are insufficient funds in the great vaults of opportunity of this nation. And so we've come to cash this check, a check that will give us upon demand the riches of freedom and the security of justice.

We have also come to this hallowed spot to remind America of the 6 fierce urgency of now. This is no time to engage in the luxury of cooling off or to take the tranquilizing drug of gradualism. Now is the time to make real the promises of democracy; now is the time to rise from the dark and desolate valley of segregation to the sunlit path of racial justice; now is the time to lift our nation from the quicksands of racial injustice to the solid rock of brotherhood; now is the time to make justice a reality for all of God's children. It would be fatal for the nation to overlook the urgency of the moment. This sweltering summer of the Negro's legitimate discontent will not pass until there is an invigorating autumn of freedom and equality.

Nineteen sixty-three is not an end, but a beginning. And those who 7 hope that the Negro needed to blow off steam and will now be content, will have a rude awakening if the nation returns to business as usual. There will be neither rest nor tranquility in America until the Negro is granted his citizenship rights. The whirlwinds of revolt will continue to shake the foundations of our nation until the bright day of justice emerges.

But there is something that I must say to my people, who stand on the 8 worn threshold which leads into the palace of justice. In the process of gaining our rightful place, we must not be guilty of wrongful deeds. Let us not seek to satisfy our thirst for freedom by drinking from the cup of bitterness and hatred. We must forever conduct our struggle on the high plain of dignity and discipline. We must not allow our creative protests to degenerate into physical violence. Again and again we must rise to the majestic heights of meeting physical force with soul force. The marvelous new militancy, which has engulfed the Negro community, must not lead us to a distrust of all white people. For many of our white brothers, as evidenced by their presence here today, have come to realize that their destiny is tied up with our destiny. And they have come to realize that their freedom is inextricably bound to our freedom. We cannot walk alone. And as we walk, we must make the pledge that we shall always march ahead. We cannot turn back.

There are those who are asking the devotees of Civil Rights, "When 9
will you be satisfied?" We can never be satisfied as long as the Negro is the
victim of the unspeakable horrors of police brutality; we can never be
satisfied as long as our bodies, heavy with the fatigue of travel, cannot gain
lodging in the motels of the highways and the hotels of the cities; we cannot
be satisfied as long as the Negro's basic mobility is from a smaller ghetto
to a larger one; we can never be satisfied as long as our children are stripped
of their selfhood and robbed of their dignity by signs stating "For Whites
Only"; we cannot be satisfied as long as the Negro in Mississippi cannot
vote and a Negro in New York believes he has nothing for which to vote.
No! No, we are not satisfied, and we will not be satisfied until "justice rolls
down like waters and righteousness like a mighty stream."

I am not unmindful that some of you have come here out of great trials 10
and tribulations. Some of you have come fresh from narrow jail cells. Some
of you have come from areas where your quest for freedom left you
battered by the storms of persecution and staggered by the winds of police
brutality. You have been the veterans of creative suffering. Continue to
work with the faith that unearned suffering is redemptive. Go back to
Mississippi. Go back to Alabama. Go back to South Carolina. Go back to
Georgia. Go back to Louisiana. Go back to the slums and ghettos of our
Northern cities, knowing that somehow this situation can and will be
changed. Let us not wallow in the valley of despair.

I say to you today, my friends, so even though we face the difficulties 11
of today and tomorrow, I still have a dream. It is a dream deeply rooted in
the American dream. I have a dream that one day this nation will rise up
and live out the true meaning of its creed, "We hold these truths to be
self-evident, that all men are created equal." I have a dream that one day
on the red hills of Georgia, sons of former slaves and the sons of former
slave owners will be able to sit down together at the table of brotherhood.
I have a dream that one day even the state of Mississippi, a state sweltering
with the heat of injustice, sweltering with the heat of oppression, will be
transformed into an oasis of freedom and justice. I have a dream that my
four little children will one day live in a nation where they will not be
judged by the color of their skin, but by the content of their character.

I HAVE A DREAM TODAY!   12

I have a dream that one day down in Alabama—with its vicious racists, 13
with its Governor having his lips dripping with the words of interposition
and nullification—one day right there in Alabama, little black boys and
black girls will be able to join hands with little white boys and white girls
as sisters and brothers.

I HAVE A DREAM TODAY!   14

I have a dream that one day every valley shall be exalted, every hill and 15
mountain shall be made low. The rough places will be plain and the crooked
places will be made straight, "and the glory of the Lord shall be revealed,
and all flesh shall see it together."

This is our hope. This is the faith that I go back to the South with. With 16
this faith we will be able to hew out of the mountain of despair, a stone of
hope. With this faith we will be able to transform the jangling discords of
our nation into a beautiful symphony of brotherhood. With this faith we
will be able to work together, to pray together, to struggle together, to go
to jail together, to stand up for freedom together, knowing that we will be
free one day. And this will be the day. This will be the day when all of God's
children will be able to sing with new meaning, "My country 'tis of thee,
sweet land of liberty, of thee I sing. Land where my father died, land of the
pilgrim's pride, from every mountain side, let freedom ring." And if
America is to be a great nation, this must become true.

So let freedom ring from the prodigious hilltops of New Hampshire; 17
let freedom ring from the mighty mountains of New York; let freedom ring
from the heightening Alleghenies of Pennsylvania; let freedom ring from
the snow-capped Rockies of Colorado; let freedom ring from the curva-
ceous slopes of California. But not only that. Let freedom ring from Stone
Mountain of Georgia; let freedom ring from Lookout Mountain of Tennessee; let freedom ring from every hill and mole hill of Mississippi. "From
every mountainside, let freedom ring."

And when this happens, and when we allow freedom to ring, when we 18
let it ring from every village and every hamlet, from every state and every
city, we will be able to speed up that day when all of God's children, black
men and white men, Jews and Gentiles, Protestants and Catholics, will be
able to join hands and sing in the words of the old Negro spiritual: "Free
at last. Free at last. Thank God Almighty, we are free at last."

❀ ❀ ❀

AFTER YOU READ

• *THINK* about the words and ideas that King repeats in his speech. What
word does King use most often? What other words or phrases are repeated
frequently?

• *EXAMINE* King's use of parallel structure to emphasize important points.
For example, in his third paragraph, King repeats four times the introduc-

tory phrase "one hundred years later, the Negro is. . . ." King follows each repeated phrase with a different point, but the drumlike—almost poetic—repetition of the similar statements emphasizes the fact that the life of African-Americans had not changed appreciably between the time of Emancipation and the time in which King was speaking. Reread King's essay carefully, looking for other places where he effectively uses repeated structures to emphasize a point.

• *EXAMINE* also the following poem, in which Gwendolyn Brooks memorializes and describes King:

Martin Luther King Jr.

A man went forth with gifts.

He was a prose poem.
He was a tragic grace.
He was a warm music.

He tried to heal the vivid volcanoes.   5
His ashes are
    reading the world.

His Dream still wishes to anoint
    the barricades of faith and of control.

His word still burns the center of the sun,   10
    above the thousands and the
    hundred thousands.

The word was Justice. It was spoken.

So it shall be spoken.
So it shall be done.   15

What gifts, or positive qualities, does Brooks attribute to King? Are these qualities similar to those you identified as you were reading King's speech? If not, can you find connections between the qualities mentioned in Brooks's poem and King's speech? What specific word does Brooks associate with King? Circle this word (or variations on it) in King's speech.

• *WRITE* your own "prose poem" describing Martin Luther King Jr. Begin by thinking of three words that you associate with King—words that describe him or his ideal. Then use these words as the basis of a series of brief sentences about King.

Unit Five: Critical Thinking and Writing Assignments

❀   ❀   ❀

EXPLORING IDEAS TOGETHER

1. Discuss with your classmates ways in which our society can protect its citizenry and yet continue to open its doors to newcomers. The selections by Victor Landa, Nathan Glazer, Joan Marie Snider, and Hendrik Hertzberg and Henry Louis Gates, Jr., can contribute to your discussion.

2. The selections by Sherman Alexie, Maxine Hong Kingston, and Marta Salinas all focus on school experiences. Discuss the special challenges that face students who are not members of the mainstream culture. What compromises must these students make? What types of problems do they encounter. What could schools do to accommodate these students?

3. Discuss "I Have a Dream" by Martin Luther King Jr. Is his dream dead or has it been realized? What do you think his dream would be if he were alive today?

4. Douglas A. Blackmon and Shelby Steele both discuss the racial phenomenon of "resegregation" and the "politics of difference" in our schools and universities (and, by implication, in our society as a whole). Although these authors both focus on resegregation, their explanations for this phenomenon differ greatly. Compare and contrast their explanations as well as their attitudes.

5. Compare the dreams discussed by Victor Landa and Martin Luther King Jr. Define each of the dreams and then discuss how they are alike and how they are different.

6. Discuss with your classmates the role of language in shaping attitudes, especially prejudice. The reading selections by Aurora Levins Morales, Sherman Alexie, Maxine Hong Kingston, and Chana Schoenberger will help you to frame your discussion and identify issues.

WRITING ESSAYS

1. Write an essay in which you argue that our diversity strengthens or weakens our society. To prepare for this essay, list the problems that result from having a diverse population and the strengths that result

from this diversity. Support your thesis with specific examples from your reading, observations, and experience.

2. Write an essay in which you describe one or more of the problems that have been caused by immigration and then propose a solution (or solutions) for the problem(s). You will find the selections by Victor Landa, Nathan Glazer, and Hendrik Hertzberg and Henry Louis Gates, Jr., useful as sources.

3. Write an essay in which you argue for or against English-only policies in the public schools. You may want to refer to the selections by Aurora Levins Morales, Sherman Alexie, and Maxine Hong Kingston.

4. Write a poem or essay about yourself, celebrating your own diversity—how you are different or unique in some way.

5. Write an essay in which you explore the relationship between language and prejudice. In addition to your own opinions and experiences, you may want to refer to the selections by Sherman Alexie, Chana Schoenberger, and Maxine Hong Kingston.

Self with Environment

Our environment is the area—the atmosphere—that surrounds us. This environment extends from the close surroundings of our homes and workplaces to the distant reaches of the entire world. Although the environment includes human and animal life, the word is often used to refer to physical conditions, especially those in nature.

As shown in the readings in this unit, the environment may be personal or distant, friendly or hostile, beautiful or ugly, awe inspiring or frightening. Moreover, in making decisions about our environment, we humans can think primarily of ourselves and our time, or we can think about future generations and their world. In our own lives, we can make ourselves aware of and responsible for our physical and natural environment, or we can impoverish our lives and the lives of others by ignoring and damaging it.

To prepare to read the selections in this unit more effectively, write about your attitude toward and knowledge of your environment. Use one of the following sets of questions as the basis for a journal entry on this topic:

1. What kind of personal environment do you enjoy? Do you like to be outside in nature or inside in an artificially cooled or heated environment? Do you prefer a rural or an urban environment? What natural surroundings do you prefer? Do you like a climate that is cool or warm? Moist or dry?

2. In what ways do you interact with your natural environment? Do you like to go on scenic drives in the mountains or the country? Do you like to walk, jog, hike, or mountain bike? Or do you prefer, for the most part, to ignore the natural environment?

3. Do you ever worry about the future of the environment? Are you concerned about the depletion of natural resources, endangered species, pollution, waste disposal, the destruction of the rain forest, or global warming? What possible danger to the environment disturbs you the most?

4. How should we balance the welfare of human beings with the protection of the environment? Are genetically engineered crops potentially beneficial or dangerous to society and the environment? Should animals be used for research for human diseases? What is the appropriate balance necessary to protect both the environment and individual property rights?

After you have written your journal entry, meet with a group of your classmates who responded to the same set of questions and discuss your responses. On what points do you agree? On what points do you disagree? Make a list of questions or concerns that you and your classmates have about the environment. As you read the selections in this unit, write your questions and reactions in the margins.

A Sense of Place

GEORGE J. DEMKO

❀

Having served as director of the U.S. Office of the Geographer and edited several scholarly books on social and political geography, George J. Demko is a respected scholar and scientist. In his book Why in the World: Adventures in Geography, *however, Demko shows that his real interest is in* people *and how they are affected by the geographical environments—or the places—in which they live. As one reviewer wrote, Demko shows that geography is "about the human race, animal and plant life, and the planet itself" (*Kirkus Reviews, *March 15, 1992). In this selection from his book, George J. Demko encourages you to take your own adventure in geography by exploring your own personal place.*

BEFORE YOU READ

▪ *THINK* about your own "sense of place." Demko believes that "When we give ourselves to a place, we put it on, the surroundings included, as if it were our very own clothing. We are truly 'in place.'" Have you given yourself to a particular place, or have you moved so much that you do not identify with one single place?

▪ *EXAMINE* the word *geography,* which occurs in the title of Demko's book. This word was created from the Greek *geo,* meaning "earth," and *graph,* meaning "write." Therefore, geography is a written record of the earth, including its changing boundaries, physical formations, oceans, weather, cities, countries, and people.

▪ *EXAMINE* also the third paragraph, in which Demko writes, "Few of us in the West envy the peoples of Third World countries, their hardships and often-hostile environments." When you think of the West, you probably think of the western United States or of cowboys and Indians associated with the Old West. However, Demko uses the word to mean the Western Hemisphere, which includes all of Europe and both North America and South America.

▪ *WRITE* a journal entry about your sense of place, or lack of it.

AS YOU READ

Underline passages that define the term "a sense of place."

Every place on Earth is unique. Each has characteristics distinguishing 1 it from all other places. Geographers usually describe places by their characteristics, both human and physical. Sometimes they group places that are somewhat similar, thereby "creating" regions, such as "the Corn Belt," or the "American South," which is a cultural region that is changing rapidly. Regions can be created from any set of places with something in common.

It is hard to think of any place that is untouched by human contact, 2 even the cruelest, most hostile environments, such as the glaciers of Antarctica and the broiling, waterless Sahara. All places bear the imprimatur of human visits and habitation, or the vestiges of such connections.

Few of us in the West envy the peoples of Third World countries, their 3 hardships and often-hostile environments. But these peoples are usually in touch with their indigenous places in a very real, a very physical sense. Changes in locales, whether in vegetation and agricultural methods or available building materials, come slowly. These peoples rarely leave their corners of the world. Neither are they uprooted by choice or necessity, as are so many Westerners. (The average American moves his residence 18 times in his lifetime.) They remain relatively unaware of the variety of places that lie outside their borders. Billions of people have never heard of the United States.

People often say of their childhood, "We were poor, but we didn't 4 know it." They may not be exaggerating. But what they are really saying, I think, is that they knew who they were, they had the security of belonging somewhere. Why else do so many of us want to go home again? When we give ourselves to a place, we put it on, the surroundings included, as if it were our very own clothing. We are truly "in place."

Too many Westerners, in their getting and spending and laying waste, 5 have lost their understanding of place in any meaningful sense. Oh, we may

remember our hometowns, the house we grew up in, the schools we went
to, where we went to college, where we got inducted into the armed
services, where we proposed marriage and spent our honeymoon. We may
be swept away on a tide of memory if we revisit these scenes, recollecting
beloved faces and good times long ago. But we do not have that sense of
the totality of place that is the essence of geography. We have static images
of places frozen in time.

"One place comprehended," Eudora Welty remarks, "can make us 6
understand other places better. A sense of space gives equilibrium, a sense
of direction."

All places change. They change in themselves and they change relative to 7
other places, and they may cause change in other places. We may imagine
there are certain places magically untouched by time or change. But we
have to turn to literature to find Shangri-la and Brigadoon.

Maps can conjure up images of strange and enchanting landscapes, 8
unintelligible languages, and rainbow-hued peoples. Tweakings of the
imagination are the magic of geography, a magic that stays with some of
us forever, enriching our lives as we travel, observe, work, and dream.

Places and their contents, and the processes that continually change 9
places and their contents, are the wondrous ingredients of geography and
the seductive potion that excites minds and imaginations. All places, even
after they have been found, described, and added to maps, can still thrill
us in their rediscovery and reexploration.

We can search for an understanding of why places are continually 10
changing and try to predict how they will change. There can be no doubt
that the Germany east of the former Berlin Wall and barbed-wire boundary
is a different place in 1999 than it was in 1989. The spatial processes
bombarding the former East Germany—migration, the flow of capital, the
flow of ideas—will transform its towns, villages, and cities, farms, landscapes, population, and industry. They will require new explorations by all
of us to know it again.

I don't believe anyone has written more sensitively about the sense of place 11
and the inevitability of change than the novelist Willa Cather. In *My
Antonia,* two characters reminisce about their childhood in a town in
Nebraska. They recall the burning summers with everything green and
billowy under a brilliant sky and the smell of heavy harvests and the
ferocious winters when the whole country was bare and gray as sheet iron.
"We agreed that no one who had not grown up in a little prairie town could

know anything about it," one of the characters remarks. "It was a kind of freemasonry, we said."

Civilization, as we know it, is the poorer when we lose the sense of place. Every piece of space is unique. Processes over space and time keep them so. A sense of place is central to our very comprehension of the world, "this spherical universe wrapped layer around layer with the cunning of nesting dolls." 12

❀   ❀   ❀

AFTER YOU READ

▪ *THINK* about how place and change are related. Why do changes in physical and social geography come slowly in Third World countries? Why do places change more rapidly in developed countries like the United States?

▪ *EXAMINE* paragraph 7. This paragraph refers to Shangri-la and Brigadoon, both of which are exotic and imaginary places. Brigadoon is the subject of a 1947 musical written by Alan Jay Lerner and Frederick Loewe. The setting of James Hilton's 1930s novel *Lost Horizons*, Shangri-la is an imaginary land of youth and peace in the mountains of Tibet. Shangri-la has become a symbol of an ideal place of refuge.

▪ *EXAMINE* also paragraphs 10 and 11. In paragraph 10, Demko lists Germany as one example of a place that has undergone major changes in "spatial processes." What specific changes have occurred there? What other countries are currently undergoing major changes in physical and cultural geography?

▪ *WRITE* an essay in which you discuss the physical environment, or place, that has given you a sense of identity, or of who you are. This place may be a location from your childhood or a place that has more recently become important to you. Use the following plan to structure your essay:

1. In your introduction, explain the importance of this particular place, or environment, to your life.
2. Describe the place.
3. Explain how and why this place has changed.
4. Discuss how your personal sense of this place has changed.

Sacred Cartography

JAN DeBLIEU

❊

After moving to Hatteras Island on the Outer Banks of North Carolina, Jan DeBlieu recorded her experiences exploring the marshes, beaches, and waters of the island in Hatteras Journal. *In this essay she explains how and why she created a personal map of the island. Continuing her focus on ecology and nature writing, DeBlieu has also written* Meant to be Wild: The Struggle to Save Endangered Animals Through Captive Breeding *and* Wind: How the Flow of Air Has Shaped Life, Myth, and the Land.

BEFORE YOU READ

▪ *THINK* about the place where you live, the place you call home. How would you give directions to your home to a friend who had never been there? If you drew a map to guide your friend, what would you draw?

▪ *EXAMINE* the title "Sacred Cartography." Derived from the French word *carte*, meaning "map," and from a Latin root meaning "write," *cartography* is the art of making maps and charts. In the previous selection, George J. Demko states that "Maps can conjure up images of strange and enchanting landscapes" (page 357), but DeBlieu is interested in mapping places that are personally significant to her. What are your associations with maps? How do you use them?

▪ *WRITE* a journal in which you draw a map of a place that is special, even sacred, to you. Then exchange maps with one of your classmates. As you examine and discuss your maps, explain the symbolic marks that you used to indicate specific sites, roads, and trails.

AS YOU READ

Underline the landmarks that DeBlieu includes in her descriptions of her maps of Hatteras and of her home on Roanoke Island.

I once drew a map to my home on the North Carolina Outer Banks for 1
a friend who wanted to visit. I was new then on Hatteras Island, new to the salt-scorched landscape and interlocking planes of earth, sea, and sky. I felt newly awakened as well, as if I had spent the previous years with my eyes and my thoughts half-lidded. Every day I set aside time to explore unfamiliar terrain and wonder at the great schools of fish, the falcons, and sea birds that migrated past the island with the tug of seasonal currents.

Since there was not much to show on my map—just a single road 2
bee-lining down a skinny arm of sand—I decorated it with my favorite landmarks. On the north end I put three arches covered with a mane of vertical lines; these were the grassy, camel-hump dunes that fronted the ocean. Halfway to my house I drew a tuxedoed heron with hot-pink legs; this marked the marshy flats where I had stumbled on a group of black-necked stilts and the messy stacks of twigs they use as nests. Last I drew a stick-figure crustacean waving a flag on a nearby beach. I went to that beach often to watch ghost crabs skirmishing, shoving each other with round, pearly claws as if locked in mortal combat. Next to the figure I penciled in "Ghost Crab Acres."

I meant the map to be comical, but also to honor places on Hatteras 3
where I had witnessed something important or particularly beautiful. I am not much of an illustrator, and the map looked like something a first-grader might have drawn. My friend called a few days after she received it. "Are these amusement parks or something?" she asked. I realized sheepishly that the connection I felt to each landmark was too personal, too powerful to be explained by a simple drawing.

Now I wish I had kept that map for myself, or made another. I wish I 4
had drawn a new map with equally foolish figures for each of my 15 years on these islands. Put together, they would compose a running chronicle of the places I have held dear here, a mental history of my courtship with the land.

I am more insular these days, too caught up in the eddies of family life 5
to do much. While I'm still curious about the natural forces that play across the islands, I no longer have the same white-hot drive to observe and learn. I live on a pine-sheltered ridge on Roanoke Island, out of sight of the

ever-shifting horizons. The latest atlas of my world would mark hide-
aways in the dunes and marshes, but also the houses of close friends, the
bookstore in nearby Manteo, and the grassy field where I take my young
son to romp. . . .

We map, each of us, mentally and physically, every day of our lives. 6
We map to keep ourselves oriented, and to keep ourselves sane. "The very
word lost in our language means much more than simple geographical
uncertainty," the urban planner Kevin Lynch once wrote. "It carries
overtones of utter disaster. . . . Let the mishap of disorientation occur, and
the sense of anxiety and even terror that accompanies it reveals to us how
closely it is linked to our sense of balance and well-being." And we map
the places we love in much more detail than the places we dislike. "The
sweet sense of home is strongest," Lynch wrote, "when home is not only
familiar but distinctive as well." . . .

. . . And so I draw maps when I should be working, seeking to tap that 7
power. Seeking to keep my bearings in a shifting world. I watch a flock of
grackles invade the pines in my yard, and I dream of Hatteras Island. As
soon as I moved from there, the sharp images I held of that landscape began
to fade. Through the years, many of the places I loved have been taken
from me. The beach I called Ghost Crab Acres was sandbagged to slow
erosion. The salt flats I nicknamed Stilt Field were flooded to attract ducks.
An overgrown road where I went to spy on night herons was sternly marked
with no trespassing signs. Yet I map with those spots still prominent in my
mind.

I map in concentric circles, my Roanoke Island home at the center. I 8
place the barrier islands, eight miles to the east, an inch from my own
bedroom, closer than the grocery store and jail that are just down the road.
When I visit Hatteras, I tip my heart to the camel-hump dunes, the flooded
marsh, the sandy ruts that lead to Pamlico Sound. Driving by, you would
not know they held anything special at all.

❀ ❀ ❀

AFTER YOU READ

- *THINK* about the landmarks that you underlined in DeBlieu's descriptions of her maps. How do they differ from the landmarks you would find
on a state highway map or on most other physical maps? Why was
DeBlieu's first map of Hatteras not very helpful to her visitor? How did

DeBlieu's maps of the Outer Banks area change when she moved from Hatteras to Roanoke? How did some parts of her mental maps of Hatteras remain the same even when the terrain itself changed?

- *EXAMINE* paragraphs 6 and 7, in which DeBlieu asserts that we each produce maps—whether mental or physical—every day of our lives. Do you believe this statement is correct? Do you regularly produce mental maps—mental visions—of certain places? According to DeBlieu, what places do we map in more detail? Why is mapping a place we love, perhaps our home, such a powerful experience?

- *WRITE* an essay in which you create a descriptive map of a place that is special to you. You might choose to focus on your home or a place you have visited. In structuring your essay, you may choose a linear organiza- tion, or you might decide to use a concentric model, beginning with a central place and then fanning out to secondary sites.

The Soul of a City

PYTHIA PEAY

❦

*Raised as a "small-town girl," in Oak Grove, Missouri,
Pythia Peay has been fascinated by cities all her life. Having
"lived in or near five American cities," she ultimately gave
her heart to Washington, D.C. In the following essay,
originally published in* The Utne Reader, *Peay uses six
different approaches to explain the unique character of our
capital.*

BEFORE YOU READ

• *THINK* about the place you consider your hometown. Is this place a large
city, a small town, or something in between? Do you consider yourself a
city person or a country person? That is, in what general environment do
you feel most at home?

• *EXAMINE* the first paragraph of the selection. What are the five cities
that have been most significant in Pythia Peay's life? How has each of these
cities shaped her character? Why has Washington, D.C., become her
favorite city?

• *WRITE* a journal entry in which you identify the most important city or
town in your life and explain briefly why it has been important to you.

AS YOU READ

Underline and number the methods Peay suggests for developing a greater
understanding of your hometown or city.

I was the proverbial small-town girl, raised in Oak Grove, Missouri. While   1
my friends looked forward to marriage and career, I yearned for big
cities. It was a dream that cast my fate and, since leaving home 30 years

ago, I have lived in or near five American cities. As much as any intimate tie to friend or family, each of these places has shaped my character. To Kansas City and St. Louis I owe my ability to stay grounded; to San Francisco, my impulse to seek out life's edge; to Santa Fe, my reliance on imagination.

But it is to Washington, D.C., the metropolis where I finally settled 14   2 years ago, that I owe a part of my soul. Transplanted from the subtle-hued desert of Santa Fe to the highly charged atmosphere of the nation's capital, I felt turmoil within myself and dreamed of going mad. With time, however, the special charm of the place—the poetry of the passing seasons and the spirit of American history that sighs invisibly through the air—opened my heart. "As soon as man has stopped wandering and stood still and looked about him," wrote the American author Eudora Welty, "he found a God in that place." And I did, too.

The idea that cities possess a soul was common among the ancients.   3 The Romans spoke of "genius loci," meaning the special spirit of a place. Indeed, until the 18th-century Enlightenment, when the sacred was severed from the secular in Western culture, cities were often built on foundations of myth and religion, and were thought to be watched over by gods and goddesses, nature spirits, saints, and angels. Belief in a city's mysteriously personal character lives on in the colorful images that arise when we think of certain places: Los Angeles is the city of angels and dreams of stardom. New Orleans is jazz and black magic. Boulder is breathtaking mountain views and spiritual exploration. Boston, founded by austere Puritans, is symbolized by the lowly bean. Even when they're repeated ad nauseam in travel brochures, these images connect us with the underground wells of myth that water a city's soul.

But does anyone today really care about the souls of our cities? Like   4 giant urban gods fallen from their pedestals, they lie dying of neglect, buried beneath asphalt and artless architecture, crushed by the weight of overwhelming social problems, their inhabitants often blind to the fact that their own souls are shaped, for better or worse, within the city's larger reality. We ignore the magic of a place—hidden beyond the real estate deals, the political squabbles, and numbing commutes—at our own peril.

I embarked on my own quest to uncover the soul of Washington, D.C.,   5 as a way to quell my distress after moving here. It dawned on me recently that if I can succeed in a city renowned for its hollow-hearted power-mongering and inside-the-beltway narcissism, then anyone anywhere could do the same. Here are a few methods to help unearth the soul of your hometown, based on my own exploration and conversations with thinkers around the country as well as with Washington historians, artists, mapmak-

ers, poets, and activists. Some may sound deceptively simple, but beware:
As your perceptions are transformed, you may find yourself living in a city
wholly transformed.

Unearth the original landscape.   The essence of a place is closely tied to 6
its landscape. According to Gail Thomas, director of the Dallas Institute
for Humanities and Culture, who studies the connection between soul and
cities, settlers initially were attracted to a site by some remarkable natural
feature—the way the wind blows, or the abundance of good underground
water. Kansas City, for example, was founded on the high bluffs overlook-
ing the Missouri River that explorers Lewis and Clark trumpeted as an
ideal location for a fort. But even though a city's topography may have
been obscured by development, maps and history books may offer a vivid
image of how it once looked.

   I was inspired to learn from a mapmaker how Washington's landscape 7
resembled the very principle of unity out of diversity that is the city's—and
the nation's—foundation. It is a geographical crossroads where the flora
and fauna of the North and the South intermingle, maples growing
alongside magnolias. Most surprising to me was learning that Washington,
so often described as a swamp, is predominantly a city of river terraces and
hills. Archetypal psychologist James Hillman, who has thought deeply
about the ties between soul and city for more than two decades, sees
significance in the way the swamp image has found its way into Washington's cultural imagination. He calls it a psychologically apt metaphor that
captures the way our politicians' ideals inevitably become bogged down by
less noble realities.

Steep yourself in history.   Thomas Moore, author of *The Care of the Soul,* 8
writes that reflecting on the past is an important part of retrieving your
soul. Just as individuals in therapy or on a spiritual search discern new
patterns of meaning by revisiting what they've experienced, so, too, does
a city's history reveal something of its intrinsic nature.

   To know that the poet Wait Whitman once walked the streets of 9
Capitol Hill after tending wounded Civil War soldiers housed in the Patent
Office Building, and that the banks of the Anacostia River were lined for
3,000 years with settlements of the Nacotchtank Indians, opened my heart
to the ghosts of the past still haunting its modern spaces.

Stoke your imagination.   In some way, great cities are created by the artists 10
who render them immortal as much as by the planners, construction
workers, and business leaders who build them. Think of James Joyce's

Dublin, impressionist painter Camille Pissarro's Paris, or even Bruce Springsteen's Asbury Park. Washington came magically alive when I saw it through the eyes of artist Renee Butler, who showed me slides of the city's trees printed on large screens to express the way their lacy-leafed branches evoke the sacred. Delving into the works of local poets, fiction writers, columnists, memoirists, painters, photographers, folk artists, and songwriters deepens how we experience our home, imbuing commonplace reality with awareness, appreciation, and perhaps wonder.

Find the heart of town.   Ask your friends this question: Where do you go   11
to find the true heart of the city? In Seattle, many would say Pike's Place Market. In Chicago, Wrigley Field. In Madison, the lakeside beer garden at the University of Wisconsin student union. Most of the people I interviewed in Washington, D.C., located the city's soul not in the famous monuments and museums but in neighborhood streets, cafés, bookstores. John Johnson, founder of Process Work D.C.—a multicultural group that meets to discuss race and class issues—took me on a tour of his favorite spots: a tucked-away Cheers-style café near Capitol Hill that is frequented by activists, a baseball field where Hispanic families gather on Sundays for games and picnics. Others cited Kramer's Books and Afterwords, the popular Dupont Circle hangout, or ethnic restaurants with atmosphere and inexpensive menus. Nearly everyone finds at least a slice of the city's soul in Washington's surprising wealth of parks and natural areas. I expect you'd find the same in San Francisco, where many people connect with their city's soul in Golden Gate Park or on the winding trails of Mount Tamalpais, the gentle mountain rising up out of the ocean mists north of the Golden Gate Bridge.

Discover the civic wound that needs healing.   All cities have problems,   12
though they are often unacknowledged. While it's usually difficult and politically risky to draw attention to shortcomings, especially in a place that prides itself on being a city that "works," ignoring them perpetuates a state of soullessness. In Santa Fe, for example, conflicts arise between the economic bonanza of tourism and its rich historic, Hispanic character. The influx of wealthy Anglos purchasing vacation homes has come at the expense of indigenous residents—the Native Americans and Spanish—who can no longer afford to live where their grandparents and great grandparents lived.

Race, of course, is an issue affecting most American cities. Almost every   13
person I've talked with in Washington mourns the racial divide between

blacks and whites; some people describe it as a city of "two souls." To drive past abandoned buildings with the U.S. Capitol looming in the background, to see how dramatically the pollution-choked Anacostia River contrasts with the cleaner, suburban Potomac River, is to witness a visible tear in the city's soul.

Volunteering at a shelter for the homeless, throwing yourself into a   14 political reform movement, getting to know down-and-out neighborhoods, speaking out about community ills all can help you find the soul of your hometown, as well as contribute to healing it.

Find where people come together.   The polis, wrote Hannah Arendt,   15 arises out of people acting and speaking together in a "sharing of words and deeds." Thus the living force of a city's soul is most palpable in those large physical spaces—the commons—where the people of a city come together to celebrate, to protest, or simply to enjoy a Sunday afternoon. As a veteran of the anti-war movement, I fondly recall the boisterous rallies held in Kansas City's Volker Park and San Francisco's Golden Gate Park. The first place I ever felt the true beat of Washington, D.C., was at the Georgetown Flea Market, an open-air bazaar where people from every corner of the city come each Sunday to barter with vendors for produce and craftwork.

Washington, of course, is the city where the rest of the country comes   16 to make its voice heard. The open rectangle of green grass on the Mall is one of the most powerful outdoor public spaces in the modern world. It's where Martin Luther King gave his "I Have a Dream" speech and the destination for protesters about abortion, gun control, foreign policy, and countless other causes. Yet I've also enjoyed spring days strolling along the Mall while my kids clamor to pet someone's dog.

Take note of outdoor spaces where people gather to share in the   17 ordinariness of life and, in being together, keep city life vibrant. More than the physical landscape or architectural design of a city, it is people, individually and collectively, who are the true force that enlivens and empowers a place.

Ironically, commitment to saving the souls of our cities might lead to   18 greater protection of wilderness. As James Hillman has frequently pointed out, Americans tend to see their cities as the place where the innocent become corrupted and where soul is lost, rather than found. He has argued passionately on behalf of reversing this trend, thus protecting nature from too much human contact and reanimating our cities from within. For to seek soul only in nature, or within ourselves, is to miss the wondrous natural creation that is a city—a convergence of community, commerce, street life, history, nature, geography, politics, art, and people that offers a perpetually renewing source of life.

❀   ❀   ❀

AFTER YOU READ

• *THINK* about some of the cities that Peay mentions in her article: Kansas City, St. Louis, San Francisco, Santa Fe, Los Angeles, New Orleans, Boulder, Boston, Chicago, and, of course, Washington, D.C. If you have visited any of these cities, do you agree with Peay that this city has a special character or "soul"? What is another city you have visited literally or vicariously (through the media and books) that has a unique character?

• *EXAMINE* the six methods for understanding a city or hometown that you underlined in Peay's essay. Discuss these techniques with your classmates, applying them to the city or town in which your college or university is located. You might divide into six small discussion groups, with each group focusing on one technique.

• *WRITE* an essay in which you discuss the character of a city or town of your choice—perhaps your hometown, perhaps the city or town in which you are attending school. Use one or more of Peay's suggestions for finding the character of a town to help you develop your essay. For example, you could write an essay discussing the landscape or the history of the town. You could describe some of the activities found at "the heart of the town." Or you could focus on a civic wound, identifying the causes and effects of the wound and making suggestions for healing it.

Weather Reports

KATHLEEN NORRIS

❀

In the mid-1970s, poet Kathleen Norris returned to a small town on the border between North and South Dakota to live in a house built by her grandparents. Here she explored not only the isolated, elemental landscape of the region but also the values, customs, and faith of this land from which her family had come. The result was a book she entitled Dakota: A Spiritual Geography. *Interspersed between the chapters of the book are short pieces called "Weather Reports." Read in sequence, these reports form a poetic narrative of the year she spent in this small North Dakota town.*

BEFORE YOU READ

▪ *THINK* about the information we get from weather reports. What do weather reports tell us about a region and the people who inhabit it?

▪ *EXAMINE* the dates of these reports. At what intervals were they written, and what period of time do they span?

▪ *WRITE* in your journal an objective description of the weather you are currently experiencing.

AS YOU READ

Notice that Norris provides a strong sense of time as well as place in her weather reports. Underline details that suggest the changing of the seasons during this year in her life.

WEATHER REPORT: JANUARY 17

Encircled. The sea that stretched out before me in Maili, on the Waianae   1
coast of Oahu, as this month began, has been transformed into the
plains of North Dakota. I am riding a Greyhound bus to the small town
where I'll be teaching writing to schoolchildren for the next two weeks.
Snow in the fields has crusted over; wind-lines, restless as waves, flash like
the ocean in sunlight.

"Never turn your back on the sea," is Hawaii's wisdom. "Or the sky,"   2
we Plains folk might add. Like sailors, we learn to read cloud banks coming
from the west. We watch for sundogs and count rings around the moon.

I have turned with the circle: away from gentle air and birdsong, the   3
Waianae Range unfolding like a fan in mist, toward a wind gritty with spent
soil burning my tongue, a freezing rain that stings my hands and face.

In the schoolyard, a snow angel's wings are torn, caught in grass   4
exposed by the sudden thaw. In the stuffy classroom, a little girl, restless
and distracted, probably a bad student, becomes White Buffalo Calf
Woman, speaking of a world in which all people are warm in winter and
have enough to eat.

"They sing, 'the rain is new,'" she writes, "'the rain is always new.'"   5

WEATHER REPORT: FEBRUARY 10

I walk downtown, wearing a good many of the clothes I own, keeping my   6
head down and breathing through several thicknesses of a wool scarf. A
day so cold it hurts to breathe; dry enough to freeze spit. Kids crack it on
the sidewalk.

Walking with care, snow barely covering the patches of ice, I begin to   7
recall a canticle or a psalm—I can't remember which—and my body keeps
time:

> Cold and chill, bless the Lord
> Dew and rain, bless the Lord
> Frost and chill, bless the Lord
> Ice and snow, bless the Lord
> Nights and days, bless the Lord
> Light and darkness, bless the Lord.

Another line comes to mind: "at the breath of God's mouth the waters   8
flow." Spring seems far off, impossible, but it is coming. Already there is

dusk instead of darkness at five in the afternoon; already hope is stirring at the edges of the day.

WEATHER REPORT: MARCH 25

Mud and new grass push up through melting snow. Lilacs in bud by my 9 front door, bent low by last week's ice storm, begin to rise again in today's cold rain. Thin clouds scatter in a loud wind.

Suddenly, fir trees seem like tired old women stooped under winter 10 coats. I want to be light, to cast off impediments, and push like a tulip through a muddy smear of snow. I want to take the rain to heart, let it move like possibility, the idea of change.

WEATHER REPORT: JUNE 30

I get started early, before six. It promises to be a good laundry day: a steady 11 wind but not too strong. I come by my love of laundry honestly: my earliest memory is of my mother pulling clothes in from the sky on a line that ran out our apartment window in Washington, D.C.

Hanging up wet clothes while it is still cool, I think of her. Though 12 she's lived in Honolulu for more than thirty years, she's a plainswoman at heart; her backyard clothesline is a dead giveaway. The challenge of drying clothes in a tropical valley agrees with her; mountain rains sweep down at least once a day, and she must be vigilant.

Here no rain is likely, unless, as so often happens, our most beautiful 13 summer days turn dark and violent in late afternoon, thunderstorms pelting us with rain or hail. I think of a friend who was dying, who had saved up all her laundry for my visit. "I can't trust my husband with it," she whispered conspiratorially. "Men don't understand that clothes must be hung on a line."

She was right. Hanging up wet clothes gives me time alone under the 14 sky to think, to grieve, and gathering the clean clothes in, smelling the sunlight on them, is victory.

WEATHER REPORT: JULY 3

Rains came late in June and haying was delayed. But today it was 65 degrees 15 by six A.M., and that means a hot day, 100 degrees or more; it means haying can't wait.

It's one of the miracles of nature that this empty-looking land can be 16
of such great use, that cattle can convert its grasses to milk and meat.

I know that the brome and wheatgrass will lose its value as feed if it 17
isn't hayed soon, but ever since I moved to Dakota I've felt a kind of grief
at haying time. I hate to see the high grass fall.

Alfalfa and clover still stand tall by the road, smelling sweet and clean, 18
like a milkfed infant's breath. In a few days these vigorous plants will be
coffin-size heaps in the ditch.

WEATHER REPORT: OCTOBER 2

"When my third snail died," the little girl writes, sitting halfway in, halfway 19
out of her desk, one leg swinging in air, "I said, 'I'm through with snails.'"
She sits up to let me pass down the aisle, the visiting poet working with the
third grade: in this dying school, this dying town, we are writing about our
lives. I'm hungry, looking forward to the lefse I bought for lunch at the
Norwegian Food Festival sponsored by the Senior Citizen Center, one of
the few busy places on Main Street. That and the post office, the café, the
grocery. The other buildings are empty.

The teacher's writing too. Yesterday she told me that when I asked the 20
kids to make silence and the room was suddenly quiet, she thought of her
mother. "She's been dead for years," she said, adding almost apologetically,
"I don't know why I thought of her. But then I just had to write." She told
me about the smells, how this time of year the lingering scent of pickling
spices in the house would gradually give way to cinnamon, peppermint,
cloves, the smells of Christmas baking. "It was the candy I loved most,"
she wrote, "nut fudge, caramels, divinity."

The sunsets here have been extraordinary, blazing up like distant fire 21
in the window of the old boarding house where the school has put me.
Last night I was reading when the light changed: I looked up and gasped
at the intensity of color, a slash of gold and scarlet on the long scribble of
horizon.

I was reading one of the old ones who said, "One who keeps death 22
before his eyes conquers despair." The little girl calls me, holding up her
paper for me to read:

When my third snail died, I said,
"I'm through with snails."
But I didn't mean it.

WEATHER REPORT: NOVEMBER 2

Wind prowled the monastery grounds, giving night silence an increased air   23
of watchfulness. Glass shook in the window frames and sleep was slow in
coming.

   We had prayed at vespers for the deceased members of the community,   24
from Isidore who died in 1898 to Michael who died last year. We sang of
"the narrow stream of death," as if the distance were not so far. I woke to
find the ground dusted with snow, the Killdeer Mountains looming white
on the horizon, a distance of forty-five miles.

   All Souls', blustery and chill. I hear them before I see them, six lines   25
scribbling across the white sky. I look up at the tiny crosses beating above
me. The pain is new each year, and I'm surprised, even though I expect it:
the sudden cold, the geese passing over.

❀   ❀   ❀

AFTER YOU READ

• *THINK* about how the author changed during the year she describes in
these reports. What did she learn from her experiences?

• *EXAMINE* the events recorded in the final weather report (November 2).
Next describe the tone of this report. Finally identify the weather images
the author includes in this report. How do these images reinforce the tone?

• *WRITE* a weather report similar to those included in this reading selection. Describe current weather conditions but include subjective as well as
objective details. In your report use vivid images that appeal to your
reader's sense of touch and hearing as well as sight. Begin or end your
report with an account of a single event that is related in some way to the
weather conditions you describe.

Weather Collage

BARRY HANNAH, JANE SMILEY,
and
E. ANNIE PROULX

❀

This series of readings combines George J. Demko's focus on a sense of place with Kathleen Norris's interest in the weather. Here, three acclaimed fiction writers focus on memorable weather events in three different regions of the country. Barry Hannah, whose novels include Geronimo Rex *and* High Lonesome, *describes an ice storm that shocks the Deep South. Jane Smiley, winner of the Pulitzer Prize and a National Book Critics Circle Award for* A Thousand Acres *and the author of* Moo *and* Horse Heaven, *remembers her fear of tornadoes when she was growing up in the Midwest. And E. Annie Proulx, winner of the Pulitzer Prize for* The Shipping News *and author of* Postcards *and* Accordion Crimes, *paints a New England sky with lightning flashes.*

BEFORE YOU READ

▪ *THINK* about the severe weather that is most likely to occur in your geographical area. Are you most concerned about tornadoes, hurricanes, floods, earthquakes, ice storms, or droughts? What do you do to protect yourself from this type of weather?

▪ *EXAMINE* the title "Weather Collage." A *collage* is a work of art composed of various images that form a unified whole in spite of their differences. Thus, this trio of readings describes different personal experiences that are tied together by the theme of the weather.

▪ *EXAMINE* also the titles of each of the short essays that make up this collage of readings. Which weather phenomenon would frighten you the most and why? Which phenomenon would result, in your opinion, in the most spectacular images?

- *WRITE* a journal entry about one of your own experiences with severe weather.

AS YOU READ

Identify and underline the reactions that each writer has to the weather he or she is describing.

The Ice Storm

BARRY HANNAH

❀

Here in Oxford, Mississippi, most of the leaves are fallen and this place 1
looks bombed all over again. Last February the ice storm of the century passed through the Arkansas delta into north Mississippi and lower Tennessee up to Nashville. Eleven at night, I was out in the front yard waiting for it, led by a special alarm, even horror, in the voice of the television weathercaster. Like a Jeremiah just miles ahead of the storm and pointing backward down the road, raving. The edge of the storm came on in feather-light little BB's, then began to drive and pile. The glass on the west of the house went pecking as if attacked by a gale of birds. Under the streetlights the swirls of white-silver turned almost opaque. It was a determined blizzard. A southerner doesn't see such driving ice more than twice in a lifetime. But at one I went to bed pleasantly aroused, rich as a caveman with the weather outside.

When my wife and I awoke, civilization as we knew it had mainly shut 2
down. Luckily we had gas heaters. All electricity and water were gone; no telephone, all local radio stations kaput. Outside, the trees were draped sculptures in white, but in their quietness, a whole new storm of ghouls.

I am an addict of great weathers. Had I been in Hurricane Camille, 3
which struck the Mississippi coast in 1969, I would be dead. I would have
been the leading fool in some motel party hoisting a silver mug, crying
havoc, hailing and adoring the wind until blasted off like a kite. Twelve
years ago I decided I wanted Oxford for my home when I was having coffee
at the Hoka, a café in a warehouse with a tin roof. A violent rainstorm came
up. The sound of it thrashing on the tin moved something deep within me,
a memory of another storm, my pals and me in a barn sleeping on hay when
I was a boy: That tin roof was the margin against everything dangerous.

But at noon when limbs and then whole trees began falling around me, 4
nothing was nice. The picturesque had turned into terror. Whatever we
were, whatever good and rotten had transpired in this, our little jewel of
a city, these trees had witnessed it. Now they were splitting apart and falling
wholesale with mournful cracks and awful thuds. They were coming in the
window glass like dead uncles. Next door, an 80-foot tree fell on a neighbor
woman's Mercedes, the fetish of her life. She came out into the driveway
wailing as I've never heard a white person wail. But you see a whole tree
go over like that, and your grip on the universe goes. A small mob of
slackers came down the block and stood around the big tree over the
Mercedes. They grinned, sort of worshiping the event. But the woods
running down a hill to the east went into an exploding mutual collapse too
much like the end of the world, and everyone fled back inside.

All of these old trees were like family in the act of dying, their agony 5
was more terrible than the storm itself. We had been confident, even
arrogant, with them around us, I realized. They'd been comforting brothers
and sisters. Now the town was suddenly half as tall.

In the next weeks, trucks and electricians from four states poured into 6
town. You would drive around very stupidly and like a zombie point to
another great oak down, another smashed roof: Look at that, Sue. A vast
pile of debris burned like the end of a war out on the west edge of town.

You hear a fatuous volume about growing, nurturing, and blossoming 7
as a person nowadays. But great subtractions must be granted, too. There
is not always more of us, growing, flapping leaves around like idiot vines.

Here under a rare storm of ice we got our comeuppance. The leaves 8
are gone, and we see it all over again. Lessness rules. But in the South we've
been used to that for quite a while.

❀   ❀   ❀

Tornadoes

JANE SMILEY

❦

By the time I was 25 and living in Iowa City, my fear of tornadoes was 1
a significant fact of my inner life. I had spent my childhood in the heart
of tornado country reading every stormy sky for the signs—greenness, hail,
the anvil cloud, the black finger dropping down to make its mark upon the
earth. When it came, I knew, it would drive straws into the trunks of trees,
carry tractors five or ten miles, twirl us up and spray us out over the
landscape, sucking the breath from our bodies and tearing us limb from
limb.

We lived on a hill east of Iowa City. A half-mile away, down a long, 2
gentle slope of corn and bean fields, freight trains ran between Iowa City
and Cedar Rapids. One of them passed every morning about two o'clock.
I was always grateful to hear it, and I always thought of the tornado cutting
it in two, how the sound would be a half-mile's warning.

The night the tornado finally came, I was alone, and I knew what I 3
wanted to save. My banjo. My recorders. My typewriter. The Great Dane
and the cats. My boyfriend's 12-string Gibson. That was all. No clothes.
No dishes. No major appliances. As I ran from my bedroom, the wind
howled louder and louder. Air pressure seemed to change inside the house,
swelling the walls outward, pressing my skill inward. That was enough
evidence for me.

Safe in the basement, I uncased the banjo and played a few songs. It 4
was getting close to two, so I stopped and listened for the train, though all
sounds were lost in the sounds of the house rattling and groaning in the
wind. I sang louder. When the moment came that the house above me
would be ripped from its foundations and smashed into the next township,
I'd watch it go with equanimity (at least a little bit). The wind beat against
the basement windowpanes.

Outside my boyfriend pulled up in his old pickup, finished with his 5
night's work tending bar. He's fond of the wind. He sat on the running
board of the truck and lit a cigarette. He took a few drags, relaxed, heard

the train go by. He glanced at the house and wondered why the basement light was on.

The tornado, of course, never came. It was the conventional wisdom 6 in Iowa City that tornadoes simply never struck there.

Will it ever come? It might. I would save the children and the dogs and 7 the backup disk of whatever novel I am working on. My husband has too many guitars to carry in a single panicked load into the basement. And what if I were at the stable, my husband on the golf course, the 16-year-old at high school, the 12-year-old at grammar school, and the two-year-old at day care? How would I save us all then?

Perhaps because we're all too much to save now, or perhaps simply 8 because of age, I'm no longer convinced that big weather has my name on it. Sometime during my thirties, the dread that governed my youth slipped away, took its place among all the other dreads. My husband's love of wind has reassured me, and I've produced a daughter whose favorite sleeping arrangements include a thunderstorm outside and a fan blowing on her face. And we are always forewarned. We subscribe to the Weather Channel and have three weather radios. But actually I miss the drama.

❁   ❁   ❁

Lightning

E. ANNIE PROULX

❁

What a fiery summer, no rain, the well gone dry. I was trying to finish 1 the house. Spent the day on a ladder sloshing stain on clapboards that radiated heat like a bed of coals, the breathless air so thick I could scratch it with my fingernails.

"Lightning" by E. Annie Proulx, *Outside Magazine*. March 1995. Reprinted by permission of Darhansoff, Verrill, Feldman Literary Agents, NY.

Around five I got off the ladder, fixed a mason jar full of ice and gin, 2
and sat on the back steps. The slack sky was bruised up. I could hear rumbles
like a truck going over a plank bridge. By the last tilt of the mason jar the
sky was in mood indigo. To the north, west, and south, nothing but
lightning jelly and thunder roll and a strange cloud, underside studded with
immense dusky udders. The west leaned forward, shot out snake tongues.

When the first rain belted down, when the wind hit, I went inside to 3
watch the storm through the open door. The rain clicked into pea-size hail,
a tympani section on metal roof, truck, wheelbarrow, flagstones. Storm in,
power out.

A glaring blue flash and the ionized air exploded in a stunning 4
thunderclap. Another and another. I slammed the door. Lightning erupted
in a shuttering, wild, demented carnival of raw electricity, streamers and
leaders, streaks, forks, bolts, and arcs, until the atmosphere itself burned
and the hail pearls glowed. Window ghastly white as though dashed with
a bucket of milk. There was the roar of cloudburst, windburst, and a tearing
sound as a tree fell against the side of the house. Scientists say lightning
strikes the earth a hundred times a second: if that is so, the rest of the world
was safe for a few hours.

I recognize the major flaw in my house—huge windows in every wall. 5
No room, no corner, no stairwell escaped the white sizzle of lightning
peaking at 200,000 amps per bolt just beyond the glass. If we get out of
this, I said to the mason jar, if the house don't blow down or blow up, some
of these naked windows are gone, hello walls.

And that's why they went. What you don't see can't hurt you.   6

❀   ❀   ❀

AFTER YOU READ

▪ *THINK* about the power of nature as shown in these three experiences.
How does each writer show this power? How does each writer feel in
comparison to the power of the ice, the tornadic wind, and the lightning?

▪ *EXAMINE* these three essays for effective sensory images—descriptions
that appeal to one of the five senses. What are two images that Hannah
uses to show how the ice looks and sounds? What are two images that
Smiley employs to explain how the wind storm felt and sounded? What
are two images that Proulx uses to portray the sights and sounds of the
lightning storm?

▪ *WRITE* an evaluation of the essay you believe is the most effective. Use the following questions to help you write your evaluation:

1. What is the main idea of this essay?
2. What is the mood created by the essay—terror, awe, excitement, or what? How is this mood created?
3. What are the most effective descriptive passages in the essay?

Overall, why do you believe this essay is so effective in describing an experience of severe weather? Include specific quotations from the essay in the body of your paper to support your opinion. Or *WRITE* an essay in which you describe more fully the experience with severe weather that you wrote about in your journal entry. In your essay, be sure to use—as these writers do—vivid imagery and specific details to show the sights, sounds, and feelings that you experienced.

The End of Nature

BILL McKIBBEN

❀

This reading by Bill McKibben and the one by Charles Krauthammer that follows provide parallel explorations of the relationship between humanity and the environment. A dedicated hiker and camper, Bill McKibben has been a staff writer and editor for The New Yorker *and has published several books on environmental issues. In his best-known work,* The End of Nature, *McKibben writes about environmental dangers, such as ozone depletion and global warming, and warns about their potentially devastating effects on the planet. In the following selection, which is the title essay from this book, McKibben alludes clearly to these environmental problems. Furthermore, McKibben warns not only that weather patterns discussed in the previous selections may be changed but also that nature as we know it may be destroyed if humanity does not drastically alter its treatment of the environment.*

BEFORE YOU READ

▪ *THINK* about the two environmental dangers identified in the introduction: ozone depletion and global warming. The ozone is a protective layer in the atmosphere that shields the Earth from the most harmful rays of the sun. Global warming is a gradual increase in the temperature of the Earth caused by, among other things, an increase in carbon dioxide in the atmosphere resulting from fossil fuels. Global warming could result not only in disastrous changes in climate but also in melting glaciers and devastating floods.

▪ *EXAMINE* the image of the chain saw in the first paragraph. McKibben uses the chain saw and its snarling sound as a symbol of how human actions destroy the peace and harmony of nature.

▪ *WRITE* a journal entry in which you speculate about "the end of nature." In your opinion, what could possibly "end" nature? Describe the results that you imagine.

AS YOU READ

Underline references McKibben makes to the ways people have endangered nature or destroyed the experience of nature for others.

Almost every day, I hike up the hill out my back door. Within a hundred yards the woods swallows me up, and there is nothing to remind me of human society—no trash, no stumps, no fence, not even a real path. Looking out from the high places, you can't see road or house; it is a world apart from man. But once in a while someone will be cutting wood farther down the valley, and the snarl of a chain saw will fill the woods. It is harder on those days to get caught up in the timeless meaning of the forest, for man is nearby. The sound of the chain saw doesn't blot out all the noises of the forest or drive the animals away, but it does drive away the feeling that you are in another, separate, timeless, wild sphere.

Now that we have changed the most basic forces around us, the noise of that chain saw will always be in the woods. We have changed the atmosphere, and that will change the weather. The temperature and rainfall are no longer to be entirely the work of some separate, uncivilizable force, but instead in part a product of our habits, our economies, our ways of life. Even in the most remote wilderness, where the strictest laws forbid the felling of a single tree, the sound of that saw will be clear, and a walk in the woods will be changed—tainted—by its whine. The world outdoors will mean much the same thing as the world indoors, the hill the same thing as the house.

An idea, a relationship, can go extinct, just like an animal or a plant. The idea in this case is "nature," the separate and wild province, the world apart from man to which he adapted, under whose rules he was born and died. In the past, we spoiled and polluted parts of that nature, inflicted environmental "damage." But that was like stabbing a man with toothpicks: though it hurt, annoyed, degraded, it did not touch vital organs, block the path of the lymph or blood. We never thought that we had wrecked nature. Deep down, we never really thought we could: it was too big and too old; its forces—the wind, the rain, the sun—were too strong, too elemental.

But, quite by accident, it turned out that the carbon dioxide and other ₄ gases we were producing in our pursuit of a better life—in pursuit of warm houses and eternal economic growth and of agriculture so productive it would free most of us from farming—*could* alter the power of the sun, could increase its heat. And that increase *could* change the patterns of moisture and dryness, breed storms in new places, breed deserts. Those things may or may not have yet begun to happen, but it is too late to altogether prevent them from happening. We have produced the carbon dioxide—we are ending nature.

We have not ended rainfall or sunlight; in fact, rainfall and sunlight ₅ may become more important forces in our lives. It is too early to tell exactly how much harder the wind will blow, how much hotter the sun will shine. That is for the future. But the *meaning* of the wind, the sun, the rain—of nature—has already changed. Yes, the wind still blows—but no longer from some other sphere, some inhuman place.

In the summer, my wife and I bike down to the lake nearly every ₆ afternoon for a swim. It is a dogleg Adirondack lake, with three beaver lodges, a blue heron, some otter, a family of mergansers, the occasional loon. A few summer houses cluster at one end, but mostly it is surrounded by wild state land. During the week we swim across and back, a trip of maybe forty minutes—plenty of time to forget everything but the feel of the water around your body and the rippling, muscular joy of a hard kick and the pull of your arms.

But on the weekends, more and more often, someone will bring a boat ₇ out for waterskiing, and make pass after pass up and down the lake. And then the whole experience changes, changes entirely. Instead of being able to forget everything but yourself, and even yourself except for the muscles and the skin, you must be alert, looking up every dozen strokes to see where the boat is, thinking about what you will do if it comes near. It is not so much the danger—few swimmers, I imagine, ever die by Evinrude. It's not even so much the blue smoke that hangs low over the water. It's that the motorboat gets in your mind. You're forced to think, not feel—to think of human society and of people. The lake is utterly different on these days, just as the planet is utterly different now.

❀   ❀   ❀

AFTER YOU READ

- *THINK* about the problem of pollution, which McKibben discusses in paragraph 3. What image does he use to describe the "environmental 'damage'" of various types of pollution? How serious a problem does he believe pollution to be?

- *EXAMINE* paragraphs 2 and 4, in which McKibben discusses how certain environmental changes affect weather patterns. For example, the statement in paragraph 2 that "We have changed the atmosphere, and that will change the weather" probably refers to the depletion of the ozone layer. In paragraph 4, McKibben mentions not only carbon dioxide and other gases that damage the ozone layer but also the possibility of increased temperatures that could cause global warming.

- *EXAMINE* also the statement that "an idea, a relationship, can go extinct, just like an animal or a plant" (paragraph 3). How does McKibben develop this statement in paragraphs 5 and 6?

- *WRITE* an essay explaining how the planet is "utterly different now" than it was twenty, fifteen, ten, or even five years ago. What are two or three specific changes that you have observed? What do you think caused these changes?

Saving Nature, But Only for Man

CHARLES KRAUTHAMMER

❀

A conservative columnist and commentator, Charles Krauthammer won the Pulitzer Prize for journalism in 1991 for his commentary in the Washington Post. *Currently a regular contributor to* Time, *Krauthammer is also the author of* Cutting Edges: Making Sense of the Eighties. *In the following essay from* Time, *he continues the debate about the rights and responsibilities of humanity in relationship to the environment.*

BEFORE YOU READ

▪ *THINK* again about the relationship between humanity and the environment that McKibben discusses in the previous reading. In your opinion, what responsibilities do human beings have to the environment? What rights do human beings have regarding the environment?

▪ *EXAMINE* the word *anthropocentric,* which occurs in paragraph 5. Derived from the Greek roots *anthropo-,* meaning "man," and *centric,* meaning "center," the word literally means "man centered," or interpreting the world in terms of human experiences and values.

▪ *WRITE* a journal response to Krauthammer's title "Saving Nature, But Only for Man." In your opinion, why should nature by saved? Should it be saved primarily for humanity's sake or for its own sake?

AS YOU READ

Look for the paragraphs in which Krauthammer defines "a sane environmentalism." Put a check mark beside each of these paragraphs.

© 1991 Time Inc. Reprinted by permission.

Environmental sensitivity is now as required an attitude in polite society 1
as is, say, belief in democracy or aversion to polyester. But now that
everyone from Ted Turner to George Bush, Dow to Exxon has professed
love for Mother Earth, how are we to choose among the dozens of
conflicting proposals, restrictions, projects, regulations and laws advanced
in the name of the environment? Clearly not everything with an environmental claim is worth doing. How to choose?

There is a simple way. First, distinguish between environmental luxu- 2
ries and environmental necessities. Luxuries are those things it would be
nice to have if costless. Necessities are those things we must have regardless.
Then apply a rule. Call it the fundamental axiom of sane environmentalism: Combatting ecological change that directly threatens the health and
safety of people is an environmental necessity. All else is luxury.

For example: preserving the atmosphere—stopping ozone depletion 3
and the greenhouse effect—is an environmental necessity. In April scientists
reported that ozone damage is far worse than previously thought. Ozone
depletion not only causes skin cancer and eye cataracts, it also destroys
plankton, the beginning of the food chain atop which we humans sit.

The reality of the greenhouse effect is more speculative, though its 4
possible consequences are far deadlier: melting ice caps, flooded coastlines,
disrupted climate, parched plains and, ultimately, empty breadbaskets. The
American Midwest feeds the world. Are we prepared to see Iowa acquire
New Mexico's desert climate? And Siberia acquire Iowa's?

Ozone depletion and the greenhouse effect are human disasters. They 5
happen to occur in the environment. But they are urgent because they
directly threaten man. A sane environmentalism, the only kind of environmentalism that will win universal public support, begins by unashamedly
declaring that nature is here to serve man. A sane environmentalism is
entirely anthropocentric: it enjoins man to preserve nature, but on the
grounds of self-preservation.

A sane environmentalism does not sentimentalize the earth. It does not 6
ask people to sacrifice in the name of other creatures. After all, it is hard
enough to ask people to sacrifice in the name of other humans. (Think of
the chronic public resistance to foreign aid and welfare.) Ask hardworking
voters to sacrifice in the name of the snail darter, and, if they are feeling
polite, they will give you a shrug.

Of course, this anthropocentrism runs against the grain of a contem- 7
porary environmentalism that indulges in earth worship to the point of
idolatry. One scientific theory—Gaia theory—actually claims that Earth is
a living organism. This kind of environmentalism likes to consider itself
spiritual. It is nothing more than sentimental. It takes, for example, a highly

selective view of the benignity of nature. My nature worship stops with the April twister that came through Kansas or the May cyclone that killed more than 125,000 Bengalis and left 10 million (!) homeless.

A nonsentimental environmentalism is one founded on Protagoras' maxim that "Man is the measure of all things." Such a principle helps us through the thicket of environmental argument. Take the current debate raging over oil drilling in a corner of the Alaska National Wildlife Refuge. Environmentalists, mobilizing against a bill working its way through the U.S. Congress to permit such exploration, argue that Americans should be conserving energy instead of drilling for it. This is a false either/or proposition. The U.S. does need a sizable energy tax to reduce consumption. But it needs more production too. Government estimates indicate a nearly fifty-fifty chance that under the ANWR lies one of the five largest oil fields ever discovered in America. 8

The U.S. has just come through a war fought in part over oil [the 1991 Gulf War]. Energy dependence costs Americans not just dollars but lives. It is a bizarre sentimentalism that would deny oil that is peacefully attainable because it risks disrupting the calving grounds of Arctic caribou. 9

I like the caribou as much as the next man. And I would be rather sorry if their mating patterns are disturbed. But you can't have everything. And if the choice is between the welfare of caribou and reducing an oil dependency that gets people killed in wars, I choose man over caribou every time. 10

Similarly the spotted owl in Oregon. I am no enemy of the owl. If it could be preserved at no or little cost, I would agree: the variety of nature is a good, a high aesthetic good. But it is no more than that. And sometimes aesthetic goods have to be sacrificed to the more fundamental ones. If the 11

By permission of John Deering and Creators Syndicate.

cost of preserving the spotted owl is the loss of livelihood for 30,000 logging families, I choose family over owl.

The important distinction is between those environmental goods that   12 are fundamental and those that are merely aesthetic. Nature is our ward. It is not our master. It is to be respected and even cultivated. But it is man's world. And when man has to choose between his well-being and that of nature, nature will have to accommodate.

Man should accommodate only when his fate and that of nature are in-   13 extricably bound up. The most urgent accommodation must be made when the very integrity of man's habitat—e.g., atmospheric ozone—is threat- ened. When the threat to man is of a lesser order (say, the pollutants from coal- and oil-fired generators that cause death from disease but not fatal damage to the ecosystem), a more modulated accommodation that balances economic against health concerns is in order. But in either case the principle is the same: protect the environment—because it is man's environment.

The sentimental environmentalists will call this saving nature with a   14 totally wrong frame of mind. Exactly. A sane—a humanistic—environmen- talism does it not for nature's sake but for our own.

❀ ❀ ❀

AFTER YOU READ

▪ *THINK* about how Krauthammer defines "a sane environmentalism," especially in paragraphs 6 and 8. What is his definition? Do you agree or disagree with him? Why do you feel as you do?

▪ *EXAMINE* paragraphs 2–5 to determine what Krauthammer believes to be an environmental necessity. What particular environmental concern(s) does Krauthammer consider necessities rather than luxuries? Why does he consider these environmental problems to be so important?

▪ *EXAMINE* also the cartoon on p. 387 to determine the attitude it ex- presses toward humanity's relationship with the environment. What is its theme, or message? Do you think Krauthammer would agree or disagree with the message expressed in this cartoon? Support your opinion with direct quotations from Krauthammer's essay, paying particular attention to paragraph 11.

▪ *WRITE* an essay that states and develops your own definition of "a sane environmentalism." Include in your definition direct quotations from Krauthammer's essay. Be sure to indicate whether you agree or disagree with the statements you use.

Grains of Hope

J. MADELEINE NASH

❖

J. Madeleine Nash has been a correspondent for Time *since 1974. Her interest in the environment is evident not only in many of her articles but also in her book,* El Nino: Unlocking the Secrets of the Master Weather-Maker *(2002). In the following essay, originally published in* Time, *Nash poses questions about the potential dangers and values of genetically engineered crops—specifically a new "golden rice."*

BEFORE YOU READ

- *THINK* about the idea of genetically engineered food crops in which the genetic structure has been modified in some way to increase yield or resistance to pests or herbicides. Do you think such genetic alteration is dangerous, or do you think genetic modification of crops can be used for positive purposes?

- *EXAMINE* the word "Frankenfood," the term many opponents of genetic engineering use to describe crops grown by this process. This word derives from Mary W. Shelley's novel *Frankenstein,* in which an uncontrollable monster ultimately destroys its creator. What warning is suggested by the term "Frankenfood"?

- *EXAMINE* also the title "Grains of Hope." What attitude toward genetic engineering is implied in this title? In her essay, Nash explains that the alteration of DNA through genetic engineering has been used to create not only crops that are resistant to insects and/or weed-controlling herbicides but also a new golden rice that contains the nutrient beta-carotene.

- *WRITE* a journal entry in which you explain how you feel about genetically engineered crops. Do you object to eating foods produced by genetic engineering? Why or why not?

© 2000 Time Inc. Reprinted by permission.

Attempt to answer the question implied in Nash's introductory paragraph. That is, do you think increased production of genetically engineered crops will "revolutionize farming" or "destroy the ecosystem"?

Genetically engineered crops could revolutionize farming. Protesters 1 fear they could also destroy the ecosystem. You decide.

At first, the grains of rice that Ingo Potrykus sifted through his fingers 2 did not seem at all special, but that was because they were still encased in their dark, crinkly husks. Once those drab coverings were stripped away and the interiors polished to a glossy sheen, Potrykus and his colleagues would behold the seeds' golden secret. At their core, these grains were not pearly white, as ordinary rice is, but a very pale yellow—courtesy of beta-carotene, the nutrient that serves as a building block for vitamin A.

Potrykus was elated. For more than a decade he had dreamed of 3 creating such a rice: a golden rice that would improve the lives of millions of the poorest people in the world. He'd visualized peasant farmers wading into paddies to set out the tender seedlings and winnowing the grain at harvest time in handwoven baskets. He'd pictured small children consuming the golden gruel their mothers would make, knowing that it would sharpen their eyesight and strengthen their resistance to infectious diseases.

And he saw his rice as the first modest start of a new green revolution, 4 in which ancient food crops would acquire all manner of useful properties: bananas that wouldn't rot on the way to market; corn that could supply its own fertilizer; wheat that could thrive in drought-ridden soil.

But imagining a golden rice, Potrykus soon found, was one thing and 5 bringing one into existence quite another. Year after year, he and his colleagues ran into one unexpected obstacle after another, beginning with the finicky growing habits of the rice they transplanted to a greenhouse near the foothills of the Swiss Alps. When success finally came, in the spring of 1999, Potrykus was 65 and about to retire as a full professor at the Swiss Federal Institute of Technology in Zurich. At that point, he tackled an even more formidable challenge.

Having created golden rice, Potrykus wanted to make sure it reached 6 those for whom it was intended: malnourished children of the developing world. And that, he knew, was not likely to be easy. Why? Because in addition to a full complement of genes from Oryza sativa—the Latin name for the most commonly consumed species of rice—the golden grains also contained snippets of DNA borrowed from bacteria and daffodils. It was what some would call Frankenfood, a product of genetic engineering. As such, it was entangled in a web of hopes and fears and political baggage, not to mention a fistful of ironclad patents.

For about a year now—ever since Potrykus and his chief collaborator, 7 Peter Beyer of the University of Freiburg in Germany, announced their achievement—their golden grain has illuminated an increasingly polarized public debate. At issue is the question of what genetically engineered crops represent. Are they, as their proponents argue, a technological leap forward that will bestow incalculable benefits on the world and its people? Or do they represent a perilous step down a slippery slope that will lead to ecological and agricultural ruin? Is genetic engineering just a more efficient way to do the business of conventional crossbreeding? Or does the ability to mix the genes of any species—even plants and animals—give man more power than he should have?

The debate erupted the moment genetically engineered crops made 8 their commercial debut in the mid-1990s, and it has escalated ever since. First to launch major protests against biotechnology were European environmentalists and consumer-advocacy groups. They were soon followed by their U.S. counterparts, who made a big splash at last fall's World Trade Organization meeting in Seattle and last week launched an offensive designed to target one company after another. Over the coming months, charges that transgenic crops pose grave dangers will be raised in petitions, editorials, mass mailings and protest marches. As a result, golden rice, despite its humanitarian intent, will probably be subjected to the same kind of hostile scrutiny that has already led to curbs on the commercialization of these crops in Britain, Germany, Switzerland and Brazil.

The hostility is understandable. Most of the genetically engineered 9 crops introduced so far represent minor variations on the same two themes: resistance to insect pests and to herbicides used to control the growth of weeds. And they are often marketed by large, multinational corporations that produce and sell the very agricultural chemicals farmers are spraying on their fields. So while many farmers have embraced such crops as Monsanto's Roundup Ready soybeans, with their genetically engineered resistance to Monsanto's Roundup-brand herbicide, that let them spray weed killer without harming crops, consumers have come to regard such things with mounting suspicion. Why resort to a strange new technology that might harm the biosphere, they ask, when the benefits of doing so seem small?

Indeed, the benefits have seemed small—until golden rice came along 10
to suggest otherwise. Golden rice is clearly not the moral equivalent of
Roundup Ready beans. Quite the contrary, it is an example—the first
compelling example—of a genetically engineered crop that may benefit not
just the farmers who grow it but also the consumers who eat it. In this case,
the consumers include at least a million children who die every year because
they are weakened by vitamin-A deficiency and an additional 350,000 who
go blind.

No wonder the biotech industry sees golden rice as a powerful ally in 11
its struggle to win public acceptance. No wonder its critics see it as a cynical
ploy. And no wonder so many of those concerned about the twin evils of
poverty and hunger look at golden rice and see reflected in it their own
passionate conviction that genetically engineered crops can be made to
serve the greater public good—that in fact such crops have a critical role
to play in feeding a world that is about to add to its present population of
6 billion. As former President Jimmy Carter put it, "Responsible biotechnology is not the enemy; starvation is."

Indeed, by the year 2020, the demand for grain, both for human 12
consumption and for animal feed, is projected to go up by nearly half, while
the amount of arable land available to satisfy that demand will not only
grow much more slowly but also, in some areas, will probably dwindle.
Add to that the need to conserve overstressed water resources and reduce
the use of polluting chemicals, and the enormity of the challenge becomes
apparent. In order to meet it, believes Gordon Conway, the agricultural
ecologist who heads the Rockefeller Foundation, 21st century farmers will
have to draw on every arrow in their agricultural quiver, including genetic
engineering. And contrary to public perception, he says, those who have
the least to lose and the most to gain are not well-fed Americans and
Europeans but the hollow-bellied citizens of the developing world.

❀   ❀   ❀

AFTER YOU READ

▪ *THINK* about the potential benefit of golden rice to poor and overpopu-
lated countries, especially countries whose citizens subsist primarily on a
diet deficient in Vitamin A. According to Nash, what are the effects of this
deficiency on children? Think also about the world's growing need for
grain for both animals and humans described in Nash's last paragraph. Do

"well-fed Americans and Europeans" have the moral right to curb or ban genetically engineered crops?

• *EXAMINE* the questions posed in paragraph 7 and discuss your responses with your classmates. Ultimately, do you think the potential benefits of genetically engineered crops outweigh the dangers? Why or why not?

• *WRITE* an essay in which you argue for or against genetically modified food crops. Include references to Nash's article as well as your own observations and opinions.

Is a Lab Rat's Fate More Poignant Than a Child's?

JANE MCCABE

We Must Find Alternatives to Animals in Research

ROGER CARAS

※

These two articles, which present opposing viewpoints about using animals in research, appeared together in Newsweek. *Jane McCabe, living with her husband and daughter Claire in northern California, writes from personal experience. In contrast, Roger Caras (1928–2001) writes from a more scientific point of view. He is the author of more than fifty books for adults and children on nature, wildlife, and domestic animals, including* A Perfect Harmony: The Intertwining Lives of Animals and Humans Throughout History. *Caras reported on the environment and on animals for* ABC-TV News *and often appeared on* The Today Show, World News Tonight, Nightline, 20/20, *and* Good Morning America.

BEFORE YOU READ

▪ *THINK* about your own view on the use of animals in medical research. Do you think animals should be used in research for cures for human diseases such as cancer, heart disease, cystic fibrosis, Alzheimer's, and AIDS? Do you consider human rights more important than animal rights? Or do you think scientists should strive for alternative methods of research?

- *EXAMINE* the titles of these two articles. Do the titles suggest that these articles will be informative or persuasive? What approach and appeal do you think McCabe will make in her article? What approach and appeal do you think Caras will make?

- *WRITE* in your journal a list of reasons for continuing animal research. Then write another list of reasons for discontinuing animal research or seeking alternate methods.

AS YOU READ

Decide which article appeals more to your sense of reason and which appeals more to your emotions. Then decide which appeal is more effective.

Is a Lab Rat's Fate More Poignant Than a Child's?

I see the debate about using animals in medical research in stark terms. 1 If you had to choose between saving a very cute dog or my equally cute, blond, brown-eyed daughter, whose life would you choose? It's not a difficult choice, is it? My daughter has cystic fibrosis. Her only hope for a normal life is that researchers, some of them using animals, will find a cure. Don't misunderstand. It's not that I don't love animals, it's just that I love Claire more.

Nine years ago I had no idea that I would be joining the fraternity of 2 those who have a vital interest in seeing that medical research continues. I was a very pregnant woman in labor; with my husband beside me I gave birth to a 7-pound 1-ounce daughter. It all seemed so easy. But for the next four months she could not gain weight. She was a textbook case of failure to thrive. Finally a hospital test of the salt content in her sweat led to the diagnosis of cystic fibrosis.

The doctor gave us a little reason for hope. "Your daughter will not 3 have a long life, but for most of the time, it will be a good life. Her life expectancy is about 13 years, though it could be longer or shorter. As research continues, we're keeping them alive longer."

"As research continues." It's not a lot to rely on but what's our 4 alternative? We haven't waited passively. We learned how to take care of our little girl; her medical problems affect her digestion and lungs. We protected her from colds, learned about supplemental vitamins and antibiotics. We moved to California where the winters aren't so harsh and the cold and flu season isn't so severe. Our new doctor told us that the children at his center were surviving, on the average, to age 21. So far, our daughter is doing well. She is a fast runner and plays a mean first base. She loves her friends and is, in general, a happy little girl. All things considered, I feel very lucky.

How has research using animals helped those with CF? Three times a 5 day my daughter uses enzymes from the pancreas of pigs to digest her food. She takes antibiotics tested on rats before they are tried on humans. As an adult, she will probably develop diabetes and need insulin—a drug developed by research on dogs and rabbits. If she ever needs a heart-lung transplant, one might be possible because of the cows that surgeons practiced on. There is no animal model to help CF research, but once the CF gene is located, new gene-splicing techniques may create a family of mice afflicted with the disease. Researchers would first learn to cure the mice with drugs, then cautiously try with humans.

There are only about 10,000 people with CF in the United States. But 6 the number of people dependent on research is much larger. Walk with me through Children's Hospital at Stanford University: here are the youngsters fighting cancer, rare genetic illnesses, immunological diseases. Amid their laughter and desperate attempts to retain a semblance of childhood, there is suffering.

I think the motivation of animal-rights activists is to cut down on the 7 suffering in this world, but I have yet to hear them acknowledge that people—young and old—suffer, too. Why is a laboratory rat's fate more poignant than that of an incurably ill child?

There are advocates for animals who only seek to cut down on 8 "unnecessary research." They don't specify how to decide what is unnecessary, but they do create an atmosphere in which doing medical research is seen as distasteful work. I think that's wrong. Researchers should be thanked, not hassled.

Every time I see a bumper sticker that says "Lab animals never have a 9 nice day," a fantasy plays in my brain. I get out of my car, tap on the driver's window and ask to talk. In my fantasy, the other driver gets out, we find a coffee shop and I show her photos of my kids. I ask her if she has ever visited Children's Hospital. I am so eloquent that her eyes fill with tears and she promises to think of the children who are wasting away as she considers the whole complicated issue of suffering.

I have other fantasies, too, that a cure is found for what ails my   10 daughter, that she marries and gives us some grandchildren, and does great work in her chosen profession, which at this moment appears to be cartooning or computer programming. We can still hope—as long as the research continues.

We Must Find Alternatives to Animals in Research

I believe that animals have rights which, although different from our own,   1 are just as inalienable. I believe animals have the right not to have pain, fear or physical deprivation inflicted upon them by us. Even if they are on the way to the slaughterhouse, animals have the right to food and water and shelter if it is needed. They have the right not to be brutalized in any way as food resources, for entertainment or any other purpose.

Since animals must be classified as property if we are to have the power   2 of life and death over them (and we must, even over our pets), there is a vast philosophical/legal rift to be negotiated. No other property has rights, yet animals must. It is going to take some fine legal minds to work out the details so that we can get across that gulch.

One of the most difficult problems is our unrelenting use of animals   3 in biomedical research. Until recently the arguments between biomedical researchers and the humane movement centered on the conditions under which laboratory animals are maintained. Lately, in keeping with our "age of activism," it has become a raging name-calling contest over whether one species, ours, has the right to use other species to solve our own health problems. If tens of millions of people elect to smoke and expose themselves to the risks of cancer and heart disease, do we have the right to subject animals that would never smoke to those same cancers and heart diseases?

A great many researchers I have met would love to have alternatives.   4 They are against vivisection in spirit but believe that today's research protocols require—and grant money goes to—research involving animals. Often they are right. What's more, the use of animals in research is not limited to the good of humans. Vaccines used on animals were developed using animals. Animal-rights advocates who decry using animals for research on human diseases have not made it clear what models should have been used for canine distemper, parvovirus or feline leukemia.

Animal-rights activists say that far too little effort has gone into seeking ₅ substitute methods such as cell culture and computer modeling. They are right. Finding a substitute for animals in research has only recently become an imperative in the scientific community. And that change has coincided with a change in the techniques employed by the militant animal-rights movement. When leaflets and picket signs were replaced by night raiders and bombers, science sat up and paid attention. Personally, I decry terrorism as the solution to any problem.

Many laboratories provide too little in the way of creature comforts ₆ (no pun intended) for laboratory animals. That has to change and in many places it is. Jane Goodall has fought to upgrade the psychological environment provided for chimpanzees. For an animal as bright as a chimp (its genetic package varies from our own by no more than 1 percent, most researchers agree), boredom and lack of social interaction is nothing less than cruelty, according to Goodall.

Much of the research done on chimps involves their immune systems, ₇ current work on AIDS being an obvious example. Since scientists know that stress alters any animal's power to respond to invading organisms, why do they stress chimps by confining them in isolation when the research protocol doesn't demand it?

What has happened is analogous to current geopolitical problems. ₈ Everybody is so angry at everybody else nobody is really listening. The animal-rights groups are at odds with each other. That could be because they are all looking for the same membership dollars, the same bequests. Then, of course, there are the antivivisectionists vs. the provivisectionists. They are so busy shrieking at each other no one can be heard.

One day animals will not be used in the laboratory. How soon that day ₉ comes depends on how soon people stop screaming and make the search for alternatives a major research imperative. As long as conferences on the subject sound like feeding time in the monkey house, monkeys along with millions of other animals are going to stay right where they are now—in the laboratory.

❁   ❁   ❁

AFTER YOU READ

▪ *THINK* about the difference in purpose in the two articles. How does each author suit his or her primary method of appeal to his or her purpose? Would a logical appeal have been as effective for McCabe's article as her emotional appeal? Would an emotional appeal have been as effective for Caras's article? Why or why not?

▪ *EXAMINE* the details and examples that each writer uses. How do these details differ? Identify several of the most effective supporting details used by each author. Which details and examples are most convincing to you? Does either essay contain examples of weak or illogical reasoning?

▪ *WRITE* a persuasive letter on the subject of animal research. As you write, imagine a specific audience for your letter. You might write to the editor of *Newsweek*, the magazine in which these readings appeared. Or you might try to persuade McCabe to support alternate methods of research or Caras to support the use of animals in research. If possible, use your own personal knowledge and experiences as well as the knowledge you have gained from reading these articles.

Dice or Doves?

CINDY CAMBURN

❀

This essay by Cindy Camburn was one of several she included in the portfolio she submitted for her freshman composition course. Having lived on the Gulf Coast all of her life, Camburn had mixed emotions when offshore gambling became legal a few years ago. Her essay focuses on the environmental effects of the coming of gambling casinos to that area.

BEFORE YOU READ

▪ *THINK* about the environmental cost of progress. Identify several examples that illustrate this cost. Is progress always harmful to the environment? If the choice is between protecting the environment and providing a community or region with economic security (new jobs, more money for schools, increased incomes, and so on), which would you choose? Are there other options?

▪ *EXAMINE* the following sentence from the second paragraph:

> Even so, I am aware of a beam of light that washes across the backyard, penetrates the closed blinds, and bounces off my mirror every thirty seconds.

Notice how Camburn's choice of strong verbs (*washes, penetrates,* and *bounces*) and her use of parallelism combine to make this an effective sentence.

▪ *EXAMINE* also the word *holograph* in paragraph 8. In this context, a holograph (or hologram) is a three-dimensional image produced by laser photography.

▪ *WRITE* a journal entry in which you tell about a change that has occurred in the environment of a place you know well.

AS YOU READ

Notice how Camburn combines her own experiences with information
from other sources to lead her readers to her point of view.

One of my earliest memories of growing up on the Mississippi Gulf   1
Coast is waking every morning to the sounds of birds in the trees
around the feeder. The types of birds varied with the season, but the most
common visitors were a pair of doves with distinctive markings. Some
mornings the doves would not be there, but they always eventually
reappeared. I would watch them walk slowly around the deck, one bird
pecking at the seeds which had fallen from the feeder while the other stayed
alert for danger. At breakfast on these mornings, my mother would always
say, "My doves are back." I was constantly surprised that the birds were
hers because I felt they had returned for me.

Now when I go home for a visit, I always close the blinds before I go   2
to bed. Even so, I am aware of a beam of light that washes across the
backyard, penetrates the closed blinds, and bounces off my mirror every
thirty seconds. That beam comes from the laser show at Palace Casino, ten
miles across the bay from my home. The Palace is one of fifteen casinos
which have opened on the twenty-six mile stretch of coast in the last two
years, creating an economic boom for the area. "Things couldn't be better,"
according to George Lammons, editor of the *Coast Business Journal*. The
Coast, he explains is "enjoying robust economic growth. The biggest reason
for our turnaround and one of the biggest reasons for the expectation of a
good, long-term outlook is probably our newest industry—casino gambling." Lammons adds that the casinos have "put smiles on the faces of
coastians."

If Lammons were to look a little more closely, he would find that many   3
coastians are not smiling. They feel that their quality of life has been
destroyed. These casinos have turned the coast highway into a perpetual
construction project and traffic jam. Their employees dump trash and waste
water into the Mississippi River sound. Their six-story parking garages
have replaced the palm trees and shrimp fleets and blocked the views of
the beach. The casinos have changed the entire face of the Coast. In
particular, they have changed the habitat of one of the coast's greatest
attractions, its flocks of birds.

According to Becky Gillette in the *Coast Business Journal*, the Wildlife   4
and Nature Preservation Society Center is already citing a large increase in

orphaned and injured wildlife due to habitat destruction caused by the
rapid growth that has accompanied the new casino industry. In "Silence of
the Songbirds" in the June 1993 issue of *National Geographic,* Les Line
puts the problem in a larger perspective. "Thirty years ago," he says, "when
Rachel Carson wrote of 'a spring without voices' and the silence of the
dawn without the chorus of robins, catbirds, doves, jays, and wrens, we
thought the culprit was TOXINS. Now," he adds, "we know that habitat
destruction is an even greater threat" (79–80). He explains

> Each spring, from mid-March to mid-May, [the birds] come north across
> the Gulf of Mexico in great waves, riding flows of warm humid air on a
> flight launched shortly after sunset from staging areas like the Yucatán
> Peninsula. Under the best conditions the . . . larger, faster fliers . . . will
> reach the coast by mid-morning after a 600-mile journey; smaller birds .
> . . lag behind. The travelers' goal is to make a rest stop in the first line of
> extensive forest on the mainland, perhaps 30 miles inland. But if they are
> buffeted by head winds or storms en route, they will drop exhausted into
> remnant scrub woodlands along the coast. . . . (72)

When the rest and recovery areas of forests and shrubs have been 5
replaced by buildings and concrete parking areas, many exhausted birds
die. The survivors, who would have rested on the coast, cannot reproduce.
In the early 60s, "Thirty thousand [migrating birds] would cross a given
mile of coast . . . every hour for five hours" (Line 73) every day during the
peak season in April. Today, however, those numbers have already been
reduced by more than forty percent (Line 74).

In addition to losing their natural resting and nesting areas, birds 6
arriving on the Mississippi Gulf Coast face another hazard, the casinos'
laser lights. The Palace Casino's lights are considered to be hazardous
within 2,000 feet because they cause "temporary flash blindness and/or
permanent retina damage" (Gillette). Local wildlife specialists feel that the
threat to birds is even greater. Judith Toups, a local ornithologist, says any
strong beam of light is a major hazard for migrating birds, especially in
foggy or stormy weather, because birds get disoriented and head toward
the light (Gillette). Janet Miller, president of the Mississippi Gulf Coast
Audubon Society, adds, "We end up with migrating birds being attracted
to the bright lights of the casinos and then having their eyesight damaged
by the laser shows" (Gillette).

Of course, casino officials are quick to defend their lasers. "The laser 7
show draws people," explains the chief executive of Palace Casino. "The
lights can be seen as far as fifty miles away. We receive lots of compliments
and have had very few complaints" (Gillette).

I am complaining. The laser shows and the economic boom the casinos 8
represent do not put a smile on my face. If the unrestrained development
continues, the Mississippi Gulf Coast will have to depend on the lasers to
produce holographs of birds. Then the casino officials can receive compliments on how real the holographic birds look. I do not want the laser
versions. I want my (and my mother's) doves to keep reappearing.

Works Cited

Gillette, Becky. "Will It Harm Birds? Will It Harm Planes?" *Coast Business
    Journal* 1 August 1994: 1, 31+.
Lammons, George. "State of the Coast: Taking Off After Tough Times."
    Coast Business Journal 15 February 1993: 4.
Line, Les. "Silence of the Songbirds." *National Geographic* June 1993:
    68–92.

❀   ❀   ❀

AFTER YOU READ

▪ *THINK* about the relationship between change and progress. People often
resist change, especially changes that transform a familiar scene from
childhood into something new and strange. Does Camburn's attitude
toward the changes that she has witnessed on the Gulf Coast seem to be
simple resistance to change, or does she convince you that these changes
have altered not only the birds' quality of life but also that of the residents
of that area? How does she make her own experience one that readers can
understand?

▪ *THINK* also about Camburn's concession that the gambling casinos have
brought economic prosperity to the Gulf Coast. Does this concession
strengthen or weaken her argument? Why does it have this effect?

▪ *EXAMINE* Camburn's list of Works Cited, in which she identifies and
gives credit to her sources. Notice that each entry begins with the author's
name (last name first, comma, first name) and then gives the title of the
article in quotation marks, the title of the journal italicized, the date, and
the page numbers of the entire article. Notice also how these entries are
arranged and punctuated.

▪ *WRITE* an essay in which you identify an environmental problem in your
area and suggest a reasonable, fair solution.

Whistling Swan

TERRY TEMPEST WILLIAMS

❀

Describing herself as "a naturalist first and a writer sec-
ond" (Gale Literary Databases), Terry Tempest Williams
has nevertheless written children's books, essays, poetry,
fiction, and nonfiction. Her work is deeply tied to natural
spaces, especially to the region around Salt Lake City,
Utah, where she grew up in a traditional Mormon family.
This selection, which is from Refuge: An Unnatural History of Family and Place, *weaves together the parallel*
stories of her mother's death from ovarian cancer and the
threat to a nearby bird sanctuary from the rising of the
Great Salt Lake. Implicit in the book is Williams's activist
concern about the effect of nuclear tests on the people and
ecosystems of Nevada and Utah, but the more direct
themes in the book are those of change and the wholeness
and spirituality of the natural world. In the following
selection Williams, who has been a bird watcher since her
childhood, poignantly expresses her grief about her
mother's terminal illness through her equally intense grief
for the death of the swan.

BEFORE YOU READ

• *THINK* about the title "Refuge." What is a refuge? Where do you find
refuge from your problems, fears, and losses? Before the events described
in her book, Williams had found refuge with her family and in nature.
However, in the spring of 1983 Williams faced two personal tragedies.
First, she learned that her mother was dying of cancer. Second, the Bear
River Migratory Bird Refuge, which had been a sanctuary for her, was
devastated by the flooding of the Great Salt Lake because of increased
rainfall and climatic fluctuations. Contemplating her losses, Williams is

forced to ask the question, "How do we find refuge in the midst of change?"
How do you answer this question?

▪ *EXAMINE* the first two paragraphs in the selection, noticing that these
paragraphs introduce Williams's parallel themes of her mother's illness and
the natural cycle of life and death. How do the images of the snow and the
apples relate to the theme of death? Notice also that Williams's style
combines the use of such concrete poetic images as the descriptions of the
snow and apples with factual details about the wooden benches in the
chapel.

▪ *WRITE* a journal entry in which you describe a place that provides you
with a refuge from your problems—a place where you feel at peace.

AS YOU READ

Identify and underline the services that Williams performs for the dead
swan. What do these actions tell you about her feelings for the swan?

The snow continues to fall. Red apples cling to bare branches.   1

    I just returned from Tamra Crocker Pulsifer's funeral. It was a   2
reunion of childhood friends and family. Our neighborhood sat on wooden
benches row after row in the chapel. I sat next to Mother and wondered
how much time we had left together.

Walking the wrackline of Great Salt Lake after a storm is quite different   3
from walking along the seashore after high tide. There are no shells, no
popping kelp or crabs. What remains is a bleached narrative of feathers,
bones, occasional birds encrusted in salt and deep piles of brine among the
scattered driftwood. There is little human debris among the remote beaches
of Great Salt Lake, except for the shotgun shells that wash up after the
duck-hunting season.

    Yesterday, I walked along the north shore of Stansbury Island. Great   4
Salt Lake mirrored the plumage of immature gulls as they skimmed its
surface. It was cold and windy. Small waves hissed each time they broke
on shore. Up ahead, I noticed a large, white mound a few feet from where
the lake was breaking.

    It was a dead swan. Its body lay contorted on the beach like an   5
abandoned lover. I looked at the bird for a long time. There was no blood
on its feathers, no sight of gunshot. Most likely, a late migrant from the

north slapped silly by a ravenous Great Salt Lake. The swan may have drowned.

I knelt beside the bird, took off my deerskin gloves, and began 6 smoothing feathers. Its body was still limp—the swan had not been dead long. I lifted both wings out from under its belly and spread them on the sand. Untangling the long neck which was wrapped around itself was more difficult, but finally I was able to straighten it, resting the swan's chin flat against the shore.

The small dark eyes had sunk behind the yellow lores. It was a whistling 7 swan. I looked for two black stones, found them, and placed them over the eyes like coins. They held. And, using my own saliva as my mother and grandmother had done to wash my face, I washed the swan's black bill and feet until they shone like patent leather.

I have no idea of the amount of time that passed in the preparation of 8 the swan. What I remember most is lying next to its body and imagining the great white bird in flight.

I imagined the great heart that propelled the bird forward day after 9 day, night after night. Imagined the deep breaths taken as it lifted from the arctic tundra, the camaraderie within the flock. I imagined the stars seen and recognized on clear autumn nights as they navigated south. Imagined their silhouettes passing in front of the full face of the harvest moon. And I imagined the shimmering Great Salt Lake calling the swans down like a mother, the suddenness of the storm, the anguish of its separation.

And I tried to listen to the stillness of its body.   10

At dusk, I left the swan like a crucifix on the sand. I did not look back.   11

❀   ❀   ❀

AFTER YOU READ

▪ *THINK* about the loving services that Williams performs for the swan. (If necessary, reread the passages that you underlined.) What do these actions suggest about Williams's feelings for the dead swan? For nature in general? For life in general? Where do you think she ultimately seeks refuge—in nature, in herself, or in both? Explain.

▪ *EXAMINE* paragraph 8, especially the use of the word *preparation*. Of what does Williams's "preparation of the swan" remind you? You might be interested to know that when Williams's mother dies later in the book, she prepares her body for burial in a manner similar to her preparation of the swan.

▪ *EXAMINE* also the very last paragraph of the selection, which describes the dead swan as lying "like a crucifix on the sand." A *crucifix* is a cross, a Christian religious symbol. Williams uses this image to connect nature and humanity into a spiritual whole.

▪ *WRITE* an essay in which you describe the place or environment in which you find personal refuge. You may find your earlier journal entry helpful in writing this essay.

Unit Six: Critical Thinking and Writing Assignments

❀   ❀   ❀

EXPLORING IDEAS TOGETHER

1. With a group of your classmates, discuss significant recent effects of the weather on the environment and on the people who live in it. Have you had severe weather—such as a flood, tornado, or hurricane—in your area recently? Have you read about such severe weather in another locale? What were the effects? You may even want to bring newspaper accounts to share with your group members.

2. Meet with a group of your classmates to discuss the major environmental issues that your generation faces. First, make a list of the different issues about which you are concerned. Then identify the one or two issues that concern you the most and explain to the remainder of the class why these issues are so disturbing.

3. Several of the readings in this unit, especially those by Bill McKibben and Charles Krauthammer, discuss the relationship between the rights and responsibilities human beings have toward the environment. With a group of your classmates, make two lists—one of rights and one of responsibilities.

4. As suggested by Cindy Camburn's essay, a vigorous debate exists about how to protect both the environment and property rights. In class, debate this issue with one group arguing for the rights of property owners and another group arguing for the protection of the environment, perhaps specifically for endangered species. Is it possible for our society to respect both the environment and property rights? How? For example, do many property owners, including farmers, take special care of the land?

5. Jan DeBlieu and Kathleen Norris both describe a natural, rural environment whereas Pythia Peay analyzes an urban environment. Working with a group of your classmates, compare rural life with city life. What are the advantages of living in each environment? What are the disadvantages? Which do you ultimately prefer?

WRITING ESSAYS

1. The essays by Kathleen Norris, Barry Hannah, Jane Smiley, and E. Annie Proulx focus on how the weather affects the environment and

the people in it. Write an essay in which you discuss how you have been affected by the weather—either by the changing seasons as in "Weather Reports" or by a particular incident as in "Weather Collage."

2. Write a brief narrative describing some possible effects of global temperatures rising to a dangerous level. Use your imagination to describe how climates might change in certain areas. In your narrative, you might focus on the area where you live.

3. Write a letter to a citizen of a Third World country in which you argue for or against the use of genetic engineering to modify food crops. Try to include reasons and support for your position that would be convincing to such an audience. In writing your essay, you may want to review "Grains of Hope" by J. Madeleine Nash.

4. Human beings share a relationship not only with the physical environment but also with the animals and plants that live in this environment. Write an essay in which you describe an instance of an ideal relationship between a human being and an animal.

5. Entering into the general debate about whether or not nature is primarily for the use of human beings, Jane McCabe and Roger Caras focus on the issue of using animals for medical research for humans. Take a position on this issue, arguing for or against using animals in medical research.

6. Cindy Camburn and Terry Tempest Williams both focus on animals—doves and a swan—that have been harmed or reduced in numbers because their habitats have been changed by human interference or a natural catastrophe. Select another animal that is threatened or endangered because of changes to the environment and write a report in which you explain the problem and suggest a possible solution. You may want to do some research on the animal you select.

7. Identify a local environmental issue that you can investigate or that you already know something about. Then write an informative report or persuasive essay on this topic.

8. Write an essay in which you respond to *one* of the reading selections in this unit. You may agree or disagree with the author's position. Begin your essay by summarizing briefly the essay to which you are responding. Be sure you identify the title and author's name in your summary.

Self with Technology

Technology. This unit focuses on your relationship to something that is not living—to the machines and gadgets that you use each day and perhaps take for granted. Your days and nights are filled with machines that make your life easier and more pleasant. An alarm clock or radio wakes you each morning, a coffeemaker brews your coffee, a dishwasher washes the mug, a hair dryer styles your hair, a car or bus or truck transports you to school or work, a radio or stereo keeps you company during the day, computers perform many of the routine tasks that you once did manually, a washing machine launders your clothes, a microwave or at least a stove cooks your dinner, a television entertains you in the evening, and a VCR may even record shows for you while you sleep.

Technology affects not only how you live your life but how you relate to other people. As a teenager, you probably spent countless hours with your friends riding around in a car or talking about cars. You maintain long-distance relationships by talking on the telephone or sending messages by email or fax machines. And if your family is typical, you gather around a television set in the evenings. In fact, the television set has become the focal point of many homes, replacing the fireplace and kitchen table that once served this purpose.

In addition to the role that technology assumes in your relationships with other people, you may also establish relationships with certain machines. You may not have thought of a machine as something with which

411

you could have a relationship, and certainly you do not relate to machines in the same way that you do to people, yet there are similarities. Although many of the machines you use may evoke little emotional response from you, you may love some and hate others. For example, do you remember your first bicycle or car or stereo and how you loved it? Or your excitement when you first had a telephone of your own? Perhaps you are one of millions of Americans who depends on the television or the Internet to keep you company. You may have even made new friends or chatted with old ones on the Internet.

But all of your relationships with machines may not be love relationships. You may also hate certain machines—the computer that has a mind of its own, the car that will not start, the toaster that always burns your toast, the vending machine that robs you of your money. Although machines are usually designed to make your life easier, they may also, on occasion, make your life frustrating if not miserable. Machines certainly contribute to much that is bad in our lives: Guns contribute to the high crime rate; automobiles increase air pollution and cause accidents; computers reduce human interaction to blips on a screen; and machines in general often put people out of work. As shown in the cartoon on the next page, machines often seem to control our lives: yet, no one is eager to do without machines. Having become used to them, to the convenience and entertainment and stimulation they provide, people cannot imagine a life in which machines do not play a major role.

So it is likely that you will continue your complex relationship with machines and technology—sometimes even loving and hating the same form of technology at different times. This unit explores those relationships. Some of the reading selections focus on the close, almost intimate relationships people establish with the machines that are important to them. Others tell of negative feelings that machines and technology in general evoke in people at times. And still others explain the effects, both positive and negative, that technology has on our society, especially on education and physical and mental health.

As you prepare to read the selections in this unit, think about your own attitude toward machines. Is there a particular machine or form of technology that you love? If you could keep only one machine, which one would it be? In general, are you a gadget lover or a gadget hater? To answer this last question, do the following exercise: On a blank piece of paper, write your name in the center and draw a circle around it. Now list on the paper around your name all the gadgets, machines, and other forms of technology that you use routinely. Circle those that you view positively and

© 1987 by Matt Groening. All Rights Reserved. Reprinted by permission of Acme Features Syndicate.

draw a box around those that you view negatively. Now determine whether your relationship with technology is generally positive or negative.

As you read the selections in this unit, your attitude toward technology may change. Certainly, you should begin to understand more clearly the force that technology represents and how it shapes your life.

The Plot Against People

RUSSELL BAKER

❁

A writer of multiple talents, Russell Baker has twice won the Pulitzer Prize, first for his distinguished journalistic commentary in his "Observer" column in the New York Times *and second for his autobiographical memoir* Growing Up. *You may have read Baker's "Observer" column, which is syndicated throughout the United States, or you may have seen him hosting* Masterpiece Theater *on PBS. Baker's shrewd social and political commentary is particularly distinguished by its wit and humor. In the following essay about humanity's daily struggle with inanimate objects—or simple machines—Baker shows us how to survive by laughing at ourselves and our frustrations.*

BEFORE YOU READ

• *THINK* about how machines could "plot against people." Do you sometimes feel that one of your machines—your alarm clock, your computer, or your automobile—has a personality and a voice of its own? Have you ever actually "named" a machine such as an automobile? Is it understandable, if not realistic, to personify inanimate objects?

• *EXAMINE* the first paragraph. Into what three major categories does Baker classify inanimate objects? What makes these categories funny? Are these categories really "scientific"?

• *WRITE* in your journal a humorous story about a time a machine "plotted" against you.

AS YOU READ

Identify and number in the body of this essay the three categories of inanimate objects that Baker gives in his introduction. How many paragraphs does Baker devote to each category?

Inanimate objects are classified scientifically into three major categories— 1
those that break down, those that get lost, and those that don't work.

The goal of all inanimate objects is to resist man and ultimately to 2
defeat him, and the three major classifications are based on the method
each object uses to achieve its purpose. As a general rule, any object capable
of breaking down at the moment when it is most needed will do so. The
automobile is typical of the category.

With the cunning peculiar to its breed, the automobile never breaks 3
down while entering a filling station which has a large staff of idle
mechanics. It waits until it reaches a downtown intersection in the middle
of the rush hour, or until it is fully loaded with family and luggage on the
Ohio Turnpike. Thus it creates maximum inconvenience, frustration, and
irritability, thereby reducing its owner's lifespan.

Washing machines, garbage disposals, lawn mowers, furnaces, TV sets, 4
tape recorders, slide projectors—all are in league with the automobile to
take their turn at breaking down whenever life threatens to flow smoothly
for their enemies.

Many inanimate objects, of course, find it extremely difficult to break 5
down. Pliers, for example, and gloves and keys are almost totally incapable
of breaking down. Therefore, they have had to evolve a different technique
for resisting man.

They get lost. Science has still not solved the mystery of how they do 6
it, and no man has ever caught one of them in the act. The most plausible
theory is that they have developed a secret method of locomotion which
they are able to conceal from human eyes.

It is not uncommon for a pair of pliers to climb all the way from the 7
cellar to the attic in its single-minded determination to raise its owner's
blood pressure. Keys have been known to burrow three feet under mat-
tresses. Women's purses, despite their great weight, frequently travel
through six or seven rooms to find hiding space under a couch.

Scientists have been struck by the fact that things that break down 8
virtually never get lost, while things that get lost hardly ever break down.
A furnace, for example, will invariably break down at the depth of the first
winter cold wave, but it will never get lost. A woman's purse hardly ever
breaks down; it almost invariably chooses to get lost.

Some persons believe this constitutes evidence that inanimate objects 9
are not entirely hostile to man. After all, they point out, a furnace could
infuriate a man even more thoroughly by getting lost than by breaking
down, just as a glove could upset him far more by breaking down than by
getting lost.

Not everyone agrees, however, that this indicates a conciliatory atti- 10
tude. Many say it merely proves that furnaces, gloves and pliers are
incredibly stupid.

The third class of objects—those that don't work—is the most curious 11
of all. These include such objects as barometers, car clocks, cigarette
lighters, flashlights and toy-train locomotives. It is inaccurate, of course,
to say that they *never* work. They work once, usually for the first few hours
after being brought home, and then quit. Thereafter, they never work again.

In fact, it is widely assumed that they are built for the purpose of not 12
working. Some people have reached advanced ages without ever seeing
some of these objects—barometers, for example—in working order.

Science is utterly baffled by the entire category. There are many 13
theories about it. The most interesting holds that the things that don't work
have attained the highest state possible for an inanimate object, the state
to which things that break down and things that get lost can still only aspire.

They have truly defeated man by conditioning him never to expect 14
anything of them. When his cigarette lighter won't light or his flashlight
fails to illuminate, it does not raise his blood pressure. Objects that don't
work have given man the only peace he receives from inanimate society.

❀   ❀   ❀

AFTER YOU READ

▪ *THINK* about your own experiences with inanimate objects and simple
machines. Which of Baker's three categories of inanimate objects frustrates
you the most? Those that break down? Those that get lost? Or those that
do not work? Why is this category particularly frustrating for you? What
particular object in this category causes you the most trouble?

▪ *EXAMINE* the three categories that you identified and numbered in the
body of the essay. In each section, underline the inanimate objects you
consider to be machines. Remember that in its simplest form, a machine is
a gadget designed to do some sort of work.

▪ *WRITE* an essay in which you provide your own classification of machines. In planning your essay, list all of the machines you use. Then study
your list and try to think of an original method of classification that makes
an interesting point. Be sure your categories include all of the machines
you listed and that each machine fits into only one category.

The Beep Goes On

CAROL ORLOCK

❀

Carol Orlock's first novel, The Goddess Letters, *won the Pacific Northwest Bookseller's Award. Since then, she has also written* Inner Time: The Science of Body Clocks and What Makes Us Tick *and* The End of Aging: How Medical Science Is Changing Our Concept of Old Age. *The following essay appeared in* Lear's, *a magazine intended primarily for women. In the essay, Orlock identifies—but expresses reservations about—a number of machines generally seen as beneficial to society. Most of the authors in this unit take a position on how technology affects individuals' experiences. Orlock expresses her concerns and hopes about the effect machines have on society as a whole. In fact, Orlock suggests that machines can even affect the future of the world.*

BEFORE YOU READ

▪ *THINK* about how many machines you use in a single day. How many of these machines make your life easier or more pleasant? How many make your life more tedious or frustrating?

▪ *EXAMINE* the following words, which appear in the essay and may be unfamiliar to you:

Terra incognita: "The *terra incognita* at our fingertips is made up of buttons and dials, registers that dance with prickles of electricity, diodes that blip, and switches smooth and effortless as sleep."

This Latin phrase means "unknown land" but is used by Orlock metaphorically, not literally. That is, she is not referring to a geographical place, to real land, but to the unknown territory created by modern technology. (Notice that the word *territory* comes from the Latin word *terra.*)

417

Elliptical: "Creatures from this land breed among themselves and speak a language only they can comprehend—CD-ROM, fully buffered RAM, Ethernet . . . phrases brief and *elliptical* as an electron's leap toward the future."

When writers want to indicate that material has been omitted from a text, they use ellipses—three spaced periods. Thus the word *elliptical* means "containing or characterized by ellipsis." But it can also be used to refer to a writing style that is characterized by economy or obscurity of expression. Which of these definitions applies to the word as it is used by Orlock?

Inaudible: "This device emits an *inaudible* sound. . . ."

If something is audible, it can be heard. Thus an *inaudible* sound is one that cannot be heard.

Unfathomable: "Then there are *unfathomable* miracles—like the machines that can keep me alive."

A fathom is a unit of length equal to six feet. It is used primarily to measure the depth of water. However, as a verb, fathom means not only "to determine the depth of" but also "to get to the bottom of and understand." Thus *unfathomable* means "not capable of being understood." Notice that the prefixes *in* (as in *inaudible*) and *un* (as in *unfathomable*) can both mean "not."

Proliferation: "I have seen the *proliferation* of electronic transmissions. . . ."

The word *proliferation* means "rapid growth," but it applies to all types of rapid expansion, not just the growth of living things. Thus *prolific* means "rapidly growing," and *proliferate* means "to grow rapidly."

▪ *WRITE* a list of the machines you typically use each day. Make your list as accurate and complete as possible.

AS YOU READ

Keep two lists—one that includes the machines Orlock is positive toward and one that includes the machines she thinks are useless or silly.

They gleam—cool aluminum servants more agile than their masters. They flash reflections, fractionalizing our lives in segmented lines on black plastic and chrome. They are tech toys and tech tools, born at the rate of some 60 electronic patents each day. If these inventions are exhilarating, they are also eerie. Occasionally they are down-right silly.

The terra incognita at our fingertips is made up of buttons and dials, 2 registers that dance with prickles of electricity, diodes that blip, and switches smooth and effortless as sleep. Creatures from this land breed among themselves and speak a language only they can comprehend—CD-ROM, fully buffered RAM, Ethernet . . . phrases brief and elliptical as an electron's leap toward the future. As these creatures enter our world with accelerating velocity, we perform quick sleights of mind to absorb the latest miracle.

A few of these miracles strike absurd notes. It is possible, for example, 3 to purchase a battery-powered ultrasonic canine flea collar. This device emits an inaudible sound field around the at-risk pet, giving perimeter protection against midair insects hopping in its direction. Lacking the dog, I still crave the device, with a lust I inherited from my ancestors who tamed wolves. They too must have craved the new; in their case it was probably sharper flint.

Equally absurd, but no less desirable, is the latest hand-held language 4 translator. With this polyglot computer, and a Eurailpass, I can manage pleasantries in five languages. My hostess may doze off while I input FIND WORD: GOOD NIGHT AND THANKS FOR THE STRUDEL, but I will have been polite as well as postmodern.

Alongside the absurdities, there are useful miracles. Ever since my son, 5 who is in sales, installed the cellular phone in his car, I no longer pay for groceries to be delivered. I call his number, and he stops between appointments to pick up what we need. There are drawbacks, of course. If my son is out of his car, I must dictate my list to a real, live mobile-intercept operator, who is notoriously poor at distinguishing the word *cases* from *cans*. But we like stewed tomatoes and expect to use them up before next autumn.

Likewise, I appreciate bar-code pricing in supermarkets. At least I think 6 I do. But if I ever see short black stripes worked into the mottling on a zucchini, I will immediately flee the market screaming.

I definitely like cash machines. I like the snap of a plastic card slipping 7 like a tongue into a dark mouth of a machine, and I like to imagine chips pondering my secret code and thoughtfully checking my balance. I like when the money comes out. I like that best. I have hoodwinked my creditors, gotten ahead of the signatory on my paycheck, and possibly mortgaged my future, but for a brief electronic instant no one knew. It is a secret between the machine and me, and when it asks whether I want a report on my balance, I always punch *No*.

Then there are unfathomable miracles—like the machines that can 8
keep me alive. I walk past a hospital and see through porthole windows
the shining surfaces and serpentine wiring of these medical wonders. Or I
can hear a screaming siren and believe a life is about to be saved. The value
of that life cannot be calculated, yet the miracle of saving it is played out
in numbers: starting with the digits *911,* transmitted as an address and an
estimated time of arrival, figured as a pulse rate and a blood pressure,
calibrated for tomography and sonography, measured into millimeters,
minute dosages, and statistics regarding recovery. I will never understand
all this but I'm reassured knowing it is there.

I have seen men walking on the moon via live television. I have watched 9
a brain cell actually grow threads as it was stimulated toward a new memory
trace. I have seen the banded pattern from a DNA test display the unique
secretions of a rapist. I have seen the proliferation of electronic transmissions and have felt, on some days, as though it were all aimed at me.

We covet the new technology because, like an unclimbed mountain, it 10
is there. We fear it because, as in toxic-waste dumps and acid rain, it is here.

The everyday can become terrifying: I see myself standing in a grocery 11
line while the bar-code reader goes *peep-peep-peep.* The checker angles his
wrist, sliding my purchases past a red pencil of light, and the register prints
out exactly what I bought and exactly when, right down to the date, the
hour, and the minute. Will I ever have to prove I was buying figs at precisely
10:02 the morning of the 24th? I save receipts. The blue vein on the
checker's wrist passes over the red light, reminding me that we can now
read genetic codes from blood samples. These codes are not yet legible to
the masses, but they will be one day. What will happen to us when a single
drop of blood reveals our ancestry? Divulges our diet? Predicts our appeal
to certain viruses?

Meanwhile, the new science of molecular psychology studies brain 12
chemistry to explain mood and behavior. When the chemical formula for
the experience of pure terror is understood, surely some dictator will want
to purchase the ingredients. The day may come when defense systems will
have to guard our hearts and minds on the molecular level.

On better days I persuade myself I will actually be protected by laser 13
weapons in space. If I open my arms wide and throw my head back to drink
in a blue September afternoon, the machinery is too distant to imagine. On
such days the approaching clouds are shaped like Sunday school cutouts.
Will they reconfigure to dark, slouching beasts when I know that a
silicon-and-steel "miracle" is actually out there, watching over me? I feel
unable to prepare, except to think up better uses for the new technology.

If we can all talk to one another—instantly—and if we can all understand one another—anthropologically, linguistically, genetically—let's all get on the wire together one fine day. Let's talk peace.

❀ ❀ ❀

AFTER YOU READ

- *THINK* about Orlock's statement that "We covet the new technology because, like an unclimbed mountain, it is there. We fear it because, as in toxic-waste dumps and acid rain, it is here." What do you think she means by this statement?

- *EXAMINE* the machines Orlock thinks are silly or useless and those she thinks are helpful. What do the "good" machines have in common? Why does she like them?

- *EXAMINE* also Orlock's last paragraph, especially her last sentence. Despite her reservations, what is Orlock's hope for the future of technology? Do you share her hope? Are you optimistic or pessimistic about this hope being fulfilled?

- *WRITE* a summary of this essay. Begin by stating Orlock's thesis. Include in your summary only the main points that she makes to support her thesis. Then argue for or against this thesis. Or *WRITE* an essay in which you express your "hopes" for the future of technology.

Television Addiction

MARIE WINN

❀

We hear a great deal these days about different forms of addiction, but we don't usually think of our television viewing habits as a form of addiction. However, Marie Winn, who was born in Czechoslovakia and educated at Radcliffe, suggests just that in her classic book Television: The Plug-in Drug *(1977). This reading selection, in which Winn defines television addiction, was taken from that book.*

BEFORE YOU READ

- *THINK* about your own television viewing habits. How many hours a day do you typically spend in front of a television set? How would you react if you suddenly had to give up watching television? Would you describe yourself as television dependent or television addicted?

- *EXAMINE* the words *passive* and *enervated,* which Winn uses to describe certain types of television viewers. A *passive* person is not involved or not active, and to be *enervated* means to be physically weakened. Do these words have negative connotations? That is, do they suggest negative rather than positive qualities?

- *WRITE* in your journal a brief description of a person who is addicted to television. How does this person (yourself or someone you know) think, look, and act? How does this person react to others?

AS YOU READ

Focus on Winn's comparison of television addiction with other types of addiction. Mark the text as you read to highlight her definition of television addiction.

The word "addiction" is often used loosely and wryly in conversation. 1
People will refer to themselves as "mystery book addicts" or "cookie
addicts." E. B. White writes of his annual surge of interest in gardening:
"We are hooked and are making an attempt to kick the habit." Yet nobody
really believes that reading mysteries or ordering seeds by catalogue is
serious enough to be compared with addictions to heroin or alcohol. The
word "addiction" is here used jokingly to denote a tendency to overindulge
in some pleasurable activity.

People often refer to being "hooked on TV." Does this, too, fall into 2
the lighthearted category of cookie eating and other pleasures that people
pursue with unusual intensity, or is there a kind of television viewing that
falls into the more serious category of destructive addiction?

When we think about addiction to drugs or alcohol, we frequently 3
focus on negative aspects, ignoring the pleasures that accompany drinking
or drug-taking. And yet the essence of any serious addiction is a pursuit of
pleasure, a search for a "high" that normal life does not supply. It is only
the inability to function without the addictive substance that is dismaying,
the dependence of the organism upon a certain experience and an increasing inability to function normally without it. Thus a person will take two
or three drinks at the end of the day not merely for the pleasure drinking
provides, but also because he "doesn't feel normal" without them.

Real addicts do not merely pursue a pleasurable experience one time in 4
order to function normally. They need to *repeat* it again and again. Something about that particular experience makes life without it less than complete. Other potentially pleasurable experiences are no longer possible, for
under the spell of the addictive experience, their lives are peculiarly distorted. The addict craves an experience and yet is never really satisfied.
The organism may be temporarily sated, but soon it begins to crave again.

Finally a serious addiction is distinguished from a harmless pursuit of 5
pleasure by its distinctly destructive elements. Heroin addicts, for instance,
lead damaged lives: their increasing need for heroin in increasing doses
prevents them from working, from maintaining relationships, from developing in human ways. Similarly alcoholics' lives are narrowed and dehumanized by their dependence on alcohol.

Let us consider television viewing in the light of the conditions that 6
define serious addictions.

Not unlike drugs or alcohol, the television experience allows the 7
participant to blot out the real world and enter into a pleasurable and
passive mental state. The worries and anxieties of reality are as effectively
deferred by becoming absorbed in a television program as by going on a

"trip" induced by drugs or alcohol. And just as alcoholics are only vaguely aware of their addiction, feeling that they control their drinking more than they really do ("I can cut it out any time I want—I just like to have three or four drinks before dinner"), people similarly overestimate their control over television watching. Even as they put off other activities to spend hour after hour watching television, they feel they could easily resume living in a different, less passive style. But somehow or other while the television set is present in their homes, the click doesn't sound. With television pleasures available, those other experiences seem less attractive, more difficult somehow.

A heavy viewer (a college English instructor) observes: "I find televi- 8 sion almost irresistible. When the set is on, I cannot ignore it. I can't turn it off. I feel sapped, will-less, enervated. As I reach out to turn off the set, the strength goes out of my arms. So I sit there for hours and hours."

Self-confessed television addicts often feel they "ought" to do other 9 things—but the fact that they don't read and don't plant their garden or sew or crochet or play games or have conversations means that those activities are no longer as desirable as television viewing. In a way the lives of heavy viewers are as imbalanced by their television "habit" as a drug addict's or an alcoholic's. They are living in a holding pattern, as it were, passing up the activities that lead to growth or development or a sense of accomplishment. This is one reason people talk about their television viewing so ruefully, so apologetically. They are aware that it is an unproductive experience, that almost any other endeavor is more worthwhile by any human measure.

Finally it is the adverse effect of television viewing on the lives of so 10 many people that defines it as a serious addiction. The television habit distorts the sense of time. It renders other experiences vague and curiously unreal while taking on a greater reality for itself. It weakens relationships by reducing and sometimes eliminating normal opportunities for talking, for communicating.

And yet television does not satisfy, else why would the viewer continue 11 to watch hour after hour, day after day? "The measure of health," writes Lawrence Kubie, "is flexibility . . . and especially the freedom to cease when sated."* But heavy television viewers can never be sated with their television experiences—these do not provide the true nourishment that satiation requires—and thus they find that they cannot stop watching.

✿   ✿   ✿

---

*Lawrence Kubie, *Neurotic Distortion and the Creative Process* (Lawrence: University of Kansas Press, 1958).

AFTER YOU READ

- *THINK* about television viewing as a form of addiction. How is it like other addictions? How is it different? In what ways is it more harmful than other addictions? In what ways is it less harmful?

- *EXAMINE* Winn's assertion that "the essence of any serious addiction is a pursuit of pleasure, a search for a 'high' that normal life does not supply." What other forms of addiction can be viewed as "pursuits of pleasure"? According to Winn, when does an innocent pursuit of pleasure become a destructive addiction?

- *WRITE* an argument *against* Winn's thesis that extensive and habitual television viewing is a form of addiction.

Don't Touch That Dial

MADELINE DREXLER

❀

Free-lance writer Madeline Drexler published the follow-
ing analysis of the effects of television viewing in the
Boston Globe *in 1991. In contrast to Marie Winn in the*
previous essay, Drexler believes that television can have a
positive influence on its viewers—even on child viewers.

BEFORE YOU READ

▪ *THINK* about your own attitude toward television. Do you think watching television is primarily beneficial or harmful? Do you believe that its
effects on children are similar to or different from its effects on adults?

▪ *EXAMINE* the first paragraph of Drexler's essay. From this paragraph,
what do you expect her attitude toward television to be? Now read the
first sentence of the second paragraph. How does this sentence change your
expectations?

▪ *WRITE* a journal entry in which you discuss the television viewing habits
that you had as a child. How much television did you watch? What
particular television shows did you watch? Do you think your experiences
with television encouraged you to learn or prevented you from learning?

AS YOU READ

Notice that Drexler states the position, which is held by Marie Winn, that
television viewing is harmful and then argues against this position. Underline the three reasons many people believe that television is bad for children
and then evaluate Drexler's refutation of these beliefs.

426

Television acts as a narcotic on children—mesmerizing them, stunting 1
their ability to think, and displacing such wholesome activities as book
reading and family discussions. Right?

Wrong, says researcher Daniel Anderson, a psychologist at the Univer- 2
sity of Massachusetts at Amherst. Anderson doesn't have any particular
affection for *Garfield and Friends,* MTV clips, or *Gilligan's Island* reruns.
But he does believe it's important to distinguish television's impact on
children from influences of the family and the wider culture. We tend to
blame TV, he says, for problems it doesn't really cause. In the process, we
overlook our own roles in shaping children's minds.

One conventional belief about television is that it impairs a child's 3
ability to think and to interpret the world. But Anderson's own research
and reviews of the scientific literature discredit this assumption. While
watching TV, children do not merely absorb words and images. Instead,
they muse upon the meaning of what they see, its plausibility, and its
implications for the future—whether they've tuned in to a news report of
a natural disaster or an action show. Because television relies on such
cinematic techniques as montage and crosscutting, children learn early how
to draw inferences about the passage of time, character psychology, and
implied events. Even preschoolers comprehend more than just the information supplied on the tube.

Another contention about television is that it displaces reading as a 4
form of entertainment. But according to Anderson, the amount of time
spent watching television is not related to reading ability. For one thing,
TV doesn't take the place of reading for most children; it takes the place
of similar sorts of recreation, such as going to the movies, reading comic
books, listening to the radio, and playing sports. Variables such as socioeconomic status and parents' educational background exert a far stronger
influence on a child's reading. "Far and away," Anderson says, "the best
predictor of reading ability, and of how much a child reads, is how much
a parent reads."

Conventional wisdom has it that heavy television-watching lowers IQ 5
scores and hinders school performance. Since the 1960s, SAT scores have
dropped, along with state and national assessments of educational achievement. But here, too, Anderson notes that no studies have linked prolonged
television exposure in childhood to lower IQ later on. In fact, research
suggests that it's the other way around. Early IQ predicts how much TV
an older child will watch. "If you're smart young, you'll watch less TV
when you're older," Anderson says. Conversely, in the same self-selecting
process, people of lower IQ tend to be lifelong television devotees.

When parents watch TV with their young children, explaining new 6
words and ideas to them, the children comprehend far more than they
would if they were watching alone. This is due partly to the fact that when
kids expect that TV will require thought, they spend more time thinking.
What's ironic is that most parents use an educational program as an
opportunity to park their kids in front of the set and do something in
another room. "Even for parents who are generally wary of television,"
Anderson says, "*Sesame Street* is considered a show where it's perfectly
okay to leave a child alone." The program was actually intended to be
viewed by parents and children together, he says.

Because our attitudes inform TV viewing, Anderson applauds the 7
nascent trend of offering high school courses that teach students how to
"decode" television. In these classes, students learn to analyze the persuasive techniques of commercials, compare the reality of crime to its dramatic
portrayal, inquire into the economics of broadcasting, and understand the
mechanics of TV production. Such courses, Anderson contends, teach the
kind of critical thinking central to the purpose of education. "Kids can be
taught as much about television as about text or computers," he says.

If anything, Anderson's views underscore the fact that television 8
cannot be disparaged in isolation from larger forces. For years researchers
have attempted to show that television is inherently dangerous to children,
hypnotizing them with its movement and color, cutting their attention span
with its fast-paced, disconnected images, curbing intellectual development,
and taking the place of loftier pastimes.

By showing that television promotes none of these effects, Anderson 9
intends to shift the discussion to the real issue: content. That, of course, is
a thornier discussion. How should our society judge the violence of
primetime shows? The sexism of MTV? The materialism of commercials?
"I feel television is almost surely having a major social impact on the kids,
as opposed to a cognitive impact," Anderson says.

In this context, he offers some advice to parents. First, "Parents should 10
think of their kids as actively absorbing everything on television. They are
not just passively mesmerized—in one eye and out the other. Some things
on TV are probably good for children to watch, like educational TV, and
some things are bad."

Second, "If you think your kid is spending lots of time watching 11
television, think about what alternatives there are, from the child's point
of view." Does a youngster have too much free time? Are there books, toys,
games, or playmates around? "A lot of the time, kids watch TV as a default
activity: There's nothing else to do."

Finally, "If a child persists in watching too much television, the 12
question is why. It's rare that TV shows are themselves so entertaining."
More often than not, the motive is escapism. A teen-ager may be uncomfortable with his or her peers; a child may want to retreat from a home
torn by marital strife; there may be problems at school.

For children, as for adults, television can be a source of enlightenment 13
or a descent into mindlessness—depending mostly on the choices of
lucre-driven executives. But as viewers, we can't ignore what we ourselves
bring to the medium.

❀   ❀   ❀

AFTER YOU READ

▪ *THINK* about the reasons people believe television is bad for children.
Do you agree or disagree with these reasons? Now think about how Drexler
refutes these reasons. Are Drexler's arguments in support of television
convincing?

▪ *EXAMINE* the three quotations from Daniel Anderson that Drexler gives
in paragraphs 10, 11, and 12. Write the main point of each of these three
quotations in your own words. Then discuss each of these three points with
the rest of your class. Do you agree or disagree with Anderson's ideas and
advice? Why or why not?

▪ *WRITE* an essay in which you discuss the positive and negative effects of
television on children. Do you think the positive effects outweigh the
negative ones, or vice versa? In your essay, use support from the readings
by both Winn and Drexler as well as your own experiences and observations. Or *WRITE* an essay for parents of young children in which you give
them advice about how to use television as an effective learning tool in the
home. You might suggest specific shows for their children to watch as well
as specific ways for the parents and children to interact in relation to these
television shows.

Getting a Degree by E-mail

MARY LORD

❀

In this article, which appeared in U.S. News & World
Report *on October 30, 1995, Mary Lord describes how
some students are pursuing degrees by enrolling in "online
courses"—that is, college courses that can be accessed via
the Internet. Lord not only describes how to get a degree
by using email but also offers advice to students who
choose to pursue a college degree in this way.*

BEFORE YOU READ

▪ *THINK* about what it is (or would be) like to take an online course. How
are such courses like those taken at a college or university? How are they
different?

▪ *EXAMINE* the terms *online* and *on-campus.* What connotations does each
term have for you? That is, what are your emotional reactions to these two
terms?

▪ *WRITE* a journal entry in which you argue for or against the idea of online
courses.

AS YOU READ

Underline information and arguments that influence your attitude toward
this new form of education.

To advance in the Air Force, Lt. Jay Jones needs an advanced degree—no 1 small obstacle given his frequent stints underground in a nuclear missile silo in Wyoming. So three years ago he launched into an MBA program at Colorado State University that allows him to "attend" class by VCR and file homework anytime he wants.

For Patti Shank, head of patient education at a small health mainte- 2 nance organization in Columbia, Md., the challenge was to "stay ahead of the curve" in the rapidly evolving managed-care field while working 60-hour weeks and raising two children. Her solution: an online master's degree in educational technology leadership from George Washington University. She reads the same texts as her campus peers, watches lectures on satellite TV, sends papers through an electronic bulletin board and "talks" with professors and classmates during the wee hours via E-mail. At $574, online courses cost less than half the traditional program's.

The old correspondence course has stormed into the high-tech age— 3 and it's proving to be a big hit. As many as 4 million Americans are now buffing their professional credentials by padding over to their PCs and plugging into "distance learning." Need to get over your fear of public speaking? Front Range Community College near Denver will teach you the techniques over the Internet. (Note: There's no escaping four live on-campus presentations.) How about accounting? Great Britain's Open University, with nearly 150,000 students worldwide, offers a highly re-garded curriculum. The University of Massachusetts at Dartmouth recently started an online course in writing for the World Wide Web.

All told, some 75 universities and colleges offer online degree pro- 4 grams, according to a tally on CompuServe's Education Forum. "We're beginning to see a revolution in higher education," says Milton Blood, director of accreditation at the American Assembly of Collegiate Schools of Business. He calls the explosion of electronic courses "mind-boggling."

As has long been true with by-mail courses, which date back to 1890, 5 the quality of online programs varies from superb to subpar. And students have little help distinguishing the one from the other. No certification system exists for online programs, though the American Council on Education hopes to announce good-practice guidelines soon. (The Dis-tance Education and Training Council, which accredits home-study courses, can lead you to programs that pass muster—some of which include online courses.) Some courses consist solely of long-winded lectures trans-mitted over the wires or videos, with scant opportunity for interaction with a professor. The top-notch choices are as academically rigorous as their on-campus counterparts. "This is probably the best education I've gotten, but you have to be extremely self-motivated," says Shank, who read 30 books to research a recent paper on workplace technology.

Good programs use the medium itself to enhance the learning experi- 6 ence. For its cybercourse on the Holocaust, for instance, the University of Massachusetts at Dartmouth is connecting a geographically dispersed group of online students with a Nazi death camp survivor living in Israel—an experience the students would never have otherwise. In worthwhile programs, students can debate with professors on the school bulletin board and through E-mail. And they can electronically brainstorm with their peers.

Such discourse is an especially important feature of distance business 7 programs like that of Britain's Henley Management College—which counts a fishing captain off the Falkland Islands among its 7,000 MBA students. While much of Henley's courseware consists of mailed packs of videotaped lectures and case-study readings, far-flung students can work in groups by conferring via E-mail. Such teamwork is a hallmark of the best on-campus MBA programs. Online, the collaboration has the advantage of mimicking the way employees at muscular multinationals increasingly find themselves working: in "virtual teams" with colleagues around the globe.

To harried professionals, distance learning's greatest attribute may be 8 that the student decides when to hear a lecture, do a paper, graduate. "What other class can you go to in your pajamas and red fuzzy slippers?" asks Janice Norman, a sight-impaired student at Montgomery College in Rockville, Md., who welcomes the lack of prejudice online—and of intimidating class loudmouths. Instructors also benefit by having more time to ruminate over a response to a student's performance. "I'm more persnickety with my online students," says Montgomery College computer Prof. Ben Acton.

For now, the surest way to find the fussy professors and quality 9 programs is to stick with those schools whose classroom courses are accredited. "We are applying the technology to proven theories and existing courses, not developing a curriculum to fit the technology," says Bruce Heasley, associate director for student services at Pennsylvania State University, which has one of the nation's largest distance learning programs, with nearly 18,000 students. "Anyone can throw an accounting course together, but do you have enough to put four or five courses together for a certificate or degree? It has to add up and mean something."

A worthy institution also will treat credits earned on campus and at a 10 distance as interchangeable. If missile officer Jones wanted to, he would have the flexibility to attend class at Colorado State or transfer to another school. Henley managers who are assigned to jobs that lack Internet access have the option of coming to campus. Their diplomas don't distinguish between distance degrees and the on-campus kind.

Finally, for online courses, you'll want strong technical support. Along 11 with keeping the school's electronic bulletin board humming, Montgomery College's Acton fields regular calls from students with the computer-era equivalent complaint of "the dog ate my homework." Colorado State has a 24-hour hot line, while Henley includes software help in its courseware.

Remote courses won't ever shut down campus. But even people who 12 prefer the familiar ways of learning are apt to get a taste of distance education. Businesses, which currently spend $30 billion a year on formal training, are among the biggest proponents of cost-saving CD-ROM instruction, for example. Denver-based Re/Max International beams recertification courses over the company's own satellite-TV system to 25,000 real-estate brokers in North America. The U.S. Postal Service uses teleconferencing to bring far-flung mail workers up to speed on new equipment.

Even such bastions of tradition as the Harvard Business School are 13 bowing to the inevitable. Instead of wasting their first weeks plugging gaps in such fundamentals as accounting or basic computer skills, future MBAs will take an assessment test—and receive refresher exercises—over the World Wide Web.

❀   ❀   ❀

AFTER YOU READ

- *THINK* about the advantages of online courses. Then think about the disadvantages of such courses. Is the technology involved in such courses a positive feature for you or an obstacle to overcome?

- *EXAMINE* the term *distance learning,* which can apply to online courses or televised courses. Compare online courses and televised courses. Which has more potential for learning? Why? How does each compare to a course in which you are actually present in the same room with your instructor and classmates?

- *WRITE* an essay discussing the advantages and disadvantages of an online education. In your essay you may consider the effectiveness of online courses, the cost of such courses, their accessibility to students, and so on. Ultimately, would you recommend an online education to a friend?

Unplugged

DAVID GELERNTER

❦

A computer science professor at Yale University, David Gelernter was almost killed in 1993 when he opened a package that he thought was a doctoral dissertation and it exploded in his face, destroying his right hand and eye. In his book Drawing Life: Surviving the Unabomber *(1997), he describes walking to the local hospital, bleeding and "royally annoyed" but keeping time to an old Zionist marching song as he walked. Although his blood pressure was at zero when he reached the hospital, he lived to write about his experiences and to continue his commentary on the technology of our age. For example, he analyzes the role of beauty and art in computer technology in his books* Machine Beauty: Elegance and the Heart of Technology *and* The Aesthetics of Computing. *However, in the following article, originally published in the* New Republic, *Gelernter questions the current use of computers in the school system.*

BEFORE YOU READ

• *THINK* about the use of computers in educational classrooms—especially in public school classrooms. How can computers be helpful in these classrooms? How can they be harmful? You might be interested to know that some state legislators have proposed substituting laptop computers for books in the public school system. Do you think this is a good idea or a bad idea? Why do you feel as you do?

• *EXAMINE* the title "Unplugged." Based on this title, what attitude do you think Gelernter has toward computers in the classroom?

• *WRITE* in your journal two lists—one, of ways that computers can be helpful in classrooms, and the other, of ways they can be harmful.

AS YOU READ

Notice the structure of Gelernter's essay, in which he first recognizes the beneficial uses of computers in the classroom and then argues that computers are ultimately harmful to education. Identify and number in the margins the three uses of computers that Gelernter believes are especially harmful to the education of children.

Over the last decade an estimated $2 billion has been spent on more than 2 million computers for America's classrooms. That's not surprising. We constantly hear from Washington that the schools are in trouble and that computers are a godsend. Within the education establishment, in poor as well as rich schools, the machines are awaited with nearly religious awe. An inner-city principal bragged to a teacher friend of mine recently that his school "has a computer in every classroom . . . despite being in a bad neighborhood!"

Computers should be in the schools. They have the potential to accomplish great things. With the right software, they could help make science tangible or teach neglected topics like art and music. They could help students form a concrete idea of society by displaying on-screen a version of the city in which they live—a picture that tracks real life moment by moment.

In practice, however, computers make our worst educational nightmares come true. While we bemoan the decline of literacy, computers discount words in favor of pictures and pictures in favor of video. While we fret about the decreasing cogency of public debate, computers dismiss linear argument and promote fast, shallow romps across the information landscape. While we worry about basic skills, we allow into the classroom software that will do a student's arithmetic or correct his spelling.

Take multimedia. The idea of multimedia is to combine text, sound and pictures in a single package that you browse on screen. You don't just *read* Shakespeare; you watch actors performing, listen to songs, view Elizabethan buildings. What's wrong with that? By offering children candy-coated books, multimedia is guaranteed to sour them on unsweetened reading. It makes the printed page look even more boring than it used to look. Sure, books will be available in the classroom, too—but they'll have all the appeal of a dusty piano to a teen who has a Walkman handy.

So what if the little nippers don't read? If they're watching Olivier ₅
instead, what do they lose? The text, the written word along with all of its
attendant pleasures. Besides, a book is more portable than a computer, has
a higher-resolution display, can be written on and dog-eared and is com-
paratively dirt cheap.

Hypermedia, multimedia's comrade in the struggle for a brave new ₆
classroom, is just as troubling. It's a way of presenting documents on screen
without imposing a linear start-to-finish order. Disembodied paragraphs
are linked by theme; after reading one about the First World War, for
example, you might be able to choose another about the technology of
battleships, or the life of Woodrow Wilson, or hemlines in the '20s. This
is another cute idea that is good in minor ways and terrible in major ones.
Teaching children to understand the orderly unfolding of a plot or a logical
argument is a crucial part of education. Authors don't merely agglomerate
paragraphs; they work hard to make the narrative read a certain way, prove
a particular point. To turn a book or a document into hypertext is to invite
readers to ignore exactly what counts—the story.

The real problem, again, is the accentuation of already bad habits. ₇
Dynamiting documents into disjointed paragraphs is one more expression
of the sorry fact that sustained argument is not our style. If you're a
newspaper or magazine editor and your readership is dwindling, what's
the solution? Shorter pieces. If you're a politician and you want to get
elected, what do you need? Tasty sound bites. Logical presentation be
damned.

Another software species, "allow me" programs, is not much better. ₈
These programs correct spelling and, by applying canned grammatical and
stylistic rules, fix prose. In terms of promoting basic skills, though, they
have all the virtues of a pocket calculator.

In Kentucky, as *The Wall Street Journal* recently reported, students in grades ₉
K–3 are mixed together regardless of age in a relaxed environment. It works
great, the *Journal* says. Yes, scores on computation tests have dropped 10
percent at one school, but not to worry: "Drilling addition and subtraction
in an age of calculators is a waste of time," the principal reassures us.
Meanwhile, a Japanese educator informs University of Wisconsin mathe-
matician Richard Akey that in his country, "calculators are not used in
elementary or junior high school because the primary emphasis is on
helping students develop their mental abilities." No wonder Japanese kids
blow the pants off American kids in math. Do we really think "drilling
addition and subtraction in an age of calculators is a waste of time"? If we

do, then "drilling reading in an age of multimedia is a waste of time" can't be far behind.

Prose-correcting programs are also a little ghoulish, like asking a 10 computer for tips on improving your personality. On the other hand, I ran this article through a spell-checker, so how can I ban the use of such programs in schools? Because to misspell is human; to have no idea of correct spelling is to be semiliterate.

There's no denying that computers have the potential to perform 11 inspiring feats in the classroom. If we are ever to see that potential realized, however, we ought to agree on three conditions. First, there should be a completely new crop of children's software. Most of today's offerings show no imagination. There are hundreds of similar reading and geography and arithmetic programs, but almost nothing on electricity or physics or architecture. Also, they abuse the technical capacities of new media to glitz up old forms instead of creating new ones. Why not build a time-travel program that gives kids a feel for how history is structured by zooming you backward? A spectrum program that lets users twirl a frequency knob to see what happens?

Second, computers should be used only during recess or relaxation 12 periods. Treat them as fillips, not as surrogate teachers. When I was in school in the '60s, we all loved educational films. When we saw a movie in class, everybody won: teachers didn't have to teach, and pupils didn't have to learn. I suspect that classroom computers are popular today for the same reasons.

Most important, educators should learn what parents and most teach- 13 ers already know: you cannot teach a child anything unless you look him in the face. We should not forget what computers are. Like books—better in some ways, worse in others—they are devices that help children mobilize their own resources and learn for themselves. The computer's potential to do good is modestly greater than a book's in some areas. Its potential to do harm is vastly greater, across the board.

❀ ❀ ❀

AFTER YOU READ

▪ *THINK* about the use of multimedia, hypermedia, and correcting programs for educational purposes. Do you agree or disagree with Gelernter that these teaching methods can ultimately be harmful to students? Why do you feel as you do?

• *EXAMINE* the structure of the first major section of Gelernter's argument. His first paragraph provides background information and an example of computers in the classroom; his second paragraph recognizes the beneficial effects of computers in the classroom; and his third paragraph states the thesis that he will develop in the remainder of the essay. What is this thesis?

• *EXAMINE* also the last three paragraphs of Gelernter's essay in which he provides three conditions that he believes must be met if the educational potential of computers is to be realized in the classroom. What are these three conditions? With which do you agree and why? With which do you disagree and why?

• *WRITE* an essay in which you argue *for* or *against* the use of computers in the classroom. In your essay, specify particular conditions under which computers should or should not be used and your reasons for these conditions.

Internet Insecurity

ADAM COHEN

❋

A graduate of Harvard College and Harvard Law School, Adam Cohen is the coauthor of American Pharaoh: Mayor Richard Daley [and] His Battle for Chicago and the Nation, *which was a* New York Times *Notable Book of 2000. A senior writer at* Time *magazine, he has written articles on many topics, including the Microsoft antitrust case, the national economy, and various legal issues. Cohen concentrates on technology issues in his upcoming book about eBay and in many of his articles, including the following essay about problems with Internet security.*

BEFORE YOU READ

▪ *THINK* about your own use of the Internet—or about ways that you might use it as a first-year college student. Do you sometimes worry about information that others might obtain about you from your Internet usage? Do you give your credit card number when you order merchandise over the Internet? Have you ever given your address, telephone number, or social security number on the Internet?

▪ *EXAMINE* the title "Internet Insecurity," which is a clever play on words. In the second word in the title, Cohen inserts the prefix *in-* to reverse reader expectations (or perhaps hopes) about Internet security. Since the prefix *in-* literally means "not" or "no," it changes the positive definition of *security* to the negative meaning of "no security."

▪ *EXAMINE* also the first and last sections of the article. Cohen encloses his serious message about lack of Internet security within the framework of a humorous story about his "spying" on a colleague's use of the Internet. Do you think this framing adds to the essay? Why or why not?

© 2001 Time Inc. Reprinted by permission.

▪ *WRITE* a journal entry in which you discuss problems with Internet security that you have experienced or heard about from friends or on the media.

AS YOU READ

Notice Cohen's nine main points, which are numbered and printed in boldface. Put brackets around the points that seem most important to you.

M y colleague Joel Stein let drop a while back that he was working on ₁ a book proposal. I found it a bit frustrating that he wouldn't tell me the topic. Joel had been traveling a lot lately too—to Iceland to interview Björk; to Hollywood for the Oscars—but he was stingy with details. Where was he going? Whom was he hanging with, and how much money was he spending? I've also wondered what kind of websites he surfs. And, O.K., I wouldn't mind reading his e-mail.

So I did.   ₂

Joel went out of town recently, which allowed me to duck into his ₃ office and install spying software on his hard drive. You can buy commercial spyware these days, but I used VNC, which can be downloaded free. VNC was designed to help people link their own computers. But it also worked as a cheap and easy way for me to keep tabs on Joel. Soon after loading VNC onto my computer, I was rifling through Joel's hard drive.

That book proposal? With a few mouse clicks, it appeared on Joel's ₄ screen—and on mine. (*Adventures in Monogamy*, a 12-chapter comic romp starring . . . Joel. Mystery solved.) It was also easy to pore over his expense reports, checking out whom he took to dinner in L.A., and what he thinks passes for a legitimate expense. Has Björk even recorded $112.76 worth of CDs?

Then I—or should I say Joel?—hit the Internet. The great thing about ₅ controlling another person's computer is that you can surf the Web as if you were him or her. When you go to a site, his or her IP address—a kind of digital fingerprint—is the one that gets left behind, not yours.

I was going to mess with Joel. Stop by a few investing message boards, ₆ and have him break securities law by pumping stocks. Get him trapped by one of those FBI agents who patrol kiddie chat rooms, looking for predators. But in an effort to keep Joel—O.K., both of us—out of jail, I just posted a few items for him on pet newsgroups seeking poodle-grooming tips.

When Joel returned, I could look over his shoulder as he surfed the 7 Net. It was weird but oddly riveting to see his cursor click, click, click its way across my screen. But in the end, there were no busty babes, no Catholic school girls looking for trouble. He actually spent most of his time on CNN.com.

Then he started opening his e-mail. The first was from our boss, about 8 Joel's next column. I liked being a snoop in the loop. Another was from Joel's girlfriend's brother asking Joel to score free concert tickets. Then a chain e-mail from a few of our co-workers, with snarky comments about someone else on our floor they evidently don't like. Ah, isn't this what computer spying is all about?

I also had Joel's Social Security number, the keys to the kingdom. Those 9 digits would be enough on some websites to get me a driver's license in his name—and to start a full-scale identity theft. Before long, I could be ruining his credit rating, draining his bank accounts, and—well, you get the idea.

Too bad my editors, darn them, insisted that I tell Joel what I was 10 doing. (I can't help thinking he trashed some good stuff before I started spying.) Not that it would have been difficult to really spy on Joel at his home computer. I could have sent him spyware wrapped in an e-greeting card, programmed to install itself when he opened the card. He'd never know.

It has been two years since Sun Microsystems CEO Scott McNealy deliv- 11 ered his famous warning: "You have zero privacy [on the Internet] anyway. Get over it." Privacy advocates resisted that pessimistic assessment at the time. But since then, hardly a week goes by without a news story suggesting McNealy was on to something. Russian hackers breaking into e-commerce sites to steal credit-card numbers. Rings of Nigerian identity thieves. Cyberstalkers.

Just last week, Microsoft conceded that all versions of Windows 2000, 12 and early "beta" versions of its new XP operating system due out this fall, have a "serious vulnerability" that lets hackers take control of victims' machines. Microsoft, which is making patches available for Windows 2000, has urged consumers to "take action immediately" to fix the glitch. And it is promising to cure the problem before XP's rollout.

Internet users are well aware they are trading off privacy when they 13 dial up their modems. In a recent Time/CNN poll conducted by

Yankelovich Partners, 61% of respondents said they were "very concerned" or "somewhat concerned" that information about their Internet usage was being collected without their knowledge.

Yet websites that track users' movements are the least of it. Privacy 14 advocates and law enforcement are homing in on nine areas—from spyware to identity theft—where they say the Internet's threat to privacy is the greatest.

1
Someone Might Use
the Internet to Steal Your Identity

When police arrested Brooklyn, N.Y., busboy Abraham Abdallah in March, 15 he had *Forbes* magazine's issue on the 400 richest people in America, plus Social Security numbers, credit-card numbers, bank-account information and mothers' maiden names of an A list of intended victims drawn from the issue, including Steven Spielberg, Oprah Winfrey and Martha Stewart. Abdallah is accused of using websites, e-mail and off-line methods to try to steal the celebrities' identities and make off with millions in assets. One scheme that was caught in time: he allegedly sent an e-mail purporting to come from Siebel Systems founder Thomas Siebel to Merrill, Lynch, directing that $10 million be transferred to an offshore account. (Abdallah, who has yet to be indicted on federal charges, denied all wrongdoing at the time of his arrest.)

Abdallah's high-profile arrest brought national attention to identity 16 theft, which the FBI says is the nation's fastest-growing white-collar crime. An estimated 500,000 Americans have their identities stolen each year. A sign of the times: at least four insurance companies now offer ID-theft policies. The Privacy Rights Clearinghouse, which works with victims, says it takes an average victim of identity theft two years to clear his credit rating. A growing worst-case scenario: "criminal-identity theft," in which thieves use the stolen identity when they are arrested, leaving their victims with a criminal record that can be difficult to expunge.

Most identity theft still begins off-line, often in such low-tech ways as 17 a criminal sifting through garbage to find an unwanted preapproved credit card. But once an ID theft is under way, the Internet can make the work considerably easier. A particular problem: fast-proliferating websites that sell fake IDs.

It was a fake-ID seller who helped an identity thief run up $30,000 in   18
false charges to Charles Glueck, a Metarie, La., dentist. After Glueck lost
his wallet, the man who took it went online to get a driver's license with
his picture and Glueck's identity. He then used that license to get 15 credit
cards in Glueck's name and started charging. Glueck was shocked to learn
later from police that the website had not broken the law because when it
shipped the driver's license to the thief, the license was marked for
"novelty" use only. "Once you know how to work a computer, you can be
whoever you want to," Glueck says.

2

You May Be Unintentionally Revealing Information About Yourself as You Move Through Cyberspace

Surfing the Internet feels anonymous, like looking through the pages of a   19
magazine in a library. But the websites you visit can look back at you. Many
use "cookies" to collect data about your visit—where you go in the site,
what links you click on. There was a blowup last year when it appeared
that Internet advertising agency Doubleclick would match up its cookies
with data from an off-line marketing company that had names, addresses
and phone numbers of 88 million Americans. That plan, since abandoned,
would have let the company create personal profiles of individuals and
their Web-surfing habits.

Your Web browser may also be giving away information about you as   20
you travel through cyberspace. Whether you know it or not, your browser's
"preferences" menu may include your name, e-mail address and other
information that can be captured and stored by sites you visit. Your Internet
Protocol address can also give you away. Every computer on the Internet
is assigned an IP address, the online equivalent of a street address that
allows it to receive data. Dial-up connections usually assign you a new IP
address every time you connect. But if you use a fixed connection (like DSL
or cable), you may have a permanent IP address that any website you visit
can capture and, by comparing it against a database, connect to you by
name.

Sometimes the spy is an "E.T." program, so called because once it is   21
embedded in your computer it is programmed to "phone home" to its
corporate master. RealNetworks' RealJukebox program was found in 1999

to be sending back information to headquarters about what music a user listened to. The Federal Trade Commission decided in May that zBubbles, a now defunct online shopping service once owned by Amazon, probably deceived consumers when it told them that the information it collected about a user's Web surfing would remain anonymous.

3
That Personal Information You Just Provided to a Website Might Be Sold—Or Stolen

Websites, particularly e-commerce sites, collect a lot of data from visitors. 22 If you buy a book or a magazine at a bookstore and pay cash, there will be no record linking you to the purchase. But the books, magazines, music and movies you buy online are all linked to you by name. Web retailers are collecting a sizable database of information on individual purchasers. Who's buying pornography, and who's buying extreme political tracts. Who's buying cancer drugs, or contraception.

E-commerce sites routinely share your information, or sell it. The 23 Electronic Frontier Foundation launched a campaign in early June against Macys.com for giving away info from its bridal registry to its business partners. Amazon, which once permitted users to choose to keep their data confidential, rewrote its privacy policy last year to say customer data are an "asset" it may sell or transfer in the future. If an e-commerce site you bought from goes bankrupt, it could be legally required to sell your data to the highest bidder. And sites routinely sell or exchange your personal information. Privacy advocates are pushing for federal legislation requiring websites to let users opt out of sharing, as has recently happened in financial services.

Theft of personal data from websites is also growing. Egghead.com 24 sent a chilly wind through cyberspace late last year when it disclosed that hackers had broken into its system and may have accessed millions of credit-card numbers from its database. (It later found that no credit cards had been compromised.) It was a stark reminder that financial data are only as safe as every website you share them with.

There have been other recent high-profile hacks. Music retailer CD 25 Universe lost up to 300,000 credit-card numbers; Bibliofind, a subsidiary of Amazon, had the names, addresses and credit-card numbers of 98,000 customers stolen. One thing that makes online credit-card theft more tolerable than some cyberscams: if consumers find false charges, banks and merchants should pay most of the bill.

4
That Website on Which You Just Entered Your Credit-Card Number May Be a Fake

In April the FBI cracked a Russian ring and charged a pair of its members 26 with conspiracy and fraud. The hackers were also allegedly involved in website "spoofing." Federal officials said the Russians tried to create a counterfeit website mimicking the real home page of PayPal, the popular online fund-transfer service. PayPal has been hit with such spoofs several times. When a fake site was operating, hackers e-mailed PayPal users and got them to click on a hyperlink with the spoof site's domain name: *www.paypai.com.* On many computers, a capital *I* looks identical to the *l* at the end of the word PayPal.

Near-identical domain names are easy to obtain. Banks have also been 27 a frequent target of spoofers. Bank of America got *wwwbankof-america.com* taken down—its domain name, minus the dot after *www*—but not before some customers were tricked into entering financial information.

5
The Government May Be Giving Out Your Home Address, Social Security Number and Other Personal Information Online

If you live in Ohio, anyone who types your name into a county database 28 can learn your address and how much your house is worth. He can also inspect detailed floor plans of your house, showing placement of your windows, porches, and balconies. Supporters of the state's online initiative call it a breakthrough for open access to government records. Critics have another way of describing it: a breaking-and-entering handbook.

Governments around the country have been rushing to put property 29 records online. Many jurisdictions have joined Ohio in creating databases searchable by name. If you go to the Brookline, Mass., website, you can find out where Michael Dukakis lives. Miami's will tell you Janet Reno's home address.

It isn't just property databases. Wisconsin has most of its arrest and   30
court records online. (I discovered that a former law-school classmate
of mine has had two traffic violations and was a defendant in a civil
lawsuit.) The federal courts have put many of their records online through
a system called Public Access to Court Electronic Records (PACER). Among
the data available: Social Security numbers, financial assets, which often
must be revealed in court proceedings; and the names and ages of minor
children.

Critics say the government has gone too far in making data available   31
online, and there are signs the tide may be turning. California's court
system is considering new rules that would deny Internet access to certain
court records, including those of criminal, family and mental-health proceedings. "The purpose of making public records accessible is to ensure
accountability," says Chris Hoofnagle, legislative counsel for the Electronic
Privacy Information Center. That, he argues, does not require putting
details of divorce and child-custody disputes or bankruptcy proceedings on
the Internet.

6
For-Profit Companies and People Who Don't Like
You May Be Broadcasting Your Private Information
on the Internet

The murder of Amy Boyer, a 20-year-old New Hampshire dental assistant,   32
by an obsessed admirer in 1999 called attention to an obscure part of the
cybereconomy—online data brokers. Boyer's assailant paid $45 to Florida-
based Docusearch.com for her Social Security number and later purchased
the name of her employer. He then tracked her down on the job and killed
her.

Data brokers insist they are doing necessary work, providing back-   33
ground information to employers, creditors and other people who legiti-
mately need it. But many sell Social Security numbers and private financial
information to anyone willing to pay their fees. Often they are the first stop
for identity thieves and stalkers.

Data brokers get most of their information from government records.   34
Privacy advocates want governments to be more selective about what
information they allow brokers to harvest. California, for example, has a
law that permits police to release arrest data to reporters while withholding

it from businesses that would use it for commercial purposes. Privacy advocates say more jurisdictions should follow California's lead.

The Internet makes it easier for people to broker information about 35 people they don't like. In Seattle, a battle is raging over Justicefiles.org, a frequent critic of local law enforcement. The group began posting police officers' Social Security numbers on its website. A state court has ordered the group to stop, holding that it was infringing on the officers' privacy rights. Free-speech advocates are fighting the ruling, arguing that there is no basis for preventing the dissemination of truthful, legally obtained information.

7
Your Company or Your Spouse May Be Using Your Computer to Spy on You

Companies have the legal right to monitor their employees' Web surfing, 36 e-mail and instant messaging. Many do, whether they warn their workers or not—so don't count on any of it remaining private. Last month the University of Tennessee released more than 900 pages of archived e-mail between an administrator and a married college president in which the administrator wrote of her love for him and of her use of drugs and alcohol to deal with her unhappiness. Employers, including [*The New York*] *Times* and Dow Chemical, have fired workers for sending inappropriate e-mail.

But the fastest-growing area for Internet spying is the home. Spector- 37 Soft, a leading manufacturer of spyware, at first marketed its products to parents and employers. Sales jumped fivefold, however, when the company changed its pitch to target spouses and romantic partners. "In just one day of running Spector on my home PC, I was able to identify my fiancé's true personality," a testimonial on the company's website trumpets. "I found all 17 of his girlfriends."

What can you expect if someone puts SpectorSoft's Spector 2.2 on 38 your computer? It will secretly take hundreds of snapshots an hour of every website, chat group and e-mail that appears on your screen, and store them so that the special someone who is spying on you can review them later. A new product, SpectorSoft's eBlaster, will send the spy detailed e-mail reports updating your computer activities as often as every 30 minutes. These products work in stealth mode, so that the people being spied on are totally unaware.

SpectorSoft has sold 35,000 copies of its spyware, and it has only a   39
piece of a booming market. WinWhatWhere, another big player, sells
primarily to businesses, but what it calls the "disgruntled spouse" market
has been finding WinWhatWhere. Many smaller companies have sites that
sell relatively crude "keyloggers," software that records every keystroke
typed on a computer.

Isn't all this spying on loved ones a little creepy? Not to SpectorSoft   40
president Doug Fowler. "If you're in a committed relationship and you get
caught because of evidence online, as far as I'm concerned you deserve to
be caught," he says. Richard Eaton, president of WinWhatWhere, recognizes that in a perfect world users would reveal that they have placed
monitoring software on a computer. But WinWhatWhere Investigator has
a feature that allows it to be completely hidden. "Our customers demanded
it," he says.

8
A Stranger May Be Using Your Computer
to Spy on You

Hackers can get into your computer and look through everything on it if   41
your defenses are down. Computers hooked up to the Internet through
cable or DSL connections, which are always on, rather than dial-up
services, are particularly vulnerable. A home firewall is the best protection
against these sneak attacks.

Another prime method of turning your computer against you is   42
tricking you into downloading spyware. Hence the name Trojan horse. This
software's danger is hidden inside a benign exterior. That's why so many
viruses—like last year's "I Love You," and recent ones promising photos of
Anna Kournikova and Jennifer Lopez—are wrapped in appealing packages.

A lot of viruses are designed to damage computers, but some are aimed   43
at stealing information. The "I Love You" virus retrieved passwords from
victims' computers to send back to its creator. Other viruses are programmed to strip e-mail addresses from your address book. Back Orifice,
a notorious piece of software created a few years ago by a hacking group
called Cult of the Dead Cow, takes over a host computer completely.
Among its privacy-invading features: it can dig up passwords and monitor
every keystroke typed into it.

Computer worms and viruses can dig through the files on your hard   44
drive. VBS.Noped.A@mm invades computers and searches for child por-

nography. If it finds picture files with suspect-sounding names, it notifies the police and e-mails some of the files to them—and sends copies of itself to addresses in the victim's e-mail address book. A big problem with Noped, in addition to the privacy concerns: it's often wrong.

Back Orifice is freely available online, along with newer hackware like   45 SubSeven. There are sites like *hack.co.za* and *astalavista.box.sk* that hold a hacker's hand as he plans an assault on your computer. And there are mailing lists like BugTraq that offer up the latest viruses. As a hacker posted at *astalavista.box.sk:* "Nowadays, every idiot knowing how to press buttons is able to take control over your computer if you are not careful."

9
You May Have a Cyberstalker

When a woman in North Hollywood, Calif., spurned Gary Dellapenta's   46 advances, the 50-year-old security guard got back at her via the Internet. Using her name, he posted personal ads describing fantasies of a "home-invasion rape." Six men appeared at her apartment over five months to take her up on Dellapenta's offer. Sentenced to six years in prison in 1999, he was the first person jailed for cyberstalking.

Dellapenta met his victim off-line, at church, but more often the first   47 encounter occurs online. There are few hard statistics on cyberstalking. But Working to Halt Online Abuse, a group that helps cyberstalking victims, says it receives reports of nearly 100 cases a week. The stalkers meet their victims, according to the group, mainly via e-mail, chat groups, newsgroups and instant messaging.

Jayne Hitchcock, president of WHOA, believes that her cyberstalker   48 found her when she got into a controversy in a writers' newsgroup. Her stalker sent sexually explicit e-mails with forged addresses purporting to be from her. One contained her home address and phone number and said she was interested in sado-sexual fantasies. At one point, Hitchcock was getting 30 phone calls a day. She was repeatedly mail-bombed—barraged with enough e-mails to shut down her computer. Her stalker also mail-bombed her husband, her literary agent and her colleagues at the University of Maryland.

Hitchcock is lobbying states to enact specialized cyberstalking laws. So   49 far, 33 have. In most of the cases that WHOA tracks, contacting the offender's Internet service provider is enough to make the activity stop. But more than 16% of the time, victims have to go to the police.

When I was done spying on Joel, I gave him a quick rundown on what I 50
had seen. He was fine about the book proposal. He'd been having second
thoughts about it anyway. He had an explanation for the $112.76 that
involved the high price of American CDs in Iceland. And he pointed out
that he had not added to the snarky e-mail about our co-worker. All he did
was read it. Then he told me that for the good stuff I should have spied on
his home PC. That's where he does his most interesting web surfing, he
said. He went off on a brief discourse about the various kinds of hard-core
pornographic pop-ups that show up when he visits soft-core sites. Joel also
told me that he keeps all his financial data on his home computer.
Interesting. Come to think of it, I've always wondered about his salary.
Joel, I owe you an e-birthday card. Be sure to open it at home.

❀   ❀   ❀

AFTER YOU READ

▪ *THINK* about how you would feel if you knew that someone were
invading your privacy on the Internet. Would your feelings be the same as
if someone were opening your mail or listening to your telephone conversations? According to Cohen, how easy is it for a hacker to invade the
security of Internet users? In most cases, do Internet users know when their
privacy has been invaded?

▪ *EXAMINE* the nine breaches of Internet security that Cohen identifies.
Which types of invasion do you think are most common? Which are most
harmful to Internet users? Which types are you most susceptible to
personally?

▪ *WRITE* an essay in which you compare invasion of privacy on the Internet
to other types of invasion of privacy, such as personal eavesdropping,
unsolicited telemarketing calls, and/or phone tapping. Which concerns you
more and why? Or *WRITE* an essay in which you focus on the effects of one
or more of the breaches of Internet security that Cohen discusses. For
example, you might discuss the problems you could have if someone used
the Internet to steal your identity, to spy on you, or to stalk you. Develop
your essay with specific support from Cohen's essay as well as with
examples from your own experience or reading.

Fraternities of Netheads:
Internet Addiction on Campus

KIMBERLY S. YOUNG

❀

Kimberly S. Young is a faculty member of the Psychology Department at the University of Pittsburgh, Bradford. She is also the founder of the Center for On-Line Addiction, which provides consultations on misuse of the Internet to educational institutions, mental health facilities, and corporations. Young has spoken about Internet abuse on network news programs and has published articles on the subject in The New York Times, *the* Wall Street Journal, Newsweek, *and* U.S. News & World Report. *The following selection is taken from her book* Caught in the Net: How to Recognize the Signs of Internet Addiction—and a Winning Strategy for Recovery *(1998).*

BEFORE YOU READ

▪ *THINK* about the problem of Internet addiction, of being "Caught in the Net," as Young phrases it. An addiction is a compulsive commitment to a particular substance or activity; hence, Internet addiction is compulsive use of the Internet. Do you think Internet addiction is a serious problem on college campuses? Do you spend large blocks of time online? Do you have friends or classmates who are frequent Internet users? Would you consider yourself, or anyone you know, to be "addicted" to the Internet?

▪ *EXAMINE* the description of the party in the first paragraph of the essay. How is this party like other parties you have experienced or heard about? Then examine both paragraphs 1 and 2 to see how this party differs from most late-night campus socials. Can you guess what type of party Young is describing?

• *WRITE* a journal entry in which you describe the Internet usage on your campus. How do most students use the Internet? That is, do they spend time sending personal or academic e-mail messages, participating in chat rooms, playing games, ordering merchandise, or doing research for their classes? How much time do most students spend on these activities? How much time do you spend?

AS YOU READ

Number the factors that contribute to Internet overuse and think about which of these factors are present on your campus.

It's after midnight at an upstate New York university, and there's a party 1 on—lots of food and drink, lively conversation, juicy gossip, boyfriends and girlfriends retreating to private corners to pour out their affections. New friendships are forming between students who delight in learning of the many interests and beliefs they share despite coming from separate states or even different countries. The lights stay on at this campus hot spot all night, and by dawn most partygoers slink bleary-eyed back to their dorm rooms. Vampires, some call them. And when darkness descends the next day, they're back. The party cranks up again.

Let's take a closer look at this party, symbolic of what's fast becoming 2 the most popular college activity of the late '90s. While the chips and cookies might resemble the same munchies of parties in decades past, we see that instead of beer, the drink of choice tends to be the nonalcoholic Jolt, selected because of its extra dose of caffeine to keep participants awake and alert. We also notice how this party is eerily quiet—no blaring music, no outrageous dancing, no shouting or singing to keep other students awake or arouse the suspicions of campus security making late-night rounds.

In fact, these party animals seldom leave their seats. No, they're not 3 passing joints around, either. Usually, they don't interact with their fellow partygoers seated beside them at all. That lively conversation, juicy gossip, secret romancing, and new bonds with friends from afar—it's all happening through their individual computer terminals. This is, after all, a gathering of a typical fraternity of netheads, those Internet-obsessed students who every night fill the large computer labs sprinkled throughout campus. Seated in row upon row of terminals all hooked up to the Internet, these busy young men and women are taking advantage of their free and unlimited on-line access—their ticket to one continuous, semester-long party.

The parties aren't happening only in the computer labs. During the 4 last several years, the demand for instant Internet availability has spread so rapidly that many colleges with crowded computer labs now ship hundreds of additional terminals and modems into newly created computer residence halls. These designated lounges are stationed right inside the dormitories, so students need no longer even walk across campus to plug into their favorite chat room. Some colleges even provide a modem and free Internet access in students' individual rooms. Most computer residence halls have replaced TV lounges or other open meeting spaces, but few students protest. As we near the dawn of a new century, TV is out. The Net is in.

"Staying up late at night on the Internet is the best time I have at 5 school," reveals Kim, a sophomore physics major and regular attendee of the kind of party we just witnessed. "After awhile, it was all I wanted to do, all I thought about. It was all so fascinating. In the chat rooms, I met a woman from Ottawa, Canada, who was a physics major at a university there. I don't see many women physics majors where I am. And I became close friends with a guy living in England, who was actually an exchange student from California. We connected over everything in life!"

Kim got so engrossed in her Net world that she ignored her studies. A 6 former math and science whiz in high school with serious career ambitions, she allowed her grades to crash before recognizing that her new obsession was sabotaging her goals. When we met Kim . . . she just had tried and failed to quit the Internet cold turkey before understanding the power of this addiction. Now she's seeking help through a campus counselor and . . . recovery strategies . . . .

At least Kim recognized the problem. Most netheads, sadly, do not. 7 And as their numbers continue to soar, colleges may be becoming the major breeding ground of Internet addiction. For example, when the dropout rate at Alfred University in Alfred, New York, more than doubled recently, Provost W. Richard Ott wanted to find out why. He couldn't see any logical explanation for why so many students who had arrived in college with SAT scores of 1,200 or higher would fail so quickly. An in-house survey revealed that 43 percent of these dropouts had been staying up late at night logged on to the Internet. "It's ironic," Ott said, "we've put all this money in for an educational tool, and some students are using it for self-destruction." Connie Beckman, director of Alfred's computing services, said "through educational programs designed to increase awareness of the danger of Net abuse, heavy pattern use dropped to 19 percent in this year's freshman class."

Here's a quick look at the contributing factors to such rampant Internet 8
overuse:

- *Free and unlimited Internet access.*   When freshmen register today, 9
  they get a student ID card, a meal card, and most important, a free
  personal e-mail account. They've got no on-line service fees to pay,
  no limits to their time logged on, and computer labs open for their
  convenience round-the-clock. It's an Internet user's dream.

- *Huge blocks of unstructured time.*   Most college students attend 10
  classes for 12 to 16 hours per week. The rest of the time is their
  own to read, study, go to movies or parties, join clubs, or explore the new environment outside their campus walls. Many forget all those other activities and concentrate on one thing: the
  Internet.

- *Newly experienced freedom from parental control.*   Away from 11
  home and their parent's watchful eyes, college students long have
  exercised their new freedom by engaging in pranks, talking to
  friends to all hours of the night, sleeping with their boyfriends and
  girlfriends, and eating and drinking things Mom and Dad would
  not approve of. Today, they utilize that freedom by hanging out in
  the MUDs and chat rooms of cyberspace, and no parent can
  complain about on-line service fees or their refusal to eat dinner
  with the family or help out with chores.

- *No monitoring or censoring of what they say or do on-line.*   When 12
  they move on to the job world, college students may find suspicious
  bosses peeking over their shoulder or even monitoring their online
  time and usage. Even e-mail to coworkers could be intercepted by
  the wrong party. In college, no one's watching. Computer lab
  monitors tend to be student volunteers whose only responsibility is
  to assist anyone who needs help understanding how to use the
  Internet, not tell them what they can or cannot do on it.

- *Full encouragement from faculty and administrators.*   Students 13
  understand that their school's administration and faculty want them
  to make full use of the Internet's vast resources. Abstaining from all
  Net use is seldom an option; in some large classes, professors place
  required course materials solely on the Net and engage in their only
  one-on-one contact with students through e-mail! Administrators,
  of course, want to see their major investments in computers and
  Internet access justified.

- *Adolescent training in similar activities.* By the time most kids get 14
  to college, they will have spent years staring at video game terminals, closing off the world around them with Walkmans, and
  engaging in that rapid-fire clicking of the TV remote. Even if they
  didn't get introduced to the Internet in high school, those other
  activities have made students well suited to slide into aimless Web
  surfing, skill-testing MUDs, and rat-a-tat-tat chat-room dialogue.

- *The desire to escape college stressors.* Students feel the pressures 15
  of making top grades, fulfilling parental expectations, and, upon
  graduation, facing fierce competition for good jobs. The Internet,
  ideally, would help make it easier for them to do their necessary
  course work as quickly and efficiently as possible. Instead, many
  students turn to their Net friends to hide from their difficult feelings
  of fear, anxiety, and depression.

- *Social intimidation and alienation.* With as many as 30,000 stu- 16
  dents on some campuses, students can easily get lost in the crowd.
  When they try to reach out, they often run into even tighter [cliques]
  than the in crowds of high school. Maybe they don't dress right or
  look right. But when they join the faceless community of the
  Internet, they find that with little effort they can become popular
  with new "friends" throughout the United States and in England,
  Australia, Germany, France, Hungary, Japan, New Zealand, and
  China. Why bother trying to socialize on campus?

- *A higher legal drinking age.* With the drinking age at 21 in most 17
  states, undergraduate students can't openly drink alcohol and socialize in bars. So the Internet becomes a substitute drug of choice
  for many: no ID required and no closing hour!

With so many signs on campus pointing toward heavy reliance on the 18
Internet, it's little wonder that when respondents to my Internet addiction
survey were asked to name their main complications from excess on-line
usage, academic problems ranked No. 1. When I asked respondents to
identify which problem areas they would rate severe, 58 percent mentioned
academic woes. Fifty-three percent referred to relationship issues, 52
percent cited Internet-related financial burdens, and 51 percent said their
jobs were impacted. Internet addiction, clearly, has hit college students
especially hard.

❀   ❀   ❀

AFTER YOU READ

- *THINK* about the factors identified in the article that contribute to Internet overuse. What can students and college administrators do to reduce the number of factors leading to Internet overuse and abuse?

- *EXAMINE* paragraphs 5 and 6, which describe Kim's struggle with Internet addiction. What were the major causes of Kim's getting "caught in the Net"?

- *EXAMINE* the last paragraph of the selection, which discusses the complications students experience from excessive Internet use. What are the major problems caused by spending too much time online?

- *WRITE* a report about Internet use on your campus. In your report, focus on one of these questions:

  1. For what purpose(s) do most students use the Internet? How beneficial or harmful to students are these purposes?
  2. What are the positive and negative effects of Internet use on your campus? Which effects are more dominant?
  3. Is Internet addiction a problem on your campus? If so, what are the major reasons?

Before writing your essay, you may want to interview three or four students—perhaps students who are actually working in a computer lab on your campus. Use the questions above and the information in Young's essay to help you formulate your interview questions. Or *WRITE* an essay in which you compare the Internet party described by Young with a regular campus party. In your opinion, which would be more fun? Which would be more beneficial? More harmful? Explain.

The Perfect Baby: A Pragmatic Approach to Genetics

GLENN McGEE

❀

Renowned bioethicist Glenn McGee is Associate Director for Education at the Penn Center for Bioethics and a faculty member in Penn's School of Medicine. Editor of The Human Cloning Debate *and coeditor of* Pragmatic Bioethics *and* The New Immortality: Science and Speculation About Extending Life Forever, *McGee has also authored numerous articles in scholarly journals, newspapers, and encyclopedias and has appeared on national news programs on both CNN and PBS to discuss bioethics, genetics, and cloning. In the following selection from his book* The Perfect Baby: A Pragmatic Approach to Genetics *(2000), Glenn expresses his hopes that genetic enhancement and cloning will in the future create a "perfect baby."*

BEFORE YOU READ

▪ *THINK* about the rapid changes that have occurred the last few years in human genetics. You have probably heard of the Human Genome Project, to which McGee refers in his article. Begun in 1990 under the sponsorship of the National Institutes of Health and the U.S. Department of Energy, this project proposed to identify the chromosomal location of all human genes and to analyze the exact chemical structure of each gene to determine its function. On June 26, 2000, the Human Genome Project announced that it had completed 90 percent of the sequencing of the human genome.

▪ *EXAMINE* the title "The Perfect Baby." Do you think that it is possible to create a perfect baby? If such a goal were possible, do you think it would be desirable to create perfect babies? Why or why not?

457

• *WRITE* a journal entry in which you make two lists, one of the advantages and one of the disadvantages of using genetic enhancement in the development of a baby. Or *WRITE* an entry describing the "perfect baby."

AS YOU READ

Identify and underline some of the genetic changes that McGee argues could improve humanity.

The popular literature can hardly mention the word "genetic" without   1
including a description of engineered, perfect babies of the future. The description of 1990s-style, consumer-culture perfection in humanity is repeated in virtually every major news journal's coverage of genetic advances: 6 feet tall, weighing in at 185 pounds, without hereditary disease. His brain is engineered to an IQ of 150, with special aptitudes in biomedical science. He has blond hair, blue eyes, archetypal beauty, and poise. Neurotic and addictive tendencies have been engineered out, as has any criminal urge, but in the male model, aggressiveness is retained as part of the "athleticism" package: muscular and quick, he is competitive and can play professional level basketball, football, and hockey. He also has the "sensitivity" package, and enjoys poetry from several cultures and periods.

But much better babies are not only the stuff of *Brave New World* and   2
Time. The new portfolio of reproductive choices is at least in part what makes for the attractiveness of genetic engineering in the popular press: parents could participate in the scientific and systematic construction of their perfect baby. How might parents make these decisions? The choice faced by the Salvanos, shopping for a sperm donor, offers a clue. At the Repository for Germinal Choice in California, the sperm of "geniuses" and "athletes" is stored in a special bank, teaming the technologies of in vitro fertilization with the hopes of genetic enhancement. The sperm of a luminary or jock can be placed in a petri dish with your egg; several of the fertilized embryos can then be implanted in your uterus. And you don't even have to ask the donor out on a date or read his latest book.

Similar sperm donor choices have already found their way into more   3
mundane in vitro fertilization (IVF) centers across the country. Parents in some medical centers may request information about sperm donors, including religion, age, ethnicity, and a variety of bodily and medical char-

acteristics. This has placed IVF physicians in the position of choosing whether to dispense entirely nontherapeutic information. The power to make that choice enlarged their social role considerably. Even if an IVF team refuses to release certain donor information, it still can and chooses not to. Thus the power to decide about release of information pits a physician's desire to protect autonomy against the physician's own judgment concerning the privacy, inheritability, and desirability of donor traits. No matter how the physician decides, she will still have made the important decision. There is virtually no law regulating IVF.

Decision making about IVF donor information opens the door to other 4 decisions physicians will soon make concerning the use of reproductive technologies. Patients may request tests to screen for a host of conditions. Hamer's homosexuality study involved the creation of a diagnostic probe that physicians could use to look for these markers. Physicians must decide whether to perform this nontherapeutic diagnostic procedure for patients who request information about their fetus's sexual orientation. Whatever their decision, the ability to perform the procedure gives new powers to physicians, power that either enlarges the territory of medicine by pathologizing homosexuality or gives the physician the new, nonmedical position of being reproductive adviser and technician.

Little or no technical modification will be required for physicians to 5 take on these new powers in the area of reproduction. Physicians would use the same sorts of procedures to diagnose homosexuality or aggressive tendencies that are used to diagnose cystic fibrosis or Alzheimer's. The same informed consent provisions would apply, requiring the physician to explain that these procedures may not effectively diagnose the desired condition, and that there may be social or economic implications. The momentum will be toward including some of these new tests in a one-shot "panel" of genetic tests, alongside the many other diseases for which genes have been identified.

As we will discuss at length later, the only real shift would involve the 6 understanding of what physicians may properly do for, and to, patients and society. If a physician agrees to dispense these technologies, it will have the effect of bringing these technologies into the realm of medical practice— even if we call the traits we test for "conditions" rather than "pathologies." The American community's faith, and long-standing covenant, holds that what physicians do is to cure the sick. If a physician concerns himself or herself with nontherapeutic traits and conditions, while acting as a physician in the medical context, the net effect is that the definition of pathology (and thus of medicine) is expanded to include the new area of concern.

Beyond new diagnostic choices for parents and physicians lies the   7
possibility of genetic enhancements through gene therapy. Images of gene
therapy for enhancement are everywhere in our culture, though the reality
is that genetic tests for the purpose of enhancement will be just about the
only genetic enhancement available in the next twenty-five years. Still,
engineering the human species through direct and systematic modification
holds such imaginative potential that gene therapy enhancement has been
celebrated by innumerable writers, each of whom emphasizes the potential
for a "human canvas" on which to draw a better being.

Social theorist Brian Stableford is one such writer. Stableford endorses   8
a "new quest for better human beings." Society is ready, he writes, to
progress from our present stage of social engineering, which he (following
Daniel Dennett) terms "second phase Darwinism." The present stage began
when we became aware of the role of forces of evolution in human conduct:

> In the second phase, most of our achievements in controlling the evolution
> of other species were accomplished haphazardly. Our ancestors had only
> a vague notion of what they were doing as they bred all the special strains
> of domestic plants and animals. . . . Now that we are beginning to
> understand how DNA works, we are also acquiring technologies for
> tinkering with its workings, which will enable us to become genetic
> engineers, and take control of the living machinery of cells and organisms.

The capacity to make adjustments to evolution will hoist humanity into   9
the "third stage" of human biological power. "Men will become masters of
evolution, and will be empowered to control their own evolution as well
as that of other species." Our activities during the final stage begin with
"external activities," such as the cloning of human organs for transplantation, and "curative activities," such as the removal of heritable pathologies
from the genome. After these activities are mastered, human biological
engineering can move to the active advancement of evolutionary development.

Stableford makes many specific suggestions for the improvement of   10
human bodies through genetic modification. First, we fix frailty. Because
we are so vulnerable to the loss of oxygen during trauma, often causing
brain damage and death, he proposes "small extra lungs, with a tiny heart
and blood vessels . . . added to the throat, to keep the brain oxygenated
when the major blood-system is injured." Using animal DNA, we might
splice in a better backbone to protect us from strain and fatigue. Regenera-
tive hands could be added, to protect us from accidents with knives and
chain saws. And the skin, so frail around our vital organs, could be made

tougher. Cellulose-digesting stomachs would allow us to eat "lower on the food chain," so that we could make more of foods like grasses—perhaps helping to alleviate world hunger problems. And we have too much small intestine, an organ he favors truncating genetically.

The new world of human life will extend beyond repairs of existing   11
defects. Why not engineer the eyes of a fly into humans, so that we might be able to perceive a greater spectrum in lower light? The owl can see in virtual darkness. The flashlight fish lights its own way—we could engineer similar luminous bacterial colonies on our cheeks. The bat and whale "see" with an aural efficiency we have only roughly begun to duplicate with technology—why not splice in sonar? And hearing has been all but perfected in a variety of different animal forms. We might study these in search of augmentary modifications as well.

With "better protection against cold and some kind of physiological   12
protection against caisson sickness [the bends]," we might live underwater. Stableford literally draws a picture of such a proposed person for the reader: the genitals may be withdrawn for protection against the cold, the skin is tough and scaly, feet are webbed, and a second breathing apparatus is added. It looks like one of the aliens we see landing on Earth in our Hollywood science fiction fantasies. "With underwater houses and factories made of non-ferrous materials, our descendants might have little cause to visit the land of their ancestors. Two separate worlds could develop. . . ." Stableford also puts new humans in space, with sealed skin and eyes and new oxygen and food storage capacity. To live in zero gravity, a different skeletal composition would be needed.

Studies of the correlation of heredity and intelligence are central to   13
genetic mapping efforts, and hopes for genetic alteration of intelligence are shared by many of the genome project's most distinguished researchers. Naturally, speculation about how this kind of engineering might take place is subject not only to potential limitations of the project, but also to those of cognitive neuroscience. What the mind actually is, and how it works, is as hotly contested among molecular geneticists as among philosophers of mind and psychiatrists. At least since the famous exchange between Edward O. Wilson and Richard Lewontin in the mid-1970s, molecular geneticists have wondered how much hereditary control exists over intelligence. For many, optimism about the biological etiology of intelligence culminates in the hope for much brighter children able to solve problems with élan and speed. The same drive that has led parents to give their gifted children Prozac and Ritalin, the drive to obtain better scores that lead to Harvard admission, presses the drive for genetic improvement of cognition.

French experimental biologist Jean Rostand is among those who 14
believe that genetics ought to be put to an even more constructive social
use, one that improves on Stableford's piecemeal bodily repairs and on the
improved brain. He writes of a new *kind* of human, the human engineered
to embody as many perfections as possible. Rostand's future "super"
human

> has been the dream of philosophers from Nietzsche's *Zarathustra,* to
> Renan's *Dialogues philosophiques* . . . it is probable that [through genetic
> engineering] we would get, in a few generations, men of more than
> average intelligence, and possible that among them would be found men
> superior to anything we have known.

Although Rostand, as do most of the writers who cite Friedrich 15
Nietzsche as an example of "superman" ideology, mistakenly attributes to
Nietzsche some sort of biological plan for better people, the general point
is well taken: everywhere in constructive thought since Socrates, the dream
of a better kind of person has been central to metaphysics, religion, and
social thought.

The faith in our ability to socially engineer human natures leads 16
Rostand to endorse a hereditary division of labor. Naturally it favors the
university professor. Super-thinkers could spend their time thinking things
through, with huge brains and visionary creativity. The thinkers would not
have to fight for their ideas; a more aggressive species of warriors might
perform that purpose. In justification of this schema, Rostand points to the
fact that our society is already stratified. More pointedly, present-day
children frequently inherit the occupations of parents. Rostand's scheme
is to enlarge parenthood, so that all of the mothers and fathers collectively
make decisions about who will inherit which lifestyle and body style.
Rostand argues that the moral leap from societal and parental pressure to
genetic specialization is a small one.

One specific technology to extend this social control of human nature 17
is *cloning.* Cloning is instrumental in a variety of plans for the improvement of humanity, dating to the earliest science fiction novels. Present
technology allows the virtually unlimited duplication of an embryo. The
difference, though, between a clone of a two-cell zygote and the clone of
a 10,000,000,000,000-cell adult is quite momentous. It is not currently
possible to clone an adult or even a child. Advances in cloning technology,
it is hoped, will come closer to what we mean when we say "clones"—the
duplicate of an adult human individual, possessing all of the extant features
of the original. In the clone of science fiction, the brow lines earned during

a long summer of writing about a new issue are preserved, as is the acidic sense of humor developed to cope with graduate school. A real clone requires us to duplicate not only structures of intelligence or character, but the total person. Your clone *is* you, copied, as if by a photocopy machine.

Such a clone seems to be the key to Rostand's tiered society, stratified 18 by function and form. Cloning eviscerates nature's hold on randomness—a condition that presently plays a major role in reproduction. In this sense, cloning holds a whole range of new possibilities for social and parental control. It also involves the development of a kind of technology popularized in the 1960s by the "transporter" technology used in the *Star Trek* television series: a person can be reduced to molecular energy, then reconstructed—"beamed up." Such a technology makes of a whole person a collection of information, which seems to get right at the heart of the hopes many hold for the Human Genome Project, hopes for the perfect baby.

❀   ❀   ❀

AFTER YOU READ

▪ *THINK* about the genetic modifications in human beings that McGee and other scientists argue may be possible in the future. Which of these seem desirable to you? Which seem frightening?

▪ *EXAMINE* the last two paragraphs in which McGee discusses human cloning. What is a human clone? What is McGee's view about creating human clones? What is your view?

▪ *WRITE* an essay in which you argue for or against the use of genetic engineering to try to create what parents consider a perfect baby. Refer to your journal entry as well as to McGee's article.

Techno-Utopia or Techno-Hell?

DINESH D'SOUZA

❀

In clear contrast to Glenn McGee's argument in the previous selection, Dinesh D'Souza issues both practical and moral warnings about genetic enhancement and human cloning. A former senior domestic policy adviser to President Ronald Reagan, D'Souza is currently a John M. Olin research fellow at the American Enterprise Institute. He has authored Illiberal Education: The Politics of Race and Sex on Campus, Ronald Reagan: How an Ordinary Man Became an Extraordinary Leader, *and, most recently,* The Virtue of Prosperity: Finding Values in an Age of Techno-Affluence, *in which he analyzes issues similar to those discussed in the following essay. This essay appeared in* The American Enterprise *in December of 2000.*

BEFORE YOU READ

- *THINK* about the contrast in philosophies suggested in the title, "Techno-Utopia or Techno-Hell?". A utopia is a perfect society; hell is a place of pain, punishment, and death. What are some of the positive and negative effects that could arise from the ongoing research into the human genetic code?

- *EXAMINE* the reference to "techno-Nietzscheanism" in the second paragraph. Friedrich Nietzsche (1844–1900) was a German philosopher who supported the idea of intellectual or scientific supermen who were, he felt, exempt from the laws and moral restraints of ordinary human beings.

- *WRITE* a journal in which you make two lists, one of positive applications that might derive from genetic research and another of possible negative applications.

AS YOU READ

Circle and number in the left margin applications of genetic research that you consider desirable; underline and number in the right margin applications of this research that seem inappropriate, dangerous, or even immoral to you.

With human genes being mapped, the cloning of large mammals becoming common, and other startling innovations on the way, a triumphant ideology is beginning to take root among many scientists, doctors, and computer whizzes. Princeton biologist Lee Silver declares that if we only have the will, we can take over the reins of evolution and choose the genetic code we want for our children, collectively determining the composition of our species. "We will liberate future generations from today's limitations and offer them a much wider scope of freedom," exults biotech journalist Ronald Bailey. Physicist Gregory Benford is no less rapturous. Nature "for billions of years has tossed off variations on its themes like a careless, prolific Picasso. Now Nature finds that one of its casual creations has come back with a piercing, searching vision, and its own pictures to paint." 1

Despite their claims of scientific neutrality, there is a hidden ideology behind these visions. It's a kind of man-as-superman ethic one might call techno-Nietzscheanism. Nietzsche was the German philosopher who, after announcing that "God is dead," urged the "natural aristocracy" at the top of human society to "live dangerously" and follow their creative passions and "will to power" in order to remake the world. These scientific supermen, Nietzsche urged, would need to go "beyond good and evil" and all conventional morality, and redirect the "weak herd" of everyday citizens. 2

Having spent a couple of years researching a book on the implications of today's high-tech wealth, I am struck by the prevalence of techno-Nietzschean doctrines among today's technology elites. The techno-Nietzscheans view humans as just molecules, but molecules that know how to rebel! In their view, our moral principles derive not from nature or nature's God—as the Declaration of Independence puts it—but from the arbitrary force of our wills and desires. And soon our wills will be able to make the most momentous choice ever—to relinquish our humanity. 3

Why should we remain subject to the constraints of our mortality, techno-Nietzscheans wonder? Wealth and technology have given us the 4 keys to unlimited, indeed godlike, power. Let us proceed with the conquest of our own limitations. From now on our children can be products of our own design. Down with our human nature! Up to something greater! Immortality here we come.

The techno-Nietzschean doctrines now winning many high-tech con- 5 verts are also gathering critics. One of the most prominent is bioethicist Leon Kass, a medical doctor and philosopher at the University of Chicago, and adjunct scholar at Washington, D.C.'s American Enterprise Institute.

The trouble with techno-Nietzscheans is not that they themselves are 6 scary, Kass emphasizes. Many "are quite cheerful and nice. But they speak of terrible things like designing and manufacturing children, or changing the nature of humanity, with grins on their faces. They are intoxicated by power, but they show no evidence of responsibility. This is why they are so dangerous." We are being led down new paths "by people who have no moral sense of what is at stake."

Part of the problem, Kass says, is with the nature of modern science 7 itself. "The ancients conceived of science as the understanding of nature, pursued for its own sake," Kass writes. "We moderns view science as power, as control over nature." Modern science assumes the only valid knowledge is scientific knowledge. But that presumption, Kass says, forces us to "shut our eyes to the most important human questions: What is good, what is bad, what is beautiful, what is happiness?" Technology gives man unprecedented power, but it does not say—it cannot say—what this power is for.

Traditionally, Kass writes in his *Toward a More Natural Science,* the 8 purpose of medicine was to restore health to the standard supplied by nature. Modern medicine has gone way beyond this. A couple wants to abort a female fetus because they prefer to have a boy. A woman wants her breasts enlarged to attract male attention, or reduced because they interfere with her golf swing. A man seeks prescription drugs to alter his moods: Prozac when he is down, Ritalin when he is up. Bored with life, a person asks for a lethal injection so he can die a painless death. None of these cases, Kass notes, involve producing better health; in fact some conscript the doctor in undermining, even destroying health.

The stated justification for advances in biotechnology, such as cloning 9 and genetic engineering, is that they will help people to live longer and healthier lives, and to give birth to children who can do the same. Kass concedes the legitimacy of this: "Who would not welcome surgery to correct the genetic defects that lead to sickle-cell anemia, Huntington's disease, and breast cancer, or to protect against the immune deficiency caused by the AIDS virus." I asked Kass if his child needed gene therapy to recover from a deadly disease, would he pursue it? Unhesitatingly, he answered yes.

But precisely the benefits of these technologies, Kass hastened to add, 10 blind us to their dangers. "It is easy to recognize evil pure and simple. It's much harder to recognize the evil in things that are partly good." So what is the danger? The first involves the means used to achieve biotechnology's noble objectives. Kass recites a litany of modern laboratory techniques: experimentation on embryos and cadavers, sperm banks, organ transplantation, test-tube babies, surrogate wombs, sex-change operations, mind-altering drugs, and now cloning and genetic surgery. Many of these are standard practice, Kass says, and yet in thoughtful and decent human beings they violate some visceral sense of what is right and proper, what he calls a "wisdom of repugnance."

Repugnance, he concedes, is not by itself an argument. Someone may, 11 for example, be revolted at the idea of his daughter dating someone of a different race; it does not follow that this feeling is morally justified. But though repugnance may sometimes reflect prejudice, Kass says it usually reflects "a deep natural revulsion to violations we dare not condone." He gives an example: Incest is universally considered an abomination, but why? Can we give adequate logical reasons for this? Not really. Certainly incest may increase the chance for defective offspring, but if this were the sole problem, we should approve of sexual relations between brothers and sisters, and also between parents and children, so long as contraception is used. The horror of incest, Kass says, goes beyond a regard for the health of offspring to a profound natural wisdom no less wise because we cannot justify it scientifically.

But with practices like dissecting cadavers, freezing embryos, trans- 12 planting organs, and making babies in test tubes now so common, can they any longer be resisted? Kass admits there is no way to go back. But he hopes "a heightened awareness of what we have been doing" will prevent us from making more serious mistakes in the future. Even freely chosen uses of our biological powers, Kass warns, "carry dangers of degradation, depersonalization, and enfeeblement of soul." We don't choose to be dehumanized, of course. We choose to "fight illness, and then to extend life, and then to pursue immortality, and then to design our children, and then to remake our species." Little by little, Kass says, "we are trading away our basic humanity."

But what is wrong, I ask, with seeking to extend life, perhaps even 13 indefinitely? "I don't have a problem with finding cures for diseases that kill people," Kass says. "But now we hear that aging and death are themselves diseases." In an essay subtitled "The Virtue of Finitude" Kass argues that mortality and the natural life cycle are the foundation of our deepest and most meaningful experiences—the basis for taking life seriously, living it passionately, and finding fulfillment in it. "To number our days," Kass writes, "is the condition of making them count." Kass suggests that, in a profound and inexplicable way, the beauty of flowers and sunsets is connected to their passing; the rose that never withered and the sun that hovered endlessly on the horizon would cease to command our astonishment and awe. Thus the project to extend life indefinitely carries with it the danger of "extending the body while diminishing the soul."

Kass's real targets are human cloning and genetic engineering. He 14 recognizes the distinction between gene therapy, aimed at curing diseases, and gene enhancement, aimed at improving human beings, but says that in practice no bright line separates the two. If it's O.K. to administer genes that increase height to midgets and dwarves, why isn't it O.K. for you to obtain them for your son who is three inches below average? It will be hard to say no to parents who believe height confers confidence and other advantages, and are willing to pay for their offspring to be taller. Kass points out that plastic surgery, developed to aid accident victims, rapidly became a cosmetic industry.

Producing clones and genetically engineering our children are "inher- 15 ently despotic" practices, Kass argues, because they reflect our desire to make other people in accordance with our wills. In such situations, children are no longer surprises to their parents and to the world. Rather, they become "custom ordered products" to be judged according to their conformity to the traits others have picked out for them. Cloning and genetic selection are thus exercises in narcissism that amount to "a new form of child abuse."

He points out several possible uses of cloning that make the clone a 16 mere instrument to fulfill someone else's desire: A sick child needs an organ transplant; so a clone is produced to provide one. A dying child is cloned to provide a close replacement. Clones are produced for the purpose of medical research, or to send on space missions, or on dangerous military expeditions. These may sound like abuses of cloning, but Kass notes that these very possibilities have been suggested by advocates of cloning. And even more benign goals like providing a cloned child for an infertile couple reduce clones to the object of other people's desires, he adds.

I ask Kass whether some of those same motives aren't already present 17 today: A couple may want a child because they think it will help their faltering relationship. A tennis fan may seek out an athletic mate with the aim of raising a professional tennis player. These distressing cases exist, Kass admits, but nature often frustrates the desires of parents to use their children as instruments. Cloning, he says, would make an existing social problem immeasurably worse.

Kass charges that cloning would represent a complete redefinition of 18 the relationship between parents and their children. He worries about a "confounding of all normal understandings" of father, mother, sibling, and grandparent, and of all the moral relationships implied by those terms. With cloning, "the usually sad situation of the single parent is here deliberately planned." Further, the clone has a bizarre biological relationship to her single parent. Since the clone is, biologically speaking, an identical twin, she and her mother are twin sisters. The clone's biological parents are her grandparents! When the clone grows up and has children, her children will also be her mother's children!

Cloning, Kass argues, represents a radical assault on the already fragile 19 institution of the family.

When parents attempt to design their children, they are in Kass's view 20 committing a similar abomination. What makes us think we are wise enough to decide such questions? What makes us think we know better than our descendants how their lives should turn out? Perhaps the well-meaning father who gives his daughter brown eyes confronts an angry teenager many years later who says, "Daddy, I can't believe you gave me brown eyes. I want blue eyes." Against this perversity, Kass offers a very different understanding of the role of parents. "When a couple now chooses to procreate, the partners are saying yes to the emergence of a new life in its novelty, saying yes not only to having a child but also, tacitly, to having whatever child the child turns out to be. In accepting our finitude and opening ourselves to our replacement, we are tacitly confessing the limits of our control."

This means our children "are not our property, nor our possessions. 21 Neither are they supposed to live our lives for us, or anyone's life but their own. To be sure, we seek to guide them on their way, imparting to them not just life but nurturing, love, and a way of life; to be sure, they bear our hopes that they will live fine and flourishing lives. . . . Still, in their genetic distinctiveness and independence are the natural foreshadowing of the deep truth that they have their own and never-before-enacted lives to live."

So where does this leave us? Kass argues that in our endless scientific 22 quest for power over nature, we have lost sight of the ends this power is meant to serve. And so we strive desperately for control—control over nature, control over our lives, control over death, control over our children, control over our species. In Kass's view this pursuit is a response to "a deep human longing that is not fully satisfied with earthly life," and so we labor to extend it and change human nature in the hope we will find true happiness, true wholeness. But we haven't found it yet, and Kass says we are not going to.

In fact, he insists, the path we are on is the path to self-destruction. 23 True progress in such a situation can only mean turning back.

❁   ❁   ❁

AFTER YOU READ

• *THINK* about Leon Kass's argument, quoted in paragraph 13, that "mortality and the natural life cycle are the foundation of our deepest and most meaningful experiences—the basis for taking life seriously, living it passionately, and finding fulfillment in it." Do you agree that the awareness of death makes life more meaningful? If technology were able to provide human beings assurance of a very long life, how would people react? Would they become more or less selfish? More or less caring about their fellow human beings? More or less appreciative of life itself?

• *EXAMINE* paragraph 14 to define the terms *gene therapy* and *gene enhancement*. According to D'Souza, why is it sometimes difficult to separate these two procedures?

• *EXAMINE* also paragraphs 15–21 in which D'Souza discusses the practices of cloning and genetic engineering (or enhancement). Why does he consider cloning immoral? What practical and moral problems does he see in the future if parents are able to "design" their own children? What problems, if any, do you see with these practices?

• *WRITE* an essay in which you agree or disagree with D'Souza's concluding statement that in pursuing genetic engineering and cloning "we are on . . . the path to self-destruction. True progress in such a situation can only mean turning back." In your essay, you may also want to include references to the previous essay by Glenn McGee. Or *WRITE* an essay in which you argue for or against human cloning. Recognize and refute the opposing position in addition to giving your reasons for your own position.

Technology and the Hearing Impaired

TAMMY HOLM

❀

The semester Tammy Holm wrote the following essay, she was enrolled in both a composition course and an audiology course. She was able to use the information she had learned in the audiology course to write an essay for her composition course. Her essay explains how technology has both hurt and helped people with hearing impairments.

BEFORE YOU READ

▪ *THINK* about the noise pollution that results from different forms of technology. What negative effects can result from noise pollution?

▪ *EXAMINE* the way in which Holm defines technical terms in the context of her essay. For example, in the second paragraph she includes the following sentence:

> Located in the middle ear is the eardrum and a number of tiny bones which convey the vibrations of the noise to the cochlea.

In the next sentence, she defines the term *cochlea:*

> The cochlea is a spinal canal in the inner ear that is lined with thousands of cells with microscopic hairs.

Do her definitions help you understand the process she is describing?

▪ *WRITE* a journal entry in which you identify a particular form of technology (for example, automobiles, telephones, computers) and explain how it both helps and hurts people.

AS YOU READ

Notice that Holm defines the technical terms she uses. Underline the terms that she defines and circle the terms for which you need to guess or look up the meaning.

In 1989, 22 million Americans had lost some or all of their hearing. Some of this hearing loss is due to genetic defects, damage to the developing fetus, infections, physical problems, and the natural process of aging, but more and more cases of hearing loss are due to the loud noises Americans' ears are exposed to daily.

Diesel trucks, loud music, and factory machinery are all examples of noises we hear daily that cause damage to our hearing. The noises travel to the middle ear via the ear canal. Located in the middle ear is the eardrum and a number of tiny bones which convey the vibrations of the noise to the cochlea. The cochlea is a spinal canal in the inner ear that is lined with thousands of cells with microscopic hairs. The response of the cells to the noise causes the hairs to vibrate. These hairs are the stimulant of the auditory nerves. When the nerves are stimulated, they send the message to the areas of the brain that are responsible for sound perception. The loud noises we expose our ears to damage the tiny hairs. When these hairs are damaged, the high frequencies are not sensed and the auditory nerve is not stimulated. This lack of stimulation stops the message of high frequencies from arriving at the brain. The damage may be immediate or it may develop slowly. It may also be temporary or permanent. Repeated exposure to loud noises may enhance the hearing loss associated with age.

Even though technological advances indirectly cause some hearing loss, they can also be the cure or a source of improvement for hearing loss. Technological advances have been used to develop a more advanced hearing aid called the Phoenix. New improvements in technology have also led to the development of a cochlear transplant. Other advancements include the use of computers to help hearing impaired people learn to speak and make phone calls and the development of closed caption for television viewing purposes.

First, the Phoenix hearing aid helps a person hear higher frequencies such as some consonants in speech. With hearing aids developed before the Phoenix, a person would hear lower frequencies such as an air conditioner and the quiet conversation of other patrons in a restaurant over the spoken words of the person's companion. The difference between the Phoenix and other hearing aids is that the Phoenix has a computer circuitry which analyzes the incoming sounds to determine their frequency, rhythms, and loudness. Then it suppresses background noise and enhances speech by using the results from the analysis. Even though the Phoenix costs more and is bulkier, it works better than regular hearing aids.

If a person's hearing loss is so great that a digital hearing aid such as 5 the Phoenix does not improve hearing, the person may want to consider a cochlear transplant. A cochlear transplant is an electronic prosthesis that acts as a substitute for hair cells that have been damaged by loud noises or other causes. When a person has a cochlear transplant, a microphone is worn behind the ear. The microphone transmits sounds to a computer, which then transforms the sound into an electronic signal. The signal is sent to a device located behind the ear and then to one or more of the twenty-two electrodes implanted in the cochlea. The electrodes function like hairs, protruding out of the cells and stimulating the auditory nerves. The stimulation causes the sounds to be perceived. The sounds may be distorted, but people report that there is improvement in the sounds they hear.

With the help of the cochlear transplant, people who lost their hearing 6 after they learned to speak may be able to learn to speak again by the use of sensors and computers. Hearing impaired people are fitted with sensors that are placed on their nose and inside their mouth. A speech pathologist is fitted with these same types of sensors. The sensors are hooked to a computer that generates an image on a video screen which illustrates the vibration of the speech pathologist's nose, the tongue position within the mouth, and the intensity of the speech pathologist's voice when he or she speaks sounds or words. The hearing impaired person then tries to duplicate the items on the video screen.

Once hearing impaired people learn to speak, they can communicate 7 via telephone with the use of a keyboard that allows messages to be sent over the telephone lines to a small videoscreen or a printer. In addition, they need a telecommunication device for the deaf (T.D.D.). At one time, both people communicating had to have the T.D.D., but now an operator acts as a go-between for someone using the T.D.D. and someone with a normal phone. The hearing impaired person types a message into the T.D.D., and this message appears on the operator's computer. The operator then reads the message to the other person, who types a response back to the hearing impaired person's T.D.D.

Another technological advancement is closed caption, the process of 8 displaying dialogue on a television screen. A digital code, activated by a computer chip, prints the words of the television show on the screen. Closed caption has become more available in the past ten years due to the Television Decoder Circuitry Act, passed by Congress in 1990. The act states that any television set with a screen larger than 33 centimeters (13 inches) must have a built-in closed caption decoder by July 1, 1993. After this time, any production without the decoder will be declared illegal.

By reducing the noises we hear to under ninety decibels or by taking ⁹ simple precautions such as wearing ear plugs when working around loud equipment, we can prevent damage to our hearing. The inconveniences of hearing loss far outweigh the inconveniences of prevention. The sense of hearing is important for survival and should be taken care of just as we take care of our lives. More and more advances are being developed every year to improve hearing problems that could have been prevented, but they are expensive and do not always cure the problem. Prevention is the only one hundred percent cure for hearing impairments.

❀ ❀ ❀

AFTER YOU READ

▪ *THINK* about both the positive and negative effects of technology on not only the hearing impaired but everyone in our society. Do the positive effects outweigh the negative ones? Why or why not?

▪ *EXAMINE* the causes of hearing loss that Holm identifies in paragraph 2. Which of these noises have you experienced? Can you identify other noises that could lead to hearing loss?

▪ *WRITE* an essay in which you argue that some form of technology has ultimately been detrimental to our society in general or to some segment of society. In your introduction, explain its benefits to society and then in the body of your essay argue that it also has harmful effects. Or *WRITE* an essay in which you explain how a particular type of technology has been used to solve a problem—perhaps a health problem or an environmental problem.

Could You Live with Less?

STEPHANIE MILLS

❁

Stephanie Mills' career and writings reflect her dedication to environmental and ecological issues. A correspondent for Wild Earth *and the winner of a 1987 award from the Friends of the United Nations Environment Program, Mills was vice president of the Earth First! Foundation from 1986 to 1989 and has served on the advisory boards of various environmental organizations. She is the author of* Whatever Happened to Ecology? *(1989) and* In Service of the Wild: Restoring and Reinhabiting Damaged Land *(1995). Her concern about the relationship between technology and the environment, the subject of the following essay from the May 1998 issue of* Glamour *magazine, is also the focus of the* Neoluddite Papers, *which she is currently editing for publication.*

BEFORE YOU READ

▪ *THINK* about the term "Neoluddite," which is mentioned in the headnote. The original Luddites were an organized group of English weavers who attempted to protect their jobs and way of life by destroying the mechanical looms that were being installed in textile mills in the early nineteenth century. Today's rapidly growing neo-Luddite movement began in the early 1990s. Bound together by their common opposition to technology and its perceived dangers, the neo-Luddites encompass religious groups such as the Quakers and the Amish as well as extreme environmentalists.

▪ *EXAMINE* the question posed in the title. Think about the material possessions you have, especially those that involve technology. Which of these are really necessary to your life? Which could you live without?

▪ *WRITE* a journal entry in which you answer Mills's question, "Could You Live with Less?"

AS YOU READ

Underline the technological products or services that Mills has chosen to live without.

Compared to the lifestyle of the average person on Earth, my days are 1
lush with comfort and convenience: I have a warm home, enough to eat, my own car. But compared to most of my urban American contemporaries, I live a monastically simple life.

Since 1984 I've made my home outside a small city in lower Michigan, 2
where the winters are snowy but not severely cold. My snug 720-square-foot house is solar- and wood-heated. No thermostat, just a cast-iron stove. There's electric lighting, indoor plumbing, a tankless water heater, a secondhand refrigerator and range—but no microwave oven, no dishwasher, no blow-dryer, no cordless phone. My gas-sipping compact station wagon has 140,000 miles on it and spreading patches of rust. I've never owned a television set. My home entertainment center consists of a thousand books, a stereo system, a picture window and two cats.

Part of the reason I live the way I do is that as a freelance writer, my 3
income is unpredictable and at best fairly unspectacular. Thus it behooves me to keep in mind the difference between wants and needs. Like all human beings, I have some needs that are absolute: about 2,000 calories a day, a half a gallon of water to drink, a sanitary means of disposing of my bodily wastes, water to bathe in, something muscular to do for part of the day and a warm, dry place to sleep. To stay sane I need contact with people and with nature, meaningful work and the opportunity to love and be loved.

I don't need, nor do I want, to complicate my life with gadgets. I want 4
to keep technology at the periphery rather than at the center of my life, to treat it like meat in Chinese cuisine—as a condiment rather than as a staple food. Technology should abet my life, not dominate or redefine it. A really good tool—like a sharp kitchen knife, a wheelbarrow or a baby carrier, all of which have been with us in some form for thousands of years—makes a useful difference but doesn't displace human intelligence, character or contact the way higher technologies sometimes do. Working people need the tools of their trade, and as a writer, I do have a fax, but I've resisted

the pressure to buy a personal computer. A manual typewriter has worked well for me so far. Noticing that the most computer-savvy people I know are always pining for more megabytes and better software, I've decided not to climb on the purchasing treadmill of planned obsolescence.

Doing with less is easier when I remember that emotional needs often 5 get expressed as material wants, but can never, finally, be satisfied that way. If I feel disconnected from others, a cellular phone won't cure that. If I feel like I'm getting a little dowdy, hours on a tanning bed can't eradicate self-doubt.

Why live in a snowy region when I don't use central heat? I moved 6 here for love several years ago, and while that love was brief, my affection for this place has grown and grown. I like the roots I've put down; living like Goldilocks, moving from chair to chair, seems like not much of a life to me.

Being willfully backward about technology suits my taste—I like living 7 this way. Wood heat feels good, better than the other kinds. (Central heating would make my home feel like it was just anywhere.) Fetching firewood gets me outdoors and breathing (sometimes gasping) fresh air in the wintertime when it's easy to go stale. It's hard, achy work to split and stack the 8 or 12 cords of stove wood I burn annually. I've been known to seek help to get it done. But the more of it I do myself, the more I can brag to my city friends.

My strongest motivation for living the way I do is my knowledge, deep 8 and abiding, that technology comes at a serious cost to the planet and most of its people. Burning fossil fuels has changed the Earth's climate. Plastics and pesticides have left endocrine-disrupting chemicals everywhere—in us and in wildlife, affecting reproductive systems. According to Northwest Environment Watch in Seattle, the "clean" computer industry typically generates 139 pounds of waste, 49 of them toxic, in the manufacture of each 55-pound computer.

I refuse to live as if that weren't so. In this, I'm not unique. There are 9 many thousands of Americans living simply, questioning technology, fighting to preserve what remains of nature. We're bucking the tide, acting consciously and succeeding only a little. Yet living this way helps me feel decent within myself—and that, I find, is one luxury worth having.

❀   ❀   ❀

AFTER YOU READ

▪ *THINK* about Mills's distinction between needs and wants. What does she consider necessary to sustain a healthy and happy life? What does she put in the category of unnecessary wants? What products of technology do you need in your own life? Which ones do you want?

▪ *EXAMINE* paragraph 8, which reveals Mills's "strongest motivation" for living the way she lives. What is this motivation? Do you agree with her belief that "technology comes at a serious cost to the planet and most of its people"? What are the human and environmental costs of technology?

▪ *WRITE* an essay in which you describe what life would be like with little or no technology. How would it be better? How would it be worse? In your essay, you may want to use ideas from a journal entry you wrote before reading this selection.

Unit Seven: Critical Thinking and Writing Assignments

❀ ❀ ❀

EXPLORING IDEAS TOGETHER

1. Technology has affected not only modern life but also modern language. Our vocabulary is full of words that are associated with commonly used machines. Working as a group, select a particular type of machine or technology (such as the airplane or the computer) and brainstorm on the words that this technology has added to our vocabulary.

2. Discuss with your group the effects of technology on individuals as opposed to its effects on society as a whole. That is, is it possible that a certain technology or machine may benefit an individual yet harm society? For example, cars make life easier on individuals but create problems (pollution, dependency on oil-producing nations, deteriorating highways, and so on) for our society. Make a list of different technologies and machines, and decide whether each benefits both individuals and society or just individuals.

3. Working with the members of your group, write a brief technical definition of a particular simple machine, identifying its function, describing it, and telling how it differs from other machines with similar functions. For example, you might define a hammer, a stapler, or a pair of pliers or scissors. Be as factual and objective as possible in this definition.

4. Writers often *personify* the machines about which they are writing. That is, they give the machines the attributes and characteristics of a human. Work with a group of your classmates to write a brief narrative or description of a common machine (such as a computer, a car, a vending machine, an alarm clock, or a microwave oven), personifying it by giving it a name and other human characteristics. Exaggerate your narrative for humorous effect.

WRITING ESSAYS

1. Imagine that all the machines on which you depend were suddenly destroyed or inoperative. Write an imaginative narrative describing what a typical day in your life would be like if this were to happen.

2. Write a humorous essay about a time when you were frustrated by a certain machine (for example, when your car would not start, a

vending machine would not give you your selection or return your money, your smoke alarm kept going off, or your microwave burned your dinner).

3. Write an essay about a time when you skillfully operated a machine. How did you overcome the challenges of the task, and how did you feel during and after the process?

4. Write an essay analyzing either the positive or negative effects of computers as tools in the educational process. You may want to use support from Mary Lord, David Gelernter, and Kimberly S. Young.

5. Write an essay in which you argue for or against the idea that men are more fascinated by machines and technology than women are. Before you write, decide whether you are writing for an audience of males, females, or both.

6. Write an essay in which you discuss either the causes or the effects of addiction to some form of technology, such as television, video games, or the Internet. You may want to limit this topic further, focusing on e-mail or chat rooms, for example.

7. Write an essay in which you discuss how the Internet has changed— and will continue to change—our lives. You might focus on its use in daily activities such as shopping and keeping up with the news, its use for educational research or business applications such as paying bills and buying stocks, or its use for entertainment or socializing. In this particular area of life, is the effect of the Internet primarily positive or negative? Why? (Before writing your essay, you may want to review the selections by Mary Lord, Adam Cohen, and Kimberly S. Young.)

8. Write an essay in which you take a position on whether some forms of technology, especially computers and television, create a sense of isolation *or* a feeling of community. (You may want to review the essays by Mary Lord, Kimberly S. Young, Marie Winn, and Madeline Drexler.)

9. Write an essay in which you argue that the effects of a particular type or use of technology—such as television, computers, or gene research—are either positive or negative. Use support from readings in this unit that are relevant to your topic. You might focus your topic more, arguing, for example, for the positive or negative effects of television on some aspect of children's lives—their education, their imagination, or their values.

10. Using the selections in this unit as sources, write an essay in which you argue for or against the assertion that technology has improved our lives.

Self with Heroes

Most of us have heroes—people whom we admire because they have done something we consider noble, brave, or generous. Traditionally, heroes were male figures who performed remarkable feats of bravery. These traditional heroes slew dragons, fought in battles, embarked on exciting adventures, or went on long, difficult quests.

During the last quarter of the twentieth century, however, political scandals and the media's close scrutiny of public figures took a heavy toll on society's belief in contemporary heroes. Simultaneously, historians and teachers began calling attention to the human faults of traditional heroes such as Christopher Columbus, George Washington, Thomas Jefferson, John F. Kennedy, and Martin Luther King, Jr. In searching for new heroes, people have increasingly focused on celebrities, such as models, movie stars, and sports figures. As a result, before the events of September 11, 2001, we were in danger of becoming a "world without heroes."

The many heroic responses to the devastation created by the terrorists who transformed four fuel-filled passenger planes into lethal weapons against the Pentagon and the World Trade Center have forever changed the way we view heroes. These individuals—including firefighters, policemen, ordinary citizens, and the passengers who crashed their plane into the Pennsylvania countryside rather than allowing it to be used as another missile—have restored and enlarged our faith in heroism. In the aftermath of the terrorist attack, we recognize heroes not just on the battlefield but also in our daily lives. Quiet and unassuming, many heroes today are displaying a courage that is moral and emotional as well as physical.

In this unit you will read about male and female heroes, about heroes and role models, about traditional heroes and nontraditional heroes, and about the previous decline of heroes. You will consider how society's view of its heroes is affected by the media, and you will discover that heroes can be ordinary as well as extraordinary. Finally, you will turn your focus back to yourself as a potential hero, considering yourself in the context of the heroes and heroic acts that you have read about.

Before reading the selections in this unit, consider the following questions. You may want to respond to one or more of these questions in the form of a journal entry or freewriting. Or you may want to discuss one or more of them with a group of your classmates.

1. How do you define a hero? What qualities do you associate with a hero? Is a hero the same as a role model or something quite different?

2. Do you define male and female heroes in the same way? Are the terms *female* hero and *heroine* interchangeable? How would you react to the terms *heroes* and *sheroes*?

3. Does our society have more male heroes than female heroes? Why? Does this situation reflect the basic heroism of men and women or the beliefs and traditions of our society?

4. How do the media portray heroes? Do the media confuse heroes with celebrities and role models?

5. Are heroes born or made? In other words, is character a qualification for heroes, or is the act of heroism the issue?

6. Have you ever witnessed a heroic act? What was this act and why was it heroic? What do heroic acts have in common?

7. Are heroes perfect or imperfect? Have you ever been disappointed with or disillusioned by someone you considered a hero? How?

8. Do you believe that our society has more or fewer heroes today than in the past? Why or why not? Have your ideas about heroes and heroism changed since September 11, 2001? If so, how?

9. Who is your favorite hero? Why did you select this person?

10. Have you ever been a hero? Do you think you could be? Why or why not?

As you read the following selections, remember to *interact* with your reading by underlining passages, writing questions and comments in the margins, and relating what you read to your own personal life.

We believe you will discover from this unit that heroes influence our beliefs and goals and even shape the people we become, showing us the potential for goodness that lies within us all. Ultimately, heroes teach us as much about who we are as about who they are. Clearly, we still need heroes.

Larger Than Life

PHIL SUDO

❀

Phil (Philip Toshio) Sudo is a Japanese-American musician, black-belt martial artist, and the author of four books, including Zen Guitar *and* Zen 24/7. *After working as a journalist in New York, Sudo spent twelve years in Japan studying Zen, a branch of Buddhism that focuses on individual potential to achieve enlightenment, and five years on the island of Maui writing and raising a family. Currently fighting the stomach cancer with which he was diagnosed in 2001, Sudo exemplifies the fact that real heroes exist not only in legend and history but also in real life. The following essay, written while Sudo was managing editor for* Scholastic, *provides a definition of the word* hero *and argues that we can learn much about the values of a society from its heroes.*

BEFORE YOU READ

• *THINK* about your own heroes. That is, think about the men and women you look up to as heroes. Do you look up to these people because they are attractive, famous, or wealthy? Or do you look up to them because they have performed some great good, not for themselves but for humanity?

• *EXAMINE* the title "Larger Than Life." What does this title suggest about Sudo's view of heroes? Examine also the headings that Sudo uses. What do these headings suggest about Sudo's definition of a hero?

• *WRITE* a journal entry listing some living men and women whom you consider to be heroes.

AS YOU READ

Underline Sudo's definitions of *hero*.

When Nelson Mandela visited the United States in June [1990], 1
cheering throngs of Americans hailed him as a hero. His decades-
long struggle against South Africa's system of racial separation, unwavering
through years of imprisonment, was inspiring not only to South Africans,
but to freedom-loving people in this country as well.

Imagine if Iraqi leader Saddam Hussein were to visit the United States. 2
The crowds would still turn out—only they'd be hostile. Many here view
him as a murderous, ruthless dictator. And yet, in his own part of the world,
Hussein is as big a hero as Mandela is in South Africa.

How can Mandela and Hussein—one admired in this country, the 3
other despised—*both* be heroes? . . .

COURAGE AND LOYALTY

The word "hero" comes from the Greek word *heros,* meaning to protect 4
or to serve. Originally, the term applied only to mythical figures—gods or
semidivine beings, such as Hercules and Perseus, who excelled in battle and
embodied such values as courage and loyalty. The ancient Greeks developed an entire tradition of literature around such heroes; in classic epics
like the *Iliad* and the *Odyssey,* Homer spun tales of the brave Odysseus and
other warriors, whose adventures were first passed down orally, then later
through the written word.

The notion of heroes was not unique to the West. Other early societies, 5
such as China and India, developed similar traditions, around heroes such
as Kuan Ti and epics like the *Mahabharata.*

Over time, historians began to look upon real people as heroes—Simón 6
Bolívar, Sun Yat-sen, George Washington—larger-than-life individuals
who founded countries or dedicated their lives to liberation. These were
the rare men and women who embodied, as one historian wrote, "the
perfect expression of the ideal of a group, in whom all human virtues
unite."

Learning the tales of these greats helps forge values and a cultural 7
identity. When you read the story of George Washington cutting down a
cherry tree and saying, "I cannot tell a lie," you learn the value of honesty
in American society. In Japan, when schoolchildren read the tale of the 47
Ronin, a band of samurai who stick together through years of hardship to
avenge their master's death, they learn the value of loyalty and group
togetherness. . . .

In this country, some educators believe our heroes are too one-sided. 8
U.S. history books, they say, are filled with the accomplishments of white
European males to the exclusion of women and minorities.

In fact, many Americans today are beginning to question the very 9
definition of a "hero." These days, we bestow the honor mainly on sports
figures, movie stars, musicians, and comedians. "The word 'hero' is a
debased word," says Michael Lesy, a professor at Hampshire College in
Amherst, Mass., and author of the . . . book *Rescues*. It has become
confused with "celebrity," "role model," and "idol," he says. . . .

WHAT MAKES A HERO?

But if there is argument over what constitutes a "hero," few among us fail 10
to admire heroic acts. Thwarting a robbery, rescuing a drowning man,
pulling a child from a burning house—these are all unquestionable acts of
heroism. And while the brave souls who perform them may never become
famous or reap rewards, they are certainly heroes.

In fact, the one trait of heroes that transcends all cultural boundaries, 11
Lesy says, is the willingness to risk one's life for the good of others. "It's
not an American trait, it's not Japanese, it's not Iraqi, it's the bottom-line
of the human species," he says.

Consider the words of Nelson Mandela: "I have cherished the idea of 12
a democratic and free society. It is an ideal which I hope to live for and to
achieve. But if needs be, it is an ideal for which I am prepared to die."

And these words from slain civil rights leader Martin Luther King, Jr.: 13
"If a man hasn't found something he will die for, he isn't fit to live."

POTENTIAL WITHIN US ALL

We hail these men as heroes because their courage gives us strength, their 14
ideals give us vision, and their spirit enlarges our own. But keep in mind
that, extraordinary as these heroes may seem, they are still human beings
like you and me. And as such, they demonstrate that within all of us, there
is the potential to become heroes ourselves.

Look around you, at your friends, your family, your school. Is there 15
someone among them that you'd call a hero? Probably so.

Now take a look in the mirror. What do you see?   16
What do you *want* to see?   17

❀ ❀ ❀

AFTER YOU READ

- *THINK* about the question that Sudo asks in the third paragraph: "How can Mandela and Hussein—one admired in this country, the other despised—*both* be heroes?" How would you answer this question?

- *EXAMINE* this statement: "In this country, some educators believe our heroes are too one-sided. U.S. history books, they say, are filled with the accomplishments of white European males to the exclusion of women and minorities" (paragraph 8). Do you agree or disagree with educators who hold this belief? Why do you feel as you do?

- *EXAMINE* also the last section of the reading, subtitled "Potential Within Us All." Do you see a potential hero in the mirror? How do you think you could become more heroic? Would you have to save someone's life to become a hero, or could you perform heroic acts and make heroic decisions in your daily life?

- *WRITE* a paragraph giving your own definition of *hero*. That is, answer Sudo's question, "What makes a hero?" Before you write your definition, review the list of heroes that you wrote before reading the selection. What qualities do these people have in common? How is your definition similar to or different from Sudo's definition? (*Note:* If you quote from Sudo's article, be sure to include his words within quotation marks.)

September 11, 2001:
Answering the Call

BILL MOON

❊

On September 11, 2001, the members of an interdisciplinary class on the topic of "Heroes in Ancient and Modern Society" gathered to begin their discussion of Joseph Campbell's The Hero with a Thousand Faces *while the shock and grief of the morning's terrorist attack on the Pentagon and the World Trade Center was still fresh on their minds. Over the next several weeks, the students discussed developing events, constantly relating them to their reading of Campbell. Out of that experience, Bill Moon developed the following essay primarily expressing his own feelings and reactions to the tragedy but also reflecting some of the ideas expressed by the class as a whole, especially by fellow students Gina Allemang and Denise Bryson-Hurley. Moon, an English major, was a junior at Texas A&M University–Commerce when he wrote the essay.*

BEFORE YOU READ

▪ *THINK* about where you were when you heard about the September 11 attack on the World Trade Center and the Pentagon. What were your first thoughts? How did you adjust to the news as it kept pouring in?

▪ *EXAMINE* the title of the selection. In your opinion, what was the "call" issued on September 11, 2001? Who do you think answered this call most heroically? Why do you consider these individuals to be heroic? Are individuals still answering the call issued on that day? How?

▪ *WRITE* a journal entry in which you describe where you were and how you reacted when you heard of the terrorist attack.

AS YOU READ

Identify the individuals who, according to Moon, answered the call to heroism most effectively on September 11.

When the Pentagon was seriously damaged and the twin towers of the   1
World Trade Center were physically leveled by the terrorist attack on September 11, 2001, I was emotionally leveled myself. Hearing that terrorists had flown fuel-filled passenger planes into these buildings, my fellow students and I were outraged, believing that the terrorism that occurs on a daily basis in many places could not happen *here*. As Americans, we are not accustomed to being on the defensive. We pick and choose our battles, deciding when and where we will have a confrontation. But we didn't have that option on that fateful Tuesday.

In spite of the initial shock, or perhaps because of it, this tragic event   2
has become an enormous opportunity for the renewal of heroism, patriotism, and unity in our nation. Indeed, the events surrounding those first shocking moments have helped us all see not only the heroic actions of our fellow citizens but also the heroic potential within ourselves. In his book *The Hero with a Thousand Faces*, Joseph Campbell describes the pattern of heroic action—a pattern that begins with a call to action, a "summons [that] may be to live . . . or to die," but one that "rings up the curtain, always, on a mystery of transfiguration—a rite, or moment, of spiritual passage, which, when complete, amounts to a dying and a rebirth" (51). The attacks on America were indeed a call to action on the part of our nation. Those involved—from the firefighters to the police officers to the passengers on Flight 93—had a choice between accepting or refusing the call. An amazing number of individuals answered the call, and the reactions of these many heroic individuals are an inspiration to all of us as we continue to attempt to understand exactly what occurred and why.

Many of the heroes of September 11 are nameless faces on the pages   3
of weekly news magazines and local newspapers: people who donated blood, money, or water for the victims and workers; the doctors and nurses who worked around the clock to provide medical attention for those who needed it most; and the crews who dug for weeks to clear away the smoldering razor-sharp debris and recover the remains of the dead. The very wise author Anonymous once said, "Character is made up of small duties faithfully performed—of self-denials, of self-sacrifices, of kindly acts of love and duty." On that terrible day the most memorable heroic

responses came from two particular groups who indeed sacrificed themselves for love and duty—the firefighters and rescue personnel of the cities involved and the passengers on United Airlines Flight 93.

On that terrible day, firefighters and rescue personnel rushed to the   4 scenes at the Pentagon and the World Trade Center, but it was at the WTC where the most lives—about 3,000—were lost. Two of the over 300 firefighters who lost their lives at what has come to be known as "Ground Zero" were Ray Downey and the Rev. Mychal Judge. The chief of special operations in New York City, 63-year-old Downey was in the first tower trying to save those still trapped inside when the second tower collapsed and he disappeared. Downey had a history of being a hero: in 1993 he answered the call at the first World Trade Center bombing; in 1995 he was in Oklahoma City answering the call there; and in 1996 he had responded at the TWA Flight 800 explosion. He stepped into the crumpled Trade Center on September 11 knowing full well what potential danger lay ahead, but he also knew that there were people in the building who needed to be rescued ("Facing" 75). He answered the call. The Rev. Mychal Judge also responded to the call to heroism on September 11. When a fellow Franciscan monk told him about the attack, he immediately rushed to where he could be of most service. Eyewitnesses say that he was administering last rites and comforting the wounded when he was killed by falling rubble ("Courage" 40–41). He, too, answered the call.

Another group of individuals called into action on September 11 were   5 the passengers on United Airlines Flight 93 who apparently rushed hijackers who had also taken over their plane with intentions to use it as another missile. We don't know—and may never know—exactly what went on during those few minutes before the plane slammed into a rural Pennsylvania field. However, we can be fairly sure that a few courageous passengers saved the lives of hundreds of potential terrorist targets—many of whom may have been government officials—and perhaps preserved an American landmark such as the White House. In phone calls to relatives, Jeremy Glick, Tom Burnett, and Mark Bingham all revealed their plans to rush the hijackers ("Facing" 68), and Todd Beamer was heard on an onboard phone call giving the signal, "Let's roll." These men also answered the call, sacrificing their lives in the process.

After accepting the call to service, the potential hero undergoes a   6 rigorous challenge. The firefighters literally had to go through what Campbell describes as "dark and devious ways" (21) as they climbed through the ruins of the Pentagon and the World Trade Center. Because they had more time to think about their decision, the passengers of Flight 93 must have traveled the hero path that Campbell says is "fundamentally inward rather than outward." But all of these heroes left their comfort zones, giving their lives unselfishly, unswervingly. They pressed on into dark, frightening places. Some crawled through black, billowing smoke and falling debris into tight airless passages to pull out victims; others grappled both physically and psychologically with crazed and determined terrorists, wrestling them and therefore the plane itself to the ground. All faced death.

In the traditional hero tale, the successful adventurer returns to his or   7 her society with a "boon" of some kind—either physical treasure or spiritual knowledge. The stories of many of the heroes of September 11 do not have happy endings for the individuals involved, for in giving of themselves, many gave the ultimate sacrifice of their lives. However, the gift they bestowed on society is greater far than anything they could have lived for. Drawing on their own inner resources, these heroes revived the heroic potential in all of us and made it available for "the transfiguration of the world" (Campbell 29). Even though they died in the process, these heroes live on in our memories, in the lives of those they saved, and in the renewed sense of patriotism our nation has experienced.

Indeed, those individuals who answered the call on September 11 have   8 renewed our belief in heroism itself. Campbell believes that the hero of the fairy tale "prevails over his personal oppressors" whereas the hero of myth "brings back from his adventure the means for the regeneration of his society as a whole" (38). As countless numbers of quiet heroes continue to sift through the ashes of the World Trade Center and as Americans throughout the country give of their blood, tears, and prayers, we need both kinds of heroes. Our country must prevail over our attackers, and our citizens must have the courage, diligence, and faith to continue the process of regeneration our society has already begun.

WORKS CITED

Campbell, Joseph. *The Hero with a Thousand Faces,* 2nd ed. Bollingen
    Series 42, Princeton, NJ: Princeton University Press, 1968.
"Courage Under Terrible Fire." *U S. News and World Report, Special Issue,*
    24 September 2001: 40–43.
"Facing the End." *Time, Special Issue,* 24 September 2001: 68–77.

❀   ❀   ❀

AFTER YOU READ

▪ *THINK* about the two different groups of heroes that Moon identifies in the third paragraph: the firefighters and the passengers on United Airlines Flight 93. What qualities did these heroes have in common? What was unique and special about each group?

▪ *EXAMINE* Moon's claim in paragraph 7 that "Drawing on their own inner resources, these heroes revived the heroic potential in all of us and made it available for 'the transfiguration of the world' (Campbell 29)." On what inner resources do you think the heroes of September 11 relied? Do you agree that the heroic response to the terrorist attack has "transfigured" American society? If so how?

▪ *WRITE* an essay in which you describe what you believe to have been the most heroic response to the terrorist attack. Or *WRITE* an essay in which you discuss the effects the terrorist attack of September 11 has had on *either* (1) the values of our society or (2) our society's view of heroes.

Martin Luther King

JACK E. WHITE

❀

Phil Sudo's definition of a hero as a "larger-than-life" individual who is willing to risk his life "for the good of others" certainly applies to African-American civil rights leader Martin Luther King Jr. Throughout his all-too-brief career, King worked with the Southern Christian Leadership Conference to gain for African-Americans the freedom and justice promised all Americans in the Constitution but denied for many years to its non-white citizens. King was assassinated in Memphis in 1968, but he left a rich heritage of courage and faith for all of us. This heritage is explored in the following article, which was published in 1998 in a special issue of Time *on "Leaders and Revolutionaries of the 20th Century." The author of the article, Jack E. White, is a* Time *correspondent who has covered civil rights issues for more than thirty years.*

BEFORE YOU READ

▪ *THINK* about what life was like for African-Americans during Martin Luther King, Jr.'s lifetime. What kind of hopes and dreams did King and other civil rights leaders have then? How has our society changed since that time? Do you think some of the improvements in civil rights were directly influenced by King? If so, did King contribute to these changes? Have civil rights for African-Americans (and others) improved enough since King's lifetime?

▪ *EXAMINE* the first paragraph of White's article. Do you agree or disagree that King's achievements are less appreciated by whites than by African-Americans? Why might white Americans owe King just as much as—if not more than—African-Americans?

© 1998 Time Inc. Reprinted by permission.

▪ *WRITE* a journal entry in which you discuss the contributions that King made to American society in general—to whites as well as to African-Americans. How is he a "larger-than-life" figure?

AS YOU READ

Identify and underline the reasons Jack E. White thinks King was "the right man at the right time."

It is a testament to the greatness of Martin Luther King Jr. that nearly 1 every major city in the U.S. has a street or school named after him. It is a measure of how sorely his achievements are misunderstood that most of them are located in black neighborhoods.

Three decades after King was gunned down on a motel balcony in 2 Memphis, Tenn., he is still regarded mainly as the *black* leader of a movement for *black* equality. That assessment, while accurate, is far too restrictive. For all King did to free blacks from the yoke of segregation, whites may owe him the greatest debt, for liberating them from the burden of America's centuries-old hypocrisy about race. It is only because of King and the movement that he led that the U.S. can claim to be the leader of the "free world" without inviting smirks of disdain and disbelief. Had he and the blacks and whites who marched beside him failed, vast regions of the U.S. would have remained morally indistinguishable from South Africa under apartheid, with terrible consequences for America's standing among nations. How could America have convincingly inveighed against the Iron Curtain while an equally oppressive Cotton Curtain remained draped across the South?

Even after the Supreme Court struck down segregation in 1954, what 3 the world now calls human-rights offenses were both law and custom in much of America. Before King and his movement, a tired and thoroughly respectable Negro seamstress like Rosa Parks could be thrown into jail and fined simply because she refused to give up her seat on an Alabama bus so a white man could sit down. A six-year-old black girl like Ruby Bridges could be hectored and spit on by a white New Orleans mob simply because she wanted to go to the same school as white children. A 14-year-old black boy like Emmett Till could be hunted down and murdered by a Mississippi gang simply because he had supposedly made suggestive remarks to a white woman. Even highly educated blacks were routinely denied the right to vote or serve on juries. They could not eat at lunch counters, register in motels or use whites-only rest rooms; they could not buy or rent a home wherever they chose. In some rural enclaves in the South, they were even compelled to get off the sidewalk and stand in the street if a Caucasian walked by.

The movement that King led swept all that away. Its victory was so 4 complete that even though those outrages took place within the living memory of the baby boomers, they seem like ancient history. And though this revolution was the product of two centuries of agitation by thousands upon thousands of courageous men and women, King was its culmination. It is impossible to think of the movement unfolding as it did without him at its helm. He was, as the cliché has it, the right man at the right time.

To begin with, King was a preacher who spoke in biblical cadences 5 ideally suited to leading a stride toward freedom that found its inspiration in the Old Testament story of the Israelites and the New Testament gospel of Jesus Christ. Being a minister not only put King in touch with the spirit of the black masses but also gave him a base within the black church, then and now the strongest and most independent of black institutions.

Moreover, King was a man of extraordinary physical courage whose 6 belief in nonviolence never swerved. From the time he assumed leadership of the Montgomery, Ala., bus boycott in 1955 to his murder 13 years later, he faced hundreds of death threats. His home in Montgomery was bombed, with his wife and young children inside. He was hounded by J. Edgar Hoover's FBI, which bugged his telephone and hotel rooms, circulated salacious gossip about him and even tried to force him into committing suicide after he won the Nobel Peace Prize in 1964. As King told the story, the defining moment of his life came during the early days of the bus boycott. A threatening telephone call at midnight alarmed him: "Nigger, we are tired of you and your mess now. And if you aren't out of this town in three days, we're going to blow your brains out and blow up your house." Shaken, King went to the kitchen to pray. "I could hear an inner voice saying to me, 'Martin Luther, stand up for righteousness. Stand up for justice. Stand up for truth. And lo I will be with you, even until the end of the world.'"

In recent years, however, King's most quoted line—"I have a dream 7 that my four little children will one day live in a nation where they will not be judged by the color of their skin but by the content of their character"— has been put to uses he would never have endorsed. It has become the slogan for opponents of affirmative action like California's Ward Connerly, who insist, incredibly, that had King lived he would have been marching

alongside them. Connerly even chose King's birthday last year to announce
the creation of his nationwide crusade against "racial preferences."

Such would-be kidnappers of King's legacy have chosen a highly 8
selective interpretation of his message. They have filtered out his radicalism
and sense of urgency. That most famous speech was studded with demands.
"We have come to our nation's capital to cash a check," King admonished.
"When the architects of our Republic wrote the magnificent words of the
Constitution and the Declaration of Independence, they were signing a
promissory note to which every American was to fall heir," King said.
"Instead of honoring this sacred obligation, America has given the Negro
people a bad check; a check which has come back marked 'insufficient
funds.'" These were not the words of a cardboard saint advocating a
Hallmark card-style version of brotherhood. They were the stinging
phrases of a prophet, a man demanding justice not just in the hereafter, but
in the here and now.

❀   ❀   ❀

AFTER YOU READ

▪ *THINK* about the challenges that King faced in his fight for civil rights.
Even before his assassination, how was King physically and mentally
threatened? Based on these threats and on what had happened to other
African-Americans fighting for their civil rights, what fears must he and his
family have had? How did he conquer these fears and continue with his
work?

▪ *EXAMINE* the quotations from King's "I Have a Dream" speech in
paragraphs 7 and 8 of White's article. How does White describe the tone
and purpose of these statements? How does he believe King's words have
been misused? Do you agree or disagree with White's opinions? (*Note:* You
may also want to reread, or review, King's entire "I Have a Dream" speech
on pp. 344–349.)

▪ *WRITE* a letter to the mayor or city council in your hometown arguing
that a particular street or building should (or should not) be named for
Martin Luther King Jr. You may use ideas from your journal entry about
King as a "larger-than-life" figure as well as ideas from White's essay. If you
do use information from the reading, be sure to give the author credit and
to enclose quotations within quotation marks.

Freedom's Daughter: Pauli Murray

LYNNE OLSON

❀

Lynne Olson is the coauthor of The Murrow Boys: Pioneers on the Front Lines of Broadcast Journalism. *In her more recent book,* Freedom's Daughters *(2001), from which this selection was taken, Olson argues that the civil rights movement from 1830 to 1970 had many "unsung heroines" who deserve far more recognition than they have received. These heroines include Rosa Parks, who not only sparked a social revolution when in December of 1955 she refused to leave her seat in the front of a bus in Montgomery, Alabama, but who had also been a civil rights activist since the 1940s; Daisy Bates, who shepherded nine African-American teenagers through the traumatic experience of defying segregation at Little Rock's Central High School in 1957; and many other brave and little-known African-American women. One of these remarkable women was Pauli Murray, a student at Howard University who planned and carried out a sit-in at an all-white restaurant in Washington, D.C., in the mid-1940s.*

BEFORE YOU READ

- *THINK* about the fact that many African-Americans fought and died for their country during World War II (1941–1945), yet returning African-American veterans were not allowed such basic freedoms as eating in restaurants of their choice. How would African-American men and women have felt about this ironic situation? What do you think you would have done in a similar situation?

▪ *EXAMINE* the title and the first paragraph—particularly the last sentence—of the selection. What kind of liberation do you think Pauli Murray had in mind?

▪ *WRITE* a journal entry describing a time when you were treated differently in some way from other people. How did that experience affect you?

AS YOU READ

Compare Pauli Murray's actions with those of other civil rights activists, particularly Martin Luther King, Jr. How was her situation similar to King's? How was it different?

It was April 22, 1944, a warm Saturday in Washington, D.C. The skies 1
threatened rain, but the cherry trees near the Jefferson Memorial were in bloom, and hundreds of people, many of them soldiers and sailors in uniform, strolled the banks of the Tidal Basin to admire the lacy pink and white foam of the blossoms. News from the war was mostly good: The Marines had recently captured blood-soaked Iwo Jima, the Fifth Army was about to liberate Rome. In the capital city of the United States, however, a small, thin black woman named Pauli Murray had a different sort of liberation in mind.

Murray, due to graduate in June from Howard University Law School, 2
was standing with some other Howard students outside Thompson's cafeteria, a few blocks northeast of the Tidal Basin. She watched as her fellow students slipped, two and three at a time, inside the cafeteria. Finally, Murray took a deep breath and joined them. Once inside, she picked up a tray and entered the serving line. When the stone-faced employees behind the steam tables refused to serve her, as they refused to serve any black, Murray silently carried her empty tray to a table and sat down among the other black students who had been turned away.

The silent demonstration at Thompson's cafeteria, led by Murray and 3
three other Howard activists on a cloudy afternoon in wartime Washington, was a harbinger. But it did more than prefigure many similar actions almost two decades later. It also symbolized the importance of women to a movement that always *seemed* to be dominated by men. Of the approximately fifty black students who sat in that day at Thompson's, most were women, and *all* of the leaders were. Together, they had stepped from behind a historical curtain and, for the moment, were deferring to no one.

Sitting at Thompson's table, waiting to be served, they read textbooks and poetry. Some were glancing at the latest issue of the liberal tabloid newspaper *P.M.* Others watched apprehensively through the windows as a crowd of whites gathered on the sidewalk, where another group of students walked a picket line, carrying placards. One of the placards read: "Are You for HITLER'S Way (Race Supremacy) or the AMERICAN Way (Equality)? Make Up Your Mind!" And another: "We Die Together. Why Can't We Eat Together?" Some soldiers jeered and taunted the pickets. A woman spat at them. Through it all, "[o]ur demonstrators were thoroughly disciplined," Murray wrote to her friend Eleanor Roosevelt several days later. "No response was made to any taunt. . . . We clamped down on our teeth and kept our eyes straight ahead."

The manager of Thompson's pleaded with the students to leave, but 4 they replied, politely, that they would stay till they could eat. By dinnertime, the cafeteria's trade had dropped by half. After several desperate telephone calls from Thompson's manager to his superiors, an order finally came down from the chain's national headquarters: Serve the demonstrators. Even with that, two of Thompson's waitresses refused, so the manager and the chain's district supervisor quickly filled in. For the first time since Reconstruction, a downtown whites-only eating establishment in Washington, D.C., was serving black customers.

"It is difficult to describe the exhilaration of that brief moment of 5 victory," Murray wrote long afterward. The sit-in at Thompson's was the culmination of months of intense planning and training. The participating students had been carefully selected, then rigorously schooled in the nonviolent principles and tactics of Mahatma Gandhi. Each student had signed a pledge not to retaliate against harassment or violence. And it had all worked! Soon, however, the glow of victory vanished. The press wasn't much interested, and the president of Howard University, fearing a backlash from a Congress dominated by Southern racists, ordered the students to suspend further action. Murray was furious that the students' "brief act of imaginative defiance, a commando raid against entrenched racism . . . which, if expanded, could have brought new hope to millions of black Americans," was so abruptly and completely throttled. But throttled it was, and, with the pressure lifted, Thompson's went back to "no Negroes allowed."

Not until sixteen years later would civil rights demonstrators use the 6 same kind of nonviolent resistance employed by Murray and her fellow students. By then most activists didn't even know who Pauli Murray was. When Eleanor Holmes, a brilliant young Yale law student and member of the Student Nonviolent Coordinating Committee, returned to Yale for classes after a summer of civil rights work in 1963, she met Murray, who was then studying for her doctorate in law. Holmes, who as Eleanor Holmes Norton would later become a noted civil rights lawyer and the chair of the Equal Employment Opportunity Commission, had never heard of the 1944 Howard sit-in. She recalled being stunned on learning about the "nerve and bravery of this little woman who had already done what we were only beginning to do [but without] the safety and protection of the full-blown movement and reformist national mood that cushioned our risk."

Important as Murray was to the history of the early civil rights 7 movement in the United States, she and the other Howard women with whom she demonstrated were merely in the middle of a long line of female soldiers of change, black and white, that stretched from the nineteenth-century abolitionist movement forward to twentieth-century civil rights and feminism. Indeed, the interconnections between race and gender, and between racism and misogyny, have helped place women at the very center of social ferment and conflict over the last two centuries of American history. Pauli Murray thus stands as a bridge between present and past. The granddaughter of a slave and great-granddaughter of a slave owner, she sprang from a family whose history, like the histories of countless others, illustrates how far the United States has come since the days of slavery, unbridled racism, and pernicious sexism—and how far it has still to go.

❀ ❀ ❀

AFTER YOU READ

▪ *THINK* about Pauli Murray's courageous actions and relate them to the bravery of Martin Luther King, Jr. How would you compare their overall abilities, achievements, and effects on society? Why do you think King is better known than Murray? Do you agree with Olson that Murray is not well-known today primarily because she was a *female* civil rights activist, or do you think the question is more complex? Do you, nevertheless, think that female civil rights leaders such as Murray and Rosa Parks should receive more attention from historians, the media, and the general public than they have?

▪ *EXAMINE* paragraphs 5 and 6 of the essay. How did Murray plan and prepare for her sit-in? How did she conduct herself during the sit-in? How effective was the sit-in? Why wasn't it even more effective? Look back at paragraphs 3 and 4 of Jack E. White's essay on "Martin Luther King." How was the situation that King and his followers encountered similar to that which Murray and her friends faced? How was it different? What is the significance of White's statement that King was "the right man at the right time" in explaining King's greater success? What unique personal qualities contributed to his success?

▪ *WRITE* an essay in which you compare and contrast Pauli Murray and Martin Luther King, Jr. In your essay, consider the situations in which Murray and King found themselves as well as their personal qualities.

A World Without Heroes

GEORGE ROCHE

❀

Phil Sudo describes a world of heroes, but for many years people believed that heroes were scarce in modern American society. In his essay "A World Without Heroes," based on his book of the same title, George Roche analyzes the importance of heroes and explains why he believes heroes seemed so rare in the latter part of the twentieth century. A respected historian, Roche has served as president of Hillsdale College in Michigan.

BEFORE YOU READ

▪ *THINK* about the title of the selection. What would "a world without heroes" be like?

▪ *THINK* about your own heroes. That is, think about the men and women you look up to as heroes. Do you look up to these people because they are attractive, famous, or wealthy? Or do you look up to them because they have performed some great good, not for themselves, but for humanity?

▪ *EXAMINE* the following italicized words from the selection.

Warmonger: "If our knight-errant rode out and slew a dragon, half the editorials the next day would brand him . . . an outright *warmonger.*"

The word *monger* means a "dealer" in a specific commodity. You may have heard the term *scandalmonger,* which means "one who spreads scandal or gossip." Thus, a *warmonger* is "one who deals in, or tries to start, a war."

Invincible: "Galileo's is an ancient faith . . . but reanimated by the seemingly *invincible* science. . . ."

Although you probably know that the prefix *in-* often means "not," you are not likely to know that the Latin *vincere* means "to conquer." With this information, however, you can deduce that *invincible* means "unconquerable" or "unbeatable."

Autonomous: "It is the vision of man without God, of man at the center of being, *antonomous,* free of external controls and in command of his own destiny."

Think for a moment about what *autobiography, autograph, automat,* and *automobile* have in common. You can quickly see that each word uses the prefix *auto-,* and you may be able to infer that this prefix means "self." Thus, an *autonomous* person is self-reliant, self-governing, independent.

Atheists, agnostics: "Even the *atheists* and *agnostics* among us admit they believe that 'something' out there in the cosmos is bigger than all of us."

These two words are best understood in relation to one another. Both words begin with the prefix *a-,* which means "without." *Atheist* is further based on the root *the* or *theo* (god), and *agnostic* is based on the root *gnosis* (knowledge). Thus, an *atheist* is one who is without god, or one who does not believe in the existence of a Supreme Being; an *agnostic* is one who is without knowledge of God, a skeptic, or a doubter.

Iconoclast: "He is generally an *iconoclastic,* angry young man. . . ."

The word *iconoclast* is an interesting word because it literally means "image breaker." Thus, to be iconoclastic is to destroy or attack sacred or respected images and traditions.

▪ *WRITE* a list in your journal of some living people who are considered heroes today. Include the names of people that you personally think of as heroes as well as the names of people who are considered heroes by a large segment of our society. You might want to compare your list with those of your fellow students, perhaps adding or deleting names after discussing various individuals. Or *WRITE* a journal entry describing "a world without heroes." What would life be like in such a world? What conditions could create such a world?

AS YOU READ

Underline the words and phrases and even sentences that Roche uses to define a "real hero." As you read, use the title of the essay and the words you have underlined to help you formulate Roche's thesis.

"It is an unhappy country that has no heroes," says Andrea Sarti, puzzlingly, 1 in Bertolt Brecht's 1939 play, "Galileo." Odder still is the fictional

Galileo's reproach: "It is an unhappy country that needs heroes." What are we—dwellers in a world without heroes—to make of this? . . .

THE LESSONS OF HEROES

Who are our heroes, and how can they make us happier? Heroes are a 2 fading memory in our times, but we still can recall a little about them. We know, at least, that what sets the hero apart is some extraordinary achievement. Whatever this feat, it is such as to be recognized at once by everyone as a good thing; and somehow, the achieving of it seems larger than life. The hero, furthermore, overcomes the ordinary and attains greatness by serving some great good. His example very nearly rebukes us, telling us that we fail, not by aiming too high in life, but by aiming far too low. Moreover, it tells us we are mistaken in supposing that happiness is a right or an end in itself. The hero seeks not happiness, but goodness, and his fulfillment lies in achieving it. In truth, the question is less about heroes than about the framework of belief in which they can, and can not, flourish. In the end, it concerns what we ourselves believe in and what we ask of life. What the hero gives us is a completely fresh, unfailed way of looking at life and, perhaps, the answer to our pervasive, mysterious unhappiness. Heroes, by their example, remind us that to pursue happiness for its own sake is the surest way to lose it.

Modern experience certainly bears this out. If nothing else, then, the 3 hero yanks us out of the old rut and bids us to reexamine our values and goals. At the same time, he shows us by his own example that higher purposes in life, far from being an illusion, are the key to our richest potentials. Already, this is much more than the how-to books can promise.

Real heroism requires courage. It entails peril or pain. The dictionary 4 says heroes are "distinguished by valor or enterprise in danger, or fortitude in suffering." Plainly, heroism also has a selfless quality. The hero's deed is ennobled not by courage alone, but by the call to duty or by service to others. In this, it gains a larger symbolic value that can inspire and bind a whole nation. The hero acts for what is common and precious to all, and thereby replenishes the strength of our shared convictions.

Our debt to heroes is no metaphor, but the very substance of a free 5 society. Our duty to one another and to moral law is exemplified by the hero's selflessness, but we have not kept our end of the bargain. The very words we need to think about when we discuss heroes—valor, magnanimity, fortitude, gallantry—rust from disuse.

If I were to depart from this theoretical discussion of heroes for a 6
moment and ask you to name a dozen who are living today who generally
are recognized as heroes, who would you name? It ought to be an easy list
to make, but, on the contrary, most people can not think of half-a-dozen
who fulfill the requirements I have outlined. Rock stars, movie idols, sports
figures, and political celebrities, as well as the occasional ordinary person
who acts bravely in an emergency, are the substitutes for absent heroes and
are thus a symptom of a paralyzing moral division in America.

If our knight-errant rode out and slew a dragon, half the editorials the 7
next day would brand him "insensitive," if not an outright warmonger, and
they would remind us that dragons are on the endangered species list. If
we can not agree that dragons are evil, we will have no dragon-fighters.
Unhappy is the country that loses its moral bearings. Unhappy the many,
bereft of spiritual leadership, who are doomed to cling to the self as the
only reality in an unfathomable existence. Small wonder that we fling
ourselves on the treadmills of sensation and turn for our redemption to the
purveyors of clinically tested, guilt-free selves. . . .

The heroes we recognize all affirm, by their very deeds, the larger 8
spiritual dimension to life. Materialist conceptions may purport to tell us
what we are, but can not touch our souls because, in the last analysis, they
can not tell us what we should be. There is no "should" in the materialist
cosmos, nor can it produce heroes. In Brecht's play, Galileo says that "it is
an unhappy country that needs heroes." He is telling mankind, "it is your
own reason and determination which control your destiny." . . .

Galileo's is an ancient faith, man's second oldest, as old as Eden, but 9
reanimated by the seemingly invincible science of the 19th century: "ye
shall be as gods." It is the vision of man without God, of man at the center
of being, autonomous, free of external controls and in command of his
own destiny. It is the promise of a new man and of a new world given
purpose and plan by man, the new Creator. . . .

By its own view and the Christian alike, "good" is the one thing the 10
vision and its works cannot be. The natural universe, according to the
vision, is all there is, and there is no good or evil in it, only natural events.
What, then, makes a priest or an artist or a teacher or even a politician
choose his vocation when he knows he can receive greater material rewards
doing something else? What, then, drives men and women to suffer and
die for their family, their country, their beliefs? Don't these acts suggest
that man may have a spiritual side, if not a pervasively spiritual nature?

A great many experts will tell you that the materialist vision is stone 11
dead today, an empty husk. The purely scientific explanation of man is no

longer viable in popular or intellectual circles. Even the atheists and
agnostics among us admit they believe that "something" out there in the
cosmos is bigger than all of us. The clearest expression of this sentiment is
to be found in the enormously successful "Star Wars" films. There is a Force
in the universe. It is all-powerful, it is mystical, it can only be tapped by
those who have enough faith to believe in it. So far as it goes, this is not a
bad message, but it is a limited one and it can not be regarded as an adequate
repudiation of the materialistic view. . . .

This is why we need heroes so desperately. By deed and symbol, they   12
replenish our spiritual strength. They are tangible proof that man does not
live by reason alone—that he has a moral conscience which is divinely
inspired, that he freely may choose virtue over sin, heroism over cowardice
or resignation.

THE DOMINANCE OF THE ANTIHERO

However, another kind of image has become dominant in the 20th century;   13
it is that of the antihero. While you may have had trouble thinking of
genuine heroes, you will probably have no trouble recalling names in this
case. In literature and in the movie industry, the antihero is a common
phenomenon and, more often than not, he is a smash hit. Modern Western
culture has been inundated with the antihero in various shades. He is
generally an iconoclastic, angry young man who cynically writes off
religion (except for some vague thing such as the Force) as a tool of the
Establishment. For him, God can not be an authority because he is against
all authority, and he owes no responsibility or allegiance to anyone except
himself or those under his immediate protection. He may exhibit many
heroic qualities like bravery and self-sacrifice, but he does not recognize
purpose in human life. He is a complete cynic.

Quite conversely, the genuine hero tells us that life *can* be what it   14
should be; that bravery and self-sacrifice occur because there are beliefs
and responsibilities which warrant bravery and self-sacrifice. The hero tells
us there is indeed purpose in human life.

❋   ❋   ❋

AFTER YOU READ

▪ *THINK* carefully about the following statements from Roche's essay. How
are the ideas expressed in these statements similar? How does Roche define
a true hero?

The hero . . . overcomes the ordinary and attains greatness by serving some great good. (paragraph 2)

The hero seeks not happiness, but goodness. (paragraph 2)

Heroes, by their example, remind us that to pursue happiness for its own sake is the surest way to lose it. (paragraph 2)

Real heroism requires courage . . . [and] entails peril or pain. (paragraph 4)

Plainly, heroism also has a selfless quality. (paragraph 4)

The hero acts for what is common and precious to all, and thereby replenishes the strength of our shared convictions. (paragraph 4)

By deed and symbol, they [heroes] replenish our spiritual strength. (paragraph 12)

The hero tells us there is indeed purpose in human life. (paragraph 14)

▪ *EXAMINE* Roche's references to Galileo in paragraphs 1, 8, and 9. According to Bertolt Brecht's fictional character Galileo, based on the prominent sixteenth-century scientist, "It is an unhappy country that needs heroes." Do you agree or disagree with his statement? Do you agree or disagree with Sarti's statement in the first paragraph that "It is an unhappy country that has no heroes." Why do you feel as you do?

▪ *EXAMINE* also the list of heroes you made before reading Roche's essay. According to Roche, which of these individuals qualify as true heroes? Why? Which ones do not? Why? Do you agree with Roche's definition? Why or why not?

▪ *WRITE* a summary of the main ideas of Roche's essay. Before writing your summary, you might want to reread the sentences in the *THINK* section above, but you should also review the entire essay for other main points. Or *WRITE* an essay about one of the individuals included in your earlier list of heroes, explaining in detail why you think he or she is a hero. Your own definition of a hero may be similar to that of Roche, or it may be quite different.

George Washington: A Hero
for American Students?

ERVIN L. JORDAN, JR.
and
CLIFFORD T. BENNETT

❀

Heroes can have a unique relationship to a nation, a cultural group, or an individual. As Phil Sudo explains in "Larger Than Life," George Washington is usually considered one of our national heroes, one of those "larger-than-life individuals who founded countries or dedicated their lives to liberation" (p. 485). In the following essay, however, Ervin L. Jordan and Clifford T. Bennett raise questions about Washington as a hero. Their revisionist view of Washington, which was published in 1997 as part of The Social Studies *special issue on Washington, is shared by many other contemporary historians who argue that traditional national heroes such as Christopher Columbus and Washington do not deserve heroic status because of the way they treated Native Americans and African-Americans. An archivist-historian and associate professor at the University of Virginia, Jordan has published numerous articles and three books, including* Black Confederates and Afro-Yankees in Civil War Virginia *(1995). Bennett, who is an associate professor in the Curry School of Education at the University of Virginia, has been elected chair of the Association of African American Educators of Social Studies.*

BEFORE YOU READ

▪ *THINK* about what you know about George Washington. What do you consider to be his most important accomplishments? Have you ever heard or read anything negative about Washington? If so, what?

▪ *EXAMINE* the title of this selection, noticing that it ends in a question mark. What does the question mark suggest about the authors' view of Washington as a hero? What is your view about his heroic status?

▪ *WRITE* in your journal a list of three individuals who have been treated as national heroes in your history textbooks. Then think about each name on your list. Do you agree that each is a hero? Write a few sentences about each, explaining why you believe this individual is or is not a hero.

AS YOU READ

Notice that Jordan and Bennett follow the classic persuasive structure by first providing background information and arguments for the opposing position (paragraphs 1–4), then giving arguments for their own position (paragraphs 5–9), and finally providing a conclusion (paragraph 10).

George Washington (1732–1799), soldier, slaveholder, and statesman, is undoubtedly an American hero. One state, thirty counties, naval vessels, and countless geographical features are named in his honor. The site he personally selected as the nation's capital bears his name: Washington, D.C.

GEORGE WASHINGTON'S IMPORTANCE TO AMERICAN HISTORY

Any summary of his sixty-seven years could barely cover his venerated fame. Born in Westmoreland County, Virginia, in February 1732, Washington served as a British officer during the French and Indian War and in the Virginia House of Burgesses where he led opposition to Great Britain's colonial policies. He served as a delegate to the First and Second Continental Congresses until selected to be commander-in-chief of the Continental Army during the American Revolution. Afterward he served as president at the Constitutional Convention, said little but lent his prestige to the proceedings, and supported the creation of a strong central government.

Washington, elected the first president of the United States (1789– 3
1797), was the only one elected unanimously. He defined the character of
the American presidency and the development of the federal government
(Carpenter 1976). After his death, one of his officers memorialized him as
"first in war, first in peace, and first in the hearts of his countrymen." Mason
Locke "Parson" Weems's laudatory and exaggerated biography of him
falsely established the cherry tree legend familiar to schoolchildren and
Washington's supposed declaration that he could not tell a lie (Weems
1808). The Mount Vernon tomb, jointly guarded by Confederate and
Union soldiers, was neutral ground during the American Civil War. Southerners inaugurated a "permanent" Confederate government on February
22, 1862, the 130th anniversary of Washington's birth, and an equestrian
portrait of him appeared on the Confederacy's Great Seal.

Washington is the subject of more books and articles than any other 4
president, with the possible exceptions of Abraham Lincoln, Franklin D.
Roosevelt, and John F. Kennedy. His birthday is a federal holiday, his
likeness appears on federal currency and postage stamps, and he is the first
of four presidents depicted on Mount Rushmore.

WASHINGTON, THE SLAVEHOLDER

Four of America's first five presidents were Virginia slaveholders. As one 5
of those slaveholders, Washington signed the 1774 Fairfax Resolves that
prohibited the importation and sale of Africans in Virginia, but he did not
free any of his own slaves (Christian 1995). The "Squire of Mount Vernon"
owned 317 slaves on five farms. Of those, a third were married slave
couples who were separated from their spouses because Washington,
ignoring slave family ties, assigned them to separate farms according to
their skills. One example was the Slammin Joe family. Joe's family, including his wife Priscilla and their six children, toiled at the Dogue Run Farm
while Joe was assigned to the Mansion House as a ditcher. That separation
caused emotional and psychological stress on the Joe family's domestic life
(Stevenson 1996).

Washington often attempted to get more work out of his slaves by 6
personally observing them, and he concluded that slaves were habitual
shirkers and liars. He considered them to be property rather than people
(Franklin and Moss 1994). During the 1790s, when he became more

concerned about controlling costs than with their needs as human beings, he coolly reduced their rations. He estimated that eleven pounds of corn, two pounds of fish, and a pound and a half of meat were sufficient weekly rations for twenty-three slaves on one of his farms. He also limited doctors' visits to six times annually for the treatment of sick slaves and encouraged his slaves to raise chickens and vegetables for their own consumption (Fitzpatrick 1944). Limited evidence does suggest that his slave ownership and betrayal of the Revolution's freedom and liberty rhetoric occasionally troubled his conscience. However, from cradle to grave, Washington owned or directly benefited from the ownership of slaves. He was a man bound by the racial and political mores of his time.

WASHINGTON'S RACIAL VIEWS

The 1933 novel *Princess Malah* includes a scene in which Virginia's [7] governor asks what is to be done with the slaves. A troubled George Washington answers: "The other question is constantly on my mind. What will this race of slaves do to the whites of America?" (Hill 1933). A racial conservative, Washington did not believe blacks were the equals of whites. He accepted slavery and the supposed inferiority of blacks. Although he managed personally to meet and praise African American poet Phillis Wheatley for her poetry (Bennett 1987; Christian 1995), Washington's relations with blacks were typical of an elite white male slaveholder. He was their superior by any social, economic, or civil standard. Washington strongly opposed the enlistment of free blacks or slaves in the Continental Army until the British began recruiting slaves as soldiers with promises of freedom (Bennett 1987; Franklin and Moss 1994). Described by historian Matthew Taylor Mellon as a stern and "racist disciplinarian, an anti-black, licentious adventurer who fathered black children by his slaves," Washington hoped America might gradually abolish slavery (Mellon 1969; O'Reilly 1995).

Nevertheless, slaves made up the bulk of his personal wealth, and he [8] did not emancipate any until after his death. Washington believed whites had an unequivocal right to own slaves; before, during, and after his presidency, he refused to participate in any activities that might benefit and increase the number of free blacks. He remained silent on the slavery question and never publicly stated his personal opposition to it (O'Reilly 1995). When one of his slaves escaped in 1795, President Washington placed newspaper advertisements seeking his return, but he did not allow his name to appear in versions printed in Northern newspapers. Washington denied that runaway slaves had a natural right to escape (McColley 1973; Franklin and Moss 1994).

In his will, he stipulated that 124 slaves were to be freed after his wife 9 Martha's death, excepting his body servant William Lee whom he immediately freed with an annual pension of thirty dollars. Slaves aged twenty to forty were to be freed first, aged or infirm slaves received a pension, slaves aged seventeen to thirty-nine had to serve at least seven years, and those sixteen and under had to serve Martha Washington until they reached age twenty-five. The Washington slaves received their freedom over a period of forty years after his death, and many became the progenitors of free black families (McColley 1973; Collins and Weaver 1976; Smith 1984).

CONCLUSION

A surprisingly phallic Washington Monument, white and straight, points 10 skyward on the Mall in the national capital as coincidental and symbolic recognition of Washington as "the Father of His Country." George Washington is a larger than life hero-saint, and not just because of the marble statues scattered across the land (Carpenter 1976). His name will be honored as long as America shall endure. African American scholars acknowledge Washington's greatness and heroic stature in American history. Nonetheless, he will continue to be condemned by most as an anti-black, racist slaveholder and a false apostle of liberty rather than as a true freedom-fighter and crusader for democracy (Mellon 1969; Carpenter 1976; Bennett 1987; Christian 1995).[1]

❀ ❀ ❀

AFTER YOU READ

▪ *THINK* about what is required for a person to be a national hero. Can a person have personal faults and still be a hero? Are there certain human qualities that a hero should have regardless of the historical period? If so,

---

[1]For a complete list of citations, see *The Social Studies* 88 (July/August 1997): 154–156.

AS YOU READ

Keep in mind Firstenberg's thesis that "film and television have had enormous impact on the evolution of the modern hero" (paragraph 1). Underline the media's portrayals of heroes at different times.

S torytellers, bards, and dramatists have always shared with us the legends 1
of our heroes. And in this era of the moving image, filmmakers have become the prime chroniclers of the twentieth-century experience. As a result, the images of film and television have had enormous impact on the evolution of the modern hero.

Our earliest heroes were god figures from mythology, later half-divine 2 and half-man (or half-animal); then heroes became men, which is to say "persons"—like you and me. Or perhaps not quite like you and me, because, as the great scholar Joseph Campbell tells us in his book *The Hero with a Thousand Faces,* in every incarnation, and age, certain recurrent characteristics have defined the hero and set him apart from ordinary men.

"The hero ventures forth from the world of common day," Campbell 3 says, "into a region of supernatural wonder; fabulous forces are there encountered and a decisive victory is won; the hero comes back from this mysterious journey with the power to bestow boons on his fellow man."

With minor variations, this classic heroic adventure has been related 4 in myths, folk legends, and fairy tales for thousands of years. It is only in the last two hundred years that we've modified the formula to downplay its "supernatural" and "fabulous" elements and recast our heroes to reflect the changes that modernization has wrought. Clearly, the nature of a hero changes with, and mirrors, the values of the times.

In the forties and fifties, Americans still embraced heroes who were 5 "larger than life." John Wayne, Gary Cooper, Jimmy Stewart, and Henry Fonda obeyed most of the traditional heroic rules: overcoming "evil"— rustlers, venal politicians, and other forms of corruption—in order to create a new order, as Campbell would have it.

But by the midfifties, and for the next fifteen to twenty years, huge 6 advances in technology and increased sophistication in the audiences shouldered these supermen aside in favor of what has been called the "antihero"—an ordinary man with recognizable frailties. Dustin Hoffman in *The Graduate,* Paul Newman in *Hud* and *Cool Hand Luke,* Alan Arkin in *Catch-22,* Al Pacino in *Dog Day Afternoon,* and Woody Allen in all his films personified a modern hero whose biggest victory was frequently the mere fact of his survival in a mechanized world that often seemed unhealthy for children and other living things.

By the late seventies, the war in Vietnam and the Watergate affair had 7 taken their toll on the American spirit, leaving a need for the old-school heroes again—larger-than-life types like Rocky and even those with supernatural qualities like Luke Skywalker and Superman.

Recently, however, the immediacy and intimacy of the media have 8 somehow confused the issue of heroism, blurring the traditional criteria by which we measure our heroes and allowing mere exposure—that is, "fame"—to precede, and occasionally preempt, "worthiness" as a qualification for heroism.

It was also during the late seventies that television-news coverage, 9 assisted by the new satellite technology, began to bring "instant news" into our living rooms. Before that, Walter Cronkite, with his thoughtful objectivity and measured delivery, had been the most trusted man in America—Dante's Virgil guiding us through the confusion and chaos of the day's events. Now we often find ourselves abandoned, watching the news along with the commentator as it unfolds. The laurels for broadcast journalism often seem to be going to the first, as opposed to the "best," coverage.

And paralleling the trend in movies and fictional television, the em- 10 phasis in news began to shift away from analysis and toward action: We could watch a hostage crisis unfold right on the runway, see crash victims hoisted from an icy river, watch firemen spray water on a burning hotel. News began to resemble drama, except that with drama, the hero is readily identified, and in reality, he often is not.

Have we in fact begun to create heroes in order to make reality more 11 dramatic? . . . Debates over Sen. Gary Hart, Jim and Tammy Bakker, and Lt. Col. Oliver North should have made abundantly clear to us that we need to take a long, hard look at the role the media has begun to play in creating/evaluating/rejecting/destroying contemporary heroes.

Are we now confusing fiction with fact and imbuing people who simply 12 have wide media exposure with the heroic ideals that fictional figures represent? Against what criteria are we measuring their "victories" and what "boons have they bestowed on [their] fellow men"? These are disturbing thoughts, but ones that we should all begin to consider. If we don't know where reality ends and fiction begins, I think we need to be concerned with our visual literacy.

❀   ❀   ❀

AFTER YOU READ

▪ *THINK* about individuals who have become your heroes through the influence of television or movies? Why do you consider these people heroes?

▪ *EXAMINE* the reading selection carefully to identify the categories into which Firstenberg groups heroes. Her first category is based on Joseph Campbell's definition of a godlike figure who "ventures forth from the world of common day into a region of supernatural wonder," encounters "fabulous forces" and wins a victory, and then "comes back from this mysterious journey with the power to bestow boons [gifts] on his fellow man." Firstenberg's later categories, however, are often associated with how heroes have been presented by the media during certain historical periods, dating through the late 1980s, when this essay was first published.

▪ *WRITE* a description of "the hero" as created or portrayed by the media in recent years, being sure to give several specific examples or one extended example. How does this hero differ from those in previous periods as described by Firstenberg? What does this hero have in common with other periods? Does this hero have more in common with the traditional hero or the antihero? Or *WRITE* an essay in which you discuss the role the media have played in "creating/evaluating/rejecting/destroying" some prominent figure as a hero.

Lenny Skutnik: Accidental Hero

RICHARD SHEREIKIS

❀

Whether it is rescuing someone from an assailant, an accident, a fire, or some other disaster, many individual acts of heroism occur that go unrecognized. Indeed, although we know about many heroic deeds during the terrorist attack of September 11, 2001, there were no doubt numerous heroic sacrifices about which we will never know. In the following article, originally published in The Hero in Transition, *Richard Shereikis focuses not only on one of these acts—a heroic rescue that occurred during the Air Florida crash in Washington, D.C. in the winter of 1982—but also on the relationship between heroism and fame discussed by Firstenberg in the previous selection.*

BEFORE YOU READ

▪ *THINK* about what you would do if you saw someone—perhaps a stranger—in great danger and were in a position to help. Do you think you would have the strength and courage to act quickly and decisively?

▪ *EXAMINE* the title of this article. You might be interested to know that the complete original title of this essay was "Heroes Don't Need Zip Codes: Lenny Skutnik—Accidental Hero." What questions does this title suggest?

▪ *EXAMINE* also the following italicized words from the selection:

Lionized: "He's been toasted by governors, *lionized* by legislators and proclaimed a savior by our President."

The surrounding context should help you realize that to *lionize* a person is to treat that person as if he or she were a famous and important person, a celebrity. This word derives from the use of the word *lion* to mean a "celebrity or an important person," a meaning that probably derived from the idea of the lion as the king of the beasts.

Subliminal: "If the name sounds familiar, it's because, like one of those *subliminal* messages that hidden persuaders can put into movies, Lenny blipped his way into the national consciousness for one brief shining moment on a dismal day in January 1982."

Word structure provides you with a clue to the meaning of this word. From such words as *subway* and *submerge,* you probably know that the prefix *sub* means "under." You may not, however, know the Latin root *limin,* which means "threshold." These word parts suggest that a *subliminal* message is one that is below the level or "under the threshold" of consciousness.

Specious: "He's justly proud of his heroism, but he recognizes mere celebrity for the *specious* and fleeting thing it is."

You probably cannot define this word from the context, but *specious* refers to something that is not what it appears to be, to something that only seems to be fair or true.

Quasi-illusion: "In this life of illusion and *quasi-illusion,* the person with solid virtues who can be admired for something more substantial than his well-knownness often proves to be the unsung hero. . . ."

The Latin root *quasi* means "almost," and thus a *quasi-illusion* is a near-illusion. Remember that, in contrast to *allusion* (which means "a reference to literature or history"), an *illusion* is a fantasy or a dream—even a delusion.

▪ *WRITE* in your journal several reasons that, as suggested in the original title, "Heroes Don't Need Zip Codes."

AS YOU READ

Underline passages that specifically describe Lenny's *heroism* (not the reaction to it) both during and after the crash.

Lenny Skutnik. It's a name you think you remember. Maybe a utility 1
infielder for the Cubs or Phillies back in the '50s. Scrappy little guy. Got his uniform dirty a lot. Batted maybe .230 lifetime in a short career. Or maybe a guy from your old high school. Kind of an average student. Wrestled at one of the lighter weight divisions and worked hard to keep in shape. Even when people hear the name for the first time, they furrow

brows and rummage in their memories. "Lenny Skutnik. Lenny Skutnik. I'm sure I know the guy, but I just can't place him." It's that kind of name.

But however unromantic the name may sound, Martin Leonard Skut- 2 nik III is an American hero. He's been toasted by governors, lionized by legislators and proclaimed a savior by our President. Millions have seen him on television, short and sturdy with dark brown hair that is cut most unromantically. For a hero, he's quiet and modest and really very shy, which makes his appearances before large and distinguished groups a bit of a trial for him. "In school," he remembers, "I'd go up to do an oral report and hide behind the paper and just start reading it without any punctuation. And the teacher would tell me to sit down because I was making a fool of myself." But recently he's talked to huge audiences that have included politicians and other public figures. "Sometimes I'll say to myself after-wards, 'How am I doing this? I just talked to 800 people. How am I doing this?'" But the audiences, big and important, hang on his few and simple words, and Lenny has grown easier in the mantle of fame which has been thrust upon him willy-nilly.

If the name sounds familiar, it's because, like one of those subliminal 3 messages that hidden persuaders can put into movies, Lenny blipped his way into the national consciousness for one brief shining moment on a dismal day in January 1982. On Wednesday, January 13, Lenny was the one who leaped into the freezing Potomac River to save a sinking victim of the crash of Air Florida Flight 90. The 737 had gone down soon after take-off at 4:00 p.m. from Washington's National Airport, ripping into the 14th Street bridge and crashing into the Potomac. Seventy-four passengers and four people on the bridge were killed in the disaster, and Priscilla Tirado, 23, would have been among them had it not been for Lenny's quick and decisive act.

Along with other commuters who were snarled in the traffic caused by 4 the crash and the swirling snowstorm that hit Washington that day, Lenny and the others in his carpool had gone down to the shore to see what the problem was. Lenny and the others had watched as a U.S. Park Police helicopter had first lowered a ring to Priscilla and another man who were somehow, miraculously, afloat on the ice. They had watched as Priscilla had let go soon after the lift, her frozen hands unable to hold on. She had fallen back to the ice while the helicopter had dropped the man safely ashore. The copter tried again, and again Priscilla had grabbed, but this time, too, she had slipped off, now splashing into the freezing water about 20 feet from shore.

Lenny didn't think about what he ought to do, about the cold or about   5
his lack of lifesaving skills. He kicked off his boots, shed his jacket, and
dived in, swimming surely as he'd learned to do in his youth in Upper
Michigan, where his father, an army man, had been stationed for a while.
"I just did what I had to do," Lenny says quietly, as is his way. "I got out
behind her and then I kinda pushed and stroked, pushed and stroked, until
we got to shore. Her eyes were rolling back in her head, and she looked
real bad." When they got Priscilla to the hospital, her body temperature
was 81 degrees, Lenny recalls. If he had hesitated even slightly, she might
have perished with her husband, Jose, 23, and her two-month-old son
Jason, both of whom were lost in the crash.

It was a noble and courageous act. Lenny had risked his life to save a   6
life. He had responded like a hero. A hero, as opposed to the mere celebrity,
as outlined by Daniel Boorstin, is "a human figure—real or imaginary or
both—who has shown greatness in some achievement. He is a man or
woman of great deeds."*

But Lenny's deed alone, as selfless as it was, would not have been   7
enough to change his life as it has been changed since that awful winter
afternoon. There was another force involved, and that was what pushed
Lenny so vigorously into the spotlight of celebrity he endured in the months
following his heroic act. There was a television camera on shore that day,
and Lenny's deed was beamed across the country. That made all the
difference. "The hero created himself," says Boorstin. "The celebrity is
created by the media" (p. 61).

As Lenny himself says, these kinds of things are not rare. "You hear of   8
firemen who go into burning buildings and come out with a kid under each
arm. It happens daily. It's just that the cameras aren't there all the time. It
was just that that day, that place, everything was so dramatic and unexpected, it was a big deal."

But that day, because it was in the nation's capital and the cameras were   9
there, Lenny Skutnik, 28, a $14,000-a-year service assistant at the Con-
gressional Budget Office, a family man and a former painter and supermarket porter and Burger Chef cook and worker in a meat packing plant and
furniture factory, became a national figure. Because the cameras were there,
Lenny Skutnik the hero also became Lenny Skutnik the celebrity—a

---

*Daniel Boorstin, *The Image: or What Happened to the American Dream* (New York:
Atheneum, 1974), 49. Subsequent references to this work will be made parenthetically in the
body of the text.

"person who is known for his well-knownness," as Boorstin expresses it. On that bleak and tragic day, Lenny had seized the moment, given the country something to cheer about, something to admire; but because the cameras were there, he was also threatened by the danger of celebrity.

He got nearly 1600 pieces of mail in the first few weeks, some of it 10 addressed to "Lenny Skutnik, Hero of the Potomac." Heroes don't need zip codes. The letters came from everywhere, according to Skutnik, mostly "short, real personal notes, telling how it made them feel. How they were watching TV and saw the girl and started screaming, 'Somebody save that girl!' They came from young, old, elementary school kids, classrooms, from all walks of life. Anybody and everybody."

Other, more public tributes came quickly over those same weeks. The 11 state of Mississippi, where Lenny was born, celebrated "Lenny Skutnik Day" on February 10, and Lenny was flown there in the governor's private plane. Columbia, Mississippi, the home town of Lenny's mother, had used February 9 to celebrate another "Lenny Skutnik Day." He was honored by the Virginia legislature and had lunch with Governor Charles Robb. . . . The walls of his living room in Lorton, Virginia, are lined with over 20 handsome plaques and framed testimonials and citations. . . . He's had other honors and gifts, too. An anonymous check for $7000 came from somewhere in Virginia, telling Lenny to pay his rent or buy a car or whatever he wanted with the money. A Washington, D.C., auto dealer offered him the use of a car for a year. . . . But most prominent and suggestive in his collection of awards and tributes is a picture that hangs in the middle of the living room wall above his television set. It's a large framed color photograph of Lenny and his wife Linda, standing with Nancy Reagan during the President's State of the Union message. During the speech on national television, the President had paid special tribute to Lenny, who had stood to acknowledge the generous applause which the distinguished audience had given him. . . .

But with Lenny Skutnik we should also remind ourselves of another 12 kind of heroism, which may be more precious and more rare than the courage he showed in the Potomac. It isn't really embodied in the act of saving another human life, as important as that act was. Lenny's real heroism lies in how he's handled the mantle of celebrity that was flung at him so unexpectedly. It lies, too, in his ability to realize the real significance of his act. It lies in his ability to maintain his sense of basic human decency even while those around him, starting with the journalists, are losing theirs.

A few days after the crash, for example, he was called by CBS News 13 and asked if he would be interested in meeting Priscilla's father, Beirne

Keefer, of Clearwater, Florida. The man had just lost his grandson and son-in-law, and Lenny had misgivings about the appropriateness of such a meeting. "I had a weird feeling about that," Lenny recalls. "I thought, 'Well this is too soon.' But I finally said, 'Well, if it's all right with him, OK.'"

Ike Pappas, the CBS newsman, warned Lenny not to tell any other 14 reporters about the meeting, or else he'd have a hundred of them invading his house, as they had on another occasion, a day or two earlier. Lenny didn't want any more disruptions of his life or his living room, so he agreed, and only the CBS camera crew waited outside his town house, preparing to capture the meeting between the hero and the father of the person he saved. Later, Lenny learned that Mr. Keefer had not expected any cameras there, that he was expecting only a simple, personal meeting arranged by Pappas, who was an acquaintance of his from their days in the service. In any case, Lenny knew it was all wrong as soon as he saw Mr. Keefer. "The minute I laid eyes on him, I could tell he was in no condition, that he shouldn't even be there," Lenny says.

And then, after they were all seated, and the cameras were rolling, 15 Pappas asked the time-honored tasteless question: "Mr. Skutnik, how do you feel about meeting Priscilla's father?"

Lenny recalls his shock at the banality of the question. "Here's the 16 man, his eyes all swelled up, he's all emotional. How can you answer something stupid like that? What can you say? And I told him [Pappas], I said, 'What kind of question is that?' I said that. And I just gave him short snappy answers to the rest of the questions he asked." That act alone should make Lenny a hero, a defender of some little nook of privacy against the ravages of the media.

There's something heroic and very telling, too, about Lenny's criteria 17 for accepting the trips and vacations he's been offered over the months which followed his deed. "If there's family there, I'll go," he says quite simply. "If there isn't, I won't." Hence his acceptance of those trips to Mississippi, to Chicago, and Philadelphia, and his rejection of the ones to Hawaii, Germany and Canada, where he wouldn't feel comfortable because he wouldn't know anyone. The heroic restraint seems refreshing, in these times when "Where's mine?" has become all but a national motto.

Finally, there's his heroically sensible and modest perspective on the 18 act he performed and the subsequent handling of it by the press and other media. "They embarrassed me," he says, "because what they were doing is they were bragging on me, which I never did and don't do. I just did what I had to do. And they're trying to make a macho man out of me." They tried to turn a hero into a mere celebrity, in other words, and Lenny has been Olympian in his resistance. . . .

He pauses, sorting through his thoughts and feelings about all the fuss ₁₉ and attention. "It's a big deal to me personally that I saved someone's life. That's important," he says softly. "Other than that, all this that's come about is mostly . . ." and his voice trails off before he can say anything too negative or nasty, which would be against his nature. He's justly proud of his heroism, but he recognizes mere celebrity for the specious and fleeting thing it is.

Other words of Boorstin's come to mind. "In our world of big names, ₂₀ curiously, our true heroes tend to be anonymous. In this life of illusion and quasi-illusion, the person with solid virtues who can be admired for something more substantial than his well-knownness often proves to be the unsung hero" (p. 76).

So it is with Lenny Skutnik, now that the blinding light of his celebrity ₂₁ has dimmed, and we can see his virtues clear.

❀   ❀   ❀

AFTER YOU READ

▪ *THINK* about how Lenny Skutnik reacted to the crisis in the Potomac and then about how he reacted to his fame. Which reaction was more admirable and why?

▪ *EXAMINE* the actions of the newspeople as described in the selection. How do you view these actions? Were they necessary and appropriate? Were they sensitive or insensitive? How would you have reacted if you had been Lenny or the father?

▪ *WRITE* a persuasive essay about the origin of heroism. In your opinion, does a person become a hero because of qualities that he or she possesses or because of specific circumstances? What was the source of Lenny Skutnik's heroism? What other examples support your point of view?

The Man in the Water

ROGER ROSENBLATT

❀

This essay, which was first published in Time, *focuses on the same air tragedy that was the subject of the previous essay by Richard Shereikis. Indeed, Shereikis provides an excellent connection to this related article when he quotes Daniel Boorstin's statement that "In our world of big names, curiously, our true heroes tend to be anonymous."* Although Shereikis's essay focuses on an initially anonymous hero whose identity later becomes well known, the hero of Rosenblatt's essay remains anonymous. The author of several books, Rosenblatt is an award-winning journalist who has written for the* New Republic, *the* Washington Post, U.S. News and World Report, *and* Time.

BEFORE YOU READ

- *THINK* about how the title of this selection differs from the title of the previous selection. The two readings focus on specific—but different—heroes of the 1982 Air Florida crash in Washington, D.C. At least one important piece of information that is available in the title "Lenny Skutnik: Accidental Hero," however, is absent in the title "The Man in the Water." What is this information?

- *EXAMINE* the first paragraph of the selection. Notice that the first sentence states that "as disasters go, this one was terrible, but not unique, certainly not among the worst on the roster of U.S. air crashes." And yet Rosenblatt goes on to list several details that help to make this crash

---

*Daniel Boorstin, *The Image: or What Happened to the American Dream* (New York: Atheneum, 1974), 76.

© 1982 Time Inc. Reprinted by permission.

different. Notice that Rosenblatt concludes this paragraph with a question that increases our interest in the remainder of the article.

▪ *EXAMINE* also the following words from the selection:

Emblemized: "The jets from Washington National Airport . . . are, for the moment, *emblemized* by the one that fell. . . ."

As you probably know, an emblem is an object or symbol that represents a particular idea, concept, company, country, and so on. For example, the American flag is an emblem of America. To *emblemize,* then, would be to use such an object to represent the idea associated with it.

Anonymity: "His selflessness was one reason the story held national attention; his *anonymity* another."

Anonymity is literally the state of being without a name or identity (*a* = "without," *onym* = "name"). In this sentence, Rosenblatt introduces one of his major points in the essay, for he continues by saying that "The fact that he went unidentified invested him with a universal character."

Implacable: "The man in the water pitted himself against an *implacable,* impersonal enemy; he fought it with charity; and he held it to a standoff."

You may have heard the word *placate* (pronounced PLAY′ kate), which means "to calm or to appease." Someone who is *placable* (pronounced PLAK′ able) can be calmed or appeased easily, but an *implacable* enemy is not easily appeased, will not yield or give up.

▪ *WRITE* in your journal, based on your preview of the first paragraph and the vocabulary sentences, your prediction of why this crash was different from most other air crashes.

AS YOU READ

Underline passages that help explain why Rosenblatt chose to call his essay "The Man in the Water."

As disasters go, this one was terrible, but not unique, certainly not among the worst on the roster of U.S. air crashes. There was the unusual element of the bridge, of course, and the fact that the plane clipped it at a moment of high traffic, one routine thus intersecting another and disrupting both. Then, too, there was the location of the event. Washington, the city of form and regulations, turned chaotic, deregulated, by a blast of real winter and a single slap of metal on metal. The jets from Washington National Airport that normally swoop around the presidential monuments like famished gulls are, for the moment, emblemized by the one that fell; so there is that detail. And there was the aesthetic clash as well—blue-and-green Air Florida, the name a flying garden, sunk down among gray chunks in a black river. All that was worth noticing, to be sure. Still, there was nothing very special in any of it, except death, which, while always special, does not necessarily bring millions to tears or to attention. Why, then, the shock here?

Perhaps because the nation saw in this disaster something more than a 2 mechanical failure. Perhaps because people saw in it no failure at all, but rather something successful about their makeup. Here, after all, were two forms of nature in collision: the elements and human character. Last Wednesday, the elements, indifferent as ever, brought down Flight 90. And on that same afternoon, human nature—groping and flailing in mysteries of its own—rose to the occasion.

Of the four acknowledged heroes of the event, three are able to 3 account for their behavior. Donald Usher and Eugene Windsor, a park police helicopter team, risked their lives every time they dipped the skids into the water to pick up survivors. On television, side by side in bright blue jumpsuits, they described their courage as all in the line of duty. Lenny Skutnik, a 28-year-old employee of the Congressional Budget Office, said: "It's something I never thought I would do"—referring to his jumping into the water to drag an injured woman to shore. Skutnik added that "somebody had to go in the water," delivering every hero's line that is no less admirable for its repetitions. In fact, nobody had to go into the water. That somebody actually did so is part of the reason this particular tragedy sticks in the mind.

But the person most responsible for the emotional impact of the 4 disaster is the one known at first simply as "the man in the water." (Balding, probably in his 50s, an extravagant mustache.) He was seen clinging with five other survivors to the tail section of the airplane. This man was described by Usher and Windsor as appearing alert and in control. Every time they lowered a lifeline and flotation ring to him, he passed it on to another of the passengers. "In a mass casualty, you'll find people like him," said Windsor. "But I've never seen one with that commitment." When the helicopter came back for him, the man had gone under. His selflessness was one reason the story held national attention; his anonymity another. The fact that he went unidentified invested him with a universal character. For a while he was Everyman, and thus proof (as if one needed it) that no man is ordinary.

Still, he could never have imagined such a capacity in himself. Only 5 minutes before his character was tested, he was sitting in the ordinary plane among the ordinary passengers, dutifully listening to the stewardess telling him to fasten his seat belt and saying something about the "no smoking sign." So our man relaxed with the others, some of whom would owe their lives to him. Perhaps he started to read, or to doze, or to regret some harsh remark made in the office that morning. Then suddenly he knew that the trip would not be ordinary. Like every other person on that flight, he was desperate to live, which makes his final act so stunning.

For at some moment in the water he must have realized that he would 6 not live if he continued to hand over the rope and ring to others. He *had* to know it, no matter how gradual the effect of the cold. In his judgment he had no choice. When the helicopter took off with what was to be the last survivor, he watched everything in the world move away from him, and he deliberately let it happen.

Yet there was something else about our man that kept our thoughts on 7 him, and which keeps our thoughts on him still. He was *there,* in the essential, classic circumstance. Man in nature. The man in the water. For its part, nature cared nothing about the five passengers. Our man, on the other hand, cared totally. So the timeless battle commenced in the Potomac. For as long as that man could last, they went at each other, nature and man; the one making no distinctions of good and evil, acting on no principles, offering no lifelines; the other acting wholly on distinctions, principles and, one supposes, on faith.

Since it was he who lost the fight, we ought to come again to the 8 conclusion that people are powerless in the world. In reality, we believe the reverse, and it takes the act of the man in the water to remind us of our true feelings in this matter. It is not to say that everyone would have acted as he did, or as Usher, Windsor and Skutnik. Yet whatever moved these men to challenge death on behalf of their fellows is not peculiar to them. Everyone feels the possibility in himself. That is the abiding wonder of the story. That is why we would not let go of it. If the man in the water gave a lifeline to the people gasping for survival, he was likewise giving a lifeline to those who observed him.

The odd thing is that we do not even really believe that the man in the 9 water lost his fight. "Everything in Nature contains all the powers of Nature," said Emerson. Exactly. So the man in the water had his own natural powers. He could not make ice storms, or freeze the water until it froze the blood. But he could hand life over to a stranger, and that is a power of nature too. The man in the water pitted himself against an implacable, impersonal enemy; he fought it with charity; and he held it to a standoff. He was the best we can do.

❀ ❀ ❀

AFTER YOU READ

- *THINK* about what "the man in the water" comes to symbolize to those who observe his actions. How is he an "Everyman hero"? Why is such a hero especially important to society? Would the man's heroism have been as effective if his identity had been known? Why or why not?

- *EXAMINE* the conflict between nature and "the man in the water," especially as shown in paragraphs 2, 7, and 9. What strengths does nature have? What strengths does "the man in the water" have? Who, or what, is victorious? How?

- *WRITE* an essay in which you describe a selfless act that you have observed.

Heroines and Role Models

MAXINE F. SINGER

❈

In the following essay, which was presented as a commencement address at Barnard College in New York City, Maxine F. Singer distinguishes between heroines and role models. Currently president of the Carnegie Institution for Research in Washington, D.C., Singer has been a leading scientist in cancer research and in the field of human genetics and has been a spokesperson for the responsible and ethical use of such research. An editorial board member and frequent contributor to Science *magazine, she writes for both the specialist and the general reader.*

BEFORE YOU READ

▪ *THINK* about the terms *heroine* and *role model*. How would you define a heroine? How would you define a role model? How are a heroine and a role model similar? How are they different?

▪ *EXAMINE* Singer's first paragraph. Does the label "role model" bother you as it does Singer? Do you think role models are as important to our society as heroines? Why or why not?

▪ *EXAMINE* also the following words from the selection and the definitions that follow them:

Emulate: "And none of us would want to *emulate* her disregard for the known dangers of radiation, a disregard that ended in the destruction of her life."

To *emulate* is to copy, follow, or imitate. Thus Singer says that we would not want to imitate Curie's disregard for danger but implies that we may want to model some of her other qualities.

Exemplars: "Still, these heroines are more worthy *exemplars* than contemporary women occupying the roles to which young American women aspire."

530

As suggested by the context of this sentence, an *exemplar* is an ideal example or a model worthy of being imitated.

Proximal: "For one thing, a heroine is distant while a role model's *proximal* reality encourages too close scrutiny. . . ."

The context of this sentence suggests that *proximal* means the opposite of "distant." Thus *proximal* means "near or nearest." *Proximal* is an adjective form of *proximity,* which means the state of being near; closeness.

▪ *WRITE* in your journal a list of women whom you consider heroines. Then write another list of women whom you consider role models. Discuss your lists, comparing them with those of your classmates.

AS YOU READ

Underline Singer's definitions of *heroine* and *role model.* How are her definitions similar to or different from your own?

The label "role model" is well intended, and the concept is useful. Yet, 1 the term is bothersome. Why?

Young women in the 1930s and '40s, when I grew up, had real 2 heroines. Isadora Duncan and Martha Graham were among them. Their extraordinary talents made dance into an original art form. They initiated schools, had followers, were leaders; their unconventional personal lives were romantic. Heroines, yes, but role models? Most American women of my generation could not have imagined an unconventional personal life, and most lacked the talents of Duncan and Graham, not to mention their courage.

Marie Curie was another heroine of ours. The biography of Curie, 3 written by her daughter Eve, inspired scientifically inclined young women in an age when heroism still mattered and not many women were scientists. Through the book, and the famous movie based on it, we were touched by the image of Marie and Pierre Curie stirring great vats of pitchblend in their dark shed of a laboratory. Nor could anyone forget that this hard physical work led to two Nobel prizes: one in physics in 1903, shared by Marie and Pierre Curie with Antoine Bequerel, and another in 1911, for Marie alone in chemistry for the discovery of radium.

The description in Eve Curie's book is of a heroine, not a role model. 4 No young American woman could imagine the sacrifice of the lonely years Marie Curie spent in Poland as a governess, sending money to her sister who was studying medicine in Paris, saving what was left for her own eventual opportunity to study. And none of us would want to emulate her disregard for the known dangers of radiation, a disregard that ended in the destruction of her life.

Still, these heroines are more worthy exemplars than contemporary 5 women occupying the roles to which young American women aspire. For one thing, a heroine is distant while a role model's proximal reality encourages too close scrutiny and a destructive mimicry of both public and private behavior. More importantly a heroine is, by definition, known for courage and nobility of purpose, thereby uplifting our own ambitions out of narrow, self-centered concerns.

Why then do young women now speak so often of role models and so 6 rarely of heroines? Why are heroines and even heroes so out of fashion? Nobility of purpose is not currently admired; our society is afraid that following such a leader will extract too high a cost from us as individuals or as a nation. Rather, we deny greatness and seek instead a false image of equality. In our compulsive effort to make everyone ordinary we assume license to delve into personal matters, from the trivial to the profound; unsurprisingly, the glorious images are tarnished. And for those who are truly great, where the effort to make them ordinary cannot succeed, we strive to make them evil. Not even the giants of our world can escape. Consider the sad efforts to tarnish Martin Luther King's image, as if that could undermine his greatness.

Technology makes this program easier. Television is unforgiving in its 7 ability to reveal the personal flaws of everyone from athletic stars to scientists. Modern high-speed journalism sometimes seems to make the whole world into a soap opera.

People have always known that heroines and heroes are imperfect. But 8 they chose to ignore the warts so that the greatness could inspire new achievement. We are all diminished by the disappearance of heroism. Role models will be for naught if there are no heroines and heroes from whom to learn about courage, about noble purpose, about how to reach within and beyond ourselves to find greatness.

Young women now have more freedom to shape themselves than 9 young women anywhere or at anytime in history. That freedom is a lonely and difficult burden, but it is also a blessing. The burden cannot be conquered nor the blessing realized by standing in anyone's shadow. But both can be achieved by standing on the shoulders of the great heroines.

❀ ❀ ❀

AFTER YOU READ

▪ *THINK* about the distinctions that Singer makes between heroines and role models. With a group of your classmates, make one list of the qualities that she associates with heroines and another list of the qualities that she associates with role models. In Singer's opinion, who are the more vital to a society—heroines or role models?

▪ *EXAMINE* the questions that Singer asks at the beginning of paragraph 6: "Why then do young women now speak so often of role models and so rarely of heroines? Why are heroines and even heroes so out of fashion?" How does Singer answer these questions? How would you answer them? Do you agree or disagree with Singer?

▪ *WRITE* an essay comparing a contemporary heroine with a contemporary female role model. You may want to begin with definitions of a heroine and a role model. For these definitions, use your own ideas as well as the list of qualities you made in the "*THINK* about" assignment above.

Christa McAuliffe:
An Ordinary Hero

MIKE PRIDE

❀

*Many heroic individuals have participated in the U.S.
space program. Alan B. Shepard, Jr., was the first U.S.
astronaut to enter space; John Glenn was the first American to orbit the earth; and Neil A. Armstrong was the first
human being to set foot on the moon. Chosen by NASA in
1984 for the teacher-in-space program and a crewmember
of the space shuttle* Challenger, *Christa McAuliffe was
supposed to become the first teacher (and one of the first
women) in space. However, McAuliffe's own heroic journey was cut tragically short when the* Challenger *exploded
immediately after takeoff from Cape Canaveral, Florida,
in January 1986. In the following editorial from
McAuliffe's hometown newspaper* The Concord Monitor,
*editor Mike Pride remembers McAuliffe and comments
about her heroism.*

BEFORE YOU READ

• *THINK* about the idea of women as heroes. In his essay "Larger Than
Life," Phil Sudo calls attention to the small number of women treated as
heroes in American history. In your opinion, why do we have so few female
heroes? Are women more likely to be viewed as role models than as heroes?
How does a female hero differ from a female role model? From what you
know about Christa McAuliffe, would you consider her a hero? Why or
why not?

• *EXAMINE* the use of the word *odyssey* in the second paragraph: "From
before that July day until the moment she disappeared in a pink-white puff
on the newsroom television screen, we helped her neighbors follow her
odyssey." The word *odyssey* can be traced back to Odysseus, a mythical

534

Greek hero. Because of Odysseus's epic quest for his homeland, the word *odyssey* now means a personal journey or search.

▪ *WRITE* a journal entry explaining why you think our society has so few female heroes.

AS YOU READ

Determine whether Christa McAuliffe was a hero or a role model. As you read, underline passages that help you decide on your response.

In the journal I keep, the entry for July 20, 1985, begins: "Yesterday was an incredible day to be editor of the local paper." The day before at the White House, Christa McAuliffe, from my hometown, Concord, N.H., had been named the teacher in space. Near the end of my journal entry is this quotation from her: "I think the students will say that an ordinary person is contributing to history, and if they can make that connection, they are going to get excited about history and about the future." 1

Christa made the future—space—an area we covered in the small newspaper I edit. From before that July day until the moment she disappeared in a pink-white puff on the newsroom television screen, we helped her neighbors follow her odyssey. Last week we had a different job. There had been a death in the family, and we groped, with our readers, for what it meant. 2

Christa made Concord proud. The people in our city saw in her the best that we have to offer. Concord is a family town, and it cares about education. A mother, a wife, and a teacher, Christa spoke out for her profession. She was robust and confident; she played volleyball and loved the outdoors. She was a volunteer in a city that seems at times to be run by volunteers. She also taught what Roman Catholics used to call a catechism class. She let no one forget that when she was growing up, teaching was one of the few fields open to women. She was a role model, bringing home the message again and again: if I can do this, think what you can do. 3

And she became a media darling. In front of a semicircle of TV cameras, she would describe deadpan how the shuttle's toilet worked. The people of Concord, of course, knew that Christa was not performing for the media. The camera didn't lie, and Christa didn't act. This was the real *her*. Whether she was waving Paul Giles's baton to conduct Nevers' Band—it dates back 4

to the Civil War—or chatting with her son's hockey teammates at the
Everett Arena, she was the same vibrant, positive person the rest of America
saw on TV.

CRAZY ABOUT CHRISTA

It is assumed in our society that people who capture the nation, as Christa 5
had, go on to fame and fortune. Those who knew her best knew that Christa
had no such intention. She would have used her celebrity to advocate causes
she believed in, but she could hardly wait to get back to her classroom at
Concord High. She had chosen the profession and chosen Concord, and
her selection as teacher in space had done nothing but affirm those choices.

If Christa liked Concord, Concord was crazy about Christa. It made 6
her the grand marshal in a parade. It gave her a day. Her high school sent
her off to Houston with a banner that read "Good luck from the Class of
'86 . . . Mrs. McAuliffe . . . Have a blast!" A committee made big plans for
her homecoming. New Year's Eve, the city featured ice sculptures of rocket
ships and stars on the New Hampshire State House lawn.

Bob Hohler, our paper's columnist, became Christa's shadow, sending 7
back dispatches from Washington, Houston, and finally, Cape Canaveral.
Her beaming face graced our front page countless times, floating weightless
during training, dwarfed by *Challenger* before an earlier launch, grinning
with her husband, Steve. Her story always seemed too good to be true, and
too American. No one is really the girl next door. No one rides in a parade
down Main Street on a bright, sunny Saturday afternoon. No one equates
a modern venture with the pioneers crossing the plains in Conestoga
wagons.

In the journal I keep, the entry for Jan. 28, 1986, begins: "What a 8
tragic day for Concord." Tears have flowed in my city for days—long,
wearying days. Words have flowed, too, in verse, in letters to the editor,
on radio talk shows.

INTENSE AND PERSONAL

All the media people who have interviewed me and others at the newspaper 9
want to know how it feels here. Our pain is more intense and personal, I
tell them, but we know we are not alone; nearly everyone I know was
consoled by a call from someone. Ordinary people, the kind McAuliffe's
mission had intended to reach, have called from out of the blue. One man
from Alberta, Canada, told me that his family felt terrible and needed to

speak with someone here because if they felt that bad, he said, we must feel much worse.

I thought at first that Christa's death would be hardest on the children. They had learned all about the shuttle, and in an age without heroes, they had found one in her. Most had witnessed the dreadful moment. Yet times like these remind us that children are resilient. Age robs us of the instinct to go forward without a backward glance. I even suspect now that we have tried too hard to make our children feel what we want them to feel. It is the adults in Concord who still have swollen eyes and stricken looks. They comprehend what was lost, and what was lost was a part of them. It is not a myth to say that everyone in town knew Christa. She was easy to meet, easy to talk to. Even those who never had the chance felt as though they had.

Since we picked up Christa McAuliffe's trail, our town has traversed from the green, fertile days of midsummer to the cold heart of winter. The subtle daily changes of nature have played tricks on us; sometimes, at this time of year, it can seem as if summer might never come again.

Many people have compared Christa's death with the assassination of John F. Kennedy, the inspiration of her youth. There are differences, but for the people of Concord—even for the nation as a whole—the comparison is valid. She stood for what was best in us at a time when we wanted to believe that the American spirit was reborn. That makes her death hard.

❀   ❀   ❀

AFTER YOU READ

- *THINK* about the statement Pride makes in paragraph 10 that "in an age without heroes, they [the children] had found one in her [McAuliffe]." Do you agree with George Roche (see pp. 502–507) and Pride that the late twentieth century was without heroes? Explain your response.

- *EXAMINE* the title "Christa McAuliffe: An Ordinary Hero." How many times does Pride use the word *ordinary* in his essay? What does he mean by the phrase "an ordinary hero"? How was McAuliffe an ordinary hero? How was she an extraordinary hero?

- *WRITE* an essay arguing whether Christa McAuliffe was *primarily* a hero or a role model. Begin your paragraph with a definition of the category into which you place McAuliffe. Then develop your essay by discussing how McAuliffe fits your definition.

A Higher Cause

FRANK LALLI

✿

On April 19, 1995, a bomb ripped apart the Alfred P. Murrah Federal Building in Oklahoma City, not only killing and maiming many innocent individuals but also damaging forever our feelings of security within the borders of our own country. As in the terrorist attack on the World Trade Center in September 2001, many unsung heroes emerged that day—police and fire department officers, medical personnel, and private citizens. One of the heroes in Oklahoma City was Rebecca Anderson, a nurse who answered her own internal call to aid the victims and, in the process, lost her own life. In the following essay, Frank Lalli reports her story.

BEFORE YOU READ

• *THINK* about the Oklahoma bombing, about the terrorist attack on September 11, 2001, or about some other national disaster in which several lives were lost or endangered. How did people in the vicinity of the disaster respond? If you had been on the scene, how do you think you would have responded?

• *EXAMINE* the first paragraph. According to Lalli, what message were the bombers trying to send? Instead, what truth did they unwittingly reveal to us? Do you agree or disagree with this final "truth"?

• *WRITE* a journal entry in which you describe how you *think* you would react in a traumatic situation such as a car wreck, a fire, or a national disaster such as an earthquake or a bombing.

AS YOU READ

Underline the passages that convince you of Rebecca Anderson's heroism.

The twisted souls who blew up the Alfred P. Murrah Federal Building
in Oklahoma City, killing 167 including 19 children under age six,
were apparently trying to send a message that the government is the
enemy of the people. Instead, they reminded us that the government is the
people.

People like Rebecca Anderson. She was one of 20,000 volunteers from
all corners of the land who joined the 2,000 professional emergency
workers combing through the rubble to rescue the living and recover the
dead. Rebecca, like so many others, reacted instinctively to the April 19
blast. The moment she saw the obscene TV image of the building's north
face ripped open by a terrorist bomb, she went to her bedroom, pulled on
a pair of jeans and rushed to the scene. She wanted to help.

In many ways, Rebecca's story is much like other volunteers', except
for one detail: Though they all risked their lives when they entered the
crumbling hulk of mangled metal and shattered cement, she was the only
one who died. At 37, this newly remarried mother of four gave her life
trying to save six ordinary people like herself.

Since they lived only nine miles away in Midwest City, Rebecca and
her husband Fred, 37, a Coca-Cola trucker, drove up to the building in
their pickup about half an hour after the 9:02 a.m. blast. She jumped out
and, without a helmet, quickly pulled two survivors out of the wreckage.
She went back in a third time and again led a victim to safety.

But then another volunteer, Glenn Sheppard, 34, a local security guard,
noticed that Rebecca was hurt. "She was dazed," he says. Rebecca, a newly
accredited nurse, told him she had gotten hit on the head, apparently by a
falling chunk of the structure. There was no blood, but her head was
throbbing.

"You wouldn't believe this woman," says Sheppard. "What made her
so special is that she was hurt badly, but she persisted in helping." Five
minutes later someone screamed that a woman had fainted. "I saw that it
was Rebecca," Sheppard adds.

At first doctors at nearby University Hospital were hopeful. But a small
fistlike clot formed in her right frontal lobe and her brain swelled against
her cranium. Despite two operations, she slipped into a coma and was
pronounced brain dead four days later. Then she saved a fourth and fifth
life and nearly a sixth.

Months before, she had told Fred that if she died suddenly she wanted
her organs donated. Hours after doctors ruled that her brain had stopped
functioning, her heart was transplanted to a 54-year-old casino supervisor
who secured an emergency Coast Guard flight from Louisiana to get to the

hospital. Unfortunately, he died 10 days later. But Rebecca's kidneys were also transplanted in two lifesaving operations. Both patients survived.

Those who knew her best weren't at all surprised by her sacrifices. 9 "I've seen Rebecca step into the middle of a busy road to rescue a little bird," says her 59-year-old mother, Doris Needham of Fort Smith, Ark. Then she recalls another detail with a pride any mother can appreciate: "And she always left the kitchen clean."

No one in her family—not her four brothers, her sister, her two sons, 10 her two daughters or her husband of nine months—could make sense of her death. They have not yet absorbed the tragedy. In a two-hour conversation with *Money* reporter Karen Hube, Fred kept talking about Rebecca in the present tense, then awkwardly correcting himself.

However, one of Rebecca's nursing school friends, Dorene McCam- 11 mon, 28, also of Midwest City, offers these thoughts: "When you think about it, this antigovernment movement—these bombers—is really a movement against the people. We as American citizens and voters hire our government officials. They work for us. I can see that, in the bombers' maniacal minds, this bombing of a federal office building is a political act. But I think most people see it as murder, plain and simple—mass murder of ordinary working people and their children."

Americans also saw something even more significant than the isolated 12 act of terrorism. They watched countless fellow citizens respond with an outpouring of bravery and generosity that amounted to a reassuring display of national heroism. Hundreds of thousands of us, if not millions, reached out spontaneously to help the victims any way we could because in a very real sense we identified with them as members of our family, the American family. We all wanted to help. Rebecca Anderson happened to die doing it. One can only add that in a democracy like ours, you can't give your life for any higher cause.

❀   ❀   ❀

AFTER YOU READ

▪ *THINK* about Rebecca Anderson's heroism, perhaps reviewing the passages that you underlined as you read. In addition to her actions after the Oklahoma City bombing, what other heroic decisions or actions did she accomplish during her life?

• *EXAMINE* the last paragraph of the essay. For what "higher cause" did Anderson give her life?

• *EXAMINE* also paragraph 11 (p. 486) of Phil Sudo's essay. According to Sudo, what trait do all heroes have in common? How does Anderson exhibit this trait? How is this trait related to the "higher cause" that Lalli identifies? What other higher causes can you identify?

• *WRITE* an essay in which you identify and discuss one or more higher causes for which heroes have been willing to risk their lives and property. Support your essay with one extended example or several briefer examples of people who have devoted themselves to the cause(s) you are discussing.

True Grit

BARRY TARGAN

❀

The award-winning author Barry Targan is a man of many interests and talents. In addition to publishing several collections of poetry and short stories and three novels, Kingdoms, The Tangerine Tango Equation, *and* The Ark of Marindor, *Targan has been—among other things—a teacher, a violinist, a photographer, a naturalist, a sailor, a gardener, and a potter. His stories have won the Pushcart Prize and the O. Henry Award and have been anthologized in* Best American Short Stories. *As shown in the following autobiographical essay, one of Targan's main themes is an individual's heroic and loving commitment to his or her family, work, or art.*

BEFORE YOU READ

• *THINK* about the title "True Grit," which is an allusion to a 1969 John Wayne movie. In the movie, Wayne's "true grit" is shown through physical courage, but this term can also refer to other types of courage. Does it also require "true grit" to sacrifice for one's family? To go to work when one is sick or in pain?

• *EXAMINE* the following words that occur in this essay and the definitions that are provided for you:

Virulent: "Recently I came down with a cold, what is called a common cold, although this cold felt to me to be uncommon, particularly virulent" (paragraph 1).

Virulent means particularly harsh, hateful, or even poisonous; thus Targan felt that his cold was unusually severe.

Validate: "The time had come for me to assume a greater responsibility than slicing cold cuts or marking prices on cans; now I had to *validate* his life by *validating* my own" (paragraph 14).

To *validate* something is to make it valid, sound, or convincing; therefore, Targan's father believes his life will have been meaningful if he has helped his son to succeed.

Rancid: "So, when I left, I did not slink away dragging a bundle of second and third thoughts or *rancid* misgivings, but like a darling I went forth, well armed with my father's strength and resolve and gaiety" (paragraph 15).

Meaning disagreeable or offensive in smell or taste, *rancid* is used here to show that Targan has no negative feelings as he leaves his father.

Chimera: "The worst my father could imagine befalling him was not the short-term robber but the long-term inability to provide for those he loved. Against that *chimera* guns could not prevail" (paragraph 20).

In Greek mythology, a *chimera* was a terrible monster—part lion, part goat, and part serpent—that terrorized the land and was killed by the hero Bellerophon. By referring to a chimera, Targan suggests that his father is a hero for successfully fighting against the fear or possibility of failing to provide for his family.

▪ *WRITE* a journal entry in which you describe how someone you know has shown "true grit" in his or her daily life.

AS YOU READ

Notice that the way Targan's father deals with a cold in paragraph 3 becomes representative of how he deals with other challenges in life. Underline other challenges that he faces and bracket the ways in which he reacts to these challenges.

Recently I came down with a cold, what is called a common cold, although this cold felt to me to be uncommon, particularly virulent, on the edge of something worse. I considered a doctor but let it go. I have a strong constitution, and I have often gone without a cold for a year or two or even three. Colds for me had become Abstractions, what the caricatures in the TV ads suffer from before they pop the sorcerer's pill that enables them in mere minutes to regain their world and its required momentum. But healthy people are all healthy in the same way: sickness is unique, private, solitary. The rattle in my chest, the thickness in my hearing, the cottony tongue in the tarnished metal case my mouth has turned into—these are mine, my infection to do with what I will.

I am well now, back on my feet, as active as ever. This past weekend ₂
my wife and I went cross-country skiing.

And now I think about my father. What did he do when he had a cold? ₃
It occurs to me with particular force that he could do nothing about it, only
endure it and go on. Other than aspirin he had nothing to help him.
Certainly none of the current antihistamines and various cold remedies and
certainly none of the powerful drugs that do work against bacterial
infections. No vaccinations against the various flus. But, even more to the
point, he simply could not stop. He could not, as I can, step out of his life
for a day or two or longer to rest and heal or maybe only suffer less. In all
his long working life of six-day weeks (six and a half days in the summer),
I never knew him to miss a day of work because of sickness or pain of any
sort. Except once. That was the day he had all his teeth pulled.

In 1899 my father came from Russia at the age of eight months. He ₄
was orphaned in Philadelphia at the age of six years. He was raised
thereafter in an orphanage until he was thirteen. Then he went to work
and never stopped working until he died in 1989.

I doubt that he ever saw a dentist who filled a cavity. In his early life ₅
that would have been an unimaginable indulgence. For him, as for most
like him, you went to the dentist to have a bad tooth pulled, not filled.
Dentists cost money. He had to wait for the development of sufficient
(though limited) personal means to support such a system of dental care.
But even then, before his own teeth, there were the teeth of his children
and wife to be attended to. By the time his turn came, it was too late. Finally
most of his teeth were too badly decayed to be saved. Those few that were
still sound would only get in the way of a full set of dentures. The
disadvantages outweighed their slight usefulness. They all had to go and,
my father decided, all at once. Most of the details I do not know; I was
very young. In later years he would answer my questions about all sorts of
things: what I thought to ask, what he remembered. But I did not ask him
about that day.

What I do remember with etched vividness was my father coming home ₆
around noon and getting into bed. I did not know what to make of that,
and I did not even know what to make of my confusion. I was frightened
in a profound, soul-deep way, not like the quick and immediate terrors of
being chased by a bully dog in the neighborhood, and certainly not like the
scariness of the Shadow on the radio. This was a fear that I could not even
name as fear. I did not know how to inquire after it. Something was greatly
wrong. Something had gone wrong. My father was in bed in a darkened
room, my mother ministering to him. I was admonished to make no noise
at all. But I was silent of my own accord.

The next morning when I awoke he was gone. Back to work. He was 7
the owner of a small food store. Not yet a grocery or a butcher shop. In
those days in the 1940s there were no supermarkets as we now know them
and not even combination stores. Shopping for food was more on the
European model—specialized. My father sold vegetables and fruit. To do
this, he had to rise early enough to get to the farmers' market on the edge
of the city near dawn to be ready when, at six o'clock, by general agreement
amongst the farmers, the selling would start. Then he would go to his store
in the city and prepare: trimming the lettuce that he would soak in the ice
water in old bathtubs in the back of the store, or unwrapping the oranges
to make handsome displays of them (oranges and lemons came in thin,
beautiful tissue paper), or sorting through the delicate, thin-skinned tomatoes shipped in from Texas to separate the green ones from the ripe ones,
and from those the tomatoes that were rotting. There was always something he had to do. The tomatoes could not wait, nor could the spinach,
the beans. Between tending to his customers—weighing out peas, cutting
a watermelon into halves or quarters or slices to sell whatever his customers
could afford—he rushed at the beets whose tops were turning slimy or into
the nests of mold deep within the boxes of grapes from California.
Everywhere and constantly he raced against the autolysis of vegetables, the
ripening of fruit.

What did he do when he had a cold? What could he do? If he was not 8
there to open his store, there was no store. No money that day. If he was
not there to trim and soak and ice his ware, his loss increased. So there was
no alternative. He was doing what he had to do: he was working to create
a life that he wanted. He had a wife and three sons and a means to feed
and clothe them—and even, in time, to educate them handsomely.

I never heard him complain about anything except the lack of business. 9
My father never complained about his hard work. Nor did he express in
other ways any self-pity or resentment or quiet desperation. Indeed I
remember him as an unfailingly cheerful man, friendly and optimistic. And
years later, when I looked back from my educated heights, I could understand where his optimism came from—imagination. Even when his little
business did begin to crumble before the juggernauts of A&P and ACME
and the like, his impulse was to battle back, not in anger but in a kind of
delight (as odd as that may sound), because he could imagine not victory
over the A&P but the possibilities within the combat itself: the chance to
outsmart and beat them, even if beating them meant little more than
surviving. But more he did not ask. He explained his response. He would
stay open at night, a convenience that the supermarkets then did not offer.
He would get the special tax license required to sell cigarettes and candy.

He had by 1950 added a grocery section and meat to his store, but after a few relatively prosperous years the mounting competition ground his business down: he did not sell enough to buy enough. Then, wonder of wonders, he found wholesalers who would sell him half and even quarter cases of applesauce and peanut butter, canned peas and baked beans, or half of a lamb, a hindquarter of beef. A dozen packages of Fordhook limas, six of frozen strawberries. He had a sign made that he posted in his window—FREE DELIVERY, and hired neighborhood boys. Let the A&P compete with that! He extended credit to his customers. Still his business faltered and shrank—wilted like the lettuce in July.

Surely he was able to consider defeat. He was not foolish; he was, in 10 fact, quite intelligent and, incredibly, a passionate reader within the limits of his education and the scarce hours available to him. So he did not minimize the supermarket threat. He measured it against his needs and possibilities, but never against his means. By now his three sons, in the 1950s, were beyond his financial responsibility. Social Security had come into being for the self-employed. But, although the little house we had finally moved to from the apartment was nearly paid for, as was a modest insurance policy, he could not afford to work less or begin to contemplate an eventual gentle retirement. And his two elder sons, just beginning their own families, could not help him. Not that he asked or expected. He asked for nothing and demanded nothing except the opportunity to do what he could. And that is what he did: go on. What hope he had was vested in a future beyond his own—in his children. What dreams he permitted himself were dreams of their prosperity. The only explanation of his life I ever heard from him was this: I sell potatoes, he said to me one day, so that you won't have to.

I returned early in summer in 1956 from the University of Chicago 11 with my freshly minted master's degree, and within a day I was in my apron in the store, cleaning and cutting up chickens, boning beef to grind for hamburger, putting up stock, checking out the occasional customer, and delivering orders in the neighborhood on the now rickety bicycle that the store had purchased new years ago. It was the same summer that I had lived over and over again for twelve years, more than half my life: his righthand man. But it was the wrong summer now for me to do this any longer. I would do it, of course, and not with resentment. After all I had no immediate plans, certainly no firm prospects. And the old harness that I had sweated into my shape over the years was comfortable enough. And, most important, he was nearly alone in the store with the summer coming, his only chance to make a little money. I would stay.

But we both knew that it was wrong for me to stay. The time had come   12
for me to leave. I was twenty-two.

But I could not. Business was now worse than it had ever been. The   13
area was changing. Even the supermarkets were leaving, following the
families that were leaving. He could no longer afford a full-time butcher
and not even a full-time worker. He patched together and limped along.
Often he was entirely alone. He sold the truck and used the old family
car instead. He turned off one and then a second of his three refrigerated
cases. He stayed open later than ever. Never had he had a greater need for
help.

But he also had a much greater need, and that was for me, his youngest   14
son, to go on out into my life free and clear, with not the merest
encumbrance of guilt. The time had come for me to not sell potatoes. The
time had come for me to assume a greater responsibility than slicing cold
cuts or marking prices on cans; now I had to validate his life by validating
my own. But I could not leave. With every day, every hour of inaction as
the business shriveled, it became more my determination to stay by him.
Until one evening on our way home he told me that he wanted me to go.
I protested. But he insisted. What he told me was simply this: he worried
more about me staying with him than he worried about the business. The
business could not fail, only he could fail, and that had nothing to do with
the business. But what truly convinced me was his enthusiasm for my going.
Just as he had faced A&P with vigorous imagination, so now he looked
toward my future. What was waiting out there? What would I make of it?
That I was a student of literature and had pretensions to write thrilled him.
Thrilled is the accurate word. That his son would read all the books that
he had wanted to read and then write about them! That his son might
someday write books of his own! Was this not a world full of wonder? That
out of onions and carrots he had made this possible?

So, when I left, I did not slink away dragging a bundle of second and   15
third thoughts or rancid misgivings, but like a darling I went forth, well
armed with my father's strength and resolve and gaiety.

He was, all in all, a man who made and met his life with as much grace   16
and dignity as any of us, the best of us, is capable.

Hector, heavyweight champions, Lindbergh, soldiers in combat, pulling   17
guards, inner-city vigilantes, astronauts, Texas Rangers . . . heroes all.
Maybe.

On the other hand, I think of my father, who arose each morning to   18
go forth compelled by no ideology or creed or belief or quest for self-glory

or the need to impose some truth upon others and certainly not by any sense of martyrdom. He was compelled only by the beautiful necessity to do what his life required of him. No magical Excalibur singing in his hand, only a small sharp knife with which to trim the icy lettuce. Unlike the abstract courage embodied in the mythicized hero, my father's courage was rooted in the truly extraordinary strength of the uncompromising love that defends and takes personal responsibility for the lives that it creates.

That is heroic courage. It is discovered not in a single act of heroism 19 or in a victory of some sort or by demonstrations of physical bravery; truly heroic courage might include such things, but it transcends them. Such heroic courage is determined by the quality and magnitude of what is lived for, the worth of what is lived for. My father lived for what he loved, for what is profoundly and fundamentally worth loving. Against such values nothing can be compared.

I do not know if my father was a physically brave man. In his little 20 store as the neighborhood around him disintegrated and became more and more dangerous, he refused to keep a gun under the counter. It was not his style. But I think he understood intuitively that what defended him was his invincible faith in his own determination. He would not give in to A&P or to the threatening violence that began to rise around him. Or to fear. I think he believed at some level that fear, like victory, was actually a kind of metaphor: fear, like victory, stood for something else. If you were afraid of someone, some entity, then you got a gun. If you strove for a victory, it had to be a victory over someone or something, a person or a nation or an idea or a baseball team. But my father was not afraid of such entities, and he did not conceive of his victory in such limited terms. The worst my father could imagine befalling him was not the short-term robber but the long-term inability to provide for those he loved. Against that chimera guns could not prevail. Only his effort, his work. What victories he imagined had nothing to do with such abstractions as prestige or status or with such tangibles as an expensive car or well-cut clothing or a vacation in Florida. The only victory my father sought was to have "enough," even if only just enough.

Such attitudes, such values, gave him considerable advantages. My 21 father was, it seemed, entirely without envy. For businesses that succeeded as his did not, he had only admiration. For those that failed, businesses or people, he had always pity, an empathetic compassion. He simply did not have the time, certainly not the psychic energy, to spend on anything that would not create for him his requisites. Which does not mean that he was a narrow man limited in his concerns. He had fiercely passionate political feelings, but not so much an allegiance to party or platform. His was more an attitude, an orientation. His stand was for humane justice, for the underdog, for social equity. For a genuine freedom for people. In his youth he had been a Wobblie, had demonstrated for Eugene Debs. A lifetime later he had not moved much from that position.

In the last correspondence I had with him shortly before his death he 22 enclosed in the letter an editorial that had recently appeared in the *Philadelphia Bulletin.* The editorial excoriated the conduct of Judge Julius Hoffman, who was presiding at the trial of the Chicago Seven. The editorial, while coming down hard on the accused, yet was much harder on the judge, for it was he, the judge, in whose hands all our justice rested. His conduct was dangerous and inexcusable. My father had underlined in blue pencil all the good parts, the hardest condemnations, to emphasize his agreement. That was my father.

Perhaps, in the general scheme of things, there is still need for the 23 traditional idealized hero—or, rather, a need to idealize in the warrior (or warrior-athlete) those virtues we still consider to be the highest, most honorable virtues. But if our human civilization is to endure—to triumph, then my father's quiet but relentless heroism, that of the uncommon man, is the heroism that ultimately and alone will sustain us.

❀   ❀   ❀

AFTER YOU READ

▪ *THINK* about people you have known who exhibit the same kind of courage shown by Targan's father. Have your parents, or parents of your friends, shown this kind of courage? Do you know other owners of small businesses who have tried to survive the modern competition of supermarkets and discount stores? Do you consider these people heroic? Why or why not?

▪ *EXAMINE* also the names Hector (paragraph 17), Lindbergh (paragraph 17), and Excalibur (paragraph 18) from the selection. Each of these names relates to a mythic or national hero. Hector was the greatest of the Trojan heroes in the Trojan war described in Homer's *Iliad.* Charles Lindbergh was an American aviator who made the first nonstop solo transatlantic flight, flying his monoplane *Spirit of St. Louis* from New York to Paris in 1927. And Excalibur was King Arthur's sword, which he magically pulled out of a stone to prove that he was the true king of England.

▪ *EXAMINE* also Targan's definition of courage, or "true grit," in paragraphs 18, 19, and 23. Rewrite this definition in your own words and then discuss it with your classmates.

▪ *WRITE* an essay in which you first summarize Targan's definition of courage and then agree or disagree with it, explaining why you feel as you do. Support your essay with brief quotations from "True Grit" as well as specific examples from your personal experience.

Nani

ALBERTO RÍOS

❀

Like Barry Targan in the previous essay, Alberto Ríos pays tribute in "Nani" to a family member whose giving nature elevated her to heroic stature in his life. The son of an English mother and a Mexican father, Ríos grew up in Nogales, Arizona, on the Mexican border. Encouraged to speak only English as a child, he did not discover his Mexican heritage until he was nearly grown. In fact, one person who helped him to gain a greater awareness of his Hispanic heritage was his "Nani," or grandmother, who, in this poem, also represents a universal heroine—the eternal mother figure. Ríos has published The Iguana Killer: Twelve Stories of the Heart *and several collections of poetry, including* Whispering to Fool the Wind *(1982), in which "Nani" appears. His most recent collection of stories is* The Curtain of Trees: Stories *(1999).*

BEFORE YOU READ

▪ *THINK* about the most important female figure in your life—perhaps a grandmother, a mother, or a sister. Would you call this person a heroine for her contributions to your life and the lives of others? What is heroic about her life?

▪ *EXAMINE* the word *Nani,* which in Spanish is an affectionate term for a grandmother. How do you like the looks and sound of this word as compared with the English term *Grandma* or *Grandmother*?

▪ *WRITE* in your journal a one-paragraph description of the most important female figure in your life and of your relationship to her.

AS YOU READ

Underline the Spanish words in the poem. Can you figure out the meanings
of these words from the context of the poem?

Nani

Sitting at her table, she serves
the sopa de arroz to me
instinctively, and I watch her,
the absolute *mamá,* and eat words
I might have had to say more   5
out of embarrassment. To speak,
now-foreign words I used to speak,
too, dribble down her mouth as she serves
me albóndigas. No more
than a third are easy to me.   10
By the stove she does something with words
and looks at me only with her
back. I am full. I tell her
I taste the mint, and watch her speak
smiles at the stove. All my words   15
make her smile. Nani never serves
herself, she only watches me
with her skin, her hair. I ask for more.

I watch the *mamá* warming more
tortillas for me. I watch her   20
fingers in the flame for me.
Near her mouth, I see a wrinkle speak
of a man whose body serves
the ants like she serves me, then more words
about this and that, flowing more   25
easily from these other mouths. Each serves
as a tremendous string around her,
holding her together. They speak
Nani was this and that to me
and I wonder just how much of me   30
will die with her, what were the words
I could have been, was. Her insides speak

through a hundred wrinkles, now, more
than she can bear, steel around her,
shouting, then, What is this thing she serves?   35

She asks me if I want more.
I own no words to stop her.
Even before I speak, she serves.

❀   ❀   ❀

AFTER YOU READ

• *THINK* about the character of the poet's grandmother, Nani. How does she reveal her unselfishness, generosity, and love? Are these qualities in some way heroic? Why or why not?

• *THINK* also about the phrase "the absolute *mamá*" in line 4 of the poem. This term suggests a kind of eternal mother figure who gives completely of herself. In addition to food, what kind of life does Nani give the speaker in Ríos's poem? How is this gift connected to the language that Nani speaks?

• *EXAMINE* the Spanish words that you underlined as you read the poem. These words are defined for you below:

> *sopa de arroz* (line 2): rice that is cooked and then steamed in soup
> *albóndigas* (line 9): spiced meatballs
> *mamá* (lines 4 and 19): mother

How many of these words were you able to figure out from the context of the poem?

• *EXAMINE* also lines 22–24, which are confusing to some readers. Literally, these lines reveal that Ríos's grandfather, Nani's husband, is dead. Symbolically, however, this statement suggests that in the cycle of life, one organism "serves," or contributes, to another. Nani shares her life and love with her grandson just as the body of the grandfather contributes to the organic richness of nature.

• *WRITE* a character sketch of the most important mother figure in your life. Explain in your essay why this person is so important—perhaps even heroic—to you. (You may want to expand or include ideas from the journal you wrote earlier in this lesson.)

A Song of Greatness
(from the Chippewa)

MARY AUSTIN

❀

*American nature writer and novelist Mary Austin is best
known for her works about the American Southwest,
especially her first book and acknowledged masterpiece,*
The Land of Little Rain *(1903). In 1888, when she was
twenty years old, she moved to Southern California to
homestead with her mother, and this move transformed
her life. Austin not only grew to love the Southwestern
landscape but also developed great sympathy and understanding for Native American cultures. By retelling many
stories and chants from various tribes throughout the
United States, she helped to preserve these vanishing cultures. "A Song of Greatness" comes from the Chippewa, or
Ojibway, tribe of the far Northeast, which was also
Austin's home for a while. This Native American chant
connects the theme of heroes with the theme of self,
completing the circle of investigation that you began in the
first chapter of* Interactions.

BEFORE YOU READ

- *THINK* about how the idea of heroism relates to you. Do you consider—
or have you ever considered—yourself a hero? Why or why not? What
would it take for you to become a hero in your own eyes?

- *EXAMINE* the title of the chant. Does the title suggest a positive or a
negative view of life and humanity?

- *WRITE* a journal entry in which you define greatness.

AS YOU READ

Notice that each stanza concludes by focusing on the speaker. What effects do these stories have on the speaker?

When I hear the old men
Telling of heroes,
Telling of great deeds
Of ancient days,
When I hear that telling   5
Then I think within me
I too am one of these.

When I hear the people
Praising the great ones,
Then I know that I too   10
Shall be esteemed,
I too when my time comes
Shall do mightily.

❀ ❀ ❀

AFTER YOU READ

▪ *THINK* about the speaker's growing self-confidence that he (or she) will also "be esteemed" and "do mightily." What causes the speaker to become more confident?

▪ *EXAMINE* the last line of the first stanza: "I too am one of these." Notice that this line suggests the growing feeling of community, of oneness, that the speaker feels. How does such a feeling of community contribute to an individual's self-confidence and belief in his or her potential?

▪ *WRITE* about yourself as a hero or a heroine. Do you consider yourself or some aspect of your life to be heroic? If so, how? If not, how might you become heroic?

Unit Eight: Critical Thinking and Writing Assignments

❀ ❀ ❀

EXPLORING IDEAS TOGETHER

1. With a group of your classmates, make a list of all the heroes—male and female—that you have read about in this unit. Then categorize, or group, these heroes. What categories do you have? Which qualities distinguish the heroes of each category? Into which category, or categories, do most heroes fit?

2. The main characters of many movies from the last ten or fifteen years are what George Roche and Jean Picker Firstenberg call antiheroes—people who do not exhibit the traditional strength and courage of heroes. For example, Clark Kent is the antihero who corresponds to the traditional hero Superman. With a group of your classmates, brainstorm about the main characters of movies you have seen recently. How many of these characters are true heroes? How many are antiheroes? Which type of hero do you prefer? Why?

3. With a group of your classmates, discuss the relationship between celebrities and heroes. (You may want to review the readings by Phil Sudo, Jean Picker Firstenberg, Richard Shereikis, and Maxine F. Singer.) After you have discussed this issue with your group, write a collaborative statement explaining your position.

4. In their essays—all written before September 11, 2001—George Roche and Mike Pride believe that we live in a "world without heroes," while Ervin L. Jordan, Jr. and Clifford T. Bennett question the heroic status of George Washington, one of our traditional heroes. Do you agree with these writers that the belief in heroes declined in the latter part of the twentieth century? If so, why do you think this was so? How did September 11 change our view of heroes? Discuss these issues with a small group of your classmates.

WRITING ESSAYS

1. Several readings in this unit—most notably those by Richard Shereikis, Mike Pride, Barry Targan, and Alberto Ríos—focus on the concept of the "ordinary hero." Write an essay about an ordinary person whom you consider a hero.

2. The reading selections by Maxine F. Singer, Mike Pride, Frank Lalli, and Alberto Ríos all focus on female heroes. What woman do you consider a hero? Write an essay about this person.

3. Write an essay in which you compare the heroic actions of Lenny Skutnik and "the man in the water." In your conclusion, state who—in your opinion—was the more heroic and why.

4. Write an essay in which you argue for or against the idea that a sports figure or an entertainer can be a true hero. Remember to use specific support.

5. Jean Picker Firstenberg, Richard Shereikis, and Roger Rosenblatt focus on the influence of the media on our perception of heroes. Write an essay in which you argue that this influence is negative or positive. Be sure to use specific supporting details.

6. Several of the readings in this unit, including those by Jack E. White, Lynne Olson, and Alberto Ríos, focus on heroes of particular ethnic groups. Write an essay about a hero who has contributed to a particular culture. If necessary, do some research on this person before writing your essay.

7. Write an essay in which you answer the question "Are heroes born or made?" That is, which element is more crucial in determining whether or not an individual becomes a hero—the individual's character or the critical situation in which he or she is involved? In your essay, you may want to consider how different individuals responded to national crises such as the Oklahoma City bombing or the terrorist attack on the Pentagon and the World Trade Center on September 11, 2001.

8. Many movies, both classic and modern, focus on a hero figure. Write a review of one of these movies, focusing on its portrayal of the hero.

9. Write a letter (or an essay) recommending someone you know for a Medal of Valor. Your purpose is to persuade the committee awarding the medal to select your nominee. Therefore, you should include specific supporting details as well as examples that will convince your audience.

10. Write an essay in which you evaluate yourself as a hero (or a role model). Begin by providing your definition of a hero and then show how you do, or do not, fit that definition. In your evaluation, you may want to consider how you have lived your daily life as well as whether or not you have performed "heroic" actions. Whether or not you find heroism in your earlier life, do you think you have the potential for heroism? How can you further develop your heroic potential?

Acknowledgments

❀

Text Credits

From Edward Abbey, *Desert Solitaire: A Season in the Wilderness*. Reprinted by permission of Don Congdon Associates Inc. Copyright © 1968 by Edward Abbey. Copyright renewed 1996 by Clarke Abbey. Pages 4–5.

"My Name" from *The House on Mango Street* by Sandra Cisneros. Copyright © 1984, 1988 by Sandra Cisneros. All rights and inquiries: Sandra Cisneros, c/o Susan Bergholz Literary Service, 340 W. 72nd St., NYC 10023. Page 19.

Copyright © 1986 by the New York Times Co. Reprinted by permission. Page 22.

Adapted from "Race Needs Other Option," by Lylah M. Alphonse, *Boston Globe*, October 5, 1996. Copyright © 1996. Reprinted courtesy of The Boston Globe. Page 26.

From *The Effects of Knut Hamsun on a Fresno Boy: Recollections and Short Essays* by Gary Soto. Copyright © 1983, 2000 by Gary Soto. Reprinted by permission of Persea Books, Inc. (New York) Page 29.

"Salvation," from *The Big Sea* by Langston Hughes. Copyright © 1940 by Langston Hughes. Copyright renewed 1968 by Arna Bontemps and George Houston Bass. Reprinted by permission of Hill and Wang, a division of Farrar, Straus and Giroux, LLC. Page 34.

"Nobody Listens When I Talk" by Annette Sanford, *Descent*, reprinted in *Best American Short Stories*, 2001. Reprinted by permission of the author. Page 38.

Reprinted with the permission of The Free Press, a Division of Simon & Schuster, Inc., from *Lives on the Boundary: The Struggles and Achievements of America's Underprepared* by Mike Rose. Copyright © 1989 by Mike Rose. Page 43.

From *Newsweek*, April 1988 © 1988 Newsweek, Inc. All rights reserved. Reprinted by permission. Page 51.

From *Newsweek*, May 23, 1994 © 1994 Newsweek, Inc. All rights reserved. Reprinted by permission. Page 55.

Adapted from Spencer A. Rathus and Jeffrey S. Nevid, *Adjustment and Growth: The Challenges of Life*, 3rd edition, pp. 100–103; Copyright © 1986. This material is used by permission of John Wiley & Sons, Inc. Page 59.

From *All God's Children Need Traveling Shoes* by Maya Angelou. Copyright © 1986 by Maya Angelou. Used by permission of Random House, Inc. Page 62.

"Getting Started" from *Voices of the Rainbow* by Janet Campbell Hale, Kenneth Rosen, Ed., Viking Penguin. Reprinted by permission of the author. Page 66.

559

"No Snapshots in the Attic: A Granddaughter's Search for a Cherokee Past" by Connie May Fowler, *The New York Times Book Review*, Vol. 99, May 22, 1994, pp. 49–50. Reprinted by permission of the author. Page 73.

Copyright © 1992 by Julia Alvarez. First published in the *New York Times Magazine*, January 12, 1992. Reprinted by permission of Susan Bergholz Literary Services, New York. All rights reserved. Page 82.

"Keepsakes," by Steve Sherwood, from *New Texas*, pp. 133–140. Copyright © 1992. Reprinted by permission of the author. Page 87.

© Francine Klagsburn. Reprinted by permission of the Charlotte Sheedy Literary Agency. Page 96.

Copyright © 1993 by the Antioch Review, Inc. First appeared in the *Antioch Review*, Vol. 51, no. 1, Reprinted by permission of the Editors. Page 103.

"Two Kinds," from *The Joy Luck Club* by Amy Tan. Copyright © 1989 by Amy Tan. Used by permission of G.P. Putnam's Sons, a division of Penguin Putnam, Inc. Page 110.

"A Parent's Journey Out of the Closet," by Agnes G. Herman, *Reconstructionist*, Vol. 51, No. 2, October 1985. Reprinted by permission. Page 122.

Kristin St. John, "Adoption Should Be Color Blind," from *Parents*, volume 70, July 1995, p. 152. Copyright © 1995 Gruner & Jahr USA Publishing. Reprinted from PARENTS magazine by permission. Page 140.

"Those Winter Sundays." Copyright © 1966 by Robert Hayden, from *Collected Poems of Robert Hayden* by Robert Hayden, edited by Frederick Glaysher. Used by permission of Liveright Publishing Corporation. Page 143.

From FATHERLESS AMERICA by DAVID BLANKENHORN. Copyright © 1995 by the Institute for American Values. Reprinted by permission of Basic Books, a member of Perseus Books, L.L.C. Page 146.

Copyright © 1992 by the New York Times Co. Reprinted by permission. Page 153.

"A Simple Gift" by Robert J. Matthews excerpted from *Travelers' Tales Nepal*, edited by Rajendra S. Khadka. Copyright © 1997 by Robert J. Matthews. Reprinted by permission of Travelers' Tales and the author. Page 165.

Reprinted with the permission of Simon & Schuster from *I Know Just What You Mean*. Copyright © 2000 by Ellen Goodman and Patricia O'Brien. Page 173.

Reprinted by permission of The Wendy Weil Agency, Inc. Poseidon Press. Copyright © 1989 by Phillip Lopate. Page 178.

From *Front Porch to Back Seat: Courtship in Twentieth-Century America*, pp. 13–17. Copyright © 1988. Reprinted by permission of the Johns Hopkins University Press. Page 187.

From *The Effects of Knut Hamsun on a Fresno Boy: Recollections and Short Essays* by Gary Soto. Copyright © 1982, 1988, 2000 by Gary Soto. Reprinted by permission of Perseus Books, Inc. (New York) Page 192.

The Ledge Between the Streams, by Ved Mehta. Copyright © 1982, 1983, 1984 by Ved Mehta. Reprinted by permission of George Borchardt, Inc., on behalf of the author. Page 196.

Text was submitted from *You Just Don't Understand* by Deborah Tannen. Copyright © 1990 by Deborah Tannen. Reprinted by permission of HarperCollins Publishers Inc. Page 211.

From *Newsweek*, June 3, 1996. Copyright © 1996 Newsweek, Inc. All rights reserved. Reprinted by permission. Page 218.

From *Newsweek*, June 3, 1996. Copyright © 1996 Newsweek, Inc. All rights reserved. Reprinted by permission. Page 222.

Nickie McWhirter. "What You Do Is What You Are." Originally published in *The Detroit Free Press*. Reprinted by permission of the author. Page 231.

Tom Brokaw, "The Way We Worked," *Modern Maturity*, May-June 1999, pp. 43–44. Reprinted by permission of the author. Page 234.

Copyright © 1995 by *Harper's Magazine*. All rights reserved. Reproduced from the June issue by special permission. Page 239.

"Memoir of a Girl in the Oven," by Sarah Jeanette Smith. The *TCU Magazine*, Summer 2001, pp. 24–26. Reprinted by permission of the *TCU Magazine* and the author. Page 247.

"My Mother Enters the Workforce" first published in *USA Weekend*. July 14–16, 1995, p. 14. Also published in *On the Bus with Rosa Parks*, W.W. Norton. Copyright © 1999 by Rita Dove. Reprinted by permission of the author. Page 252.

Copyright © 2000 by Donald Antrim. Originally published in *The New Yorker*. Reprinted by permission of Melanie Jackson Agency, L.L.C. Page 255.

Mary Leonard, "It's About Time." Reprinted courtesy of the *Boston Globe*. Page 259.

"Less is More: A Call for Shorter Work Hours," by Barbara Brandt. Reprinted by permission of the author, for the Shorter Work-Time Group. Page 264.

From *How to Tell When You're Tired: A Brief Examination of Work* by Reg Theriault. Copyright © 1995 by Reg Theriault. Used by permission of W. W. Norton & Company, Inc. Page 274.

Copyright © 1989 by *Harper's Magazine*. All rights reserved. Reproduced from the April issue by special permission. Page 278.

Copyright © 1995 by *Harper's Magazine*. All rights reserved. Reproduced from the March issue with special permission. Page 284.

"Child of the Americas," by Aurora Levins Morales from *Getting Home Alive* by Aurora Levins Morales. Copyright © 1986. Reprinted by permission of Firebrand Books, Mitford, Connecticut. Page 291.

From *The Lone Ranger and Tonto Fistfight in Heaven* by Sherman Alexis. Copyright © 1993 by Sherman Alexie. Used by permission of Grove/Atlantic, Inc. Page 294.

From *The Woman Warrior* by Maxine Hong Kingston. Used by permission of Alfred A. Knopf, a division of Random House, Inc. Page 301.

"The Scholarship Jacket," by Marta Salinas. *Nosotras: Latina Literature Today*, edited by Maria del Carmen Boza, Beverly Silva, and Carmen Valle. Copyright

© 1986 by Bilingual Press/Editorial Bilingue, Arizona State University. Tempe, AZ. Page 306.

From *Newsweek*, September 20, 1993. Copyright © 1993 Newsweek, Inc. All rights reserved. Reprinted by permission. Page 312.

"Cultural Diversity" by Joan M. Snider. Reprinted by permission of the author. Page 316.

Victor Landa, "Anonymous victims of dreams and a river," *Fort Worth Star-Telegram*. September 14, 1997, Sec. E, p. 5. Reprinted by permission of the author. Page 319.

Reprinted by permission of *The New Republic*. Copyright © 1997, The New Republic, Inc. Page 322.

"The African-American Century" by Hendrik Hertzberg and Henry Louis Gates, Jr. Copyright © 1996 by Hendrik Hertzberg and Henry Louis Gates, Jr. Originally published in *The New Yorker*. Reprinted by permission of the authors. Page 326.

Reprinted by permission of the author. Page 331.

Copyright © 1990 by Shelby Steele. From *Content of Our Character* by Shelby Steele. Reprinted by permission of St. Martin's Press, LLC. Page 338.

Reprinted by arrangement with the Estate of Martin Luther King, Jr. c/o Writers House as agent for the proprietor. Copyright Martin Luther King 1963, copyright renewed 1991 Coretta Scott King. Page 344.

"Martin Luther King Jr." by Gwendolyn Brooks. *A Brother's Treasury*, edited by Gwendolyn Brooks. Used by permission of Broadside Press. Page 349.

From *Why in the World* by George J. Demko, with Jerome Agel and Eugene Boe, produced by Jerome Agel. First published by Anchor, Doubleday. Copyright © 1992. Reprinted by permission of Jerome B. Agel Publishing Company. Page 355.

"Sacred Cartography: Mapping Your Most Intimate Terrain" by Jan DeBlieu, from *Utne Reader Online*. Reprinted by permission of the author. Page 359.

"Soul Searching" by Pythia Peay, from *Utne Reader Online*. Reprinted by permission of the author. Pythia Peay is an award-winning journalist in the field of spirituality and psychology. She is the author of *Soul Sisters: The Five Divine Qualities of a Woman's Soul* (Tarcher/Putnam). Page 363.

"Weather Reports," from *Dakota*. Copyright © 1993 by Kathleen Norris. Reprinted by permission of Ticknor & Fields/Houghton Mifflin Co. All rights reserved. Page 369.

Barry Hannah, "The Ice Storm," *Outside Magazine*, March 1995. Reprinted by permission of the author. Page 375.

"Tornadoes," by Jane Smiley. *Outside Magazine*, March 1995. Reprinted by permission. Page 377.

"Lightning" by E. Annie Proulx, *Outside Magazine*, March 1995. Reprinted by permission of Darhansoff, Verrill, Feldman Literary Agents, NY. Page 378.

From *The End of Nature* by William McKibben. Copyright © 1989 by William McKibben. Used by permission of Random House, Inc. Page 381.

"Is a Lab Rat's Fate More Poignant Than a Child's?" by Jane McCabe, *Newsweek*, December 26, 1988. Reprinted by permission of the author. Page 394.

"We Must Find Alternatives to Animals in Research" by Roger Caras, *Newsweek*, December 26, 1988. Reprinted by permission of Roger Caras, PRES., EMER., ASPCA. Page 397.

From *Refuge: An Unnatural History of Family and Place* by Terry Tempest Williams, copyright © 1991 by Terry Tempest Williams. Use by permission of Pantheon Books, a division of Random House, Inc. Page 404.

Originally published in the *New York Times*, June 18, 1968. Copyright © 1968 by the New York Times Co. Reprinted by permission. Page 414.

"The Beep Goes On" by Carol Orlock first published in *Lear's* November 1989. Used by permission of the author. Page 417.

"Television Addiction," from *The Plug-in Drug, Revised Edition* by Marie Winn, copyright © 1977, 1985 by Marie Winn Miller. Use by permission of Viking Penguin, a division of Penguin Putnam, Inc. Page 422.

"Don't Touch That Dial" by Madeline Drexler, *Boston Globe*, July 28, 1991. Reprinted by permission of the author. Page 426.

Copyright © 1995 *U.S. News and World Report* L.P. Reprinted with permission. Page 430.

Reprinted by permission of *The New Republic*, © 1994, The New Republic, Inc. Page 434.

From Kimberly Young, *Caught in the Net*. Copyright © 1998 by John Wiley & Sons, Inc. This material is used by permission of John Wiley & Sons, Inc. Page 451.

From *The Perfect Baby: Parenthood in the New World of Cloning & Genetics*, 2/e, by Glenn McGee, pp. 38–43. Page 457.

Dinesh D'Souza, "Techno-utopia or techno-hell?," *American Enterprise*, Vol. 11, No. 8, December 2000, pp. 36–38. Reprinted by permission of the author. Page 464.

"Could You Live With Less?" by Stephanie Mills first appeared in *Glamour*, May 1998. Reprinted with permission of the author. Page 475.

From *Scholastic Update*, November 1990 issue. Copyright © 1990 by Scholastic Inc. Reprinted by permission of Scholastic Inc. Page 484.

Reprinted with the permission of Scribner, a division of Simon & Schuster, Inc., from *Freedom's Daughter's* by Lynne Olson. Copyright © 2001 by Lynne Olson. Page 497.

"World Without Heroes" by George Roche, *USA Today Magazine*, November 1988. Reprinted by permission. Page 502.

The Social Studies, Vol. 8, pp. 154–156, July/August 1997. Reprinted with permission of the Helen Dwight Reid Educational Foundation. Published by Heldref

Publications, 1319 Eighteenth St., NW, Washington, DC 20036-1802. Copyright © 1997. Page 508.

Copyright © 1987 American Film. Reprinted by permission of Jean Picker Firstenberg. Page 514.

Extracts from "Heroes Don't Need Zip Codes: Lenny Skutnik—Accidental Hero" by Richard Shereikis. Reprinted from *The Hero in Transition*, Ray B. Browne & Marshall W. Fishwick, eds., by permission Bowling Green University Popular Press and by permission of the author. Page 518.

"Heroines and Role Models" by Maxine F. Singer. *Science*, Vol. 253, July 19, 1991. Reprinted by permission of the author. Page 530.

Reprinted by permission of the author. Page 534.

From "What We Ought to Remember About the Oklahoma Bombing is the Heroism, Not the Terrorism" by Frank Lalli, *Money*, June 1995, p. 13. © 1995 Time Inc. All rights reserved. Page 538.

First published in the *Sewance Review*, vol. 103, no. 4, Fall 1995. Copyright © 1995 by Barry Targan. Reprinted with permission of the editor and the author. Page 542.

"Nani" by Alberto Ríos, *Whispering to Fool the Wind*. Copyright © 1982. Reprinted by permission of the author. Page 551.

"A Song of Greatness," from *The Children Sing in the Far West* by Mary Austin. Copyright © 1928 by Mary Austin, © renewed 1956 by Kenneth M. Chapman and Mary C. Wheelwright. Reprinted by permission of Houghton Mifflin Co. All rights reserved. Page 554.

Index

❀